Contents

SECOND EDITION

Edited by **Phil Hubbard and Rob Kitchin**

Key Thinkers on Space and Place

Los Angeles | London | New Delhi
Singapore | Washington DC

Editorial arrangement and Introduction © Phil Hubbard
    and Rob Kitchin 2011
Chapter 1 and 56 © Euan Hague 2011
Chapter 2 © Peter Merriman 2011
Chapter 3 © Suzanne Reimer 2011
Chapters 4, 5 and 60 © David B. Clarke and
    Marcus A. Doel 2011
Chapter 6 © Lewis Holloway 2011
Chapter 7 © Gordon L. Clark 2011
Chapter 8 © Constantina Papoulias 2011
Chapter 9 © Gary Bridge 2011
Chapters 10, 44 and 49 © Minelle Mahtani 2011
Chapter 11 © Tom Mels 2011
Chapter 12 © Phil Hubbard 2011
Chapter 13 © Mike Crang 2011
Chapter 14 © Simon Batterbury 2011
Chapter 15 and 30 © Keith Lilley 2011
Chapter 16 © Donald McNeill 2011
Chapter 17 © Donald McNeill and
    Mark Tewdwr-Jones 2011
Chapter 18 © Marcus A. Doel and David B.
    Clarke 2011
Chapter 19 © Jonathan A. Beaverstock 2011
Chapters 20 and 48 © Simon Batterbury and
    Jude Fernando 2011
Chapter 21 © Chris Philo 2011
Chapter 22 © Wendy Larner 2011
Chapter 23, 25 and 55 © Barney Warf 2011

Chapter 24 © Rob Kitchin 2011
Chapters 26, 27 and 57 © Robin Flowerdew 2011
Chapter 28 and 34 © Don Mitchell 2011
Chapter 29 © Lewis Holloway 2011
Chapter 31 and 50 © Noel Castree 2011
Chapter 32 © Katherine McKittrick 2011
Chapter 33 © Hayden Lorimer 2011
Chapter 35 © Tracey Skelton 2011
Chapter 36 © Eric Laurier 2011
Chapter 37 © Rob Shields 2011
Chapters 38 and 58 © Paul Rodaway 2011
Chapter 39 © John R. Gold 2011
Chapters 40 and 66 © Felicity Callard 2011
Chapter 41 © Sarah Hall 2011
Chapter 42 © Rhys Jones 2011
Chapter 43 and 51 © Alan Latham 2011
Chapter 45 © Karen Morin 2011
Chapter 46 © James Faulconbridge 2011
Chapter 47 © Andy C. Pratt 2011
Chapter 52 © Robina Mohammad and
    James D. Sidaway 2011
Chapter 53 © Suzanne Reimer 2011
Chapter 54 and 61 © Jim Glassman 2011
Chapter 59 © Peter Adey 2011
Chapter 62 © Thomas Perreault 2011
Chapter 63 © Roland Lippuner 2011
Chapter 64 © Don Mitchell and Carrie Breitbach 2011
Chapter 65 © Graham Clarke 2011

This edition first published 2011
First edition published 2004. Reprinted 2005, 2006, 2007, 2008, 2009

SAGE Publications Ltd
1 Oliver's Yard
55 City Road
London EC1Y 1SP

SAGE Publications Inc.
2455 Teller Road
Thousand Oaks, California 91320

SAGE Publications India Pvt Ltd
B 1/I 1 Mohan Cooperative Industrial Area
Mathura Road
New Delhi 110 044

SAGE Publications Asia-Pacific Pte Ltd
3 Church Street
10-04 Samsung Hub
Singapore 049483

Library of Congress Control Number: 2010923241

British Library Cataloguing in Publication data

A catalogue record for this book is available from the British Library

ISBN 978-1-84920-101-8
ISBN 978-1-84920-102-5 (pbk)

Typeset by C&M Digitals (P) Ltd, Chennai, India
Printed and bound by CPI Group (UK) Ltd, Croydon, CR0 4YY
Printed on paper from sustainable resources

Key Thinkers on Space and Place

SAGE has been part of the global academic community since 1965, supporting high quality research and learning that transforms society and our understanding of individuals, groups, and cultures. SAGE is the independent, innovative, natural home for authors, editors and societies who share our commitment and passion for the social sciences.

Find out more at: **www.sagepublications.com**

Notes on Contributors

Peter Adey, Research Institute for Law, Politics and Justice, Keele University, UK

Simon Batterbury, School of Land and Environment, University of Melbourne, Australia

Jonathan A. Beaverstock, Department of Geography, University of Nottingham, UK

Carrie Breitbach, Department of Geography, Chicago State University, USA

Gary Bridge, School of Policy Studies, Bristol University, UK

Felicity Callard, Department of Geography, Queen Mary, University of London, UK

Noel Castree, School of Environment and Development, University of Manchester, UK

David B. Clarke, School of the Environment and Society, Swansea University, UK

Gordon L. Clarke, School of Geography and the Environment, University of Oxford, UK

Mike Crang, Department of Geography, Durham University, UK

Marcus A. Doel, School of the Environment and Society, Swansea University, UK

James Faulconbridge, The Lancaster Environment Centre, Lancaster University, UK

Jude Fernando, Department of International Development, Community and Environment, Clark University, USA

Robin Flowerdew, School of Geography, University of St. Andrews, UK

Jim Glassman, Department of Geography, University of British Columbia, Canada

John Gold, School of Social Sciences and Law, Oxford Brookes University, UK

Euan Hague, Department of Geography, DePaul University, USA

Sarah Hall, School of Geography, University of Nottingham, UK

Lewis Holloway, Department of Geography, University of Hull, UK

Phil Hubbard, Department of Geography, University of Kent, UK

Rhys Jones, Institute of Geography and Earth Sciences, Aberystwyth University, UK

Rob Kitchin, Department of Geography, National University of Ireland, Maynooth, UK

Wendy Larner, School of Geographical Sciences, Bristol University, UK

Peter Merriman, School of Geography, Aberystwyth University, UK

Alan Latham, Department of Geography, University College London, UK

Eric Laurier, School of Geosciences, University of Edinburgh, UK

Keith Lilley, School of Geography, Queen's University, Belfast, Northern Ireland

Roland Lippuner, Friedrich-Schiller-Universität Jena, School of Geography, Germany

Hayden Lorimer, Department of Geographical and Earth Sciences, University of Glasgow, UK

Minelle Mahtani, Faculty of Geography and Planning, University of Toronto, Canada

Katherine McKittrick, Department of Gender Studies, Queen's University, Canada

Don McNeill, Urban Research Centre, University of Western Sydney, Australia

Tom Mels, Faculty of Human Geography, Gotland University, Sweden

Peter Merriman, Institute of Geography and Earth Sciences, Aberystwyth University, UK

Don Mitchell, Maxwell School at Syracuse University, USA

Robina Mohammad, Department of Geography and Environmental Science, University of Reading, UK

Karen M. Morin, Bucknell University, USA

Constantina Papoulias, School of Arts and Education, Middlesex University, UK

Thomas Perreault, Center for Environmental Policy and Administration, Maxwell School at Syracuse University, USA

Chris Philo, Department of Geographical and Earth Sciences, University of Glasgow, UK

Andy C. Pratt, King's College University, UK

Suzanne Reimer, School of Geography, University of Southampton, UK

Paul Rodaway, Lancaster University, UK

Rob Shields, University of Alberta, Canada

James D. Sidaway, University of Amsterdam

Tracey Skelton, Department of Geography, National University of Singapore

Mark Tewdwr-Jones, Bartlett School of Planning, University College London, UK

Barney Warf, Department of Geography, University of Kansas, USA

Preface to the Second Edition

We were delighted when Sage asked us to update and extend the original edition of *Key Thinkers on Space and Place*. We were gratified that the original book had found an interdisciplinary audience and that there seemed to be a demand for a second edition, confirming our belief that a biographically-orientated approach is both a valid and valuable way of considering philosophical and theoretical debates on the nature of space and place. Indeed, our original intention was not to provide a reader's guide to the 'great and the good' in the discipline of Geography (a veritable 'Who's Who') that would be of interest to practising geographers keen to see if their friends, colleagues, supervisors or lecturers had entered the 'canon'; rather, we set out to use a biographical approach to show that different ways of thinking about space and place always emerge from a complex weft of contextual relations, being entangled in the personal politics and life stories of individual scholars. As many of the entries demonstrate, key ideas often appear to take on a life of their own – becoming associated with broad 'schools', movements or paradigms – yet always remain associated with key individuals. Foregrounding the scholar is for us a valuable way to understand the social production of knowledge, in this case ways of thinking about the nature of space and place.

The invitation also aroused other emotions as well, chiefly anxiety. The process of preparing the first edition, whilst enjoyable and stimulating, was also fraught as we grappled with questions about the book's pedagogical value, its range of chapters and possible reception. In particular, we agonised long and hard about balancing the coverage of different philosophical approaches to space and place with the inclusion of certain thinkers, and with constraints of space inevitably some difficult choices had to be made as to whom to include and exclude. The publication of the first edition confirmed that others shared our concerns, and we quickly received feedback that told us that the book evoked some controversy (see review section of *Environment and Planning A* 2005; Johnston, 2006). Much of this revolved around a misunderstanding of our intentions – that we were trying to compile a guide to the most influential, cited or celebrated spatial thinkers, rather than provide a selection that highlighted the value of a biographical approach and introduced a broad range of thinking on space and place from across disciplines. Moreover, we were accused of being somewhat unreflexive in our choice of thinkers, being complicit in the privileging of a white, Anglophone and masculinist worldview and marginalising other ways of seeing and theorising the world (this despite Gill Valentine being a leading feminist scholar). Related to this was a sense that we were seeking to manage disciplinary boundaries, excluding those whose understandings of space and place were not 'geographical' enough, or developed outside the academy. At the heart of such criticisms was the concern that we had not sufficiently addressed our own positionality, producing a volume that said more about our own prejudices and preferences than it might say about the state-of-the-art in cross-disciplinary, international efforts to theorise space and place. One memorable review even went so far as to imagine that we casually drew up the list of thinkers one night in a conference bar, accusing us of exercising a 'careless' approach to selection in which we never stopped to consider whether we had the right to make decisions about who is a 'key' thinker.

Such criticisms are, we feel, worth making, however misplaced some of them might have been (we actually spent weeks working out and debating whom to include and conducted extensive consultation with colleagues, despite how it might have appeared to critics). *Key Thinkers on Space and Place* – like the other handbooks, encyclopedias, and dictionaries that litter contemporary academia – has its partialities, blindspots and exclusions. It indeed serves to foreground particular individuals and push others to the periphery. Such is the nature of the project: no matter if we had listed those entries we might have included, or wanted to include, the fact is that this extended list would have been equally partial and selective. In a real sense then we are privileging particular people, certain ways of thinking, and highlighting certain stories. Whether or not this is an act borne of arrogance and 'careless power' is open to debate, we would suggest. Certainly, we concede that our editorship needs to be situated in the context of our own white, middle-aged worldviews; our own commitment to critical geographical research; our own limited language abilities and Anglophone-bias; our professional positioning as geographers and our emplacement within positions of authority within higher education establishments. It also needs to be understood within the constraints of the pedagogic remit that we established: i.e. that the book was written in the main for English speaking students and therefore we chose thinkers whose canon was available in English; that we wanted to include thinkers from a range of disciplines; that we wanted to cover as many philosophical approaches as possible; and we wanted to concentrate on the contemporary period of the last 50 years.

In these respects, we are guilty as charged. Our editorship resulted in a volume that did reproduce the hegemony of a particular way of thinking space and place; arguably the same malestream, disciplined and Anglophone geography that we had been exposed to, in different ways, in our own undergraduate studies. Despite the variations in the types of people profiled in the first edition, one could not escape a bias towards male thinkers, predominantly white, assumed heterosexual, and writing predominantly in English (or their works have been translated). The majority, too, trained and identified as geographers (although roughly half were from other disciplines), with a large number having been educated at a relatively small set of 'elite' institutions. In this respect, *Key Thinkers* is complicit in reflecting the dominant ways of thinking spatially in the social sciences, rather than what it might be or could have been.

As such, we approached the writing of the second edition with trepidation. We are making ourselves hostages to fortune once more by producing a volume that many might consider as a 'definitive' list of *the* key thinkers on space and place, effectively setting in stone those whose ideas are worthy of scrutiny, and those whose are not. We would certainly countenance against such a view, and would hope that those reading and teaching with this volume will do so with a critical eye. Indeed, we would argue that questions as to why certain ideas of space and place have come to be predominant in the discipline can indeed be addressed by considering the privileges and power obtained by certain key individuals, and relating this to their life-paths is a useful way of considering the roots of exclusion within the academy. Rather than simply noting who is not included in this volume, and noting the omission of certain traditions within and beyond geography, we hope that readers will reflect critically on why such thinkers have not been included in what is, perhaps, a view 'from the centre'.

Eagle-eyed readers will note that in this edition we have not just updated existing entries, along with our introductory essay, but also added a select number of new entries. Due to space constraints we have not been able to include as many new people as we would like (just 14). In selecting these thinkers we have been guided by a number of considerations – to address issues in the disciplinary make-up and international siting/tradition of thinkers, philosophical approach, and gender. This is both a deliberate reaction to the reviews of the first edition but is also, we would argue, a reflection of the changing composition of faculty and the cross-disciplinary nature of significant work on space and place. These selections go some way towards redressing certain balances in the original selection, although we admit the collection as a whole is still guilty of certain biases for the reasons outlined above.

Despite these shortcomings, we present this second edition hoping that educators and students alike will find it a useful, accessible and timely collection that helps them think through questions about how individual life stories might inform the development of ideas about the world. Furthermore, we hope that it will continue to provoke healthy debate and critical reaction on the production of knowledge given such debate is vital if we are ever to untangle the value of key ideas from the messy situatedness of the individuals that are making them.

REFERENCES

Boyle, M., Peet, R., Minca, C., Samers, M., Simonsen, K., Purcell, M., Graham, E., Hubbard, P., Kitchin, R. and Valentine, G. (2005) 'Review Essay on "Key Thinkers on Space and Place"', *Environment and Planning A*, 37 (1): 161–87.

Johnston, R. J. (2006) 'The Politics of Changing Human Geography's Agenda: Textbooks and the Representation of Increasing Diversity', *Transactions, Institute of British Geographers*, 31 (3): 286–303.

Phil Hubbard and Rob Kitchin, November 2009

Introduction: Why Key Thinkers?

As 1999 slowly but surely gave way to 2000, and we entered a new millennium, a not altogether surprising phenomenon emerged: the media's preoccupation with cataloguing the cultural, economic and social achievements not only of the last century, but the preceding 1000 years. Examples of this encylopaedism are legion, with in the UK critics' lists of the best album of all time, polls of the most significant British figure, polls of the greatest film ever made, and readers' surveys of the most important works of fiction (for anyone interested: The Beatles' *Sgt Pepper's Lonely Hearts Club Band*; Winston Churchill; Orson Welles' *Citizen Kane*, and Cervantes' *Don Quixote* – at least according to some polls). It was against this background of post-millennial 'listomania' that we began compiling the initial edition of this book, which was intended as a comprehensive and critical guide to a limited selection of important thinkers and intellectuals influencing the contemporary development of spatial theory. From the outset, however, we were determined that this book should amount to more than an exercise in nostalgia, and that rather than looking backward to profile the figures who have done so much to establish key ideas about space and place, this volume would be forward-looking, highlighting those thinkers who are currently doing most to shape the way that we think about the world around us – and, by inference, will undoubtedly

shape debates about space and place in the immediate future.

Given this remit, this volume is designed to offer a critical discussion of a selection of figures who have been influential in debates about space and place in the past 50 years or so. Our key criterion has been to select those who, in our opinion, have contributed significantly to *theoretical* discussions of the importance of space and place in shaping cultural, social, economic and political life in recent years. These include those working in important intellectual traditions such as positivism, phenomenology, Marxism, feminism, post-structural, queer, post-colonial, post-modern and subaltern theory (for the uninitiated, these terms are defined in the **glossary**) as well as those who have moved between, or among, theoretical and philosophical traditions. Indeed, one of our strategies of selection has been to include thinkers advocating different conceptions and approaches in order to highlight the diverse ways in which space and place have been theorised and debated. It is not then a list of the most important thinkers (although all of our selections have been influential), but rather a selection designed, on the one hand, to illustrate the utility of a biographical approach to understanding knowledge production, and on the other to demonstrate the plethora of ways of thinking spatially.

Given our disciplinary background and the key concepts at the heart of the book – space and place - it is perhaps unsurprising that geographers dominate our list; given the inequalities that characterise academic geography (as well as other forms of intellectual labour – see Sidaway, 2000), it is also unsurprising that white, Anglo-American academics are most numerous. Yet in seeking to recognise the diverse intellectual traditions and ideas that are shaping the way that we conceive of and write about space and place, our list includes many working beyond the Anglo-American academy, and includes several figures who blur the lines between academic thought, scholarly writing and critical praxis. Furthermore, our selection includes anthropologists, sociologists, economists, historians, political theorists, philosophers and planners (as well as many who elude easy disciplinary categorisation). The fact that nearly half of the thinkers profiled here are not conventionally defined as 'geographers' is an acknowledgement of the centrality of space in social theory and the significance of the so-called 'spatial turn' in disciplines such as sociology, cultural studies, and literary studies over the past 30 years, alongside the 'cultural turn' in geography that has seen a broad engagement with social theory by geographers (see Hubbard et al., 2002).

While it is easy for geographers to overstate the extent to which this spatial turn has transformed the social sciences and humanities, as the entries that follow demonstrate, space and place have become totemic concepts for those exploring social, cultural, economic and political relations. For example, many anthropological readings of the tactics of everyday life have foregrounded place in setting the rhythms of social conduct (see entries on **Marc Augé, Tim Ingold** and **Michel de Certeau**) whilst many of the key ideas in contemporary cultural studies concerning representation (such as those associated with **Edward Said, Stuart Hall, Benedict Anderson** and **Raymond Williams** to name but a few) have stressed the importance of space as a framing device in the creation of cultural imaginaries. Writing on globalisation and the informational society has also located the concepts of space and place at the centre of economic thought, with **Anthony Giddens, Manuel Castells, Saskia Sassen**, and **Amartya Sen** among numerous other 'global gurus', all offering their own distinctive takes on the importance of (virtual and real) space in creating new forms of (crisis-prone) capitalism. Post 9/11, important work on the contours of the 'war on terror' also makes great play of geo-political imaginations, with thinkers as diverse as **Jean Baudrillard, Gerard Ó Tuathail, Paul Virilio** and **Judith Butler** all drawing on a rich repository of spatial thought when arguing for the importance of mediated images of war and terror in contemporary international relations.

Crang and Thrift (2000: 1) consequently suggest that '[s]pace is the everywhere of modern thought'. The consequence of this is that academics outside the discipline have begun to theorise space in ways that have appeal for geographers. This means their work is being imported into geographical thought in a variety of ways. Conversely, work by geographers is increasingly being used and read by those in other social sciences and humanities. In part, this explains why so many of the theorists profiled in this book would not necessarily consider themselves to be 'geographers', even though their work is inherently geographical or has been adapted and reworked by geographers. On the other hand, the book profiles a number of thinkers who would certainly identify as geographers. What is evident here, however, is that our choice of key thinkers in the geographical tradition is entirely biased towards human geographers, despite the apparent common ground shared between physical and human geographers as they explore the constitutive role of space-time in the making of the world around us (see Massey, 1999). Yet despite occasional conversations between physical and human geographers (see Raper and Livingston, 1997; Harrison and Dunham, 1998), and sporadic attempts to unite the discipline through the forging of a shared philosophy and method (e.g., Haggett and Chorley, 1969), it remains the case that physical geography has remained relatively untroubled by theoretical debates about the nature of space and place. As **Doreen Massey** (1999) notes, for physical geographers the notion of *absolute space* still predominates, with phenomena seen to pre-exist their location in space. While this version of spatiality still informs certain human geographical writing – see entries on **Brian Berry**, **Reg Golledge**, **Peter Haggett**, **Waldo Tobler** and **Alan Wilson** in particular – the more widespread understanding of space among human geographers is that social, economic and political phenomena are the product of spatial-temporal locality, and that the articulation of inter-relations brings space into being. For example, **Nigel Thrift** offers the following definition:

> As with terms like 'society' and 'nature', space is not a commonsense external background to human and social action. Rather, it is the outcome of a series of highly problematic temporary settlements that divide and connect things up into different kinds of collectives which are slowly provided with the means which render them durable and sustainable.
>
> (Thrift, 2003: 95)

Hence, while there are physical geographers who are attempting to contribute to unfolding theoretical debates about the nature of space and place (Kent, 2003), most physical geographers have ignored postmodern, postcolonial or post-structural attempts to deconstruct, critique or reconstruct languages of space and place, and have only made marginal contributions to the literatures problematising concepts such as globalisation. As such, our selection of thinkers does not include any who would identify themselves as a physical geographer, but hopefully does not ignore physical geography, as many of the thinkers here offer food for thought for those in the natural as well as the social sciences (for some, notably **Bruno Latour** and **Donna Haraway**, the distinction often made between 'objective' hard science and the 'subjective' social sciences is a problematic one in any case).

Notwithstanding our decision to focus on those who are presently some of the most influential in theoretical debates over space and place, there are still many thinkers – both dead and alive – who act as key reference points in debates over the spatiality of social, economic and political life. As in Elliott and Turner's (2001) excellent *Profiles in Contemporary Social Theory*, our most difficult decision has therefore been selecting whom to omit (starting with a long shortlist of several hundred names that had to be pared down to a more manageable 66). In the final analysis, we have attempted to include a *representative* rather than exhaustive selection of names, and while we are keen to stress that each of the thinkers profiled here is relevant to contemporary *theoretical* understandings of space and place, there are of course many others who have made significant interventions in geographic debates through their empirical, practical and synoptic contributions. Hence, our choice of key thinkers should not be regarded as some barometer of influence for those for whom space and place are central foci of analysis, as it ignores many (and it would perhaps be invidious to mention names here) who have made significant contributions in applied geography, Geographic Information Systems, policy-oriented studies, action research and cartography, as well as the many whose prime contribution to geography is their empirical research (whether on environmental issues, the economy, social processes, politics, the country or the city) and those that act as key synthesisers drawing together materials into pedagogically orientated texts. In this sense, our selection of thinkers should not be read as a guide to who's currently hot (and who's not) in human geography (after all, there are plenty of citation analyses around for those who want a guide to which practitioners exercise most influence within, and beyond, the discipline – see Yeung, 2002). Rather, it stands as a user-friendly guide to *some* of the more important thinkers informing current debates about *space* and *place*. In the following section, therefore, we seek to outline why these concepts are fundamental in theoretical debates in geography and across the social sciences – and begin to show why their definition is variously problematised and clarified by the existence of different traditions of social, economic and political thought – from positivism to critical theory, from feminism to psychoanalysis, and from postmodernism to post-structuralism.

THINKING SPACE AND PLACE

Geography ... has meant different things to different people at different times and in different places.

(Livingstone, 1992: 7)

In popular discourse, space and place are often regarded as synonymous with terms including region, area and landscape. For geographers, however, these twin terms have provided the building blocks of an intellectual (and *disciplinary*) enterprise that stretches back many centuries. Yet, as Livingstone intimates, the theoretical specification of space and place has remained a matter of some dispute, being transformed as new ways of 'thinking geographically' have developed. Rather than reiterate Livingstone's analysis of how the 'geographical tradition' developed and mutated from an era of early modern navigation, through Enlightenment exploration and on to the institutional geographies of the nineteenth and twentieth centuries (see Heffernan, 2003), we want to focus here on the more recent history of spatial thinking in human geography to illustrate the diverse ways in which space and place are presently conceptualised and analytically employed to make sense of the world.

As noted above, many physical geographers remain fairly uninterested in problematising the idea that space is straightforwardly empirical, objective and *mappable*. Likewise, until the 1970s, most human geographers considered space to be a neutral container, a blank canvas which is filled in by human activity. Here, space is defined and understood through Euclidean geometry (with x, y and z dimensions) and, for analytical purposes, treated as 'an absolute container of static, though movable, objects and dynamic flows of behaviour' (Gleeson, 1996: 390). This absolute or 'empirico-physical' conception suggested that space can be conceived as outside human existence; rather than playing an active role in shaping social life, it is regarded as a backdrop against which human behaviour is played out (an idea explicitly addressed in **Torsten Hägerstrand**'s time-space modelling). In the 1950s and 1960s this conception of space was refined by a number of practitioners who sought to re-style geography as a positivist spatial science, seeking to construct theory or 'spatial laws' on the basis of statistical analysis (Robinson, 1998). This was reflected in the publication of texts covering the principles of statistical analysis to geographers (e.g. Gregory, 1963), and, later, those that sketched out the principles of spatial statistics based on regression, clustering and autocorrelation (Abler et al., 1971). For many, the ultimate promise of this progressive process of statistical testing and theory-building was the construction of predictive spatial models (with **Waldo Tobler**, **Peter Haggett**, **Brian Berry** and **Alan Wilson** as leading practitioners).

Retrospectively, this period is thus described as representing a pivotal moment in the history of the discipline– geography's 'Quantitative Revolution' (Bird, 1989; **Barnes**, 2001a) – and while many geographers were not swept up in the enthusiasm for quantification, hypothesis-testing and statistical analysis, this new 'scientific' paradigm was nonetheless responsible for ushering in a new conceptualisation of space which became widespread among even those geographers resistant to the notion of quantification. In effect, this was to conceive of space as a surface on which the relationships between (measurable) things were played out. Looking towards other disciplines, notably neo-classical economics and physics, this placed emphasis on the importance of three related concepts – direction, distance and connection. In short, it became axiomatic that the relationships between things on the Earth's surface could be explained in terms of these key concepts, and that it was possible to discern regular patterns that could be mapped and modelled (**Wilson**, 1999).

This heralded a new language of spatial physics where human activities and phenomena could be reduced to movements, networks, nodes or hierarchies played out on the Earth's surface.

Reacting against this rabidly objective type of analysis, some scholars took inspiration from psychology, developing a behavioural perspective that explored the role of the conscious mind in shaping human spatial behaviour (see **Kevin Lynch** and **Reg Golledge**). While this perspective held to the tenets of positivist inquiry, merely replacing concepts of absolute distance with notions of subjective distance, the historical and geographical materialism which emerged in the 1970s ushered in a rather different interpretation of spatiality, whereby space was deemed to be inherently caught up in social relations, both socially produced and consumed. Here, 'new' urban sociologists joined forces with geographers to document the role of urbanisation in capitalist society, with **Manuel Castells**, **David Harvey** and **Neil Smith** arguing that the city concretised certain class inequalities. On a different scale, economic geographers (e.g., **Peter Dicken**, **Michael Storper** and **Linda McDowell**) and those working in the 'localities tradition' (e.g. **Doreen Massey** and **Andrew Sayer**) sought to expose the way that spatial divisions of labour perpetuated capitalist structures, while political theorists (such as **Immanuel Wallerstein**, **Stuart Corbridge** and **Peter Taylor**) wrote of the international division of labour that was secured through particular geopolitical and territorial strategies. Yet, it was arguably not until the work of the Marxist theorist **Henri Lefebvre** (1991) that this notion of space as socially produced was convincingly (if sometimes obtusely) articulated.

Lefebvre implied that absolute space cannot exist because, at the moment it is colonised through social activity, it becomes relativised and historicised space. Insisting every society, and every mode of production produces its own space, he further distinguished between the abstract spaces of capitalism, the sacred spaces of the religious societies that proceeded it, and the contradictory and differential spaces yet to come. In outlining this history of space, Lefebvre implied that conceiving and represent-ing space as absolute (as had been com-mon in geography and across the social sciences) was in fact implicated in the production of relativised abstract space (i.e., the space of capitalism). Rejecting this, he proposed a trialectics of spatiality which explores the differential entwining of cultural practices, representations and imaginations. Moving away from an anal-ysis of things in space, this is an account that sees space as 'made up' through a three-way dialectic between perceived, conceived and lived space (see also **Ed Soja**). Here, place emerges as a particular form of space, one that is created through acts of naming as well as the distinctive activities and imaginings associated with particular social spaces.

For many geographers, place thus rep-resents a distinctive (and more-or-less bounded) type of space which is defined by (and constructed in terms of) the lived experiences of people. As such, places are seen as fundamental in expressing a sense of belonging for those who live in them, and are seen as providing a locus for identity. As with space, within regional and quantitative approaches place was conceived in absolute terms, simply as a largely self-contained gathering of people in a bounded locale (territory). This understanding of place was chal-lenged by humanistic geographers who, in the 1970s, sought to supplant the 'people-less' geographies of positivist spatial science with an approach to human geography that fed off alternative philosophies – notably existentialism and phenomenology (Hol-loway and Hubbard, 2001). Focusing on the experiential properties of space, the writings of David Lowenthal, **Anne Buttimer**, **David Ley**, Edward Relph and **Yi-Fu Tuan** in particular were of great value in reminding geographers that people do not live in a framework of geometric relationships but in a world of meaning. For example, **Tuan**'s (1977) poetic writings stressed that place does not have any particular scale associated with it, but is created and maintained through the 'fields of care' that result from people's emotional attachment. Using the notions of *topophilia* and *topophobia* to refer to the desires and fears which people associate with specific places, his work alerted geographers to the sensual, aesthetic and emotional dimensions of space. The humanistic tradition that these thinkers developed conceptualised place as subjectively defined. As such, what constituted a place was seen to be largely individualistic, although attachments and meanings were often shared (simply put, a place meant different things to different people).

As **Thrift** (2003) contends, one thing that does seem to be widely agreed is that place is involved with *embodiment*. The humanistic use of methods that evoke the multisensory experience of place (i.e., its visual, aural, and tactile elements, as well as its smells and tastes) provides one means by which this bodily geography of place has been evoked, though the rela-tionship between the human body and highly meaningful places is often more complex than even these methods can reveal (Holloway and Hubbard, 2001). Indeed, being 'in place' involves a range of cognitive (mental) and physical (cor-poreal) performances that are constantly evolving as people encounter place. In **Nigel Thrift**'s work on practice and affect it is suggested that these encounters cannot be adequately registered through language and discourse (hence, his talk of 'non-representational' theory). Stressing the importance of the pre-cognitive nature of being in the world (i.e., the way we intuitively inhabit places that are close and familiar to us without even thinking about it), Thrift alerts us to the practical knowledges and awarenesses that are deployed in everyday life. Other commentators suggest these skills come easier to some than others, with the geographies of embodiment implicated in the making of class (see **Pierre Bourdieu**), gender (see **Judith Butler**, **Linda McDowell**, **Cindi Katz**) and racial divides (see **bell hooks**, **Allan Pred**). Either way, place is seen to be made through the rhythms of being that confirm and naturalise the existence of certain spaces (a point made by **Henri Lefebvre** in his *rhythmanalyses* of modern life, **Marc Augé** in his reading of the spaces of transit, and in **Tim Ingold's** work on path-making).

While places have generally been theorised as authentic, close and *lived* spaces, those adopting structuralist and critical approaches have argued that places are complex entities situated within and shaped by forces from well beyond their own notional boundaries. Here, there is a recognition that places should not be romanticised as pre-political entities but that they are shaped by often oppressive institutional forces and social relationships. This is an idea explored extensively by thinkers such as **Doreen Massey** through her notion of a progressive sense of place. For her, a place is the locus of complex intersections and outcomes of power geometries that operate across many spatial scales from the body to the global. Places are thus constituted of multiple, intersecting social, political, and economic relations, giving rise to a myriad spatialities. Places and the social relations within and between them are

the results of particular arrangements of power, whether it is individual and institutional, or imaginative and material. Such a formulation recognises the open and porous boundaries of place as well as the myriad interlinkages and interdependencies among places. Places are thus relational and contingent, experienced and understood differently by different people; they are multiple, contested, fluid and uncertain (rather than fixed territorial units). The work of **John Urry**, Tim Cresswell and others, furthers these ideas, focusing on how the social, and its spatial expression as place, is composed of the ceaseless flow of people and materials across and between spaces, reconceiving social relations as a dense assemblage of mobilities. From such insights has developed the emergence of *relational geographies* as one of the key buzz concepts of twenty-first century geography (Jones, 2009).

As detailed in the discussion so far, given the different ways space and place have been operationalised, they remain relatively diffuse, ill-defined and inchoate concepts. Yet, they also remain fundamental to the geographical imagination, providing the basis of a discipline which is united primarily by its insistence on 'grounding' analyses of social, economic and political phenomena in their appropriate geographical context. In social and cultural geography, this focus on space and place has been further complicated by the adoption of different theoretical and methodological traditions. Crucial here is the continuing influence of two very different strands of geographic enquiry – on the one hand, Marxist accounts that explore the role of culture in the making of spaces of domination and resistance, and, on the other, the landscape studies of Carl Sauer and the Berkeley School (as well as the less celebrated German *Landschaft* tradition) with their emphasis on 'place-making' (evident in the ways of life that are inscribed on the landscape). Yet, far from holding these literatures in abeyance, 'new' cultural geographers have worked with them, creating a productive dialogue between them as they endeavour to examine how the world is invested with cultural meanings: the work of **Denis Cosgrove** on the role of landscape in creating social and cultural orders is a case in point, while **Gillian Rose**'s feminist critique of the landscape motif offered an influential perspective on the gendering of space and place. As Baldwin et al. (1999) suggest, cultural geographers accordingly regard both space *and* place as culturally produced, recognising the importance of both in the making of culture.

The idea that culture not only takes place, but makes place, is now manifest in a bewildering variety of work (including research into how the worlds of money, work, politics and production are enculturated). Reviewing this, Baldwin et al. (1999) assert that this coalesces around two key issues – firstly, the power and resistance played out in the everyday and, secondly, the politics of representation. Such concerns are certainly evident in those texts that were most significant in marking out the contours of a 'new' cultural geography. **Peter Jackson**'s (1989) *Maps of Meaning*, for instance, offered a distinctive take on the cultural politics of place by emphasising the discursive construction of people and place via language. Here, Antonio Gramsci's notion of hegemony was used to stress that such representations were crucial in the making of social and cultural orders, while **Raymond Williams**' close attention to spatialised language was also an important influence. Drawing on similar theoretical sources of inspiration, as well as more traditional urban sociology, scholars in the so-called LA school (**Michael Dear**, **Ed Soja**, **Michael Storper** and **Mike**

Davis, among others) showed how such close attention to the material and discursive workings of power could be used to illuminate the 'struggle' for the city. Again, a key assertion was that the meaning of place is fought over in the realms of cultural politics, being fundamental in the making (and re-making) of identity and difference. Writing in the context of Los Angeles, held up as the exemplary postmodern city (and 'capital of the twentieth century'), such authors developed the idea that the class divides that characterised the modern industrial city were being recast and redrawn in the late capitalist era as capital and culture entwined to produce an entirely new city. Characterised as decentred, fragmented and carceral, this postmodern city is one where categories of belonging are problematised, and where notions of a politics of difference take on heightened significance (as **Iris Marion Young** shows).

This attention to the making of cultural identities through cultural practices of boundary maintenance also highlights how concepts of place (and space) have been problematised and challenged by postmodern and post-structural theories that emphasise the slipperiness and instability of language. Rejecting universal definitions of 'place', such notions stress that places are real-and-imagined assemblages constituted via language. As such, the boundaries of place are deemed contingent, their seeming solidity, authenticity or permanence a (temporary) achievement of cultural systems of signification that are open to multiple interpretations and readings. Within geography, significant attention has therefore been devoted to the way that some taken-for-granted ways of representing the world (e.g., maps, atlases and aerial photographs) are in fact partial, distorted and selective, offering a particular 'way of seeing': **Brian Harley**'s influential deconstruction of maps, for instance, showing how cartography is implicated in the making of the world, not just its representation. Likewise, **Trevor Barnes'** ongoing explorations of the making of economic geographies have done much to demonstrate the way that spatial practices produce different spaces and places. This attention to the contingent nature of space and place has also problematised the taken-for-granted (binary) distinctions that often structure cultural understandings of the world – e.g., the distinction of self and other, near and far, black and white, nature and culture, etc. Most powerfully, perhaps, work on the construction of global North and South, often scripted in terms of an opposition of Oriental and Occidental values, has shown (through the writing of **Edward Said** and **Homi Bhabha** in particular) that geopolitical processes of power and resistance (including 'global terrorism') rely on the spatial metaphors. While geographers may be keen to take potshots at those corporations and individuals most obviously involved in the stigmatisation of the South (including those involved in the development 'industry' – see **Amartya Sen** and **Michael Watts**), **Derek Gregory**'s writing on spatial imaginaries of 'Otherness' squarely implicates geographers in this process. In response, there has been a widespread geographical engagement with postmodern ideas about reflexivity, polyvocality and the need to acknowledge the fluid identities of place, not least through the promotion of subaltern studies (as championed by **Gayatri Spivak**).

On occasion, this focus on language and representation has shifted the attention of geographers from the making of social, political and economic worlds to the making of individual subjectivities, though an obvious tension remains between those accounts which focus on the role of spatialised language in the construction of self (via **Michel Foucault**'s ideas about the imbrication of power and knowledge) and those that borrow from psychoanalytical theories (e.g., the work of Melanie Klein, Julia Kristeva, Derek Winnicott and **Judith Butler**) to explore the projection of the self into places that are part real, part fantasy (see **David Sibley**). This psychoanalytical perspective offers yet another take on space and place, whereby the unconscious mind is seen to 'map' itself onto space in ways that have important consequences in the constitution of gender and sexual identities. Here, as **Gillian Rose** (1993) contends, it is argued that the negotiation of the self, and its complex amalgam of desire, anxiety, aggression, guilt and love, takes place within and through the material and symbolic geographies of everyday life, with the psyche employing strategies to sustain its structure and relationship with the world.

Beyond this focus on the contested nature of space and place, elucidating the relationship *between* space and place remains a strong area of interest for geographers, particularly in the literature on *scale* (see **Neil Smith**, 2000). One key strand here is scrutiny of the way places are being transformed through processes of globalisation. Though alert to the entwining of local and global, and the creation of cultural hybridity, a key motif in such work has been that of global homogeneity. Claiming that a 'global space of flows' (to use **Manuel Castells'** terminology) is increasingly responsible for disseminating a standardised repertoire of consumer goods, images and lifestyles worldwide, the implication is that 'local' ways of life and place identities are being undermined by the logic of global capital accumulation as space is annihilated by time. Recently, a number of geographers have cited the work of anthropologist **Marc Augé** (1996), whose discussions of the familiar spaces of the supermarket, shopping mall, airport, highway and multiplex cinema revolve around the idea that these are 'non-places', symptoms of a super-modern and accelerated global society. Drawing obvious parallels with humanistic geographers' work on placelessness, he appears to suggest that there are now many 'non-places' which are solely associated with the accelerated flow of people and goods around the world and do not act as localised sites for the celebration of 'real' cultures.

The cultural theorist **Zygmunt Bauman** (2000) similarly writes of these as 'places without place', making an explicit link to the spatial strategies of purification and exclusion that are at the heart of consumer society (simultaneously condemning the shallow and banal sociality evident in so many sites of consumption). As **Peter Taylor** (1999) has spelt out, the implication here is that local place is being obliterated by global space, while on a different scale, several leading commentators have argued for the redundancy of the nation-state in an era where global corporations are key makers of the global economy (as **Peter Dicken**'s work on transnationalism demonstrates). In extreme 'globalist' accounts, as well as in the sometimes apocalyptic writings of **Paul Virilio** and **Jean Baudrillard**, these changes appear to signify not just the 'end of history', but the death of geography.

Exploring the way real and imagined place identities are bound up with the ways in which we experience and represent time and space, **David Harvey**'s (1989) discussion of the condition of postmodernity (rather than super-modernity) offers a more nuanced account of place-making under conditions of globalisation. Drawing on the ideas of Lefebvre in particular, Harvey explores how places are constructed and experienced as material

artefacts, how they are represented in discourse and how they are used as representations in themselves, relating these changing cultural identities to processes of time-space compression that encourage homogenisation *and* differentiation. In doing so, he points out the contradictory manner in which place is becoming more, rather than less, important in a period of globalisation, stressing that the specificity of place (in terms of its history, culture, environment and so on) is crucial in perpetuating processes of capital accumulation.

Such arguments have also been addressed by geographers (albeit in a different manner) in the context of locality studies and regional geography. For example, **Benno Werlen** and **Anssi Paasi** have extensively explored the process of regionalisation and how regions are discursively and materially produced through the interplay of local and global processes. Further, the attempt by **Doreen Massey** (1991), as noted above, to interrogate a 'progressive sense of place' has also been influential for those exploring the equation between globalisation and place identity. For example, several authors including **J.K.Gibson-Graham**, **Linda McDowell**, **David Harvey** and **Saskia Sassen**, who have explored the economic geographies wrought in an era of globalisation, have sought to explore the tensions between fixity and mobility, noting that place, if anything, is becoming more, rather than less, important in an economy where 'image is everything'. Literatures on economic agglomeration, location and specialism across a wide variety of sectors (e.g., high-tech industry, advanced producer services, finance and banking) all thus point to the importance of face-to-face contact, quality of life and placed proximity in the creation of new 'global' industries. In the literature on global cities, for example, scholars such as **Peter Taylor**, **Michael Storper** and **Saskia Sassen** have developed **Castells'** take on global space of flows by demonstrating that key world cities have become more important in a global era as they are the strategic 'places to be' for those who seek to control the global economy. As **Nigel Thrift**'s work on performance and the 'non-representational' nature of space emphasises, these are also places where knowledge is embodied and acted upon by those who are, in effect, the 'fast subjects' of global society (see also **Linda McDowell** on 'capital cultures').

In **Peter Jackson**'s (1999) summation, the emergence of new place identities through hybridisation denies any simple equation between globalisation and the homogenisation of space. Instead, he argues that the meaning (and hence value) of different goods and cultures is created and negotiated by consumers in different places, with the 'traffic in things' across space implicated in the making of social relations. In many ways, this echoes work in anthropology concerning the meaning of material artefacts, but adds a distinctive geographic focus via notions of displacement, movement and speed. Far from asserting the death of place (or, conversely, its resurgence), this points to a geography that is open to notions of difference and the post-structural insistence (expressed forcefully by **Gilles Deleuze**) that the world is constantly being territorialised, de-territorialised and re-territorialised in unexpected ways. For some commentators, the corollary of this is that space and place need to become conceived of as fragile entities, constantly made and remade through the *actor networks* that **Bruno Latour** insists involve people, things, languages and representations. We might speculate that it is through the creation of shared notions of place – and common understandings of space – that networks gain their power. Economic, political and social orders are thus immanent in these networks, being reinforced or re-made as 'material' moves through the network and takes different (commodity) forms in different contexts. Hence, there is no 'constitutive outside' which explains an 'inside'; place is not a location whose character can be explained through reference to wider spatial processes. Instead, such perspectives interpret both space and place as entities always becoming, in process and unavoidably caught up in power relations.

INTELLECTUAL AND DISCIPLINARY GENEALOGIES

As should be clear from the above discussion, there are many varying opinions on how to theorise and study the world. In particular, there is much debate between proponents of different theoretical traditions (positivism, Marxism, feminism, post-structuralism and so on) as they seek to develop and use concepts to think spatially. Of course, how such knowledge is produced is itself theorised, with a number of commentators developing disciplinary and conceptual histories that trace out the development and adoption of spatial ideas and approaches (for example, see Bird, 1989; Cloke et al., 1991; Hubbard et al., 2002; Johnston, 1986; 1991; 2000; Livingstone, 1992; Peet, 1998; Unwin, 1992). These most commonly are genealogical projects that seek to explain spatial thinking at the time of writing – mapping the present – by charting the conceptual paths followed by spatial theorists.

The most popular approach to date has been, following Kuhn (1962; 1970), to focus on identifying different geographic traditions that come to dominate spatial thinking through a particular period – becoming the dominant paradigm; and to document the transition – a paradigm shift – between traditions as new philosophical approaches emerge to challenge previous ways of thinking. Indeed, the pages of academic journals and books are full of debates in which the authors claim that their 'new' way of looking at the world represents the most meaningful, progressive and correct way of doing geography, rejecting existing modes of exploration and explanation out of hand and inviting others to adopt and develop their 'new' approach. These paradigm shifts, Johnston (1996) has argued, are the by-product of generational transitions. He suggests that as new schools of thought emerge, they are embraced at first by younger academics. As the productivity of earlier generations, schooled in different approaches to geography declines, the emerging generation become co-opted into the geographical establishment taking over the editing of journals, incorporating their ideas into teaching and writing textbooks. In this way, Johnston (1996) contends that academics of different age cohorts become socialised through different paradigms so that education and training produces generational shifts in ways of thinking about space and place.

It is common for those adopting such a paradigmatic approach to plot the intellectual development of Geography (e.g., Johnston, 1996) to argue that positivist spatial science emerged in the late 1950s to challenge – and ultimately supplant – a regional tradition concerned with describing and mapping (see especially the entries on **Brian Berry**, **Torsten Hägerstrand**, **Peter Haggett**, **Waldo**

Tobler and **Alan Wilson**). This positivist paradigm was itself challenged in the early 1970s by other approaches such as behavioural geography (see entry on **Reg Golledge**), humanist traditions (see entries on **Anne Buttimer**, **David Ley** and **Yi-Fu Tuan**), and structural approaches, such as Marxism (see entries on **David Harvey**, **Neil Smith** and **Michael Watts**) and feminism (see entries on **Gillian Rose**, **Doreen Massey**, **Linda McDowell** and **J.K. Gibson-Graham**). From a paradigm perspective, we might suggest that these dominant ways of thinking space and place were challenged in the 1990s by postmodern (see entries on **Michael Dear** and **Ed Soja**) and post-structural perspectives (see entries on **Jean Baudrillard**, **Judith Butler**, **Gilles Deleuze**, and **Michel Foucault**). Into the 2000s, geographers appear to have become fixated on questions of non-representation and affect, with **Nigel Thrift**'s work being particularly suggestive of new ways of doing geographies that are faithful to the multiplicity and immanence of the world – a notion also captured in the notion of 'relational space' central to the work of **Doreen Massey** and others.

However, the notion of paradigm shifts has been subject to critique as it has become more apparent that different approaches to geography are never completely overthrown (Mayhew, 2001; Hubbard et al.,2002). While it is true that institutional arenas of publishing outlets, departments, professional organisations, and informal socio-academic networks can reinforce the interests or agendas of particular academic communities, nonetheless there are always dissenting voices. Different ways of thinking about space and place are always concurrent rather than consecutive even if at particular moments some are more fashionable than others. The danger of a paradigmatic approach to understanding the geographical tradition is that it creates a linear narrative that suggests that spatial thought has developed through unified (and generational) paradigms when in reality consensus has seldom been complete or stable (something that Johnston acknowledges when he employs the pardigm concept). The notion of sequential progress thus creates a false consistency in which contributions that deviate from the dominant narrative are omitted. Noting this tendency, **Sibley** (1995) has documented the ways in which the geographies and histories of women, people of colour, those in developing countries, and other oppressed groups, have tended to be written from certain dominant positions, thereby silencing their voices and providing selective and partial geographical accounts.

Further, a paradigmatic approach often fails to fully explore the mechanisms by which ideas are constructed and knowledge is generated. As such, they often trace out trajectories of thought while glossing over the nuances in how intellectual ideas are developed within complex social and institutional structures and practices. Indeed, as **Donna Haraway** (1991) and **Pierre Bourdieu** (1988) explain in their own distinctive manners, spatial thought is not developed in a vacuum, but is rather constructed by individuals (and individuals collaborating) and situated within their own personal and political beliefs, the culture of academia, and institutional and social structures. From this perspective ideas are never 'pure' but rather emerge and become legitimated and contested according to particular material and social contexts.

Accordingly, an understanding of how ideas emerge, how they are adopted and how they evolve, requires an approach that acknowledges the situation and conditions in which they are constructed. The approach adopted in this book – biographical essays on key thinkers – seeks to provide such an analysis. While such a biographical approach does not reveal a broad historicisation of spatial thought, it is very useful for demonstrating the genealogy of intellectual ideas, revealing for example the ways in which personal history affects intellectual development, as the entries for **Edward Said**, **bell hooks** and **Anssi Paasi** demonstrate. Edward Said's experiences of being born into a Christian-Arab family in Palestine during British administration, and his subsequent fight throughout his adult-life for Palestinian self-determination, undoubtedly shaped his thinking about the relationship between culture and imperialism. Likewise, bell hooks has attributed her attempt to theorise the problems of black patriarchy, sexism, and gender subordination to her childhood experiences of growing up as a young black woman in Kentucky (United States) during the 1950s and early 1960s. And **Anssi Paasi**'s thinking on regions and regional geography has been shaped by the nature of Finnish academia and his strong empirical focus on Finland (see also Moss, 2001, on autobiographical accounts of the intellectual development of geographers).

Consequently, a biographical approach reveals how individual thinkers engage with a rich legacy of ideas drawn from past generations (as well as the influence of their contemporaries). Indeed, it should be clear from the cross-referencing between entries that no theorist develops their view of the world in an intellectual vacuum. The courses they took as students, discussions with their mentors and colleagues, the texts that they have read, and papers they have heard, all expose them to a multitude of ideas that shape their own intellectual development. Such development can be traced across thinkers to reveal a rough genealogy of ideas. For example, **Gillian Rose**'s ideas about the privileging of male ways of conceiving of space and place have been heavily influenced by psychoanalytic and post-structural writings. One major source of inspiration here has been the works of the feminist philosopher **Judith Butler**. Judith Butler, in turn, while again drawing from a diverse set of philosophical texts, has extensively utilised the writings of **Michel Foucault**. Likewise, when developing his critical philosophy, Foucault was influenced by (amongst others) the German philosophers Friedrich Nietzsche and Martin Heidegger. Of course, Gillian Rose is not the end point in this lineage but is rather a node in a complex web of interconnections, with her theorisation in turn no doubt providing influence and inspiration for a generation of feminist and cultural geographers. Moreover, Foucault has inspired many other spatial theorists in ways that are quite strikingly different to the performative analyses of Butler and Rose: for example, **Arturo Escobar** has used his writings on power to study international development, while **Brian Harley** cited Foucault extensively in his deconstruction of the map as a spatial language.

Indeed, it is clear from many of the entries that the same source of inspiration can be interpreted and used in different ways. For example, both **Ed Soja** and **David Harvey** draw upon **Henri Lefebvre**'s seminal text *The Production of Space* to develop their own ideas about the workings of capital, but differ in the interpretation and weight they place on Lefebvre's argument. Of course, a particular thinker can also influence different audiences because their own thoughts have transformed over time as they themselves come into contact with the thoughts of others and develop new lines of argument. For example, **David Harvey** remains a key influence on spatial science due to his book *Explanation in Geography* (1969), which provided a theoretical blueprint for positivist geography. At the same time, he is also a key source of inspiration and ideas for Marxist geographers who draw upon his 1973 book *Social Justice and the City* (and subsequent work) which utilised the writings of Karl Marx to construct structural explanations for socio-spatial inequality. Indeed, his 1982 text *The Limits to Capital* remains perhaps the most important statement by a geographer on the uneven production of space under capitalism.

A situated approach to understanding the production of spatial thought also, of course, reveals the extent to which place makes a difference to knowledge creation. For example, groupings of particular scholars in particular universities at particular periods can produce cross-generational schools of thinking. While Paris so often seems to be the locus of social theory (see **Jean Baudrillard, Manuel Castells, Gilles Deleuze, Michel Foucault, Marc Augé, Henri Lefebvre**, also Gane, 2003), other centres also emerge if we search for key locations in the theorisation of space and place. For example, Carl Sauer inspired the Berkeley school of cultural geography that influenced several generations of American geographers; **Stuart Hall** was a key actor in establishing Birmingham's Centre for Contemporary Cultural Studies whose work did much to shape 'new' cultural geography; the 1950s Washington graduate class (including **Brian Berry** and **Waldo Tobler**) are widely acknowledged as fuelling the so-called 'quantitative revolution'; and the writings of **Michael Dear, Ed Soja, Michael Storper, Mike Davis** and colleagues means that Southern California is widely acknowledged as the home of post-modern urbanism. On the other hand, the development of an individual's ideas can represent a reaction *against* the place where they are/were located. For example, to return to **Gillian Rose**, her book *Feminism and Geography* (1993) is widely acknowledged to have grown out of her critique of the Cambridge school of geography in which she was educated. A biographical approach thus alerts to the significant role of disciplinary spaces of eduction, as well as the often neglected sites of the *field*, the *body* and the *act of dissemination* by which knowledge is produced and circulated (Dewsbury and Naylor, 2002; see also Driver, 1995). As such, the biographical approach adopted in this volume focuses on both the *roots* (origins) and *routes* (directions they have evolved) of thinking on space and place. While not providing an exhaustive account, the following entries ultimately allow us to discern the many roots and routes – the intellectual genealogies – that explain why space and place have come to mean such different things to different people in different places.

CONCLUSION

At a time when some are rightly suspicious of the concentration of academic power and influence in the higher education sector (see Short, 2002), and others are seeking to resist the logic of the auditing procedures that relies on measures of individual research output (see Sidaway, 2000), there are some dangers inherent in compiling a list of key thinkers. Yet, as we have shown in our introduction, our intention is not to identify the most important or influential theorists, but to provide a guide to some (but inevitably not all) of those figures who have progressed our *theoretical* understanding – in some important way – of space and place,

at the same time as illustrating the diverse traditions of geographical thinking. While choosing just a few thinkers inevitably privileges them as key conduits of theorising and practising geographical analyses – and simultaneously marginalises and silences other thinkers and their theories – it is important to appreciate the ways in which knowledge is produced through intellectual encounters and dialogues (as illustrated in the previous section).

Given our intention to highlight the theoretical contribution these figures have made, the entries here do not offer a thorough or balanced overview of the career of each thinker. Instead, each follows a common format, starting with an overview of each subject's academic scholarship alongside some basic biographic information. While this overview is, of necessity, cursory, it hopefully provides an understanding of how each thinker developed their ideas in particular social, spatial and temporal contexts. This contextual material is followed by a summary of the way that each has conceived of space and place, aiming to identify why each is regarded as an important and influential thinker in debates on space and place. In a final section, each contributor offers a critical reflection on the work of each thinker, outlining some of the key controversies that adhere to each thinker's work (while showing how their work has been adapted by those working in different geographical and theoretical traditions). Each entry concludes with two reference lists: the first being a guide to each thinker's most important 'key' works. Here, the most important and key works by each thinker are listed, with an emphasis on those works that are most readily and widely available (hence, where there are multiple editions of one book in existence, we have tended to list the most recent English version rather than the first edition). The second reading list contains minor books, papers and chapters (where these are cited in the text), as well as a range of secondary sources. It is our hope that each entry inspires readers to explore these references, and develop their own take on the varied geographical imaginations deployed by these key thinkers on space and place.

REFERENCES

Abler, R., Adam, J. and Gould, P. (1971) *Spatial Organisation: The Geographer's View of The World.* New Jersey: Prentice Hall.

Augé, M. (1996) *Non-places: Introduction to an Anthropology of Supermodernity.* London: Verso.

Baldwin, E., Longhurst, B., McCracken, S., Ogborn, M. and Smith, G. (1999) *Introducing Cultural Studies.* Harlow: Prentice Hall.

Barnes, T. (2001a) 'Retheorizing economic geography: from the quantitative revolution to the cultural turn', *Annals, The Association of American Geographers,* 91: 546–65.

Barnes, T. (2001b) 'Lives lived and tales told: biographies of geography's quantitative revolution', *Environment and Planning D – Society and Space,* 19: 409–29.

Barnett, C. (1998) 'The cultural turn: fashion or progress in human geography', *Antipode,* 30: 379–94.

Bauman, Z. (2000) *Liquid Modernities.* Cambridge: Polity.

Benko, G. and Strohmeyer, U. (1997) *Space and Social Theory.* Oxford: Blackwell.

Bingham, N. (1996) 'Objections: from technological determinism to towards geographies of relations', *Envronment and Planning D – Society and Space,* 14: 635–57.

Bird, J. (1989) *The Changing World of Geography.* Oxford: Clarendon Press.

Blunt, A. and Wills, J. (2000) *Dissident Geographies: An Introduction to Radical Ideas and Practice.* London: Prentice Hall.

Bourdieu, P. (1988) *Homo Academicus.* Oxford: Blackwells.

Cloke, P., Philo, C. and Sadler, D. (1991) *Approaching Human Geography.* Liverpool: PCP Press.

Crang, M. and Thrift, N. (2000) 'Introduction; in M. Crang and N. Thrift (eds), *Thinking Space.* London: Routledge. pp. 1–30.

Cresswell, T. (1996) *In Place/Out of Place: Geography, Ideology and Transgression.* Minneapolis: University of Minnesota Press.

Dear, M. (1988) 'The postmodern challenge: reconstructing human geography', *Transactions of the Institute of British Geographers,* 13: 262–74.

Dear, M. (2000) *The Postmodern Urban Condition.* Oxford: Blackwell.

Dewsbury, J.D. and Naylor, S. (2002) 'Praticising geographical knowledge: fields, bodies and dissemination', *Area,* 34: 253–60.

Doel, M. (1999) *Postructuralist Geographies: The Diabolical Art of Spatial Science.* Edinburgh: Edinburgh University Press.

Driver, F. (1995) 'Geographical traditions: thinking the history of geography' , *Transactions of the Institute of British Geographers,* 20: 403–04.

Elliott, A. and Turner, B.(eds) (2001) *Profiles in Contempory Social Theory.* London : Sage.

Gane, M. (2003) *French Social Theory.* London: Sage.

Gibson-Graham, J.K. (2000) 'Poststructural interventions', in T. Barnes and R. Sheppard (eds), *A Companion to Economic Geography.* Oxford: Blackwells. pp 95–111.

Gleeson, B.(1996) 'A geography for disabled people', *Transactions of the Institute of British Geographers,* 23 : 387–96.

Gregory, D. (1994) 'Social theory and human geography', in D. Gregory, R. Martin, and G. Smith (eds), *Human Geography: Society, Space and Social Science.* London: Macmillan. pp. 78–109.

Gregory, S. (1963) *Statistical Methods and the Geographer.* London: Longman.

Haggett, P. and Chorley, R.J. (1969) *Network Analysis in Geography.* London: Arnold.

Haraway, D. (1991) *Simians, Cyborgs, and Women : The Reinvention of Nature.* London: Free Association Books.

Harrison, S. and Dunham, P. (1998) 'Decoherence, quantum theory and their implications for the philosophy of geomorphology', *Transactions of the Institute of British Geographers,* 23: 501–14.

Harvey, D. (1969) *Explanation in Geography.* London : Edward Arnold.

Harvey, D. (1973) *Social Justice and the City.* Oxford : Arnold

Harvey, D. (1982) *The Limits to Capital.* Oxford: Blackwell.

Harvey, D. (1989) *The Condition of Post-modernity.* Oxford: Blackwell.

Heffernan, M. (2003) 'Histories of geography', in S.L. Holloway, S. Rice and G. Valentine (eds), *Key Concepts in Geography.* Sage: London. pp. 3–23.

Holloway, L. and Hubbard, P. (2001) *People and Place: The Extraordinary Geographies of Everyday Life.* Harlow: Prentice Hall.

Hubbard , P., Kitchin R., Bartley, B. and Fuller, D. (2002) *Thinking Geographically: Space, Theory and Contemporary Human Geography.* London: Continuum.

Jackson, P. (1989) *Maps of Meaning.* London: Routledge.

Jackson, P. (1999) 'Commodity cultures: the traffic in things', *Transactions of the Institute of British Geographers,* 24: 95–108.

Johnston, R.J. (1986) *On Human Geography.* Oxford: Basil Blackwell.

Johnston, R.J. (1991) *Geography and Geographers: Anglo-American Geography since 1945.* London: Edward Arnold.

Johnston, R.J. (1996) 'Paradigms and revolution or evolution?', in J. Agnew, D. Livingstone and A. Rogers (eds), *Human Geography.* Oxford: Blackwell. pp 37–53.

Johnston, R.J. (2000) 'Authors, editors and authority in the postmodern academy', *Antipode, 32:* 271–91.

Johnston, R.J. (2006) 'The politics of changing human geography's agenda: textbooks and the representation of increasing diversity, *Transactions of the Institute of British Geographers,* 31(3): 286–303.

Jones, M. (2009) 'Phase space: geography, relational thinking and beyond', *Progress in Human Geography,* 33 (4): 487–502.

Kent, M. (2003) 'Space: making room for space in physical geography', in S.L, Holloway, S. Rice and G. Valentine (eds), *Key Concepts in Geography.* Sage: London. pp 109–130.

Kuhn, T.S. (1962) *The Structure of Scientific Revolutions* (1st edition). Chicago: University of Chicago Press (2nd edition 1970).

Lefebvre, H. (1991) *The Production of Space.* Oxford: Blackwell.

Livingstone, D. (1992) *The Geographical Tradition.* Oxford: Blackwell.

Massey, D. (1991) 'The political place of locality studies', *Environment and Planning A,* 23: 267–81.

Massey, D. (1999) 'Space-time, science and the relationship between physical and human geography', *Transactions of the Institute of British Geographers,* 24: 261–76.

Mayhew, R. (2000) The effacement of early modern geography : a historiographical essay', *Progress in Human Geography,* 25(3): 383–401.

Moss, P. (2001) *Placing Autobiography.* Syracuse: Syracuse University Press.

Olwig, K.R. (2002) 'The duplicity of space: German *raum* and Swedish *rum* in English language geography', *Geografiska Annaler; B 84B* 1, 1–17.

Peet, R. (1998) *Modern Geographic Thought.* Oxford: Blackwell.

Raper, J. and Livingstone, D. (2001) 'Let's get real: spatio-temporal identity and geographic entities', *Transactions of the Institute of British Geographers,* 26: 237–42.

Relph, E. (1976) *Place and Placelessness.* London: Pion.

Robinson, G. (1998) *Methods and Techniques in Human Geography.* Chichester: John Wiley.

Rose,G.(1993) *Feminism and Geography.* Cambridge: Polity Press.

Shields, R. (1991) *Places on the Margin.* London: Routledge.

Short, J.R. (2002) 'The disturbing case of the concentration of power in human geography', *Area,* 34: 323–4.

Sibley, D. (1995) *Geographies of Exclusion: Society and Difference in the West.* London: Routledge.

Sidaway, J. (1997) 'The production of British geography', *Transactions of the Institute of British Geographers,* 22: 488–504.

Sidaway, J. (2000) 'Recontextualising positionality: geographical research and academic fields of power', *Antipode, 32(3):* 260–70.

Smith, N. (2000) 'Scale', in R. Johnston, D. Gregory, G. Pratt, and M. Watts (eds), *The Dictionary of Human Geography* (4th edition). Blackwell: Oxford. pp. 724–27.

Taylor, P. (1999) 'World cities and territorial states under conditions of contemporary globalization', *Third World Planning Review,* 21(3): 3–10.

Thrift, N. (2003) 'Space: the fundamental stuff of geography', in S.L.Holloway, S. Rice and G. Valentine (eds), *Key Concepts in Geography.* Sage: London. pp. 95–108.

Tuan, Yi-Fu (1977) *Space and Place: The Perspective of Experience.* Minneapolis: University of Minnesota Press.

Unwin, T. (1992) *The Place of Geography.* Harlow: Longman.

Urry, J. (1995) *Consuming Place.* London: Routledge.

Wilson, A.G. (2000) *Complex Spatial Systems: The Modelling Foundations of Urban and Regional Analysis.* Harlow: Pearson.

Yeung, H. (2002) 'Deciphering citations', *Environment and Planning A,* 34: 2093–106.

Phil Hubbard and Rob Kitchin

1 Benedict Anderson

BIOGRAPHICAL DETAILS AND THEORETICAL CONTEXT

Author of one of the most important concepts in political geography, that of nations being 'imagined communities', Benedict Richard O'Gorman Anderson was born in Kunming, China in 1936. Brother of political theorist Perry Anderson and an Irish citizen whose father was an official with Imperial Maritime Customs, he grew up in California and Ireland before attending Cambridge University. Studying briefly under Eric Hobsbawm, Anderson graduated with a First Class degree in Classics in 1957. He moved to Cornell University in 1958 to pursue PhD research on Indonesia where he was influenced by George Kahin, John Echols and Claire Holt (Anderson, 1998; 1999). In 1965 Indonesia's military leader Suharto foiled an alleged coup attempt by communist soldiers, purged the army, and massacred civilians. Working with two other graduate students, Anderson analysed Suharto's version of events, questioning their veracity. Their assessment reached the Indonesian military who in 1967 and 1968 invited Anderson to the country to persuade him of the errors in this monograph, then known as the 'Cornell Paper'. Failing to be convinced, Anderson was denounced by the Indonesian regime.

Following formal publication of the allegations (Anderson et al., 1971), Indonesian authorities barred Anderson from Indonesia for what became the duration of Suharto's regime (though Anderson returned to Indonesia in 1999 following the dictator's death).

Anderson completed his PhD, *The Pemuda Revolution: Indonesian Politics, 1945–46* in 1967 and taught in the Department of Government at Cornell University until retirement in 2002. Editor of the interdisciplinary journal *Indonesia* between 1966 and 1984, Anderson studied topics as diverse as Indonesia's government, politics and international relations (e.g., 1964), human rights (e.g., 1976) and role in East Timor (e.g., 1980). An expert on South East Asia, military conflicts between Cambodia, Vietnam and China in the late-1970s stimulated Anderson to analyse the importance of, and political attraction to, nationalist politics. The result was *Imagined Communities – Reflections on the Origin and Spread of Nationalism* (1983; 1991; 2006).

In this work, Anderson maintained that major theoretical approaches had largely ignored nationalism, merely accepting it as the way things are:

> Nation, nationality, nationalism – all have proved notoriously difficult to define, let alone analyse. In contrast to the immense influence that nationalism has exerted on the modern world, plausible theory about it is conspicuously meager. (Anderson, 2006: 3)

Particularly culpable in this respect was Marxism, the relationship between it and nationalism being the subject of debate in *New Left Review* in the 1970s (e.g., Nairn, 1975; Löwy, 1976; Debray, 1977; see Anderson, 2006: 208–9). In this climate, Anderson (2006: 3; original emphasis) argued Marxist thought had not ignored nationalism but that 'nationalism has proved an uncomfortable *anomaly* for Marxist theory and, precisely for that reason, has been largely elided, rather than confronted'. *Imagined Communities* was an effort to reconcile theories of Marxism and nationalism, and counter what Anderson envisaged as a skewed context for the assessment of nationalism, namely an almost wholly European focus, to the detriment of understanding the colonial antecedents of modern nationalist politics. Drawing on case studies of colonialism in Latin America and Indonesia, Anderson (2006: 5–6) proposed 'the following definition of the nation: it is an imagined political community – and imagined as both inherently limited and sovereign'.

SPATIAL CONTRIBUTIONS

Anderson's concept of nations being 'imagined communities' has become standard within books reviewing geographical thought (e.g., Crang, 1998; Cloke et al., 2001; Anderson et al., 2003; Oakes and Price, 2008). The contention that a nation is 'imagined' does not mean that a nation is false, unreal or to be distinguished from true (unimagined) communities. Rather Anderson is proposing that a nation is constructed from popular processes through which residents share nationality in common:

> It is *imagined* because the members of even the smallest nation will never know most of their fellow-members, meet them, or even hear of them, yet in the minds of each lives the image of their communion.

(Anderson, 2006: 6; original emphasis)

This understanding both shapes and is shaped by political and cultural institutions as people 'imagine' they share general beliefs, attitudes and recognise a collective national populace as having similar opinions and sentiments to their own. Secondly:

> The nation is imagined as *limited* because even the largest of them, encompassing perhaps a billion living human beings, has finite, if elastic, boundaries, beyond which lie other nations.

(Anderson, 2006: 7; original emphasis)

To have one nation means there must be another nation against which self-definition can be constructed. Anderson is thus arguing for the social construction of nations as political entities that have a limited spatial and demographic extent, rather than organic, eternal entities. Further:

> It is imagined as *sovereign* because the concept was born in an age in which Enlightenment and Revolution were destroying the legitimacy of the divinely-ordained, hierarchical dynastic realm ... nations dream of being free ... The gage and emblem of this freedom is the sovereign state.

(Anderson, 2006: 7; original emphasis)

Anderson argues that the concept of the nation emerged in the late-eighteenth century as a societal structure to replace previous monarchical or religious orders. In this manner, a nation was a new way of conceptualising state sovereignty and rule. This rule would be limited to a defined population and territory over which the state, in the name of nationality, could exercise power:

Finally, it is imagined as a *community*, because, regardless of the actual inequality and exploitation that may prevail in each, the nation is always conceived as a deep, horizontal comradeship. Ultimately it is this fraternity that makes it possible, over the past two centuries, for so many millions of people, not so much to kill, as willingly to die for such limited imaginings.

(Anderson, 2006: 7; original emphasis)

Nations hold such power over imaginations, claims Anderson, that patriotic calls to arms are understood as the duty of all national residents. Further, in war, national citizens are equal and class boundaries are eroded in the communal struggle for national survival and greatness.

Anderson's second key aspect of the development of nationalism is what he identifies as the role of 'creole pioneers'. In both North and South America, those who fought for national independence in the eighteenth and nineteenth centuries had the same ancestries, languages and traditions as the colonising powers they opposed. Anderson (2006: 47) argues these 'creole pioneers' developed nationalist politics *before* Europe, because colonies were largely self-administrating territorial units. Thus, residents conceived of their belonging to a common and potentially sovereign community, a sentiment enhanced by provincial newspapers raising debate about intercontinental political and administrative relationships. Anderson stakes much of his thesis on 'print-capitalism'; novels and newspapers, he claims, 'made it possible for rapidly growing numbers of people to think about themselves, and to relate themselves to others, in profoundly new ways' (Anderson, 2006: 36). In addition, standardised national calendars, language and clocks generated a sense of simultaneous national experiences and national difference from elsewhere. Disparate occurrences thus became bound

together as *national* experiences as people felt that all national residents were reading the same publications. Thus, 'the convergence of capitalism and print technology ... created the possibility of a new form of imagined community, which in its basic morphology set the stage for the modern nation' (Anderson, 2006: 46).

The worldwide impact of *Imagined Communities* across academic disciplines led to revised editions in 1991 and 2006. In the enlarged 1991 edition Anderson noted that he had '[become] uneasily aware that what I had believed to be a significantly new contribution to thinking about nationalism – changing apprehensions of time – patently lacked its necessary coordinate: changing apprehensions of space' (2006: xiii–xiv). Utilising South East Asian examples, Anderson corrected this omission by including chapters addressing the construction of national memories and the roles of national census, museums, biographies and maps. Drawing on a 1988 PhD dissertation by Thongchai Winichakul about nineteenth-century Siam/Thailand (published as Winichakul, 1994), Anderson (2006: xiv) argued that maps contribute to the 'logoization of political space' and their myriad reproductions familiarise people with the limitations of national sovereignty and community.

Having examined mass communication with his thesis of print-capitalism, Anderson subsequently turned to the legacy of migration:

The two most significant factors generating nationalism and ethnicity are both linked closely to the rise of capitalism. They can be described summarily as mass communications and mass migrations.

(Anderson, 1992: 7)

Maintaining that nationalist movements were/are often initiated by expatriates, noting again the 'creole pioneers' of Latin

America and financial contributions to the Irish Republican Army and ethno-nationalist factions in the Balkan Wars of the early 1990s from overseas, Anderson assesses:

> It may well be that we are faced here with a new type of nationalist: the 'long-distance nationalist' one might perhaps call him (fn. "Him" because this type of politics seems to attract males more than females). For while technically a citizen of the state in which he comfortably lives, but to which he may feel little attachment, he finds it tempting to play identity politics by participating (via propaganda, money, weapons, any way but voting) in the conflicts of his imagined *Heimat* – now only fax-time away.

> (Anderson, 1992: 13)

Thus nationalism exists in an 'undivorcible marriage to internationalism' (Anderson, 2006: 207). Drawing primarily on anti-colonial nationalisms in South East Asia, Anderson's (1998; 2005) work demonstrates that, since the nineteenth century, political activists have engaged in multilingual global debates about the possibilities of nationalist revolution. Often expatriates, these individuals imagined their putative national communities by, amongst other things, writing novels and anthropological treatises that articulated the belief that indigenous peoples, often understood by colonial powers to be divided by tribal and ethnic difference, comprised a nation with common roots, traditions and aspirations.

Translated into dozens of languages and arguably the most regularly cited scholar on the topic of nationalism, Anderson has appeared on television, addressed committees of the United Nations and US Congress regarding Indonesia and East Timor, and raised questions about human rights abuses in South East Asia (e.g., Anderson, 1976; 1980; see also 1998: 20–2). One of the most influential scholars of his generation, although not a geographer by training or career, issues of space, territory and place, critical to nationalist politics, have led to Anderson's work being widely utilised within geographical research.

KEY ADVANCES AND CONTROVERSIES

Imagined Communities received little attention from geographers upon its publication. Largely without review in major geography journals, Anderson's concepts entered geographical debate through their impact on interdisciplinary studies of nationalism. Indeed, Spencer and Wollman (2002: 37) claim that such is the regularity with which articles about nationalism routinely cite *Imagined Communities* that Anderson's conceptualisation 'has become one of the commonest clichés of the literature' the result being that 'invocation has, in some cases, been a substitute for analysis'. Geographers have not been immune to this (see, *inter alia*, **Jackson** and Penrose, 1993; Smith and Jackson, 1999) and prolonged geographical assessments of Anderson's contentions are few: Blaut (1987), for example, does not assess Anderson's work in his review of Marxist theories of nationalism and Short's (1991: 226) *Imagined Country* simply proposes Anderson's *Imagined Communities* as additional reading. Some geographers, however, explicitly built upon Anderson's contentions: Sidaway (2002), for example, offering an exploration of 'imagined regional communities'. Arguably the most sustained geographical utilisation of Anderson's concept is

Radcliffe and Westwood's (1996: 2) study of how a national imagined community is 'generated, sustained and fractured' in Ecuador. They maintain that Anderson's 'geographical imagination ... permits him to link themes of space, mobility and the nation', but comment that he fails to fully acknowledge or develop the implications of this within his work (Radcliffe and Westwood, 1996: 118). Other geographers extend Anderson's initial thesis to understand imagined *and material* communities of nations and nationalisms. Angela Martin (1997: 90) maintains that although 'intellectuals have been given the power to "imagine" the nation or national community, ... the material dimension, or political economy, of nationalism and the nation have been ignored.' Her assessment of late-nineteenth century Irish nationalism argues for a 'corporeal approach to the nation' to interrogate how gender roles were constructed both in the Irish national imagination and how they restricted behaviour in everyday life (Martin, 1997: 91). Studying the construction of a Swiss heritage community in New Glarus, Wisconsin, Steven Hoeschler (1999: 538) invokes Anderson to explain that specific 'forms of imagining' are utilised by elites to produce place and community identities. These local 'imagined communities' are, Hoeschler demonstrates, often contested by non-elite groups.

The strongest challenges to Anderson's arguments come from post-colonial scholars. Drawing a contrast with Anderson's spatially bounded explorations of nations, **Stuart Hall** (2008: 273) offers a fluid understanding of 'diaspora' as 'an alternative framework for thinking about "imagined communities"' which recognises that many individuals feel allegiances to numerous locations and connections with people who are dispersed globally, not solely nationally. **Edward Said** (1993), in turn, contends that Anderson is too linear

in claiming that political structures and institutions change from dynasties to sovereign nations through the standardising influence of print-capitalism. Scholars of Latin America, although applauding the 'imagined communities' concept, have contended that Anderson's analyses of proto-nationalist creole pioneers and colonial newspapers assume too much homogeneity across the region. Castro-Klarén (2003: 163), for example, suggests the diversity of Latin American nationalisms necessitates 'more complex explanations' than Anderson offers. As historians reassess the chronology of nation formation that Anderson proposes, the assertions made in *Imagined Communities* appear to be, for Guerra (2003: 4, 5), at best 'problematical', and in some instances, 'false'. Such errors in the Latin American case studies do not weaken the utility of the 'imagined communities' theory, and may be partly due, maintains Chasteen (2003: xviii), to Anderson's reliance on a small number of 'egregiously outdated' sources about Latin America.

Arguably, Anderson's most vocal critic has been Partha Chatterjee (1993) who contends that the imagination of political communities has been limited by European colonialism. In imposing specifically nationalist institutional forms on their colonies, upon independence these areas had no option but to follow European paths, with Western powers ready to prevent any seemingly dangerous deviations. 'Even our imaginations', asserts Chatterjee (1993: 5) 'must remain forever colonized.' Nationalism and nations, Chatterjee maintains, operate only within limits formulated in Europe, thus can only be conceptualised within these European strictures. Anti-colonial nationalisms thus typically opposed colonialism using the same nationalist arguments as the colonists. Distinction could not be made through political or economic conceptualisation due to the European dominance of these realms and thus the limited sovereignty and territory of the colony was already imagined for the colonised by the colonisers. Consequently, anti-colonial nationalism could only be imagined through cultural processes and practices. Echoing other critics, Chatterjee challenges that although the processes of print-capitalism were important, Anderson's formulation of them as standardising language, time and territorial extent is too simplistic to impose on the diverse, multilingual and asymmetrical power relations of the colonial situation.

A second major critique of *Imagined Communities* comes from a feminist perspective. With a focus on the 'fraternity' experienced by members of a nation (Anderson, 2006: 7), the protagonists in Anderson's conceptions of nationalism are typically assumed to be male. Mayer (2000: 6) argues that Anderson envisions 'a hetero-male project ... imagined as a brotherhood', eliding gender, class and racial structures within and between national communities and **McDowell** (1999: 195) demonstrates that although seemingly neutral, 'the very term horizontal comradeship ... brings with it connotations of masculine solidarity.' Subsequently, McClintock (1995: 353) laments that sustained 'explorations of the gendering of the national imagination have been conspicuously paltry.'

A third challenge comes from Don Mitchell who argues that as well as *imagining* communities, there must be attention to:

> The *practices* and exercises of power through which these bonds are produced and reproduced. The questions this raises are ones about who defines the nation, how it is defined, how that definition is reproduced and contested, and, crucially, how the nation has developed and changed over time... The question is not what common imagination *exists*, but what common imagination is *forged*.

(Mitchell, 2000: 269; original emphasis)

Anderson's proposal, therefore, is constrained by its narrowness. What does it matter that a nation is an imagined community? The issue must be to show the work needed to produce and maintain that imagination, how this impacts on people's lives, and how power to enforce the national community that is imagined shapes behaviours across time and space. Anderson's latter work moves in these directions. He notes constructions of gender and sexuality in the nationalist imagination and describes how Filipino nationalist imaginings were internationally produced, promoted, opposed and challenged – with often deadly consequences – by individuals in the nineteenth-century Filipino diaspora (Anderson, 1998; 2005). There is hence much to commend in the concept of imagined communities, although there remains a need to explore power relations inherent in the processes Anderson describes to elucidate their material impacts, be these founded on gender, racial, ethnic, class, sexual or other aspects of individual identity.

ANDERSON'S KEY WORKS

Anderson, B., McVey, R. T. and Bunnell, F. P. (1971) *A Preliminary Analysis of the October 1, 1965 Coup in Indonesia*. Ithaca: Cornell Modern Indonesia Project, Publication No. 52.

Anderson, B. (1972) *Java in a Time of Revolution: Occupation and Resistance, 1944–1946*. Ithaca: Cornell University Press.

Anderson, B. (1983) *Imagined Communities: Reflections on the Origin and Spread of Nationalism*. London: Verso.

Anderson, B. (1990) *Language and Power: Exploring Political Cultures in Indonesia*. Ithaca: Cornell University Press.

Anderson, B. (1991) *Imagined Communities: Reflections on the Origin and Spread of Nationalism* (revised and enlarged edition). London: Verso.
Anderson, B. (1998) *The Spectre of Comparisons: Nationalism, Southeast Asia and The World.* London: Verso.
Anderson, B. (2005*)* *Under Three Flags: Anarchism and the Anti-Colonial Imagination.* London: Verso.
Anderson, B. (2006) *Imagined Communities: Reflections on the Origin and Spread of Nationalism* (revised edition). London: Verso.

Secondary Sources and References

Anderson, B. (1964) 'Indonesia and Malaysia', *New Left Review*, 28: 4–32.
Anderson, B. (1967) '*The Pemuda Revolution: Indonesian Politics, 1945–1946*'. Unpublished PhD dissertation, Ithaca, Cornell University.
Anderson, B. (1976) 'Prepared testimony on human rights in Indonesia,' in *Human Rights in Indonesia and the Philippines.* Washington, DC: US Government Printing Office. pp. 72–80.
Anderson, B. (1980) 'Prepared testimony on human rights in Indonesia and East Timor,' in *Human Rights in Asia: Noncommunist Countries.* Washington, DC: US Government Printing Office. pp. 231–62 and 275–7.
Anderson, B. (1992) 'The new world disorder,' *New Left Review*, 193: 3–13.
Anderson, B. (1999) 'The spectre of comparisons', *Cornell University College of Arts and Sciences Newsletter*, 20 (2) online: www.arts.cornell.edu/newsletr/spring99/spectre.htm (accessed 2 October 2002).
Anderson, K., Domosh, M., Thrift, N. and Pile, S. (eds) (2003) *The Handbook of Cultural Geography.* London and Thousand Oaks: Sage.
Blaut, J. M. (1987) *The National Question: Decolonising the Theory of Nationalism.* London: Zed Books.
Castro-Klarén, S. (2003) 'The nation in ruins: archaeology and the rise of the nation', in S. Castro-Klarén and J. C. Chasteen (eds) *Beyond Imagined Communities: Reading and Writing the Nation in Nineteenth-century Latin America.* Baltimore: Johns Hopkins University Press. pp. 161–95.
Chasteen, J. C. (2003) 'Introduction', in S. Castro-Klarén and J. C. Chasteen (eds), *Beyond Imagined Communities: Reading and Writing the Nation in Nineteenth-century Latin America.* Baltimore: Johns Hopkins University Press. pp. ix–xxv.
Chatterjee, P. (1993) *The Nation and its Fragments: Colonial and Postcolonial Histories.* Princeton: Princeton University Press.
Cloke, P., Crang, P. and Goodwin, M. (eds) (2001) *Introducing Human Geographies.* London: Arnold.
Crang, M. (1998) *Cultural Geography.* London: Routledge.
Debray, R. (1977) 'Marxism and the national question', *New Left Review*, 105: 25–41.
Guerra, F–X. (2003) 'Forms of communication, political spaces, and cultural identities in the creation of Spanish American nations', in S. Castro-Klarén and J. C. Chasteen (eds) *Beyond Imagined Communities: Reading and Writing the Nation in Nineteenth-century Latin America.* Baltimore: Johns Hopkins University Press. pp. 3–32.
Hall, S. (2008 [1995]) 'New cultures for old', in T. S. Oakes and P. L. Price (eds), *The Cultural Geography Reader.* London and New York: Routledge. pp. 264–74.
Hoelscher, S. (1999) 'From sedition to patriotism: performance, place, and the reinterpretation of American ethnic identity', *Journal of Historical Geography*, 25 (4): 534–58.
Jackson, P. and Penrose, J. (1993) 'Introduction: placing "race" and nation', in P. Jackson and J. Penrose (eds), *Constructions of Race, Place and Nation.* Minneapolis: University of Minnesota Press. pp. 1–23.
Löwy, M. (1976) 'Marxists and the national question', *New Left Review*, 96: 81–100.
Martin, A. K. (1997) 'The practice of identity and an Irish sense of place', *Gender, Place and Culture*, 4: 89–113.
Mayer, T. (2000) 'Gender ironies of nationalism: setting the stage', in T. Mayer (ed.), *Gender Ironies of Nationalism: Sexing The Nation.* London: Routledge. pp. 1–22.
McClintock, A. (1995) *Imperial Leather: Race, Gender and Sexuality in the Colonial Contest.* London: Routledge.
McDowell, L. (1999) *Gender, Identity and Place: Introducing Feminist Geographies.* Minneapolis: University of Minnesota Press.
Mitchell, D. (2000) *Cultural Geography: A Critical Introduction.* Oxford: Blackwell.
Nairn, T. (1975) 'The modern Janus', *New Left Review*, 94: 3–29.
Oakes, T. S. and Price, P.L. (eds) (2008) *The Cultural Geography Reader.* London and New York: Routledge.
Radcliffe, S. and Westwood, S. (1996) *Remaking the Nation: Place, Identity and Politics in Latin America.* London: Routledge.
Said, E. W. (1993) *Culture and Imperialism.* New York: Vintage.

Short, J. R. (1991) *Imagined Country: Society, Culture and Environment.* London: Routledge.

Sidaway, J. D. (2002) *Imagined Regional Communities: Integration and Sovereignty in the Global South.* London and New York: Routledge.

Smith, G. and Jackson, P. (1999) 'Narrating the nation – the "imagined community" of Ukranians in Bradford', *Journal of Historical Geography*, 25 (3): 367–87.

Spencer, P. and Wollman, H. (2002) *Nationalism: A Critical Introduction.* Sage: London.

Winichakul, T. (1994) *Siam Mapped: A History of the Geo-Body of a Nation.* Honolulu: University of Hawaii Press.

Euan Hague, DePaul University

2   Marc Augé

Marc Augé was born in Poitiers in west central France in 1935. He attended the prestigious Lycée Louis-Le-Grand in Paris, before studying literature at the École Normale Supérieure (1957–1961). After obtaining his Agrégation des Lettres Classiques and undertaking a year of military service in Algeria (1961–62), Augé pursued his interest in anthropology and ethnology, working for the Office de la Recherche Scientifique et Technique Outre-Mer, Paris (ORSTOM, now L'Institut de Recherche pour le Développement) until 1970, and gaining his doctorat de troisième cycle from the École Pratique des Hautes Études in Paris in 1967. He subsequently received his thèse d'état from the Sorbonne (University of Paris V) in 1973, where he was supervised by the influential Africanist sociologist and founder of the Centre d'Études Africaines, Georges Balandier. Augé emerged as one of France's most prominent Africanists in the late 1960s and 1970s, and since the mid-1980s he has gained international renown as an anthropologist of the contemporary West and for his ethnologies of everyday practices, spaces and 'non-places'. Augé became a Professor at the École des Hautes Études en Sciences Sociales (EHESS) in 1970, where he later served as President (1985–1995), and Director of the Centre d'Anthropologie des Mondes Contemporains.

Between the mid-1960s and mid-1980s Augé undertook extensive anthropological fieldwork in the West African former French colonies of Ivory Coast and Togo. Drawing upon prevailing anthropological theories and methods shaped by the structuralist and Marxist writings of Claude Lévi-Strauss, Marcel Mauss, Emile Durkheim, Cornelius Castoriadis and Louis Althusser, Augé focused his attention on the Alladian peoples of the lagoon region in Ivory Coast, west of Abidjan. An initial eighteen-month visit resulted in his doctorat de troisième cycle (1967) and his first book, Le Rivage Alladian (1969), in which he examined the history of the Alladian region, the spatial organisation of Alladian family, village and economic life, local spirituality, and Alladian mediations of white Western cultural practices. A second book Théorie des Pouvoirs et Idéologie (1975), which originated as his thèse d'état (1973), provided a structural-Marxist analysis of the ideological networks of power in Alladian, Avikam and Ebrié lagoon societies; tracing these through traditional understandings of the family, village, religion, witchcraft, and sickness, and analysing shifts in these understandings under the influence of colonial and post-colonial cultural and religious forces. A third study, *Pouvoirs de Vie, Pouvoirs de Mort* (1977), explored attitudes to life, death and spirituality in Bregbo, the village of the renowned Ebrié Christian prophet-healer Albert Atcho (b.1903). These studies marked Augé out as a leading anthropologist of health and spirituality, and he went on to develop these themes in subsequent studies in the early 1980s (Augé, 1985b; Augé and Herzlich, 1995).

In the mid-1970s, Augé contributed to the interdisciplinary journal *Traverses*, which published work on everyday spatial practices and whose editorial board included **Jean Baudrillard**, **Michel de Certeau** and **Paul Virilio** (Andermatt Conley, 2001). Following this, he began to pay increasing attention to social and cultural life in the contemporary West, authoring a series of 'self-ethnologies' that emerged amidst a broader movement towards 'proximate ethnographies' or 'anthropologies of the near' (Augé, 1995; Sheringham, 2006). In *Génie du Paganisme* (1982b) Augé analysed the pagan spiritualities present in both Ivorian and European cultures, but it was in *La Traversée du Luxembourg* (1985a) that he first adopted the part-autobiographical, part-fictional, essayistic anthropological approach that was to serve as the template for many of his subsequent studies of the everyday spaces and cultural practices of the contemporary West, particularly contemporary France and Paris.

In *La Traversée du Luxembourg*, subtitled an 'ethno-novel of a French day', Augé provides a 'critical autobiography' (Conley, 2002b: 74) of his travels through Paris on 20th July 1984; from waking up to the news on the radio and his walk across the Jardins du Luxembourg to his doctor's surgery, to his thoughts on future lectures, current research, and speculations on the anthropology of life in the

Paris métro (the underground railway) (Augé, 1985a). This was followed, a year later, by his important book-length essay *Un Ethnologue dans le Métro* (1986; translated as *In the Metro*, 2002a), in which Augé examined the embodied techniques, practices, solitudes, rituals and itineraries of the métro traveller in this 'strange public place' (2002a: 29), as well as meditating on the function of the métro map and the history of station names. A third book on modern France, *Domaines et Châteaux* (1989), examines how upmarket glossy magazines present images of country properties and rural living to wealthy urbanites.

Augé most fully articulated the conceptual basis for undertaking anthropologies of contemporary Western spaces, practices and cultures in what is probably his most widely read and acclaimed book, *Non-Lieux* (1992; translated as *Non-Places: Introduction to an Anthropology of Supermodernity*, 1995). Here, Augé provides a largely theoretical discussion of the changing characteristics of space, time, individuality and place in an excessively modern or 'supermodern' world that is characterised by 'an excess of simultaneous events ... acceleration of history ... the shrinking of the planet ... excess individualism' and a proliferation of non-places (1998a: 104). While a predominantly conceptual book, *Non-Lieux* opens with a fictional (or perhaps autobiographical) account of a journey to Charles de Gaulle airport through the non-places of suburban Paris, and he went on to develop this fictional, ethnological approach in subsequent anthropological monographs (Augé, 1999a, 2000a) as well as his first novel *La Mère d'Arthur* (Augé, 2005; see O'Beirne, 2006a, 2006b).

In a number of recent books Augé has addressed themes of temporality and memory. He has argued that 'oblivion' is as necessary as 'memory' in contemporary culture (Augé, 2004a), and he has explored the impact of film on collective and personal memories, discussing the impact of the American romantic drama *Casablanca* (1942) on his recollections of war-time and post-war France (Augé, 2009b). Over the past decade or so Augé has authored books on a vast array of subjects, including tourism and tourism imagery (1997), mobility, borders and globalisation (1999a, 2009a), globalisation and 9/11 (2002b), cycling (2008b), the death of the future (2008a), and questions surrounding the meaning of life (2003b), as well as contributing notable essays to edited collections on the death of Princess Diana (Augé et al., 1998) and human cloning (Atlan et al., 1999). Nevertheless, he has not limited his output to traditional academic publications. In addition to authoring a novel, Augé has collaborated with filmmakers, photographers and artists. This includes eight films and two books with his anthropologist colleague Paul Colleyn (Augé and Colleyn, 1990, 2006; *L'Homme*, 2008: 446-7), and four collaborative books on the spaces and landscapes of Paris: one on Parisian gardens with photographer Claire de Virieu (Augé and de Virieu, 2008); a book of photographs of 1930s Paris from the Roger-Viollet photographic archives (Augé, 1996a); and two books on the hidden gardens and spaces of Paris with distinguished photographer Jean Mounicq (Augé and Mounicq, 1995; Mounicq and Augé, 1992). His other 'art' books include: one with Jean Mounicq on Venice (Mounicq and Augé, 1998); a book on the prominent Icelandic modern artist and Paris resident Erró (Augé, 1994b); a book on the French architects Denis Valode and Jean Pistre (Augé 1998b); and a book on airports and the experiences of the frequent flyer with Italian photographer, business executive and frequent

flyer Francesco Cianciotta (Augé and Cianciotta, 2009). Augé's books have been translated into at least 15 different languages.

SPATIAL CONTRIBUTIONS

Africa helps us think space.

(Augé, 1994a: 86)

In his African anthropologies, Augé revealed the spatial organisation of Alladian societies, tracing the 'therapeutic itineraries' or journeys to sites of cure undertaken by the sick, examining how social order was reflected in 'rules of residence' and the spaces of village life, and revealing how 'the prophet-medicine man organises a space which is specific to him', a 'place apart' (2004b: 539–40). As he later reflected:

> Africa taught me several lessons which took the form of genuine theories: a theory of space, a theory of the person, a theory of the event and a theory of mediation.
>
> (Augé, 2004b: 537)

It is, however, in his later studies of contemporary France – his 'anthropologies of the near' – that his spatial imagination and attention to spatial practices is most evident. *La Traversée du Luxembourg* (1985a) and *Un Ethnologue dans le Métro* (1986; English 2002a) provide part-autobiographical, part-fictional, reflexive ethnologies of an anthropologist's journeys through contemporary Paris; focusing attention on everyday spaces, events, practices and ruses in a manner familiar to readers of **Michel de Certeau**, **Henri Lefebvre**,

Roland Barthes and Georges Perec (Sheringham, 2006). Augé addresses a wide range of anthropological and 'sociological questions in "spatial" terms' (1996b: 175), and it was in *Non-Lieux* (1992; *Non-Places*, 1995) that he most systematically outlined these conceptual dimensions to his approach to space, place and non-place.

In *Non-Places* Augé (1995) characterises place or 'anthropological place' as localised, occupied, familiar, organic, historical and meaningful to its occupants and visitors, 'a space where identities, relationships and a story can be made out' (2000b: 8). The archetypal 'anthropological place' would be a historic village or town which is distinctive and easily 'read', a place of continuous dwelling with a clear sense of history. Place, here, is associated with prolonged fixities and practices of dwelling; echoing humanistic ideas and those associated with Martin Heidegger, as well as popular constructions of local place as always under threat from external global forces. Augé suggests that place is undergoing a transformation in an increasingly 'supermodern' Western world characterised by a speed-up of communications, an excess of images and simultaneous events, an 'excess of individualism' and a 'shrinking of the planet' (1998a: 104); excesses which are mediatised, concretised or experienced in what he terms *non-lieux* or non-places:

> the spaces of circulation, communication and consumption, where solitudes coexist without creating any social bond or even a social emotion.
>
> (Augé, 1996b: 178)

Individual users are passified, fabricated by signs, texts and interfaces, becoming 'merely a gaze' (Augé, 1998a: 103). These users are solitary individuals, temporarily dwelling in archetypal non-places such as motorways, airports, shopping centres, hotels, theme parks or cyberspace. In utilising the concept of non-place Augé was deliberately playing with the French legal term *non-lieu*: the court judgement that denies the proceedings, where there is no evidence of implication, no place to judge (Bosteels, 2003; O'Beirne, 2006a). In *non-lieu* there is a denial of the event, of the space. Non-place is a 'space completely emptied out of eventfulness' (Bosteels, 2003: 136).

KEY ADVANCES AND CONTROVERSIES

Augé's arguments about the proliferation of non-places in the contemporary West have had a significant impact across the social sciences and humanities, regularly surfacing in anthropology, geography, urban studies, sociology, cultural studies, architectural theory, contemporary philosophy, and literary studies. In one sense, his writings echo Edward Relph's (1976) earlier writings on the proliferation of agents of 'placelessness' in the West, and, before that, Melvin Webber's (1964) focus on the significance of interaction and process rather than localised and fixed places in the emergence of stretched out communities in 'the non-place urban realm'. However, Augé is neither as directly critical or judgemental of placelessness as Relph, nor a distanced and dispassionate observer like Webber. Augé recognises that the ubiquitous familiarity of non-places is comforting to many users and consumers (O'Beirne, 2006a), and he provides an effective and powerful description of the feelings of distraction and indifference which some, perhaps many, travellers and consumers appear to experience in such spaces.

Academic engagements with Augé's writings on non-places have tended to either affirm his observations on the proliferation of non-places in the contemporary West, or criticise him for neglecting the myriad ways in which individuals consume and inhabit sites such as motorways and airports *as places*. This is partly due to the style of *Non-Places* (1995), which reads more like a theoretical anthropology of the contemporary West, than as the kind of context-specific, part-autobiographical, part-fictional ethnology that he deployed in earlier and later studies (e.g. Augé, 1985a, 2000a, 2002a). Indeed, Augé clearly states that non-place 'never exists in pure form':

> places reconstitute themselves in it; relations are restored and resumed in it; ... Place and non-place are rather like opposed polarities: the first is never completely erased, the second never totally completed; they are like palimpsests on which the scrambled game of identity and relations is ceaselessly rewritten.
>
> (Augé, 1995: 78–9)

Place and non-place are relational, contingent and in process, but it was only in later writings that he was to more strongly assert that airports, motorways and other spaces are often simultaneously experienced as both places and non-places (Augé, 1996b, 1998a, 1999b), while he was to most fully develop his fictional (perhaps semi-autobiographical) exposition of non-places in his novel *La Mère d'Arthur* (Augé, 2005; O'Beirne 2006b). Nevertheless, Augé has justifiably been criticised for not adequately explaining the relationship between the objective and subjective, social and material, quantifiable and qualitative dimensions of places and non-places (Merriman, 2004). Augé variously describes non-places as 'empirically

measurable' (1995: 115) 'physical spaces' *and* as reflecting individual experiences and perceptions of such spaces, but he fails to adequately resolve this tension (Merriman, 2004; O'Beirne, 2006a).

Other criticisms relate to his theoretical approach to place and his use of the term non-place. Augé has been criticised for constructing 'anthropological place' as rooted, organic and static, and for unnecessarily coining a new kind of space – the rather negative and polarised 'non-place' – to account for feelings of boredom, solitariness and detachment which some travellers may experience in spaces of consumption and mobility (Merriman, 2007). Augé's arguments appear in contrast to geographers such as **Doreen Massey** and **Nigel Thrift** who account for movement, globalisation and transient relations by utilising more relational, open, dynamic and inclusive conceptions of place (Massey, 1991; Thrift, 1999). What is more, feelings of solitariness and detachment are evidently not limited to archetypal non-places; they can emerge in any space, e.g. at home or at work. Augé has been criticised for his characterisation of sociality and solitariness as functions of face-to-face human interaction, neglecting the processes and materialities that facilitate the movements of travellers and consumers, the heterogeneity of the social relations he is studying, and 'the ways in which virtual or highly mediated social relations... [can] construct a familiar sociality' (Frow, 1997: 77). As **Bruno Latour** remarked of *Un Ethnologue dans le Métro*, Augé 'limited himself to studying the most superficial aspects of the metro', whereas 'a symmetrical Marc Augé would have studied the sociotechnological network of the metro itself ... simply doing at home what he had always done elsewhere' (Latour, 1993: 100–1).

Augé's descriptions of the excesses of supermodernity in the late twentieth century echo the arguments of scholars such as **David Harvey**, Fredric Jameson, **Manuel Castells** and **Anthony Giddens** surrounding the processes of speeding-up, shrinkage, disembedding, and globalisation in an era of advanced/late capitalism, late/high modernity or postmodernity. Like these scholars, Augé at times overstates the novelty of the processes and registers he is discussing, for his observations on the detachment, boredom and illegibility of travelling could just as easily be applied to nineteenth-century railway travel as to contemporary air or motorway travel (Thrift, 1995; Frow, 1997; Merriman, 2004). Finally, Augé's semi-autobiographical approach could be criticised for neglecting to discuss the privileged position and highly specific experiences he has as a relatively affluent, western, white, male anthropologist-traveller. Augé claims that he cannot rely on distance, difference and exoticism as he is 'like every other man' (1996b: 176), but not only does he overlook the differences of diverse users and travellers in these spaces, but this unprivileged position disappears once we learn that the anthropologist is able to interpret non-places which 'human beings do not recognise themselves in ...' (1996c: 82).

AUGÉ'S KEY WORKS

Augé, M. (1969) *Le Rivage Alladian: Organisation et Évolution des Villages Alladians*. Paris: Office de la Recherche Scientifique et Technique Outre-Mer.

Augé, M. (1975) *Théorie des Pouvoirs et Idéologie: Étude de Cas en Côte d'Ivoire*. Paris: Hermann.

Augé, M. (1977) *Pouvoirs de Vie, Pouvoirs de Mort: Introduction à une Anthropologie de la Répression*. Paris: Flammarion.

Augé, M. (1982a) *The Anthropological Circle: Symbol, Function, History*. Cambridge: Cambridge University Press [French 1979].

Augé, M. (1982b) *Génie du Paganisme*. Paris: Gallimard.

Augé, M. (1985a) *La Traversée du Luxembourg, Paris, 20 Juillet 1984: Ethno-Roman d'une Journée Française Considérée sous L'Angle des Moeurs, de la Théorie, et du Bonheur*. Paris: Hachette.

Augé, M. (1989) *Domaines et Châteaux*. Paris: Éditions du Seuil.

Augé, M. (1995) *Non-Places: Introduction to an Anthropology of Supermodernity*. London: Verso [French 1992].

Augé, M. (1998a) *A Sense for the Other*. Stanford, CA: Stanford University Press [French 1994].

Augé, M. (1999a) *The War of Dreams: Exercises in Ethno-Fiction*. London: Pluto Press [French 1997].

Augé, M. (1999b) *An Anthropology for Contemporaneous Worlds*. Stanford, CA: Stanford University Press [French 1994].

Augé, M. (2002a) *In the Metro*. Minneapolis, MN: University of Minnesota Press [French 1986, Revisited 2008].

Augé, M. (2004a) *Oblivion*. Minneapolis, MN: University of Minnesota Press [French 1998].

Augé, M. (2005) *La Mère d'Arthur*. Paris: Fayard.

Secondary Sources and References

Andermatt Conley, V. (2001) 'Processual practices', *The South Atlantic Quarterly*, 100 (2): 483–500.

Atlan, H., Augé, M., Delmas-Marty, M., Droit, R-P., Fresco, N. (1999) *Le Clonage Humain*. Paris: Éditions du Seuil.

Augé, M. (1967) *Organisation et Évolution des Villages Alladians*. Unpublished *doctorat de troisième cycle*, École Pratique des Hautes Études, Paris.

Augé, M. (1973) *La Vie en Double: Theorie des Pouvoirs et Ideologie du Pouvoir en Basse Côte D'Ivoire*. Unpublished *thèse d'état*, University of Paris V.

Augé, M. (ed.)(1985b) 'Interpreting illness (special issue)', *History and Anthropology*, 2(1): i–205.

Augé, M. (1988) *Le Dieu Objet*. Paris: Flammarion.

Augé, M. (1994a) 'Home made strange [interviewed by Jean-Pierre Criqui]', *Artforum*, 32 (10): 84–8/114/117.

Augé, M. (1994b) *Erró, Peintre Mythique*. Paris: Le Lit du Vent.

Augé, M. (1996a) *Paris Années 30: Roger-Viollet*. Paris: Hazan (Fernand) Éditions.

Augé, M. (1996b) 'Paris and the Ethnography of the Contemporary World', in M. Sheringham (ed.) *Parisian Fields*. London: Reaktion. pp. 175–81.

Augé, M. (1996c) 'About Non-Places', *Architectural Design*, 66 (121): 82–3.

Augé, M. (1997) *L'Impossible Voyage: Le Tourisme et ses Images*. Paris: Éditions Payot et Rivages.

Augé, M. (1998b) *Valode et Pistre*. Paris: Éditions du Regard.

Augé, M. (2000a) *Fictions Fin de Siècle, Suivi de Que se Passe-t-il ? (29 Février, 31 Mars, 30 Avril 2000)*. Paris: Fayard.

Augé, M. (2000b) 'Airports', 'Roundabouts', 'Yellow lines', in S. Pile and N. Thrift (eds), *City A-Z*. London: Routledge. pp. 8–9, 206–7, 297–8.

Augé, M. (2002b) *Journal de Guerre*. Paris: Galilée.

Augé, M. (2003a) *Le Temps en Ruines*. Paris: Galilée.

Augé, M. (2003b) *Pour Quoi Vivons-Nous?* Paris: Fayard.

Augé, M. (2004b) 'An itinerary', *Ethnos*, 69 (4): 534–51.

Augé, M. (2006) *Le Métier d'Anthropologue: Sens et Liberté*. Paris: Galilée.

Augé, M. (2008a) *Où est Passé l'Avenir?* Paris: Éditions du Panama.

Augé, M. (2008b) *Éloge de la Bicyclette*. Paris: Éditions Payot et Rivages.

Augé, M. (2009a) *Pour une Anthropologie de la Mobilité*. Paris: Éditions Payot et Rivages.

Augé, M. (2009b) *Casablanca: Movies and Memory*. Minneapolis, MN: University of Minnesota Press [French 2007].

Augé, M., Bougnoux, D., Debray, R., Gaillard, F., Morin, E. and Rushdie, S. (1998) *Diana Crash*. Paris: Descartes et Cie.

Augé, M. and Cianciotta, F. (2009) *A Journey Apart: Inside and Outside Airports*. Milan: Motta.

Augé, M. and Colleyn, J-P. (1990) *N'kpiti: La Rancune et le Prophète*. Paris: Éditions de L'EHESS.

Augé, M. and Colleyn, J-P. (2006) *The World of the Anthropologist*. Oxford: Berg [French 2004].

Augé, M. and Herzlich, C. (eds) (1995) *The Meaning of Illness: Anthropology, History and Sociology*. Luxembourg: Harwood Academic Publishers [French 1983].

Augé, M. and Mounicq, J. (1995) *Paris Ouvert*. Paris: Imprimerie Nationale.

Augé, M. and de Virieu, C. (2008) *Paris Jardins*. Paris: Actes Sud.

Bessis, R. (2004) *Dialogue avec Marc Augé Autour d'une Anthropologie de la Mondialisation*. Paris: L'Harmattan.

Bosteels, B. (2003) 'Nonplaces: an anecdoted topography of contemporary French theory', *Diacritics*, 33 (3/4): 117–39.

Conley, T. (2002a) 'Introduction: Marc Augé, "A Little History"', in M. Augé, *In the Metro*. Minneapolis, MN: University of Minnesota Press. pp. vii–xxii.

Conley, T. (2002b) 'Afterword: riding the subway with Marc Augé', in M. Augé, *In the Metro*. Minneapolis, MN: University of Minnesota Press. pp. 73–113.

Frow, J. (1997) *Time and Commodity Culture*. Oxford: Oxford University Press.

Latour, B. (1993) *We Have Never Been Modern*. Harlow: Prentice Hall.

L'Homme: Revue Française D'Anthropologie (2008) 'Special issue on Marc Augé and anthropologies of the present', 185–6: 7–447.

Massey, D. (1991) 'A global sense of place', *Marxism Today*, June: 24–9.

Merriman, P. (2004) 'Driving places: Marc Augé, non-places and the geographies of England's M1 motorway', *Theory, Culture, and Society*, 21 (4–5): 145–67.

Merriman, P. (2007) *Driving Spaces*. Oxford: Blackwell Publishing.

Mounicq, J. and Augé, M. (1992) *Paris Retraversé*. Paris: Imprimerie Nationale.

Mounicq, J. and Augé, M. (1998) *Venise d'Eau et de Pierre*. Paris: Imprimerie Nationale.

O'Beirne, E (2006a) 'Mapping the *non-lieu* in Marc Augé's writings', *Forum for Modern Language Studies*, 42 (1): 38–50.

O'Beirne, E (2006b) 'Navigating non-lieux in contemporary French fiction: Houellebecq, Darrieussecq, Echenoz, and Augé', *Modern Language Review*, 101 (2): 391–405.

Relph, E. (1976) *Place and Placelessness*. London: Pion.

Sheringham, M. (1995) 'Marc Augé and the Ethno-Analysis of Contemporary Life', *Paragraph*, 18 (2): 210–22.

Sheringham, M. (2006) *Everyday Life: Theories and Practices from Surrealism to the Present*. Oxford: Oxford University Press.

Thrift, N. (1995) 'A hyperactive world', in R. J. Johnston, P. J. Taylor and M. J. Watts (eds), *Geographies of Global Change*. Oxford: Blackwell. pp. 18–35.

Thrift, N. (1999) 'Steps to an ecology of place', in D. Massey, J. Allen and P. Sarre (eds), *Human Geography Today*. Cambridge: Polity Press. pp. 295–322.

Webber, M. (1964) 'The urban place and the nonplace urban realm', in M.M. Webber, J.W. Dyckman, D.L. Foley, A.Z. Guttenberg, W.L.C. Wheaton and C.B. Wurster (eds), *Explorations into Urban Structure*. Philadelphia: University of Pennsylvania Press, pp. 79–153.

Peter Merriman, Aberystwyth University

3   Trevor Barnes

BIOGRAPHICAL DETAILS AND THEORETICAL CONTEXT

Trevor Barnes was born in London, England in 1956. Having grown up in Cornwall, he studied Economics and Geography at University College London from 1975 to 1978. Barnes completed MA and PhD degrees in Geography at the University of Minnesota under the supervision of Eric Sheppard; and since 1983 has taught at the University of British Columbia in Vancouver, Canada. Barnes' work extends across theories of economic value; analytical political economy; flexibility and industrial restructuring; and, latterly, the 'theoretical histories' of Anglo-American economic geography. He also sought to make key statements on the position of economic geography at the end of the millennium through a number of important edited volumes (Barnes and Gertler, 1999; Barnes and Sheppard, 2000) as well as reviews of political economic approaches in the journal *Progress in Human Geography* (e.g., Barnes, 1998).

Although perhaps giving the appearance of a relatively divergent set of themes, there are strong threads running through Barnes' research and writing interests. He has long been captivated by the work of the economist Piero Sraffa, for example.

In Barnes' view, Sraffa's terse expositions on value in *Production of Commodities by Means of Commodities* (via a set of simultaneous production equations) usefully speak both to rigorous abstract theorists as well as scholars who are more interested in the contextual and the concrete (1996, chapter 7; 1989). Barnes views anti-essentialist accounts such as Sraffa's as a useful means of critiquing both classical Marxist accounts of the labour theory of value (which essentialise the role and nature of labour power) as well as neoclassical utility theory.

Together with Eric Sheppard (Sheppard and Barnes, 1990), Barnes has sought to ground political economy in space and place through the development of analytical approaches. Engaging with, but also developing a substantial critique of, analytical Marxism, such approaches use 'both mathematical reasoning and rigorous, formal statistical testing to determine logically how space and place make a difference both to the definition of social processes and to their relation to the economy' (Barnes and Sheppard, 2000: 5). Although cursory readings (particularly if solely focused upon the use of formal mathematical language) might discern in his analytical approaches a preference for the abstract over the concrete and contextual, Barnes would refute such a contention.

Barnes' engagement with debates surrounding flexible production has drawn upon research on the forestry industry in British Columbia conducted with Roger Hayter (Barnes and Hayter, 1992; Hayter and Barnes 1992). Whilst many accounts of flexibility through the 1980s and 1990s centred upon developments in 'new industrial spaces', Barnes and Hayter sought to extend conceputalisations of flexibility through a consideration of 'in situ' restructuring in the context of a marginal resource economy. The theoretical and the political are closely connected in Barnes' use of the work of Canadian economic historian Harold Innis to understand 'the dependency and disruptions' that have emerged in British Columbia (Barnes, 2001a: 4; see Barnes et al., 2001). Barnes' explicit concern has been to confront the profound devastation of lives and communities wrought by the decline of the forest products sector in British Columbia (Barnes, 2001a).

Over the course of his career, Barnes (1992; 1996; 2002a) has become increasingly interested in tracing the social and political connections that produced the spatial scientific narratives that came to dominate geography – and particularly economic geography – during the 1950s and 1960s. Drawing in part upon studies in the sociology of scientific knowledge (including the work of **Bruno Latour**), Barnes has been keen to read changes in the nature of Anglo-American economic geography as transformations in attitudes towards theory itself. For Barnes, the most significant aspect of geography's quantitative revolution was, ironically, not that it ushered in a set of new methodologies – in fact 'geography had been quantitative from the time of its formal institutionalisation as a discipline in the nineteenth century' (Barnes, 2001c: 552) – but rather that it involved a shift in theoretical sensibilities. This is not to say that the practices of geography

remained static: computerisation and 'even more complex statistical methods' (Barnes, 2001c: 553) became increasingly paramount. New 'scientific' vocabularies were important in the valorisation of new technical competencies, but most significantly the quantitative revolution sought to produce foundational understandings of the world in which the truthfulness of representation was guaranteed (Barnes, 2001c: 553; see also Barnes, 2009).

In researching the connections between and among spatial scientists in North America, Barnes (2001b; 2001c) was concerned to reflect upon the socially embedded nature of geography's quantitative revolution. Crucially, transformations in geographical thinking emerged as 'local affairs' within particular institutional sites (Barnes, 2001c: 552). Again, his perspective is informed by philosophy of science literatures and particularly by the notion of externalism, or 'the belief that ... knowledge is intimately related to the local context in which it develops' (Barnes, 2003: 70). This contrasts sharply from an internalist perspective, which presumes that 'there is a deep-seated, autonomous and universal principle that guides theoretical development' (Barnes, 2003: 70)

Barnes' interest in understanding the production of knowledge derives at least in part from a desire to be conscious of the social power and interests that shape such knowledge. In Barnes' (1996: 250) view, 'from the moment we enter the academy, we are socialised into pre-existing networks of knowledge and power that, whether we are conscious of them or not, come with various sets of interests.' Shifting and changing interests are inextricably bound up with transformations in knowledge itself, as demonstrated in Barnes' accounts of the relationships between geographers and the military during the Cold War (Barnes and Farish 2006; Barnes 2008). Writing about the use of locational analysis in geography, Barnes reflects upon 'the duration of ... principles, that is, how long people were willing to continue using and elaborating them, to pass them on and to defend them' (Barnes, 2003: 91). He suggests that the persistence of particular knowledges 'is a social (and geographical) process, and has as much to do with local context as any inherent quality of the principles themselves' (Barnes, 2003: 91).

SPATIAL CONTRIBUTIONS

One of the key contributions provided by Barnes' examination of the histories of economic geography lies in his provision of a more nuanced story of the discipline than narrations of strict succession and progression of knowledge generally would suggest. The notion of a quantitative *revolution* in geography itself obviously implies a move beyond pre-existing theoretical perspectives – and indeed post-spatial science approaches such as Marxism, feminism, locality studies and accounts of flexible production explicitly 'were an attempt to create something different from the past' (Barnes, 1996: 4). However, Barnes (1996: 4-5) argues that economic geography through the 1970s and 1980s remained in the grip of a strong Enlightenment view which sought certainties and foundations. Despite seeking to distance themselves from both the language and practice of spatial science, most analysts ultimately were unable to escape the legacy of the seventeenth century.

Excavating the subdisciplinary histories of economic geography might at first glance seem a somewhat atavistic project. However, Barnes explicitly argues that:

> Only by understanding ... earlier issues can we both comprehend the shape of contemporary discussions in economic geography and, more important, define a real alternative to the Enlightenment view that hitherto has dominated the discipline.

(Barnes, 1996: 6)

Barnes characterises such emergent alternatives as 'post'-prefixed economic geographies that reject the search for a singular order. Exemplary work includes post-structuralist feminist economic geographies (e.g., **J.K.Gibson-Graham**, 1996); feminist work on local labour markets (Hanson and Pratt, 1995; see also Pratt 1999); and development geography informed by post-colonial sensibilities. Barnes (2002b: 95) also has exhorted researchers to strive for a more 'edgy' engagement with their topic: to '[attempt] to undo formerly fixed conceptual categories of economic geography, and put them together again in different ways, and add new ones as well.' In the same way that he has sought to use the work of Sraffa (amongst others) to demonstrate the possibility of 'embrac[ing] openness, context and reflexivity', Barnes hopes that other economic geographers similarly will shun 'closure, universals and dogmatism' (Barnes, 1996: 251).

Such a stance correspondingly informs Barnes' own thinking about space and place. Moving beyond singular conceptions of economic space as (for example) surface or territory, he has sought to argue that 'there is neither a single origin point for enquiry *or* a singular logic, spatial or otherwise' (Barnes, 1996: 250, emphasis mine). Elsewhere, constrasting 'old' and 'new' economic theory, he has argued that the former – which drew heavily upon the work of von Thunen, Christaller and Weber – demonstrated that 'one should not explain events or phenomena by reducing them to fundamental entities taken as natural, or at least lying outside the social' (Barnes, 2001c: 559). Barnes' (2001b; 2001d; 2002a) considerations of the performances of networks of actors (including, for example, economic geographers as well as textbooks) represent attempts to work with and through anti-essentialist conceptualisations of space and place. His work thus has contributed substantially to the reconfiguration of economic-geographical approaches which seek new theoretical understandings of space and place but which at the same time reject a 'single route from here to there' (Barnes, 1998: 101).

KEY ADVANCES AND CONTROVERSIES

One of Barnes' first statements about the importance of knowledge production was presented in a short editorial written for the journal *Environment and Planning A* (Barnes, 1993). Taking his cue from emergent debates surrounding the sociology of scientific knowledge (see entry on **Bruno Latour**), Barnes argued for specific examinations of the sociological construction of *geographical* knowledges, suggesting that geographers should be more reflexive both about the form and nature of the explanations they use as well as the strategies they adopt in presenting these explanations to their audiences. Such arguments prompted considerable reaction. For example, Bassett (1994)

expressed concern about the implications of increased reflexivity in research and writing and argued (*contra* Barnes) that certain 'rational' or 'foundational' standpoints might be necessary for the achievement of social justice, for example. Interestingly, Barnes' contribution to the debate utilised a multiply-positioned narrative structure in order to support his case, arguing that 'there are many different ways to make a convincing argument, [but] there is no formal commonality among them' (1994: 1657). Thus Barnes' writing strategy ('replying' in five different ways) was a deliberate attempt to take seriously a key tenet of sociology of scientific knowledge: that the meanings of any particular 'reality' are 'constructed within a wider social network of meanings' (1994: 1655).

Certain commentators have been sceptical of Barnes' approach to the history of economic geographies and of his interest in the economic landscapes created through the use of metaphor (Barnes, 1992). Scott (2000: 495), for example, is uncomfortable with Barnes' emphasis upon the subdiscipline's fissures and dislocations, preferring to foreground 'evident continuities' in economic geography. Scott (2000: 495) also is concerned that attention to the textual effects of metaphors is 'rather off target' when compared to a need to address 'the immensely real substantive issues and purposive human practices that have always been and still are fundamentally at stake.' As is visible in his reviews of geographical work in political economy, however (see particularly Barnes, 1998), Barnes certainly does not eschew a focus on worlds of (for example) production, class divides and labour market change.

Much of Barnes' writing (see especially 2002b) has sought to contest the drawing of lines around the coherent entities of 'economy', 'politics' and 'culture'. He has, for example, considered the performances of two classic economic geography textbooks (via the networks through which they moved) as a means of developing 'a cultural geography of economic geography and economic geographers' (2002a: 496). In narrating multilayered histories of economic geography, Barnes is critical of attempts to police where different 'types' of geography are allowed to be and where they cannot. He acknowledges:

> There are critics like Harvey (2000) and Storper (2001) who argue that the focus on culture distracts too much from 'the "hard world" of production and things'

(Hall, 1988), and economic geographers would be better off if they devoted their energies to them.

(Barnes, 2002b: 95)

At the same time, he maintains that economic geographers would do better to overturn and rupture existing categories. For Barnes, recognition that there is no single road to truth is essential in developing critical theories. Further, we need a range of imaginative approaches particularly because of the potential role they can play in 'reconfigur[ing] the world and our place within it' (Barnes, 2001a: 12).

BARNES' KEY WORKS

Sheppard, E. and Barnes, T.J. (1990) *The Capitalist Space Economy: Geographical Analysis After Ricardo, Marx and Sraffa.* London: Unwin Hyman.

Barnes, T.J. and Duncan, D.S. (eds) (1992) *Writing Worlds: Texts, Discourses and Metaphors in the Interpretation of Landscape.* London: Routledge.

Barnes, T.J. (1996) *The Logics of Dislocation: Models, Metaphors and Meanings of Economic Space.* New York: Guildford.

Barnes, T.J. and Gertler, M. (1999) *The New Industrial Geography: Regions, Institutions and Regulation.* London: Routledge.

Barnes, T.J. and Sheppard, E. (2000) *A Companion to Economic Geography.* Oxford: Blackwell.

Barnes, T.J. (2003) 'The place of locational analysis: a selective and interpretive history', *Progress in Human Geography*, 27: 69–95.

Secondary Sources and References

Barnes, T.J. (1989) 'Place, space and theories of economic value: contextualism and essentialism in economic geography', *Transactions of the Institute of British Geographers*, 14: 299–316.

Barnes, T.J. (1992) 'Reading the texts of theoretical economic geography: the role of physical and biological metaphors', in T.J. Barnes and J.S. Duncan (eds), *Writing Worlds: Texts, Discourses and Metaphors in the Interpretation of Landscape.* London: Routledge. pp. 118–35.

Barnes, T.J. (1993) 'Whatever happened to the philosophy of science?', *Environment and Planning A*, 25: 301–4.

Barnes, T.J. (1994) 'Five ways to leave your critic: a sociological scientific experiment in replying', *Environment and Planning A*, 26: 1653–8.

Barnes, T.J. (1998) 'Political economy III: confessions of a political economist, *Progress in Human Geography*, 22: 94–104.

Barnes, T.J. (2001a) 'Critical notes on economic geography from an ageing radical. Or radical notes on economic geography from a critical age', *ACME: an International E-Journal for Critical Geographies*, 1 (at www.acme-journal.org).

Barnes, T.J. (2001b) 'Lives lived and lives told: biographies of geography's quantitative revolution', *Environment and Planning D: Society and Space*, 19: 409–29.

Barnes, T.J. (2001c) 'Retheorising economic geography from the quantitiative revolution to the cultural turn', *Annals of the Association of American Geographers*, 91: 546–65.

Barnes, T.J. (2001d) '"In the beginning was economic geography" – a science studies approach to disciplinary history', *Progress in Human Geography*, 25: 521–44.

Barnes, T.J. (2002a) 'Performing economic geography: two men, two books, and a cast of thousands', *Environment and Planning A*, 34: 487–44.

Barnes, T.J. (2002b) '"Never mind the economy. Here's culture." Economic geography goes punk', in K. Anderson, M. Domosh, S. Pile and N.J. Thrift (eds) *Handbook of Cultural Geography*. London: Sage. pp. 89–97.

Barnes, T.J. (2008) 'Geography's underworld: the military-industrial complex, mathematical modelling, and the quantitative revolution', *Geoforum*, 39: 3–16.

Barnes, T.J. (2009) '"Not only . . . but also": quantitative and critical geography', *The Professional Geographer*, 61: 1–9.

Barnes, T. J. and Faris, M. (2006) 'Between regions: science, militarism, and American geography from World War to Cold War', *Annals of the Association of American Geographers*, 96: 807–26.

Barnes, T.J. and Hayter, R (1992) '"The little town that did": flexible production and community response in Chemainus, BC', *Regional Studies*, 26: 647–63.

Barnes, T.J., Hayter, R. and Hay, E. (2001) 'Stormy weather: cyclones, Harold Innis and Port Alberni, BC', *Environment and Planning A*, 33: 2127–47.

Bassett, K. (1994) '"Whatever happened to the philosophy of science?": some comments on Barnes' , *Environment and Planning A*, 26: 343–60.

Gibson-Graham, J.K. (1996) *The End of Capitalism (As We Knew It): a Feminist Critique of Political Economy.* Oxford: Blackwell.

Hall, S. (1988) 'Brave new world', *Marxism Today*, 24–29 October.

Hanson, S. and Pratt, G. (1995) *Gender, Work and Space.* London: Routledge.

Harvey, D. (2000) *Spaces of Hope.* Berkeley: University of California Press.

Hayter, R. and Barnes, T.J. (1992) 'Labour market segmentation, flexibility and recession: a British Columbia study', *Environment and Planning C: Government and Policy,* 10: 333–53.

Pratt, G . (1999) 'From Registered Nurse to registered nanny: diverse geographies of Filipina domestic workers in Vancouver, BC', *Economic Geography,* 75: 215–36.

Scott, A.J. (2000) 'Economic geography: the great half-century', *Cambridge Journal of Economics,* 24: 483–504.

Sraffa, Piero (1960) *Production of Commodities by Means of Commodities: Prelude to a Unique of Economic Theory.* Cambridge: Cambridge University Press.

Storper, M. (2001) 'The poverty of radical theory today: from the false promises of Marxism to the mirage of the cultural turn', *International Journal of Urban and Regional Research,* 25: 155–79.

Suzanne Reimer, Southampton University

4 Jean Baudrillard

BIOGRAPHICAL DETAILS AND THEORETICAL CONTEXT

Jean Baudrillard was born in Reims in 1929. He died in Paris in 2007. Baudrillard completed a doctorate at Université de Paris X – Nanterre under the direction of **Henri Lefebvre** in 1966, taking up a teaching post there in the same year. Despite completing his 'habilitation' in 1986, Baudrillard was never awarded a Chair at Nanterre. Instead, he was 'detached' to the Université de Paris IX – Dauphine, where he spent the remaining years of his academic career (at the Interdisciplinary Research Institute in Socio-economics (IRIS), an associate body of the Centre National de la Recherche Scientifique (CNRS)). He retired from the academic system in 1990, at the earliest opportunity. Baudrillard was a key intellectual figure during the political ferment of May 1968, and took pleasure in distancing himself from the formalities of university life – famously provoking French academe with his publication of *Oublier Foucault* [*Forget Foucault*] in 1977, at the height of **Michel Foucault's** influence. 'Foucault's discourse is a mirror of the powers it describes,' he wrote (Baudrillard, 1987a: 10). 'It is there that its strength and its seduction lie, and not at all in its "truth index," which is only its leitmotiv: these procedures of truth are of no importance, for Foucault's discourse is no truer than any other.' In this relatively early text one can already see three crucial aspects of Baudrillard's theoretical disposition: his indifference to truth and power; his dismissal of critique as an act of complicity (mirroring) rather than subversion (undermining); and his preference for a strategy of seduction rather than production.

Though he was described as a postmodernist, post-structuralist, lapsed Marxist or the French Marshall McLuhan, Baudrillard regarded himself as a 'fatal' theorist: 'Pataphysician at twenty – situationist at thirty – utopian at forty – transversal at fifty – and viral and metaleptic at sixty – my complete history' (Baudrillard, 1996b: 83). Mike Gane (1991) notes that Baudrillard's radicalism consisted in his shift from critical theory (in his case, Marxism) to 'fatal theory' (Clarke et al., 2009). Rather than adopting the critical strategy of comparing theories with reality and turning theories against themselves in order to precipitate their subversion and transgression (e.g. ideological critique, dialectical critique or deconstruction), Baudrillard favoured the fatal strategy of pushing theories beyond themselves in order to glimpse what is on the other side: nothing – or what he prefers to call the 'objective indifference' of the world:

Unlike the discourse of the real, which gambles on the fact of there being something rather than nothing, and aspires to being founded on the guarantee of an objective and decipherable world, radical thought, for its part, wagers on the illusion of the world. It aspires to the status of illusion, restoring the non-veracity of facts, the non-signification of the world, proposing the opposite hypothesis that there is nothing rather than something.

(Baudrillard, 1996c: 97–8)

Given that Western thought has been actively producing different versions of the real for millennia, one can appreciate why Baudrillard's work of annulling reality has been so badly misunderstood. To put it bluntly, he did not wish to produce yet another version of reality. Rather, he was interested in what makes the reality that we have conjured up for ourselves continually withdraw and disappear. Like Friedrich Nietzsche, who claimed to have pushed only that which wanted to fall, Baudrillard was fascinated by the complete cycle of appearance *and disappearance*. By focusing only on the 'mode of production' (of truth, power, reality, desire, knowledge, meaning, value, etc.), he argued that critical theory blinded itself to the other half of the game: the 'mode of disappearance'. This explains Baudrillard's penchant for the *double game* of appearance and disappearance, which he pursued through a strategy of seduction that testifies to the inseparability of perception and deception. (Baudrillard reminds us that to produce is to make appear and move forward [*producere*], whilst to seduce is to lead astray and make disappear [*se-ducere*].) And just as modes of production have mutated over space and time (cf. Karl Marx, Michel Foucault, and Jacques Lacan), so too have modes of disappearance. This is why Baudrillard (1988c) characterised his

work as a 'double spiral'. 'If it is nihilistic to be obsessed by the mode of disappearance, and no longer by the mode of production, then I am a nihilist' (Baudrillard, 1994a: 162).

Although Baudrillard was influenced by Lefebvre's focus on everyday life in a 'bureaucratic society of controlled consumption', he rejected his humanistic brand of Marxism, written under the signs of 'alienation' and 'dis-alienation'. In seeking to replace the 'tottery Marxist denture with new, sharp and high-tech teeth, better fit to bite critically into the brave new world of consumption' (Bauman, 1992: 153), Baudrillard evidently found Roland Barthes' structuralist-cum-semiotic framework for *Mythologies* and *The Fashion System* inspirational during the writing of *The Consumer Society* and *The System of Objects*. Nonetheless, Baudrillard took Lefebvre's anti-structuralism seriously; rejecting the possibility that structuralism might represent a neutral, scientific, and objective approach. What structuralism gave Baudrillard was not a discourse of truth, but a means to explode the 'reality principle' upon which the entire Marxist edifice rested.

In Baudrillard's reading, Marx regarded exchange-value (defined in terms of relations between people misconstrued as relations between things, and exemplified by money) as an artificial supplement to use-value (defined in relation to nature as the self-evident usefulness of things), which under capitalism has all but eclipsed use-value. For Marx, overcoming capitalist alienation and reification therefore required a return to use-value, famously sloganized as 'From each according to his ability; to each according to his need.' For Baudrillard, however, the very *notion* of use-value was an effect of exchange-value. Use-value (and the associated notion of 'need') is not the natural state of things, but a semiological projection onto an indifferent world. The idea that pre-capitalist or primitive-communist societies were based on use-value and the satisfaction of need is a nostalgic myth: such societies had as little room for use-value as they had for exchange-value. Marcel Mauss's analysis of 'gift exchange', Georges Bataille's 'general economy', and Thorstein Veblen's account of 'conspicuous consumption' reveal the existence of an entirely different logic, marginalised by capitalism and ignored by Marx: the logic of *symbolic exchange* (Baudrillard, 1993a). In moving beyond Marx, Baudrillard alighted upon 'another, potentially more radical, critique of capitalist consumption as corrosive not of human relations ... but of more fundamental symbolic exchange relations' (Gane, 1991: 5). Indeed, he offers his fatal theory as a form of symbolic exchange: 'The absolute rule is to give back more than you were given. Never less, always more. The absolute rule of thought is to give back the world as it was given to us – unintelligible. And, if possible, to render it a little more unintelligible' (Baudrillard, 1996c: 105).

Symbolic exchange, then, does not refer to the fact that commodities transmit meanings alongside their material qualities. Certainly, all commodities function as signs, and modern consumers are expected to manipulate these 'commodity-signs' in order to fashion their own identity – thus forming a powerful productive force for the expanded reproduction of capitalism into which countless millions are now routinely socialised. Yet, this sign system as a mode of production and seduction, naturalised in the ideology of consumption, disavows the symbolic principle. Baudrillard gives the example of the sun. As a sign, the sun differentiates itself from other weather types: its unequivocal meaning, evident in countless holiday brochures, is 'not rain'. For the Aztecs, however, the sun was not a meaningful sign but an ambivalent force: both beneficent and cruel; saviour and destroyer; giver of life and requirer of death. Precisely because of its own enormous generosity, it demands a sacrificial offering in return: every gift solicits a counter-gift. This logic of reciprocity – which involves challenge, obligation, and the escalation of stakes – is what Baudrillard means by symbolic exchange. For him, fatal theory does not aspire to truth. 'In my opinion, theory is simply a challenge to the real. A challenge to the world to exist' (Baudrillard, 1987a: 124).

To refashion Marxism for the 'age of affluence', Baudrillard eagerly employed the insights and lexicon of structuralism to demonstrate that capitalism and consumerism were sign systems, and therefore modes of seduction (Baudrillard, 1975, 1981, 1996a, 1998a). Rather than a structural *return* to Marx *à la* Louis Althusser, however, Baudrillard found himself *beyond* Marx. Re-reading Marxism in the light of structuralism, Baudrillard began to detect fundamental problems in Marx. His shocking conclusion was that Marxism represented little more than a reflection of capitalism: a *mirror* of production. By remaining caught in the very code of capitalism (the production of meaning and value), the reversal of terms (e.g. use-value over exchange-value, need over desire, work over labour, and production over circulation) changed nothing. Whether it was dressed up in humanistic or structuralist guise, Marxism remained the alibi (mirror) of capital. Or as McLuhan famously put it: 'The medium is the message.' Moreover, Baudrillard argued that insofar as capitalism is a sign system, it can neutralise and incorporate *any* opposition that continues to invest in meaning and significance, in the same way that the art establishment can incorporate any form of 'anti-art,' and politics any form of 'anti-politics' (even 'nonsense' can be taken up by an interpretative gesture). The fundamental lesson Baudrillard drew from this was that it is futile to confront a sign system in terms of its mode of production. The only glimmer of hope is to confront its mode of seduction (Baudrillard, 1990a, 1990b). However, from that point on, Baudrillard's fatal strategy has more often than not been woefully misunderstood.

In parallel to this fatal response to Marxism, Baudrillard has developed a fatal strategy in response to modernity and the Enlightenment project more generally. Following Max Weber, Baudrillard holds that modernity involved the 'disenchantment' of the world through the imposition of a 'reality principle'. The pre-modern world was experienced as an enchanted realm in which fate reigned supreme. Modernity took this world to task and attempted to knock it into shape. It aimed to destroy flighty, deceptive appearances in the name of solid, trustworthy reality; to replace ambivalence with equivalence. Modernity's goal was 'an unconditional realization of the world' (Baudrillard, 1996c: 25), which it pursued through 'the radical destruction of appearances, the disenchantment of the world and its abandonment to the violence of interpretation and of history' (Baudrillard, 1994a: 160). But in keeping with Baudrillard's appreciation for the *other side* of the game, he was also attentive to postmodernity – 'the immense process of the destruction of meaning, equal to the earlier destruction of appearances' (Baudrillard, 1994a: 161).

It is in this context that Baudrillard (1994a) offers his infamous 'genealogy of the image': from reflection (the servile image); through perversion (the diabolical image); via dissimulation (the duplicitous image); to the simulacrum (the liberated image). In addition, Baudrillard (1990b) offers an account of three 'orders of appearance (or simulacra),' which demonstrates how modernity's commitment to the reality principle has been repeatedly 'geared up:' from first-order counterfeiting (a fake reality based on the natural law of value: an inferior copy that is *distinct from* a unique original); via second-order production (a serial reality based on the commercial law of value: a mechanical reproduction that is *equivalent to* its prototype); to third-order simulation (an encoded reality based on the structural law of value: that which is generated by models and codes; that which is always already reproduced – the *hyperreal*). In the third order, the mode of production is enveloped by the mode of seduction. For when everything is real, reality loses its specificity (*just as when all words in a clause are italicized, italics no longer add emphasis*). Ironically, only that which is reproducible is accorded the status of reality. Our reality would be nothing without the mirror that makes it the reality *of* the image. So, it is not that everything becomes unreal, inauthentic, and fake (*less* than real). On the contrary, everything becomes hyperreal (*more* real than real) – thus becoming enigmatic (enchanted) once again. 'The irony of the facts, in their wretched reality, is precisely that they are only what they are,' says Baudrillard (1996c: 98). '[N]othing is wholly obvious without becoming enigmatic'. Such is the diabolical 'obscenity' into which realism plunges: '*verifying to the point of giddiness the useless objectivity of things*' (Baudrillard, 1988c: 31–2). Hereinafter, the obscenity of hyperrealism has immunised itself against all second-order critiques, such as Marxism and Freudianism. Once again, Baudrillard maintains that the only way to confront hyperreality is by recourse to the 'superior irrationalism' of the mode of seduction and symbolic exchange.

SPATIAL CONTRIBUTIONS

As one might expect of a former student of Lefebvre, and from his early involvement with the journal *Utopie* (Baudrillard, 2001a), Baudrillard always attempted to think through his ideas in spatialised terms. From his initial examination of the effects of consumerism on domestic space (Baudrillard, 1996a) to his tour of hyperreal America (Baudrillard, 1988b), Baudrillard's interest in space, architecture, and the built environment remained constant. There can be few theorists who have written on the significance of both the construction and destruction of New York's World Trade Center (Baudrillard, 1981, 2002a). Yet Baudrillard's spatial imagination is frequently reduced to a handful of throwaway remarks. Baudrillard's sardonic take on Disneyland features amongst his best-known comments:

> Disneyland is presented as imaginary in order to make us believe that the rest is real, whereas all of Los Angeles and the America that surrounds it are no longer real, but belong to the hyperreal order and to the order of simulation. ... The imaginary of Disneyland is neither true nor false, it is a deterrence machine set up in order to rejuvenate the fiction of the real in the opposite camp.

(Baudrillard, 1994a: 12–13)

In another discussion of hyperreality, Baudrillard (1994a: 1) drew on a short story by Jorge Luis Borges concerning the fate of a 1:1 scale map of a great Empire:

'the decline of the Empire witnesses the fraying of this map, little by little, and its fall into ruins, though some shreds are still discernible in the deserts.' Baudrillard inverted this second-order simulacrum to offer his most memorable hyperreal allegory: 'The territory no longer precedes the map, nor does it survive it. ... [T]oday it is the territory whose shreds slowly rot across the extent of the map. It is the real, and not the map, whose vestiges persist here and there in the deserts that are no longer those of the Empire, but ours. *The desert of the real itself.*' Of course, Baudrillard was hardly satisfied with such an analogy, which preserved a critical distance between map and territory – representation and reality – that has actually been abolished: 'Only the allegory of the Empire, perhaps, remains.'

In marshalling the forces of seduction and symbolic exchange against third-order simulacra, Baudrillard developed a sustained theorisation of space and time under conditions of hyperreality (Clarke, 2003). Modernity was committed to *linear* (spatialised) time: time with a sense of direction. Linear time allowed modernity to forget the past, lament the present, and hope for a better future, instating a canonical morality of 'progress'. If the idea of an end (in the sense of a goal) is a function of linear time, linear time lends another sense to the end. Linear time is the *time of no return*. Every moment that passes is a finality – once it is gone, it is gone for good. In modernity, time is scarce. Likewise with space. In contrast, *cyclical* time – the time of seduction and symbolic exchange – is the *time of eternal return*: the rhythm of the seasons, for instance, gives every reason for supposing that what has come to an end will, in due course, return. In short, cyclical time is manifold. Rather than a scarcity of time and space, there is an *abundance* of spaces and times. And if linear time has always been subject to a secret curvature, the end can no longer be seen as a mere finality: 'in a non-linear, non-Euclidean space of history the end cannot be located' (Baudrillard, 1994b: 110). In other words, finality is illusory, despite modernity's best efforts to instil a sense of direction. What we might call postmodernity amounts to the situation we face *beyond* the attempt to accomplish a final solution. Baudrillard acknowledged that the journey never ends; that modernity's vain attempt to guide us to a final destination (*telos*) has plunged us into a strange *hyper-telic* universe – characterised, amongst other things, by hysteresis (the continuation of the effect in the absence of the cause). Space and time no longer provide a stable framework for tracing out an orderly trajectory across the desert of the real. They mutate in strange, unstable, and obscene ways, and in so doing become fatal and fractal (a fourth order of simulacra). Such is the 'objective irony' through which radicality has passed into events. Like a cancerous cell or a viral infection, when things are deprived of their finality they proliferate uncontrollably towards the saturation of a limitless space.

KEY ADVANCES AND CONTROVERSIES

Baudrillard's (1987a: 126) account of a world in which there is 'no more system of reference to tell us what happened to the geography of things' has been much misunderstood. His critics fail to appreciate that his is not a celebration of modernity's furtive destiny, but an exposé of the murder of reality by its own hand (Baudrillard, 1996c). Baudrillard is not dealing with a case where the dominant position of reality is simply usurped by representations, images, and signs (a reversion to a situation where the appearance of the world holds sway). On the contrary, the distinction between appearance and reality dissolves in the opposite direction, in the direction of hyperreality. The sense of 'simulation' proper to hyperreality does not imply a degree of dissimulation, falsity or deception – which would be to obliquely construe the presence of a solid and durable reality elsewhere. It marks the irruption of an obscene world characterised by 'the total promiscuity of things' (Baudrillard, 1993c: 60). If the common response to this situation is nostalgia, lamentation, or out-and-out denial, Baudrillard (1987a: 127) insists that 'The only thing you can do is let it run all the way to the end.'

BAUDRILLARD'S KEY WORKS

Baudrillard, J. (1981) *For a Critique of the Political Economy of the Sign.* Trans. C. Levin. St. Louis: Telos [1972].

Baudrillard, J. (1988b) *America.* Trans. C. Turner. London: Verso [1986].

Baudrillard, J. (1990a) *Seduction.* Trans. B. Singer. London: Macmillan [1979].

Baudrillard, J. (1990b) *Fatal Strategies.* Trans. P. Bietchman and W. G. J. Niesluchowski. London: Pluto [1983].

Baudrillard, J. (1993a) *Symbolic Exchange and Death*. Trans. I. H. Grant. London: Sage [1976].
Baudrillard, J. (1994a) *Simulacra and Simulation*. Trans. S. F. Glaser. Ann Arbor: University of Michigan Press [1981].
Baudrillard, J. (1995) *The Gulf War Did Not Take Place*. Trans. P. Patton. Sydney: Power Publications [1991].
Baudrillard, J. (1996a) *The System of Objects*. Trans. J. Benedict. London: Verso [1968].
Baudrillard, J. (1998a) *The Consumer Society: Myths and Structures*. Trans. C. Turner. London: Sage [1970].
Baudrillard, J. (2002a) *The Spirit of Terrorism and Requiem for the Twin Towers*. Trans. C. Turner. London: Verso [2002]
Baudrillard, J. (2005a) *The Intelligence of Evil or The Lucidity Pact. Trans*. C. Turner. London: Berg [2004].

Secondary Sources and References

Barthes, R. (1973) *Mythologies*. Trans. A. Lavers. St Albans: Paladin.
Barthes, R. (1983) *The Fashion System*. Trans. M. Ward and R. Howard. New York: Hill and Wang.
Baudrillard, J. (1975) *The Mirror of Production*. Trans. M. Poster. St. Louis: Telos [1973].
Baudrillard, J. (1983) *In the Shadow of the Silent Majorities*. Trans. P. Foss, P. Patton, and J. Johnston. New York: Semiotext(e) [1978].
Baudrillard, J. (1987a) *Forget Foucault: Forget Baudrillard*. Trans. P. Beitchman, N. Dufresne, L. Hildreth and M. Polizzotti. New York: Semiotext(e) [1977].
Baudrillard, J. (1988c) *The Ecstasy of Communication*. Trans. B. Schutze and C. Schutze. New York: Semiotext(e) [1987].
Baudrillard, J. (1990c) *Cool Memories*. Trans. C. Turner. London: Verso [1987].
Baudrillard, J. (1993b) *The Transparency of Evil: Essays on Extreme Phenomena*. Trans. J. Benedict. London: Verso [1990].
Baudrillard, J. (1993c) *Baudrillard Live: Selected Interviews*. Ed. M Gane. London: Verso.
Baudrillard, J. (1994b) *The Illusion of the End*. Trans. C. Turner. Cambridge: Polity [1992].
Baudrillard, J. (1996b) *Cool Memories II, 1987–90*. Trans. C. Turner. Cambridge: Polity [1990].
Baudrillard, J. (1996c) *The Perfect Crime*. Trans. C Turner. London: Verso [1995].
Baudrillard, J. (1997) *Fragments, Cool Memories III, 1991–1995*. Trans. C. Turner. London: Verso [1995].
Baudrillard, J. (1998b) *Paroxysm: Interviews with Philippe Petit*. Trans. C. Turner. London: Verso [1997].
Baudrillard, J. (2000) *The Vital Illusion*. New York: Columbia University Press.
Baudrillard, J. (2001a) *Impossible Exchange*. Trans. C. Turner. London: Verso [1999].
Baudrillard, J. (2001b) *The Uncollected Baudrillard*. Ed. G. Genosko. London: Sage.
Baudrillard, J. (2002b) *Screened Out*. Trans. C. Turner. London: Verso [2000].
Baudrillard, J. (2003a) *Cool Memories IV, 1995–2000*. Trans. C. Turner. London: Verso [2000].
Baudrillard, J. (2003b) *Passwords*. Trans. C. Turner. London: Verso [2000].
Baudrillard, J. (2005b) *The Conspiracy of Art: Manifestos, Texts, Interviews*. Ed. S. Lotringer. New York: Semiotext(e)/MIT.
Baudrillard, J. (2006a) *Cool Memories V (2000–2005)*. Trans. C. Turner Cambridge: Polity [2005].
Baudrillard, J. (2006b) *Utopia Deferred: Writings from Utopie (1967–1978)*. Trans. S. Kendall. New York: Semiotext(e).
Baudrillard, J. and Guillaume, M. (2008) *Radical Alterity*. Trans. A. Hodges. New York: Semiotext(e) [1994].
Bauman, Z. (1992) 'The world according to Jean Baudrillard', *in Intimations of Postmodernity*. London: Routledge. pp. 149–55.
Butler, R. (1999) *Jean Baudrillard: The Defence of the Real*. London: Sage.
Clarke, D. B. (2003) *The Consumer Society and the Postmodern City*. London: Routledge.
Clarke, D. B., Doel, M. A., Merrin, W. and Smith, R. G. (eds) (2009) *Jean Baudrillard: Fatal Theories*. London: Routledge.
Gane, M. (1991) *Baudrillard: Critical and Fatal Theory*. London: Routledge.
Kellner, D. (ed.) (1994) *Baudrillard: A Critical Reader*. Oxford: Blackwell.
Rojek, C. and Turner, B. S. (eds) (1993) *Forget Baudrillard?* London: Routledge.
Zurbrugg, N. (ed.) (1997) *Jean Baudrillard: Art and Artefact*. London: Sage.
Baudrillard, J. with Noailles, E.V. (2007) *Exiles From Dialogue*. Trans. C. Turner. Cambridge: Polity [2005].

David B. Clarke, Swansea University/Prifysgol Abertawe
and Marcus A. Doel, Swansea University/Prifysgol Abertawe

5　Zygmunt Bauman

BIOGRAPHICAL DETAILS AND THEORETICAL CONTEXT

Zygmunt Bauman is a sociologist. He was born into a Jewish family in Poland in 1925. The Nazi invasion of 1939 forced his family to flee their homeland. Bauman joined the exiled Polish Army in 1943 and saw action on the Russian front fighting against the Nazis. Returning to Poland after the war, he took up a post at the University of Warsaw in the early 1950s, his army career having been abruptly ended by anti-Semitic elements. In 1968, however, he was forced into exile after the communist authorities fabricated political charges against him during a campaign heavily imbued with anti-Semitism. By way of Tel Aviv and Canberra, Bauman finally settled in England (where he had previously held visiting scholarships at the London School of Economics and University of Manchester), taking up a Chair of Sociology at the University of Leeds in 1972. He retired in 1990. At around the same time, the collapse of the Eastern bloc saw him reconciled with his Alma Mater. Since then, he has been Emeritus Professor of Sociology at both the University of Leeds and the University of Warsaw. Bauman continues to write prolifically, on themes that are often held to reflect his life-experience. As Tester (in Bauman and Tester 2001: 3) cautions, however, 'if we explain Bauman's thought by reference to his biography we are actually making ourselves completely incapable of understanding what he has to say.' Not only does Bauman eschew the cult of personality he holds responsible for undermining public life, he maintains that the human condition is *necessarily* one of exile. We are all outsiders, strangers even to ourselves. Bauman's insights should not, therefore, simply be referred back to their author – the last person one should quiz about the significance of his work.

Even a cursory glance at the sweep of Bauman's *oeuvre* reveals the breadth of his interests. Amongst other things, he has produced studies of social movements, socialism, and class; critical theory, culture, and hermeneutics; modernity, ambivalence, and the Holocaust; post-modernity, consumerism, globalisation and community; and liquid modernity, uncertainty, and life. Bauman constantly elucidates the dilemmas that human society is forced to deal with in the absence of a guidebook or instruction manual, thus ensuring a multitude of actual and possible solutions, each offering different opportunities in terms of freedom, politics, and morality. Bauman's influences are equally varied: Theodor Adorno, Hannah Arendt, **Jean Baudrillard**, **Pierre Bourdieu**, Cornelius Castoriadis,

Mary Douglas, Norbert Elias, **Michel Foucault**, Antonio Gramsci, Jürgen Habermas, Emmanuel Lévinas, Claude Lévi-Strauss, Jean-François Lyotard, Karl Marx, Richard Rorty, Richard Sennett, Georg Simmel; and, of course, his wife, Janina, whose *Winter in the Morning* (1986) precipitated the moral turn that began with *Modernity and the Holocaust* (Bauman, 1989). *Modernity and the Holocaust* embodies one of the changes of perspective that characterise Bauman's work, casting previous conceptions in a new light:

> What had happened ... to my thinking between *Socialism: the Active Utopia* [1976a] and *Modernity and the Holocaust* [1989] was that the perspective from which I viewed beauty and humiliation and ugliness widened. Gradually, the victims of economic injustice began to appear to me as a particular case of a much wider, more ubiquitous and stubborn problem of the 'stranger'.
>
> (Bauman, in Bauman and Tester, 2001: 52)

The plight of the worker under industrial capitalism was perceived as but a 'peculiar, and historically limited, form of the social production of outcasts'. Bauman had come to recognise that modernity's obsession with imposing order *necessarily* produced outcasts – requiring that the entire mythology of modernity, and not just the ideology of capitalism, be stripped away. He was on the threshold of this realisation in addressing the socialist utopia, but it took a fuller analysis of modernity for the pieces finally to fall into place. Recognition that the gas chambers and industrial crematoria of the Holocaust were made in the image of modernity – that order, efficiency, and rationality could just as readily be harnessed to evil as good – triggered this broadening of perspective; although

Bauman has examined modernity from all angles (Bauman, 1982; 1987; 1988; 1989; 1991; 1992a). 'Postmodernity' was, for Bauman, a concept offering the opportunity for extending that analysis.

Bauman, like Baudrillard and Lyotard, was never an apologist for postmodernity, as some have erroneously believed. As an *outgrowth* of modernity – as the unanticipated result of modernity's impossible bid for mastery – postmodernity was always part of modernity, even if this realisation could only take shape as the Owl of Minerva spread her wings and faith in modernity waned. Bauman's dazzling series of conceptions of postmodernity are simultaneously conceptions of modernity, since 'postmodernity' is nothing other than modernity's posthumous form. Whilst Bauman frequently deploys suggestive contrasts, modernity and postmodernity are not to be regarded as forming an identifiable, historical sequence. Each conception of postmodernity implies contradiction of modernity without implying its transcendence, typically involving the return of everything that modernity tried to repress. Following Lyotard (1984), Bauman's (1987; 1992b) initial conceptions focused on the modern alignment and postmodern decoupling of power and knowledge – on the shift from a *repressive* form of social control, reliant on force and violence, to a *seductive* form, guided by consumerist desires. Later formulations trace the decomposition of a modern world of transient permanence (driven by the deconstruction of mortality) into a postmodern world of permanent transience (characterised by the deconstruction of immortality) (Bauman, 1992a). Or, following Sigmund Freud (1930), modernity is seen to involve relinquishing a degree of freedom in exchange for an increased sense of security, postmodernity seeing that trade-off reversed

(Bauman, 1997). Perhaps the most significant aspect of Bauman's engagement with postmodernity, however, has been in terms of morality (Bauman, 1993a; 1995).

Modernity, as the Holocaust clearly revealed, 'out-rationalized' (adiaphorised) the moral impulse, unburdening individuals of moral responsibility by delegating it to a higher authority. The bureaucratisation of decision-making – the hallmark of modernity, according to Max Weber – promoted the idea that moral responsibility would be taken care of elsewhere: that 'I am not responsible'. So it was that the 'desk killer' became a chief perpetrator of the Holocaust; the 'banality of evil' being redoubled by the 'rationality of evil'. Yet, if the dark side of modernity has been exposed, postmodernity should not be prematurely eulogised. It does not necessarily improve matters. Postmodernity 'out-aestheticizes' the moral impulse. It holds moral sentiment at bay by refusing to 'choose as its points of reference and orientation the traits and qualities possessed by or ascribed to the objects of spacing' (Bauman, 1995: 101). It selects, instead, 'the attributes of the spacing subject (like interest, excitement, satisfaction or pleasure)' as the measure of the world: what matters to us is us, not them. Indeed, the pinnacle of moral responsibility becomes: let them be. Insofar as obligations interfere with enjoyment, the postmodern world is as inhospitable to morality as the modern world. Following Lévinas' maxim that 'ethics comes before ontology', Bauman (in Bauman and Tester, 2001: 54) finds modernity *and* postmodernity guilty of producing moral indifference: 'since in a world with ethics but without ontology there is no "before" or "later," but only "better" and "worse" ... it is the socially produced reality which needs to justify itself at the tribunal of ethics, instead of usurping the right to decide what is and what is not moral.' Postmodernity is perhaps all the more pernicious, being programmatically geared towards the (an)aesthetisation of politics (Bauman, 1999). The current reduction of politics to little more than managerialism and opinion-polling – its fragmentation into single-issue politics that are purportedly 'beyond Left and Right' – speaks of a society that has lost the ability to ensure both 'the autonomy of society (the ability to change things) and the autonomy of its members (the ability to select things that need to be changed)' that 'are each other's indispensable conditions' (Bauman, 2002: 57), without which politics would not be what it is. Personal survival under postmodern conditions relies on the *refusal* of social solidarity. In stark contrast to modernity, postmodernity prevents disaffection from building up into collective calls for the system to be overhauled by co-opting dissent: 'Postmodernity enlists its discontents as its most dedicated storm-troopers' (Bauman 1993b: 44).

Bauman has latterly dismissed the term 'postmodernity'. It has, he insists, been wrung dry. His preferred term is now, appropriately, 'liquid modernity' – a fluid form resulting from the meltdown of modernity's previously solid, durable nature. For Émile Durkheim, it seemed obvious that society outlasted the individual, offering 'shelter from the horror of one's own transience' (Bauman, 2000: 183). Today, suggests Bauman, bodily mortality no longer seems so fleeting and fickle, given the increasing ephemerality of institutional forms: 'The body ... has become the last shelter and sanctuary of continuity and duration.'

In a fluid situation, one can no longer count on things remaining in place or staying the way they are. Consequently, it makes little sense to behave in a way that regards commitment, loyalty, or any other form exhibiting permanence as likely to be forthcoming from the world or as virtues to be nurtured in oneself. 'No strings attached' has become the most sought-after quality in the liquid-modern world; 'until further notice' the only rational expectation. The consequences of this world – our world of globalisation (Bauman, 1998b), consumerism (Bauman, 1998a), and individualism (Bauman, 2001a; 2001b) – require constant vigilance, but vigilance itself is under permanent attack. The erosion of the sense that one can do anything about forces operative at a global scale, coupled with the feeling that looking after number one has become a full-time job, is perhaps the greatest threat – and also the greatest challenge – that society has yet faced (Bauman, 2002).

SPATIAL CONTRIBUTIONS

Drawing on Alfred Schütz (Schütz and Luckmann, 1974), Bauman (1993a: 145) maintains that our very sense of objective, physical space derives from the 'phenomenological reduction of daily experience to pure quantity, during which distance is "depopulated" and "extemporalized"'. What we objectify as 'pure space' is but an abstraction, freed of 'content relative to time and circumstance', deriving from 'social space' (from our relations with others). In commonsensical terms, talk of 'social distance' appears reliant on a metaphorical transference from real, 'objective distance'. Yet apprehension of the objective world is itself actually achieved

through notions 'coined originally to "map" the qualitatively diversified relations with other humans' (Bauman, 1993a: 145). Social differentiation – stratified by degrees of intimacy and anonymity, familiarity and strangeness – is the basis of all purportedly empty and objective notions of proximity and distance. Modernity, however, tore apart the connection between social interaction and physical proximity.

The appearance of the 'stranger' on the modern stage was a direct consequence of the dissociation of social space and physical space: the stranger was an alien presence within the lifeworld; a figure proximate in physical space, yet socially distant. Whilst modernity thrived on relations with strangers – particularly in terms of the proliferation of anonymous monetary transactions – their otherness could not but arouse anxiety. Neither friend nor enemy, the stranger defied accepted categories. The proliferation of strangers thus prompted an effort to construct, 'intellectually, by acquisition and distribution of knowledge', an ordered, bounded, and mappable 'cognitive space' (Bauman, 1993a: 146) within which the stranger could be contained, monitored, and normalised. Yet, if cognitive spacing was driven by such concerns, modernity gave rise to other forms of social spacing: 'aesthetic space is plotted affectively, by the attention guided by curiosity and the search for experimental intensity, while moral space is "constructed" through an uneven distribution of felt/assumed responsibility' (Bauman, 1993a: 146).

Cognitive spacing derives from modernity's desire to master space; to determine a place for everything and ensure that everything is in its place – so that surveillance might readily reveal whatever or whomever is 'out of place'. It is a function of knowledge; a tool of the powerful; part and parcel of modernity's desire for order and abhorrence of ambivalence. But since the stranger is necessarily an ambivalent, boundary-straddling character, all efforts of cognitive spacing will ultimately be in vain. Cognitive spacing employs a repressive, 'anthropoemic' strategy – 'aimed at the exile or annihilation of *the others*' (Bauman, 2000: 101). Yet, since the other always lies within, modernity would gradually transfer its allegiance to a seductive, 'anthropophagic' strategy – 'aimed at the suspension or annihilation of *their otherness*' (Bauman, 2000: 101). The roots of this strategy lie in a different response to being in the company of strangers. That archetypal city-stroller, the nineteenth-century Parisian *flâneur* – another footloose character on the modern scene – embodied a diametrically opposed attitude to the proteophobia (fear of strangers) responsible for gestating cognitive space. Amongst the urban crowd, the *flâneur* managed to keep his distance socially by transforming physical proximity into *aesthetic* proximity – by opening up another dimension, hidden to others. Purely for his own satisfaction, he narrated the world around him without letting reality interfere with the plot, coming to enjoy the strange and unfamiliar. 'One may say that if proteophobia is the driving force of cognitive space – *proteophilia* prompts the efforts of aesthetic spacing' (Bauman, 1993a: 168). Yet, the pleasures of aesthetic space would not remain a private affair. The *flâneur*'s ludic world was gradually transformed into a *managed* playground: modernity appropriated the pleasures of *flânerie*, putting them into the service of consumerism. The result was the shift away from a repressive mode of social control (forcibly maintaining the order of cognitive space) towards a new seductive mode (guided by the contours of aesthetic space) (Clarke, 2003). Neither spares much room for morality. Moral space is hardly commensurate with

cognitive space. The unconditional demand to be *for* the other is incompatible with the suppression of moral responsibility promoted by the normalising designs of cognitive space. Aesthetic space is also inhospitable to moral sensibilities. Moral responsibility demands the kind of serious attention that conflicts with the free play of attention on which aesthetic spacing thrives. Yet, there is always hope for morality. Being *with* others opens up a possibility for the ethically prior mode of being *for* others. The construction of a space of moral responsibility is never guaranteed. 'But it does happen, daily, and repeatedly – each time that people care, love, and bring succour to those who need it' (Bauman, 1993a: 185). Nevertheless, being *with* – let alone being *for* – others has become subject to a profound transformation. In an era of globalisation, 'Proximity no longer requires physical closeness; but physical closeness no longer determines proximity' (Bauman, 2003: 62). Indeed, globalisation 'divides as much as it unites; it divides as it unites – the causes of the division being identical with those that promote the uniformity of the globe' (Bauman, 1998b: 2).

The social roots of globalisation, Bauman maintains, lie in the liquidation of modernity's formerly resilient, solid form (e.g., nation states, industrial society, and cultural hegemony), and in the liquidation of modernity's erstwhile universalising ambitions (e.g., THE law, THE truth, THE future). Globalisation conveys the precise opposite of universalisation: effects rather than intentions, consequences rather than undertakings, untameable rather than tameable forces. It implies that 'jungle law' has broken out once more, this time in what **Anthony Giddens** refers to as the 'manufactured jungle' – the wilderness that unintentionally results from modernity's ordering drive. It also implies that the institutions once holding that wilderness at bay have been rendered increasingly impotent, not least the nation-state. Drawing on Michel Crozier's (1964) principle that being in control rests on minimising uncertainty for oneself whilst maximising it for others, Bauman discusses the essential compatibility of the *deterritorialisation* of economic activity (its increasing extraterritoriality, aided and abetted by advances in information technology – see entry on **Peter Dicken**) with the seemingly paradoxical *reterritorialisation* of the nation-state (evident in the clamour to form new nation-states from those whose collective identities were formerly subjugated to invented national traditions, now that the traditional tests of economic viability and military capability have been relaxed). Extraterritorial, hypermobile capital has a vested interest in the weak states associated with 'the *morcellement* of the world scene' (Bauman, cited in Beilharz, 2001: 303). The consequences of this complex spatial restructuring are glossed over by talk of 'time–space compression': '*rather than homogenizing the human condition, the technological annulment of temporal/spatial distances tends to polarize it*' (Bauman, 1998b: 18, italics in original).

Globalisation, Bauman maintains, is best thought of as *glocalisation* – which implies more than deterritorialisation and reterritorialisation occurring simultaneously, or the reassertion of place in the midst of space–time compression. It implies a worldwide restratification of society based on freedom of movement (or lack thereof). Glocalisation polarises mobility, or polarises society in terms of differential mobility: 'Some inhabit the globe; others are chained to place' (Bauman, cited in Beilharz, 2001: 307). Glocalisation means *globalisation for some; localisation for others*. The ability to use time to overcome the limitations of space is the prerogative of the globals.

The locals remain tied to place – where, for many, time is increasingly abundant *and* redundant. Localised existence was hardly a problem when this was the norm, and the means of giving meaning to that existence were within reach. Being merely local in a glocalised world, however, is automatically rendered a secondary existence, since the means for giving meaning to existence have been placed out of reach. It is tantamount to confinement without the need for prison walls. The polarisation of freedom of movement thus serves to redefine all other freedoms, adding a new dimension to deprivation.

KEY ADVANCES AND CONTROVERSIES

Bauman's reflections on the evolution of modernity, its key characteristics, and subsequent meltdown, offer numerous lessons for those interested in space and place, not least in relation to globalisation. Whilst Bauman (1998b: 1) readily accepts that term's status as 'a fad word fast turning into a shibboleth, a magic incantation, a pass-key meant to unlock the gates to all present and future mysteries', he nonetheless pinpoints its consequences with startling accuracy. For the first time in human history, we face a situation where the consequences of our collective cohabitation on the same planet are inescapable: '*il n'y a pas hors du monde*' ['there is nothing outside the world'] (Bauman, 2002: 12). Yet, if globalisation means that rich and poor, globals and locals, no longer sit at the same distributive table of the nation-state, Bauman's position is valuable in its oblique refusal of what the globalised world likes to regard as a *fait accompli*. 'Bauman,' says Beck (2000: 57), 'may be said to overlook himself. For at least in *his* perspective as observer, he *binds together* what he depicts as irrevocably disintegrated in trans-state world society: namely, the framework, the *minima moralia*, which make the poor appear as *our* poor, and the rich as *our* rich.'

BAUMAN'S KEY WORKS

Bauman, Z. (1973) *Culture as Praxis*. London: Routledge and Kegan Paul (new edition, 1999).
Bauman, Z. (1987) *Legislators and Interpreters: On Modernity, Post-modernity and Intellectuals.* Cambridge: Polity.
Bauman, Z. (1989) *Modernity and the Holocaust.* Cambridge: Polity.
Bauman, Z. (1991) *Modernity and Ambivalence.* Cambridge: Polity.
Bauman, Z. (1992a) *Mortality, Immortality and Other Life Strategies.* Cambridge: Polity.
Bauman, Z. (1993a) *Postmodern Ethics.* Oxford: Blackwell.
Bauman, Z. (1998a) *Work, Consumerism and the New Poor.* Milton Keynes: Open University Press.
Bauman, Z. (1998b) *Globalization: The Human Consequences.* Cambridge: Polity.
Bauman, Z. (2000) *Liquid Modernity.* Cambridge: Polity.
Bauman, Z. (2002) *Society Under Siege.* Cambridge: Polity.
Bauman, Z. (2005) *Liquid Life.* Cambridge: Polity.
Bauman, Z. (2008) *The Art of Life.* Cambridge: Polity.

Secondary Sources and References

Bauman, J. (1986) *Winter in the Morning: A Young Girl's Life in the Warsaw Ghetto and Beyond.* London: Virago.
Bauman, Z. (1972) *Between Class and Élite. The Evolution of the British Labour Movement: A Sociological Study.* Manchester: Manchester University Press.
Bauman, Z. (1976a) *Socialism: The Active Utopia.* London: George Allen and Unwin.
Bauman, Z. (1976b) *Towards a Critical Sociology: An Essay on Common-sense and Emancipation.* London: Routledge and Kegan Paul.
Bauman, Z. (1978) *Hermeneutics and Social Science: Approaches to Understanding.* London: Hutchinson.
Bauman, Z. (1982) *Memories of Class: The Pre-history and After-life of Class.* London: Routledge and Kegan Paul.
Bauman, Z. (1988) *Freedom.* Milton Keynes: Open University Press.
Bauman, Z. (1990) *Thinking Sociologically.* Oxford: Blackwell (2nd edition, with May, T., 2001).
Bauman, Z. (1992b) *Intimations of Postmodernity.* London: Routledge.
Bauman, Z. (1993b) 'The sweet scent of decomposition', in C. Rojek and B.S. Turner (eds), *Forget Baudrillard?* London: Routledge. pp. 22–46.
Bauman, Z. (1995) *Life in Fragments: Essays in Postmodern Morality.* Oxford: Blackwell.
Bauman, Z. (1997) *Postmodernity and its Discontents.* Cambridge: Polity.
Bauman, Z. (1999) *In Search of Politics.* Cambridge: Polity.
Bauman, Z. (2001a) *Community: Seeking Safety in an Insecure World.* Cambridge: Polity.
Bauman, Z. (2001b) *The Individualized Society.* Cambridge: Polity.
Bauman, Z. (2003) *Liquid Love: On the Frailty of Human Bonds.* Cambridge: Polity.
Bauman, Z. (2004) *Wasted Lives. Modernity and Its Outcasts.* Cambridge: Polity
Bauman, Z. (2004) *Europe: An Unfinished Adventure.* Cambridge: Polity.
Bauman, Z. (2006) *Liquid Fear.* Cambridge: Polity.
Bauman, Z. (2006) *Liquid Times: Living in an Age of Uncertainty.* Cambridge: Polity.

Bauman, Z. (2007) *Consuming Life.* Cambridge: Polity.

Bauman, Z. (2009) *Living on Borrowed Time: Conversations with Citlali Rovirosa-Madrazo.* London: Wiley.

Bauman, Z. and Tester, K. (2001) *Conversations with Zygmunt Bauman.* Cambridge: Polity.

Beck, U. (2000) *What is Globalization?* Cambridge: Polity.

Beilharz, P. (2000) *Zygmunt Bauman: Dialectic of Modernity.* London: Sage.

Beilharz, P. (ed.) (2001) *The Bauman Reader.* Oxford: Blackwell.

Beilharz, P. (ed.) (2002) *Zygmunt Bauman* (4 Volumes) London: Sage.

Clarke, D. B. (2003) *The Consumer Society and the Postmodern City.* London: Routledge.

Crozier, M. (1964) *The Bureaucratic Phenomenon.* Chicago: University of Chicago Press.

Freud, S. (1930) *Civilization and its Discontents.* Trans. J. Rivière. London: Hogarth Press.

Kilminster, R. and Varcoe, I. (eds) (1996) *Culture, Modernity and Revolution: Essays in Honour of Zygmunt Bauman.* London: Routledge.

Lyotard, J.–F. (1984) *The Postmodern Condition: A Report on Knowledge.* Trans. G. Bennington and B. Massumi. Manchester: Manchester University Press.

Schütz, A. and Luckmann, T. (1974) *The Structures of the Lifeworld.* Trans. R. M. Zaner and H. T. Engelhardt Jr. London: Heinemann.

Smith, D. (1999) *Zygmunt Bauman: Prophet of Postmodernity.* Cambridge: Polity.

Tester, K. and Jacobsen, M. H. (2006) *Bauman Before Postmodernity: Invitation, Conversations and Annotated Bibliography 1953–1989.* Aalborg: Aalborg University Press.

Tester, K., Jacobsen, M. H., and Marshman, S. (2007) *Bauman Beyond Postmodernity: Conversations, Critiques and Annotated Bibliography 1989–2005.* Aalborg: Aalborg University Press.

David B. Clarke, Swansea University/Prifysgol Abertawe
and Marcus A. Doel, Swansea University/Prifysgol Abertawe

6   Ulrich Beck

BIOGRAPHICAL DETAILS AND THEORETICAL CONTEXT

Ulrich Beck's sociology of 'late modernity' has been influential on geographical thinking on subjects as diverse as environmental hazards, globalisation and the changing relationships between individuals and social institutions. Like **Anthony Giddens**, Beck is broadly concerned with how human social experience is changing as modern industrial societies face periods of uncertainty and restructuring brought about by problems inherent to their constitution. Beck's writing can also be understood as an agenda for new forms of political action, and his influence has thus gone beyond academic circles; like Giddens, Beck is noted for publishing articles for non-academic audiences (e.g. Beck, 2001). Notably, and in contrast with some critical theorists such as **Michel Foucault**, Beck at times presents a rather optimistic account of how people might engage in radical and liberating forms of political action, suggesting that many of the economic, political, social and ecological crises he identifies may be circumvented.

Beck was born in 1944, growing up in Hanover, in the then West Germany. By the mid-1980s he was Professor of Sociology at the small town of Bamberg, later obtaining Chairs in Sociology at the University of Munich and the London School of Economics and Political Science. During this time, his sociology has sought to make sense of a series of seemingly unrelated global phenomena in the latter part of the twentieth and early twenty-first centuries, including the emergence of particular sorts of environmental hazards, global economic instability and the threat of global terrorism. Beck has attempted to theorise these phenomena together, working with terminology which has become iconic in debates over the nature and future of late modernity. Hypothesising a transition from 'first modernity' to 'second modernity', Beck's central theme has been the emergence of a so-called 'risk society'. It is this notion which underpins his key publications, including *Risk Society: Towards a New Modernity* (1992); *Ecological Politics in the Age of Risk* (1995); *The Reinvention of Politics: Rethinking Modernity in the Global Social Order* (1997), *World Risk Society* (1999) and *World at Risk* (2008).

Beck's notion of the 'risk society' refers broadly to a sense in which there has been a transition from an industrial society (in which 'natural hazards' could be regarded as fate and 'human-made' hazards could be understood within a frame of calculability which rendered them insurable and thus manageable), to a late-modern society where some hazards produced by the way society operates are incalculable, perhaps unknowable. Risk society is thus still an industrial society, yet the hazards produced by that society take on a heightened importance in human consciousness. Thus:

> Threats from civilisation are bringing about a new kind of 'shadow kingdom' comparable to the realm of the gods and demons in antiquity, which is hidden behind the visible world and threatens human life on this Earth. People no longer correspond today with spirits residing in things, but find themselves exposed to 'radiation', ingest 'toxic levels' and are pursued into their very dreams by the anxieties of a nuclear holocaust.

(Beck, 1992: 72)

In relation to ecological hazards, Beck argues that scientific and economic 'progress' is overshadowed by forms of risk produced by the very processes involved in such progress (Lash and Wynne, 1992); as he puts it, the 'production of *wealth* is systematically accompanied by the social production of *risks*' (Beck, 1992: 19). These new risks (e.g., pollution, climate change) can be thought about in three ways. First, they result *from* science and technology, rather than being just something to which science can be applied as a solution. Second, the risks produced may have impacts over greater spatial and temporal scales than was the case in earlier industrial society; in particular, these forms of risk affect people and places not directly involved in their causes. Third, they are often not immediately sensible to individuals; indeed, they require the 'sensory organs of science – *theories, experiments, measuring instruments – in order to become visible or interpretable as hazards at all'* (Beck, 1995: 27). However, in the case of risks like climate change, science can be limited in predicting effects and proposing solutions.

According to Beck, late-modern, techno-scientific, industrial, capitalist society is systematically affected by risks caused by the fundamental conditions of its establishment.

In addition to ecological threats, Beck's concept of risk society encompasses the economic and political instabilities associated with global change. A key dimension of Beck's sociology is to consider the implications of these multiple risks for social institutions and individual lives. He thus argues that the social and economic stabilities people learned to expect under conditions of 'first modernity' have been challenged by new instabilities associated with various processes of change:

> [T]he collective patterns of life, progress and controllability, full employment and exploitation of nature that were typical of this first modernity have now been undermined by five interlinked processes: globalization, individualization, gender revolution, underemployment and global risks (as ecological crisis and the crash of global financial markets).

(Beck, 1999: 2)

Beck (1992) accordingly describes the contemporary social experience as one of 'reflexive modernization', with society continually evolving through a series of institutional changes in response to unanticipated risks. This fundamental change in society is associated with a shift in the role of politics. In first modernity, politics was principally concerned with the social distribution of 'goods' (such as wealth). In late-modern risk society, however, it is increasingly having to be concerned with the distribution of 'bads': biohazards, environmental degradation or the negative effects of economic globalisation (e.g. unemployment, labour casualisation or disinvestment). For Beck, this requirement to deal with late-modern 'bads' has produced a crisis in many conventional institutions (e.g. national governments) responsible for their management – a crisis related to two characteristics of contemporary risk. First, as already suggested, many of the new risks are unpredictable, perhaps unknowable, and have incalculable long-term and geographically widespread consequences. Although there is an unequal socio-spatial distribution of such risks (the poorest people and places tend to be worst afflicted), these are nevertheless hazards which potentially affect anybody. Second, both the new risks (e.g., radiation leaks, regional financial collapse), and the emergence of other formations, such as multinational corporations or international terrorist networks, have effects which extend beyond the remit of those institutions conventionally bound by national frontiers: they are transnational.

SPATIAL CONTRIBUTIONS

Beck's writing has emphasised the shifting relationships between individuals and society on a variety of scales in relation to a range of issues, and it is unsurprising that his ideas have influenced geographers. Indeed, Beck's notion of reflexive modernisation implies a process of constant revision of social activity, at the institutional and individual levels, with both changing how they function in response to the existence of an uncertain and risky world. Both are held to be caught up in a process of consciously reflecting upon more uncertain, risky and hazardous existences, and, in response, changing the ways they function. In part this process is driven by the constant production of highly specialised

knowledges by scientific, technical and expert organisations. In turn, this information reflects the ambiguities and complexities surrounding the types of risk that are being dealt with; that is, it is often unclear what exact causal links are responsible for ecological degradation or financial meltdown, and if that is unclear, then it is also unclear who or what is accountable. For example, are there risks involved in introducing Genetically Modified Organisms (GMOs)? If such risks become apparent only over a longer time scale or across national boundaries, who or what should or could take responsibility? Science, industry and politics seem incapable of supplying definitive answers to such questions, yet GMOs are increasingly used in agriculture and enter human food chains. Institutional and individual responses to this confusing and sometimes incomprehensible or contradictory state of affairs and the possible international political conflicts they might engender become part of wider processes of socio-spatial change:

> This is what I mean by talking about 'reflexive modernization'. Radicalised modernisation undermines the foundations of the first modernity and changes its frame of reference, often in a way that is neither desired nor anticipated ... A new kind of capitalism, a new kind of economy, a new kind of global order, a new kind of society and a new kind of personal life are coming into being.
>
> (Beck, 1999: 2)

One particular impact of this process is in the workplace. For Beck (1992), our working lives are one arena in which we experience risk (Allen and Henry, 1997). Late-modern working practices stress flexibility, which is often translated into processes of work casualisation, short-term contracts and periods of unemployment. Similarly, globalisation has allowed companies to disinvest from some places and reinvest in others, so that the availability of work in particular places is fluid and uncertain. At the same time, institutions allowing collective bargaining (e.g., trades unions), associated with first modernity, have become less significant in a world of transitory and flexible working relationships. Work is thus an important sphere in which institutions and the individual meet under late-modern, risky conditions:

> The new power-play between territorially fixed political actors (government, parliament, unions) and non-territorial economic actors (representatives of capital, finance, trade) is the central element expressed in the political economics of uncertainty and risk ... capital is global, work is local.
>
> (Beck, 1999: 11)

Such situations lead to another of Beck's key themes. This is the process of 'individualization', a progressive disassociation of individuals from social institutions such as employers, unions, religions or conventional political agencies. Individualisation is a structural process, implying a changing relationship between individuals and institutions. Individualisation is partly something which is done to people by economic and political institutions which wish to divest themselves of responsibility for those people. Simultaneously, it is something people want for themselves as part of the process of reflexive modernisation, recognising that conventional social institutions are limited in responding to the risks they face. Individuals are increasingly sceptical of the authority of governing, moralising or employing institutions, and of ways of aggregating people into social classes or communities, which went relatively unquestioned in first modernity. In late modernity, then, 'People are invited

to constitute themselves as individuals: to plan, understand, design themselves as individuals, and should they fail, to blame themselves' (Beck, 1999: 9). Life is thus increasingly lived as an individual project, in which an individual's bonds of love and friendship become more important than the relationships with social institutions which structured their sense of identity in first modernity (Beck and Beck-Gernsheim, 1995). Beck's emphasis is on how individuals' life-projects are forged through their personal experiences of fear and risk, and that while this might produce defensive or paralysing reactions (counter-modernisation–a reactionary demand for a return to traditional certainties and securities), it might instead reflexively produce new forms of ethical and political engagement with the world, and new forms of ethical and political community which might connect people in geographically disparate places, and be centred around, for example, ecological issues.

Beck sets these more radical possibilities in the context of what he calls 'subpolitics'. Subpolitics take place in 'sites which were previously considered unpolitical' (Beck, 1999: 93), and implicate individuals and a range of non-governmental institutions in new forms of political practice.

> The concept of 'subpolitics' refers to politics outside and beyond the representative institutions of the political systems of nation-states ... Subpolitics means *'direct'* politics –that is, *ad hoc* individual participation in political decisions, bypassing the institutions of representative opinion-formation (political parties, parliaments) and often even lacking the protection of the law. In other words, subpolitics means the shaping of society from below. Economy, science, career, everyday existence, private life, all become caught up in the storms of political debate ... Crucially, however, subpolitics sets politics free by changing the rules and boundaries of the

political so that it becomes more open and susceptible to new linkages –as well as capable of being negotiated and reshaped.

(Beck, 1999: 39–0)

Beck points to the role of organizations such as Greenpeace in subpolitical debate, arguing that individualisation and subpolitical agency are part of a more critical attitude towards scientific, economic and (conventional) political authorities as regards issues like 'development' and 'progress'. They are, too, associated with a re-emerging public sphere; a space for more democratic dialogue about reshaping society.

In addition to his work on politics, of major significance for geographers is Beck's work on transnationalism and 'reflexive cosmopolitization' (e.g. Beck, 1996; 1999; 2000; 2001). Beck draws a distinction between 'simple globalization', which envisages interconnections between nation states that otherwise continue to exist as bounded, independent entities, and transnational or cosmopolitan visions of globalisation which, potentially, both disrupt the assumed stability of the state and create new forms of interconnectedness:

> The cosmopolitan gaze opens wide and focuses – stimulated by the post-modern mix of boundaries between cultures and identities, accelerated by the dynamics of capital and consumption, empowered by capitalism undermining national borders, excited by the global audience of transnational social movements, and guided and encouraged by the evidence of world-wide communication ... World-wide public perception and debate of global ecological danger or global risks of a technological and economic nature ('Frankenstein food') have laid open the cosmopolitan significance of fear.

(Beck, 2000: 79)

This might involve the creation of new, spatially non-contiguous, communities of interest ('risk communities'), and simultaneously affect the nature of political and social life within states. Beck identifies many such globalised communities of interest in the contemporary world: 'Models of post-national risk communities may be found, for example, in the regional ecological treaties ... in transnational communities, non-governmental organizations, or global movements, such as ecological or feminist networks' (Beck, 1999: 16).

For Beck, the idea of cosmopolitisation involves the emergence of new forms of geographical imagination. Individualised human subjects, living and thinking transnationally, are capable of greater awareness of their mutually being affected by global issues, and have the potential to use subpolitical agency in order to influence, and take responsibility for, social change. Thus,

> The ethic of individual self-fulfilment and achievement ... [might provide] the basis for a new cosmopolitanism, by placing globality at the heart of political imagination, action and organization.

(Beck, 1999: 9)

Beck has also applied his theoretical position to the risks associated with global terrorism, linking this threat to the other ecological, social and economic issues which exemplify his attitude to late modernity. He thus argues that:

> In the face of the menace of global terrorism (but also of climate change, of migration, of toxins in food, or organised crime) the only path to national security is by way of transnational co-operation. The following paradoxical principle holds true: States must de-nationalise and trans-nationalise themselves for the sake of their own national interest, that is, relinquish sovereignty, in order, in a globalized world, to deal with their national problems.

(Beck, 2001: unpaginated)

KEY ADVANCES AND CONTROVERSIES

Beck's key achievement has been to formulate a theory of late modernity which is able to encompass a diverse range of phenomena. He has been a social commentator, writing for a larger public-sphere audience, as well as an academic theorist. Simultaneously, Beck's work is partly an agenda for political and social change. However, his attempt to explain everything under the 'risk society' meta-narrative is also problematic. Critique of Beck's sociology has focused on both the underlying principles on which his theories are based, and the potential for radical change and new forms of political activity which he suggests might emerge as responses to, or within, risk society.

First, although Beck's analysis of risk society has become important in responses to contemporary environmental issues, it has been criticised from social constructivist and post-structuralist positions (see Eden, 1998; Whatmore, 2002). Here, critics have claimed that Beck maintains a distinction between the social and the natural that is questioned by other theorists (e.g., **Bruno Latour** or **Donna Haraway**) and unrealistic given the social-natural hybrids (like GMOs) that increasingly populate our world. Wynne (1996), for example, notes Beck's acceptance of a model of the environment (and its hazards) as an externality affecting society. Beck is criticised for neglecting cultural dimensions of social responses to risk, and for accepting 'expert' constructions of environmental problems. Wynne suggests that Beck contributes to reproducing an expert–lay dichotomy in analysis of environmental issues and to the exclusion of lay understandings of those issues.

Second, Beck is accused of not paying enough attention to geographical and cultural difference, despite his focus on transnational and cosmopolitan trends. It has been suggested that more consideration needs to be given to how different cultural groups, in different places, make sense of and respond to risks. Risks are not simply matters of fact, but become parts of cultural discourse and embedded in social practice. It is further argued that in this sense, the 'new' risks identified by Beck are not necessarily that different to forms of risk (disease, famine etc.) not related to industrial society. These hazards too were differentially interpreted and responded to. While Beck does recognise geographical difference in his work, for example in acknowledging that the wealthy are more able to defend themselves against risk, he is accused (see, for example, Bulkeley, 2001) of the global extension of a theoretical framework which is actually based in the specific conditions of Western Europe.

Third, there is criticism of Beck's perceived over-optimism as regards potential new forms of political activism. Here, Beck is accused of uncritically supporting a progressive, Enlightenment view of a move towards a situation of rational consensus, where reflexive modernisation produces effective responses to global risks. Redclift (1997), for example, focusing on questions of ecological sustainability, argues that Beck's vision requires the existence of a politically aware and active citizenry, as yet not present. Similarly, Hinchliffe (1997) is critical of notions that alternative political groupings will form in the ways Beck suggests, and that they could necessarily be more politically effective than earlier forms of protest and activism. Hinchliffe imagines a different possible future, in which an increasingly uncertain world produces new forms of authority and control, rather than individual and political liberation.

This alternative view of the future of modernity marks a contrast between what is taken as Beck's optimism and other, bleaker, perspectives. For example, Bulkeley's (2001) study of government responses to possible climate change in Australia suggests that far from radical political formations becoming influential, conventional government–industry links are reinforced by the regulatory structures being proposed. Bulkeley is thus critical of Beck for not engaging with how risks and responsibilities remain negotiated within existing arenas of power. Such criticism of Beck's optimism is perhaps somewhat unfair, given that his own understanding of reflexive modernisation (e.g., Beck, 1999) makes it clear that the reflexive process only *might* produce the positive effects he suggests. The decisions made by individuals or in institutions might instead be reactionary or selfish, not 'rational' and cosmopolitan. The nature of politics and society in an individualised, yet globalised, future is not certain; indeed for Beck, this uncertainty is characteristic of reflexive modernisation and risk society. Thus, we may conclude by citing Beck's assertion that the human condition is now characterised by 'fundamentally ambivalent contingencies, complexities, uncertainties and risks which, conceptually and empirically, still have to be uncovered and understood' (Beck, 2000: 81).

BECK'S KEY WORKS

Beck, U. (1992) *Risk Society: Towards a New Modernity*. London: Sage.
Beck, U. (1995) *Ecological Politics in the Age of Risk*. Cambridge: Polity Press.
Beck, U. (1997) *The Reinvention of Politics: Rethinking Modernity in the Global Social Order*. Cambridge: Polity Press.
Beck, U. (1998) *Democracy Without Enemies*. Cambridge: Polity Press.
Beck, U. (1999) *World Risk Society*. Cambridge: Polity Press.
Beck, U. and Willms, J. (2003) *Conversations with Ulrich Beck*. Cambridge: Polity Press.
Beck, U. (2005) *Power in the Global Age*. Cambridge: Polity Press.
Beck, U. (2006) *Cosmopolitan Vision*. Cambridge: Polity Press.
Beck, U. and Edgar, G. (2007) *Cosmopolitan Europe*. Cambridge: Polity Press.
Beck, U. (2008) *World at Risk*. Cambridge: Polity Press.

Secondary Sources and References

Allen, J. and Henry, N. (1997) 'Ulrich Beck's *Risk Society* at work: labour and employment in the contract service industries', *Transactions of the Institute of British Geographers*, 22, 180–96.
Beck, U. (1996) 'World risk society as cosmopolitan society?', *Theory, Culture and Society*, 13, 4: 1–32.
Beck, U. (2000) 'The cosmopolitan perspective: sociology of the second age of modernity', *British Journal of Sociology*, 51, (1): 79–105.
Beck, U. (2001) 'The cosmopolitan state. Towards a realistic utopia', www.eurozine.com/article/2001-12-05-beck-en.html
Beck, U. and Beck-Gernsheim, E. (1995) *The Normal Chaos of Love*. Cambridge: Polity Press.
Bulkeley, H. (2001) 'Governing climate change: the politics of risk society?', *Transactions of the Institute of British Geographers*, 26: 430–47.

Eden, S. (1998) 'Environmental issues: knowledge, uncertainty and the environment', *Progress in Human Geography,* 22: 425–432.

Hinchliffe, S. (1997) 'Locating risk: energy use in the 'ideal' home and the non-ideal world', *Transactions of the Institute of British Geographers,* 22: 197–209.

Lash, S. and Wynne, B. (1992) 'Introduction', in U. Beck, *Risk Society: Towards a New Modernity.* London: Sage. pp. 1–8.

Redclift, M. (1997) 'Sustainability and theory: an agenda for action', in D.Goodman, and M.Watts (eds), *Globalizing Food: Agrarian Questions and Global Restructuring.* London: Routledge. pp. 333–43.

Whatmore, S. (2002) *Hybrid Geographies: Natures Cultures Spaces.* London: Sage.

Wynne, B. (1996) 'May the sheep safely graze? A reflexive view of the expert–lay knowledge divide', in S. Lash, B. Szerszynski and B.Wynne (eds), *Risk, Environment and Modernity: Towards a New Ecology.* London: Sage. pp. 44–83.

Lewis Holloway, University of Hull

BIOGRAPHICAL DETAILS AND THEORETICAL CONTEXT

Brian Berry is perhaps the most important of a handful of people who transformed human geography over the second half of the twentieth century. His immediate peers and contemporaries were **Peter Haggett** and **David Harvey**. This group (along with others including **Reg Golledge**, Peter Gould, and Leslie J. King) effectively initiated and led the 'quantitative revolution' in human geography from the early 1960s through to the 1980s. In this sense, Brian Berry has had an enormous and lasting impact on the discipline, being for nearly 20 years the world's most cited geographer and no less importantly the reference point for successive generations of graduate students in North America, the United Kingdom, and Australasia. While intimately associated with spatial analysis and quantitative revolution, his work has continued to develop and evolve encompassing urbanism, public policy, and long waves of innovation and development. The scope of his academic career and research publications is astounding, identifying him as one of the world's leading social scientists.

Brian Berry was born on 16 February 1934 in Stafford, England to Joe and Gwendoline (neé Lobley) Berry. Brian spent his formative early years in the East Midlands and Lincolnshire, areas associated with the Berry family for more than four hundred years (tracing his roots back to these areas has been one thread of his intellectual and emotional journey). Berry was one of a small number of children from lower middle-class and working-class families who came through the British selective grammar school system to go on to university in the 1950s. At a time when few children made it through to high-school matriculation, and even fewer went to university, Berry's subsequent progress through what was then a highly stratified and elitist society to outstanding academic success at University College London and the University of Washington (Seattle) was the result of enormous ability, determination and, perhaps paradoxically, opportunity. On completing his PhD at Washington (1958) he joined the University of Chicago before moving to Harvard (1976–1981), becoming Williams Professor of City and Regional Planning and Dean of the Heinz School of Public Policy and Management and University Professor at Carnegie Mellon University (1981–86). In addition, he was the youngest social scientist ever elected to the US National Academy of Sciences (1975). In 1991, Brian Berry became the Lloyd Viel Berkner Regental Professor and Professor of Political Economy at the University of Texas at

Richardson, Dallas, later (2005) becoming Dean of the School of Economic, Political and Policy Sciences. Berry also served on the council of the National Academy of Sciences (1999–2002).

Whereas he is primarily known as a geographer and social scientist, he is also an accomplished family historian and genealogist. Since the late 1980s and early 1990s he has published a large number of books, pamphlets and papers on his own family, his wife's family, and related families (Berry married Janet Shapley in 1958, having a family of four children, and a larger number of grandchildren). Characteristically, these genealogical projects combine close attention to empirical detail with a sure feel for the historical geography of trans-Atlantic economic relations. A geographer by intuition and inclination, he has approached research and scholarship with a strong grasp of his own agenda and a clear commitment to the principles he believes to be appropriate in understanding economic and social processes and their place in the broad sweep of history and geography. In turn, unfashionable, fashionable, and now again unfashionable, he has promoted a social scientific and analytical style of research. He stood by his views and opinions in the face of great social turbulence and dissent during the 1970s and 1980s, and restated his agenda in relation to the identity politics and post-modern angst of the 1990s and early years of the twenty-first century. If politically conservative and egalitarian by instinct, he is surely a radical when it comes to poking fun at orthodoxy whatever its origins. By this account, Berry's ambition has given many geographers the space in which to flourish and contribute to the growth of the discipline.

SPATIAL CONTRIBUTIONS

It is difficult to do justice to Berry's role in the quantitative revolution that swept through human geography in the 1960s and 1970s (though for his own assessment of his role in this intellectual revolution, see Berry, 1993). In this respect, it is worth repeating that Berry's generation took aim at the very core of geography, deliberately setting out to provide new issues and themes, and an analytical approach in contradiction to the cultural and regional geography that dominated the practice of US human geography. His earliest papers in the *Annals of the Association of American Geographers* (Berry, 1958; Berry, 1959; Berry, 1960) were remarkable for their agenda-setting, their social science form and format, and their engagement with the processes driving the development of the urban economic landscape. These papers were especially significant given the personal fiefdoms, patronage, and prejudice at work in what was a small and marginal discipline in the US. There is a certain irony, then, in seeing contemporary cultural geographers re-discover many of the leading figures of North American post-war geography who were so active in resisting Berry's call for relevance.

Berry's early work focused upon crucial theoretical issues in urban economic geography, using the tools and methods of the social sciences (especially economics) to develop empirically-informed explanations of urban patterns and processes, and led the discipline into contemporary issues including housing, race, planning and US urban policy. Moreover, the remarkable *Geography of Market Centres and Retail Distribution* (1967) had an enormous impact in the social sciences, going beyond geography and the English-speaking world to symbolise the ambition and scope of an urban geography rooted in the 'Chicago School': Wrigley and Matthews (1986) identified it as a citation 'classic' of the twentieth century. At the time, it stood against William Alonso's (1964) own attempt to set the agenda for urban economic research. Whereas Alonso's book sought to provide a theoretical framework consistent with the axioms and methods of neo-classical economics Berry's book sought to establish empirical principles and regularities that could account for the observed urban hierarchy and patterns of development (see Yeates, 2001, for a sympathetic assessment). In this respect, Berry's approach and his relationship to economics are issues replayed in recent commentaries on the 'new' economic geography associated with Paul Krugman (1991) and others (see also Clark et al., 2000).

By the early 1970s, however, a number of factors conspired to undermine Berry's project, and the more general project of spatial analysis and quantitative urban economic geography. One was obviously the arrival in higher education and post-graduate study of the 'baby boom' generation. Ironically, again, whereas Berry, Haggett, and Harvey and their colleagues opened opportunities and set broad intellectual horizons at the interface between geography and other social sciences, their work was the stepping-off point for a new generation of would-be academics who hardly understood the intellectual battles fought and won in the late 1950s and 1960s. The 'baby boom' generation were deeply affected by the Vietnam War and the political leaders who were fighting the Cold War with the lives of the baby boom generation. As a result, this generation was also very suspicious of any social science agenda that put analytical rigour ahead of political and economic realities. Indeed, the close association between social science, the war effort and status and progress through US academic disciplines reinforced a ready-made schism between Berry's generation and the baby boom generation.

A related factor that drove human geography away from spatial analysis and the quantitative revolution was the search for social theory that could, firstly, better understand urban and economic geography in relation to capitalist dynamics, and, secondly, appreciate the sources of social and especially racial inequality in US cities – cities increasingly being pulled apart by market forces of differentiation and middle-class distinction. Here, there was fertile ground for dissent and disagreement but equally fertile ground for great misunderstanding and easily made enmities. Whether by accident or design, the debate between Berry and David Harvey about 'relevance' in leading journals in geography crystallised for a whole generation many of the limits of social science as an analytical priesthood. Just as Brian Berry had been the reference point for a new generation striving to leave behind a conservative and confining geography, David Harvey (1973; 1982) and his form of Marxist social and economic geography (set out in *Social Justice and the City* and *The Limits to Capital*) were clarion calls for a new generation.

If Berry was disenchanted by the forces of change and dissent, his resolve to contribute to the formation of public policy and urban justice did not waver. Indeed, his papers, reports, and books over the period 1975 to 1990 were a testament to his deeply held belief that social science should make a constructive and purposeful difference to the structure and design of cities and the lived experience of those who dwell therein. In 1976, he published two books that set the agenda for urban studies and public policy across the world, namely *Urbanisation and Counter-urbanisation* and *Chicago: Transformations of an Urban System*. Together, these volumes spelt out Berry's approach to understanding inter- and intra-urban hierarchies, issues placed on the national stage while he taught at Harvard University and later as Dean of the School of Urban Public Affairs at Carnegie Mellon University. In this way, Brian Berry became truly an advocate and citizen of social science, consistently portraying social science as a means of solving pressing public policy concerns. This was reflected, for example, in his contributions to the NAS (1982) report *Critical Issues for National Urban Policy*. Throughout this period, Berry's brand of social science became widely recognised throughout US social science and in sociology in particular.

Remarkably, from the 1990s onwards Berry embarked on an ambitious and important intellectual project: understanding and empirically specifying so-called long waves of development. Whereas this topic was associated with discredited views attributed to Kondratiev (a Russian economist of the early twentieth century), Brian Berry has been able to remake the issue into his own bringing to bear his characteristic close attention to empirical detail, respect for the historical record, and sense of the personal and collective histories of English-speaking people (in particular but not exclusively) over the past 400 years. Setting the stage for this intellectual project was his (1991) book *Long-Wave Rhythms in Economic Development and Political Behaviour*. A succession of papers and monographs developing themes related to this project have been published integrating what he has termed 'long-wave macro-history' with urbanisation, innovation, technological change, and social and political movements. If less appreciated and less well known in

geography, these contributions to understanding the broad sweep of history have had a ready audience across the rest of North American social sciences. Here, demography, politics and economics have been brought together in a quite remarkable synthesis of time and space – a genuine historiography of capitalism.

KEY ADVANCES AND CONTROVERSIES

Berry has confronted recent developments in geography and the social sciences, and the challenges posed by postmodernism in its various forms, voices and themes. He has used his position as editor-in-chief of *Urban Geography* to engage and argue with anyone who will listen – especially younger generations of human geographers. Again, characteristically, he has not been afraid to make plain his own views in contradiction to current fads and fashions as well as others' strongly-held and deeply-committed views about the proper path of geography as a social science. For example, his attack (Berry, 1998b) upon a paper by **Michael Dear** and Steven Flusty (1998), published in the *Annals of the Association American Geographers*, combines his outspoken commitment to analytical and theoretical clarity with his vision of the proper role and place of social scientists in the world at large. He attacks these authors for not understanding the implications of their own argument while suggesting there are analytical methods available for the rigorous study of urban complexity and diversity. Berry's strongly held views make for entertaining reading. Those who are the targets of his attention may be offended by his scornful remarks, but Berry's project has never been one of currying favour.

In a related commentary, Berry (1998a: 95) reviewed Edward O. Wilson's argument in favour of reconciliation that 'refers to the convergence of facts and theory to form a common network of explanation across scientific disciplines'. Sharing Wilson's concern about the narrowness and reductionist logic that informs much of the social sciences and especially economics, Berry goes on to suggest that Wilson's mandate is one that geography (among other disciplines) should emulate. In doing so, Berry (1998a: 96) sets out his own template for social science – a mode of explanation wherein 'our findings are repeatable and expressed with economy'. Insisting 'mensuration is unambiguous', Berry stresses we are all 'continually engaged in heuristics, fully committed to the delights of scientific discovery' (Berry, 1998a: 96). There is little doubt the vast majority of human geographers are deeply suspicious of the rational utility maximising model that dominates his explanations of human agency and decision-making. But, at present, there is little in the way of consensus about the proper mode of research practice and the ultimate objectives of human geography. His agenda is one of many that co-exist in an uneasy coalition of shared disciplinary anxiety.

Brian Berry remains committed to understanding the spatial organisation of economy and society. Over the first decade of the twenty-first century he has pressed the case for 'geospatial science' with willing collaborators inside and outside of geography (e.g. Berry et al., 2008). If this means transcending the discipline as it has been practised over past decades, Berry argues that we should not be squeamish about seeking an integrated science of geographical understanding. This is a challenge to those who have fashioned their careers out of playing the game within the conventional norms of the discipline. And it is a challenge to those who would wish to police the accepted borders of the cultural consensus – as each generation claims intellectual ascendancy over the past, so too do the forces of resistance and transformation begin to germinate and eat away at the consensus. In a way, the current state-of-play in the discipline reminds us of the challenge Berry made to the discipline to be more responsive 50 years ago. Like all challenges that come from people with integrity and ability, it is a challenge that can not be easily ignored. Whether human geography will embrace "geoscience" is perhaps less important than the need to follow his lead and seek engagement and reinvigoration.

BERRY'S KEY WORKS

Berry, B. J. L. (1958) 'A note concerning methods of classification', *Annals, Association of American Geographers*, 48: 300–3.

Berry, B. J. L. (1959) 'Ribbon developments in the urban business pattern', *Annals, Association of American Geographers*, 49: 145–55.

Berry, B. J. L. (1960) 'The impact of expanding metropolitan communities upon the central place hierarchy', *Annals, Association of American Geographers*, 50: 112–16.

Berry, B. J. L. (1967) *Geography of Market Centres and Retail Distribution*. Englewood Cliffs: Prentice-Hall.

Berry, B. J. L. (1976a) *Urbanisation and Counter-urbanisation*. London: Sage.

Berry, B. J. L. (1976b) *Chicago: Transformations of an Urban System*. Cambridge, MA: Ballinger.

Berry, B. J. L. (1991) *Long-Wave Rhythms in Economic Development and Political Behaviour.* Baltimore: Johns Hopkins University Press.
Berry, B. J. L. (1993) 'Geography's quantitative revolution: initial conditions, 1954–1960 – a personal memoir', *Urban Geography,* 14: 434–41.

Secondary Sources and References

Alonso, W. (1964) *Location and Land Use.* Cambridge, MA: Harvard University Press.
Berry, B. J. L. (1998a) 'On consilience', *Urban Geography,* 19: 95–7.
Berry, B. J. L. (1998b) 'Wallerstein's middle ground' ,*Urban Geography,* 19: 393–4.
Berry, B.J.L., Griffith, D.A. and Tiefelsdorf, M.R. (2008) 'From spatial analysis to geospatial science', *Geographical Analysis,* 40: 229–38.
Clark, G. L., Feldman, M. and Gertler, M.S. (eds) (2000) *The Oxford Handbook of Economic Geography.* Oxford: Oxford University Press.
Dear, M. J. and Flusty, S. (1998) 'Post-modern urbanism', *Annals, Association of American Geographers,* 88: 50–72.
Harvey, D. (1973) *Social Justice and the City.* Baltimore: Johns Hopkins University Press.
Harvey, D. (1982) *The Limits to Capital.* Chicago: University of Chicago Press.
Krugman, P. (1991) *Geography of Trade.* Cambridge, MA: MIT Press.
National Academy of Sciences (1982) *Critical Issues for National Urban Policy.* Washington DC: NAS (with Royce Hanson and others).
Wrigley, N. and Matthews, S. (1986) 'Citation classics and citation levels in geography', *Area,* 18: 185–94.
Yeates, M. (2001) 'Yesterday as tomorrow's song: the contributions of the 1960s "Chicago School" to urban geography', *Urban Geography,* 22: 514–29.

Gordon L. Clark, University of Oxford

8 Homi K. Bhabha

Homi K. Bhabha was born to an English and Gujarati speaking Parsi family in the newly independent India of 1949. Parsis, a minority of Persian descent, were instrumental in the emergence of an urban middle class in nineteenth-century Imperial India and in this capacity often functioned as mediators between the Indians and the British. Because of their dispersion – Parsis live in small clusters in a number of different host cultures – they derive their cultural cohesion partly from their Zoroastrian faith and partly from a negotiation of their host cultures' traits. Thus, Parsis offer a striking example of the hybridised, cosmopolitan minorities at the centre of Bhabha's work; indeed Bhabha has often linked his intellectual preoccupations to the specificity of his origins.

Bhabha spent his childhood and early adulthood in Bombay where he received a BA in English from Bombay University. Shortly after the completion of his undergraduate degree, Bhabha left India to read English at Christ Church College Oxford where he took an MA, MPhil, and DPhil. While at Oxford, he wrote his doctoral thesis on the Trinidadian writer V.S. Naipaul, whose thematisation of the 'mimic' identity of colonised populations remained a central reference point in Bhabha's subsequent development. In 1978, Bhabha gained a lectureship at Sussex University where he remained until 1994. This position was to be decisive for the young academic: in the late 1970s and 1980s the Sussex English department functioned as a privileged site for the importation and appropriation of French and Continental theory into British academic work. Bhabha's work is a palimpsest of this traffic in theory, and his texts resonate with allusions to Derridean deconstruction, Lacanian psychoanalysis and – perhaps most profoundly of all – the work of **Michel Foucault.**

Between the mid-1980s and the early 1990s Bhabha held visiting fellowships at Princeton, Dartmouth College and the University of Pennsylvania. During this time Bhabha produced several articles published in the journals *Critical Inquiry*, *Screen* and *October* through which he first established himself as a distinct voice within the emergent field of postcolonial studies. In 1986 he wrote the introduction to the English translation of Frantz Fanon's *Black Skin, White Masks*, in which he argued for the salience of the Martiniquan psychiatrist's writings on the psychology of the colonised for contemporary political practice. During the late 1980s Bhabha joined a number of academics in seeking an engaged understanding of the cultural forces shaping Thatcher's Britain. In this context he argued for the symbolic centrality of cultural minorities for national discourse. In the wake of the 1989 fatwa on Salman Rushdie for his book *The Satanic Verses*, Bhabha wrote a series of position pieces for the left-affiliated weekly *The New Statesman* in which he castigated the Western liberal representation of Muslim populations prompted by the Rushdie affair. Through these engagements, Bhabha's writings turned more decisively towards discussions of the place of migrant and displaced populations in the geographies of the new world order. His first edited collection – *Nation and Narration* (1990a) – brought together a number of scholars who sought to analyse the discourses through which nations find their coherence as collective bodies.

Bhabha's reputation was cemented in 1994 through the publication of *The Location of Culture*, a collection of most of his earlier essays in revised form. In the same year, he became Professor in the Humanities at the University of Chicago. While in Chicago, Bhabha taught Art History as well as English and became a regular contributor to the journal *Artforum*. Following his move to the US, Bhabha became more substantially engaged with visual culture, and he advises several leading cultural institutions in New York, namely the Whitney and the Rockefeller Foundation. His later work moved in two related directions: the potential of a new, vernacular cosmopolitanism (the subject of his forthcoming book, *A Measure of Dwelling*) and the question of minority rights in discussions of multiculturalism (to be considered in another ongoing book project, *The Right to Narrate*). Bhabha became Anne F. Rothenberg Professor of Humanities in the Department of English at Harvard University in 2001,

and continues to lecture on post-colonial and literary theory.

SPATIAL CONTRIBUTIONS

Bhabha's early essays intervened in the emerging analyses of colonial discourse following **Edward Said's** installation of this term in *Orientalism*. While Bhabha agreed with Said's mobilisation of **Michel Foucault's** writings on discourse for an analysis of colonial knowledge formations, he countered Said's claim that colonial discourse imposed a firm distinction between European and native identities. Instead, Bhabha suggested that colonial texts both assumed such a distinction and continuously cast it into doubt. Bhabha proposed that the colonisers' stereotypes of the colonised were characterised by *ambivalence*, in other words, that stereotypes were 'a form of knowledge and identification that vacillates between what is always "in place", already known, and something that must be anxiously repeated' (Bhabha, 1994: 66). Stereotypes revealed both the authority of colonial discourse and the limits of this authority: their aim was to fix the colonised through a series of characterisations (e.g. the 'lazy African', the 'lascivious Oriental') but their constant reiteration suggested that such a fixity was impossible.

In a series of essays published in the mid-1980s, Bhabha extended his psychoanalytic and deconstructive readings to an elaboration of native resistance against colonialism. In so doing, Bhabha returned to the writings of V.S. Naipaul and refashioned them in the light of Frantz Fanon's understanding of the colonised psyche. While Naipaul had produced the seemingly pessimistic diagnosis that the colonised is nothing but a 'mimic man' living on the borrowed culture of the colonising powers, in Bhabha's hands this diagnosis became tinged with subversive potential. Bhabha claimed that the colonial 'mimic men' represent a paradox at the heart of the Imperial mission: to wit, that the Imperial project depended both on the coloniser's wish for the native to become Europeanised and on his fear that – in so becoming – the native may become too much like the coloniser. Mimicry, for Bhabha, is thus premised upon the missionary desire to make the colonised 'almost the same *but not quite*' (Bhabha, 1994c: 86). However, the mimicry of the colonised also confronts the coloniser with an uncanny version of himself, a parodic re-enactment of European distinctiveness. Such a re-enactment has the potential to dislodge the very authenticity assumed by the European and to undermine its originality. Bhabha's arguments here anticipate the later discussions of performativity in the work of **Judith Butler**: for Bhabha, the colonised is not a second-rate European but rather a disturbance to the European's dream of authority and authenticity.

Bhabha's early essays thus contained a double challenge to the understanding of colonial identity formations. On the one hand, they involved the claim that Western discourses of Othering inevitably become fractured and split at the point of their application, and that it is precisely these applications that enabled the resistance of the colonised. On the other hand, however, these essays also troubled understandings of the political implications of such resistance. If the coloniser becomes a split, ambivalent figure, then so does the colonised: the latter possesses no authentic self beneath the mask of mimicry bequeathed by the coloniser. Therefore, any political resistance to colonial rule has to be understood not as the oppressed population's straightforward rejection of the coloniser's legacy, but rather as a much more ambiguous process in which that legacy is both refused and desired.

Bhabha later refined his concept of ambivalence, giving it a decidedly spatial cast. From the late 1980s on, and beginning with his articles for *The New Statesman*, Bhabha urged for a more nuanced reading of cultural identities within the post-colonial geographies of migration and diaspora. In these articles – some of his most elegant and lucid writings to date – Bhabha deplored the binary thinking which pitted the cultural spaces of Western liberal states against the minority enclaves of Islamic populations living within them. He claimed that these categories remained blind to the complex dynamics of negotiation through which displaced populations make sense of their lives across contesting cultural values and traditions. For Bhabha such experiences should not be seen to form a distinct and self-contained cultural *space* but to signal a *process* of 'cultural translation' between traditions (Bhabha, 1989).

In the 1990s, Bhabha continued his elaboration of 'cultural translation' as a process which has inevitably accompanied the installation of modernity through the legacies of colonisation. Bhabha called for a post-colonial revision of modernity and a rejection of the social-scientific vocabulary of development and underdevelopment, of First and Third Worlds. In the place of such totalising explanations, Bhabha called for partial and localised strategies of analysis capable of recognising the liminality and instability of cultural and political practices.

In accord with the insights of other post-colonial theorists, Bhabha's work too insists that we cannot think the spatialities of modernity outside those produced through Imperial projects; that the cultural present inevitably testifies to a sedimentation of colonial histories. But while some post-colonial theorists have claimed that communities and identities are therefore shaped through boundaries between 'us' and 'them', 'self' and 'other', Bhabha has proposed instead that identities are inevitably hybridised, because the spaces of social life are formed through a *rupturing* of boundaries and through flows of illicit border traffic. Bhabha has employed a number of terms, such as 'hybridity', 'the in-between', 'cultural translation' and 'third space' to describe this rupturing. These terms are neither intended to be synonymous nor do they point to discrete types of spatiality. Rather, they represent Bhabha's attempt to problematise the spatio-temporal coordinates routinely employed by social scientists. The proliferation of such terms in Bhabha's writings enacts the slipperiness of the spatialities he is attempting to evoke, and their irreducibility to conventional types of mapping. In the context of the 'cultural turn' within geography and the social sciences more broadly, the work of Homi Bhabha, along with that of **Gayatri Spivak** and **Edward Said**, has thus provided a methodological compass for geographers engaging with the spatial legacies of colonization (though, as noted in the next section, not always without criticism).

KEY ADVANCES AND CONTROVERSIES

The distinctiveness of Bhabha's work can be gauged by the amount of criticism his essays have generated. One focus of such criticism and debate has been Bhabha's

attempt to redefine culture by submitting it to a 'radical' spatialisation. What this means is that while for Bhabha culture is primarily spatial, he suggests it cannot be conceptualised through the oppositions between tradition and modernity, or east and west. Instead, Bhabha suggests that a cultural space is the location of shared practices which, while generated in response to particular historical and geographical conditions, cannot simply be said to belong to one discrete culture or another. It is with reference to such practices that Bhabha initially used the term 'third space'. In Bhabha's discussion of the Rushdie affair, 'third space' described the hybrid cultural practices of British Muslims and other displaced populations who negotiate often irreconcilable fragments of different traditions and make their temporary home at their limits. The identities generated within such spatialities cannot be authentically Muslim or authentically British, but are both and neither at the same time. Bhabha further proposed that the presence of migrant populations disturbs normative understandings of social space and of national culture. Hybridised spaces are omnipresent in the shifting demographies of actual nations, produced by the 'wandering peoples who ... are themselves the marks of a shifting boundary that alienates the frontiers of the modern nation (Bhabha, 1990a: 315).

This definition of 'third space' has proved particularly attractive to geographers who wish to engage with the complex and shifting experiences in contemporary global spaces. Steve Pile, for example, has read Bhabha's 'third space' as a call for an overcoming of dualistic epistemologies. For Pile, Bhabha gestured to the emergence of a new politics through 'a space which avoids the politics of polarity and enables the construction of new radical allegiances to oppose structures of authority' (Pile, 1994: 271). Similarly, **Gillian Rose** has employed Bhabha's work in her discussions of the kinds of collective solidarity that do not rely on exclusionary tactics. Both Pile and Rose have thus praised Bhabha's problematisation of space as 'something which must itself be made different' (Rose, 1995: 369).

In tandem with this identification of 'third space' as the cultural location of hybrid communities, Bhabha has also maintained a rather different usage of the term. This second usage, while equally central in Bhabha's texts, has generated a less amiable reception. In his essay 'The commitment to theory' published in *The Location of Culture* (1994a) for example, 'third space' does not refer solely to a spatiality produced by particular populations, but, in addition, to the 'general conditions of language' within which hegemonic discourses are elaborated (Bhabha, 1994: 36). Briefly, Bhabha uses the term to suggest that every time particular cultural traditions and discourses are performed, the outcome is something in excess of what had been intended, so that the enactment of cultural practices always necessarily displaces them. Here, 'third space' designates both specific hybridised cultural practices and an aspect of all cultural life. 'Third space' is thus both the space between cultures and the non-coincidence of a *single* culture with itself. This generalisation of 'third space' has provoked severe criticism from a number of academic locales. Within post-colonial studies, Robert Young claimed that Bhabha lacked historical and geographical specificity insofar as his formulations made ambivalence and hybridity into conditions inherent in cultural practice rather than specific to particular impositions of colonial power (1990). More recently, Moore-Gilbert has similarly concluded that Bhabha's uncritical use of psychoanalysis leads him to homogenise

discrete geopolitical formations under a Western set of categories (1997). In addition, a number of Marxist critics have castigated Bhabha for his deprioritisation of class dynamics in his accounts of spatiality (e.g. Ahmad, 1992).

Bhabha's work has also generated ambivalent responses among geographers engaging with post-colonial theory. His predilection for gnomic pronouncements and his fondness for a rhetoric of exhortation has meant that he quickly became eminently quotable by many academics seeking a theoretical language attentive to the spatial heterogeneities of cultural life. Thus, for example, while **Ed Soja** quotes Bhabha extensively in his book *ThirdSpace*, he also makes it clear that his work owes more to **Henri Lefebvre** and to the African American cultural critic **bell hooks** than it does to Bhabha (Soja 1996). While Soja discusses Bhabha's work at length, he suggests that Lefebvre's and hooks' perspectives are more immediately engaged with the production of spatiality and the politics of marginalised people respectively.

Indeed, a number of geographers have taken issue with the level of abstraction and generality in Bhabha's claims. **Gillian Rose** has used Bhabha's work while also critiquing Bhabha's inattention to the actual effectivity of political struggles. For Rose, this is a serious problem of Bhabha's methodology. In her otherwise favourable review of *The Location of Culture*, Rose suggested that it is because of his central thesis concerning the ambivalence of hegemonic discourses, that Bhabha fails to adequately address historical specificity. In other words, insofar as Bhabha claims that dominant discourses (such as discourses of 'nation' or 'Empire') contain their own failure within themselves, he cannot throw light on how *some* powerful discourses *remain* powerful while others fail (see Rose, 1995; Sparke, 1998).

Other geographers have suggested that hybridity is not always related to a failure of dominant discourses – at least not as far as economic discourses are concerned. In other words, while hybridity may upset the cultural ideologies of nationalism, it gives perfect sustenance to the ideologies of capitalism. For example, Katharyne Mitchell's research on Hong Kong entrepreneurs in Vancouver, Canada, has demonstrated how 'hybrid subject positions ... and liminal and partial sites can be used for the purposes of capital accumulation' (Mitchell, 1997: 534).

These contestations of Bhabha's approach may be symptomatic of wider tendencies characterising current research on location and social practice. Bhabha's work militates against the critique of 'theory' launched by many social scientists who privilege the local and geographically specific. As geographers turn increasingly to the politics of experience, they castigate Bhabha's use of hybridity as a catch-all category which, in their view, ignores the specificity and irreducibility of different experiences of marginalisation. However, Homi Bhabha's approach does not necessarily entail an indifference to politics and to material practices. Rather, by suggesting that such practices are divided and conflictual, Bhabha's writings may facilitate our questioning of the distinctions between theory and politics, or between resistance and complicity, by recommending an attentiveness to the in-between spaces of everyday life. Recent work by Jane M. Jacobs and Lisa

Law illustrates this alternative reading of Bhabha.

In her research on Filipina sex workers, Lisa Law uses 'third space' as a way of thinking the politics of location together with the ambivalence of psychic life. By refusing to dichotomise between western sex-tourists as oppressors and Asian prostitutes as their victims, Law claims instead that 'comprehending the political economic and colonial realities of sex tourism does not necessarily provide an understanding of the personalized modes of identification which form around issues of race, gender and sexuality' (Law, 1997: 109). Here, 'third space' refers to the dynamics of psychic life, and to the way in which these dynamics engage particular dominant discourses.

Jane M. Jacobs' book, *Edge of Empire*, argues that the spatial legacies of British Imperialism cannot simply be seen as the outcome of imperial impositions, or as the effect of native resistance (1996). The analysis of such spatialities, Jacobs claims, requires a double vision. On the one hand, geographers must be attentive to how local dynamics translated imperial projects. On the other hand, they must also perceive the imperial projects themselves as ambivalent formations (split between the imperative to civilise and the desire to violate the other). In other words, Jacobs suggests that it is possible and, indeed, necessary for geographers to hold on to both a general understanding of culture as 'third space' (as proposed by Bhabha) while also remaining attentive to the specificity of experiences of cultural life.

BHABHA'S KEY WORKS

Bhabha, H. K. (1986) 'Remember Fanon: Self, psyche and the colonial conditional', Foreword to Frantz Fanon *Black Skin, White Masks*. London: Pluto Press. pp.vii–xvi.
Bhabha, H.K. (1989) 'Beyond fundamentalism and liberalism', *The New Statesman and Society*, 2 (39): 34–5.

Bhabha, H.K. (1990a) *Nation and Narration*. London and New York: Routledge.

Bhabha, H.K. (1990b) 'The third space: interview with Homi K. Bhabha', in J. Rutherford (ed.) *Identity: Community, Culture, Difference*. London: Lawrence and Wishart. pp. 207–21.

Bhabha, H.K. (1994) *The Location of Culture*. New York and London: Routledge.

Bhabha, H. K. (1994a) 'The commitment to theory', in *The Location of Culture*. New York and London: Routledge. pp. 19–39 (revision of essay published in 1988).

Bhabha, H. K. (1994b) 'The other question: sterotype, discrimination and the discourse of colonialism', in *The Location of Culture*. New York and London : Routledge. pp. 66–84 (revision of essay published in 1983).

Bhabha, H. K. (1994c) 'Of mimicry and man: the ambivalence of colonial discourse', in *The Location of Culture*. New York and London : Routledge. pp. 85–92 (revision of essay published in 1984).

Bhabha, H. K. (1994d) 'How newness enters the world: postmodern space, post-colonial times and the trials of cultural translation', in *The Location of Culture*. New York and London: Routledge. pp. 212–35.

Bhabha, H.K. (1995) 'Translator translated: conversation with Homi Bhabha', *Artforum* 33 (7): 80–83, 110, 114, 118–19.

Bhabha, H. and W.J.T. Mitchell (eds) (2004) *Edward Said: Continuing the Conversation*. Chicago: The University of Chicago Press.

Bhabha, H. K. (forthcoming) *A Measure of Dwelling: Reflections on Vernacular Cosmopolitanism*. Cambridge, MA : Harvard UP.

Secondary Sources and References

Ahmad, A. (1992) *In Theory: Classes, Nations, Literatures*. London: Verso.

Jacobs, J.M. (1996) *Edge of Empire: Postcolonialism and the City*. London: Routledge.

Law, L. (1997) 'Dancing on the bar: sex, money and the uneasy politics of third space,' in S .Pile and M. Keith (eds), *Geographies of Resistance*. London: Routledge. pp. 107–123.

Mitchell, K. (1997) 'Different diasporas and the hype of hybridity,' *Environment and Planning D: Society and Space*, 15: 533–53.

Moore, D.S. (1997) 'Remapping resistance: "Ground for struggle" and the politics of place', in S. Pile and M. Keith (eds), *Geographies of Resistance*. London: Routledge. pp. 87–106.

Moore-Gilbert, B. (1997) *Postcolonial Theory: Contexts, Practices, Politics*. London: Verso.

Pile, S. (1994) 'Masculinism, the use of dualistic epistemologies and third spaces', *Antipode*, 26: 255–77.

Rose, G. (1994) 'The cultural politics of place: local representation and oppositional discourse in two films', *Transactions of the Institute of British Geographers*, 19: 46–60.

Rose, G. (1995) 'The interstitial perspective: a review essay of Homi Bhabha's *The Location of Culture*', *Environment and Planning D: Society and Space*, 13: 365–73.

Rose, G. (1997) 'Spatialities of community, power and change: the imagined geographies of community arts projects', *Cultural Studies*, 11: 1–16.

Routledge, P. (1996) 'The third space as critical engagement', *Antipode*, 28: 399–419.

Said, E. (1978) *Orientalism*. London: Routledge and Kegan Paul.

Soja, E. (1996) *ThirdSpace: Journeys to Los Angeles and Other Real-and-imagined Places*. Oxford: Blackwell.

Sparke, M. (1998) 'A map that roared and an original atlas: Canada, cartography, and the narration of nation', *Annals of the Association of American Geographers*, 88: 463–95.

Young, R. (1990) *White Mythologies: Writing History and the West*. London: Routledge.

Young, R. (1995) *Colonial Desire: Hybridity in Theory, Culture and Race*. London: Routledge.

Constantina Papoulias, Nottingham Trent University

9 Pierre Bourdieu

BIOGRAPHICAL DETAILS AND THEORETICAL CONTEXT

Pierre Bourdieu was born in 1930 in a small village in south-west France. When he finished high school (as a star pupil and rugby player) he moved to Paris where he studied philosophy at the elite École Normale Supérieure. After graduating he worked as a teacher for a year before being drafted into the army to fight in the Algerian War between 1956 and 1958. His experiences in Algeria (a conflict over French colonialism that he subsequently described as 'an appalling war') turned him away from philosophy and towards sociology and anthropology, and he remained in Algeria after the conflict to teach at the University of Algiers while conducting fieldwork among the Kabyle of the North East region. In 1960 he returned to France and held posts at the University of Paris-Sorbonne, the University of Lille and in 1964 became Director of Studies at the École des Hautes Études en Sciences Sociales. In 1968 he launched the Centre for European Sociology and later established the journal *Actes de la Recherche en Sciences Sociale*, devoted to understanding cultural reproduction and class domination. Bourdieu was elected to a chair at the

prestigious Collège de France in 1981. He died in 2002.

Over his distinguished career Bourdieu published over 40 books and more than 400 articles. These range from early anthropological texts – such as *The Algerians* (1962) – and related theoretical contributions – most notably, *Outline of a Theory of Practice* (1977) – through to definitive contributions to our understanding of class reproduction (*Distinction: A Social Critique of the Judgement of Taste*, 1984); the sociology of education (*The Inheritors*, 1979; *Reproduction in Education, Society and Culture*, 1977) and theorisations of action in everyday life (*Practical Reason*, 1998). Bourdieu was also engaged in a critique of the politics of globalisation rendered in the voices of those dispossessed by the neo-liberal global regime (*The Weight of the World*, 1999). This is also reflected in later work (*The Social Structures of the Economy*, 2005) in which he stressed the significance of local circumstances against the discourse of a universal market.

Bourdieu's leading theoretical claim was that his work transcended the dualism between explanations that attributed social change and social reproduction to certain over-arching structures and theorisations that privileged individual subjective intention or experience. He drew on existentialism to emphasise the importance of practical action and existence (praxis) in understanding the human

individual whilst simultaneously rejecting the highly conscious, subjectivist
elements of Sartre's existentialism which
sees authentic existence as an act of self-
creation. At the same time Bourdieu's
work has affinities with American pragmatism (especially Mead and Dewey) in
his social conception of mind and agency
and emphasis on the body as a site of
socially instilled habit (see Aboulafia,
1999; Bridge, 2005). This response to
the dualisms of objectivism and subjectivism constituted Bourdieu's 'theory of
practice'. This is the idea that ongoing,
practical everyday activities – articulated
through bodies – contain prior cultural
dispositions that weigh upon, but not
definitively so, ongoing actions. This mix
of activities and ways of acting tends
to encompass distinctive deployments
of different forms of capital. Hence,
Bourdieu's innovation is to argue that
forms of capital include cultural assets:
the ability to 'consume' rare objects, such
as certain works of art, might demand
skills of taste and appreciation that are
derived from family background and/or
via institutionalised education (hence his
interest in the sociology of education).

Cultural capital involves the embodied
dispositions and resources of habitus. It
includes competences that are incorporated via education, as well as symbolic
power, which is the power of a certain
class to legitimise their 'natural' tastes
and so dominate the social order. Cultural
and symbolic capital has relations with
social capital (based on social networks)
and the economic capital. Different combinations of forms of capital operate in
'fields' (economic, political or artistic,
for example). If social life is thought of
as a 'game' (an analogy Bourdieu used
often) then fields are the playing board.
Embodied dispositions provide the 'feel
for the game', which cannot be explained
wholly by the rules of the game. Crucially, Bourdieu argued that the feel for
the game varies over social space (a term
he used to suggest a 'force field' of conflicting social power). Moreover, he suggested that strategies tend to coalesce
in relatively enduring combinations and
embodied dispositions that he termed
habitus. A crucial concept at the heart of
Bourdieu's sociology, habitus is an array
of inherited dispositions that condition
bodily movement, tastes and judgements,
according to class position (Bourdieu,
1984).

SPATIAL CONTRIBUTIONS

As Joe Painter (2000) has pointed out, the
take up of Bourdieu's ideas in geography
has been patchy. That is not to say that he
is not frequently cited, but that sustained
and direct engagement of geographers
with Bourdieu's work has been surprisingly rare. There are some early skir-
mishes, most notably Parkes and Thrift's
(1980) use of the idea of 'social time' from
Bourdieu's study of the Kabyle people in
Algeria. In this work Bourdieu analyses
how the cultural and economic rhythms
of Kabyle life constitute time in that society. Bourdieu's analysis of the times and
spaces of the Kabyle house also provides
David Harvey (1989) with an example of
the structuring of space and time that is
non-capitalist. For Harvey, the Kabyle
example shows that time and space can
be orientated socially around the body
in ways that have deep cultural resonance. Harvey ends his consideration of
Bourdieu by questioning the degree to
which this socio-cultural time/space can

survive the increasingly global reach of capitalism – an ordering of time and space that relies on the abstraction of place in accordance with the logic of capital accumulation.

This vague definition of habitus as some kind of authentic, culturally rich, 'place', resisting what Henri Lefebvre calls the 'abstract space' of capitalism, accounts for many of those citations of Bourdieu that make no direct engagement with his ideas. Against this, there has also been a much more explicit exploration of the links between habitus and place which, although not located centrally in geography, does involve geographers and urbanists and has significant implications for geographers' engagement with Bourdieu's work. The overall purpose of the edited collection by Jean Hillier and Emma Rooksby *Habitus: A Sense of Place* (2002) is to ask if the idea of habitus is still relevant in a rapidly globalising world. The book tackles this question at a number of levels, from national and subnational political fields and their relationship to symbolic capital and domination, through discussions of post-colonialism and habitus as resistance, through to the role of the built environment in the reproduction of habitus. Specific contributions in geography include Joe Painter's drawing together of the idea of habitus and Foucault's notion of governmentality in the discursive construction of place as a space for politics, and chapters by Steve Pile, Neil Leach and Kim Dovey that start to articulate the connections between the largely unconscious nature of habitus and psychoanalytic insights into the formation of identity. Leach and Dovey locate this in the domination effects of architecture as built form, and the architectural profession as an intellectual field, in reproducing dominant social divisions through place-making. Pile explores the more unpredictable effects of feelings of

the uncanny in the formation of habitus as sense of place through ideas of ghostliness and being haunted by places in the city.

Recognising another important departure Painter (2000) argues that Nigel Thrift (1996) in part takes inspiration from Bourdieu's definition of practice as a means of 'going on in the world' but pursues it through non-representational modes of knowing. In Thrift's non-representational geography (Thrift, 2007), practice, practical sense and 'a feel for the game' can never be fully captured and represented. If that is acknowledged then the spatialities of practice can give rise to the possibility of other ways of being in the world. The spatialities of practice have been taken in another direction by Tim Cresswell (1996) who shows that the geographical 'facts of life' (place, territory, landscape) are constitutive of social life because they relate the body to space through habitus. Cresswell demonstrates the power of these geographical ordering devices by exploring reactions to their transgression (for instance, by New York graffiti artists, Greenham Common peace protestors and new age travellers). Emphasising geographies of mobility, Cresswell thus offers an elegant geographic elaboration of Bourdieu's ideas (describing Bourdieu's influence on his work in a glowing appreciation of his legacy – see Cresswell, 2002).

The concept of habitus has in recent years been most evident in the analysis of urban space. A range of studies of have used Bourdieu's work on habitus to explain socio-spatial changes in the city. Tim Butler and Garry Robson argue for a distinct 'metropolitan habitus' of middle-class gentrifiers in London (Butler, 1997; Butler and Robson, 2003) and the way that distinct neighbourhoods reflect different fractions of the middle classes and the ways they defend their class habitus (over schooling, for example). Other work stresses the importance of aesthetics in 'loft living' (Podmore, 1998) or the adaptation of artistic practice into the gentrification aesthetic (Ley, 2003), how it links to constructions of cosmopolitanism (Hage, 2000; May, 1996) and to the changing aesthetics of middle-class gentrifiers more generally (Wynne and O'Connor, 1998). My own strand of work has looked at the relationship between cultural capital and urban space and the way various components of cultural capital (especially education and aesthetics) work together or are in conflict in the trajectories of middle-class residents through houses and neighbourhoods in the city and beyond (Bridge, 2001a; 2001b; 2003; 2006a; 2006b). Chris Allen's research has looked at the relationship between working-class habitus and belonging in neighbourhood in the context of the class politics of ideas of urban regeneration (Allen, 2008).

The ideas of the relationship between space, social trajectories and identity have been investigated comprehensively from a Bourdian perspective in a large-scale research programme at the UK Centre for Research on Socio-Cultural Change (CRESC). CRESC researchers have conducted a comprehensive habitus mapping across a wide range of neighbourhoods in the UK to investigate the changing nature of class relations, culture and identity in Britain (Bennett et al., 2009). As well as recording the contemporary relevance of different forms of capital and habitus in a geographical context they also adapt Bourdieu's analysis to inform new ideas of habitus, such as the significance of 'elective belonging' to neighbourhood as part of an ongoing social/spatial trajectory of middle-class habitus (Savage et al., 2005).

Bourdieu's ideas have gained currency in contemporary human geography as part of the rising concern with the body

and embodiment in the social theory as a whole. Foucault's work considered the body as the site of the operation of disciplinary power. Maurice Merleau-Ponty (1962) saw the body as locus of primary sociality, incarnated activities that exist prior to abstract cognition. From a Marxist perspective Lefebvre saw the body as the possibility of sensual and expressive 'lived space' in resistance to the instrumentalisation of the body in the abstract space of capitalism. Bourdieu's ideas are absorbed as part of this wider set of discourses about the body as a class/cultural process (Dowling, 1998), and, more specifically, as an orientation in space.

KEY ADVANCES AND CONTROVERSIES

There are long-standing and ongoing debates about the degree to which Bourdieu's canon manages to transcend the dualism of objectivism or subjectivism (for example, Jenkins, 1992; Honneth, 1986). Equally, his idea of habitus has come under fire for being too 1960s, too limited to the French social structure and too static. Another weakness for geographers is the paucity of references to space or place in Bourdieu's work, but, as we have seen, more recent developments in urban studies have started to use the spatial elements of Bourdieu's theories more explicitly. This discovery of the spatial aspects of Bourdieu's work as well as the use of Bourdieu's work in an explicitly spatial context should prove to be a rich vein of future research. There is the direct influence of his early anthropology of the Kabyle and later theorisations of practice that relate to 'social' time and space. Then there is a more diffuse, but no less pervasive, set of influences that ripple out from the idea of the body as strategy of capital accumulation: for example, the idea of the body as the locus of class reproduction; the role of the body in the making of social space and the embodied construction of socio-spatial order. Although the classed body has received least attention from geographers, the idea of the body as the site of cultural reproduction is being pursued strongly.

Future flowerings of Bourdieu's geographies are in prospect through ideas of practice and everyday spatialities, and the subconscious sensitivities to space and place. There is one other lesson that Bourdieu leaves us with and that is the richness and value of combining theoretical advances with comprehensive and careful empirical work, finding the place for the self-critical voice of the academic, alongside the voices of the subjects of knowledge. This is fitting legacy for such a 'great and original figure of contemporary sociology', as Jacques Derrida put it (in French newspaper *Le Monde* 24/1/02), when leading the tributes of the French academy and wider society mourning the death of one of its greatest public intellectuals.

BOURDIEU'S KEY WORKS

Bourdieu, P. (1962) *The Algerians.* Trans. A. Ross. Boston, MA: Beacon Press.
Bourdieu, P. (1977) *Outline of a Theory of Practice.* Cambridge: Cambridge University Press.
Bourdieu, P. (1977) *Reproduction in Education, Society and Culture.* Trans R. Nice. London: Sage.
Bourdieu, P. (1979) *The Inheritors: French Students and Their Relation to Culture.* Trans R. Nice. Chicago: Chicago University Press.
Bourdieu, P. (1984) *Distinction: A Social Critique of the Judgement of Taste.* London: Routledge and Kegan Paul.
Bourdieu, P. (1988) *Homo Academicus.* Cambridge: Polity.
Bourdieu, P. (1990) *The Logic of Practice.* Cambridge: Polity.
Bourdieu, P. (1991) *Language and Symbolic Power.* Trans. G. Raymond and M. Adamson, Cambridge: Polity.
Bourdieu, P. and Wacquant, L. (1992) *An Invitation to Reflexive Sociology.* Cambridge: Polity.
Bourdieu, P (1994) *The Rules of Art.* Cambridge: Polity.
Bourdieu, P. (1998) *Practical Reason.* Cambridge: Polity.
Bourdieu, P. (1999) The *Weight of the World: Social Suffering in Contemporary Society.* Palo Alto, CA: Stanford University Press.
Bourdieu, P (1999) *On Television.* New York: New Press.
Bourdieu, P (1999) *Acts of Resistance: Against the Tyranny of the Market.* New York: New Press.
Bourdieu, P (2000) *Pascalian Meditations.* Cambridge: Polity.
Bourdieu P (2005) *The Social Structures of the Economy.* Cambridge: Polity.
Bourdieu, P (2008) *The Batchelor's Ball.* Cambridge: Polity.
Bourdieu, P (2008) *Sketches Towards Self Analysis.* Cambridge: Polity.

Secondary Sources and References

Aboulafia, M. (1999) 'A (neo) American in Paris: Bourdieu, Mead, and pragmatism', in R. Shusterman (ed.), *Bourdieu: A Critical Reader.* Oxford: Blackwell. pp. 153–76.
Allen, C. (2008) *Housing Market Renewal and Social Class.* London: Routledge.
Bennett, T., Savage, M., Silva, E., Warde, A., Gayo-Cal, M. and Wright, D. (2009) *Culture, Class, Distinction.* London: Routledge.
Bridge, G. (2001a) 'Estate agents as interpreters of economic and cultural capital: the "gentrification premium" in the Sydney housing market', *International Journal of Urban and Regional Research,* 25: 81–101.

Bridge, G. (2001b) 'Bourdieu, rational action and the time-space strategy of gentrification', *Transactions of the Institute of British Geographers*, NS 26: 205–16.

Bridge, G. (2003) 'Time-space trajectories in provincial gentrification', *Urban Studies* Special Issue: The Gentry in the City, 40 (12): 2545–56.

Bridge, G. (2006a) 'It's not just a question of taste: gentrification, the neighbourhood and cultural capital', *Environment and Planning A*, 38: 1965–78.

Bridge, G. (2006b) 'Perspectives on the neighbourhood and cultural capital', *Urban Studies,* 43: 719–30.

Bridge, G (2005) *Reason in the City of Difference: Pragmatism, Communicative Action and Contemporary Urbanism.* London: Routledge.

Butler, T. (1997) *Gentrification and the Middle Classes.* Aldershot: Ashgate.

Calhoun, C., LiPuma, E.and Postone, M. (eds) (1993) *Bourdieu: Critical Perspectives.* Cambridge: Polity.

Butler T. and Robson, G. (2003) *London Calling: The Middle Class and the Remaking of Inner London.* London: Berg.

Cresswell, T. (1996) *In Place/Out of Place: Geography, Ideology and Transgression.* Minneapolis: University of Minnesota Press.

Cresswell, T. (2002) Guest editorial: Bourdieu's geographies: in memoriam', *Environment and Planning D: Society and Space,* 20: 379–382.

Dovey, K. (2002) 'The silent complicity of architecture', in Hillier , J. and Rooksby, E. (eds), Habits: A Sense of Place. Aldershot: Ashgate. pp. 283–96.

Dowling, R. (1999) 'Classing the body', *Environment and Planning D: Society and Space,* 17(5): 511–14.

Fowler, B. (1997) *Pierre Bourdieu and Cultural Theory.* London: Sage.

Grenfell, M. and Kelly, M. (eds) (2001) *Pierre Bourdieu; Language, Culture and Education – Theory into Practice.* London: Peter Lang.

Grenfell, M. (2008) *Pierre Bourdieu: Key Concepts.* London: Acumen Press.

Guillory, J. (1993) *Cultural Capital.* Chicago: University of Chicago Press.

Hage, G. (2000) *White Nation: Fantasies of White Supremacy in a Multicultural Nation.* London: Routledge.

Harker, R., Mahar, C. and Wilkes, C. (eds) (1990) *An Introduction to the Works of Pierre Bourdieu.* London: Macmillan.

Harvey, D. (1989) *The Condition of Postmodernity.* Oxford: Blackwell.

Hillier, J. and Rooksby, E. (2002) *Habitus: A Sense of Place.* Aldershot: Ashgate.

Honneth, A. (1986) 'The fragmented world of symbolic forms: reflections on Pierre Bourdieu's sociology of culture', *Theory, Culture and Society* 3: 55–66.

Jenkins, R. (1992) *Pierre Bourdieu.* London: Routledge.

Lane, J.F. (2000) *Pierre Bourdieu: A Critical Introduction.* London: Pluto Press.

Leach, N. (2002) 'Belonging: towards a theory of identification with space', in J. Hillier and E. Rooksby (eds), *Habitus: A Sense of Place.* Aldershot: Ashgate. pp. 297–315.

Ley, D. (2003) 'Artists, aestheticisation and the field of gentrification', *Urban Studies*, 40(12): 2527–44.

Merleau-Ponty, M. (1962) *Phenomenology of Perception.* Trans. C. Smith, London: Routledge.

May, J. (1996) 'Globalisation and the politics of place and identity in an inner London neighbourhood', *Transactions of the Institute of British Geographers*, NS 21: 194–215.

Painter, J. (2000) 'Pierre Bourdieu', in M. Crang, and N. Thrift (eds), *Thinking Space.* London: Routledge. pp. 240–55.

Painter, J. (2002) 'Governmentality and regional economic strategies', in J. Hillier and E. Rooksby (eds), *Habitus: A Sense of Place* Aldershot: Ashgate. pp. 131–256.

Parkes, D. and Thrift, N. (1980) *Times, Spaces and Places: A Chronogeographic Perspective.* Chichester: Wiley.

Pile, S. (2002) 'Spectral cities: where the repressed returns and other short stories', in J. Hillier and E. Rooksby (eds), *Habitus: A Sense of Place,* Aldershot: Ashgate. pp. 235–57.

Podmore, J. (1998) '(Re)reading the "loft living" habitus in Montreal's inner city', *International Journal of Urban and Regional Research,* 22: 283–302.

Savage, M., Bagnall, G. and Longhurst, B. (2005) *Globalisation and Belonging.* London: Sage.

Shusterman, R. (ed.) (1999) *Bourdieu: A Critical Reader.* Oxford: Blackwell.

Swartz, D. (1997) *Culture and Power.* Chicago: University of Chicago Press.

Thrift, N. (1996) *Spatial Formations.* London: Sage.

Thrift, N. (2007) *Non-representational Theory: Space, Politics, Affect.* London: Routledge.

Wacquant, L. (2005) *Pierre Bourdieu and Democratic Politics.* Cambridge: Polity.

Webb, J., Schirato, T., and Danaher, G. (2002) *Understanding Bourdieu.* London: Sage.

Wynne, D. and O'Connor, J. (1998) 'Consumption and the postmodern city', *Urban Studies,* 5–6: 841–64.

Gary Bridge, Bristol University

10 Judith Butler

Judith Butler was born in 1956. She attended Bennington College and then Yale University, where she received her BA and PhD in Philosophy (1984). She taught at Wesleyan and Johns Hopkins universities before becoming Maxine Elliot Professor of Rhetoric and Comparative Literature at the University of California at Berkeley. Butler has written extensively on questions of identity politics, gender, and sexuality, and is largely considered the originator of modern queer theory, although she herself has resisted this label for her work (see Gauntlett, 2002). Her work has critiqued traditional feminist theory for remaining within the confines of a male/female binary and argued that gendered subjectivity needs to be understood as a socially constituted and context dependent fluid performance. Her key contributions include *Gender Trouble* (1990), *Bodies that Matter* (1993), *Excitable Speech* (1997), the collection *Undoing Gender* (2004a) and *Frames of War* (2009) among other publications. The latter demonstrates an increasing focus in her work on questions of violence, especially the relationship between Zionism and oppression, in the context of 'the war on terror'.

Although Judith Butler herself has very little to say about space or place her ideas about performativity and subject formation have been very influential for a critical geography 'concerned to denaturalize taken-for-granted social practices' (Gregson and Rose, 2000: 434). First, Butler's theorisation of gender has reshaped geographers' understandings of identities/bodies and their spatialities. Second, her notion of performativity has been recast to theorise the concept of space. Third, her work has influenced critical geographers' engagement with non-representational theory. Fourth, her conceptualisation of performativity has upset feminist methodological debates about reflexivity and positionality.

Trying to summarise *Gender Trouble*, Butler's most influential work, is a challenging task, primarily because Butler herself has commented on the difficulty of its style and content (Butler 1990: xviii). However, although well acknowledged as a dense text, Butler's (1990) analysis of gender ontologies clearly questions the naturalness of sex/gender binaries. The essence of her argument is that gender identities (masculinity and femininity) are assumed to be grounded in, and defined in relation to, two 'natural' biological sexes: male and female. This binary opposition is also the basis of heterosexual desire (i.e attraction is towards the opposite sex/gender). However, in *Gender Trouble* Butler challenges the assumptions that masculine and feminine gender identities inevitably correspond with 'male' and 'female' bodies (e.g., masculine may just as well signify a female body as a male one). Moreover, she argues that the two sexes themselves are also social constructions so that there is nothing 'natural' about everybody being defined in terms of one sex or the other. Rather than gender identities corresponding to a biological essence or articulating an authentic or core self, Butler theorises them as an effect or 'performance'.

Butler makes this argument by drawing upon the work of linguistic philosopher J. L. Austin (1955) in discussing the process of subject formation. She starts by interrogating the category of 'woman' as the subject of feminism, questioning de Beauvoir's maxim that one is not born a woman, but rather, becomes one (de Beauvoir, 1949). Butler (1990) believes that any identity is the system of a logic of power and language which generates identities as a function of binary oppositions (i.e. self/other), and which seeks to conceal its own workings by making those identities appear to be natural. Notably, she theorises identity as performative, arguing that:

> gender is the repeated stylisation of the body, a set of repeated acts within a highly rigid regulatory framework that congeal over time to produce the appearance of substance, of a natural sort of being ... The effect of gender ... hence, must be understood as the mundane way in which bodily gestures, movements, and styles of various kinds constitute the illusion of an abiding gendered self.
>
> (Butler, 1990: 33 and 140)

In challenging the notion of biology as the bedrock that underlies social categories such as gender, Butler allows for the possibility of transformed gender roles outside the traditional cartographies of discursive patriarchal power relations.

Most notably, she uses a reading of drag balls to argue that the parodic repetition and mimicry of heterosexual identities at these events disrupts dominant sex and gender identities because the performers' supposed 'natural' identities (as male) do not correspond with the signs produced within the performance (e.g., feminine body, language and dress). Thus 'by disrupting the assumed correspondence between a "real" interior and its surface markers (clothes, walk, hair etc.) drag balls make explicit the way in which *all* gender and sexual identifications are ritually performed in daily life' (Nelson 1999: 339).

Thus Butler (1990) insists that if we come to grips with the fact that gender is merely an inscription of discursive imperatives, that is to say, an elaborate, socially constructed fabrication, we open up the possibilities of displacing dominant discourses. She explains:

> Because gender is not a fact, the various acts of gender create the idea of gender, and without those acts, there would be no gender at all. Gender, is thus, a construction that regularly conceals its genesis; the tacit collective agreement to perform, produce and sustain discrete and polar genders as cultural fictions is obscured by the credibility of those productions.
>
> (Butler, 1990: 140)

In *Bodies That Matter*, Butler (1993) clarifies some of the ideas outlined in *Gender Trouble*, and tackles many of the critiques which emerged from her early analysis of the sex/gender binary. In particular, she further analyses the relationship between performativity and the material body. Performativity is explained in more detail and is linked with the notion of citationality. Butler (1993: 18) herself represents *Bodies that Matter* as 'a poststructuralist rewriting of discursive performativity as it operates in the materialization of sex'.

Indeed, Butler (1993: ix) explains to the reader that the book was conceived as a way to respond to the question, 'What about the materiality of the body, Judy?' Butler demonstrates how the unstable sexed body presents a challenge to the boundaries of discursive intelligibility. She also examines the racialization of gender norms by drawing from Nella Larsen's novel *Passing*.

Butler's ideas about sex as an effect rather than a cause are repeated here from *Gender Trouble*, but Butler plays with that argument to articulate how the supposedly 'natural' body can be a 'naturalized effect' of discourse (Salih, 2002). In exploring the limits of performativity, Butler is predominantly concerned with the question of what produces the effect of a stable core of gender. Relying upon a theory of the performative taken from speech act theory and involving ongoing actualisation of gender meanings in the present, Butler argues that performativity is not a single or even deliberate act, but rather 'the reiterative and citational practice by which discourse produces the effects that it names' (Butler, 1993:2).

Her next book, *Excitable Speech: Politics of the Performance* (1997), analysed name-calling or hate speech as both a social injury and the way in which individuals are called into action for political purposes and considered subject categories in the context of language. In this way, it is important to conceptualise Butler's musings as building blocks, where she returns and revisits themes of the sex/gender binary, performativity, citationality, speech theory, and subjectivity, among other arenas. Notably, her own understanding of her work has shifted since she wrote *Gender Trouble*. She admits that she has dramatically revised some of her theoretical positionings since its publication, being compelled to revise her arguments because of increasing political

engagements, which in turn forced her to reconceptualise the notion of the term 'universality':

> [In *Gender Trouble*] I tend to conceive of the claim of 'universality' in exclusive negative and exclusionary terms. However, I came to see the term has important strategic use precisely as a non-substantial and open ended category.
>
> (Butler, 1993: xvii)

She has also clarified what she means by a genuinely 'radical' act, insisting that 'we are never fully determined by the categories that construct us' but yet at the same time, one can dissent from the norms of society by 'occupying the very categories by which one is constituted and turning them in another direction or giving them a future they weren't supposed to have' (Butler, cited in Wallace, 1998:16).

Such questions on the limits of the subject arise again in *Giving an Account of Oneself* (2005), which draws on diverse post-structural thought (especially **Foucault**, Levinas and Nietzsche) to explore an ethics of being based on an appreciation of the construction of Selfhood:

> If I try to give an account of myself, if I try to make myself recognizable and understandable, then I might begin with a narrative account of my life, but this narrative will be disoriented by what is not mine, or what is not mine alone. And I will, to some degree, have to make myself substitutable in order to make myself recognizable. The narrative authority of the 'I'' must give way to the perspective and temporality of a set of norms that contest the singularity of my story.
>
> (Butler, 2001: 15)

From this position she argues that identity formation is not just suffused with individual notions of pleasure and pain but can be complicit in violence: in effect, she suggests that there is a need for a shared awareness of the vulnerability, humility and responsibility that can derive from our susceptibility to the 'unwilled address' of Others. Emerging from this is her consideration of how we can develop 'liveable lives' – and hence minimise the possibility of 'unbearable life' – a theme powerfully explored in what has widely been acclaimed as one of her most accessible (and controversial) works, *Precarious Life: The Power of Mourning and Violence* (2004b). Questioning whose lives are regarded as grievable, this book seeks to counter the arguments for the power of censorship and military intervention in the wake of 9/11 by suggesting that the type of treatment meted out to prisoners at Guananamo Bay, for example, is only comprehensible as a mass reaction to grief in which some lives are dehumanised and made less grievable. The question as to whether grief and loss can result in anything but a call to violence and war was pushed further in *Frames of War* (2009), which foregrounded issues and images of bodily terror and violence to develop a distinctively critical take on 'war' informed by both geopolitical and psychoanalytic theory. In 2009, Butler won a $1.5 million Mellon award which she planned to devote to further consideration of these questions.

SPATIAL CONTRIBUTIONS

From her earlist work on gender through to later work on war and terror, Butler's notions of performativity and subjecthood have been drawn on by many geographers who have considered their ramifications for understanding the body as it is lived and spatially constituted.

This engagement with Butler reflected the upsurge of interest in the body within the discipline that occurred at the turn of the millennium. Callard (1998: 387) observes that 'geographers are now taking the problematic of corporeality seriously ... "The body" is becoming a preoccupation in the geographical literature, and is a central figure around which to base political demands, social analyses and theoretical investigations.' For example, Butler's work has been used by Cream (1995) to think about how gender is inscribed on the space of the body, by Johnson (1995) to consider how women body-builders destabilise traditional notions of femininity and by Bell and Valentine (1995) to theorise the transgressive pleasures of body modification. In the context of the workplace both Crang (1994) and McDowell (1995, 1997) have shown how in restaurants and banking respectively, the performances of particular gender and sexual identities are integral to selling different types of 'interactive' service products. Some feminist geographers, have also focused on psychic and emotional processes to examine the ways in which bodies themselves are imagined as spaces, and the spaces which they are imagined as inhabiting (Rose 1993, 1996, 1999).

Other geographers have drawn upon the language of performativity to talk about identities. For example, in terms of the ways in which hegemonic discourses inscribe nationalist identities (Sharp 1996) and to examine the subject and spatial politics embedded in Cartesian maps (Kirby 1996). But perhaps the most sustained engagement by geographers with Butler's work on gender has been in relation to the theorisation of sexualised space. In the inaugural issue of the feminist journal *Gender, Place and Culture*, Bell et al. (1994) took Butler's understanding that there is a potential for transgressive politics within the parodying of heterosexual constructs, to suggest that a similar argument can be made for the production of space. Bell et al. (1994) draw on examples of the lipstick lesbian and gay skinhead to question the 'unnaturalness' of not just day-to-day heteronormative space, but also the masculine and feminine identities associated with their practice in those spaces (Bell et al., 1994). In a similar vein, Lewis and Pile (1996), writing about the Rio Carnival, consider what effects bodily performances may have on understandings of space and place. Thus, instead of thinking about space and place as pre-existing sites which occur, these studies have argued that bodily performances themselves constitute or (re)produce space.

However, these attempts to apply Butler's theory of performativity in specific everyday contexts have led to accusations that geographers have been too enthusiastic to engage with Butler and in process have often used the language of performativity uncritically and without regard to its limitations; or have misread and therefore misapplied Butler's ideas (e.g. Walker 1995, Nelson, 1999; Gregson and Rose 2000). In particular, Bell et al.'s (1994) paper sparked accusations that they had inserted the notion of choice and intentionality into their reading of the performance of lipstick lesbian and gay skinhead identities, thus presupposing human agency when Butler is at pains to deny that there is 'a *doer* behind the deed' (Nelson, 1999: 324) (these criticisms are also repeated of other geographers' attempts to deploy Butler's theorisation of performativity). Walker, for example, explains:

> The problem with the rhetoric of intentionality that creeps into Bell et al.'s discussion of how we can self-consciously perform genders in subversive ways is not just that it falls back on philosophical essentialisms about subjectivity. The problem is also that, as Butler argues,

an account of subjectivity that relies too heavily on intentionality does not take into account how people are compelled and constrained by the very regulatory norms of gender identity that are the condition of our resistance. This means that many of us do not experience our gender identities as being very fluid or available to choice.

(Walker, 1995: 76)

Subsequently, other geographers have sought to rework and elaborate on the implications of performativity for geographical understandings of space. Gregson and Rose (2000), for example, draw on two very different research projects, one with community arts workers and projects and the other on car-boot sales as alternative spaces of consumption, to develop the complexity and instability of notion of performances and performed spaces.

As the limits of Butler's notion of performativity are interrogated some geographers are linking it together with non-representational theory (drawing heavily from the work of theorists such as **Deleuze** and Guattari) to develop a wider set of ideas about performativity and body-practices (Thrift, 2000; Dewsbury, 2000). Most notably **Thrift** (1997: 125) uses dance, which he describes as 'a concentrated example of the expressive nature of embodiment', as a way to develop different ideas of the use of performance (see also Thrift, 2000).

Latterly, Butler's work on war and ethics has been inspirational in relation to geographical debates on sovereignty. Taking a somewhat different stance to **Foucault** and Agamben on biopolitics, Butler's explorations of the ways in which some lives are made less liveable (and, indeed, judged of less worth) than others have figured large in discussions of biosecurity, border surveillance and the geopolitics of the state, albeit she begins from a focus on the body and self which emphasises the subjectivity of the subject and its exposure. In the work of **Derek Gregory** (2007) on terror, for example, Butler's notions of uninhabitability and unliveable lives become animated through a consideration of the 'camp' and the prison as spaces located outside and beyond international law, suggestive of important connections both to Agamben's notions of 'bare life' as well as to emerging work on legal geography.

Butler's ideas have not only been applied by geographers in relation to theoretical, but also methodological debates. In a review of feminist writing about positionality, **Rose** (1997) has critiqued feminist geographers' attempts to define their positionality and be reflexive about their relationships with informants. Rather, drawing on Butler, Rose (1997) argues that our positionings in relation to our interviewees are never a priori. Rather an interviewer and interviewee fashion a particular performance of self through their interaction and thus it is impossible to identify a transparent, knowable self in the research process (see also Valentine, 2002).

KEY ADVANCES AND CONTROVERSIES

Although hugely influential, Butler's work has also generated many critiques and some scepticism across the social sciences. Most famously, she has been criticised for her obscure and abstract writing style, which she is accused of using to create an 'aura of importance' (Nussbaum, 1999: 6). Indeed, an extract from *Gender Trouble* won an annual Bad Writing Contest sponsored by the journal *Philosophy and Literature*. Geographers in particular have insisted that there is a disturbingly metaphysical quality to Butler's writing, which is often biased in favour of the literary (Brown, 2000, Rose, 1996). Moreover, Butler has also been accused of making allusions throughout her writing to other theorists from very contradictory theoretical traditions (including Foucault, Lacan, Freud, Althusser etc.) without any attempt to acknowledge, address or resolve these conflicts or incongruities (Nussbaum, 1999).

Butler's own theorisation has also been attacked from a number of different perspectives, including its racial blindness. Race is only mentioned in a cursory fashion in discussions of performativity in both *Gender Trouble* and *Bodies That Matter* (Mahtani, 2002) although Butler is quick to note in the anniversary issue of *Gender Trouble* that she never meant to ignore race, rather she is much more interested in asking, 'what happens to [my theory of performativity] when it tries to come to grips with race' (Butler, 1990: xvi). In a rather different sense, Butler has also been criticised for her explorations of Zionist oppression, and has been forced to debate and defend her own positionality as an American of Jewish origins (indeed, she has argued that it is completely erroneous to equate Zionism and Jewishness).

Another repeated criticism of Butler's theorisation, is that she deconstructs agency without effectively putting forth a useful alternative to humanist versions of the concept (Nelson, 1999). She is also challenged as to how collective notions of resistance (resistance is only described by Butler in terms of an individualised paraodic performance) and oppression can be conceptualised within her theory of performativity. For example, **Gillian Rose** (1996: 73), has insisted that performances never offer 'an escape from masculinist discourses', while Mahtani

(2002) shares similar concerns in her analysis of the performances among 'mixed race' women, insisting that the total sum of the effects of performances are incalculable (Mahtani, 2002). This said, Mitch Rose (2002) has provided an important counterpart to these criticisms by drawing from Butler to effectively demonstrate that practices of both resistance and domination are enactments. Likewise, in developing an alternative reading of the 'place' of performativity in geography, Houston and Pulido (2002) suggest that contemplating performativity as a form of embodied dialectical praxis creates a space for progressive social change.

More generally, Butler has been charged with inspiring a turn within feminism away from the material (poverty, violence, illiteracy etc.) towards a verbal and symbolic politics that has little connections with the everyday lives of 'real' women. Probyn (1995: 108), for example, has cautioned against the celebration of Butler's work, reminding us about the 'nasty realities of the heterosexist and homosocial society where most of us continue to live and be gendered as either women or men'. Within geography, Butler's work has also been evoked as an example of the kind of abstract theorisation that has induced a radical shift in the pattern of research and scholarship within 'new cultural geography', away from a concern with the material and the political towards a heightened concern with language, meanings and representation (see Barnett, 1998). For all this, it has proved highly influential and, with Butler's increasing focus on war and terror, it appears that her distinctive psycho-social perspectives will continue to inspire geographical engagements.

BUTLER'S KEY WORKS

Butler, J. (1990) *Gender Trouble*. London: Routledge.
Butler, J. (1992a) 'Contingent foundations: feminism and the question of "postmodernism"', in J. Butler and J.W. Scott (eds) *Feminists Theorize the Political*. New York: Routledge. pp. 3–22.
Butler, J. and Scott, J.W. (eds) (1992b) *Feminists Theorize the Political*. New York: Routledge.
Butler, J. (1992c) 'The body you want', *Artforum*, November 82–9.
Butler, J. (1993) *Bodies That Matter*. London: Routledge.
Benhabib, S., Butler, J., Cornell, D. and Fraser, N. (1995) *Feminist Contentions: A Philosophical Exchange*. London: Routledge.
Butler, J. (1997) *Excitable Speech*. London: Routledge.
Butler, J., Laclau, E. and Zizek, S. (2000) *Contingency, Hegemony, Universality: Contemporary Dialogues on the Left*. London: Verso.
Butler, J., Guillory, J. and Thomas, K. (2000) *What's Left of Theory? New Work on the Politics of Literary Theory*. London: Routledge.
Butler, J. (2004a) *Undoing Gender*. London: Routledge.
Butler, J. (2004b) *Precarious Life: The Power of Mourning and Violence*. London: Verso.
Butler, J. (2005) *Giving an Account of Oneself*. Fordham: Fordham University Press.
Butler, J. (2009) *Frames of War*. London: Verso.

Secondary Sources and References

Austin, J. (1955) *How to Do Things with Words*. Cambridge: Harvard University Press.
Awkward, M. (1995) *Negotiating Difference: Race, Gender and the Politics of Positionality*. Chicago: University of Chicago Press.

Barnett, C. (1998) 'The cultural turn: fashion or progress in human geography?', *Antipode*, 30: 379–94.

Bell, D., Binnie, J., Cream, J. and Valentine, G. (1994) 'All hyped up and no place to go', *Gender, Place and Culture*, 1: 31–48.

Bell, D. and Valentine, G. (1995) 'The sexed self: strategies of performance, sites of resistance', in S. Pile and N. Thrift (eds), *Mapping the Subject*. London: Routledge. pp. 143–57.

Brown, M. (2000) *Closet Space: Geographies of Metaphor From the Body to the Globe*. London: Routledge.

Butler, J. (2001) 'Giving an account of one's Self', *Diacritics*, 31 (4): 22–40.

Callard, F. (1998) 'The body in theory ', *Environment and Planning D: Society and Space*, 16: 387–400.

Crang, P. (1994) 'It's showtime: on the workplace geographies of display in a restaurant in southeast England', *Environment and Planning D: Society and Space*, 12: 675–704.

Cream, J. (1995) 'Resolving riddles: the sexed body', in D. Bell and G. Valentine (eds), *Mapping Desire*. London: Routledge. pp. 31–40.

de Beauvoir, S. (1949) *The Second Sex*. London: Everyman.

Dewsbury, J. (2000) 'Performativity and the event: enacting a philosophy of difference', *Environment and Planning D: Society and Space*, 18: 473–96.

Gauntlett, D. (2002) *Media, Gender and Identity*. London: Routledge.

Gregory, D. (2007) 'Law, violence and exception in the global war prison', in D. Gregory and A. Pred (eds), *Violent Geographies: Fear, Terror and Political Violence*. New York: Routledge. pp. 205–36.

Gregson, N. and Rose, G. (2000) 'Taking Butler elsewhere: performativities, spatialities and subjectivities', *Environment and Planning D: Society and Space*, 18: 433–52.

Hood-Williams, J. and Harrison, C.W (1998) 'Trouble with gender', *Sociological Review*, 46: 73–94.

Houston, D. and Pulido, L. (2002) 'The work of performativity: staging social justice at the University of Southern California', *Environment and Planning D: Society and Space*, 20: 379-504.

Johnston, L. (1995) 'The politics of the pump: hard core gyms and women body builders', *New Zealand Geographer*, 51: 16–29.

Kirby, K. (1996) 'Cartographic vision and the limits of politics', in N. Duncan (ed.), *Bodyspace: Destabilizing Geographies of Gender and Sexuality*. London: Routledge.

Lewis, C. and Pile S. (1996) 'Women, body, space: Rio Carnival and the politics of performance', *Gender, Place and Culture*, 3: 453–72.

Larsen, N. (1929) *Passing*. New York: WW Norton.

Longhurst, R. (2000) 'Corporeographies of pregnancy: bikini babes', *Environment and Planning D: Society and Space*, 19: 453–72.

Mahtani, M. (2002) 'Tricking the border guards: performing race', *Environment and Planning D: Society and Space*, 20: 425–40.

McDowell, L. (1995) 'Body work: heterosexual gender performances in city workplaces', in D. Bell, and G. Valentine (eds), *Mapping Desire: Geographies of Sexualities*. London: Routledge.

McDowell, L. (1997) *Capital Culture: Gender At Work in the City*. Oxford: Blackwell.

Nelson, L. (1999) 'Bodies (and spaces) do matter: the limits of performativity', *Gender, Place and Culture*, 6: 331–53.

Nussbaum, M. (1999) 'The professor of parody', www.tnr.com/archive/0299/022299/nussbaum0222,99.html Accessed 29 December 2002.

Probyn, E. (1995) 'Lesbians in space: gender, sex and the structure of missing', *Gender, Place and Culture*, 2: 107–9.

Rose, G. (1993) *Feminism and Geography: The Limits of Geographical Knowledge*. Cambridge: Polity.

Rose, G. (1996) 'As if the mirrors had bled: masculine dwelling, masculinist theory and feminist masquerade', in N. Duncan (ed.), *BodySpace*. London: Routledge. pp. 56–74.

Rose, G. (1997) 'Situating knowledges: positionality, reflexivities and other tactics', *Progress in Human Geography*, 21, 305–20.

Rose, G. (1999) 'Performing space', in D. Massey, J. Allen, and P. Sarre (eds), *Human Geography Today*. Cambridge: Polity. pp 247–59.

Rose, G. and Gregson, N. (2000) 'Taking Butler elsewhere: performativities, spatialities and subjectivities', *Environment and Planning D: Society and Space*, 18: 422–52.

Rose, M. (2002) 'The seduction of resistance: power, politics, and a performative style of systems', *Environment and Planning D: Society and Space*, 20: 383–400.

Salih, S. (2002) *Judith Butler*. London: Routledge.

Sharp, J. (1996) 'Gendering motherhood: a feminist engagement with national identity', in N. Duncan (ed.), *BodySpace*. London: Routledge. pp. 97–108.

Thrift, N. (1997) 'The still point: resistance, expressive embodiment and dance', in S. Pile, and M. Keith (eds), *Geographies of Resistance*. London: Routledge. pp 124–51.

Thrift, N. (2000) 'Afterwards', *Environment and Planning D: Society and Space*, 18: 213–55.

Valentine, G. (2002) 'People like us: negotiating sameness and difference in the research process', in Moss, P. (eds), *Feminist Geography in Practice*. Oxford: Blackwell. pp. 116–26.

Wallace, J. (1998) 'What does it mean to be a woman?', *The Times Higher Education Supplement*, May 8, 1998.

Walker, L. (1995) 'More than just skin-deep: fem(me)ininity and the subversion of identity', *Gender, Place and Culture*, 1: 71–7.

Minelle Mahtani, University of Toronto

11 Anne Buttimer

BIOGRAPHICAL DETAILS AND THEORETICAL CONTEXT

It was a rediscovery of earlier geographical writing attuned to the humanities and a heightened attentiveness to cultural differences in environmental knowledge and perception that inspired the rise of humanistic thought within geography during the 1960s and 1970s. The Irish geographer, Anne Buttimer, born in 1938, is generally recognised as one of the key promoters of this humanist turn. Her association with humanism in geography can be traced back to an early interest in phenomenology and existentialism, and a concomitant focus on human experience, lifeworld, and dwelling. Her work has left an imprint on three broad fields of research: geographical thought and practice; the experience of place, space and movement; and the relationships between science and policy.

Early in her professional life, Buttimer developed an interest in the practice, history and philosophy of geography. After graduation from University College Cork with a BA in Mathematics, Latin, and Geography (1957) and MA in Geography (1958), Buttimer joined the Dominican Order and moved to Seattle. The Dominican principle of 'sharing with others the fruits of one's own contemplation', would provide direction and motivation of her work during and subsequent to the 17 years she spent in the Order. Throughout her career, Buttimer also held on to the principle of alternating between attention to reflective issues and empirical concerns.

Her doctoral studies (1962–1964) at the University of Washington came to focus on social geography, especially in the French tradition – a field of research then barely considered in American academia (Buttimer, 1971). Returning to Europe as a post-doctoral fellow of the Belgian American Foundation, she devoted the late 1960s to studies in phenomenology and existentialism at the University of Louvain (1965–1966), visiting France to gain a better grasp of how social space could be used in empirical work, and lastly got involved in the evaluation of urban planning standards and residential area design in Scotland (1968–1970). In Glasgow, Buttimer interviewed working-class households that had been relocated from central city slum clearance districts to modern housing estates. Her aspiration was to understand everyday life experiences, and dimensions of social space which were not seriously considered in conventional practice. Results from the study claimed that social reference systems and collective memory were of crucial importance to how groups assigned meaning to space (Buttimer 1972). Where the Glasgow study still showed traces of a positivist approach, its general tenor was also influenced by existentialist and phenomenological ideas from the earlier sojourn in Belgium. Subsequently, this resulted in a more full-fledged philosophical surge in Buttimer's work that inspired several doctoral theses on environmental perception at Clark University, Worcester, Massachusetts, where she worked from 1970 onwards (Buttimer and Seamon 1980).

With 'Values in geography' (1974) Buttimer pioneered the now commonly accepted point that knowledge always emanates from, and is legitimised by particular sets of values and social commitments. This essay argued that conventional models, theories and practices in the discipline of geography were often insensitive to contextual differences and even had a clear affinity with imperialism and the conquest of the earth. Buttimer would later describe the essay as 'an emancipatory turning point; many contradictions and inconsistencies which I had unmasked in my own life and thought became challenges to confront. Integrity demanded, among other things, transcending those comfortable "-isms", "-ologies" and *a priori* biases, seeking the spirit rather than the letter, the ethos rather than the structure in whatever life situation' (Buttimer, 1987: 313).

While spelling out her position, Buttimer began a collaboration with the Swedish geographer **Torsten Hägerstrand** – one of the commentators of her 'Values' paper. Buttimer's subject-oriented position on human experience obviously differed from the more material and objective approach of time-geography as developed by Hägerstrand, but they shared an interest in temporal and spatial aspects of everyday life. Joining Hägerstrand at Lund University, Buttimer sought to integrate a temporal dimension to her understanding of social space. A subsequent

exploratory essay (1976), heavily resting on existentialism and phenomenology, proposed rethinking geography in terms of lived time-space rhythms. Buttimer and Hägerstrand also commenced an international project aiming at 'knowledge integration', which Buttimer translated into a process of storytelling by individuals. The so-called *Dialogue Project* lasted from 1977 to 1988 and involved a substantial number of video-recorded autobiographical interviews with senior and retired professionals. Shared career experiences and the identification of grounds for self- and mutual understanding were central themes, but the project also explored intellectual history, the social construction of geographically-situated knowledge, humanism, values, and the relationships between natural and social sciences.

The Dialogue Project yielded a wealth of new empirical knowledge about people, places and events – unique material on which Buttimer's major conceptual reading of disciplinary history and practice was subsequently built. Her *Practice of Geography* (1983b) portrayed the career trajectories of an international selection of geographers as being the result of how structural and material circumstances were combined with personal values, skills and preferences, while *Geographers of Norden* (Hägerstrand and Buttimer, 1988) was a collection of essays on career experiences from Nordic geographers (more than a decade later, this was followed by a companion volume on the history of Swedish geography – Buttimer and Mels, 2006). With the publication of *Geography and the Human Spirit* (Buttimer, 1993), Buttimer shifted attention from personal accounts to a more general focus on the history, practice and societal context of geographical thinking, reading geographical inquiry as shaped over the centuries by the different guises of Western humanism.

Notwithstanding her personal connection to the Irish countryside, Buttimer's career has therefore always had a conspicuous international orientation. She served as Council Member of the Association of American Geographers 1974–77 and the Royal Geographical Society 1996–99, was elected member of *Academia Europaea* in 1993, and President of the International Geographical Union 2000–2004. In 1991, Buttimer returned to Ireland as the Chair of Geography at University College Dublin. Here, she continued working on agrarian life and sustainable development – issues which Buttimer thought required both international dialogue and the sustained integration of both physical and human geography knowledges.

SPATIAL CONTRIBUTIONS

Generally, Buttimer's thinking about space and place has been associated with a broadly defined humanistic geography. Yet, such labelling remains unavoidably indistinct and may even mistakenly suggest a clearly defined academic mission. By extension, it has more often than not obfuscated Buttimer's more imaginative intellectual contributions. Concerning the latter, Buttimer has offered an original reading of what humanism and humanistic geography entails.

Buttimer's early work revolted against the dehumanisation and abstract space in positivist science in at least three inter-related ways. First, she explored the term social space (*l'espace social*) as it was emerging in the borderland between French geography and sociology, and introduced it into Anglophone human geography. This would offer a guide for an investigation of lived experience not only in a purely sociological or psychological sense then favoured in Anglo-American writings, but also in the sense of providing a physical spatial framework. Buttimer's understanding was influenced by the French scholars Maximilien Sorre and Paul-Henri Chombart de Lauwe, who sought to integrate the 'subjective' and 'objective' components of space. Drawing on these authors, Buttimer depicted social space as a relational concept bringing out the intermingling of subjective dimensions, such as attitudes, perceptions, and experiences of place, and objective spatial environments on a variety of scales (Buttimer, 1969: 142).

Secondly, in the 1970s Buttimer was an original voice in the shaping of post-positivist thinking about space and place in the discipline of geography. By connecting to philosophical manoeuvres in existentialism and phenomenology she has played a vital role in prodding an awareness of normativity, values, the taken-for-granted, power and lived space. Inspired by diverse sources such as Bachelard, Eliade, Husserl, Heidegger, Merleau-Ponty, Schütz and others, Buttimer contributed to the rethinking of spatio-temporal experience. In contrast to conventional thinking about linear clock-calendar time, mapping patterns of overt behaviour and routines, her aim was to understand environmental experience as a whole. Time-space rhythms also included the far more complex and relative dimension of embodied experiences and biological rhythms (Mels, 2004).

As suggested, a third contribution concerns a particular reading of humanism which was developed through a contextual approach to geographical knowledge production and disciplinary history. For Buttimer, the relationships between humanism and geography are as deep-seated as they are diverse: 'For each facet of humanness – rationality or irrationality, faith, emotion, artistic genius or political prowess – there is a geography. For each geographical interpretation of the earth there are implicit assumptions about the nature of humanness' (Buttimer, 1990: 1-2). Rather than offering any clearly delineated agenda of humanistic geography, Buttimer characterises Western humanism 'as the liberation cry (cri-de-coeur) of humanity, voiced at times and places where the integrity of life or thought was in need of affirmation' (ibid. 2). In geography, this crucially translated into a dissatisfaction with what she perceived as the widespread abstraction of human beings and space in scientific writing: 'From whatever ideological stance it has emerged, the case for humanism has usually been made with the conviction that there must be more to human geography than the dance macabre of materialistically motivated robots which, in the opinion of many, was staged by the post-World War Two "scientific" reformation' (Buttimer, 1993: 47).

As such, Buttimer argued Western humanism attained distinct, though not mutually exclusive, constellations of vocational meaning in different contexts. Analytically (logos), there was a commitment to varieties of situated knowledge and discourses. Educationally (paideia) the impact of humanism involved a heightened engagement with the humanities. From an applied point of view (ergon), it has implied a firmer social and political interest in the human condition. In what is far more narrowly labelled 'humanistic geography', these different strains have intermingled in a variety of ways. However, according to Buttimer, it remains crucial to recognise that the case for humanism has typically encompassed an emphasis on critical reflection (poesis). This includes a concern with

ontological questions about the nature of reality and humanness and conventional ways of construing them. In contemporary human geography, this contextual responsiveness has emphasised the 'inextricable connections between thought and context, experience and expertise, and the adequacy of all our practices for the elucidation of contemporary reality' (Buttimer, 1996: 841).

Adapting the American philosopher Stephen Pepper's work, Buttimer continued to explore the different ways in which key metaphors (mechanism, organicism, arena/contextualism and mosaic/formism) and their poetic, cognitive and heuristic qualities were used in geography. Metaphors, as Buttimer perceived them in the 1980s, 'could be regarded as the Dramatis Personae of Western intellectual history, the actual narrative and plot of particular pieces staged in the material and ideological contexts in which scholars thought and practiced their professions' (Buttimer 1982: 91). This focus on cognitive style or basic worldview underlying research contrasts to more conventional accounts on the succession of paradigms. According to Buttimer, the appeal of a root metaphor lies in aesthetic, moral, emotional and experientially-grounded understandings of reality, not just in its epistemological claims. Buttimer's original contribution here was also to broaden what sometimes was conceived of as a mere succession of ideas and more narrowly defined metaphorical style, to a consideration of milieu, i.e., the mediation of a scholar's personal background and the structural influence of social environment, power, and public interests. Related to this is what she dubs the variation in horizons of geographical inquiry, ranging from local to global concern.

Finally, in order to explore the modes whereby the root appeal of humanism was mediated and transformed in Western history, Buttimer discerned three mytho-poetic figures: *Phoenix* (offering the symbol of new life and emancipation from the formerly taken-for-granted), *Faust* (the building of institutions and formal structures) and *Narcissus* (reflection and questioning). These symbolise what Buttimer from the 1990s onwards probed as broad themes in a cyclically-recurring drama in human experience, material life and thought. Rather than a rigid taxonomy or an expression of teleology, this heuristic trilogy of themes and cycles connected to Buttimer's earlier efforts to contextualise geographical thought and practice in society.

All of these interpretive entries (the diachronic perspective of Phoenix-Faust-Narcissus, and the synchronic Meaning-Metaphor-Milieu and Horizon) served to gain personal, contextualised and more macro-perspective understandings of geographical knowledge production. Methodologically, part of this effort was based on a self-reflexive, narrative-oriented approach, which has resulted in an oral, video-recorded history of the field complemented with an archival record of transcripts: The Dialogue Project and its subsequent offspring were instrumental for the exploration of (auto)biography and personal relationships to societal and geographical context.

Dialogue also helped shape an understanding of sustainable development. In the 1980s and 1990s, Buttimer coordinated major international research projects on sustainable landscapes, which brought out the significance of scale in the implementation of EU policies, and issues concerning communication (e.g., Buttimer, 2001). Here, questions of dialogue returned in view of the highly contrasting taken-for-granted outlooks on planning and development that were held by researchers in different European countries.

KEY ADVANCES AND CONTROVERSIES

Buttimer's earlier examination of social space and geographical experience, decades of practising the method of dialogue and (auto)biography as well as her original understanding and analytical framing of disciplinary history and change, are widely recognised as humanistically-geared contributions to thinking about space and place. They have also been subject to criticism.

Critical appraisal of Buttimer's work can be traced back to some central controversies associated with the revival of humanistic geography. According to some critics, there were antinomies involved in Buttimer's early efforts to wed existentialist and phenomenological philosophy with more conventional, largely positivist methods. This uneasy arrangement was identified in the mapping of social space, and in Buttimer's approach to time-space rhythms, which explored how the conceptual world of lived experience, dwelling and subjectivity can be explored empirically with techniques of time-geography and spatial analysis.

In partial contradiction to these criticisms, a parallel debate suggested that Buttimer tended to misconstrue phenomenology as an anti-scientific position, which is concerned with the integrity of human experience and rejects any causal subject–object relationships. Accordingly, her flexible view of phenomenology as a perspective rather than a disciplined method with clearly operational procedures for ascertaining the nature of human experience has been questioned. Finally, the central phenomenological concept of intentionality in Buttimer's work is sometimes seen as erroneously being reduced to a psychological level, which fails to get beyond the individual subject. This critique usually highlights the pervasiveness of a kind of mentalism, in which subjectivity and the world of ideas tend to underrate the importance of material practice.

This also raised more specific questions about the nature of socialisation processes, including systems of power and interest, behind particular value claims and knowledges. The increasing popularity of structuration theory in the 1980s not only welcomed a serious engagement with knowledgeable and capable human beings, but also criticised

humanists for neglecting society's structural properties involved in the reproduction of human behaviour. Several critics noted that Buttimer remained far too silent on these issues. Granted, in her work, the individual was not portrayed as an isolated being, but rather as an existentially self-aware person, immersed in social space and practice, and inevitably engaged in the creation of community and social life. Yet, as several commentators have argued, Buttimer failed to offer an explanatory moment which would try to explain how constraints were socially produced, why certain projects and orchestrations became dominant, or why and how abstractions of time and space came to dominate lived time-space. It may be worth noting that this critique tends to be aimed at Buttimer's theoretical writings, rather than her more firmly societal contextualisation of geographical knowledge production.

BUTTIMER'S KEY WORKS

Buttimer, A. (1971) *Society and Milieu in the French Geographic Tradition.* Chicago: Rand McNally.

Buttimer, A. (1972) 'Social Space and the Planning of Residential Areas', *Environment and Behaviour,* 4(3): 279–318.

Buttimer, A. (1974) 'Values in geography', *Commission of College Geography Resource Paper 24,* Washington, DC: Association of American Geographers.

Buttimer, A. and Seamon, D. (1980) *The Human Experience of Space and Place.* New York: St Martin's Press.

Buttimer, A. (1983a) *Creativity and Context.* Lund: Lund Studies in Human Geography.

Buttimer, A. (1983b) *The Practice of Geography.* London: Longman.

Buttimer, A. (1988) *The Wake of Erasmus.* Lund: Lund University Press.

Buttimer, A. (1991) *Land-Life-Lumber-Leisure.* Ottawa, Ont.: Royal Society of Canada.

Buttimer, A. (1993) *Geography and the Human Spirit.* Baltimore, MD: The Johns Hopkins University Press.

Buttimer, A., Brunn, S.D. and Wardenga, U. (eds) (1999a) *Text and Image: Social Construction of Regional Knowledges.* Leipzig: Institut für Länderkunde.

Buttimer, A. and Wallin, L. (eds.) (1999b) *Nature and Identity in Cross-cultural Perspective.* Dordrecht: Kluwer.

Buttimer, A. (ed.) (2001) *Sustainable Landscapes and Lifeways: Scale and Appropriateness.* Cork: Cork University Press.

Buttimer, A. and Mels T. (2006) *By Northern Lights: On the Making of Geography in Sweden.* Aldershot: Ashgate.

Hägerstrand, T. and Buttimer, T. (1988) *Geographers of Norden.* Lund: Lund University Press.

Secondary Sources and References

Buttimer, A. (1969) 'Social space in interdisciplinary perspective', *The Geographical Review*, 59: 417–26.

Buttimer, A. (1971) 'Health and welfare: whose responsibility?', *Antipode*, 3: 31–45.

Buttimer, A. (1976) 'Grasping the dynamism of lifeworld', *Annals of the Association of American Geographers*, 66: 277–92.

Buttimer, A. and Hägerstrand, T. (1980) 'Invitation to Dialogue', *DIA paper 1*, Lund.

Buttimer, A. (1982) 'Musing on Helicon: root metaphors in geography', *Geografiska Annaler*, 64B: 89–96.

Buttimer, A. (1987) 'A social topography of home and horizon', *Journal of Environmental Psychology*, 7: 307–19.

Buttimer, A. (1990) 'Geography, humanism and global concern', *Annals of the Association of American Geographers*, 80: 1–33.

Buttimer (1994) 'Response to commentary on "Grasping the dynamism of life-world" (1976)', *Progress in Human Geography*, 18: 501–6.

Buttimer, A. (1996a) 'Geography and humanism', in I. Douglas, R.J. Huggett, and M. Robinson, *Companion Encyclopedia of Geography*. London: Routledge.

Buttimer, A. (1996b) 'Reply to commentaries on "Values in Geography"', *Progress in Human Geography*, 20: 513–19.

Buttimer, A. (1999) 'Humanism and relevance in Geography', *Scottish Geographical Journal*, 115: 103–16.

Buttimer, A. (2005) 'Edgar Kant (1902-1978): a Baltic pioneer', *Geografiska Annaler B*, 87: 175–92.

Maddrell, A. (forthcoming) 'An interview with Anne Buttimer', *Gender, Place and Culture*.

Mels, T. (ed.) 2004 *Reanimating Places: A Geography of Rhythms*. Aldershot: Ashgate.

Tom Mels, Gotland University

12 Manuel Castells

BIOGRAPHICAL DETAILS AND THEORETICAL CONTEXT

Manuel Castells was born in Spain in 1942. As a child he grew up in Barcelona, where he completed his secondary education, going on to study law and economics at the University of Barcelona in 1958–62. As a student activist against General Franco's fascist dictatorship he had to escape to Paris, graduating from the Sorbonne's Faculty of Law and Economics in 1964. Staying on in Paris, he went on to obtain his PhD from the École des Hautes Études en Sciences Sociale in 1967, publishing his first article ('Mobilité des enterprises et structure urbaine') in the same year. Based on a statistical analysis of location strategies of high-tech industrial firms in the Paris region, this doctoral work (supervised by the renowned sociologist Alain Touraine) highlighted two issues that would continue to preoccupy Castells over the next four decades – namely, the emergence of new technologies and the changing form of cities. Working in Paris at this time unsurprisingly brought Castells into contact with leading Marxist theorists including **Henri Lefebvre**, Nicolas Poulantzas and Louis Althusser; it was thus predictable that Castells was to be caught up in the revolutionary fervour of May 1968, with one of Castells' own students at Nanterre, Daniel Cohn-Bendit, a key figure in the student uprising. Expelled by the French government for his part in the uprising, he spent periods in Chile and Canada before returning Paris in 1972 after receiving a state pardon (see Susser, 2002).

Castells first major work – *The Urban Question: A Marxist Approach* – was also published in 1972 (and first published in English in 1977). Unquestionably a product of the times, it was heralded as a remarkable and pioneering attempt to bring Marxist concepts and perspectives to bear on the 'urban question'. In essence, Castells suggested that many of those writing about the problems and challenges facing cities in the early 1970s (e.g., race riots, poverty, criminality) were locked into an ideologically-bankrupt tradition of urban sociology that could not possibly identify the answers to these urban problems. This tradition had its roots in the influential 'urban ecology' school of sociologists at the University of Chicago in the 1920s, and was manifest in the 'factorial ecologies' produced by many sociologists and social geographers in the 1960s. Rejecting this approach, Castells drew on classical Marxist theory and emerging traditions in pluralist political science to outline an urban sociology that emphasised the conflictual production of urban space within capitalist society. In his 'Epistemological introduction' to the volume, Castells noted it was born out of his astonishment that Marxist theorists had yet to analyse cities in a 'sufficiently specific way' (Castells, 1977: 2). In the event, the book was to have remarkably little influence on those working within the Marxist tradition; its chief legacy was to inspire a generation of geographers to engage with theories of political economy and to serve as a canonical text in the 'new urban sociology'. *The Urban Question* thus stands alongside **David Harvey**'s (1973) *Social Justice and the City* as a rallying call for urban researchers to utilise the insights of Marxist theory as a means to explore the urbanisation of injustice.

A pivotal figure in the formation of the *International Journal of Urban and Regional Research*, Castells thus found himself at the vanguard of the new urban sociology. By this time, Castells had moved to the Department of City and Regional Planning at the University of California, Berkeley, where he was exposed to a more empirical tradition of sociology than that prevalent in Paris. This was reflected in *The City and the Grassroots* (1983), a comparative study of urban social movements and community organisations based on fieldwork in France, Spain, Latin America, and California. This book extended the assertion developed in *The Urban Question* that one of the chief roles of cities in the capitalist-urban era is to provide collective consumption facilities (e.g., leisure, shopping and health facilities) designed to reproduce labour power. Noting the difficulties in providing equitable access to these facilities, *The City and the Grassroots* focused on the formation of protest groups and political movements seeking to improve access to such facilities. Through detailed case studies, Castells suggested such groups could exploit the tension between labour–capital to transform capitalism. Significantly,

Castells expanded his purview in this volume from exploring the issue of class-consciousness to highlight the formation of social movements seeking the emancipation of gay and lesbian groups (e.g., one of his case studies explored the formation of gay political identity in San Francisco).

For some, this focus on agency signalled a turn away from Althusser-inspired Marxism towards Weberianism (Merrifield, 2002). Yet Castells' persistent interest in technology was to inspire a return to structural metaphors in a series of influential works on the new *informational* structures of capitalism. In 1989, Castells published *The Informational City,* an analysis of the urban and regional changes brought about by information technology and economic restructuring in the United States (highlighting changes in the San Francisco bay area). This was a timely volume in so much that it highlighted changes in the nature of urban governance that were contributing to the polarised or 'dual' city where poor, immigrant workers 'serviced' a more affluent elite working in hi-tech and knowledge-rich industries. This served as precursor to his hugely ambitious 1,400-page, three-volume treatise on *The Information Age: Economy, Society and Culture*, comprising *The Rise of the Network Society* (1996), *The Power of Identity* (1997) and the *End of Millennium* (1998). Integrating his observations on the nature of urban life in both Western and non-Western contexts with an overview of key changes in the organisation of contemporary social, economic and political life, this work is in the tradition of works by Bell, Touraine, Polyani and other major social theorists in so much that it seeks to identify a profound shift in the organisation of society. Where it perhaps differs is in its attentiveness to the specificities of place.

Coupled with *The Internet Galaxy: Reflections on the Internet, Business and Society* (2001), Castells' trilogy on informational society raised his profile significantly in academic, governmental and business circles (where he has been acclaimed as a 'globalisation guru'). For example, in 2002, he was also appointed as an advisor to the United Nations Secretary General on the relationship between the UN and the international community. For all this, he continued to deny his credentials as one of the world's foremost 'public intellectuals':

> No, I am not a public intellectual, I never was, and I never wanted to be. I am a researcher. I produce knowledge. This is my role and my project. On the other hand, of course, I am a concerned citizen, and I do whatever I can to improve the world, which is in very bad shape now. But this is my private life. My public life is to be as good an academic and researcher as I can be. My main joy in life is to be helpful to my students, and, together, produce new knowledge on relevant matters that can help people to better understand their world, and then to change it according to their own values and decisions.

(Castells, cited in Qiu, 2008: 4)

In terms of the substantive nature of his work, Castells' appointment in 2003 as Professor of Communication and Wallis Annenberg Chair of Communication Technology and Society, at the University of Southern California signalled his increasing focus on questions of media and communication. Noting the putative shift from wired to wireless modes of communication, Castells indeed became more interested in the ways that individual, mobile and 'horizontal' modes of communication intersect with more traditional 'vertical' modes of mass media to enact a shift from a public sphere anchored around the nation-state to a 'public sphere constituted around the

media system' (Castells, 2008: 620). Holding to the notion of 'real virtuality', Castells has accordingly refused to differentiate between material and symbolic sources of power, insisting that the power to shape the human mind resides in the networked power of communication (hence the title of his 2009 book, *Communication Power*). From such a perspective, he argues a new round of power-making is taking place in communication space, detailing instances where 'power holders' have sought to infiltrate and control the horizontal networks of communication, whether this involves the US government seeking to control the news agenda around the Gulf War, Rupert Murdoch's NewsCorp securing its business interests through news manipulation, Chinese authorities surveying and tracking email messages or EU powers seeking to curtail the power of social networking and file exchange websites (Arsenault and Castells, 2008; Castells et al., 2006; Castells, 2007).

SPATIAL CONTRIBUTIONS

Simplifying to the extreme, both Castells' earlier and later works have exercised considerable influence on the trajectory of geographical thought, albeit that it is possible to detect an important change in Castells' own conception of space and place between (for example) *The Urban Question* and *The Information Age*. In the former, Castells was scathing of those commentators who seemingly 'fetishised' the urban, bequeathing a distinct ecology that was somehow independent of capitalist structures. This included criticism of his contemporary, **Henri Lefebvre**, whom Castells alleged granted the city an autonomy and significance that it simply did not possess. Here, he bracketed Lefebvre with members of the Chicago School (especially Louis Wirth), arguing that he naively equated spatial propinquity with social emancipation 'as if there were no institutional organization outside arrangement of space' (Castells, 1977: 90). Developing this point, he outlined the need for a structural reading of the city:

> It is a question of going beyond the description of mechanisms of interactions between activities and locations, in order to discover the structural laws of the production and functioning of the spatial forms studied ... There is no specific theory of space, but quite simply a deployment and specification of the theory of social structure, in order to account for the characteristics of the particular social form, space, and its articulation with other historically given, forms and processes.

(Castells, 1977: 124)

This structural solution to the 'urban question' thus offered a valuable corrective to the spatial determinism widely evident in urban studies at this time, whereby specific spaces were seen to shape the lives of those who inhabited them. Yet, in offering this corrective, Castells seemingly went to the other extreme: space simply became a reflection of social process (hence, his claim that 'space, like time, is a physical quantity that tells us nothing about social relations' Castells, 1977: 442). This is mirrored in Castells' definition of the city as 'a residential unit of labour power, a unit of collective consumption corresponding "more or less" to the daily organization of a section of labour power' (Castells, 1977: 148). In this sense, the city was interpreted as the outcome of the state's provision of collective means of consuming commodities, something that Castells felt could not be assured by capital but was nonetheless essential to the reproduction of capital.

In effect, Castells' radical take on the urban question shook up urban studies through its insistence that the social processes resulting in the production of the city were not distinctly urban, but endemic to capitalist society. Yet it subsequently attracted criticism from others working in the Marxist tradition for its tendency to treat space as a mere container for social relations (see especially Saunders, 1981, as well as **Ed Soja**, 1980, on the 'socio-spatial dialectic'). In fact, Castells was to later backtrack from this social determinism to suggest instead that 'space is not a reflection of society, it is society' (Castells, 1983). In his latter work on the relation between a new 'informational' mode of development and the social structures that constitute it, this was manifest in a focus on the 'transformation of socially and spatially-based relationship of production into flows of information and power that articulate the new flexible system of production and management' (Castells, 1989). Stressing social flows are inevitably also spatial flows, Castells thus offers a different take on the relations between society and space. Central here is his hypothesis that the 'informational society' is underpinned by a new socio-spatial logic – the 'space of flows' – that is truly global in scope:

> The space of flows refers to the technological and organizational possibility of organizing the simultaneity of social practices without geographical contiguity. Most dominant functions in our societies (financial markets, transnational production networks, media systems etc.) are organized around the space of flows ... However, the space of flows does include a territorial dimension, as it requires a technological infrastructure that operates from certain locations, and as it connects functions and people located in specific places.

(Castells, 2000: 14)

Elucidating the morphology of this space of flows, Castells thus suggests it consists of three prominent levels: the infrastructural, the organisational and the managerial. The first is the 'wired world', the hardware equipment linked to software that makes electronic transmissions around the world possible. The second consists of the centres of translation and organisation that make the network society operate. In Castells' (2000) account, it is prominent world cities (e.g., London, Tokyo, New York) that are the most direct illustration of organisational nodes (places where there is also an increasing divide between an informational elite and what Castells terms the 'fourth world' – those residents in World Cities who are cut off from global networks of prestige, power and wealth). Castells in fact spends much time discussing the relationships between the infrastructural layer and this hierarchical layer of hubs and nodes, directing little attention to the third layer in a space of flows: the dominant managerial elites who are the key players in the global economy. The neglect of this third layer has led some to suggest that Castells offers a disembodied conceptualisation of global process, generating a relatively thin account of identity formation (e.g., van Dijk, 1999; Bendle, 2002). Nonetheless, by hypothesising the existence of three coterminous networks, Castells (2000) powerfully demonstrates that space is the 'material support of time-sharing social practices', leading to an era where timeless time exists in tension with chronological time – and a space of flows exists in tension with a space of places. From such a perspective, one is either in global networks, or one is not:

> The key aspect of the space of flows is not its separation from the space of places, but its ability to fragment localities and reintegrate some of the components into new functional units on the basis of their

connection to the space of flows. On the ground, this creates an entirely new, non-linear pattern of land use characteristic of contemporary urban development. The analytical clarification of this key point, the emergence of a new spatial logic, expressed in the space of flows and the fragmentation of physical space in a variable geography of hyperconnection and structurally-induced 'black holes,' is one of the most substantial and original aspects of Castells' entire theory of the network society.

> (Stalder, 2006: 161)

Whether or not these ideas are somewhat redundant given the subsequent ubiquity of wireless technologies is a moot point. Irrespective, the heuristic framing of a *space of flows* as oppositional to a *space of places* has proved attractive to many geographers, and, in economic and political geography in particular, has provided a useful device for exploring the stretched-out nature of many routine flows and movements (Staeheli, 2006).

KEY ADVANCES AND CONTROVERSIES

In much the same way that *The Urban Question* revolutionised urban sociology in the 1970s (by suggesting that urban sociologists should not be afraid to engage with Marxism), invocations of Castells' 'space of flows' idea have set new agendas in the social sciences, and Castells is unquestionably one of the world's most cited thinkers. The trilogy of works on the *Informational Society* have become obligatory points of passage when exploring the rise of global communication technologies, and Castells' latter work on the 'new public sphere' has also been significant in debates around the morphologies of cyberspace. Both empirically and theoretically, Castells' emphasis on networks of flow has offered a valuable corrective to sedentary, static and bounded notions of urban process, positing that cities are characterised and defined by the flows that pass through them (see Doel et al., 2002). This interpretation is wholly in keeping with the turn in the social sciences towards a 'sociology of fluids' that emphasises the movement and mobility of social life (see especially **Urry**, 2000). Likewise, it engages with debates emerging from the globalisation literature, not least the idea that globalisation is increasingly responsible for disseminating a standardised repertoire of consumer goods, images and lifestyles worldwide. Indeed, one implication of Castells' 'space of flows' idea is that 'local' ways of life are being undermined by the (network) logic of global capital accumulation as place is annihilated by space. In his summation, this means that the world of places – consisting of bounded and meaningful places such as the home, city, region, or nation-state – is being superseded by spaces characterised by circulation, velocity and flow. Elaborating, Castells (1996: 350) points to the proliferation of serialised ahistorical and acultural building projects that undermine the 'meaningful relationship between society and architecture', citing examples ranging from international hotels, airports and supermarkets through to the 'postmodern' office buildings that punctuate the skyline of World Cities.

Superficially, there is certainly much evidence to support the idea that a space of flows is supplanting the world of places: take any city pivotal to the articulation of global financial flow, and one can find many sites that exhibit the architectural anonymity. Yet, it is also clear that the space of places has not disappeared with

the coming of network society. World Cities, for instance, might be considered to be nodes in a network but they are also distinctive places. In this sense, they are not just strategic hubs in the global system, disembedded from their region and caught up in the 'space of flows': they are also distinctive 'centres of comprehension' whose pivotal role in the global economy is a function of their social and cultural milieu. For example, the City of London is far from simply being a 'gateway' space or mere hub in networks of global capital, remaining a strongly identifiable place despite its openness to the world (see also **Nigel Thrift**, 1994, on the distinctive social and cultural milieu of London). This type of observation undermines Castells' (1996: 200) assertion that 'a place is a locale whose form, function and meaning are self-contained within the boundaries of physical contiguity' (see also Taylor, 1999, on the distinction of space/place). On a different scale, Crang (2002) insists that many of the spaces Castells cites as non-places (malls, airports, hotels, etc.) are not simply places of homogenised commodity exchange, rationalisation and flow translation: they are also emotionally charged places of desire and disgust, inclusion and exclusion, sociality and familiarity.

Viewed in this light, as well as in the context of emerging ideas about relational space (such as those developed by **Doreen Massey**), the opposition of 'space' and 'place' in Castells' work is unhelpful. Notwithstanding these critiques, identifying the network as the organising principle of the contemporary (informational) society has offered geographers and urban researchers a useful conceptual signpost towards a renewed urban sociology (see Friedman, 2000). In Castells' estimation, this is a sociology that needs to explore new patterns of communication, 'both face-to-face and electronic', and the interaction between 'physical layouts, social organisation and electronic networks' (Castells, 2002a: 399–400). He further insists that this focus will help tackle 'lingering questions of urban poverty, racial and social discrimination, and social exclusion', contrasting this with the 'futile exercises of deconstruction and reconstruction' characteristic of postmodern urban theory (Castells, 2002a: 404).

However, Castells' cavalier dismissal of much contemporary urban theory exposes the structuralist assumptions that continue to underpin (and inevitably constrain) his work. First and foremost, he devotes insufficient attention to how structure is established: it is taken as a given rather than as an ongoing achievement (e.g., he claims 'societies are organized around human processes structured by historically determined relationships of production, experience and power' Castells, 1989: 7–8). Moreover, while the concept of the network society may facilitate an increased understanding of some of the consequences of the development of a globalised informational capitalism, some have argued it is not analytically effective for exploring 'the range of risks and threats to which social and political life, and capitalist economic activity itself, have become exposed as a consequence of globalization' (Smart, 2000: 64). Highlighting this, van Dijk (1999) argues that Castells explores the conflicts between 'vertical' global networks and 'horizontal' collective movements, but makes little of the social conflicts that destabilise networks and movements *from within*.

Ultimately, it appears that the network society that Castells evokes so brilliantly is perhaps less structured than he might imagine. For all this, he remains a widely cited commentator on the spaces and socialities of information capitalism, and a leading authority on the sociologies of cyberspace. His works continue to be among the most cited works in the social sciences, eclipsing the work of geographers to reach audiences well beyond academia. Yet, as Staeheli (2006) notes, Castells' significance within geographic debates on space and place has, if anything, declined in recent times. For Staeheli, this is both a function of 'fashionability' – Castells being less 'hot' than a range of more post-structural thinkers – as well as the continuing emphasis in Castells' work on the importance of a particular type of place – the World City – as a centre of power. For Staeheli, and others, this rather Eurocentric emphasis on particular types of city as representing privileged points of power and politics is at odds with conceptions of power as diffused, relational and multifaceted, meaning that Castells' most recent writing on the power of communication looks distinctly out-of-kilter with current theoretical debates within geography.

CASTELLS' KEY WORKS

Castells, M. (1977) *The Urban Question: A Marxist Approach.* London: Edward Arnold.

Castells, M. (1983) *The City and the Grassroots: A Cross-Cultural Theory of Urban Social Movements.* Berkeley: University of California Press.

Castells, M. (1989) *The Informational City – Information Technology, Economic Restructuring and the Urban-regional Process.* Oxford: Blackwell.

Castells, M. and Hall, P. (1994) *Technopoles of the World: The Making of 21st Century Industrial Complexes.* London: Routledge.

Castells, M. (1996) *The Information Age: Economy, Society and Culture; Volume 1: The Rise of the Network Society.* Oxford: Blackwell.

Castells, M. (1997) *The Information Age: Economy, Society and Culture; Volume 2: The Power of Identity*. Oxford: Blackwell.
Castells, M. (1998) *The Information Age: Economy, Society and Culture; Volume 3: End of Millennium*. Oxford: Blackwell.
Castells, M. (2001) *The Internet Galaxy: Reflections on the Internet, Business, and Society*. Oxford: Oxford University Press.
Castells, M. (2009) *Communication Power*. Oxford: Oxford University Press.

Secondary Sources and References

Arsenault, A. and Castells, M. (2008) 'Switching power: Rupert Murdoch and the global business of media politics', *International Sociology*, 23 (4): 489–514.
Bendle, M. (2002) 'The crisis of identity in high modernity', *British Journal of Sociology*, 53 (1): 1–18.
Bromley, S. (1999) 'The space of flows and timeless time: Manuel Castells's "The Information Age"', *Radical Philosophy*, 97: 6–10.
Castells, M. (2000) 'Materials for an exploratory theory of the network society', *British Journal of Sociology*, 51 (1): 1–24.
Castells, M. (2002a) 'Urban sociology for the twenty-first century', in I. Susser (ed.), *The Castells Reader on Cities and Social Theory*. Oxford: Blackwell. pp. 390–406.
Castells, M. (2002b) 'Local and global: cities in the network society', *Tijdschrift voor Economische en Sociale Geografie*, 93 (5): 548–58.
Castells, M. (2007) 'Communication, power and counter-power in the network society', *International Journal of Communication*, 1 (1): 238–66.
Castells, M. (2008) 'The new public sphere: global civil society, communication networks, and global governance', *The Annals of the American Academy of Political and Social Science*, 616 (1): 78–93.
Castells, M., Fernandez-Ardevol, M., Qiu, J.L. and Sey, A. (2006) *Mobile Communication and Society: A Global Perspective*. Cambridge, MA: The MIT Press.
Crang, M. (2002) 'Between places: producing hubs, flows and networks', *Environment and Planning A*, 34 (4): 569–74.
Doel, M., Beaverstock, J., Taylor, P. and Hubbard, P. (2002) 'Attending to the world: co-efficiency and collaboration in the world city network', *Global Networks*, 2 (2): 96–116.
Friedman, J. (2000) 'Reading Castells: *Zeitdiagnose* and social theory', *Environment and Planning D: Society and Space*, 18 (1): 111–20.
Harvey, D. (1973) *Social Justice and the City*. London: Arnold.
Merrifield, A. (2002) *Metromarxism: A Marxist Tale of the City*. New York: Routledge.
Qiu, J.L. (2008) 'Interview with Manuel Castells', *Chinese Journal of Communication*, 1 (1): 3–6.
Smart, B. (2000) 'A political economy of new times? Critical reflections on the network society and the ethos of informational capitalism', *European Journal of Social Theory*, 3 (1): 51–65.
Soja, E. (1980) 'The socio-spatial dialectic', *Annals, The Association of American Geographers*, 70 (2): 207–25.
Saunders, P. (1981) *Social Theory and the Urban Question*. London: Hutchinson.
Staeheli, L.A (2006) 'Re-reading Castells: indifference or irrelevance twenty years on', *International Journal of Urban and Regional Research*, 30(1): 198–201.
Stalder, F. (2006) *Manuel Castells and the Theory of the Network Society*. Cambridge: Polity.
Susser, I. (2002) 'Manuel Castells: conceptualising the city in the information age', in Susser, I. (ed.), *The Castells Reader on Cities and Social Theory*. Oxford: Blackwell. pp. 1–12.
Taylor, P. (1999) 'Places, spaces and Macy's: place-space tensions in the political geography of modernities', *Progress in Human Geography*, 23 (1): 7–26.
Thrift, N. (1994b) 'On the social and cultural determinants of international financial centres', in S. Corbridge, R. Martin and N. Thrift (eds), *Money, Power and Space*. Oxford: Blackwell. pp. 327–25.
Urry, J. (2000) *Sociology beyond Societies: Mobilities for the Twenty-First Century*. London: Routledge.
Van Dijk, J. (1999) 'The one-dimensional network society of Manuel Castells', *New Media and Society*, 1 (1): 127–38.

Phil Hubbard, University of Kent

13 Michel de Certeau

BIOGRAPHICAL DETAILS AND THEORETICAL CONTEXT

Michel de Certeau (1925–1986) certainly lived an academic life less ordinary, starting as an ordained Jesuit priest working on their archives, producing enormously erudite studies of Mediaeval Mysticism with his most sustained work on the spiritual possessions of medieval Loudun and popular religious mysticism. Contrastingly, he was also a member of Jacques Lacan's *l'école Freudienne* from its start to finish. These hardly seem likely starting points for someone who has become something of a shibboleth for work on consumption. It becomes clearer if we understand that de Certeau underwent something of a personal revelation through the events in Paris in 1968 and moved his later scholarship onto more topical urban matters. Through his work on urban anthropology he became seen as the champion of the common folk, of a street-level social theory, with his key theoretical contribution a theory of practice which stresses how objects and happenings exceed our conceptualisations of them. To take an early programmatic statement:

> This essay is dedicated to the ordinary man [sic]. The common hero. Disseminated character. Untold wanderer. In invoking, at the outset of my narratives, this absent being who gives them their beginning and necessity, I question myself as to the desire of which he figures the impossible object. When we dedicate to him documents which formerly were offered in homage to divinities or to inspirational muses, what do we ask of this oracle merged with the rumor of history that will authorize us to speak or make believable what we say? This anonymous hero comes from way back. He is the murmur of societies.
>
> (de Certeau, 1980: 5)

Here lie several key elements of his project. For sure, there is clearly an attention to the everyday, and its alignment with spatial practices of walking and movement. More subtly though, is a roundaboutness to this object. De Certeau positions the everyday hero as 'impossible', yet generating rumours and inspirations. There is both the positive evaluation of the only half-heard (again not quite knowable) murmurings of social action – described through aural not visual metaphors of knowledge – and the dangerous sense of such half-heard things authorising knowledge claims. Through examining such themes de Certeau's work has been picked up for: first, how it points to a critique of urban ideologies, and especially those of planning and rationalism; second, as offering an account of life that exceeds notions of planned space in terms of a model of active practice transforming spaces; third, a sense of local 'tactics' that, fourth, form part of consumption practices.

Philosophically his work might be seen to be anchored in two great traditions. First, the anti-Parmenidean approach that sees things always as exceeding and irreducible to our conceptions of them, and second as being inspired by work on language. In terms of linguistic theories, the two great touchstones are clearly the theories of Jacques Lacan, and also those of Ludwig Wittgenstein. De Certeau used Wittgentein's analysis of ordinary language and his grounding of philosophy in everyday language to resist claims for both a special domain of expertise 'beyond language' and claims for an extra-discursive position of authority. De Certeau thus commented 'We are subject to, but not identified with, ordinary language. As in the ship of fools, we are embarked, without the possibility of an aerial view or any sort of totalization' (de Certeau, 1984: 11). His embrace of thinking from within ordinary practice follows from this and is best exemplified in his most read work – *The Practice of Everyday Life* (1984). It is in this guise that de Certeau has become a darling to some, as a counterpoint to stratospheric theory, and villain for others, as an example of taking micro-theory too far.

SPATIAL CONTRIBUTIONS

Possibly his most celebrated essay – *Walking in the City* – often reprinted from *The Practices of Everyday Life*, opens with what is now an anachronistic evocation of urban theory and its desire for an orderly view of what he calls the 'Concept city':

> Seeing Manhattan from the 110th floor of the World Trade centre. Beneath the haze stirred up by the winds, the urban island, a sea in the middle of the sea, lifts up the skyscrapers ... A wave of verticals. Its agitation momentarily arrested by vision. The gigantic mass is immobilized before the eyes. It is transformed into a texturology ... To what erotics of knowledge does the ecstasy of reading such a cosmos belong? Having taken voluptuous pleasure in it, I wonder what is the source of this pleasure of 'seeing the whole', of looking down on, totalizing the most immoderate of human texts.

(de Certeau, 1984: 91–2)

This has keyed into a whole series of critiques of urban theory – that question the subject position and viewpoint of planners, the panoptic disciplining of space and the pretensions of social theory. Here he asks us to think about the enjoyment mobilised by theoretical and management accounts that offer us a privileged and 'powerful' view of urban process – there is no innocent viewpoint and the gaze of theory offers to satisfy desires for knowledge and order. In other words, the popularity of these approaches is not just about their better insights but also how they position us as powerful knowing subjects. As such he is critical of visual metaphors for knowledge and practices of visualising society, arguing that:

> Our society is characterized by a cancerous growth of vision, measuring everything by its ability to show or be shown and transmuting communication into a visual journey. It is a sort of epic of the eye and the impulse to read.

(de Certeau, 1984: xxi)

His caution is that this converts the world into a 'texturology' that we can read, but in so doing it freezes urban life and thus occludes a great many urban practices. Thus he argues that representational art and science immobilise the city's 'opaque mobility' into a transparent text that offers only the 'empire of the evident' (1984: 204) where practices are often treated as inert contents or as cultural attributes to be measured. This leaves theory 'mourning at the tomb of the absent' speaking about the laws or structures not the actions themselves.

He suggests social theory often replicates the epistemological vision of the powerful. Thus even if its purpose is critical or oppositional, it too tends to believe in plans, regularities and structures, as though they were the limits of social life. Instead he looks to a 'scattered polytheism' of different systems of thought – the dispersed knowledges of practices that elude the gaze of theory. He does not see an aggregate sum of practices but an innumerable mass of singularities – not because they are too numerous to count, but because they are ontologically uncountable. In other words, it is not a lack of technical capacity that might be overcome by more surveys and larger datasets processed in bigger algorithms. Instead he sees tactics transforming the *places* designed by hegemonic powers and envisioned as the neat and orderly realm of the concept city, into unruly *spaces;* that is, he sees practices as spatialising places.

> Space occurs as the effect produced by the operations that orient it, situate it, temporalize it, and make it function in a polyvalent unity of conflictual programs or contractual proximities. On this view, in relation to place, space is like the word when it is spoken, that is when it is caught in the ambiguity of an actualization, transformed into a term dependent upon many conventions, situated as the act of a present (or of a time), and modified by the transformations caused by successive contexts. ... In short, *space is a practiced place.* Thus the street geometrically defined by urban planning is transformed into space by walkers.
>
> (de Certeau, 1984: 117, original emphasis)

This rather unhelpfully inverts the usual geographical usage where space is associated with the abstract form of space and place with the more lived and experiential. In part this stems from the translation of the French words *lieu* as 'place', and *espace* as space. In some sense the translation would be better with 'location' instead of place. The sense that de Certeau gives it (lieu) is clearer when we read it as 'the order (of whatever kind) in accord with which elements are distributed in relationships of coexistence. It thus excludes the possibility of two things being in the same location (place)' (de Certeau 1984: 117). Here one can see the connection with the synchronic structures of structural linguistics, and thus de Certeau's turn to 'speech acts' and the use of everyday language, after Wittgenstein, is enacting a post-structuralist move. However, this version of place also invokes a deeper ontological sense from Lacanian analysis of the 'propre' as a purified centre organising knowledge. Here then he looks to the control of space as a matter of strategy which is orientated through the construction of powerful knowledges. In contrast, there are tactics – the arts of making do, like reading, or cooking – which use what they find in multiple permutations. This practical knowledge of the city transforms and crosses spaces, creates new links, comprising mobile geographies of looks and glances as people walk through and walk by these given places. Strategy claims territory and defines place; tactics use and subvert those places.

The strategic vision of power and theory are thus transformed by small-scale tactics. Strategy, he sees, as the imposition of power through the disciplining and organisation of space – zoning activities, prescribing some activities in some places, proscribing them in others. Tactics are the 'ruses' that take the predisposition of the world and make it over, that convert it to the purposes of ordinary people. The giant order of urban planning and the concept city is thus both vast yet also strangely tenuous when set against the 'maritime immensity' of scattered practices – the city is an 'order-sieve' (1984: 143). The gaze of power transfixes objects but also thus becomes blind to a vast array of things that do not fit its categories. Thus empirically we might look at different modes of kn... he city – what he termed the '... histories' of things such as way... king, modes of dress, cooking or... od memories. These create absen... ghosts in the machine that render... truly 'habitable' and inhabited. '... e is sceptical of knowledges that... cities from a God's-eye view, and... e concerned with 'stories' as e... ogies of actually getting by in cities; and, in spatial terms, he saw walking as a form of practical narration. The city is known by walking rather than looking down at a static plan. In making this move one can see him setting himself against the geometric forms of knowledge and ordering of spaces, seeing such mathematical languages and forms of knowledge as leading inexorably to places being depicted as equivalent to one another.

His work looks at the use of objects and places rather than their ownership and production – the French title of *The Practice of Everyday Life* is '*L'art de faire*', which can also be translated as 'ways of making do'. So he turns our attention to how tactics appropriate what has been created by hegemonic knowledge systems. Thus children make jungles and castles out of apparent wasteland or 'spaces left over in planning' or street signs become associated with social memories that may reject their formal significance (instead of commemorating generals for instance they may be associated with a first kiss, a riot or something different entirely) and monuments become refigured into popular culture (statues of reclining women in fountains in both Birmingham and Dublin have earnt the local epithets of 'the floozy in the Jacuzzi').

The city for de Certeau is as much about dreams as things, and about doings not just knowings. It is through taking what is there and re-using it that locations become meaningful and inhabited. But if we were to look for conventional indicators of production or use then we would see nothing of this urban life. He has thus become associated with seeing consumption not as an end point or afterthought to producing urban spaces and service, but as an active process. Although here he points to the overall framing of hegemonic power, he sees the Brownian movements of myriad practices within that system. The plurality of practices creates a 'piling up of heterogeneous places. Each one, like the deteriorating page of a book, refers to a different mode of territorial unity, of socioeconomic distribution, of political conflicts and of identifying symbolism' (de Certeau 1984: 201); that is, multiple practices, some of which may be powerful and others residues of former systems of knowledge, overlap. Thus, for example, gentrified neighbourhoods may have been built to service factories that have disappeared, with streets named after forgotten heroes of empires that have fallen. 'The whole [is] made up of pieces that are not contemporary and still linked to totalities that have fallen into ruins' (ibid.).

If we look at de Certeau's wider corpus of work we can see that another key contribution is then analysing the organisation and production of knowledge. Here, his work draws on that notion of proper places producing organising systems of knowledge and argues instead these are largely artefacts of our ways of thinking. As he put it, 'it would be wrong to think that these tools are neutral, or their gaze inert: nothing gives itself up, everything has to be seized, and the same interpretive violence can either create or destroy' (1986: 135). Just as places are made up of different clashing symbolic systems, he comments, as social scientists or historians present evidence, they actually freeze and dissect the dynamism of practices so that that they only appear in the text in a fragmented, wounded state, as perhaps a 'ruin'. He also looks carefully at this 'place' of analysis as being one where we can accumulate knowledge by subjecting it all to the same interpretation. This he says is part of an accumulatory economy or 'Occidental capitalization of knowledge' that serves to locate a privileged knowledge 'back here' in the place of analysis and sets that against a world 'out there'. He thus offers a critique of knowledge processes, seeing a quest for purity and conceptual order as linked to both the symbolic and historic economy of dominance of the West. Instead he sees the process as more itinerant, with us moving through different material in different places, in libraries, in the field, with a sort of textual and theoretical voyaging that complements empirical travels and travails; and argues for a conceptualisation of making knowledge through fortuitous encounters and tracing connections.

KEY ADVANCES AND CONTROVERSIES

De Certeau's influence in geography has been with respect to four main areas, in perhaps roughly chronological order: rethinking urban planning; developing conceptions of consumption; postcolonial approaches to historiography; and the theorisation of space. The earliest is perhaps, quantitatively, the second most prominent. Here, de Certeau has figured in planning and geography as

against totalising planning and urban theory. He has been set against, for instance, more pessimistic readings from **Lefebvre** or the Situationists that suggest capital is colonising the lifeworld to see a continued vivacity of urban practice. He has also been taken as a statement for the importance of not producing totalising, academic accounts – of refusing the powerful gaze of theory. His works here, thus, both figure in and against, accounts such as those by **Ed Soja**, that seek to accord a liveliness to place and practices, yet continue to offer the grand vision of urban process as a whole.

The second thematic on consumption built upon his twofold move of seeing consumption as creative praxis (thus liberating its study from being an economic epiphenomena) and as being capable of resistance. His work here chimed with that of the Birmingham School of Cultural Studies and came into a confluence of work around resistance through consumption practices. It is important to recall that up until the 1990s very few studies had followed consumption beyond the point of purchase.

The third strand, in terms of post-colonial historiography, aligns his work with other historians (such as Hayden White) and emphasises that the politics of knowledge extend beyond the urban. Here his accounting of science's production of an exquisite corpse is coupled with his powerful global spatial imaginary. It is notable here that in terms of reach, while the English translation of *Practice of Everyday Life* has some 5000 citations on Google scholar, *Heterologies* has more like 500.

Finally, his determination to create a sense of place as actively constructed has been developed in theoretical accounts, especially taking his notions of the transformation of space through the conjunction of circumstances and memory – meaning its affordance change and it too is changed

(Crang and Travlou, 2001). His work has emphasised the invisible myths that do not merely ornament places but deeply structure their uses.

It is worth pausing to think about the limits of the adoption of de Certeau into social theory. He has perhaps been too easily co-opted as the champion of the common man (it is perhaps notable that it is only with Volume 2 of the practices of everyday life that he and a collaborator, Luce Giard, have chapters on cooking and neighbourhoods that really address the gendering of spaces). One might build three sets of critiques of how he has been used and especially his urban thinking. First, his conceptualisation of power tends to see a totalising and powerful form of knowledge pitted against the ordinary citizen. This lacks a more sociological sense of the mediation of power by different institutions and actors within those institutions, all of whom have their own agendas (or dare one say tactics) about their work. De Certeau stands accused of having such a powerful version of power, it is almost inoperable. Second, the opposition of tactic and strategy is thus rather more like a series of gaps or misalignments in a dance than how it is often portrayed as resistance or transgression. De Certeau's tactics are actually not politically oppositional, they are evasive of the orders and plans of the dominant knowledge rather than forming a coherent, and equally limited, resistance. Such always dispersed, limited evasions, that he refuses to say could constitute an alternative order have frustrated those seeking just such an alternative model for society. Third, his empirical connection to practices of neighbourhood life and walking the streets connects him to an imaginary of urbane life that is located in a European intellectual culture that may not reflect all urban lifestyles. Finally, these are linked in the sense that de Certeau had a coherent overall philosophical view and project, with its own language and terminology. The over-quick use of his terms and ideas in consumption studies can often sound like invocation rather than analysis and risks losing the subtleties of his work.

Where current debates might look to develop new avenues from his work is more speculative. But it seems remarkable that with the rise of non-representational work, his attention to the violence of representation has not been used, and his focus on practice chimes well where he says the ordinary actor 'always precedes texts' (1980: 4). Indeed he links the triumph of power with the triumph of vision and representation (1980: 5). But more surprising is that in that non-representational work's attentiveness to the unsaid, and the unsayable, to the felt and indeed almost spiritual, it has not found support in his work on mysticism and the unrepresentable.

DE CERTEAU'S KEY WORKS

de Certeau, M. (1980) 'On the oppositional practices of everyday life', *Social Text*, 1: 3–43.

de Certeau, M. (1984) *The Practice of Everyday Life*. Vol. 1. Berkeley, CA: California University Press. Original edition, *L'Arts de faire*, (1980) Editions Minuit.

de Certeau, M. (1986) *Heterologies: Discourses on the Other*. Manchester: Manchester University Press.

de Certeau. M. (1988) *The Writing of History*. Trans. T. Conley New York: Columbia University Press.

de Certeau, M. (1992) *The Mystic Fable: The Sixteenth and Seventeenth Centuries.* Trans. M. Smith, Chicago: University of Chicago Press.

de Certeau, M. (1997) *The Capture of Speech and other Political Writings.* Trans. T. Conley. Minneapolis: University of Minnesota Press.

de Certeau, M. (1997) *Culture in the Plural.* Trans. T. Conley Minneapolis: University of Minnesota Press.

de Certeau, M., Giard L. and Mayol, P. (1998) *The Practice of Everyday Life: Living and Cooking.* Trans. T. Tomasik. Vol. 2. Minneapolis: Minnesota University Press. Original edition, *L'Invention du quotidien II habiter, cuisiner,* 1994, Editions Gallimard.

Secondary Sources and References

Ahearne, J. (1995) *Michel de Certeau: Interpretation and Its Other.* Cambridge: Polity Press.

Buchanan, I. (2000) *Michel de Certeau: Cultural Theorist.* London: Sage.

Brammer, M. (1992) 'Thinking practice: Michel de Certeau and the theorization of mysticism', *Diacritics,* 22: 26–37.

Carrard, P. (2001) 'History as a kind of writing: Michel de Certeau and the poetics of historiography', *South Atlantic Quarterly,* 100: 465–82.

Conley, T. (1992) 'Michel de Certeau and the textual icon', *Diacritics* 22: 38–49.

Crang, M. (2000) 'Spaces of practice: the work of Michel de Certeau', in M. Crang, and N. Thrift (eds) *Thinking Space.* London: Routledge. pp. 126–40.

Crang, M. and Travlou, S.E. (2001) 'The city and topologies of memory', *Society & Space,* 19: 161–77.

Frow, J. (1992) 'Michel de Certeau and the practice of representation', *Cultural Studies,* 6: 52–60.

Giard, L. (1991) Michel de Certeau's heterology and the New World', *Representations,* 33: 212–21.

Lock, C. (1999) 'Michel de Certeau: walking the *via negative*', *Paragraph,* 22: 184–98.

Meagher, S.M. (2007) 'Philosophy in the streets', *City,* 11: 7–20.

Olwig, K. R. (2006) 'Place contra space in a morally just landscape', *Norsk Geografisk Tidsskrift – Norwegian Journal of Geography,* 60: 24–31.

Reynolds, B. and Fitzpatrick, J. (1999) 'The transversality of Michel de Certeau: Foucault's panoptic discourse and the cartographic impulse', *Diacritics,* 29: 63–80.

Mike Crang, Durham University

14 Stuart E. Corbridge

BIOGRAPHICAL DETAILS AND THEORETICAL CONTEXT

Stuart Corbridge was born in 1957 and grew up in the English West Midlands, before gaining a place at the University of Cambridge to read Geography at Sidney Sussex College, graduating in 1978. At Cambridge, Corbridge's earliest influence was **Derek Gregory**'s theoretically inspired historical geography, and he also benefited from the reworking of key ideas in development studies by other Cambridge academics, among them Polly Hill, Suzy Paine and Ajit Singh. His PhD, supervised by Bertram Hughes Farmer, combined fieldwork with archival study of a century of tribal politics in Jharkhand, India, paying particular attention to the influence of positive discrimination polices for people labelled as 'tribal' (the *adivasis*). Corbridge began publishing his Indian research in 1982, and his interest in Eastern Indian politics and development issues has been sustained over 30 years, moving between questions of agrarian change, development policy, and governance. His broader research interests revolve around geopolitics and development theory, and have entailed collaborations with colleagues at the many institutions where he has been employed. Work took him from a lectureship at Huddersfield Polytechnic (UK) to Royal Holloway (University of London), Syracuse University (US), the University of Cambridge (UK), the University of Miami, and, since 2001, the London School of Economics where he became Professor in the interdisciplinary, postgraduate Development Studies Institute.

SPATIAL CONTRIBUTIONS

In Anglophone geography, Corbridge is best known for his sustained analysis of the development process, finance, and geopolitics. His first book, *Capitalist World Development* (1986: 10), was a critical examination of radical perspectives in development thinking, particularly the then-common view among radical theorists wedded to 'deterministic models of capitalism' that theorised an inevitable conflict of interest between 'metropolitan capitalism and the development of the periphery of the modern world system' (ibid.: 3). Corbridge was at an early stage of his thinking on these issues, but nonetheless challenged existing theories of underdevelopment, as well as the counterveiling optimism of modernisation theorists. His vision of development and its potential steered a middle course that could best be described as 'cautiously optimistic'. Subsequently he has gone on to write widely on the potential for liberatory development theory and its moral basis (Corbridge, 1993b), rethinking the colonial experience, the dilemmas faced by post-colonial states in the midst of the geopolitics of the Cold War, and the role of debt in the financial system (Corbirdge, 1993; Corbridge et al., 1994). Some, but not all, of this work is phrased in the language of post-Marxism and even post-Keynesianism (Corbridge, 1988; 1990; 1994), while his work on India has recently drawn on the work of Chatterjee and Kaviraj, as well as that of **Foucault** and Gramsci.

He argues frequently, as in his second book, *Debt and Development* (1993), that the evident contradictions of global capitalism do not in themselves make the case for transcendental forms of radical politics that would seek to iron out what John Toye (1993) has called the 'dilemmas of development'. The idea of development is not, therefore, dismissed out of hand, and indeed 'there is ... a strong case for a massive expansion in aid budgets to help rescue people from levels of absolute poverty not of their own making' (Agnew and Corbridge, 1995: 216), even though important political battles have to be waged around development's meanings and practices. Corbridge's general support for aid flows, and an interest in promoting some form of economic development, sets his work apart from his Marxist critics, and particularly from the post-development theorists like **Arturo Escobar** who challenge most overtly the hegemonic power of Western development discourse (Corbridge, 1998b).

The themes raised in *Debt and Development* were followed with further work on international debt and monetary policy. For example, Corbridge's work on inflation

follows a Keynesian argument about the need for economic pragmatism and 'rigorous eclecticism' in monetary policy (1994: 88), and he engages with the geopolitics of monetary transfer and regulation in *Money, Power and Space,* which also traces the imbrications of money with social and cultural networks of power (Corbridge et al., 1994). This collection was soon followed by a book with John Agnew, *Mastering Space* (1995), which is an overview of the global political economy of the past two hundred years. In a development of his earlier position, in this text, the authors argued:

> Globalization is not only a synonym of disempowerment: it creates certain conditions for democratization, de-centralization and empowerment as well as for centralization and standardization. Globalization opens as many doors as it shuts.
>
> (Agnew and Corbridge, 1995: 219).

As **Gearóid Ó Tuathail** (1995) argues, the book demonstrated this by some deft applications of **Henri Lefebvre**'s arguments, distinguishing between flows of goods and power, the discursive representations that sustain these flows, and the 'imagined geographies' that 'inspire the future organization and articulation of spatial practices and representations of space'.

This nuanced and critical approach to geopolitics suggests the existence of three 'geopolitical orders' over time, each operating with distinct forms of hegemonic authority. The period 1815–1975, termed the *Concert of Europe,* gave way to 70 years of *Inter-Imperial Rivalry* until 1945, followed by the *Cold War* from 1945–90. The book argues that, as of the mid-1990s, the world order was missing a dominant nation state, thus 'there is always hegemony, but there are not always hegemons' (Agnew and Corbridge, 1995: 17). The argument here is prophetic: hegemony, used in a Gramscian sense to describe structures that legitimate dominant practices and organise consent, is creating:

> new conditions for 'ordered disorder' by ignoring, tidying away and/or disciplining a group of countries, regions and communities which are not party to a new regime of market-access economics or which threaten it in some way.
>
> (Agnew and Corbridge, 1995: 193)

Agnew and Corbridge argued that transnational liberalism had become dominant through the breakdown of Keynesian economic policy and the Bretton Woods agreements, as well as through the power of new transnational business and military networks. Consistent with Corbridge's stand on globalisation more generally, *Mastering Space* also argued that opposition to hegemonic discourses and practices necessarily accompanies their growth and their increased spatial reach. The millennial anti-globalisation movements and protests were anticipated in the book, but perhaps not the turns that some have taken (for example, through Islamic militancy), nor the geopolitical repercussions of 9/11.

A second major contribution is Corbridge's detailed and sustained interrogation of Indian development as an idea and in practice. From the early 1990s, he returned to studies of rural issues in the eastern Indian States of Bihar, Jharkhand, Orissa and West Bengal. Alongside new interpretations of ethno-regional politics in Jharkhand, he has worked on forest citizenship and forest management, the collection and marketing of non-timber forest products, the impacts of development policy, the politics of compensatory discrimination, and the question of how empowerment and poverty are negotiated in the modern Indian state. His book with John Harriss, *Reinventing India* (2000) analysed economic liberalisation and Hindu

nationalism as 'elite revolts' that resisted a discourse of egalitarianism in India's early post-war years. Divisive religious and economic practices have replaced the sense of nationhood that guided India at independence and Partition.

India's lack of an effective 'developmental state' is traced to the failure of national leaders to assert political control, (particularly under Indira Gandhi), and to their failure to slow the rise of heavily bureaucratic planning. Echoing the argument developed in *Mastering Space*, the depressing and violent 'centralising instincts' of Hindu nationalism will, it is suggested, continue to clash with the aspirations and social movements of lower castes and subaltern groupings. A major empirical study of state performance and empowerment issues in five Districts of Bihar and West Bengal, working with geographers Glyn Williams, Manoj Srivastava and Réne Véron, was based on substantial fieldwork and hundreds of detailed interviews (Corbridge et al., 2005). The project argued that the upward accountability of the local state (especially to political parties) is as important as downward accountability to communities in this Indian context. Participatory political decentralisation is not a panacea, because local actors can develop networks of corruption implicating civil society and local state officials alike (Corbridge et al., 2005; Sengupta and Corbridge, 2008). Corbridge has also worked with Sanjay Kumar on questions of participation and social capital in India (2002a), imperial legacies (Corbridge et al., 2003) and on the links between community, corruption and landscape in Jharkhand (2002b).

Third, Corbridge believes geographical research and teaching must draw upon, and contribute to, the social sciences and international studies more broadly, and he has made significant contributions at this interface, recently locating himself in an interdisciplinary institute rather than a geography department. He signals the importance of spatiality, geography, and the 'power' of space in explanations of geopolitical change and development, but he does not privilege them. 'Development geography', and concepts of space and place that it holds dear, must form part of ecumenical analysis and broader debate across a range of disciplines. Aside from the substantive contributions mentioned above, Corbridge has completed a substantial essay on the life and work of **Amartya Sen** (2002b), edited two Development Studies readers (1995; Chari and Corbridge 2009) and another on the global economy, and published a six-volume reference collection of readings entitled *Development: Critical Concepts* (2000) that spans the entire range of historical and contemporary key works in that field.

KEY ADVANCES AND CONTROVERSIES

In the 1980s, Corbridge's work on global capitalism and the world economy came to attention at a time when radical geographers like Richard Peet, **Neil Smith**, and **David Harvey** dominated the field. Corbridge was uneasy with the core tenets and political ramifications of the Marxist geography of the day, and countered with post-Marxist critiques of determinism, some associated with regulation theorists like Alain Lipietz. As a result, *Capitalist World Development* attracted several comradely but also vituperative ripostes, notably from **Michael Watts** (1990), who argued articulately that Marxism offers

more to the study of development than Corbridge permits it. In the same vein, Michael Johns (1990: 180) accused him of wielding a 'rather dull polemical axe'.

With these debates now two decades old, and with several of the protagonists occasionally now writing or working together (e.g. Corbridge, **Thrift** and Martin, 1994), some of Corbridge's arguments have become more accepted in development geography, while he himself has moved between post-Marxism and a critical stance on the style and substance of some mainstream development policies. Arguably (and unlike some of his protagonists), his work on the idea and the practice of 'development' is based on many years of grounded field research projects, and this enables him to speak with some authority when questioning its core values and its outcomes in particular places, and when challenging others coming from different viewpoints (notably **David Harvey**; see Corbridge, 1998a).

Corbridge's work has been taken up most directly by several geographers and former students who have worked on India, including Emma Mawdsley and Sarah Jewitt. Since the 1980s, there have been relatively few sustained criticisms of his work in the two domains of world development/geopolitics and Indian development. *Mastering Space* has made an impact among geographers and international relations scholars (it is heavy on criticism of the latter discipline). In his review, **Ó Tuathail** (1995) felt the book steered away from some of the more deconstructive ambitions of critical geopolitics, but a more substantive critique concerns the validity of the concept of 'hegemony without hegemons', and whether the term 'hegemony' masks as much as it reveals, by glossing over significant differences in the aspirations and development paths of nation states lumped together in the new neo-liberal world order (Sidaway, 1997).

These doubts about the absence of hege-monic nations emerged with renewed force in the early twenty-first century, as a result of the US's aggressive foreign pol-icy under Bush, its questionable claims to be acting multilaterally in the 'war' on terrorism, and its renewed efforts to assert a world order using both military strength and a revival of Cold-War lan-guage and discourse. Could this be her-alding a new set of hegemonic practices? In addition, Agnew and Corbridge down-played the possibility of severe economic crisis emerging in the international politi-cal economy (which of course occurred in 2008) and the real possibilities of cata-strophic violence occurring on a global scale. In their framing of the hegemonic order, Toal feels, the power of 'institu-tions to regulate the power of dictators, ethnic cleansers or fundamentalism is not evident.' Again, viewed from the early twenty-first century, these actors are still showing their colours.

Reinventing India (2000) shared some theories and concepts with *Mastering Space*, but advances an innovative idea: that a new India is being 'invented' through elite interests that serve the ends of particular classes, particularly since economic liberalisation after 1991 and the rise of Hindu nationalism (Corbridge also made this argument in his account of the politics of India's nuclear bomb (1999)). While Singh (2001) uncharita-bly accuses the authors of undue attach-ment to concepts of class-based politics, and Chari (2002) feels the Marxist and Gramscian approach to social change in *Reinventing India* gives scant attention to gender politics and feminist moments in current economic and political strug-gles, the book explains current political manoeuvres and discourses in a rich lan-guage. The concept of failed social revo-lutions led by elites ('elite revolts') goes a long way to explain India's particular

crises of nationalism and violence (Hall, 2002), and shows how good intentions turn bad.

In conclusion, Corbridge's work to date rests on several major contribu-tions. His work on post-Marxist devel-opment theory, debt, and the transitions experienced in rural India has antici-pated some of the current thinking on globalisation made by eminent interna-tional relations theorists and sociologists like **Anthony Giddens**, David Held and Fred Halliday, as well as contributing to rethinking these areas in geography. The links between the Indian state and its citizens has been re-conceived, and fleshed out with 25 years of detailed study. The notion of 'hegemony without hegemons' has contributed to the emerg-ing field of critical geopolitics (Dodds, 2001), although in the present conflict-ridden era we have seen the US aggres-sively assert the 'rightness' of democracy across the globe. However, as Corbridge and Harriss (2000) rightly note, the neo-liberal world economy has encountered resistance, for example from the sub-altern spaces and resistance to 'elite revolts', eloquently described in *Rein-venting India*. Such movements always accompany these hegemonic forces, even if they sometimes lack power. Cor-bridge shares with **Castells**, **Watts** and **Escobar** an interest in the promotion of alternatives to mainstream develop-ment, but some of these alternatives have unfortunately emerged as aggres-sively fundamentalist or nationalist in their own right (and thus are unpleasant to the sensibilities of Western activists and scholars), and not all have been able to challenge the state or the market with sufficient force. As other biographies in this volume show, development geogra-phy will have to remain attentive to the nuances of globalisation, and resistance to it.

CORBRIDGE' S KEY WORKS

Corbridge, S.E. (1986) *Capitalist World Development: A Critique of Radical Development Geography.* London: Macmillan.

Corbridge, S.E. (1993) *Debt and Development.* Oxford: Blackwell.

Corbridge, S.E., Thrift, N. and Martin, R. (eds) (1994) *Money, Power and Space.* Oxford: Blackwell.

Agnew, J. and Corbridge, S.E. (1995) *Mastering Space: Hegemony, Territory and International Political Economy.* London: Routledge.

Corbridge, S.E. (ed.) (2000) *Development: Critical Concepts in the Social Sciences.* London: Routledge. [6 Volumes]

Corbridge S.E., Jewitt, S. and Kumar, S. (2003) *Jharkhand: Environment, Development, Politics.* Delhi: Oxford University Press.

Corbridge S.E., Williams G., Srivastava, M. and Véron, R. (2005). *Seeing the State: Governance and Governmentality in Rural India.* Cambridge: Cambridge University Press.

Chari, S. and Corbridge,S. E. (eds) (2009) *The Development Reader.* London: Routledge.

Secondary Sources and References

Chari, S. (2002) 'Review of *Reinventing India*', *Annals of the Association of American Geographers*, 92 (2): 349–51.

Corbridge, S.E. (1988b) 'The ideology of tribal economy and society: politics in Jharkhand, 1950–1980', *Modern Asian Studies*, 22 (1): 1–41.

Corbridge, S.E. (1990) 'Post-Marxism and development studies: beyond the impasse', *World Development*, 18 (5): 623–39.

Corbridge, S.E. (ed.) (1993a) *World Economy.* Oxford: Oxford University Press.

Corbridge, S.E. (1993b) 'Marxisms, modernities and moralities: development praxis and the claims of distant strangers', *Environment and Planning D: Society and Space*, 11: 449–72.

Corbridge, S.E. (1994) 'Plausible worlds: Friedman, Keynes and the geography of inflation' in S. E. Corbridge, N. Thrift, and R. Martin (eds), *Money, Power and Space.* Oxford: Blackwell. pp. 63–90.

Corbridge, S.E. (1994a) 'Bretton Woods revisited: hegemony, stability and territory', *Environment and Planning A*, 26 (12): 1829–59.

Corbridge, S.E. (1998a) 'Reading David Harvey: entries, voices, loyalties', *Antipode*, 30: 43–55.

Corbridge, S.E. (1998b) 'Beneath the pavement only soil: the poverty of post-development', *Journal of Development Studies*, 34: 138–48.

Corbridge, S.E. (1999) "The militarization of all Hindudom?" The Bharatiya Janata Party, the bomb and the political spaces of Hindu nationalism', *Economy and Society*, 28: 222–55.

Corbridge, S.E. (ed.) (1995) *Development Studies: A Reader.* London: Edward Arnold.

Corbridge, S.E. (2000a) 'Competing inequalities: the Scheduled Tribes and the reservations system in India's Jharkhand', *Journal of Asian Studies*, 59 (1): 62–85.

Corbridge S.E (2002b) 'Development as freedom: the spaces of Amartya Sen', *Progress in Development Studies*, 2: 183–217.

Corbridge, S.E. and Harriss, J. (2000) *Reinventing India: Liberalization, Hindu Nationalism and Popular Democracy.* Cambridge: Polity and Delhi: Oxford University Press.

Corbridge, S.E. and Kumar, S. (2002b) 'Community, corruption, landscape: tales from the tree trade', *Political Geography*, 21: 765–88.

Dodds, K. (2001) 'Political geography III: critical geopolitics after ten years', *Progress in Human Geography*, 25 (3): 469–84.

Hall, J. (2002) 'Review of Reinventing India', *Canadian Journal of Sociology Online*. July–August. www.arts.ualberta.ca/cjscopy/reviews/india.html

Johns, M. (1990) 'Review of Capitalist World Development', *Antipode*, 22(2): 168–174.

Kumar, S. and Corbridge, S.E. (2002a) 'Programmed to fail? Development projects and the politics of participation', *Journal of Development Studies*, 39 (2): 73–103.

Muralidharan, S. (2001) 'Review of *Reinventing India*', *Frontline*, 18 (19) online www.frontlineonnet.com/fl1819/18190730.htm

Raju, S., Kumar, S. and Corbridge, S. (eds) (2006) *Colonial and Postcolonial Geographies of India.* London/New Delhi: Sage.

Sengupta, A. and Corbridge, S.E. (eds) (2008) *Democracy, Development and Decentralisation in India.* Oxford: Oxford University Press.

Sidaway, J.D. (1997) 'Review of *Mastering Space*', *Transactions of the Institute of British Geographers*, NS 22: 130–2.

Singh G. (2001) 'Review of Reinventing India', *Journal of Development Studies*, 38 (1): 71.

Toal, G. (1995) 'Political Geography I: Theorizing history, gender and world order amidst crises of global governance', *Progress in Human Geography*, 19: 260–72.

Toye, J. (1993) *Dilemmas of Development: Reflections on the Counter-Revolution in Development Theory and Policy* (2nd edition) Oxford: Blackwell.

Watts, M.J. (1990) 'Deconstructing determinism: Marxism's development theory and a comradely critique of Stuart Corbridge', *Antipode,* 20 (2): 142–70.

Simon Batterbury, University of Melbourne

15 Denis Cosgrove

In the course of an academic career spanning more than three decades, Denis Cosgrove did perhaps more than any other Anglophone academic geographer to ensure that 'landscape' continues to occupy a central place on the disciplinary 'map'. His work on the idea of landscape, which came to the fore in the 1980s especially, profoundly altered the course of landscape study in human geography through a series of theoretically-informed yet empirically-grounded books and articles (Cosgrove, 1984/1998a; 1985; 1993; Cosgrove and Daniels, 1988). In 1993 he co-founded a new journal – *Ecumene: a geographical journal of environment, culture and meaning* (later *Cultural Geographies*) – providing a forum for research within the humanities tradition of geographical scholarship. Later, in the 1990s, Cosgrove's interests moved towards broader issues of 'mapping' and representation, but his work continued to be characterised by its close attention to empirical – and particularly historical – detail, whilst continuing to engage with theoretical ideas from disciplines such as cultural studies, landscape architecture, cartographic history and creative art

(Cosgrove, 1996; 1999a; 2001a; 2001b; 2008). This blending of empirical and theoretical material is a hallmark of Cosgrove's work, and it is this that has ensured that his writing has had considerable impact on contemporary geographical thought and enquiry despite the focus of much of his work on the historical geographies of Renaissance and Enlightenment Europe.

Born in 1948, and educated in Liverpool at St Francis Xavier College and then St Catherine's College, Oxford, Cosgrove established his reputation as a leading practitioner of the 'new' cultural geography while in the Geography Division of Oxford Polytechnic (now Oxford Brookes University), where he served as Chairman (*sic*) from 1976 to 1980, and while at the Department of Geography of Loughborough University (from 1980 to 1993). Alongside those humanistic geographers in the UK and US who critiqued the positivist and quantitative basis of much of human geography, Cosgrove sought to recognise the subjectivity of geographical enquiry, and situate geography within a broader humanities tradition that acknowledged both charisma and context (Cosgrove, 1989; Freytag and Jöns, 2006). This concern with 'authorship' and 'authority' in geographical writing arguably informed Cosgrove's subsequent scholarship (Cosgrove and Domosh, 1993), and while few contemporary geographers might refer to themselves as 'humanistic', the contributions made by Cosgrove to theoretical debates in the early 1980s about the writing and representation of space have endured (see Cosgrove, 2001b). One important reason for this was Cosgrove's own enthusiasm to engage with post-modern and post-structural thought, marking him out as one of the most important sources of inspiration for those geographers seeking to interrogate the relations of knowledge and power. From 1999, resident in the US as Alexander von Humboldt Professor of Geography at the University of California at Los Angeles (UCLA), Cosgrove continued in his role as a mediator between geography, the humanities and arts, becoming Getty Distinguished Scholar for 2008–9, but died in March 2008, at the age of 59, following a prolonged illness (see Lilley, 2009). His empirical and theoretical insights in cultural and historical geography are a rich intellectual legacy that will no doubt influence future human geography widely.

SPATIAL CONTRIBUTIONS

One of Cosgrove's key contributions was to engage with key geographical concepts through the motif of *landscape*. Within the context of cultural geography in the UK, Cosgrove's engagement with ideas of 'writing' and 'reading' landscape drew upon the ideas of North American geographers such as Carl Sauer, J.B. Jackson and **Yi-Fu Tuan**, among others (see Cosgrove, 1998b). Taking one of the concepts that was central to the North American geographical imagination, Cosgrove nonetheless departed from North

American 'Berkeley' cultural tradition by exploring not just the cultural processes that shaped landscape but also the constitutive role that landscape plays in shaping the lives of those who engage with that landscape, or landscapes. In the early 1980s this was a new and radical way of viewing landscape for, up to that point, UK historical geographers were broadly concerned with 'reconstructing' past landscapes from maps, documents and fieldwork in a tradition derived from the work of W.G. Hoskins (as well as M. W. Beresford and M. R. G. Conzen) (see Wylie, 2007; Whitehand, 2001). Cosgrove offered a different approach to landscape, one that recognised that 'landscape is not merely the world we see, it is a construction, a composition of the world', in short, 'an ideological concept' (Cosgrove, 1984, 1998a: 13, 15). Cosgrove set out this thesis in his first book, *Social Formation and Symbolic Landscape*, introducing the idea that 'landscape is a way of seeing' – a means by which 'Europeans have represented to themselves and to others the world about them and their relationships with it' (Cosgrove, 1984: 1).

Looking back on this work in the 'introduction' to the book's second edition, Cosgrove reflects on its 'prime intention ... to press landscape studies, especially in Geography, towards what seemed to be specific new directions: to locate landscape interpretation within a critical historiography, to theorise the idea of landscape within a broadly Marxian understanding of culture and society, and thus to extend the treatment of landscape beyond what seemed ... a prevailing narrow focus on design and taste' (Cosgrove, 1998b: xiii). The book certainly did this, and at its heart was Cosgrove's interest in Renaissance Italy (Cosgrove, 1993). Here he found the roots of the 'landscape idea' in Western culture, which was (like the book itself) a humanistic enterprise concerned with new ways of imagining and representing landscape, of 'seeing' the land.

Cosgrove's landscape 'as a way of seeing' idea became more influential in geographical discourse following the publication in 1985 of his paper, 'Prospect, perspective and the evolution of the landscape idea' (Cosgrove, 1985), and with the publication of a collection of papers under the title *The Iconography of Landscape*, edited by Cosgrove and Daniels (1988). In both, Cosgrove reinforced the message of *Social Formation*, that landscape was 'a "way of seeing" that was bourgeois, individualist and related to the exercise of power' (Cosgrove, 1985: 45). Simultaneously, he underlined that this was connected with Renaissance Humanism and scientific advances in mapping, projection, surveying and cosmology. As a 'way of seeing', landscape is thus 'a composition and structuring of the world' that 'may be appropriated by a detached, individual spectator to whom an illusion of order and control is offered through the composition of space according to the certainties of geometry' (Cosgrove, 1985: 55). 'Landscape' was property, owned by those beholding it; capturing and controlling the land through representations of it as landscape in maps and in paintings – and through fashioning landscapes on the ground using design and architecture. The landscape, then, far from being neutral and inert, has social and cultural meanings, a symbolism – an 'iconography'. It was this 'iconography' of landscape that Cosgrove (1984) sought to elucidate, and this is perhaps the most enduring and celebrated aspect of Cosgrove's work.

In their editorial introduction to the *Iconography of Landscape,* Cosgrove and Daniels began by referring to the landscape as a 'cultural image, a pictorial way of representing, structuring or symbolising surroundings' (Daniels and Cosgrove, 1988: 1). The idea was that in order to understand the material landscape it was necessary not just to make use of 'images and verbal representations of it' for the purposes of illustration, but to recognise that such images were constitutive of 'landscape' and 'its meaning or meanings' (Daniels and Cosgrove, 1988: 1). To explore this idea, the editors capitalised on the ideas of iconography which 'sought to probe meaning in a work of art by setting it in its historical context and ... analyse the ideas implicated in its imagery' (Daniels and Cosgrove, 1988: 2) – exactly what Cosgrove had been doing with his work on the emergence of landscape as a 'way of seeing' in late-medieval and Renaissance Italy. Conceptually, this approach owed much to art history, and especially the work of Ernst Cassirer and Erwin Panofsky on Christian iconography, while at the same time the anthropologist Clifford Geertz was drawn on to provide some sense of method with his 'thick description' and 'conceptualisation of culture as a "text"', (Daniels and Cosgrove, 1988: 4). There was little advice apart from this on how to interpret landscapes iconographically. What was instead significant about this book was that it opened up new avenues for understanding 'landscape' – including both the 'imagined' landscapes of maps, literature and art, as well as the 'material' landscape (Cosgrove and Daniels, 1988). Indeed running throughout much of Cosgrove's work was his concern with 'representation' – especially visual culture, from art and architecture in fifteenth- and sixteenth-century Italy, for example, through to cartographic images of the earth and cosmos in studies of Western and Renaissance cosmography (Cosgrove 1988; 1992; 2001a; 2001b; 2006; 2007; Cosgrove et al. 1996; Atkinson and Cosgrove, 1998).

KEY ADVANCES AND CONTROVERSIES

Certainly, Cosgrove made a key contribution to spatial thought by offering a distinctive take on the interpretation and understanding of landscape. In the light of his work, landscape can no longer be considered an unproblematic geographical concept. Equally, geographers cannot now refer to landscape without referring to Cosgrove – the two becoming synonymous. Yet it would be wrong to cast Cosgrove's contributions to the thinking of space and place simply in these terms, for his approach to landscape provided a means by which geographers broached broader conceptual issues – especially in matters of subjectivity, representation, power and authority (see Cosgrove, 1988; Freytag and Jöns, 2006). These had of course been present in Cosgrove's earlier work on landscape, but in the 1980s and 1990s they were under closer scrutiny under the rubric of a 'new' cultural geography informed by critical social and cultural theory (particularly feminist and post-colonial critiques). Cosgrove addressed these issues of authority and authorship writing with Mona Domosh, noting the 'crisis of geographical representation' and stressing that 'the very structures of representation are implicated in moral and political discourse' (Cosgrove and Domosh, 1993: 30). This 'crisis' was one in which geographers began to realise that by writing about the world in the ways that they did, they were also reinforcing a particular view of the world; an institutionalised, bourgeois, male-dominated, and sometimes imperialist view. Indeed, others at this time were also becoming conscious of geography's history and duplicity in presenting and shaping the world (see Livingstone, 1992; Driver, 2001). Hence, together with the work of **Peter Jackson** (1989) and Susan Smith (1989) on the scripting of race and racism, James and Nancy Duncan on landscape as text (Duncan and Duncan, 1988; Duncan, 1990), and **Derek Gregory's** analysis of the production of geographical knowledge (Gregory, 1994), Cosgrove's idea of landscape as 'way of seeing' (and an ideologically-infused mode of representation) emerged as a key reference point in the formation of a putative 'new' cultural geography.

Though Cosgrove has been identified as a key practitioner of the 'new' cultural geography, it is important to stress that not all those implicated in the making of this 'new' cultural geography were agreed on what its definition was (Dear, 1988). Discussions in the early 1990s flowed back and forth about its newness and also concerns over its tendency to deal more with abstract theory than with the empirical world. There were those, too, who sought to argue that this 'new' cultural geography, with its concern with text, image and metaphor, was making 'landscape' more unstable and slippery (see Muir, 1999). Indeed, there seemed to be a polarisation in the way that historical and cultural geographers were treating landscape – some continuing with their empirically-grounded, largely atheoretical work on landscape history; others more inclined to see landscapes as imaginings, in poetry, art and literature (and accused of detaching these representations from their material contexts) (see Whyte, 2002). This polarisation was in part a conceptual parting of the ways, between, on the one hand, those geographers with more positivist leanings, and on the other, those concerned with taking on board critical theory. It was an empirical and historical divide too, with the focus of the latter being especially – indeed almost exclusively – on the 'modern' world, particularly the eighteenth, nineteenth and twentieth centuries. It was here that historical and cultural geographers led the field during the 1990s (Daniels, 1993; Driver, 1992; Ogborn, 1998; Driver and Gilbert, 1999; Graham and Nash, 2000), neglecting earlier periods, particularly the Middle Ages, which during the 1960s and 1970s had been such a focus for earlier landscape work in geography (see Hooke, 2000). Indeed, to read of 'landscape' in recent UK and US geography textbooks makes it all too clear that the landscape as a 'way of seeing' has won the day, for the 'landscape history' tradition that follows in the footsteps of W. G. Hoskins and J. B. Jackson is rarely if fleetingly mentioned (see Nash, 1999; Seymour, 2000). Where reaction occurred to this new approach to landscapes it was among those human geographers whose move towards 'non-representational theory', and a desire to move beyond the textual landscape, begun to open up landscapes of 'performance' (see Wylie, 2007).

It could be said then, that Cosgrove's approach to landscape was not only in and of itself highly original and novel, but that it also influenced geographers' approach to space and place more generally, as well as catalysing disciplinary changes in cultural and historical geography. Later, although landscape remained

an important element of Cosgrove's work (e.g., Cosgrove, 1993), he focused increasingly on issues of visual representation, especially mapping and aerial photography (Cosgrove, 1992; 1999b; 2006; 2008; Cosgrove and Fox, 2009). Still there was a firm historical basis to this work, and still there was theoretical insight. Thus in his editorial introduction to *Mappings*, Cosgrove (1999b: 9) discusses 'mapping' in its various guises – both literal and metaphorical – probing the 'complex accretion of cultural engagements with the world that surround and underpin the authoring of a map', questioning how maps 'may be regarded as a hinge around which pivot whole systems of meaning'. This concern with mapping and its meanings connects of course with a growing querying of the 'map' in geographical discourse, largely inspired by **Brian Harvey**'s work in the late 1980s on 'deconstructing the map' (q.v.), and the theoretical challenges laid at cartography's door during the 1990s. At the same time, Cosgrove's focus on visual imagery and mapping connected with his long-held interests in Renaissance and Enlightenment geographical knowledges, particularly the representation of the world and globe in cosmology and cosmography (Cosgrove, 2001a; 2001b; 2007). While for some Cosgrove's subject matter might appear esoteric, his approach is catholic, and from it he always spun a larger and forceful argument that provided fuel for debate within and beyond geography – a true Renaissance project.

COSGROVE'S KEY WORKS

Cosgrove, D.E. (1984/1998a) *Social Formation and Symbolic Landscape.* London: Croom Helm (second edition with additional introductory chapter, Madison: Wisconsin University Press).

Cosgrove, D.E. (1989) 'Geography is everywhere: culture and symbolism in human landscapes', in Gregory, D. and Walford, R. (eds) *Horizons in Human Geography.* Totowa, NJ: Barnes and Noble Books. pp. 118–35.

Cosgrove, D.E. (1993) *The Palladian Landscape: Geographical Change and its Cultural Representations in Sixteenth-Century Italy*. Leicester: Leicester University Press.

Cosgrove, D.E. (ed.) (1999a) *Mappings*. London: Reaktion Books.

Cosgrove, D.E. (2001a) *Apollo's Eye: A Cartographic Genealogy of the Earth in the Western Imagination*. Baltimore: Johns Hopkins University Press.

Cosgrove, D.E. (2008) *Geography and Vision: Seeing, Imagining and Representing the World*. London: I B Taurus.

Cosgrove, D.E. and Daniels, S. (eds) (1988) *The Iconography of Landscape: Essays on the Symbolic Representation, Design and Use of Past Environments*. Cambridge: Cambridge University Press.

Secondary Sources and References

Atkinson, D. and Cosgrove, D.E. (1998) 'Urban rhetoric and embodied identities: city, nation and empire at the Vittorio Emanuele II monument in Rome 1870–1945', *Annals, The Association of American Geographers*, 88: 28–49.

Cosgrove, D.E. (1985) 'Prospect perspective and the evolution of the landscape idea', *Transactions of the Institute of British Geographers*, NS 10: 45–62.

Cosgrove, D.E. (1988) 'The geometry of landscape: practical and speculative arts in 16th century Venice', in D. Cosgrove and S. Daniels (eds), *The Iconography of Landscape*. Cambridge: Cambridge University Press. pp. 254–76.

Cosgrove, D.E. (1992) 'Mapping new worlds: culture and cartography in sixteenth-century Venice', *Imago Mundi*, 44: 1–25.

Cosgrove, D.E. (1996) 'The measures of America', in J. Corner and A. MacLean (eds), *Taking Measures Across the American Landscape*. New Haven: Yale University Press. pp. 3–13.

Cosgrove, D.E. (1998b) 'Introductory essay', in D.E. Cosgrove, *Social Formation and Symbolic Landscape* (2nd edition). Madison: Wisconsin University Press. pp. xi–xxxv.

Cosgrove, D.E. (1999b) 'Mapping meanings', in D.E. Cosgrove (ed.), *Mappings*. London: Reaktion. pp. 1–23.

Cosgrove, D.E. (2001b) 'Geography's cosmos: the dream and the whole round earth', in K. Till, S. Hoelscher and P. Adams (eds), *Textures of Place*. Minneapolis: University of Minnesota Press. pp. 326–39.

Cosgrove, D.E. (2006) *Geographical Imagination and the Authority of Images* (Hettner Lecture 2005). Stuttgart: Franz Steiner Verlag.

Cosgrove, D.E. (2007) 'Renaissance cosmography 1450–1650', in D. Woodward (ed.), *The History of Cartography, Vol.3 'Renaissance cartography'*, Chicago: University of Chicago Press. pp. 55–97.

Cosgrove, D.E. and Domosh, M. (1993) 'Author and authority: writing the new cultural geography', in J. Duncan. and D. Ley (eds), *Place/culture/representation*. London: Routledge. pp 25–38.

Cosgrove, D.E. and Fox, W. (2009) *Photography and Flight*. London: Reaktion.

Cosgrove, D.E., Roscoe, B. and Rycroft, S. (1996) 'Landscape and identity at Ladybower Reservoir and Rutland Water', *Transactions of the Institute of British Geographers*. NS 21: 534–51.

Daniels, S. (1993) *Fields of Vision: Landscape Imagery and National Identity in England and the United States*. Cambridge: Polity.

Daniels, D. and Cosgrove, D.E. (1988) 'Introduction: iconography and landscape', in D.E. Cosgrove and S. Daniels (eds), *Iconography of Landscape*. Cambridge: Cambridge University Press. pp. 1–10.

Dear, M. (1988) 'The post-modern challenge: reconstructing human geography', *Transactions of the Institute of British Geographers*, NS 13: 262–74

Driver, F. (1992) 'Geography's empire: histories of geographical knowledge', *Environment and Planning D: Society and Space*, 10: 23–40.

Driver, F. (2001) *Geography Militant: Cultures of Exploration and Empire*. Oxford: Blackwell.

Driver, F. and Gilbert, D. (eds) (1999) *Imperial Cities: Landscape, Display and Identity*. Manchester: Manchester University Press.

Duncan, J. (1990) *City as Text: The Politics of Landscape Interpretation in the Kandyan Kingdom*. Cambridge: Cambridge University Press.

Duncan, J. and Duncan, N. (1988) '(Re)reading the landscape', *Environment and Planning D: Society and Space*, 6: 117–26.

Freytag, T. and Jöns, H. (2006) 'Vision and the cultural in human geography: a biographical interview with Denis Cosgrove', in D.E. Cosgrove (ed.) *Geographical Imagination and the Authority of Images* (Hettner Lecture 2005). Stuttgart: Franz Steiner Verlag. pp. 79–91.

Graham, B. and Nash, C. (eds) (2000) *Modern Historical Geographies*. Harlow: Pearson.

Gregory, D. (1994) *Geographical Imaginations*. Oxford: Blackwell.

Hooke, D. (ed.) (2000) *Landscape – The Richest Historical Record*. Oxford: Society for Landscape Studies.

Hoskins, W.G. (1955) *The Making of the English Landscape*. London: Hodder and Stoughton.

Jackson, P. (1989) *Maps of Meaning. An Introduction to Cultural Geography*. London: Unwin Hyman.

Lilley, K.D. (2009) 'Obituary: Denis E. Cosgrove, 1948-2008', *Social and Cultural Geography,* 10: 219–24.

Livingstone, D.N. (1992) *The Geographical Tradition*. Oxford: Blackwell.

Muir, D. (1999) *Approaches to Landscape*. Basingstoke: Macmillan.

Nash, C. (1999) 'Landscapes' in P. Cloke, P. Crang and M. Goodwin (eds), *Introducing Human Geographies*. London: Arnold. pp. 217–25.

Ogborn, M. (1998) *Spaces of Modernity: London's Geographies, 1680-1780*. New York: Guilford Press.

Seymour, S. (2000) 'Historical geographies of landscape', in B. Graham and C. Nash (eds), *Modern Historical Geographies*. Harlow: Pearson. pp. 193–217.

Smith, S. (1989) *The Politics of 'Race' and Residence: Citizenship, Segregation and White Supremacy in Britain*. Cambridge: Polity.

Whitehand, J.W.R. (2001) 'British urban morphology: the Conzenian tradition', *Urban Morphology,* 5: 103–9.

Whyte, I.D. (2002) *Landscape and History since 1500*. London: Reaktion.

Wylie, J. (2007) *Landscape*. London: Routledge.

Keith Lilley, Queen's University Belfast

16 Mike Davis

One of few urban scholars who have had a genuine impact outside the academy, Mike Davis is an uncompromising critic of the urban and environmental impacts of American capitalism. He owes this reputation to a prolific set of writings on the US city – *City of Quartz* (1990), *Ecology of Fear* (1998), and *Magical Urbanism* (2000) – which chart the conflictual evolution of Los Angeles over the twentieth century, and latterly, a series of polemics addressing a range of urbanized political geographies. With his writing conveying a deep sense of political immediacy – much of the material in his books began life as shorter, topical articles – he is nonetheless an urbanist with a deep sense of radical social history.

Born in Fontana, California in 1946, Davis has worked variously as a meat-packer, lorry driver, and manager of the Communist Party's Los Angeles bookshop. He was a militant in SDS (Students for a Democratic Society), but his formal academic career began in the early 1970s, when an interest in Northern Ireland took him to the UK, where he studied Irish history at the University of Edinburgh, and undertook research on Irish nationalism in Belfast. For the first half of the 1980s, Davis worked full-time for *New Left Review*, in the pages of which would appear many of his most seminal essays. His first book, *Prisoners of the American Dream* – a pessimistic but carefully theorised analysis of the American working class – appeared in 1986, yet this was quickly overshadowed by the appearance of *City of Quartz* in 1990. By 2001, when he published *Late Victorian Holocausts*, Davis had been widely acclaimed as one of the most controversial, yet also most original, urbanists.

His chosen site for his best-known work – Los Angeles – was highly conducive to enhancing his reputation, for both scholarly and political reasons. Firstly, during the 1980s and 1990s a cluster of influential urban theorists began to project Los Angeles as a prototype of how *all* cities might develop in coming years. Here, Davis sat alongside the so-called 'LA School', composed of theorists such as **Michael Dear, Ed Soja,** and Allen Scott, each of whom offered influential theories of post-Fordism and post-modernism based on readings of the changing geographies of Los Angeles. Secondly, the publication of *City of Quartz* came only a couple of years before the explosion of urban unrest in Los Angeles in 1992, following the acquittal of police officers implicated in the Rodney King beatings. For academics, journalists and politicians seeking to understand the conflagration, Davis's careful – if startlingly rendered – analysis of gangs, land-grabbing power elites, extremist polic-ing and highly poli-ticised conservative homeowners provi-ded the context of an uprising waiting to happen.

By 2000, Davis was expanding the geographical scale of his examination, seeking new places through which to explore the urban consequences of une-ven development. This work displayed a fascination with the social polar opposites of contemporary urbanism, most notably through a fiery examination of Dubai's glaring social inequalities (published in a collection on these 'evil paradises' – see Davis, 2006a; Davis and Monk, 2007). By contrast, in *Planet of Slums* (2006b), he set out a sweeping critique of the con-ditions of slum dwellers in cities world-wide, and the policies and governments that place so many in 'marginal' urban conditions. The book met with much critical praise from the liberal press, but also received significant scholarly cri-tique, as discussed below. In *The Monster at Our Door* (Davis, 2005), he provided an important urban-based analysis of the looming possibility of a globalised flu pandemic, highlighting the poor and cramped housing conditions that helped to foster close human–animal viral trans-mission. In *Buda's Wagon: A Brief History of the Car Bomb* (Davis, 2007), he provides a similarly combative 'alternative history' of urban terrorism.

Davis's academic career has been far from straightforward, arriving relatively late as a university teacher. Awarded a MacArthur Foundation grant in 1998, he has gone some way to silencing the conservative backlash against his more polemical narratives. In his university teaching role, he has followed through the radical messages of his books and articles with politically engaged fieldwork. Yet, it is through his books and articles that he has proved most influential, spawning

and provoking a series of interventions that seek to understand the politics of urbanism in our biggest cities.

SPATIAL CONTRIBUTIONS

If one were to pigeonhole Davis, it may be as a social historian, yet it is clear that he has had a wider impact on urbanism, opening up a way of seeing the city as a very real terrain of political struggle, both a microcosm and process of contem-porary capitalism. And so it is the tenor of his critique, rather than his discipli-nary location, that is most characteristic of his work. Known best for his empiri-cal work, Davis nonetheless has always had a clearly grounded theoretical frame-work through which to analyse cities. In an interview, Davis claimed that *City of Quartz* was a fusion of three competing perspectives:

> I had this daydream of Walter Benja-min finally coming to LA and sitting in a bar with Fernand Braudel and Friedrich Engels. They decide to write a book about LA and divide it into three projects. Ben-jamin is going to get at all the complex and lucid fragments about power and memory. Braudel will explore its natural history, the larger world-historical forces that made it possible. And Engels will report on LA's working classes.
>
> (Davis, cited in Schatz, 1997: no pagination)

These three themes – a fierce class con-sciousness, a stress on how long-term historical processes impact on everyday life, and a strongly humanised, even individualised, account of the impact of capitalism on the lives of Angelenos – are fundamental to an understanding of his worldview. Such a method – which fuses minute archival research, much of it newspaper-based, with acerbic observational qualities – has opened up paths to radical geographers hitherto closed off by the overwhelmingly structuralist aesthetic of much urban theory.

Such a multi-tooled approach has allowed Davis to explore themes often beyond the imagination of political-economy perspectives, without excluding the power of the latter in shaping daily landscapes and lives. *City of Quartz* is a sustained and multilayered discussion of elite power in the boosterist-*noir* representations of the city's historians and writers, in the reach of the Catholic Church, and in the political clout of the city's suburban homeowners. In *Ecology of Fear* he contrasts the differing 'fire geographies' in luxury Malibu with working-class downtown; he traces the 'literary destruction of Los Angeles' through pulp fiction and disaster movies; and he warns chillingly of the impending revenge of nature on a city always built upon the domination of the natural environment. In *Dead Cities* (2002), he sets out an eye-opening challenge to future urban geographies:

> Very large cities – those with a global not just regional environmental footprint – are thus the most dramatic end-product, in more than one sense, of human cultural evolution in the Holocene. Presumably they should be the subject of the most urgent and encompassing scientific enquiry. They are not. We know more about rainforest ecology than urban ecology ... The most urgent need, perhaps, is for large-scale conceptual templates for understanding the city–nature dialectic.

> (Davis, 2002: 363)

With this research agenda being tied to a set of dire projections about the future of urban Southern California, Davis has often been dubbed a latter-day Jeremiah,

an allusion to the Old Testament prophet of the fall of Jerusalem. His apparent pessimism about the fate of LA is also seen as disempowering by some on the Left. In *Metromarxism*, Andy Merrifield argues that 'Davis's Marxism bespeaks an urbanism that lacks public space and denies any sense of collective experience. It's a Marxist urbanism that expresses only contempt for one's own city, perhaps for good reason' (Merrifield, 2002: 171). By contrast to the quirky exuberance of Marshall Berman, apparently nourished by the cultural inflections of being a New Yorker, Merrifield detects a 'brooding, doom-laden undertow' (Merrifield, 2002: 171) to the work of Davis. However, this charge might be unfair. It is precisely because of Davis's ability to understand the sprawling contours of Los Angeles – so far away from the cohesive morphology of the Paris beloved of many of Merrifield's 'metromarxists' (such as Walter Benjamin, Guy Debord, **David Harvey**, **Henri Lefebvre**, and **Manuel Castells**) – that his work has been so influential.

KEY ADVANCES AND CONTROVERSIES

Given that Davis is better known for his empirical work than his theoretical stance on space and place, what have been the aspects of his work that have proved most influential? We can perhaps identify four: first, a remarkable ability to weave political analysis that fuses city and nature, categories often treated in isolation and even antagonism; second, a powerful statement of the centrality of class politics despite the 'cultural' turn away from structural Marxism; third, his work on the 'fortress' or 'carceral' city; and, fourth, the introduction of what could be called 'activist writing', in the sense that his approach has helped to politicise theory, and make accessible and personal some of the bigger forces that shape the contemporary city.

Davis's interest in nature is prevalent, if usually underplayed, throughout *City of Quartz*, but in *Ecology of Fear* and *Dead Cities* it moves centre stage, echoing a growing personal interest in 'shock' nature. In *Ecology of Fear* he argues that the city's urbanisation is out of step with the region's ecosystem, with its hitherto relatively benign earthquake, fire, and drought potential. Above all, he reveals himself to be increasingly interested in neo-catastrophism, the idea that sudden natural occurrences may have far-reaching consequences for both social *and* natural history. This phase of his work also began to reveal the influence of Fernand Braudel (1902–85), the famed French historian who emphasised the importance of slow, long-term shifts in climate and technology on historical development. The spectre of an urban-generated global pandemic that he anatomised in *The Monster at Our Door* has certainly come to pass, and the largely epidemiological (rather than social and political) analysis that has accompanied public debate around avian and swine flu pandemics has certainly vindicated his critique.

In relation to the second theme, Davis is perhaps most infamous for the biting renditions of Los Angeles as a 'militarised space'. In 'Fortress L.A.' (chapter four of *City of Quartz*) he sets out eight trends in the ongoing destruction of public space in Los Angeles, his acerbic style in full flow. Utilising a series of short vignettes, he argues that 'in cities like Los Angeles, on the bad edge of post-modernity, one observes an unprecedented tendency to merge urban design, architecture and the police apparatus into a single, comprehensive security effort' (Davis, 1991: 224). Some of his villains are predictable. The Los Angeles Police Department (LAPD) he presents as 'space police', combining air power (helicopters) with communications systems imported from the Californian military aerospace industries. Others are less obvious. The inner-city malls of Alexander Haagen, the employment of armies of private security guards that guard the burgeoning gated communities, the designers who contribute the rounded, sleep-proof 'barrel-shaped benches' to ward off the homeless, and the celebrity architect Frank Gehry (a 'Dirty Harry' for his provocative "Beirutized" Goldwyn library in the city), are all cited as contributors to the creation of spaces of fear in LA.

This – for many, exaggerated – vision is taken to its logical extension in 'Beyond *Blade Runner*', the concluding chapter to *Ecology of Fear*. Taking the famous Chicago School/Burgess 'concentric ring' model of the archetypal structure of the North American city, he provides an inimitable up-date: 'My remapping takes Burgess back to the future. It preserves such "ecological" determinants as income, land value, class and race but adds a decisive new factor: fear' (Davis, 1998: 363). The Davis diagram represents LA as a fragmented city, with a 'gulag rim' of privatised prisons on the distant reaches of the city, a surrounding ring of gated, affluent suburbia linked orbitally to a series of edge cities, a variegated set of inner rings dominated by suspicious blue collar communities, 'homeless containment zones', drug- and gang-free parks subject to specific legal regulation, and a downtown *scanscape*, as opposed to *landscape*, dominated by highly developed surveillance technology.

In these two chapters, undoubtedly the most frequently quoted parts of his LA work, Davis sets out a plausible account of a city fractured by the 1992 riots.

Third, Davis is strongly defensive of the importance of class politics and labour exploitation at a time when other perspectives have grown in significance for geographers. His interest in ethnicity is primarily driven by the subordinate position of Latinos or African Americans in the labour market; his exploration of the dramatic contrast between Malibu and downtown LA in terms of fire and state policy is about access to housing and policy influence; his discussion of gang culture is aligned with the Black Panthers and a 'revolutionary lumpenproletariat' which has been fractured by internecine fights over drug vending territory. Yet, in his later work he moved beyond the urban, and applied his interest in class exploitation on a grander scale. In *Late Victorian Holocausts* he argued that the droughts and famines that caused mass death in India, Brazil and China in the last quarter of the nineteenth century were exacerbated by the aggressive imperialist capitalism inflicted on a global peasantry (famine occurring at a time of unprecedented grain production in India, for example) – a searing indictment of imperialism and the birth of today's 'third world'. Such an understanding fits with Davis's dystopian take on today's 'global cities', a 'dialectic of securitised versus demonic urban places' (Davis, 2006b: 206). This is epitomised by his essay on Dubai (Davis, 2006a, also contained in Davis and Monk, 2007), which exemplifies the ambiguity that many feel towards his work. On the one hand, this is a coherent and far-reaching critique of the economic, social and political inequality that underlies the Emirate's skyscrapers, artificial islands, and shopping malls. On the other hand, it repeats the breathless, and often superficial, denunciations of this city which have become commonplace in recent years, being heavily reliant on secondary sources, and often dependent on caricature to convey its message.

As a consequence, this version of global capitalism as being polarised between a class of super-rich, shaping urban space in a way that protects their lifestyles, and a global class of marginalised slum dwellers with a weak hold on both terrain and livelihood, has been criticised from several directions. Writing from a left perspective, some critics have argued that *Planet of Slums* is overly apocalyptic, effectively depoliticising and homogenising urban slum dwellers as lacking in political agency. Angotti (2006: 962) presents an excoriating critique of this book, which he sees to be full of 'condemnation and moral outrage, not serious analysis', containing a blend of anti-urban bias and simplistic dualisms regarding slum dwellers. It is argued that his use of 'slum' as terminology is itself racialised; that he is excessively reliant on the economistic data of the World Bank in drawing his conclusions; and that he lapses too often into the apocalyptic tones that marked (or marred) much of his writing on Los Angeles (Angotti, 2006; Pithouse, 2008).

This leads to a fourth important contribution made by Davis: his trademark writing style, which has arguably become increasingly tendentious, but which certainly has helped to inspire a legion of followers. In many ways it fits into a tradition of *noir* writing on the city (Gregory, 1994), where the dark realities of political life are hidden from everyday view, only accessible through the hard-boiled, fearless detective. His writing on Los Angeles is self-consciously positioned against what he sees as the boosterist rhetoric of many orthodox LA historians, such as Kevin Starr (1991). The opening chapter of *City of Quartz* is entitled 'Sunshine or Noir?', and is the hermeneutic key to understanding the book. Davis uses this dialectic – between the promotional myths of property developers and politicians of fertile land and a better life, and the competing reading of a city built upon the exploitation of labour and the environment – to structure his narrative, as the following memorable citation demonstrates:

> Welcome to post-liberal Los Angeles, where the defense of luxury lifestyles is translated into a proliferation of new repressions in space and movement, undergirded by the ubiquitous 'armed response'. This obsession with physical security systems, and, collaterally, with the architectural policing of social boundaries, has become a zeitgeist of urban restructuring, a master narrative in the emerging built environment of the 1990s ... Hollywood's pop apocalypses and pulp science fiction have been more realistic, and politically perceptive [than contemporary urban theory] in representing the programmed hardening of the urban surface in the wake of the Reagan era.

(Davis, 1990: 223)

This style, which James Duncan (1996) calls the 'Tragic/Marxian' mode of writing, can be accused of being too muscular in its pursuit of narrative coherence and political persuasiveness. While Duncan's own critique may fall guilty of the crimes he sees inherent in the Davis approach, he nonetheless makes valid observations at how the Quartz narrative progresses:

> [Davis] clearly speaks for the underclass. We do not hear from them directly, however. In fact, the only people other than Davis that we do hear from are those whom he parades before us to speak their highly edited 'confessions' and then marches out again with a resounding 'guilty'. The implied readership who stand as jury to the author's prosecutor

shake their heads sadly at these confessions. However, it is clear that were these people not to be found guilty, they would not have been summoned to speak their lines. Such is the methodology of the show trial. While this strong narrative structure may lend illusory coherence to the plot, it may fail to produce the degree of 'reality effect' that an account more open to contradictory evidence might achieve.

(Duncan, 1996: 261)

The allegation that Davis's writing is powerful but rather tendentious is one that has been voiced by sympathisers and opponents alike. Yet what he does, for students of Marxism grown tired of struggling with abstract theoretical issues, or left doubting the relevance of the Marxian legacy for the contemporary city, is to show that theory can live in the streets of one of the world's most brutally capitalised cities, and make sense of such diverse subjects as gang warfare, urban Catholicism, street furniture and place myth.

Davis's influence on geography and the urban is perhaps still to be fully realised. It is not impossible that the current direction of his theory – with his emphasis on a radical urban ecology – may fall between several established camps. His empirical work on Los Angeles and elsewhere will continue to motivate and inform a wide range of publics, and his intellectual creativity and originality should also inspire new interest in an urban geography which is too often ignorant of the political. Ultimately, perhaps, the biggest impact of Davis may be through the vibrancy of his writing, suggesting a voice to those academics and activists who see conventional theory too heavy, or too sluggish, to convey the political immediacy of contemporary urban life.

DAVIS'S KEY WORKS

Davis, M. (1986) *Prisoners of the American Dream: Politics and Economy in the History of the US Working Class.* London: Verso.

Davis, M. (1990) *City of Quartz: Excavating the Future in Los Angeles.* London: Verso.

Davis, M. (1998) *Ecology of Fear: Los Angeles and the Imagination of Disaster.* New York: Metropolitan Books.

Davis, M. (2000) *Magical Urbanism: Latinos Reinvent the American City.* London: Verso.

Davis, M. (2001) *Late Victorian Holocausts: El Niño Famines and the Making of the Third World.* London: Verso.

Davis, M. (2002) *Dead Cities and Other Tales.* London: Verso.

Davis, M. (2005) *The Monster at Our Door: The Global Threat of Avian Flu.* New York: New Press.

Davis, M. (2006a) 'Fear and money in Dubai', *New Left Review,* 41: 47–68.

Davis, M. (2006b) *Planet of Slums.* London: Verso.

Davis, M. (2007) *Buda's Wagon: A Brief History of the Car Bomb.* London: Verso.

Davis, M. and Monk, D.B. (eds) (2007) *Evil Paradises: Dreamworlds of Neoliberalism.* The New Press: New York.

Secondary Sources and References

Angotti, T. (2006) 'Apocalyptic anti-urbanism: Mike Davis and his planet of slums', *International Journal of Urban and Regional Research,* 30 (4): 961–7.

Duncan, J. (1996) 'Me(trope)olis: Or Hayden White among the urbanists', in A.D. King (ed.), *Re-presenting the City: Ethnicity, Capital and Culture in the 21st-century Metropolis.* Basingstoke: MacMillan. pp. 253–68.

Gregory, D. (1994) *Geographical Imaginations.* Cambridge, MA: Blackwell.

MacAdams, L. (1998) 'Jeremiah among the palms: the lives and dark prophecies of Mike Davis', *LA Weekly,* 3 December (www.laweekly.com/ink/99/01/news-macadams.php).

Merrifield, A. (2002) *Metromarxism: A Marxist Tale of the City.* New York: Routledge.

Pithouse, R. (2008) 'Review of M. Davis, *Planet of Slums*', *Journal of Asian and African Studies,* 43 (5): 567–74.

Schatz, A. (1997) 'The American earthquake: Mike Davis and the politics of disaster', *Lingua Franca,* September (republished on Radical Urban Theory, www.rut.com/mdavis/americanearthquake.html).

Starr, K. (1991) *American Dreams: Southern California through the 1920s.* Oxford: Oxford University Press.

Donald McNeill, University of Western Sydney

17 Michael Dear

BIOGRAPHICAL DETAILS AND THEORETICAL CONTEXT

Michael Dear's principal research interests relate to Los Angeles, and his pursuit of a project of 'post-modern urbanism'. As founding Director of the Southern California Studies Centre at the University of Southern California, he is one of the most influential members of the 'LA School' of urban theory. While well known for his work on homelessness in Los Angeles, it has been his dogged insistence on the need for a new set of theoretical categories to account for capitalist urbanism in the LA region that has given his work some degree of renown, or notoriety.

Dear was born in Treorchy, in the Rhondda Valley of South Wales, UK. He obtained a BA in Geography from the University of Birmingham, England, in 1966, followed by an MPhil in Town Planning from University College London in 1969. He undertook graduate work at the University of Pennsylvania, obtaining an MA in Regional Science in 1972 and a PhD in 1974. It was while pursuing research at Pennsylvania that he began studying the geography of community opposition to mental health care facilities. Following his appointment to McMaster University, Hamilton, Ontario, this research

work broadened out to include aspects of the organisation of health care delivery systems, and subsequently to the study of the political economic dynamics surrounding mental health care. During the 1970s, as homelessness became particularly prevalent in the US and Canada, and in partnership with Jennifer Wolch, Dear authored two books on homelessness and the city (Dear and Wolch, 1987; Wolch and Dear, 1993), and has continued to work on stigmatisation and difference with reference to those in institutionalised care (Dear et al., 1997). In the early 1980s, he became founding editor of the journal *Environment and Planning D: Society and Space*, which has become one of the most cited academic journals in Geography and Urban Studies.

Dear – like many of his associates in the 'LA School' – is profoundly influenced by the nature of Southern Californian capitalism, experimenting with various ways of representing its particular landscapes. As with **Ed Soja**, Dear has grappled with the diffuse nature of LA urbanism and urbanisation, employing novel representational strategies to capture its heterogeneous geographies. From his earlier work on postmodernism and urbanism in the mid-1980s, through to *The Post-modern Urban Condition* in 2000, Dear has accordingly concerned himself with issues of urban (dis)order and the ability of contemporary urban theory to adequately explain or represent it. His suggested alternatives – and his manner of expressing them – have aroused fierce controversy within geography, attracting attacks from many sides (see, for example, Dear, 2000; Lake, 1999 and debates in *Urban Geography, Political Geography,* and *Annals of the Association of American Geographers*). Yet his output includes some highly respected work on very pressing social issues. In *Malign Neglect* (1997) and *Landscapes of Despair* (1993), both written with Jennifer Wolch, the massive explosion in homelessness in Southern California is analysed. Here, the authors find that these 'service-dependent' people are increasingly concentrated in well defined geographical areas of cities (including the infamous 'skid rows' of LA itself). Together, these works provided the first comprehensive analysis of these service-dependent 'ghettos', their structure and evolution, their benefits and costs and how they might change in the future. Truly inter-disciplinary in scope, these works draw upon geography, planning, social work, psychiatry and history, as well as upon the wider debates in social theory. Furthermore, by being situated within a context of neo-liberal urban policy, Dear and Wolch's work demonstrates how welfare cutbacks are profoundly shaping the life experiences of the socially disadvantaged. As such, and far from being an escapee from the pressing realities of social ills, Dear's postmodernism emerges from a politically progressive position.

SPATIAL CONTRIBUTIONS

As a prominent writer on space and social theory, Dear has consistently drawn attention to the need for new representational approaches to grasp the restructuring of contemporary urban space. Grounding such ideas in the context of Los Angeles, yet with an eye on global processes, Dear (writing with Stephen Flusty) insists that this urban disordering is exemplary of wider changes in the nature of space and time:

> Have we arrived at a radical break in the way cities are developing? Is there something called a *post-modern urbanism,* which presumes that we can identify some form of template that defines its critical dimensions? This inquiry is based on a simple premise: that just as the central tenets of modernist thought have been undermined, its core evacuated and replaced by a rush of competing epistemologies, so too have the traditional logics of earlier urbanisms evaporated, and in the absence of a single new imperative, multiple urban (ir)rationalities are competing to fill the void. It is the concretization and localization of these effects, global in scope but generated and manifested locally, that are creating the geographies of post-modern society – a new time-space fabric.
>
> (Dear and Flusty, 1998: 50, original emphasis)

The most comprehensive statement of Dear's takes on postmodern space can therefore be found in *The Post-modern Urban Condition* (2000), a compendium of much of the work that he had published over the previous decade or so. This collection alerts us to three of the most important geographical contributions Dear has made. The first is his significant contribution to an 'LA School' (alongside the likes of Allen Scott, **Michael Storper, Ed Soja, and Mike Davis**) that posits Los Angeles as the most appropriate successor to Chicago in terms of a model of an ideal type of urban spatial structure. The second, and related to this, is his attempt to provide a new lexicon for describing the new spatial forms of the postmodern metropolis (set out most provocatively in Dear and Flusty (1998)). The third, is his attempt to demonstrate the consequences of the 'post-modern turn' in the social sciences for urban theory (and Geography more generally).

In relation to the first of these, the influence of the fairly disparate group of scholars known as the 'LA School' on several fields of human geography has been pronounced. As **Mike Davis** summarises:

> During the 1980s the 'L.A. School' (based in the UCLA planning and geography faculties, but including contributors from other campuses) developed an ambitious matrix of criss-crossing approaches and case-studies. Monographs focused on the dialectics of de- and re-industrialization, the peripheralization of labor and the internationalization of capital, housing and homelessness, the environmental consequences of untrammeled development, and the discourse of growth. Although its members remain undecided about whether they should model themselves after the 'Chicago School' (named principally after its *object* of research), or the 'Frankfurt School' (a philosophical current named after its *base*), the 'L.A. School' is, in fact, a little bit of both. While surveying Los Angeles in a systematic way, the UCLA researchers are most interested in exploiting the metropolis, à la Adorno and Horkheimer, as a 'laboratory of the future'. They have made clear that they see themselves excavating the outlines of a paradigmatic postfordism, an emergent twenty-first century urbanism.

(Davis, 1992: 84)

Dear has embodied this Frankfurt–Chicago fusion by serving as the editor of a number of edited collections on the LA region (Dear et al., 1996; Dear, 2001; Leclerc et al., 1999). Despite the fact that many of these contributors are cautious about the wider applicability of LA-derived models, Dear's own work on LA urbanism frequently exceeds its local focus to make somewhat grander claims about postmodern cities. For example, in his work with Steven Flusty, the original intent to provide a loosely coherent forum for debate on the region seems to have escaped its moorings:

> Yet ultimately, we are comfortable in proclaiming the existence of a Los Angeles School of urbanism ... at present, the city is now commonly represented as indicative of new forms of urbanism augmenting (and even supplanting) the older, established forms against which Los Angeles was once judged deviant ... The body of writing about Los Angeles provides alternative models to past orthodoxies on the 'essential' nature of the city and is proving to be more successful than its detractors at explaining the form and function of urbanism in a time of globalisation.

(Dear and Flusty, 2001: 12)

Thus while Dear is aware of the 'danger that a Los Angeles School could become another panoptic fortress from whence a new totalizing urban model is manufactured and marketed' (Dear and Flusty, 2001: 13), the fact is that he has been one of the most ardent promoters of that place's precocity.

The second, related, contribution made by Dear (again, often with Flusty) is his attempt to update the work of the Chicago School in the context of the globalisation of urbanism. The basic claim made is as follows:

> The concentric ring structure of the Chicago School was essentially a concept of the city as an organic accretion around a central, organizing core. Instead, we have identified a post-modern urban process in which the urban periphery organizes the centre within the context of a globalizing capitalism ... Conventional city form, Chicago-style, is sacrificed in favour of a non-contiguous collage of parcelized, consumption-oriented landscapes devoid of conventional centres

yet wired into electronic propinquity and nominally unified by the mythologies of the disinformation superhighway.

(Dear, 2000: 158–160)

While a synoptic approach to explaining the dynamism of contemporary urban form is not unwelcome, Dear creates problems for himself in deriving his models and terms from a very limited number of places (Los Angeles, Las Vegas and Tijuana). Furthermore, he has failed to convince critics that his 'alternative model of urban structure' is anything more than a rather tired, 'top-down' Marxist theory of the city, a spatial manifestation of a tyrannical, polarising capitalism:

> As the cybergeoisie increasingly withdraw from the Fordist redistributive triad of big government, big business and big labour to establish their own micro-nations, the social support functions of the state disintegrate, along with the survivability of less-affluent citizens.

(Dear, 2000: 156-7)

Thus, Dear's argument that the contemporary city is an increasingly atomised collection of spaces echoes the concerns of many Marxist urbanists who have chosen a more conventional language of urban alienation and class conflict to describe cities, past and present.

Thirdly, as noted above, Dear's output since the mid-1980s has attempted to engage with the more general debate on postmodernism by applying it to the urban. In so doing he has made significant interventions in human geography's epistemological debates (including one of the first papers to acknowledge the postmodern challenge for the discipline – Dear, 1988). Here, and elsewhere, he has applauded the epistemological challenge of postmodernism:

> For me, the radical opening made possible by post-modernism is both invigorating

and sometimes exasperating. On one hand, it has liberated our theoretical discourse and legitimized a wide variety of different voices. We no longer need to rely on implausible doctrines of objectivity to defend our contributions to knowledge, and we can treat truth claims as arguments rather than as unassailable findings ... On the other hand, the Babel of different, newly-enfranchised voices can also be profoundly disorienting

(Dear, 2000: 32)

As a means of expanding on this, Dear (2000: 166) argues that a postmodern urban analysis must take account of two things: first, the problem of urban analysis at a time when 'the urban grows increasingly to resemble televisual and cinematic fantasy' and second, the problem of developing a radical politics in postmodern times. He thus continues to be one of the leading flag-bearers for postmodernism in Geography (Dear and Flusty, 2002).

KEY ADVANCES AND CONTROVERSIES

Dear's provocative work – not least his frequent use of neologisms – has excited significant disciplinary controversy and repudiation, as evidenced by several high-profile disciplinary debates: in the *Annals of the Association of American Geographers* (Symanski, 1994), where he is labelled as postmodern geography's 'best known Brooks Brothers, Wall Street ad man' (Symanski, 1994: 301); in the journal *Urban Geography* (1999), which includes a range of largely critical responses to his and Flusty's paper on 'Post-modern Urbanism' (see Beauregard, 1999; Lake,

1999); and a series of short responses in *Political Geography* (e.g. DeFillipis, 2001; Natter, 2001) to Dear's contention that 'vicious personal attacks are a commonplace experience among geographers' (Dear, 2001: 2). In relation to the latter, Dear cited a litany of academic and personal attacks on his work as symptomatic of a broader 'culture of hate' and destructive criticism in university culture (interestingly, some of the commentaries in the *Urban Geography* forum are listed in this latter category). The reasons for such 'gleeful poison' (Dear, 2001: 3) – whether justified or not – undoubtedly stem from the pioneering nature of Dear's work, combined with his at times grandiose claims. As noted above, these include: the suggestion that Los Angeles is a privileged site from which to study contemporary urbanism; his assertion that urban studies needs to be reinvented in a postmodern era; and his insistence that geographers need to adopt new methods and languages if they are to make sense of contemporary relations of society and space. Each of these claims has been met with considerable scepticism in the aforementioned debates, although his attempt to challenge sometimes tired terminology has been applauded:

> Applied to Los Angeles, such well-worn terms as concentric zone and uniform land surface do violence, sacrificing reality to interpretation and the post-modern world to modernist theory. Consequently, we need to break away from the prevailing language of urban analysis. Only by dislocating ourselves discursively can we open up the possibility of new and more valid interpretations.

(Beauregard, 1999: 396)

Yet even here the problem of developing theories of the urban based on knowledge of one city are apparent: as Beauregard (1999: 398) suggests, the 'recent non-reductionist turn in urban theory' where 'most theorists are less intent on parsimonious descriptions and abstract and general explanations than on evoking rich images of a single city' means that accounts often make general claims on the basis of (often superficial) case studies. Indeed, while he allows portraits of Tijuana and Las Vegas to ornament *The Post-modern Urban Condition,* Los Angeles remains the single field that grounds his theory. Whether a single city can sustain such a general model remains the subject of much debates (see Dear et al., 2008, and the related papers in the same issue of *Urban Geography*).

A second critique of Dear's work is more methodological, suggesting that it is based on an unconvincing and limited engagement with the active, purposeful individuals of the city. For example, while the Chicago School abstractions were elaborated by detailed, area-based ethnographies, **Jackson** (1999: 401) suggests that Dear's work is 'populated with the cool abstractions of social polarization and fragmentation'. While Dear and Flusty defend this – citing as an example Dear's earlier work on the homeless (written with Jennifer Wolch) – questions remain as to how such complex, contradictory qualitative work feeds into the model that they offer. In some ways, this apparent abstraction or distance from everyday life is magnified by the use of neologisms – invented fusions of existing words and terminology – in order to describe or represent the apparently novel conditions pertaining in LA. Here, what is (one presumes) a well-intentioned collection of terms at times breaches the bounds of seriousness, or worse, creates a jargonistic vocabulary that further distances interpretation from everyday life. The key terms of this postmodern urbanism are thus rendered within a framework of 'Holsteinization', and 'keno capitalism', with new social classes known as 'cyber-geoisie' and the 'protosurps', and with a model of the cities as being composed of 'commudities', 'cyburbia', 'citidel', 'in-beyond', and 'cyberia' (Dear and Flusty, 1998: 60–6). While some of these terms may have explanatory merit, they may also conceal an even worse fate for a postmodern urbanism – a reinvention of outmoded 'modernist' grand theories. For example, **Jackson** (1999: 401–2) argues that the 'Holsteinization' process, 'the process of monoculturing people as consumers so as to facilitate the harvesting of desires' (Dear and Flusty, 1998: 61) is simply restating the mass society thesis of the Frankfurt School, where brainwashed consumers passively consume the products forced upon them by corporations.

Thirdly, and related to this, the somewhat arcane terminology and neologisms coined in the Dear and Flusty 'Post-modern Urbanism' paper have been fiercely criticised. As Robert Lake argues:

> Far from succeeding in their intended role of provocative hypothesis-generators, Dear and Flusty's neologisms are simplifications at best, stereotypes at worst, and ineluctably modernist in provenance and perspective ... They proclaim a victory of style over substance, of cleverness over erudition, of word play over content, neither a new vision nor a new city but only a new style. Where 'Post-modern Urbanism' proffers the possibility of a radical break in understanding the urban, the danger is that it will only encourage an outbreak of linguistic dexterity as an end in itself.
>
> (Lake, 1999: 395)

Without further empirical analysis and theoretical development, therefore, the potential of the neologisms will remain unrealised.

Thus it is by no means certain that Dear's project of postmodern urbanism has sufficient popularity, or critical depth, to be of lasting theoretical significance. As a provocative and widely read commentator on the postmodern condition, his take on the reconfiguration of Los Angeles is an important contribution to contemporary debates on space and place. Ultimately, however, whether Dear will prove more than a parochial critic riding on the wave of his host city's fame remains to be seen.

DEAR'S KEY WORKS

Dear, M.J. (1988) 'The post-modern challenge: re-constructing human geography', *Transactions of the Institute of British Geographers,* NS 13: 262–74.

Dear, M.J. (2000) *The Post-modern Urban Condition.* Oxford: Blackwell.

Dear, M.J. and Flusty, S. (1998) 'Post-modern urbanism', *Annals of the Association of American Geographers,* 88: 50–72.

Dear, M.J. and Flusty, S. (2002) *The Spaces of Post-modernity: Readings in Human Geography.* Oxford: Blackwell.

Dear, M.J. and Wolch, J.R. (1987) *Landscapes of Despair: From Deinstitutionalization to Homelessness.* Cambridge: Polity Press.

Dear, M.J., Schockman, H.E. and Hise, G. (eds) (1996) *Rethinking Los Angeles.* Thousand Oaks: Sage.

Leclerc, G., Villa, R. and Dear, M.J. (eds) (1999) *Urban Latino Cultures: La Vida Latina en L.A.* Thousand Oaks: Sage.

Wolch, J.R. and Dear, M.J. (1993) *Malign Neglect: Homelessness in an American City.* San Francisco, CA: Jossey-Bass.

Secondary Sources and References

Beauregard, R.A. (1999) 'Breakdancing on Santa Monica Boulevard', *Urban Geography,* 20: 396–99.

Davis, M. (1992) *City of Quartz: Excavating the Future in Los Angeles.* London: Vintage.

DeFillipis, J. (2001) 'Hatred and criticism inside and outside of the academy: a response to Michael Dear', *Political Geography,* 20: 13–16.

Dear, M.J. (2001) 'The politics of geography: hate mail, rabid referees, and culture wars', *Political Geography,* 20: 1–15.

Dear, M.J. and Flusty, S. (1999) 'Engaging post-modern urbanism', *Urban Geography,* 20: 412–6.

Dear, M.J. and Flusty, S. (2001) 'The resistible rise of the LA School', in M.J. Dear (ed.) *From Chicago to LA: Making Sense of Urban Theory.* Sage: Thousand Oaks. pp. 5–16.

Dear, M.J. and Taylor, M. (1982) *Not on Our Street: Community Attitudes Toward Mental Health Care.* Leeds: Pion Ltd.

Dear, M.J., Burridge, A., Marolt, P., Peters, J. and Seymour, M. (2008) 'Critical responses to the Los Angeles school of urbanism', *Urban Geography,* 29 (2): 101–12.

Dear, M.J., Wilton, R., Gaber, S.L. and Takahashi, L. (1997) 'Seeing people differently: the socio-spatial construction of disability', *Environment and Planning D: Society and Space,* 15: 455–80.

Jackson, P. (1999) 'Post-modern urbanism and the ethnographic void', *Urban Geography,* 20: 400–2.

Lake, R.W. (1999) 'Post-modern urbanism?', *Urban Geography,* 20: 393–5.

Natter, W. (2001) 'From hate to antagonism: towards an ethics of emotion, discussion and the political', *Political Geography,* 20: 25–34.

Symanski, R. (1994) 'Why we should fear post-modernists', *Annals of the Association of American Geographers,* 84: 301–4.

**Donald McNeill, University of Western Sydney and Mark Tewdwr-Jones,
University College London**

18   Gilles Deleuze

BIOGRAPHICAL DETAILS AND THEORETICAL CONTEXT

Gilles Deleuze was born into a bourgeois and conservative Parisian family in 1925. He was made famous by his catalytic role in the uprising of French students and workers in May 1968, for his promotion of a 'desiring revolution' that would destabilise the subjugation of the individual to the social formations that feed off it (e.g., family, school, factory, office, prison, asylum), and for his part in the emergence of what has become known as post-structuralism. Deleuze died in 1995, having served most of his career as a Professor of Philosophy at Université de Paris VIII, Vincennes. He was a well-regarded teacher, and his classes were reputed to have been notable events. During his life Deleuze rarely left France, not least because he disliked the conditions under which intellectuals travelled: flitting across the globe to do what they could do at home – exchange pleasantries and talk, talk, talk. This is a good example of Deleuze's indifference to the academic crowd and his disdain for intellectual fashion.

While Deleuze was not averse to conversation (which leads who knows where), exchanges (of ideas, opinions, objections, questions and answers, points of view, etc.) were anathema to him. 'We do not lack communication' wrote Deleuze and Guattari in *What is Philosophy?* (1994: 108). 'On the contrary, we have too much of it. We lack creation. *We lack resistance to the present.*' When Deleuze collaborated with others, it was not to communicate opinions or exchange ideas, as if he were at a swap meet. Collaboration, for him, was transformatory, an act of creative de-personalisation that opens a 'line of flight' along which one becomes a stranger to oneself. 'We are no longer ourselves' announced Deleuze and Guattari (1987: 3) at the outset of *A Thousand Plateaus*. With Félix Guattari, who was a radical psychoanalyst and institutional 'schizoanalyst', Deleuze undertook a long collaboration of convergence that spanned three decades. With Alain Badiou, another French philosopher, Deleuze belatedly entered into a 'collaboration of divergence' over the nature of multiplicity (Badiou, 1999).

Although the scope of Deleuze's interests was truly enormous, he always considered himself to be a philosopher. According to Deleuze, however, there is nothing privileged about philosophy in relation to other activities, each of which is perfectly capable of thinking for itself. There is nothing 'essential' or 'fundamental' about philosophy. It is not the ground of truth, the pinnacle of reason or the font of knowledge. From a

Deleuzian perspective, such claims are at best laughable and at worst despotic. So, nobody needs a philosopher to think *for* them, but somebody may benefit from a philosopher thinking *alongside* them: a form of collaboration rather than domination (e.g., Deleuze, 1986; 1989). Nevertheless, philosophy, like every other academic discipline, has not been averse to serving sectarian interests (nations, states, capital, sexism, racism, anthropocentrism, etc.). Indeed, philosophy has often been conducted as if it were in the service of a totalitarian police state: an endless succession of interrogations, inquisitions, and critical tribunals presided over by investigators, lawyers, and legislators. Deleuze was always attentive to the social context of philosophy, and especially how philosophy could be taken up for both repressive and emancipatory ends. This is why he preferred posing problems to asking questions. So, rather than answering to a higher authority (and thereby submitting oneself to truth, reason, logic, etc.), Deleuze's radicalism consisted of problematising the world (and thereby opening up the possibility that something different might happen).

For Deleuze, then, philosophy is neither communication nor contemplation 'because no one needs philosophy to reflect on anything' (Deleuze and Guattari, 1994: 6). Like any other activity, philosophy is creative – and therefore both positive and joyful. 'It is the same in philosophy as in a film or a song: no correct ideas, just ideas' (Deleuze and Parnet, 1987: 9). Needless to say, this constructivist and non-representational attitude 'beyond good and evil' put Deleuze out of step with most other philosophers, intellectuals, and radicals, who tended to be enamoured of negativity, resentment, and sadness. Deleuze had no time for doubt, reflection, and criticism (the paranoiac disposition of modern philosophy),

and even less time for lack, scarcity, and limitation (the repressive myths of social science). 'What I detested more than anything else was Hegelianism and the Dialectic' (Deleuze, 1977: 112). For Deleuze, philosophy is not critical but creative. This is what makes it radical. Moreover, what philosophers create is addressed to both philosophers and non-philosophers, just as music is addressed to both musicians and music-lovers. Such is Deleuze's democratisation of philosophy, which is based on friendship rather than ownership, passion rather than possession, and radicalism rather than criticism.

Eschewing the intellectual snobbery that glorifies thinking by letting it lord over existence and practice, philosophy for Deleuze is simply 'a flow among others; it enjoys no special privilege and enters into relationships of current and counter-current, of backwash with other flows – the flows of shit, sperm, speech, action, eroticism, money, politics, etc.' (Deleuze, 1977: 114). Such is Deleuze's equalitarianism and anti-Platonism, which returns every hierarchy (e.g., the privileging of mind over matter, truth over error, real over possible, ideal over actual, essence over appearance, form over content, subject over object, Being over beings, identity over difference, and original over copy) to the superficial abyss whence it came (cf. Georges Bataille's 'base materialism', Jacques Derrida's 'deconstruction', and Jean-François Lyotard's 'libidinal economy'). In Deleuze's estimation, the surface – or simulacrum – not only ceases to be negative and inferior, it actually comes to take all. Superficiality goes all the way down, so to speak (cf. **Jean Baudrillard**'s 'simulation'). Additionally, while the vertical axis of hierarchy gives the illusion that identity, stability, and conservation are the rule rather than the exception, the horizontal axis of the simulacrum is always open to differentiation, instability, and transformation. Reading Deleuze is unsettling, then, because nothing is fixed in place. 'On the level of style, the reader cannot fail to be struck by the fact that Deleuze makes systematic use of division' notes Jean-Jacques Lecercle (1985: 97), 'yet the text grows and multiplies in an extremely disquieting manner.'

SPATIAL CONTRIBUTIONS

Even though philosophy is without privilege, Deleuze was keen to insist that it is not without specificity, and this specificity brings philosophy into the orbit of geography. On Deleuze's account, philosophers are responsible for creating concepts: not concepts in general (Ideas, Truths, Universals, etc.), 'globalizing' concepts, 'concepts as big as hollow teeth, THE law, THE master, THE rebel' (Deleuze, citied in Boundas, 1993: 254); but situated concepts, contextual concepts, contingent concepts; 'localizing' concepts that only have meaning, value, and efficacy in a specific place or milieu. Concepts must be articulated. This is why Deleuze treated concepts as territories and events (Bonta and Protevi, 2004). 'Deleuze the thinker is, above all, the thinker of the event and always of this event here (cet événement-ci)' wrote Derrida (1998). 'He remained the thinker of the event from beginning to end.' What Deleuze offers, then, is not a first philosophy (which would be privileged, fundamental, foundational, essential, universal, etc.) but a philosophy of the event – philosophy as an event. His philosophy responded to problems that made him think. For Deleuze, thought cannot be planned out ahead of time. To the contrary, thought is always encountered. This

is a remarkably modest disposition that chimes with the spirit of most kinds of materialism.

By attending to events, Deleuze provided a profound re-conceptualisation of space and time (Deleuze, 1988a; 1994). The Deleuzian 'event' is far removed from the commonsensical notion of something that is simply present to hand and fully given (what Derrida calls the 'metaphysics of presence'). Rather than a self-contained Now that happens once and for all (at time t), an event is an untimely Meanwhile or Meantime: a becoming-multiple (and, but) rather than a being-one (is). So, space-time does not consist of points, but of folds (Deleuze, 1993). However, although an event is never simply present, it is not at all lacking. It is full (i.e., immanent) – but it is fully distributed (cf. Derrida's quasi-concepts of différance and dissemination; and Badiou's notions of the multiple and the event). One is reminded of the 'stuttering' of events in the plays of Samuel Beckett and the 'undecidability' of events in the novels of Franz Kafka. In Deleuze's version of empiricism, then, an event is as much virtual as it is actual. In accordance with everyday usage, an event is not a matter of fact; it is extraordinary and irruptive. Events are explosive: they unsettle what appears to be Given, and breathe life into what appears spent. What Dada and Marcel Duchamp did for art, literature, and politics, Deleuze did for philosophy.

Given that modern philosophy has not been especially concerned with events (and still less with spatialisation), one can appreciate why Deleuze – looking back to the Stoics – has often been characterised as an outsider, even during his long apprenticeship in the history of philosophy, which gave rise to what he called 'monstrous' caricatures of Henri Bergson, David Hume, Gottfried Leibniz, Immanuel Kant, and Baruch Spinoza, amongst others. These anti-rationalist portraits were not so much bastardisations as 'immaculate conceptions'. Deleuze perfected the duplicitous art of differential repetition (through which one repeats in order to make different and estrange) which he rehearsed in the history of philosophy before unleashing it on the world at large (e.g., a 'clean-shaven Marx' and a 'bearded Hegel'; a 'cracked-I' and a 'stationary trip').

In the context of debates on space and place, it is noteworthy that during each 'immaculate conception' Deleuze was eager to disclose the geophilosophy that underpins the history of philosophy: multiplicities in Bergson, cartography in **Foucault**, relations in Hume, folds in Leibniz, territories in Kant, articulations in Spinoza, and differences in Nietzsche. When Deleuze began to write in his own name (in books such as *Difference and Repetition* and *The Logic of Sense*) this spatial awareness was already well developed. When he wrote with Guattari (in books such as *Anti-Oedipus*, *Kafka*, *A Thousand Plateaus*, and *What is Philosophy?*) one has the sense that there is geography, nothing but geography: maps, planes, surfaces, strata, spaces, territories, transversals, etc. (Buchanan and Lambert, 2005). And although Deleuze's work is often regarded as dry and difficult, he was fond of putting ordinary words to extraordinary use: virtual reality, becoming-woman, black holes, molecular revolution, geology of morals, Body without Organs, smooth space, etc. While this eclectic 'pop philosophy', composed of deterritorialised terms (i.e., terms that have been taken from their customary habitats in order to address problems in other domains), has been appreciated by many (not least for its humour), it has obviously given rise to much misunderstanding and even infringement claims. Indeed, Deleuze and Guattari seemed

to go out of their way to provoke incredulity when they declared such things as 'Of course there are werewolves and vampires, we say this with all our hearts' (Deleuze and Guattari, 1987: 275).

Since thought is occasioned by events, 'There is no heaven for concepts. They must be invented, fabricated, or rather created and would be nothing without their creator's signature' (Deleuze and Guattari, 1994: 5). To put it bluntly, in Deleuzian terms, communication, interpretation, explanation, representation, reflection, and criticism are more often than not a waste of time. They divert us from the 'true voyage', which is a pursuance of creative encounters. Little wonder, then, that Deleuze should have been called a 'radically horizontal' thinker of difference rather than identity; seriality rather than hierarchy; and becoming and multiplicity (and ... and ... and) rather than being and nothingness (is/is not) (cf. Badiou, 2000, 2005). As Deleuze and Guattari famously declared at the outset of their delirious by-passing of the Marxian and Freudian impasse in *Anti-Oedipus* (1984: 2), 'A schizophrenic out for a walk is a better model than a neurotic lying on the analyst's couch.' Needless to say, their promotion of 'schizophrenia as process' has elicited considerable criticism and dismay (see Guattari, 1996 and 2000, for clarification). Rather than enlist academics in the service of Inquisitions and critical tribunals (State philosophy), Deleuze would prefer to take them out into the world for a stroll (nomad thought). Consequently, he was always on the lookout for creative encounters with texts, paintings, music, films, novels, and situations. He was always on the lookout for something 'overwhelming' – an event – that would force him to think and in so doing estrange himself from himself. Such was his fondness for becoming, transformation, and shape-shifting. Life always unfolds on the edge, on the horizon, and from the midst of things. Indeed, Deleuze's devotion to the immanence and singularity of creative encounters can be gleaned from his claim to have had no 'reserve knowledge'. Everything he learnt, he learnt *for* a specific encounter, and once that encounter was exhausted, he would forget everything and have to start all over again from zero. 'Even if it is for the hundredth time, you must encounter each thing as if you have never known it before' insists Paul Auster (1989: 7). 'No matter how many times, it must always be the first time. This is next to impossible, I realize, but it is an absolute rule.'

KEY ADVANCES AND CONTROVERSIES

During the 1990s, Deleuze's ex-centric empiricism, non-dialectical conception of difference, and immanent materialism began to make ripples in human geography (e.g., Doel, 1999). Like salacious gossip or the flu, word slowly got around – especially amongst post-structuralist, post-Marxist, and other so-called 'critical' human geographers – that Deleuze created an extraordinary form of geophilosophy that proffers events for everyone (e.g., *Environment and Planning D*, 1996). Not only does this non-representational geophilosophy provide an innovative basis for rethinking the nature of space and place, it is also a fully fledged 'thinking space' in its own right: not an abstract space *for* thought (a space of consciousness, representation, reflection, theory, etc. that would claim to be removed from the play of the world), but a concrete space

of thought (a portion, region or milieu within the play of the world). Quite simply, Deleuze, like Samuel Beckett and Georges Perec, had a remarkable ability to enliven even the most barren and derelict of spaces (an exhausted text, a sparsely furnished room, a stretch of pavement ...). He showed not only that every kind of space teems with life, but that space *itself* is alive. 'He is like a cork floating on a tempestuous ocean: he no longer moves, but is in an element that moves' (Deleuze, 1997: 26).

The enlivenment of our surroundings – which is sometimes called vitalism, nomadism, materialism or immanence – is perhaps Deleuze's greatest gift to geography, a discipline that remains far too enamoured of a grey and dreary conception of the world as so much dead matter: objects, things, and their inter-relationship. We live in the terrible shadow of the eighteenth-century Enlightenment and its brutal dis-enchantment of the world, which was an expression of our collective desire to make the world around us play dead so that it would not resist being subjugated to our will. At the extreme, even people were evacuated of life. More often than not, people are reduced to data, numbers, interests, opinions, and experience. Indeed, it is tempting to say that the real dullards are those who desire a matter-of-fact world contemplated by passionless and disinterested subjects. For what they leave in their wake is a morgue dressed up as a critical tribunal. Like all of the so-called poststructralist authors (e.g., **Baudrillard**, Cixous, Derrida, **Foucault**, Kristeva, and Lyotard), Deleuze can help us to refrain from stilling life, to become sensitive to the vivacity of space, and to create new spaces for life and new ways of being. Most of all, he can help us to become worthy of the specificity of geography: enabling the event of space to take place. Little wonder, therefore, that the development of so-called 'non-representational theory' has often allied itself to Deleuze (Thrift, 2007).

We should end by noting that Deleuze had no wish to be a famous intellectual and was truly horrified by the prospect of being a 'master' thinker with followers and disciples. Given his fondness for encounters, estrangement, and transformation, Deleuze always favoured what was ex-centric (out of place and untimely), impersonal (collective and transhuman), and imperceptible (the becoming of the event). In turning to Deleuze, then, we should not turn him into a shining star that would reign over us: bright, eternal, and heavenly. Rather, we should turn to him as if we were turning towards the event horizon of a black hole. 'I dream not of being invisible, but imperceptible' (Deleuze, 1977: 112).

DELEUZE'S KEY WORKS

Deleuze, G. (1983) *Nietzsche and Philosophy.* Trans. H. Tomlinson. New York: Columbia University Press [1962].

Deleuze, G. (1988a) *Bergsonism.* Trans. H. Tomlinson and B. Habberjam. New York: Zone [1966].

Deleuze, G. (1988b) *Foucault.* Trans. S. Hand. Minneapolis: Minnesota University Press [1986].

Deleuze, G. (1990a) *Expressionism in Philosophy: Spinoza.* Trans. M. Joughin. New York: Zone [1968].

Deleuze, G. (1990b) *The Logic of Sense.* Trans. M. Lester with C. Stivale. Ed. C. V. Boundas. New York: Columbia University Press [1969].

Deleuze, G. (1993) *The Fold: Leibniz and the Baroque.* Trans. T. Conley. Minneapolis: University of Minnesota Press [1988].

Deleuze, G. (1994) *Difference and Repetition.* Trans. P. Patton. London: Athlone [1968].

Deleuze, G. and Guattari, F. (1984) *Anti-Oedipus: Capitalism and Schizophrenia.* Trans. R. Hurley, M. Seem, and H. R. Lane. London: Athlone [1972].

Deleuze, G. and Guattari, F. (1987) *A Thousand Plateaus: Capitalism and Schizophrenia.* Trans. B. Massumi. Minneapolis: University of Minnesota Press [1980].

Deleuze, G. and Guattari, F. (1994) *What is Philosophy?* Trans. G. Burchell and H. Tomlinson. London: Verso [1991].

Secondary Sources and References

Ansell Pearson, K. (ed.) (1997) *Deleuze and Philosophy: The Difference Engineer.* London: Routledge.

Auster, P. (1989) *In the Country of Last Things.* London: Faber and Faber.

Badiou, A. (2000) *Deleuze: The Clamour of Being.* Trans. L. Burchill. Minneapolis: University of Minnesota Press.

Badiou, A. (2005) *Being and Event.* Trans. O. Feltham. London: Continuum.

Bogue, R. (1989) *Deleuze and Guattari.* London: Routledge.

Bonta, M. and Protevi, J. (2004) *Deleuze and Geophilosophy: A Guide and Glossary.* Edinburgh: Edinburgh University Press.

Boundas, C. V. (ed.) (1993) *The Deleuze Reader.* New York: Columbia University Press.

Boundas, C. V. and Olkowski, D. (eds) (1994) *Gilles Deleuze and the Theatre of Philosophy.* London: Routledge.

Buchanan, I. and Lambert, G. (eds) (2005) *Deleuze and Space.* Edinburgh: Edinburgh University Press.

Colebrook, C. (2006) *Deleuze: A Guide for the Perplexed.* London: Continuum.

Deleuze, G. (1977) 'I have nothing to admit', *Semiotext(e)*, 2(3): 111–16 [1973].

Deleuze, G. (1986) *Cinema 1: The Movement-image.* Trans. H. Tomlinson and B. Habberjam. Minneapolis: Minnesota University Press [1983].

Deleuze, G. (1988c) *Spinoza: Practical Philosophy.* Trans. R. Hurley. San Francisco: City Lights [1970, expanded edition 1981].

Deleuze, G. (1989) *Cinema 2: The Time-image.* Trans. H. Tomlinson and R. Galeta. Minneapolis: Minnesota University Press [1985].

Deleuze, G. (1995) *Negotiations, 1972–1990*. Trans. M. Joughin. New York: Columbia University Press [1990].

Deleuze, G. (1997) *Essays Critical and Clinical*. Trans. D. W. Smith and M. A. Greco. Minneapolis: Minnesota University Press [1993].

Deleuze, G. and Guattari, F. (1986) *Kafka: Toward a Minor Literature*. Trans. D. Polan. Minneapolis: University of Minnesota Press [1975].

Deleuze, G. and Parnet, C. (1987) *Dialogues*. Trans. H. Tomlinson and B. Habberjam. New York: Columbia University Press [1977].

Derrida, J. (1998) 'I'll have to wander all alone' *Tympanum*, 1 www.usc.edu/dept/comp-lit/tympanum/1/derrida1.html Accessed 7 July 2009.

Doel, M. A. (1999) *Poststructuralist Geographies: The Diabolical Art of Spatial Science*. Edinburgh: Edinburgh University Press.

Environment and Planning D: Society and Space (1996) Theme issue on Deleuze and Geography. J. M. Jacobs and M. Morris (eds) volume 14(4).

Goodchild, P. (1996) *Deleuze and Guattari: An Introduction to the Politics of Desire*. London: Sage.

Guattari, F. (1996) *Chaosophy: Soft Subversions*. Trans. D. L. Sweet and C. Weiner. Ed. S. Lotringer. New York: Semiotext(e).

Guattari, F. (2000) *The Three Ecologies*. Trans. I. Pinder and P. Sutton. London: Athlone.

Hardt, M. (1993) *Gilles Deleuze: An Apprenticeship in Philosophy*. Minneapolis: University of Minnesota Press.

Kaufman, E. and Heller, K. J. (eds) (1998) *Deleuze and Guattari: New Mappings in Politics, Philosophy, and Culture*. Minneapolis: University of Minnesota Press.

Lecercle, J.-J. (1985) *Philosophy through the Looking-Glass: Language, Nonsense, Desire*. La Salle: Open Court.

Massumi, B. (1992) *A User's Guide to Capitalism and Schizophrenia: Deviations from Deleuze and Guattari*. London: MIT.

May, T. (2005) *Gilles Deleuze: An Introduction*. Cambridge: Cambridge University Press.

Patton, P. (ed.) (1996) *Deleuze: A Critical Reader*. Oxford: Blackwell.

Thrift, N. J. (2007) *Non-representational Theory: Space, Politics, Affect*. London: Routledge.

**Marcus A. Doel, Swansea University/Prifysgol Abertawe
and David B. Clarke, Swansea University/Prifysgol Abertawe**

19 Peter Dicken

BIOGRAPHICAL DETAILS AND THEORETICAL CONTEXT

Peter Dicken has been one of the most influential economic geographers in the discipline over the last 30 years or more. From the foundations of his key text *Location in Space: A Theoretical Approach to Economic Geography*, with Peter Lloyd (1972), Dicken has consistently published very high quality journal articles, book chapters and texts which have investigated: global economic geographies of industrial change; the role of transnational corporations in the world economy; economic development in East Asia (with particular focus on business networks and production chains); and global production networks. Collectively, and crucially, these works chart the effects of global economic change on different geographical scales – from the global to the local. Yet perhaps Dicken's most significant impact in the academy for both research, and teaching and learning, has been his seminal text *Global Shift* (reprinted in its fifth edition, 2007) which has provided a bedrock for scholars studying the uneven geographies of globalisation since the publication of its first edition in 1986. Though written to demonstrate the complex global articulation of *economic* production chains, *Global Shift* has proved influential beyond the subdiscipline of economic geography, standing as a key reference in debates concerning the declining sovereignty of the nation-state and the formation of a global society.

Dicken is a 'Manchester man' through and through. He joined the Department of Geography at the University of Manchester in 1966 following the successful completion of his MA from the same University, and ultimately obtained a personal Chair in 1988. In between, he was awarded his PhD from the University of Uppsala, Sweden. Over almost four decades in academia, he has held distinguished research and teaching positions at universities in Australia, Canada, Hong Kong, Mexico, Singapore and the United States, and in 1999 became a Fellow of the Swedish Collegium for Advanced Study in the Social Sciences. The quality and policy relevance of his work has resulted in appointments as the Co-Director of European Science Foundation Scientific Programme on Regional and Urban Restructuring in Europe (1989–1994), and as a consultant advisor to the UNCTAD Commission on Transnational Corporations (1993–4). He has held several editorial positions on international journal boards (including *Competition and Change, Journal of Economic Geography, Global Networks, Review of International Political Economy*), including the Managing Editor of *Progress in Human Geography*. As his work on the strategic behaviour of firms and international patterns of trade and investment criss-crosses with both management studies and international economics, he has forged successful research links outside geography. For example, a recent and notable research project has been with colleagues from Manchester Business School (Jeffrey Henderson) and the National University of Singapore (Henry Yeung) investigating global production networks in Britain, East Asia and Eastern Europe. Apart from driving global research agendas in economic geography, Dicken has also been committed to supervising graduate students (including many who have gone on to highly successful academic careers) and entertaining audiences on the international conference circuit.

A year before **David Harvey** published *Social Justice and the City* (1973), Peter Dicken and Peter Lloyd (of the University of Liverpool) published *Location in Space: A Theoretical Approach to Economic Geography*. For economic geography, it became a benchmark for the period. No stone was left unturned in the search for explaining the organisation of economy, locational analysis, regional economic development in space and the differential (rather than uneven) economic growth rates experienced in North America and Europe. In essence, this text was devoted to explicating the 'economic' in economic geography. Here, Dicken and his co-author were heavily influenced by the classical and neo-classical modelling gurus of locational theorists (e.g., Christaller, 1966; Isard, 1956; Losch, 1954) and, of course, the path-breaking work of **Peter Haggett** (for example, *Locational Analysis in Human Geography*, 1965, as well as Haggett's co-writing with Richard Chorley 1967; 1969). But, if we wind the clock on a full 18 years and read the third edition of *Location in*

Space (Dicken and Lloyd, 1990), we begin to unravel other influences on Dicken's view of the (economic) world. The neo-classical spirit of *Location in Space* is prevalent, but Dicken and Lloyd re-work the interpretation of the 'economic' in space by considering the *political economy* of location and its uneven distribution through time and space. For example, they discuss the key strategic role of transnational corporations in restructuring the world economy (as espoused by Taylor and Thrift, 1983), introduce the notion of 'chains' of business organization and location (as discussed by Porter, 1985), examine geographies of corporate organisation and control (following **Pred**, 1974), investigate geographical 'linkages' in location (see Scott, 1984) and provide a thumbnail sketch of Marx's theories on capital and labour (which are drawn from original sources and informed by Harvey (1973; 1982) and others (e.g., **Massey**, 1984; Scott and **Storper**, 1986).

In 1986, Dicken published *Global Shift: Industrial Change in a Turbulent World*. In many ways, this text stands as Dicken's definitive statement on geographies of production: it is certainly his best-known and most widely cited work. In this text, Dicken looked afresh at explaining locational change in the world and to assist him in fulfilling this project, he looked beyond the geographical community for inspiration and ideas, especially to those who studied international economics and the strategic behaviour of organisations and transnational corporations. Of significance here is Dicken's appreciation of writers like Hymer (1972) on multinational corporations, Dunning (1980) on why firms engage in international production and Michalet (1980) on international subcontracting, and the use of an array of in-depth case studies (e.g., textiles and clothing) and empirics derived from

General Agreement on Tariffs and Trade (GATT), the United Nations Centre for Transnational Corporations (UNCTC), the International Labour Organisation (ILO) and Organisation for Economic Cooperation and Development (OECD) to tease out the political economy of industrial location at global–local scales.

SPATIAL CONTRIBUTIONS

Peter Dicken has always been fascinated by economic restructuring at the global–local scale (Dicken, 2003) and in particular, investigating the role of the transnational corporation in producing uneven development as transactionally linked chains of production stretch international and global space (e.g. Dicken, 1976; 1986; Dicken and Malmberg, 2001). The contributions Dicken's work has made to advancing our understanding of the geographies of restructuring within firms, and the ways in which firms impact upon different places around the globe, are considerable. These contributions can be summarised around four main themes.

First, Dicken has provided one of the most incisive and detailed geographical analyses of transnational corporations in the world economy (e.g., Dicken, 1971; 1980; 1994). From the analysis of the foreign direct investment patterns of Japanese firms in Britain (e.g., Dicken, 1990; Dicken and Lloyd, 1980; Dicken and Tickell, 1997), to in-depth studies of different sectors (e.g., automobiles – Dicken, 1987; 1992b) or, latterly, investigations into firms' production chains and networks (e.g. business networks in the Indonesian clothing industry – Dicken

and Hassler, 2000), Dicken has been at the forefront of unpacking the organisational role and geographies of the firm in (re)producing uneven development in economy and society. Of significant interest here is Dicken's reading of how firms impinge/impact upon and restructure local economies (and the state) through their organisational strategies and 'footloose' tendencies (i.e. being able to switch capital from one location to another with little friction – see Allen, 1995).

Second, Dicken has brought us a greater understanding of the role, locational behaviour and organisation of Japanese capital (and firms) in the West. He has published very detailed analysis of Japanese foreign direct investment in Britain (see above), case study material on Nissan in Washington (Dicken, 1984) and, more importantly, introduced in great depth the organisation of Japanese trading companies (*soga shosha*) to the Anglo-American academy (Dicken and Miyamachi, 1998). Dicken's research interests in Japanese firms and their management and labour practices outside of Japan reflects a much wider interest in economic restructuring in East and Pacific Asia especially (Dicken, 1987; Dicken et al., 1999).

Third, following on from the above, Dicken's work on economic restructuring within East Asia and the Pacific Rim has provided pickings for those seeking to understand the significance of chains and network structures within not only transnational corporations, but, more importantly, within the world economy (Dicken et al., 2001). Dicken's earlier work on business networks in organisations (Dicken and Thrift, 1992) provided the foundations for us to think about the organisation of economy (and places) in terms of functionally integrated linkages, connections and flows from both traditional Western and Asian business systems (Dicken, 2000). Moreover, Dicken has conceptualised the importance of chains and networks in the global economy through ideas of territorialisation, bringing scale back onto the agenda in studies of both the firm and industrial sectors (Dicken et al., 2002).

Fourth, with colleagues from the 'Manchester School' – Neil Coe, Martin Hess, Jeffery Henderson and Henry Yeung – Dicken has been instrumental in developing the Global Production Networks (GPN) perspective for critically evaluating the relationalities and network geographies of contemporary forms of economic globalisation in the world economy (Coe et al., 2004; Dicken et al., 2002). Importantly, the GPN perspective takes forward the plethora of ideas about global commodity and value chains in a *relational* rather than linear way, which embellishes theoretical understandings of the spatial dynamism of global production in a context of transnational circulation, relationships and interactions (Coe et al., 2008).

KEY ADVANCES AND CONTROVERSIES

Dicken's key advances in the discipline have already been discussed at length, and include his innovative analysis of transnational corporations as a barometer for studying global economic change, unpacking the importance of production chains and networks in understanding contemporary patterns in economy; and examining global economic change in relation to a global–local dialectic. The reaction to this work in the discipline has been, on the whole, both positive and relatively uncontroversial. Many view

Dicken's work as at the vanguard of illustrating the manifestations of economic globalisation in contemporary society by providing neatly-crafted case studies and explanations for such patterns. Dicken has summarised his key arguments about geography, location and space as follows:

> The basis of my argument is that firms, just like all other forms of social organization, are fundamentally and intrinsically *spatial* and *territorial*. They are spatial in the sense that they are responsive to geographical distance and to spatial variations in the availability of necessary resources and of business opportunities. Such spatiality may have – indeed most often has – a territorial manifestation. Hence, firms are territorial as well as spatial in the sense that the 'surface' from which firms originate and on which they operate is most commonly made up of a tessellated structure of territorial entities arrayed along a continuum of variable and overlapping scales, including those of political governance ... For some functions of the firm the territory may be intensely local, for others it may approach the global.

(Dicken, 2002: 12, our emphasis)

Dicken elucidates this global–local perspective in *Global Shift*, from first to fifth editions (with a sixth due in 2011). *Global Shift* is Dicken's major contribution to Geography and encapsulates his advocacy of a spatialised reading of economic activity. The 2007 edition, *Global Shift: Mapping the Changing Contours of the World Economy*, has excelled itself in this regard. Not only does Dicken interpret the significant ideas offered by the likes of John Allen, Ash Amin, Gordon Clark, Meric Gertler, Ron Martin, Anders Malmberg, Jamie Peck, Erica Schoenberger, **Michael Storper**, **Nigel Thrift** and Henry Yeung, but he has once again weaved into the text theoretical contributions from a wide spectrum of business and management sources (e.g., Gereffi,

Krugman, Porter, Sklair, and Whitley) to provide a richness which could not have otherwise been achieved through a geographical lens. For example, Dicken's *geographical* explanation of the organisational capabilities and competences of transnational corporations has been greatly influenced by Bartlett and Goshal's (1998) notions of 'managing across borders', where they distinguish between transnational, multinational, global and international organisational forms of the firm. Herein lies the contribution of Dicken to the discipline and beyond, in that his ideas and approach have not only been a benchmark for other geographers, but have also been accepted in international economics and organisational studies which focus on FDI and the strategic behaviour of firms in the world economy.

DICKEN'S KEY WORKS

Dicken, P. and Lloyd, P. E. (1990) *Location in Space: Theoretical Perspectives in Economic Geography* (3rd edition). New York: Harper and Row (also see 1st and 2nd editions).

Dicken, P. (1992a) 'International production in a volatile regulatory environment: the influence of national regulatory policies on the spatial strategies of transnational corporations', *Geoforum*, 23: 303–16.

Dicken, P. (1994) 'Global–local tensions: firms and states in the global economy', *Economic Geography*, 70: 101–28.

Dicken, P. (1997) 'Transnational corporations and nation-states', *International Social Science Journal*, 151: 77–89.

Dicken, P. (2003) *Global Shift: Reshaping the Global Economic Map in the 21st Century* (4th edition). London: Sage (also see 1st to 3rd editions).

Dicken, P. (2007) *Global Shift: Mapping the Changing Contours of the World Economy* (5th edition). London: Sage.

Dicken, P. and Lloyd. P. E. (1981) *Modern Western Society: A Geographical Perspective on Work and Well-Being.* London: Harper and Row.

Dicken, P. and Miyamachi, Y. (1998) '"From noodles to satellites": the changing geography of Japanese *sogo shosha*', *Transactions of the Institute of British Geographers*, 23: 55–78.

Dicken, P. and Thrift, N. (1992) 'The organizational of production and the production of organization: why business enterprises matter in the study of geographical internationalisation', *Transactions of the Institute of British Geographers*, 17: 101–28.

Dicken, P., Kelly, P. F., Olds, K. and Yeung, H. (2001) 'Chains and networks, territories and scales: towards a relational framework for analysing the global economy', *Global Networks*, 1: 99–123.

Dicken, P., Henderson, J., Hess, M., Coe, N. and Yeung, H. (2002) 'Global production networks and the analysis of economic development', *Review of International Political Economy*, 9: 436–64.

Secondary Sources and References

Allen, J. (1995) 'Crossing borders: footloose multinationals', in J. Allen and C. Hamnett (eds), *A Shrinking World*. Oxford: Oxford University Press. pp. 55–102.

Bartlett, C. and Ghoshal, S. (1998) *Managing Across Borders: The Transnational Solution* (3rd edition). London: Random House.

Christaller, W. (1966) *Central Places in Southern Germany.* Englewood Cliffs, NJ: Prentice Hall.

Coe, N.H., Dicken, P. and Hess, M. (2008) 'Global production networks: realizing the potential', *Journal of Economic Geography*, 8: 271–95.

Coe, N.H., Hess, M., Yeung, H.W.C., Dicken, P. and Henderson, J. (2004) '"Globalizing" regional development: a global production network perspective', *Transactions of the Institute of British Geographers*, NS 29: 468–84.

Dicken, P. (1971) 'Some aspects of the decision-making behaviour of business organizations', *Economic Geography*, 47: 426–37.

Dicken, P. (1976) 'The multiplant enterprise and geographical space: some issues in the study of external control and regional development', *Regional Studies*, 10: 401–12.

Dicken, P. (1980) 'Foreign direct investment in European manufacturing industry: the changing position of the United Kingdom as a host country', *Geoforum*, 11: 289–313.

Dicken, P. (1984) 'Washington welcomes Nissan', *Geographical Magazine*, 56: 286–7.

Dicken, P. (1986) *Global Shift: Industrial Change in a Turbulent World*. New York: Harper and Row.

Dicken, P. (1987) 'Japanese penetration of the European automobile industry: the arrival of Nissan in the United Kingdom', *Tijdschrift voor Economische en Sociale Geografie*, 78: 94–107.

Dicken, P. (1990) 'Japanese industrial investment in the U.K.', *Geography*, 75: 351–4.

Dicken, P. (1992b) 'Europe 1992 and strategic change in the international automobile industry', *Environment and Planning A*, 24: 11–31.

Dicken, P. (2000) 'Places and flows: situating international investment', in G. Clark, M. Gertler and M.A. Feldman (eds), *A Handbook of Economic Geography*. Oxford: Oxford University Press. pp. 275–99.

Dicken, P. (2002) 'Placing firms, firming places: grounding the debate on the global corporation', paper presented at the Conference on 'Responding to Globalization: Societies, Groups, and Individuals', University of Colorado, Boulder.

Dicken, P. and Hassler, M. (2000) 'Organizing the Indonesian clothing industry in the global economy: the role of business networks', *Environment and Planning A*, 32: 263–80.

Dicken, P., Henderson, J., Hess, M., Coe, N. and Yeung, H. (2002) 'Global production networks and the analysis of economic development', *Review of International Political Economy*, 9: 436–64.

Dicken, P. and Lloyd, P. (1980) 'Patterns and processes of change in the spatial distribution of foreign-controlled manufacturing employment in the United Kingdom 1963–1975', *Environment and Planning A*, 12: 1405–26.

Dicken, P. and Malmberg, A. (2001) 'Firms in territories: a relational perspective', *Economic Geography*, 77: 345–63.

Dicken, P., Olds, K., Kelly, P. F., Kong, L. and Yeung, H. (eds) (1999) *Globalization and the Asian Pacific: Contested Territories*. London: Routledge.

Dicken, P. and Tickell, A. (1997) 'Putting Japanese investment in Europe in its place', *Area*, 29: 200–12.

Dunning, J. (1980) 'Towards an eclectic theory of international production: some empirical tests', *Journal of International Business Studies*, 11: 9–31.

Haggett, P. (1965) *Locational Analysis in Human Geography*. London: Edward Arnold.

Haggett, P. and Chorley, R. (eds) (1967) *Models in Geography*. London: Edward Arnold.

Haggett, P. and Chorley, R. (1969) *Network Analysis in Geography*. London: Edward Arnold.

Harvey, D. (1973) *Social Justice and the City*. London: Edward Arnold.

Harvey, D. (1982) *The Limits to Capital*. Oxford: Blackwell.

Hymer, S. (1972) 'The multinational corporation and the law of uneven development', in J.N. Bhagwati (ed.), *Economics and the World Order*. London: Macmillan. pp. 113–40.

Isard, W. (1956) *Location and Space Economy*. Cambridge, MA: MIT Press.

Lloyd, P. and Dicken, P. (1972) *Location in Space: A Theoretical Approach to Economic Geography*. London: Harper and Row.

Losch, A. (1954) *The Economics of Location*. New Haven, CT: Yale University Press.

Massey, D. (1984) *Spatial Divisions of Labour. Social Structures and the Geography of Production*. London: Macmillan.

Michalet, C-A. (1980) 'International subcontracting: a state of the art', in D. Germidis (ed.), *International Subcontracting, a New Form of Investment*. Paris: OECD. pp. 37–70.

Porter, M. (1985) *Competitive Advantage*. New York: Free Press.

Pred, A. (1974) 'Industry, information and City-system interdependencies', in F.E.I. Hamilton (ed.), *Spatial Perspectives on Industrial Organization and Decision Making*. London: Wiley. pp. 105–39.

Scott, A. (1984) 'Industrial organization and the logic of inter-metropolitan location: I. Theoretical considerations', *Economic Geography*, 59: 111–42.

Scott, A. and Storper, M. (eds) (1986) *Production, Work, Territory. A Geographical Anatomy of Industrial Capitalism*. Winchester, MA: Allen and Unwin.

Taylor, M. and Thrift, N. (1983) 'Business organization, segmentation and location', *Regional Studies*, 17: 455–65.

Jonathan V. Beaverstock, University of Nottingham

20   Arturo Escobar

BIOGRAPHICAL DETAILS AND THEORETICAL CONTEXT

Arturo Escobar was born in Manizales, Colombia, in 1952, and trained first as a chemical engineer, graduating from the Universidad del Valle in Cali in 1975. After a year of studying biochemistry, he relocated to the US, completing a Masters in Food Science and International Nutrition at Cornell University in 1978, before enrolling in an interdisciplinary PhD program at Berkeley. His interests – spurred on by the presence of **Michel Foucault** on campus – shifted towards the social sciences and questions of power, international development and planning. Doctoral work, which included a year of fieldwork in Colombia, saw early expression in a brilliant article published in the Indian journal *Alternatives*, where he applied Foucault's notions of power to the study of international development (Escobar, 1984). His theoretical argument – that development should be seen as a *discourse* of power and control – was new and challenging, and by the early 1990s Escobar was established as a leading thinker among a strong group of 'post-development' theorists including Ashis Nandy, Wolfgang Sachs and James Ferguson (Escobar, 1992; Rahnema and Bawtree, 1997). Having competed three years as a lecturer in Latin American Studies at the University of California at Santa Cruz in 1989, Escobar moved into the discipline of anthropology, beginning as assistant professor at Smith College, and then the University of Massachusetts, where he taught for five years. In 2000 he became the Kenan Distinguished Teaching Professor of Anthropology, University of North Carolina. He has spent shorter periods teaching in Colombia, the UK, and Spain.

Few twentieth-century ideas sparked as much controversy as that of international and economic development, and it was Escobar's major monograph, *Encountering Development* (1995) – an elaboration of the work he had been conducting since the 1980s – that elevated him to the status of post-development icon. For many critics, development has reached an impasse, with Escobar and other post-development theorists exposing how 'development was shown to be a pervasive cultural discourse with profound consequences for the production of social reality in the so-called Third World' (Escobar, 2000: 11). In his later work, Escobar begun to look beyond the limitations of state, market and international aid to a form of social change led by new social movements, activists, and progressive non-governmental organisations.

This second strand to Escobar's work emerged in the mid-1990s, when he conducted a year's fieldwork on the Pacific coast of Colombia, the first of several periods during which he worked with Afro-Colombians (descendants from African slaves brought to mine gold) and their activist organisations (Escobar and Pedrosa, 1996b; 2008). The coast is a hot-spot of biological diversity, and is also home to Afro-Colombian rights movements with a strong sense of place and territory. Escobar's research traverses his belief in the power of these place-based social movements as alternatives to national and Western-backed development efforts. He combines this analysis with an interest in nature, which he describes as a 'constructed' category immersed in discursive and material struggles (over the meaning of biodiversity and sustainability, for example). Some of his work in Colombia is, therefore, framed in the language of political ecology, with geographical concepts of place and territory critical to his analysis (Escobar 1996a; 1998; 2001; 2008).

SPATIAL CONTRIBUTIONS

Escobar (1995: 14) believes in the 'task of imagining alternatives', and his work is stimulating and provocative. Aside from a wide-ranging conversation that has developed around his post-development critique in anthropology and development studies, some geographers have used his analysis as a point of departure for studying social movements and development alternatives. For example, the ideas expressed in *Encountering Development*, highlighted some of the spatial outcomes of the hegemonic 'development' discourse since colonial times. The argument was

that Western 'development', particularly during the Cold War, lay behind the construction of almost all aspects of social reality in the Third World, in such a pervasive way that 'that even its opponents were obliged to phrase their critiques in development terms: another development, participatory development, socialist development, and so on' (Peet and Hartwick, 1999: 145). Discourse, he argued, had the power to influence reality, following **Edward Said**'s theory of Orientalism (Said: 1978: 3). The production of knowledge and the planning of development by Western institutions was hence something that 'third world' countries and regions find it hard to escape from. The process of dominating, restructuring, and establishing authority progresses in three stages:

1   The progressive identification of Third World problems to be treated by specific interventions. This creates a 'field of the interventions of power'.
2   The professionalisation of development; the recasting of political problems into neutral scientific terms (poverty indicators, for example), leading to a regime of truth or a 'field of the control of knowledge'.
3   The institutionalisation of development to treat these 'problems' and the formation of a network of new sites of power/knowledge that bind people to certain behaviours and rationalities (in rural development discourse, 'produce or perish' became one such norm – Escobar, 1995: 157).

The professionalisation of development in the post-Second World War period, Escobar argued, incorporated the Third World as research data in 'academic programs, conferences, consultancy services and local extension services and so on' as poverty, illiteracy and hunger 'became the basis for an industry for planners, experts and civil servants' (1995: 46). Since this industry never stops producing goods in the form of new projects and reports, but actually achieves its targets only rarely, it justifies its own existence and its considerable financing from a range of donors.

The development discourse has, therefore, created underdevelopment of the Third World in a much more subtle way than through colonial control. Escobar's words are purposely harsh, and they suggest an instrumental aim lying behind a universal (Western) paradigm in which many people, including Western geographers, anthropologists, and other social scientists, are complicit. The very idea of development is framed by the Western geopolitical imagination that seeks to 'subordinate, contain and assimilate the Third World as Other. Such Western imagination is a violation of the rights of the other societies' (Slater, 1993: 421).

As alternatives, Escobar favours the responses of indigenous/autonomous social movements, and localised strategies of development, rather than the radical overturning of western-dominated geopolitical relations by the state, as was proposed by earlier dependency theorists. Like **Stuart Corbridge** and **Michael Watts**, he argues that emancipatory possibilities exist because criticism of the 'mainstream' can translate into viable alternatives, and the types of new social movements made famous by writers like **Manual Castells** can create new conversational communities. Place-based social movements need 'territory', in which their livelihoods or life project are largely conducted, but they also operate in a 'region-territory', which is a 'political construction for the defense of the territories and their sustainability' (Escobar 2001: 162). This can include global support networks, including those

now offered by the internet; his examples include the U'wa indigenous group in Colombia who have mobilised against the Colombian government and Occidental Petroleum to oppose oil exploration (Escobar and Harcourt, 2002). Escobar follows many scholars of indigenous rights in stressing the attachment such groups feel to particular places – 'The struggle for territory is thus a cultural struggle for autonomy and self-determination. This explains why for many people of the Pacific the loss of territory would amount to a return to slavery or, worse perhaps, to becoming "common citizens"' (Escobar, 2001: 162). Social movements are therefore intimately linked to local geographies; culture resides in places, even as globalisation advances.

In his work addressing matters of nature and the environment, Escobar makes further claims which are of interest to those working around the slippery interdisciplinary field of political ecology, to which anthropologists and geographers have contributed (Escobar 1996a; 1999a; 1998; 2008). Escobar's arguments here are complex, but revolve around the view that much of nature is now artificially produced, being deeply imbricated with technology and social relations which are 'hybrid and multiform' (Escobar, 1999a: 1). He defines political ecology as 'the contingent study of the manifold articulations of history and biology and the cultural mediations through which such articulations are necessarily established' (1999a: 3). This broad-ranging definition neatly combines realists' interest in the material transformations of the natural world by human actions with the arguments of those who perceive nature as a historically- and socially-constructed category (Escobar, 2008).

Political ecology, for Escobar, should be anti-essentialist, in order to situate the complex of meanings of nature–human relations in the larger context of history and power. He identifies three distinct but interlinked nature regimes, and delineates their characteristics. The regime of organic nature is most commonly found in non-industrialised societies, and best analysed through anti-dualist conceptions of nature–culture and local knowledge. Capitalist nature is that which is commodified (as in the case of bio-prospecting operations) and governed. The third, techno-nature, is artificial, newly manipulated through biotechnology and engineering. These three regimes are not a series of linear stages towards modern life – 'They coexist and overlap' (1999a: 5) and raise substantive questions about the power of discourses about nature – even the term biodiversity resulted from a modern scientific worldview, and such activities are protected through networks, actors and strategies (Escobar, 1998). Escobar urges the creation of a balanced position that, according to David Cleveland, 'acknowledges the constructedness of nature – the fact that much of what ecologists refer to as nature is a product of culture – and nature in the real sense, that is existence of an order of nature, including the body' (Cleveland, 1999:17).

This reading of political ecology goes beyond naturalism, the common philosophical foundation of nature conservation, because nature and culture are in fact hybridised as 'cultured nature'. This analysis of hybridisation, in a non-essentialist and trans-disciplinary way, makes Escobar's study of nature distinctive. It can be glimpsed indirectly in new, critical geographical work that stresses the social construction of nature and the imposition of dominant discourses. Escobar brought together his interest in political ecology and place-based social movements and cultures in *Territories of Difference* (2008), an exhaustive account of these issues in the Colombian Pacific, as well as in

work on 'fortress conservation' and wilderness protection in Africa (Neumann, 1998) and Central America (Sundberg, 1998), and in critiques of sustainable development (Rocheleau et al., 2001) and bureaucratic forestry (Robbins, 2001). In anthropology, new varieties of political ecology are constantly evolving, with Fairhead and Leach's *Misreading the African Landscape* offering a counter to dominant Western views of forest loss (1996), and Stone's work on the perils of genetic modification offering empirical data on 'technonatures' in action (2002).

KEY ADVANCES AND CONTROVERSIES

Since Escobar's major argument has been to challenge the language, discourse, and project of mainstream development as a failed modernist project, a critical response to these ideas was inevitable, and came from several quarters. For instance, a group of critics has argued that his attack on development misses the target, since 'the problem is not so much with development, even less so with modernity, than with capitalism' (Escobar, 2000:12). Richard Peet and **Michael Watts** (2004) and most of their contributors to their book, *Liberation Ecologies*, wish to balance the attention given to discourses with analysis of the impact of material transformations, while Peet and Hartwick (1999) and Kiely (1999) were more blunt, suggesting capitalist material relations have penetrated all corners of the globe. Thus, development discourse has arisen first and foremost from the spread of capitalism (Fernando and Kamat, 2000). This critique, there-fore, sees the post-development project as requiring the transformation of the social relations that produced and that sustain this discourse, arguing for active inter-vention against capitalism (i.e., a new and revolutionary form of development itself), and global solidarity.

A related concern is that development – including the actions of the state – has, of course, long contained progressive criti-cal voices and practices, and is far from monolithic in its opposition to local and marginal voices (Gardner and Lewis, 1996; Lehmann, 1997). Lumping together progressive aid agencies or the actions of radical NGOs, with the worst techno-cratic and domineering aid projects prac-tising their craft on their 'clients', and then collectively condemning the total-ity as an instrument of Western power (as passages in *Encountering Development* came close to doing), denies these differ-ences and denigrates some of those genu-inely involved in radical praxis. It also denies the possibility that development anthropology can promote *better* devel-opment or state policies, using ethno-graphic and technical skills (Gardner and Lewis, 1996; Little and Painter, 1995). Discourse analysis may, therefore, tend to throw together contested positions of development simply because they 'share the same discursive space'. Escobar may, therefore, be practising a form of essen-tialism after all (Fernando and Kamat, 2000; Kiely, 1999).

A third question concerns the power of placed-based social movements. There is much evidence that many local activist struggles are not really about overturning the status quo or challenging the global and national power relations in which they are embedded, but are more con-cerned with gaining access to develop-ment resources, some of them modern and Western (e.g., capital, paid labour,

education, health). The argument goes that because capitalism is crisis-ridden, and it is a contradictory and uneven process, its ideology permeates almost everywhere, including to distant social movements and their members. The most convincing critique of post-development in general, and of Escobar's work in particular, is along these lines, coming from geographer Tony Bebbington in *Re-encountering Development* (2000). Bebbing-ton tries to resolve the debate between post-development, and the neo-liberal interpretations informed by neo-classical economics (pro-market, and modernising), to call for a notion of development that is alternative, critical and practicable. He argues not only that the post-development case has theoretical shortcomings, but that it falls down empirically in the Andes, when put to the test in study of peas-ant culture and livelihoods. Criticisms of development's failures in the region are too blunt: plenty of cases exist in the Andes where symbols of failed devel-opment – high levels of out-migration, increased consumption of Western com-modities, and imported knowledge and technologies – have been accompanied by 'increased indigenous control of eve-rything from municipal government, to regional textile markets, to bus compa-nies' and 'assertive and ever more ethni-cally self-conscious social organizations' (Bebbington 2000: 496). Thus, alternatives to capitalist landscapes can emerge from all sorts of 'development' activities. Inte-gral to these alternatives have been the work of the state (particularly its support of land reform), NGOs, and churches. Post-development thinking either denies, or ignores the influence of such institu-tions, and fails to seriously address what peasant farmers must do in the short-term to sustain their communities. Therefore, we need to foreground 'problems of liveli-hood and production as much as problems of politics and power' and 'emphasize negotiation and accommodation as much as resistance' (Bebbington, 2000: 449).

In addressing some of these criticisms, Escobar has voiced some sympathy with the more radical (and post-structuralist) critics of post-development thinking, but he disputes the arguments that assert the 'the primacy of the material over the discursive' – partly on the grounds that insufficient attention is usually given to the role of language and meaning in the creation of reality (Escobar, 2000:12). Nonetheless, movements form broader networks of power, and thus he sees Marxist geography as essentially correct in grounding of place and identity-based social movements in wider political coalitions. Further, he does recognise that social struggles, like those of the U'wa, form networks, particularly around gender responsibilities and rights via 'theoretical and practical action – that is, in the production of alternative discourses' (Escobar and Harcourt, 2002: 4), (the focus of some of his recent work). But he also acknowledges the valuable insights provided by a group of 'actor-oriented' sociologists and anthropologists that register power in a different way, tracing it across the interfaces between actors – for example, between peasant farmers and NGO workers, exposing their mutual constructions, sense of identity, and actions, uncovered through detailed ethnography (Arce and Long, 2000).

Francophone anthropology and work on rural politics has, in fact, taken these debates further, to highlight the subversion of development by peasant groups and the work of a whole class of 'interlocutors' who shuttle between rural communities and the development industry, representing one to the other (Batterbury, 2002; Bierschenk et al., 2000; Olivier de Sardan, 2005). Escobar also has some sympathies with Bebbington's alternative take on livelihoods and development

(Escobar, 2008). However, he refuses to respond to a persistent criticism that post-development offers no concrete political and economic programme for change. This, he says, is precisely the normative goal of most development thinking, and it is something he and his colleagues are trying escape from. The future is, then, up to people themselves, and their social movements must elaborate their own paths (Escobar, 2000; Escobar 2008).

Escobar's thoughts on political ecology and the study of nature have attracted some commentary. David Cleveland (1999:18) argues that essentialism is more difficult to escape from than Escobar makes out. For example, he says that 'in the organic regime nature is not manipulated' (Cleveland, 1999:18), but this ignores the actions of certain pre-modern peoples, who clearly did exploit natural capital to an advanced degree (see Escobar, 1998, who partially addressed this). One of the founders of the field, Piers Blaikie (2000) takes on the implicit populism and support of the underdog in post-development thinking more generally, and perceives analysis to be lacking in detailed research into development processes and policy. However, it is also true that the critical geographical studies that do employ discourse analysis have found ways to apply it quite effectively to specific development 'problems', and that there is great value in combining this type of analysis with other forms of investigation (Rocheleau et al., 2001; Neumann, 1998; Peet and Watts, 2004), some of these involving a greater degree of ecological analysis, and awareness of gender politics, than Escobar has chosen (Rocheleau, 1999).

Such critiques do not diminish the power of Escobar's key political message – local cultures, places, and territories matter (2008). The grand revisionism in the classical Marxist account of social change gives way to something much more modest and localised in his work – 'grand theorizing is part of the problem' (Escobar and Harcourt, 2002: 4). Understanding local social movements provides an important role for anthropology, a discipline that like geography has an ugly past in its dealings with hegemonic discourses and colonialism. Escobar has been instrumental in promoting 'world anthropologies' for their 'richer cosmopolitics', levelling the terrain of anthropological work and recognising non-Western scholarship (Ribiero and Escobar, 2005). Nonetheless, the stronger Marxist and post-structuralist critics of Escobar's work, who argue that the material impact of capitalism must be the main target of any critical interventions, suggest that whatever one's particular ideology of development or wish-list for change, these need to begin somewhere. Even if nature and culture are hybridised, we need to isolate some essential elements within and between these hybrid regimes, and try to rectify

them. This should not prove so difficult, we suggest, where it is clearly the case that capital, as the overarching economic system, is directly responsible for social and human injustices. This also means that we look critically at social movements themselves – they are not to be romanticised given many are nationalist, fundamentalist, or insensitive to human rights and gender difference (Keily, 1999). Escobar is, of course, well aware of this (Escobar and Harcourt, 2002).

In conclusion, Escobar's 'journey of the imagination' has taken him a long way forward in 'reconceiving and reconstructing the world from the perspective of, and along with, those subaltern groups that continue to enact a cultural politics of difference as they struggle to defend their places, ecologies, and cultures' (Escobar, 2000: 15). The sentiment is laudable and his work has thus helped to foreground the importance of local culture within thinking on development hegemonies and practices.

ESCOBAR'S KEY WORKS

Escobar, A. (1984) 'Discourse and power in development: Michel Foucault and the relevance of his work to the Third World', *Alternatives*, 10 (3): 377–400.

Alvarez, S. and Escobar, A. (eds) (1992) *The Making of Social Movements in Latin America: Identity, Strategy, and Democracy.* Boulder: Westview Press.

Escobar, A. (1995) *Encountering Development: The Making and Unmaking of the Third World.* Princeton: Princeton University Press (in Spanish, Bogotá: Editorial Norma, 1998).

Alvarez, S., Dagnino, E. and Escobar, A. (eds) (1998) *Cultures of Politics/Politics of Cultures: Revisioning Latin American Social Movements.* Boulder: Westview Press (also published in Portuguese and Spanish).

Escobar, A. (1999a) 'After nature: steps to an anti-essentialist political ecology', *Current Anthropology*, 40 (1): 1–30.

Ribeiro, G.L. and Escobar, A. (eds) (2005) *World Anthropologies: Disciplinary Transformations within Systems of Power.* Oxford: Berg.

Escobar, A. (2008) *Territories of Difference: Place, Movements, Life.* Redes, NC: Duke University Press.

Secondary Sources and References

Arce, A. and Long, N. (eds) (2000) *Anthropology, Development and Modernities.* London: Routledge.

Batterbury, S.P.J. (2002) 'Discursive review of "*Courtiers en développement: les villages africains en quête de projets*", *Environment and Planning D: Society and Space*, 20 (1): 20–5.

Bebbington, A.J. (2000) 'Re-encountering development: livelihood transitions and place transformations in the Andes', *Annals of the Association of American Geographers*, 90 (3): 495–520.

Bierschenk, T., Chauveau, J.-P. and Olivier de Sardan, J.-P. (eds) (2000) *Courtiers en développement: Les villages africains en quête de projets.* Paris: Editions Karthala.

Blaikie, P. (2000) 'Development, post-, anti-, and populist: a critical review', *Environment and Planning A*, 32 (6): 1033–50.

Cleveland, D. (1999) 'Comments on Escobar', *Current Anthropology*, 40 (1): 17–18.

Escobar, A. (1992) 'Planning', in W. Sachs (ed.), *The Development Dictionary: A Guide to Knowledge as Power.* London: Zed Books. pp. 132–45.

Escobar, A. (1996a) 'Constructing nature: elements for a poststructuralist political ecology', in R. Peet and M. Watts (eds), *Liberation Ecologies: Environment, Development, Social Movements.* London: Routledge. pp. 46–68.

Escobar, A. and Pedrosa, A. (eds) (1996b) *Pacífico, Desarrollo o Diversidad? Estado, Capital y Movimientos Sociales en el Pacífico Colombiano.* Bogotá: CEREC/Ecofondo.

Escobar, A. (1998) 'Whose knowledge, whose nature? Biodiversity, conservation, and the political ecology of social movements', *Journal of Political Ecology*, 5.

Escobar, A. (1999b) *El Final del Salvaje: Naturaleza, Cultura y Politica en las Sociedades Contemporaneas.* Bogotá: Instituto Colombiano de Antropología.

Escobar, A. (2000) 'Beyond the search for a paradigm? Post-development and beyond', *Development*, 43 (4): 11–14.

Escobar, A. (2001) 'Culture sits in places. Reflections on globalism and subaltern strategies of globalization', *Political Geography*, 20: 139–74.

Escobar, A. and Harcourt, W. (2002) 'Women and the politics of place', *Development*, 45 (1): 7–14.

Fairhead, J. and Leach, M. (1996) *Misreading the African Landscape: Society and Ecology in a Forest-Savanna Mosaic.* Cambridge: Cambridge University Press.

Fernando, J.F. and Kamat, S. (2000) 'Response to Ray Kylie and Arturo Escobar', *Development* (on line forum, www.sidint.org/journal/online).

Gardner, K. and Lewis, D. (1996) *Anthropology, Development and the Post-Modern Challenge.* London: Pluto Press.

Kiely, R. (1999) 'The last refuge of the noble savage? A critical assessment of post-development theory', *The European Journal of Development Research*, 11 (1): 30–55.

Lehmann, D. (1997) 'An opportunity lost: Escobar's deconstruction of development', *Journal of Development Studies*, 33 (4): 568–78.

Little, P. and Painter, M. (1995) 'Discourse, politics, and the development process: reflections on Escobar's *Anthropology and the Development Encounter*', *American Ethnologist*, 22 (3): 602–16.

Neumann, R. (1998) *Imposing Wilderness: Struggles over Livelihood and Nature Preservation in Africa.* Berkeley: University of California Press.

Olivier de Sardan, J-P. (2005) *Anthropology and Development: Understanding Contemporary Social Change.* London: Zed Books (original in French 1995).

Peet, R. and Hartwick, E. (1999) *Theories of Development.* New York: Guilford Press.

Peet, R. and Watts, M.J. (eds) (2004) *Liberation Ecologies: Environment, Development, Social Movements.* London: Routledge.

Pieterse, J.N. (1998) 'My paradigm or yours? Alternative development, post-development and reflexive development', *Development and Change*, 29: 343–73.

Rahnema, M. with Bawtree, V. (1997) *The Post-Development Reader.* London: Zed Books.

Robbins, P. (2001) 'Tracking invasive land covers in India or why our landscapes have never been modern', *Annals of the Association of American Geographers*, 91 (4): 637–54.

Rocheleau, D. (1999) 'Comments on Escobar', *Current Anthropology*, 40 (1): 22–3.

Rocheleau, D., Ross, L., Morrobel, J., Malaret, L., Hernandez, L. and Kominiak, T. (2001) 'Complex communities and emergent ecologies in the regional agroforest of Zambrana-Chacuey, Dominican Republic', *Ecumene*, 8 (4): 465–92.

Said, E. (1978) *Orientalism.* New York: Pantheon Books.

Sen J., Anand, A., Escobar, A. and Waterman, P. (eds) (2004) *The World Social Forum: Challenging Empires.* Delhi: Viveka.

Slater, D. (1993) 'The geopolitical imagination and the enframing of development theory', *Transactions of the Institute of British Geographers*, 18: 419–437.

Stone, G.D. (2002) 'Both sides now: fallacies in the genetic-modification wars, implications for developing countries and anthropological perspectives', *Current Anthropology*, 43 (5): 611–30.

Sundberg, J. (1998) 'Strategies for authenticity, space and place in the Maya Biosphere Reserve, Petén, Guatemala', *Conference of Latin Americanist Geographers' Yearbook*, 24: 85–96.

Simon Batterbury, University of Melbourne and Jude L. Fernando, Clark University

21　Michel Foucault

BIOGRAPHICAL DETAILS AND THEORETICAL CONTEXT

Born in Poitiers, France (1926), Michel Foucault started his education inauspiciously in local state schools where his achievements apparently left his father less than satisfied. However, spurred on by the promise that learning philosophy would reveal 'the secret of secrets' (Sheridan, 1980: 2), he did well at the Catholic school to which he was removed, passing his *baccalauréat* with credit. Securing a place at the highly prestigious École Normale Supérieure (ENS), Paris, he took his *licence de philosophie* in 1948, but quickly became disillusioned that philosophy could not, after all, reveal 'the secret of secrets'. He turned instead to psychology, taking his *licence de psychologie* in 1952 and commencing research on psycho-pathology.

The 1950s–1960s were a heady period in French intellectual and political circles, with challenges to Marxism and structuralism from various strains of existentialism and phenomenology, and certain trajectories – to do with the struggles between 'determinism' and 'freedom' – were to influence Foucault's intellectual development. Seriously reconfiguring his approach to philosophy, psychology and,

indeed, science, while wandering between jobs on the fringes of academia, Foucault eventually completed a doctoral thesis in 1959 and returned to the corridors of the academy. Two years later his first major book, *Histoire de la Folie*, appeared. In the early-1960s he returned to the ENS as Professor of Systems of Thought, an awkward term that he selected, a position that he held for many years alongside visiting professorships to institutions elsewhere. In the process he was 'globalised' as his ideas began to reach many different audiences and destinations, bequeathing a 'Foucauldian' (or 'Foucaultian') approach to social inquiry that ultimately led him to be fêted as one of the leading intellectuals of the twentieth century. He died prematurely in 1984, but having already contributed enough for Sheridan (1980: 225–6) to conclude that: 'It is difficult to conceive of any thinker having in the last quarter of our century the influence that Nietzsche exerted over its first quarter. Yet Foucault's achievement so far makes him a more likely candidate than any other.'

Foucault's reputation reflected a series of powerful theoretical interventions that problematised the production of knowledge. When asked to write a preface to the second unabridged version of his *Histoire de la Folie* (Foucault, 1972a), Foucault remarked upon the mass of 'doubles' that were by then 'swarming' around the original text. By this, he meant the many commentaries and criticisms which effectively eased the text from the grip of its author, providing it with a 'life' of its own in relation to which Foucault – who had once laboured so hard in its writing – had largely ceased to matter. Consistent with Foucault's broader intellectual position, wherein writers of all sorts were viewed as occupying predetermined 'speaking positions' rather than being conduits of peculiar inspiration, he accorded himself no special privilege in the production of his own writings. In other words, he did not suppose that he himself was the key with which to unlock the meanings of his work, and certainly did not reckon his writings to be reducible to him and his intellectual lineage. Elsewhere, in an introduction to the English edition of *The Archaeology of Knowledge*, he insisted 'do not ask me who I am and do not ask me to remain the same' (Foucault, 1972b: 17). He then added in a memorable line, 'leave it to our bureaucrats and our police to see that our papers are in order' (Foucault, 1972b: 17).

The suggestion is that he objected to intellectual 'bureaucrats and police' who wanted to nail down exactly what kind of academic he embodied. Therefore, he might be suspicious of a book such as this, wondering if it tries to pigeon-hole intellectuals in too straightforward a fashion, ossifying them as the necessary 'partners' of particular ideas from which they are not allowed to depart. Yet, if the *Histoire* preface downplays the author's role, this moment in the *Archaeology* introduction plays it up, since Foucault as the moving locus of creative thought – a maverick thinker wishing to evade the shackles of conventional reasoning – now appears to be lent an agency, indeed a significance, rendering his ideas more than just his past texts and their batteries of critical commentary. In this respect, Foucault

was apparently inviting us to take him seriously for himself, not for what the 'bureaucrats and police' might say. Putting things in this way might prompt a more favourable response from him to the notion of a book in which he is a 'key thinker'.

Emphasising these different stances strikes at the deeper interpretative tensions regarding discipline and liberty that go to the heart of much, if not all, of Foucault's endeavour. On the one hand, the author who is relatively unimportant in him- or herself, whose words are determined by forces from outside, equates with the broader focus in much of Foucault's work on how human subjects are 'produced': on how their characters, beliefs and conducts are profoundly shaped by the social and institutional settings in which they find themselves, turning them into thoroughly 'disciplined' citizens with little capacity for independent action. In this guise, Foucault appears as a pessimistic theorist, one who can readily explain why the existing orders of society are commonly reproduced, complete with the in-built inequalities that such orders often entail. 'In Foucault country', writes **Thrift** (2000: 269), 'it always seems to be raining.' Yet, the author who appears to have the opportunity to shift positions equates with a second focus on the possibilities opening up to the human subject who is 'self-produced': to individuals who just occasionally can seize a fragment of liberty to imagine and accomplish things differently, to mobilise the techniques for presenting and achieving in a 'style' differing from that of contemporaries, to pursue 'the art of a life'.

Foucault's first four major texts are usually cast as his *archaeologies*, excavating the 'discourses' (or organised bodies of knowledge) that emerged within European history as the foundations for both intellectual orthodoxy and practical endeavour. *Histoire de la Folie* (1961; translated as *Madness and Civilization*, 1965) and *Naissance de la Clinic* (1963; translated as *The Birth of the Clinic*, 1973) probed the discourses present within prevailing understandings of mental ill-health ('madness') and physical illness, revealing how these gave rise to the 'invention' of both the mental hospital ('asylum') and the modern hospital. *Les Mots et les Choses* (1966; translated as *The Order of Things*, 1970) interrogated the wider discursive formations (or *épistèmes*) present within European conceptions of language, economics and nature, laying bare subtle transitions in the scaffolding of what Europeans have taken as the root 'order' of the world (the supposed links between 'words' and 'things'). *L'Archéologie du Savoir* (1969; translated as *The Archaeology of Knowledge*, 1972b) reflected still more broadly on the making of knowledge – the text was more a topical investigation of 'what is knowledge?' than a methodological treatise on 'how to produce knowledge?' – and in so doing examined the conjoint temporality and spatiality of statements, discourses and their ordering in the 'archive'. Such texts betrayed the influence of structuralism, notably in the sense that human subjects appear to be 'spoken' by discourses rather than vice versa, but by now – and in line with his realisation that there was no 'secret of secrets' – Foucault's quest was not for the deeper truths of discourse, nor for the underlying logic of how they mutate, but merely to 'map' their eruption and effects within different phases of European history.

Foucault's next four major texts are usually cast as his *genealogies*, wherein he decided that the real 'object' of his inquiries was less discourse or knowledge and more the mechanics of power, in which case his earlier archaeologies also became

available for re-reading as more critical offerings charting how order (conceptual and substantive) arises and is maintained in the human realm. *Surveiller et Punir* (1975; translated as *Discipline and Punish*, 1976) ostensibly traced the spread of prisons and reformatories throughout later- eighteenth- and nineteenth-century Europe, but also interrogated the transition from an older regime of violent 'sovereign power' (whereby monarchies terrorised their populaces into obedience through the bloody spectacle of the scaffold) to a modern calculus of 'disciplinary power' as less an absolute possession and more a subtle – but ultimately more effective – relational play of forces between the state and its subjects. Foucault argued that the occupants of identifiable spaces (whether closed institutions or national territories) were quietly disciplined as 'docile minds and bodies' compliant with the demands of capital accumulation and civic responsibility.

The next three books in the 'sexuality' series – translated as *The History of Sexuality Volume One: An Introduction* (1978), *The History of Sexuality Volume Two: The Uses of Pleasure* (1985) *and The History of Sexuality Volume Three: The Care of the Self* (1986a) – furnished 'chapters' within a projected larger survey of how Europe has 'produced' notions of sexuality, of sexual conduct both accepted and shunned, from ancient times through to the present. Foucault demonstrated that these notions have never been fixed, but rather have differed according to the status, class, gender, age and place of the peoples concerned, and have been converted into the objects of discourse (in everything from self-help manuals to confessional whisperings) wherein the possibilities for sexual expression have been curtailed on many occasions but enlarged on others. If *Discipline and Punish* emphasised the shaping of human subjects from without, through anonymous forces inserting individuals into disciplinary apparatuses of one kind or another, *The History of Sexuality* mingled this focus with a sense of how individuals could be more knowingly, wittingly even, enlisted into their own self-fashioning not just as sexual beings but as agents consciously monitoring their overall conduct (and who appreciated the rules governing 'the (wider) conduct of conduct'). The tensions between discipline and liberty can hence be witnessed in the distinction between *Discipline and Punish* and parts of *The History of Sexuality*, a point to which we must return because there are also different geographies to be spied in the gaps between discipline and liberty.

SPATIAL CONTRIBUTIONS

It is increasingly argued that Foucault's contribution to social thought amounts to a thoroughly geographical provocation, in that he demands sustained alertness to questions of space, place, environment and landscape in a manner rarely encountered from someone who is not a professional geographer (Crampton and Elden, 2007). Indeed, Elden (2001) explicitly characterises Foucault as a practitioner of a 'spatial history', setting him in an intellectual heritage encompassing Heidegger, Nietzsche and Hölderlin, and concluding that:

> Foucault's historical studies are spatial through and through, and that this is a fundamental legacy of his work to those interested in the question of space ... Understanding how space is fundamental to the use of power and to historical research into the exercise of power allows us to recast Foucault's work not just as a history of the present but as a mapping of the present.
>
> (Elden, 2001: 152)

It is important to stress that Foucault used historical research – converting it into what Dean (1994) calls 'critical and effective histories' – as a means to understand how 'we' have arrived at where 'we' are today (in short, how modernity has been shaped, complete with all of its tangled inequalities). By teasing out how space 'works' in history, tracing the spatial configurations that expose how power and knowledge operate in countless (mal) treatments of 'the unloved', he was seemingly able to throw into relief, to 'map', many of the more questionable contours of the present.

Most abstractly, Foucault advanced a fierce critique of what he referred to as the project of *total history*: 'one that seeks to reconstitute the overall form of a civilization, the principle – material or spiritual – of a society, the significance common to all the phenomena of a period, the law that accounts for their cohesion – what is called metaphorically the "face" of a period' (Foucault, 1972b: 9). Such a project was anathema to Foucault, since its ambitions stand squarely in opposition to his own belief that 'nothing is fundamental: this is what is interesting in the analysis of society' (Foucault, 1972b: 16). As an alternative he advocated a *general history*, a 'bellicose history' (Lemert and Gillan, 1982: 39), which militates against the tidying up of the past to give neat patterns, steadfastly resisting the rush from the countless small details of lived struggle to the grander pronouncements of historians (particularly those of social scientists dabbling in the practice of history). Foucault thereby drew this distinction: 'a total description draws all phenomena around a single centre – a principle, a meaning, a spirit, a world-view, an overall shape; a general history, on the other hand, would deploy the space of a dispersion' (Foucault, 1972b: 10). These comments about 'spaces of dispersion' appeared to envisage a spa-tialised ontology of the social world: a vision of a space or plane across which all of the events and phenomena relevant to the substantive inquiry are 'dispersed' (see Philo, 1992).

Foucault's own histories were spatial not solely in the philosophical sense of offering an a priori spatialised concep-tualisation of worldly phenomena, nor because they offered an overview of changing conceptions of space (although a history of space in this guise does flicker through his famous 1967 lecture 'On other spaces': see Foucault, 1986b); instead, Elden (2001: 118) argues that Foucault's 'histories are not merely ones in which space is yet another area ana-lysed, but have space as a central part of the approach itself', meaning that 'rather than merely writing histories of space, Foucault is writing spatial histories'. In one regard, this was simply because of the insistence on bringing details of past phenomena to the fore, as he acknowl-edged when borrowing from Nietzsche's notion of 'genealogy' as 'grey, meticulous and patiently documentary':

> [It] requires patience and a knowledge of details [my emphasis], and it depends upon a vast accumulation of source mate-rial. Its 'cyclopean monuments' are con-structed from 'discreet and apparently insignificant truths and according to a rig-orous method'; they cannot be the prod-uct of 'large and well-meaning errors'.
>
> (Foucault, 1986c: 76–7)

Hutcheon duly talks about Foucault's 'assault on all the centralising forces of unity and continuity', and on his requirement – using terms that should immediately arrest

the geographer – that 'the particular, the local and the specific' be pursued in place of 'the general, the universal and the eternal' (Hutcheon, 1988: 120). Whilst no straightforward empiricist, it remains the case that taking seriously particularity, specificity and locality was fundamental to Foucault's notion of 'spaces of disper-sion', with his spatial histories furnishing systematic insights into the play of spatial relations in the historical record (as can now be further elaborated).

KEY ADVANCES AND CONTROVERSIES

In *The Order of Things*, Foucault sug-gested an opposition between 'the Same' and 'the Other' (Philo, 1986) that framed many of his major historical studies. Firstly, he identified his inquiries into dis-course and knowledge as reconstructions of what it is that a given society takes as the Same, incorporating both the leading statements of 'experts' (academics, politi-cians, moralists) and the taken-for-granted assumptions figuring the everyday lives of the populace. Secondly, he effectively identified his social histories of 'the mad, the sad and the bad' as reconstructions of what it is that a given society regards as the Other, as the unacceptable mass of activities, people and places beyond the boundaries of what is deemed as 'nor-mal' and which thereby necessitate some response of policing, removal or even eradication:

> Ostensibly, [Foucault's] project is to de-scribe the mechanisms of order and exclu-sion that have operated within European society since the sixteenth century, and

above all since the late-eighteenth century. In a motif that recalls Bataille's reflections on Hegel, Foucault sees a conflict in history against which it can define itself, just as every 'master' needs a 'slave'. When such an 'Other' is absent, it must be invented.

(Megill, 1985: 192)

For Foucault, madness, sickness and criminality, as well as sexual dissidence, were hence traced historically in their Otherness to European norms, laying out the shifting bases for their constitution as oft-feared moments of alterity.

In this respect *Madness and Civilisation* examined how 'Reason' (or the Same) has progressively identified, named, stigmatised and sought to exclude 'Unreason' (or the Other). It is telling to repeat the assessment that Serres offers of this text, since he 'interprets Foucault's categories of inclusion and exclusion in terms of spatial relationships, and ... views Foucault's concept of Unreason as a "geometry of negativities"'(Major-Poetzl, 1983: 120). Such a geometry embraces projections in which society imaginatively positions itself over and against those phenomena – especially peoples reckoned less-than-human in their madness, sickness, criminality and so on – that are supposed to transgress the limits of the sanctioned. Yet, beyond these projections, and paralleling the spatialised vocabulary deployed when charting what occurred at 'the level of the imaginary' it is also true that Foucault's spatial sensibility transferred to 'the level of the real' (Elden, 2001: 93). Thus, he was clearly interested in 'the physical divide of segregation and exclusion' that distances the Other from the Same, and for this reason he ended up 'conceiv[ing] of madness and reason, sickness and health in spatial terms, and then examin[ing] the groups that inhabit these liminal areas' (Elden, 2001: 94–5). He thereby paid repeated attention to

specific 'liminal areas', notably the bricks-and-mortar solutions of institutions such as asylums, hospitals and prisons (see also Philo, 2000; 2002; 2003) designed to confine, to 'reform' and, where appropriate, to 'cure' those displaying signs of such difference.

Cross-cutting these spatial histories are different conceptualisations of power, themselves the basis for a profound theorisation of space and power (or power/knowledge: Gordon, 1980). Most abstractly, Foucault (1976: 215) insisted that power be understood through its 'micro-physics' – 'its techniques, procedures, levels of applications, targets' – and hence in a thoroughly relational fashion that subsequent theorists have readily elaborated in terms of 'capillaries', 'transmissions' and 'relays' of power through specific spatial fields (Driver, 1985, 1993; Hannah, 1997). More empirically, Foucault (1976: 141–9) analysed 'the art of distributions' underlying a host of nineteenth-century disciplinary mechanisms, tracing the enactment of spatial innovations across all manner of institutions from Bentham's design for an ideal prison, the high-walled 'Panopticon', to the example of an unwalled reformatory at Mettray. There is a danger that many readings of *Discipline and Punish* reduce Foucault's claims to the figure of the Panopticon, failing to register the significance of his arguments about Mettray (Driver, 1990), but it remains the case that the Panopticon has now become a dramatic spatial provocation for social theorists of power. With its internal spatial arrangements allowing a constant (threat of) inspection, a surveillance that captures inmates in an overall field of visibility while prompting them to convert the external eye of the inspection tower into the internal eye of conscience (Bender, 1987), it is unsurprising that many have found here keys to unlock the broader workings of disciplinary power throughout modernity.

Leading out of *Discipline and Punish*, Foucault subsequently developed the notion of 'governmentality' (Foucault, 1979), encompassing both the government of populations, wherein states and religions seek to control the processes of life, birth and death, and the government of individuals, especially in their everyday sexual and reproductive conduct. As Dean (1994: 174) explains, governmentality 'defines a novel thought-space across the domains of ethics and politics, of what might be termed "practices of the self" and "practices of government", that weaves them together without a reduction of the one to the other.' As when describing his later genealogies, Foucault became increasingly concerned with questions surrounding 'the conduct of conduct', reconstructing past codes of conduct, notably sexual and political codes, whose effects have inevitably been ones of power (in the sense of laying down the conditions for the successful exercise of power across different domains of human endeavour). The emphasis hence alighted upon individuals who regard themselves to be free or at liberty, as opposed to the inmates of institutions who know themselves to be shut away, although the typical Foucauldian twist was to assert that liberty is itself ultimately a discursive effect, a product of a particular power/ knowledge nexus, rather than some true social state. This being said, Foucault did appear to grant the human subject more wiggle-room than before, offering the fleeting possibility, as hinted earlier, of the individual being something other than a mere drone of a pre-existing order. While he said less about space in this later thinking on power, a spatial sensitivity continued to bubble under the surface in what he said about countless specific sites – from the confessional to the late-Roman

city-state (see Sharp et al., 2000: 16–19) – that become implicated in the persuading of people (or, rather, in people persuading themselves) to take seriously 'the relationship that one ought to have with one's status, one's functions, one's activities, and one's obligations' (Foucault, 1986a: 84).

For one who has been dead for over 20 years, Foucault continues to be remarkably productive. Countless interviews, magazine articles and examples of his utterances have found their way into print over the intervening years; the first major text, *Histoire de la Folie*, now has an unabridged re-translation (*The History of Madness*, 2007); and, most important of all, his lecture courses given at the Collège de France from 1971 to 1982 are currently in the process of being reconstructed – from lecture notes and tapes – and then published first in French and subsequently in English. The latter are remarkable documents, in part containing Foucault's 'trial runs' of materials later appearing in his major books, but also offering a substantial body of both substantive history and theoretical labour that is really quite distinct from what has previously appeared. They reveal more continuity between his archaeologies and genealogies than has commonly been appreciated, not least when recovering 'subjugated local discursivities' as a resource for contestations of power (which also starts to answer critics who have queried where exactly 'resistance' lies in Foucault's *oeuvre*). These lectures also greatly enlarge our understanding of what he meant by the constructs of 'biopower' and 'biopolitics' as forms of power playing out around questions of who should 'live and die', where and when, under what regimes of supposedly 'expert' truth-telling and through what precise mechanisms of intervention in matters of national, racial and class 'hygiene'. At the same time, the sharp historico-conceptual lines drawn in the prior published work between 'sovereign' and 'disciplinary power' have become blurred, and instead we learn about multiple series of powers – now including species of 'pastoral' and 'biopower' – articulating, accommodating and being a(nta)gonistic in varying forms and spaces, from ancient Greece and Rome through to more recent (neo)liberal states. In short, there *is* arguably now a 'new' Foucault for academics to contemplate and a host of exciting new Foucauldian geographies to discern.

FOUCAULT'S KEY WORKS

Foucault, M. (1965) *Madness and Civilization: A History of Insanity in the Age of Reason.* New York: Random House.

Foucault, M. (1970) *The Order of Things: An Archaeology of the Human Sciences.* London: Tavistock Publications.

Foucault, M. (1972b) *The Archaeology of Knowledge.* London: Tavistock Publications.

Foucault, M. (1973) *The Birth of the Clinic: An Archaeology of Medical Perception.* London: Tavistock Publications.

Foucault, M. (1976) *Discipline and Punish: The Birth of the Prison.* London: Allen Lane.

Foucault, M. (1978) *The History of Sexuality, Volume 1: An Introduction.* New York: Random House.

Foucault, M. (1985) *The History of Sexuality, Volume 2: The Uses of Pleasure.* Harmondsworth: Penguin.

Foucault, M. (1986a) *The History of Sexuality, Volume 3: The Care of the Self.* Harmondsworth: Penguin.

Foucault, M. (2003–2008) English translations of the Collège de France lectures: currently available are *Psychiatric Power* (1973–1974), *Abnormal* (1974–1975), *Society Must be Defended* (1975–1976), *Security, Territory and Population* (1977–1978), *The Birth of Biopolitics* (1978–1979), and *The Hermeneutics of the Subject* (1981–1982). New York: Picador; London and New York: Verso; and Palgrave Macmillan: Basingstoke and New York.

Secondary Sources and References

Bender, J. (1987) *Imagining the Penitentiary: Fiction and the Architecture of Mind in Eighteenth-Century England.* Chicago: University of Chicago Press.

Crampton, J.W. and Elden, S. (eds) (2007) *Space, Knowledge and Power: Foucault and Geography.* Aldershot: Ashgate.

Dean, M. (1994) *Critical and Effective Histories: Foucault's Methods and Historical Sociology.* London: Routledge.

Driver, F. (1985) 'Power, space and the body: a critical assessment of *Discipline and Punish*', *Environment and Planning D: Society and Space,* 3: 425–46.

Driver, F. (1990) 'Discipline without frontiers? Representations of the Mettray Reformatory Colony in Britain, 1840–1880', *Journal of Historical Sociology,* 3: 272–93.

Driver, F. (1993) 'Bodies in space: Foucault's account of disciplinary power', in C. Jones and R. Porter (eds), *Reassessing Foucault: Power, Medicine and the Body.* London: Routledge. pp. 113–31.

Elden, S. (2001) *Mapping the Present: Heidegger, Foucault and the Project of a Spatial History.* London: Continuum.

Foucault, M. (1972a) *Histoire de la Folie à l'Age Classique* (2nd edition). Paris: Gallimard.

Foucault, M. (1979) 'Governmentality', *Ideology and Consciousness,* 6: 5–21.

Foucault, M. (1986b) 'Of other spaces', *Diacritics,* 16: 22–7.

Foucault, M. (1986c) 'Nietzsche, geneaology, history', in P. Rabinow (ed.), *The Foucault Reader.* Harmondsworth: Penguin. pp. 63–77.

Foucault, M. (2007) *The History of Madness* (Unabridged English re-translation). London: Routledge.

Gordon, C. (ed.) (1980) *Power/Knowledge: Selected Interviews and Other Writings, 1972–1977.* Hemel Hempstead: Harvester Press.

Hannah, M. (1997) 'Space and the structuring of disciplinary power: an interpretive review', *Geografiska Annaler,* 79B: 171–80.

Hutcheon, L. (1988) *A Poetics of Post-modernism: History, Theory and Fiction.* London: Routledge.

Lemert, C.C. and Gillan, G. (1982) *Michel Foucault: Social Theory as Transgression.* New York: Columbia University Press.

Major-Poetzl, P. (1983) *Michel Foucault's Archaeology of Western Culture: Towards a New Science of History.* Brighton: Harvester Press.

Megill, A. (1985) *Prophets of Extremity: Nietzsche, Heidegger, Foucault, Derrida.* San Francisco: University of California Press.

Philo, C. (1986) '"The Same and the Other": on geographies, madness and outsiders', University of Loughborough, Department of Geography, Occasional Paper No.11.

Philo, C. (1992) 'Foucault's geography', *Environment and Planning D: Society and Space,* 10: 137–62.

Philo, C. (2000) '*The Birth of the Clinic:* an unknown work of medical geography', *Area,* 32: 11–19.

Philo, C. (2002) 'Accumulating populations: bodies, spaces, institutions', *International Journal of Population Geography,* 7: 473–90.

Philo, C. (2003) *The Space Reserved for Insanity: An Historical Geography of the Mad-Business in England and Wales to the 1860s.* Lampeter: Edwin Mellen Press.

Sharp, J.P., Routledge, P., Philo, C. and Paddison, R. (2000) 'Entanglements of power: geographies of domination/resistance', in J.P. Sharp, P. Routledge, C. Philo and R. Paddison (eds), *Entanglements of Power: Geographies of Domination/Resistance.* London: Routledge. pp. 1–42.

Sheridan, A. (1980) *Michel Foucault: The Will to Truth.* London: Tavistock Press.

Thrift, N. (2000) 'Entanglements of power: shadows?', in J.P. Sharp, P. Routledge, C. Philo and R. Paddison (eds), *Entanglements of Power: Geographies of Domination/Resistance.* London: Routledge. pp. 269–78.

Chris Philo, University of Glasgow

22   J.K. Gibson-Graham

BIOGRAPHICAL DETAILS AND THEORETICAL CONTEXT

J.K. Gibson-Graham is an academic pseudonym shared by two feminist economic geographers – Katherine Gibson and Julie Graham. They first met at graduate school in the mid-1970s when they both accepted places at Clark University in Worcester, Massachusetts. Katherine Gibson is an Australian who moved to the US for doctoral study following a geography undergraduate degree from the University of Sydney, and a brief period of postgraduate study in community development at Macquarie University (also in Sydney). Julie Graham was an American whose intellectual grounding involved an English literature degree from Smith College (Massachusetts) followed by several years of freelance writing, editing and researching. Gibson has previously spoken about the shift to Clark; her intellectual pleasure on discovering the rigours of Marxian political economy, but perhaps even more importantly her meeting, and subsequent friendship, with Julie Graham in her 'beatup yellow Volkswagen' and its lasting professional and personal impact (Gibson, 1999).

From this early friendship developed an intellectual camaraderie which gave rise to one of geography's longest-standing and most intellectually influential collaborations. Both Gibson and Graham wrote doctoral theses that involved rigorous theoretical engagements with Marxian political economy and substantive empirical engagements with processes of economic and industrial restructuring in Australia and the United States respectively. In the early 1980s, following completion of these projects, they took up academic positions in economic geography in their own countries, with Katherine Gibson taking up a postdoctoral fellowship at Australian National University before moving to Geography at the University of Sydney, to Geography and Women's Studies at Monash, to Geography at the Australian National University in Canberra, and later becoming Professorial Fellow at the Centre for Citizenship and Public Policy at the University of Western Sydney. Julie Graham, on the other hand, moved to the University of Massachusetts, Amherst, subsequently becoming Professor and Associate Head of the Department of Geosciences there, and remaining until her death in 2010 at the age of 65.

Despite the substantial physical distance between the two scholars, their ongoing engagement with political economy, increasingly adventurous theoretical experimentation, and robust intellectual engagements with each other continued unabated over more than three decades. As they themselves explain; 'From the theory sluts of 1996 to the self-help junkies of 2006 we have navigated a personal path that ever enriches as new challenges of relating and thinking/writing together arise' (Gibson-Graham, 2006: xi). Their collaboration spanned both the Pacific Ocean and time differences of 14–16 hours; perhaps easier to imagine in the days of e-mail and skype than in earlier days when maintaining this level of commitment required expensive international phone calls and infrequent intercontinental visits, occasionally refreshed by intensive writing retreats (preferably on islands!). The result of these efforts was a theoretically-sophisticated feminist post-structuralist economic geography that has transformed debates both within and well beyond the discipline. Their collaboration generated an influential publication record, as well as being at the heart of a series of important engagements with a broader network of colleagues inside the University and beyond, and in a growing number of countries.

In early publications Gibson and Graham developed their individual and collective interests in Marxian political economy. Plans for a co-written book, that also involved their respective collaborators Ron Horvath and Don Shakow, were never fully realised but did give rise to a series of articles that pushed for a geographically-sensitive historical materialist account of economic transition (see, amongst others, Shakow and Graham, 1983; Gibson and Horvath, 1983; Graham et al., 1989). The first co-authored Gibson and Graham (as opposed to Gibson-Graham) article was also a Marxian theoretical intervention that developed their theory of economic restructuring to include new forms of international contract labour migration (Gibson and Graham, 1986). Further signs of wider intellectual engagements

came when Graham published an early article on postmodernism and Marxism (Graham 1988) now widely considered a disciplinary classic, and Gibson (1991) began to explicitly engage with debates around what we would now call 'positionality' by stressing the intellectual distinctiveness of 'northern and 'southern' Marxist geography and the need to take into account the empirical specificity of the Australian social formation when theorising economic change.

By the late 1980s it seemed that the appeal of structural Marxian analysis ('clear, complex and promising ... to those of us who, in the early 1970s, felt starved of good theory in geography' as Gibson (1991: 76) recollects) had begun to recede. Influenced in part by the anti-essentialist Marxist economists Stephen Resnick and Richard Wolff, who were amongst Graham's new colleagues at Amherst, they began to argue for alternative theorisations of class and capitalism. The single writing persona of Gibson-Graham was born in a dormitory room at a feminist conference at Rutgers University in 1992 (Gibson-Graham, 1996: xi). This gave rise to the first Gibson-Graham co-written article, memorably called 'Waiting for the revolution, or how to smash capitalism while working at home in your spare time', published by the influential Amherst based journal *Rethinking Marxism* (Gibson-Graham, 1993). It was followed by a series of high profile articles published across the discipline that were subsequently rewritten and drawn together in their first pathbreaking book *The End of Capitalism (as We Knew It): A Feminist Critique of Political Economy* (Gibson-Graham, 1996), now on its second edition and published in multiple languages. This was followed by co-edited collections *Class and its Others* (Gibson-Graham et al., 2000) and *Re-presenting Class* (Gibson-Graham et al., 2001) and most recently *A Postcapitalist Politics*

(Gibson-Graham, 2006). Throughout these works, Gibson-Graham move back and forth between the singular and the plural in their writing in order to remind their reader of their composite persona.

SPATIAL CONTRIBUTIONS

J.K. Gibson-Graham was best known in geography for her influential analyses of capitalism. Not content with the usual intellectual targets of geographers such as territory, space and place, Gibson-Graham's ambition was to rethink the economy itself. This is no mean feat. As she observes in the introduction to the second edition of *The End of Capitalism (As We Knew It)* (Gibson-Graham, 1996), the first edition of this book was work-shopped and published at the height of the academic obsession with capitalist globalisation, and offered a profound challenge to accepted forms of Marxism and neo-Marxism that then dominated economic geography. Indeed, as will be apparent from the biography above, Gibson-Graham herself was steeped in these intellectual and disciplinary traditions and this was reflected in an ongoing interest in theorising class in her earliest work as a single writing persona and shaped the approach taken in this first book.

The book set out to challenge theoretical discourses premised on disembodied economic forces, capitalist hegemony, and global homogenisation. Influenced in particular by anti-essentialist approaches to Marxism, the aim was to challenge the essentialism and reductionism of both mainstream and radical economic discourses, and to deconstruct the economy to show that while it is often represented as a 'bounded and unified space with a fixed capitalist identity' (Gibson-Graham, 1996: 12), it is susceptible to other interpretations. She was particularly concerned to challenge 'capitalocentrism' by making visible the multiple capitalist and non-capitalist class processes present within any particular economic formation. Moreover, by contesting the coherence and permanence of capitalism through her theorisation of the economy as a multiplicity of co-existing forms – feudalisms, slaveries, independent commodity production, household production and various forms of capitalism, her work aimed to open up conceptual space not only for multiple readings of the economy but also for a wide range of political struggles.

In retrospect, however, it was perhaps the experimentation with forms of social theory other than anti-essentialist Marxism that was to leave the most lasting impact; in particular her engagements with post-structuralist feminist and queer theory. Here one can see the respective intellectual influences of both Australian feminist theory and US literary theory. These are both scholarly domains that have long been notable for their robust theoretical and political engagements with various strands of post-structural thinking. One result is that Gibson-Graham has done more than almost anyone else to introduce new conceptual approaches to economic geography and economic geographers. This is not simply a matter of the now relatively commonplace tendency to engage with accounts of the economy found beyond the discipline in heterodox areas such as feminist economics, economic anthropology, area studies, economic sociology, and studies of the informal economy. Rather hers was initially primarily a theoretical intervention. In her first book, Irigaray, **Foucault**, **Haraway**, Grosz, Sedgwick and Derrida featured prominently alongside Althusser, Engels and Marx. While some cultural geographers may have been familiar with these theorists, at the time the work of these feminist and post-structuralist scholars was a long way away from the reading lists and intellectual concerns of most economic geographers.

Gibson-Graham also offered her economic geography colleagues broader challenges. In the early work deconstruction was her primary methodological tool, and informed her efforts to shake open the accepted narratives that shaped leftist analysis and politics. But perhaps even more important than these specific theoretical and methodological engagements was the intellectual freedom and creative manner that characterised her work. Whereas Marxism was usually so terribly serious – both in prose and politics – as an explicitly and self-consciously iconoclastic figure Gibson-Graham offered an approach that challenged many academic conventions, including those of clear attribution of authorship, while remaining theoretically rigorous and politically engaged. This was evident in their titles as well as their arguments: 'Stuffed if I Know' (Gibson-Graham, 1994) had a healthy ring of irreverence that many applauded but few would have been brave enough to offer in their published work.

This early work marked the beginnings of a broader intellectual project that has culminated in a larger ambition to produce a language and politics of economic difference. Most immediately, this has involved disrupting hegemonic conceptions of capitalism as a taken-for-granted economic and social descriptor. Even in the early work, which remained engaged with more conventional Marxist economic geographical concerns, there was a clear argument for class identities to be seen as provisional, partial and temporary

solidarities mixed with other determinations. However, in arguing that classes and class processes were never merely economic she has also opened up other arenas that were to become more important as her arguments developed over the years. Looking back now, *The End of Capitalism (as We Knew It)* also made manifest her early interest in the local as an analytical entry point, an ongoing engagement with diverse theories of subjectification, and an active search for new kinds of politics. These were themes that were to become more prominent as her thinking developed through the steady stream of publications that emerged over the next decade.

Just as *The End of Capitalism (as We Knew It)* marked the consolidation of her early work, so *A Postcapitalist Politics* consolidates these later ambitions. Building on the now well-honed Gibson-Graham imperative to look for new ways of thinking and researching, *A Postcapitalist Politics* argues that rather than continuing to reiterate gloomy stories of capitalist exploitation, powerless places and people, and increasing immiseration, economic analysts should cultivate practices of critical thinking that reconceptualise economies as multiple rather than singular, thereby opening up possibilities for new subject positions and novel identifications, and creating new spaces for collective action.

This book challenges its readers – academics and activists alike – to engage with the contemporary economic landscape in ways that foster hope rather than helplessness, connections rather than closure. This conceptual reorientation, she argues, will generate the new political and economic possibilities she calls a postcapitalist politics. It is very explicit about its politics, not only developing a conceptual account of the need for new practices of thinking and new performances of the economy, but also demonstrating what these practices and performances might look like in geographically diverse settings. In doing so, *A Postcapitalist Politics* shows how over the last decade Gibson-Graham has brought her thinking to new audiences well beyond the academy by working to actively cultivate alternative economic subjects and build community economies in the US, Australia, Papua New Guinea and the Philippines (see www.communityeconomies.org).

In the latter years of their collaboration, Gibson-Graham's attention turned to a new intellectual agenda; namely that of developing 'an economic ethics for the Anthropocene' (Gibson-Graham and Roelvink, 2010). This new agenda saw Gibson-Graham extend her ambitions to cultivate new economic and political subjects to include more-than-human actants. She argued the need to expand and multiply the hybrid research collectives who will be the political participants in the context of radical environmental instability and potential climate catastrophe. As always, this is a profoundly challenging call for nothing less than a 'world changing process' but one that begins by recognising that this political process is always already in motion.

KEY ADVANCES AND CONTROVERSIES

Gibson-Graham's conceptualisations of the non-capitalist or alternative economy became an enormously influential approach in economic geography. This was marked by engagements with an extensive network of former students and colleagues – including, amongst others,

Stephen Healy, Jenny Cameron, Kevin St Martin and Gerda Roelvink – many of whom who have also been co-authors on various and diverse Gibson-Graham contributions. Her iceberg diagram – which shows how the formal economy is only the visible tip of a submerged set of economic processes – has travelled all the way from community action research groups in the Pioneer Valley, Massachusetts to the mainstream lecture theatres of Anglo-American geography (Coe et al., 2007). The diverse economies approach is also the basis for an international intellectual community who are identifying and exploring diverse economic spaces (for an overview see Leyshon et al., 2003; Gibson-Graham, 2008). Last, but not least, they brought post-structuralist, feminist and queer theory into the heartlands of economic geography which still remains – both intellectually and socially – something of a 'boy's zone'.

Her influence also extends well beyond the discipline into fields such as cultural studies, anthropology and politics. Whereas initially the ongoing emphasis on Marxian concepts such as, for example, overdetermination and class, proved a sticking point for both those wedded to a more conventional Marxist approach to political economic processes and many of those who were more broadly sympathetic to their arguments for a post-structuralist political economy (see, for diverse examples, Glassman 2003; Kelly 2005; Walters 1999) this is no longer the case. Today Gibson-Graham is acknowledged as having made a 'homegrown' disciplinary contribution to the growing range of heterodox economic approaches, many of the proponents of which she is in conversation with, including science and technology studies, governmentality theory, feminist political economy, and cultural economy. Collectively, these approaches all work to underline the constructedness of the economic rather than seeing it as a pre-given system, base or structure.

Finally, and perhaps most significantly, Gibson-Graham encourages geographers and others to recognise the constitutive power of our analytical approaches, and to understand that we contribute to the creation and performance of the academic worlds that we inhabit. In this context, she argues for three orientations towards thinking, research and politics that we might cultivate in order to better equip ourselves: performative epistemology; an ethical understanding of social determination; and an experimental orientation to research. Nor is this simply rhetoric; it would be remiss of a review such as this not to mention by way of conclusion that Katherine Gibson and Julie Graham 'walk the walk' as well as 'talk the talk'. Both individually and collectively they are generous in spirit and dynamic in style. As the 'pollyannas' of the profession, they remain relentlessly hopeful (though not optimistic) about the possibility of political change. They have promoted a more adventurous approach to reading, writing and researching, and in addition actively supported, mentored and encouraged a generation of more heterodox scholars. In doing so, they lived up to their own desire to make manifest the Gandhian adage of: 'Be the change you wish to see.' Julie Graham's untimely death in 2010 marked the end of a truly unique academic and personal collaboration, one which was widely mourned.

GIBSON-GRAHAM'S KEY WORKS

Gibson-Graham, J.K. (1996) *The End of Capitalism (As We Knew It): A Feminist Critique of Political Economy.* Oxford, UK and Cambridge, MA: Blackwell.

Gibson-Graham, J.K., Resnick, S. and Wolff, R. (eds) (2000) *Class and Its Others.* Minneapolis: University of Minnesota Press.

Gibson-Graham, J.K., Resnick, S. and Wolff, R. (eds) (2001) *Re/presenting Class: Essays in Postmodern Marxism.* Durham, NC and London: Duke University Press.

Gibson-Graham, J.K. (2006) *A Postcapitalist Politics.* Minneapolis: University of Minnesota Press.

Secondary Sources and References

Coe, N., Kelly, P. and Yeung, H. (2007) *Economic Geography: A Contemporary Introduction.* London: Blackwell Publishing.

Gibson, K. (1991) 'Considerations on northern Marxist geography: a review from the antipodes', *Australian Geographer,* 22 (1): 75–81.

Gibson, K. (1999) 'Community economies: economic politics outside the binary frame', Paper presented at the Rethinking Economy Conference, ANU, Australia, August.

Gibson, K. and Graham, J. (1986) 'Situating migrants in theory: the case of Filipino migrant contract construction workers', *Capital and Class,* 29: 130–49.

Gibson, K. and Horvath, R. (1983) 'Global capital and the restructuring crisis in Australian manufacturing', *Economic Geography,* 59 (2): 178–94.

Gibson-Graham, J.K. (1993) 'Waiting for the Revolution, or how to smash capitalism while working at home in your spare time', *Rethinking Marxism,* 6 (2): 10–24.

Gibson-Graham, J.K. (1994) '"Stuffed if I know": reflections on postmodern feminist social research', *Gender, Place and Culture,* 1 (2): 205–24.

Gibson-Graham, J.K. (2008) 'Diverse economies: performative practices for "Other Worlds"', *Progress in Human Geography,* 32 (5): 613–32.

Gibson-Graham, J.K and Roelvink, G. (2010) 'An economic ethics for the Anthropocene', in N. Castree, P. Chatterton, N. Neynen, W. Larner and M. Wright (eds) *The Point is to Change it: Geographies of Hope and Survival in an Age of Crisis.*

Glassman, J. (2003) 'Rethinking overdetermination, structural power, and social change: a critique of Gibson-Graham, Resnick, and Wolff', *Antipode,* 35 (4): 678–98.

Graham, J. (1988) 'Postmodernism and Marxism', *Antipode* 20(1): 60–5.

Graham, J., Gibson, K., Horvath, R. and Shakow, D. (1989) 'Restructuring of U.S. manufacturing: the decline of monopoly capitalism', *Annals of the Association of American Geographers,* 78 (3): 473–90.

Kelly, P. (2005) 'Scale, power and the limits of possibilities: a commentary on J.K. Gibson-Graham's "Surplus possibilities: postdevelopment and community economies"', *Singapore Journal of Tropical Geography,* 26 (1): 39–43.

Leyshon, A., Lee, R. and Williams, C. (2003) *Alternative Economic Spaces.* London: Sage.

Shakow, D. and Graham, J. (1983) 'The impact of the changing international division of labor on the labor force in mature industrial regions', *Antipode,* 15 (2): 18–22.

Walters, W. (1999) 'De-centering the economy', *Economy and Society,* 28 (2): 312–24.

Wendy Larner, Bristol University

23 Anthony Giddens

Arguably the foremost sociologist of the last four decades, Anthony Giddens has enjoyed a long and exceptionally productive career that has made him a scholar of world renown. Born in 1938, he grew up in Edmonton, North London; he was the first person in his family to go to university or college, studying psychology and sociology at the University of Hull and graduating in 1959. Giddens then pursued an MA in Sociology at the London School of Economics and Political Science, completing his doctorate at Cambridge University in 1974. He taught at the University of Leicester from 1961 to 1969, when he became a Lecturer in Sociology at Cambridge, then fellow of King's College from 1970 to 1984, then Reader (1984 to 1986), and finally as Professor in 1987. He co-founded and directed Polity Press in 1985, which published most of his books, as well as serving as Director of the Centre for Social Research from 1989. From 1997 to 2002 he served as Director of the London School of Economics and Political Science (where he remains today as professor). Long active in Labour Party politics, he was an informal advisor to former Prime Minister Tony Blair. In 2004 he was made a peer of the House of Lords. Giddens has also held an extensive variety of visiting professorships around the world and has been the recipient of 13 honorary degrees and awards, including several doctorates and membership of the Russian Academy of Sciences and the Chinese Academy of Social Sciences. His textbook, *Sociology*, now in its sixth edition, has sold almost one million copies. His 41 authored or co-authored books, which have been translated into 30 languages, and 200 journal articles have made him a public intellectual and the subject of extensive critical and biographical commentary (Bryant and Jary, 1997; Cassell, 1993; Cohen, 1991; Held and Thompson, 1989; Mestrovic, 1998; Tucker, 1998; Kaspersen, 2000).

Giddens' early works (1971; 1973; 1979) centred around a critical analysis and reconstitution of traditional European social theory. *New Rules of Sociological Method* (1976) offered a critical translation of European social theory for North American audiences, making Giddens a rare trans-Atlantic intellectual. He argued that orthodox theory, ranging from Durkheim to Marx to Weber, lacked an adequate theory of the subject as a conscious actor possessed of the capacity to choose and to exert power. Rather, actors are often portrayed as unwitting dupes, and social change is erroneously held to occur 'above their heads' or 'behind their backs'. These works both established his credentials as an insightful analyst of social theory and laid the foundations for an original and innovative synthesis.

In the 1980s, Giddens developed and advocated the theory of structuration, a notion that has become widespread and commonplace in post-positivist social sciences. This theme begins with the phenomenological recognition that only human beings are sentient, knowledgeable agents (i.e., they know a great deal about their world, however limited, in order to function within it). Because daily life is a skilled accomplishment, everyone, in this sense, is a 'sociologist'. Giddens drew on his training in psychology and the rich humanistic and behavioural traditions concerned with perception, cognition, language, and identity. Moving beyond common, simplistic definitions of culture as the sum total of learned behaviour or a 'way of life', structuration theory portrays culture as what people take for granted, i.e., common sense, the matrix of ideologies that allow actors to negotiate their way through their everyday worlds. Culture defines what is normal and what is not, what is important and what is not, what is acceptable and what is not, within each social context. Culture is acquired through a lifelong process of socialisation from cradle to grave.

Social structures in structuration theory are seen to consist of the rules and resources that are instantiated in social systems. In their daily lives, actors draw upon these rules and resources, which in turn structure their actions; hence, the structural qualities that generate social action are continually reproduced through these very same actions. The socialisation of the individual and the reproduction of society and place are two sides of the same coin, i.e., the macrostructures of social relations are interlaced with the microstructures of everyday life. People reproduce and change the world, largely unintentionally, in their everyday lives, and in turn, the world reproduces them through socialisation. In forming their biographies, everyday ordinary inhabitants recreate and transform their social worlds, primarily without meaning to do so. In short, individuals are both produced by, and producers of, history and geography. Everyday thought and behaviour hence do not simply mirror the world, they constitute it. History (and geography) is produced through the dynamics of everyday life, the routine interactions and transient encounters through which social formations are reproduced (Giddens, 1984). Such a view dethroned long-standing teleological interpretations (e.g., structural functionalism and structural Marxism) that minimised the capacity of actors to shape their worlds.

Structuration theory jettisons the long-standing schism between micro and macro approaches that long plagued the social sciences; rather, these two dimensions of human life must be seen as mutually complementary. Thus Giddens favours a *duality* between structure and agency, in which they are simultaneously determinant and mutually recursive, rather than a simplistic dualism of opposing forces. Giddens has been widely criticised for his stance that social structures *enable* as well as constrain behaviour: structures are what actors take for granted, reproduce, and change in the *durée* of their daily lives. To view structures simply as constraints, Giddens argued, is to reify them as something other than human products. Marxists in particular were vehement in their condemnation of structuration theory as reincarnated Weberian idealism. Giddens' view of social relations was profoundly important in forcing social science to take seriously the contextual and contingent nature of human consciousness. Social change in this light is neither lawless, in the sense of being anarchical and unpredictable, nor is it so completely subject to laws that the outcomes of action are predictable with confidence; in short, social organisation and change are simultaneously structured and contingent.

Power in all of its complex, multiple forms has long played a central role in Giddens' analysis. He is insistent that as transformative capacity, power is intrinsically tied to human agency: 'Power in this relational sense, concerns the capability of actors to secure outcomes where the realisation of these outcomes depends upon the agency of others' (Giddens, 1986: 93). This view differs from traditional Weberian views that imply power only exists when the resistance of others is overcome. Rather, Giddens maintains that there are two primary structures of domination, including allocative resources (material wealth and technology) and authoritative resources (the social organisation of time, space, and the body). Giddens began his extensive critique of historical materialism in a well-received trilogy of works (1981; 1984; 1987a). These volumes both articulated his vision of social relations and extended their scope. In laying out the theory of structuration in detail, he offered a compelling analysis of how capitalism radically changed the fundamental contours of class relations and culture, extending commodity relations into various spheres of life, dramatically accelerating the tempo of production and reproduction, and marking a decisive break from the past. In pre-capitalist (class-divided) societies, he noted, power was exerted primarily through the state as a mechanism to extract surplus value and implement social control; under capitalism and the private appropriation of wealth (class societies), in contrast, these relations occur through the market, i.e.,

with an apolitical patina in which power lay in the private rather than public domain. Simultaneously, control over time and space, which are central to the exertion of power, shifted from the city-states of Italy to the incipient nation-states of northwestern Europe. *The Constitution of Society* (1984), arguably his best and most explicit summary of structuration theory, emphasises the contingent nature of social life to confront functionalist and evolutionary interpretations of historical change.

In *The Nation-State and Violence* (1987a), Giddens undertook a systematic extension of the nation-state as a 'power-container' for the expression of capitalist social relations. Far from being confined to questions of individual behaviour and everyday life, he applied structuration theory to reveal the historical emergence of the nation-state in the transition from older absolutist regimes with loosely defined boundaries to the commodified relations prevalent under industrial capitalism in which boundaries are rigidly drawn. Thus, the nation-state served as a means for the organisation of surveillance and discipline in the transition from authoritarian to bourgeois democracy and the enforcement of market relations. Within this theme, Giddens explores the roles of nationalism, citizenship, capital punishment, money, and the commodification of time, as well as the intertwined scales of the nation-state and the world-system through military conflict and war.

Subsequently, Giddens' work centred upon issues of modernity (1990; 1991). We are not in a postmodern era, Giddens says, but rather a period of late modernity characterised by the *post-traditional* nature of society. When tradition dominates, individuals rarely have cause to analyse their own actions because choices are already prescribed by their taken-for-granted world. Under the tsunami of modernity, however, traditions become revealed *as tradition*, and lose much of their power. Society becomes much more reflexive and aware of itself, and social practices are not simply taken as given but continually re-assessed in light of new circumstances. Without clear, unquestioned rules for behaviour, issues of self-identity become problematic; lacking clear-cut age, ethnic, gender, and sexual norms that are constantly in rapid flux, individuals are forced to confront themselves and their social worlds consciously. This transition is manifested at various scales ranging from the most private and individual, i.e., from sexuality and intimacy to globalisation (Giddens, 2000a). Modernity is fuelled by the growing extensibility of social relations, their stretching across increasingly global scales, particularly through the use of electronic communications. Indeed, he holds that the disembedding of experience from time and space is the definitive characteristic of modernity: globalised modernity hinges upon interactions with others who are not visibly present, giving rise to a new phenomenology of being. Giddens eschews postmodernity, arguing that the so-called postmodern world is essentially a contemporary extension of distinctly modern capitalism, a view that has earned him the sobriquet 'the last modernist' (Mestrovic, 1998).

In his later work, Giddens popularised the idea of the 'Third Way' (Giddens, 1999; 2000b), which represents a pragmatic renewal of progressive social democracy that seeks to avoid the manifest failures of Marxism and the horrors of neo-liberalism. He maintained that a new social democratic agenda is emerging, and called for a middle ground between the state-directed models of the left and the free-market orthodoxy of the right, neither of which do justice to the complexities responsible for the demonstrated success of social democratic

societies in northern Europe. Far from being rendered irrelevant, government still has an important role to play in the process of globalisation. Ultimately, Third Way politics seeks a more humane world in which the sharp edges of capitalism have been softened.

SPATIAL CONTRIBUTIONS

Giddens' works became highly popular among human geographers during the 1980s, particularly in light of sustained debates between Marxists, many of whom subscribed to structuralist variations, and a broad ensemble of humanist geographers who took as their point of departure (and often destination) human agency disembodied from any social context (cf. Duncan and Ley, 1982). This 'micro–macro' schism, which was far from unique to geography, was effectively resolved through structuration theory. While Giddens' works are primarily concerned with the ontology rather than the epistemology of the social world, structuration theory was nicely complemented by the parallel emergence of critical realism in the field (see entry on **Andrew Sayer**).

Giddens was well received in Geography largely because – rare among social theorists – he takes space seriously. This concern is reflected at several spatial scales. At the level of the individual and everyday life, he is emphatic that the routinised patterns of behaviour through which social reproduction and change occur (mostly unintentionally) are always structured temporally and spatially. In this respect, structuration theory drew heavily upon (and ultimately subsumed) an earlier tradition of time geography, which focused upon the constrained capacities of the human body to negotiate the temporal and spatial trajectories of life (**Hägerstrand**, 1970; **Pred**, 1984). Closely related to this element of structuration theory is his sustained interest in regions and places; Giddens argues (1984) that because social processes unfold contingently over time and space, place *matters*, shaping the trajectory of events over time. Structuration theory essentially enabled social theory to view regions as made, not given, i.e., as contingently produced entities continually in a state of becoming via the actions of human subjects in everyday life. Thus locales are not just passive places but active milieu that influence, and are in turn influenced by, the interactions of actors.

The differential stretching of human activities and relations across greater and lesser amounts of time and space is not only fundamental to the organisation and exertion of power in all its forms, but is itself historically specific and contingent. This process Giddens calls time-space distanciation, a notion very similar to what geographers had called time-space convergence or time-space compression. The very malleability of time and space revealed them to be not 'natural' or external to social relations, but a product (and producer of) those relations, i.e., as human constructions. Time and space are thus as plastic and mutable as the social structures of which they are a part. Time-space distanciation was understandably of great utility to geographers concerned with flows of people, goods, and information (Wilson and Huff, 1994).

Finally, Giddens is as much a geographer as sociologist in his analysis of globalisation (2000a), the expansion of the reach, volume, and velocity of international exchanges that markedly intensified interactions among places. While globalisation is not new, contemporary globalisation essentially represents the extension of modernity on a worldwide stage, a major round of time-space compression driven in large part by the deployment of telecommunications networks. Giddens is emphatic that globalisation is not simply economic in nature, but entails profound political, cultural, and ideological consequences for daily life and individual identity as well. From the standpoint of structuration theory, globalisation is simultaneously humanly produced and a force largely beyond conscious human control. While this process is undoubtedly dramatically reshaping the role of nation-states, Giddens rejects simplistic assertions that globalisation entails the death of this institution. Rather, because globalisation is a contingent and contested enterprise, it is subject to the same sort of reflexivity that characterises all of modernity.

KEY ADVANCES AND CONTROVERSIES

Giddens' works played a major role in advancing and popularising social theory in many social sciences. He drew upon both Marxist and Weberian lines of thought to articulate a coherent, unified vision of social structure and everyday life that included such diverse issues as the phenomenology of everyday life, the emergence of the nation-state, and the dynamics of the world-system. Structuration theory made contingency an integral part of social theory, and Giddens' long-term perspective – encompassing societies ranging from the Neolithic to the postmodern – significantly advanced the understanding of social relations as historically situated and dispelled simplistic notions that equated historical time with inevitable progress.

Giddens' ideas became enormously widespread, popular, and influential. His works played an important role in the formulation of a coherent alternative to both Marxism and humanist geography that emphasised the social construction of space and its contingent reproduction and transformation. Human geographers generally accepted structuration theory, weaving it into the rich stew of ideas that characterises the discipline today: in many respects, structuration theory paved the way for contemporary lines of thought such as actor–network theory.

However, some geographers who drew upon Giddens also criticised his work for an inadequately developed sense of space, including lack of attention to issues of spatial scale; his view of regionalisation, for example, is primitive compared to the multiscalar approaches of renewed regional geography (cf. **Gregory** 1989; **Thrift** 1990). Nigel Thrift criticised Giddens on several grounds, including an unconvincing account of recursivity, an over-emphasis on presence that 'never fully considers the ghost of networked others', an 'impoverished sense of the unconscious', and an inadequately developed theory of culture. Gregson (1989) likewise argued that structuration theory is so vague that it is essentially useless in guiding empirical research, although others maintain it serves as a 'sensitising device' that encourages researchers to take human consciousness and everyday life seriously.

Geographers' work moved beyond Giddens in that they came to view regions as constellations of situated social practices that drew upon and in turn reconstituted changing networks of social relations stretching from the intimately local to the global. Indeed, it is not far-fetched to claim that debates over the social construction of scale – or even its necessity in geography at all – were in no small part inspired by structuration theory's solution to debates between micro versus macro schools of thought. Without his contributions, geography's subsequent engagements with cultural studies, postfoundationalism, critical social theory, actor–network theory, discourse analysis, and similar post-structuralist lines of thought would have been seriously hampered. In this respect, Giddens ultimately and ironically became a victim of his own success.

GIDDENS' KEY WORKS

Giddens, A. (1971) *Capitalism and Modern Social Theory: An Analysis of the Writings of Marx, Durkheim and Max Weber.* Cambridge: Cambridge University Press.

Giddens, A. (1973) *The Class Structure of the Advanced Societies.* London: Hutchinson.

Giddens, A. (1976) *New Rules of Sociological Method: A Positive Critique of Interpretative Sociologies.* London: Hutchinson.

Giddens, A. (1979) *Central Problems in Social Theory: Action, Structure and Contradiction in Social Analysis.* London: Macmillan.

Giddens, A. (1981) *A Contemporary Critique of Historical Materialism.* Berkeley: University of California Press.

Giddens, A. (1984) *The Constitution of Society: Outline of the Theory of Structuration.* Berkeley: University of California Press.

Giddens, A. (1987a) *The Nation-State and Violence.* Berkeley: University of California Press.

Giddens, A. (1990) *The Consequences of Modernity.* Stanford, CA: Stanford University Press.

Giddens, A. (1991) *Modernity and Self-identity: Self and Society in the Late Modern Age.* Stanford, CA: Stanford University Press.

Giddens, A. (1999) *The Third Way: The Renewal of Social Democracy.* Malden, MA: Polity Press.

Giddens, A. (2000a) *Runaway World: How Globalisation is Reshaping Our Lives.* New York: Routledge.

Giddens, A. (ed.) (2001) *The Global Third Way Debate.* Cambridge: Polity Press.

Giddens, A. (ed.) (2003) *The Progressive Manifesto. New Ideas for the Centre-Left.* Cambridge: Polity Press.

Giddens, A. (ed.) (2005) *The New Egalitarianism.* Cambridge: Polity Press.

Giddens, A. (2009) *Sociology* (6th edition). Cambridge: Polity Press.

Secondary Sources and References

Bryant, C. and Jary, D. (1997) *Anthony Giddens: Critical Assessments* (4 volumes). London: Routledge.

Cassell, P. (1993) *The Giddens Reader.* New York: Macmillan.

Cohen, I. (1991) *Structuration Theory: Anthony Giddens and the Constitution of Social Life.* New York: Macmillan.

Duncan, J. and Ley. D. (1982) 'Structural Marxism and human geography', *Annals of the Association of American Geographers,* 72: 30–59.

Giddens, A. (1972) *Politics and Sociology in the Thought of Max Weber.* London: Macmillan.

Giddens, A. (1982) *Profiles and Critiques in Social Theory.* London: Macmillan.

Giddens, A.(ed.) (1986) *Durkheim on Politics and the State.* Cambridge: Polity Press.

Giddens, A. (1987b) *Social Theory and Modern Sociology.* Cambridge: Blackwell.

Giddens, A. (1994) *Beyond Left and Right: The Future of Radical Politics.* Stanford, CA: Stanford University Press.

Giddens, A. (1996) *In Defence of Sociology: Essays, Interpretations, and Rejoinders.* Cambridge: Polity Press.

Giddens, A. (2000b) *The Third Way and its Critics.* Cambridge: Polity Press.

Giddens, A. (2002) *Where Now for New Labour?* Cambridge: Polity Press.

Giddens, A. (2007) *Europe in the Global Age.* Cambridge: Polity Press.

Giddens, A. (2009) *The Politics of Climate Change.* Cambridge: Polity Press.

Giddens, A. and Pierson, C. (1998) *Conversations with Anthony Giddens: Making Sense of Modernity.* Stanford, CA: Stanford University Press.

Gregory, D. (1989) 'Presences and absences: time-space relations and structuration theory', in D. Held and J. Thompson (eds), *Social Theory of Modern Societies: Anthony Giddens and his Critics.* Cambridge: Cambridge University Press. pp. 185–214.

Gregson, N. (1989) 'On the (ir)relevance of structuration theory to empirical research', in D. Held and J. Thompson (eds), *Social Theory of Modern Societies: Anthony Giddens and his Critics.* Cambridge: Cambridge University Press.

Hägerstrand, T. (1970) 'What about people in regional science?' *Papers of the Regional Science Association,* 24: 7–21.

Held, D. and Thompson, J. (1989) *Social Theory of Modern Societies: Anthony Giddens and his Critics.* Cambridge: Cambridge University Press.

Hutton, W. and Giddens, A. (eds) (2000) *Global Capitalism.* New York: New Press.

Kaspersen, L. (2000) *Anthony Giddens: An Introduction to a Social Theorist.* New York: Wiley-Blackwell.

Mestrovic, S. (1998) *Anthony Giddens: The Last Modernist.* London: Routledge.

Pred, A. (1984) 'Place as historically contingent process: structuration and the time-geography of becoming places', *Annals of the Association of American Geographers,* 74: 279–97.

Sayer, A. (1992) *Method in Social Science: A Realist Approach* (2nd edition). London: Routledge.

Thrift, N. (1983) 'On the determination of social action in space and time', *Environment and Planning D: Society and Space,* 1: 23–57.

Thrift, N. (1990) 'For a new regional geography 1', *Progress in Human Geography,* 14: 272–9.

Tucker, K. (1998) *Anthony Giddens and Modern Social Theory.* Boulder: Sage.

Wilson, D. and Huff, J. (eds) (1994) *Marginalized Places and Populations: A Structurationist Agenda.* Westport, CT: Greenwood.

Barney Warf, University of Kansas

24 Reginald Golledge

Reg Golledge was born in Australia in 1937 and passed away in 2009. He completed his BA and MA in geography at the University of New England, Australia before taking up a lectureship in geography at the University of Canterbury, Christchurch in New Zealand. In 1964 he moved to North America, to take up a position as a research assistant at the University of Iowa. Drawing influence from colleagues at Iowa, notably Harold McCarty, and from other geographers such as Julian Wolpert and Peter Gould and psychologist Jean Piaget, Golledge's PhD (1966) combined learning theory and probabilistic modelling to analyse the marketing of hogs. After a year as an Assistant Professor at the University of British Columbia, Vancouver, in 1966 Golledge took up a post at the Ohio State University where he stayed until 1977. It was during his time at Ohio that he rose to prominence as a key proponent of behavioural geography, a perspective that holds to the idea that human activity can only be understood in relation to people's imperfect and partial knowledge of the world.

Always keen to collaborate with academics both within geography and other disciplines, after arriving at Ohio, Golledge started to work with geographers such as Les King, Kevin Cox, Larry Brown and John Rayner, psychologists such as Paul Isaacs and Jim Wise, and mathematicians Joseph Kruskal and Doug Carroll (both at Bell Labs) on issues relating to the modelling of spatial knowledge, and specifically spatial choice and decision-making, a topic that remained a consistent focus for his entire career. His first landmark paper, published with Briggs and Demko (1969), used statistical multidimensional scaling methods to 'map' paired-comparison distance estimates, arguing that the resulting configuration provided a 'mental map' of how the city appears to people (see also entry on **Kevin Lynch**).

Over the next several years, Golledge developed a consistent and coherent theoretical framework to support his view that the best way to understand the geographical world was to understand how people cognised the world around them and made choices and decisions on the basis of such knowledge. This was accompanied by a sustained engagement with cognitive and experimental psychology and the adaptation of quantitative statistical techniques (e.g., nonmetric multidimensional scaling and hierarchical clustering). This emphasis on quantification led to Golledge's work being described as 'analytical' behavioural geography as distinguished from a more phenomenological approach being developed by others (see Saarinen et al., 1984). Nonetheless, Golledge was a key figure in the active promotion of a broad range of behavioural approaches through his writing, as well as through organising conference sessions, taking part in debates, and supporting behavioural work through his editorship of the journals *Geographical Analysis* (1973–78) and *Urban Geography* (1978–84). This work resulted in the highly cited and influential edited collections, *Behavioural Problems in Geography: A Symposium* (1969, edited with Kevin Cox), *Environmental Knowing* (1976, edited with Gary Moore), *Cities, Space and Behaviour* (1978, written with Les King), and *Behavioural Problems in Geography Revisited* (1981, edited with Kevin Cox). While the first of these arguably established behavioural geography as a mainstream approach in human geography, the latter were written at a time when behavioural geography was coming under attack from both humanists and structuralists. Through these works, Golledge thus became one of behavioural geography's staunchest defenders, providing strong rebuttals of critiques of the behavioural perspective (see Golledge, 1981; Couclelis and Golledge, 1983).

In 1977, Golledge moved to the University of California, Santa Barbara, where he remained until his death. Again, quickly building new interdisciplinary links with psychologists, mathematicians and computer scientists he started to build what was to become the Research Unit on Spatial Cognition and Choice, continuing his development of analytical behaviouralism. In 1984 he lost his sight. This impairment which initially seemed to threaten his academic career (Golledge, 1997) instead started a remarkable collaboration with psychologists Jack Loomis and Roberta Klatzky that continued until the time of his death. Over a series of related projects, they applied what had

been Golledge's work to date to issues of visual impairment, seeking, on the one hand, to understand how people with visual impairments come to comprehend spatial relationships and use this knowledge to navigate; and, on the other to apply their findings to the development of orientation and navigation systems. This culminated in a Personal Guidance System, designed by Loomis, that combines the use of global positioning system (GPS) and a Geographic Information System (GIS), and uses a virtual auditory/ sound interface as output.

Continuing his defence and promotion of behavioural approaches, in 1987 Golledge published (with Bob Stimson) *Analytical Behavioural Geography*, updated in 1997 as *Spatial Behaviour: A Geographic Perspective'*, and was active in the National Centre for Geographic Information Analysis (NCGIA), organising and participating in several themes that apply behavioural approaches to GIS. The recipient of many awards and honours, in 1999 Golledge became the President of the Association of American Geographers, using his presidential address to call for a policy-relevant geography underpinned by a behavioural approach (Golledge, 2002).

SPATIAL CONTRIBUTIONS

Golledge's key role in the study of place and space has been his contributions to the development of analytical behavioural geography. Behavioural geography developed throughout the late 1960s and early 1970s out of dissatisfaction with the stereotyped, mechanistic and deterministic nature of many of the quantitative models being developed at that time, and a realisation that not everyone behaved in a spatially rational manner. As such, it was a direct challenge to the perceived, 'peopleless' geographies of spatial science.

Behavioural geographers argued that space is not experienced and understood in a similar manner by all individuals. Instead, it was posited that each individual potentially possesses a unique understanding of their surroundings, and that this understanding is shaped by mental processes of information gathering and organisation (Gold, 1980). Consequently, it was argued that it is misleading to analyse human spatial behaviour in relation to the objective, 'real' environment as people do not conceive of (and experience) space in this way. It was suggested that a more productive approach would be to focus on the way that people act in relation to how they cognise the world around them. Such a focus would explain why human behaviour did not fit the patterns sometimes anticipated in models of spatial science (see entries on **Peter Haggett** and **Brian Berry**). At its core then, behavioural geography is based upon the belief that the explanatory powers and understanding of social scientists can be increased by incorporating behavioural variables, along with others, within a framework that seeks to comprehend and find reasons for overt spatial behaviour, rather than describing the spatial manifestations of behaviour itself (Golledge, 1981).

By the early 1970s, divisions within behavioural geography started to emerge as to how best to theorise and measure spatial behaviour, with on the one hand the development of a phenomenological-humanist approach (exemplified in research by Lowenthal, Seamon and **David Ley**) and on the other an analytical, scientific-positivist approach (of which Golledge was the chief proponent). While both approaches were united in believing that 'we must understand the

ways in which human beings come to understand the geographical world in which they live' and that 'such understanding is best approached from the level of the individual human being' (Downs, 1981), increasingly their alliance fractured, so that by the end of the 1970s they had developed into largely separate ventures (see Saarinen et al., 1984). In the humanist branch of behavioural geography, the search for scientific laws was replaced by an interpretative and reflective search for meaning and how humans come to understand and act in the world. Golledge rejected such conceptualisations, and in particular the subjective and unscientific nature of data collection and analysis. Instead, he advocated an analytical and scientific examination of the thoughts, knowledge and decisions that underpin human action, using questionnaires and adapting measures from cognitive psychology such as perceptual tests and rating scales as a means to measure people's ability to remember, process and evaluate spatial information. The findings from these studies were used to test models of spatial choice and decision-making in relation to issues such as wayfinding, residential location, industrial agglomeration, tourist behaviour, migration, and so on. Here, geographic space is conceptualised as absolute and given (thus knowable and mappable), but analytically it is how this space is cognised that is considered most important.

Golledge's contribution to analytical behavioural geography cannot be underestimated. Over the course of his career he developed a systematic programme of research that consistently sought to deepen and strengthen the theoretical and methodological underpinnings and empirical scope of behavioural geography. So, for example, he engaged in wider ontological and epistemological debates within the discipline of geography, seeking to tighten and advance behaviouralism's theoretical tenets and to promote it to a wider audience. He developed a number of specific theories concerning the development and structuring of spatial knowledge, processes of spatial choice and decision-making (in different contexts – transportation, residential choice), and environmental learning with regard to different populations (adults, children, developmental disabilities, visual impairment, men/women). Some of these theories, such as the anchor-point model of spatial knowledge, have been widely engaged with by cognitive and environmental psychologists (see Couclelis et al., 1987). He pioneered, developed and tested a whole series of behavioural measures and analytical techniques including multidimensional scaling, psychometric testing, sketch maps, distance and direction estimates (see Golledge and Stimson, 1997, for a review), and championed a move away from the (psychology) laboratory to real world environments, challenging psychologists in particular to model spatial behaviour in naturalistic settings. Finally, he sought to apply his research findings to real world issues such as planning, transportation modelling, and, perhaps most successfully, the development of orientation and communication devices for people with visual impairments (notably tactile maps, a personal guidance system, and haptic soundscapes).

KEY ADVANCES AND CONTROVERSIES

While some researchers have used Golledge's ideas to build up a large body of behavioural research (see Golledge and Stimson, 1997), and others have sought to extend his theoretical insights by making explicit links to cognitive science and environmental psychology (see Kitchin and Freundschuh, 2000; Kitchin and Blades, 2001), his work – and behavioural geography more generally – came under a sustained critique from the late 1970s onwards. As a consequence, Cloke et al. (1991) described behavioural geography as a largely forgotten element of human geography. John Gold (1992) identified three reasons why behavioural geography was not fully embraced by the geographic fraternity (especially in the UK). First, due to structural changes in the education sector in the late 1960s early 1970s, young behavioural geographers failed to secure posts and thus a critical mass failed to develop. Second, as social and welfare issues came to the fore during the 1970s as part of a radical geographical project (see **David Harvey**), behavioural geography was perceived to be inappropriate for examining them. Third, the philosophical bases of behavioural geography, particularly of the analytical variety, were heavily criticised by other researchers from different traditions. Indeed, both humanists and structuralists criticised analytical behavioural geography – and thus the approach being advocated by Golledge – for its positivistic allegiances. They argued that instead of offering a viable alternative to the positivistic, spatial science, behavioural geography just shifted emphasis so that many of the criticisms levelled at positivism still applied. As such, Cox (1981) argued that the emergence of behavioural geography was evolutionary rather than revolutionary. Further, both groups criticised analytical behavioural geography for over-emphasising empiricism and methodology at the expense of worthwhile issues and philosophical content (Gold,

1992). For example, Cullen (1976) argued that analytical behavioural geographers borrowed uncritically from the scientific paradigm, which then determined the nature of the problems to be investigated, so that the independent–dependent variable format was over-used. Ley (1981: 211) argued that the allegiance to the scientific paradigm led to a preoccupation with measurement, operational definitions and highly formalised methodology, so that 'subjectivity has been confined to the straitjacket of logical positivism'. As such, Golledge's work was accused of offering an inadequate and mechanistic understanding of human behaviour.

While structuralists critiqued the reduction of human spatial behaviour to cognition, thus failing to take into account the influence of wider social, economic and political factors on people's everyday geography (Cox, 1981), humanistic geographers disputed the dichotomy between subject/object and fact/value and argued that research which accepted these dichotomies would only provide clues to everyday life, failing to 'conceive of life in its wholeness or for that matter of individuals in their wholeness' (Eyles, 1989: 111). They argued that subject and object could not be separated because of the intervening consciousness which imposes its own interpretations upon the objective world and thus affects behaviour (Cox, 1981). Subject/object, fact/value become infused and inseparable and need to be investigated as such, so that the methods used by analytical behavioural geographers are invalid as they assume that the investigator and investigated have the same meanings. Consequently, it was argued that Golledge's theorising ignored the contours of experience and reduced individuals to crude automations (**Thrift**, 1981), systematically detached from the social contexts of their actions, and thus meanings. Ley (1981) further argued that

behavioural geography adopts a naturalist stance that sees no essential discontinuity between people and nature and gives human consciousness little theoretical status.

In addition, Walmsley and Lewis (1993) cautioned that behavioural geographers needed to be aware of the dangers of psychologism, that is, the fallacy of explaining social phenomena purely in terms of the mental characteristics of individuals. By concentrating upon the individual, they noted that behavioural geography is susceptible to the trap of building models inductively, beginning at the level of the individual, so that outcomes can only be treated as the sum of parts (Greenburg, 1984). This is a particularly salient point because one of the main criticisms of behavioural geography has been its one dimensional look at environmental behaviour at the expense of economic, political and social considerations. Indeed, Gold (1992: 240) has argued that the attempt 'to straitjacket *all* areas within a strictly psychological paradigm' is one of the fundamental reasons for the disillusionment with behavioural approaches.

This latter point is well illustrated in critiques of Golledge's (1993) work on disability. While acknowledged as pioneering, the use of behavioural theory to articulate a geography of disability drew fierce criticism from other geographers, notably Brendan Gleeson (1996) and Rob Imrie (1996). They attacked Golledge's vision in relation to his conception of disability, the ontological and epistemological bases of his research, and his lack of ideological intent. In relation to the first, they note that Golledge adopts a medical understanding of disability in which the problems facing disabled people are seen as a function of their impairment (rather than how society treats them). This in turn positions disabled people as subjects within the research, perpetuating the dichotomy between expert researcher and passive research subject. Moreover, it fails to acknowledge the exclusionary practices of society and the role of social, political and economic processes in the reproduction of disabling environments. Thus for Gleeson and Imrie, Golledge's geography of disability falls into the trap of ablism – the reduction of disability to functional limitations and an acceptance that if we can make disabled people more like able-bodied people, their problems will be significantly reduced. Golledge was accused of reducing the problems faced by disabled people to technical issues that can be solved with technical solutions, thus depoliticising the problems disabled people face. This decontextualises disability, placing it outside of the historical and spatial transformations within which modern social relations are embedded. Instead, Gleeson and Imrie suggest a more fruitful

approach is to engage with disabled people in their quest for emancipation by exposing the oppressive structures of society.

Despite widespread criticism, Golledge was fervent in his rebuttals of the perceived shortcomings of analytical behavioural geography (see Golledge, 1981; Couclelis and Golledge, 1983; Golledge, 1996; Golledge and Stimson, 1997) and it is fair to state that behavioural geography continues to be widely practised within human geography, particularly in North America where links with cognitive and environmental psychology have been forged (see Gärling and Golledge, 1993; Golledge, 1999; Kitchin and Freundschuh, 2000; Kitchin and Blades, 2001). That said, it is clearly no longer considered at the cutting edge of geographical theory and praxis, despite the efforts of Golledge to re-inspire a return to its ideas (Golledge, 2002).

GOLLEDGE'S KEY WORKS

Cox, K.R. and Golledge, R.G. (1969) *Behavioural Problems in Geography: A Symposium.* Evanston, IL: Northwestern University Press.

Golledge, R.G., Briggs, R. and Demko, D. (1969) 'The configuration of distances in intraurban space', *Proceedings of Association of American Geographers*, 1: 60–5.

Moore, G.T. and Golledge, R.G. (eds) (1976) *Environmental Knowing.* Stroudsberg: Dowden, Hutchinson and Ross.

Golledge, R.G. and Spector, A.N. (1978) 'Comprehending the urban environment: theory and practice', *Geographical Analysis*, 9: 403–26.

Golledge, R.G. and Stimson, R.J. (1987) *Analytical Behavioural Geography.* London: Croom Helm.

Golledge, R.G. (1993) 'Geography and the disabled: a survey with special reference to vision impaired and blind populations', *Transactions of the Institute of British Geographers*, 18: 63–85.

Golledge, R.G. and Stimson, R.J. (1997) *Spatial Behaviour: A Geographic Perspective.* New York: Guilford Press.

Golledge, R.G. (2002) 'The nature of geographic knowledge', *Annals of the Association of American Geographers*, 92 (1): 1–14.

Secondary Sources and References

Cloke, P., Philo, C. and Sadler, D. (1991) *Approaching Human Geography.* London: Paul Chapman Publishing.

Couclelis, H., Golledge, R.G., Gale, N. and Tobler, W. (1987) 'Exploring the anchor-point hypothesis of spatial cognition', *Journal of Environmental Psychology*, 7: 99–122.

Cox, K.R. (1981) 'Bourgeois thought and the behavioural geography debate', in K.R. Cox and R.G. Golledge (eds), *Behavioural Problems in Geography Revisited.* Evanston, IL: Nortwestern University Press. pp. 256–79.

Cullen, I. (1976) 'Human geography, regional science, and the study of individual behaviour', *Environment and Planning A,* 8: 397–409.

Downs, R.M. (1981) 'Maps and mappings as metaphors for spatial representation', in L.S. Liben, A. Patterson and N. Newcombe (eds), *Spatial Representation and Behaviour Across the Life Span.* New York: Academic Press. pp. 143–66.

Eyles, J. (1989) 'The geography of everyday life', in D. Gregory and R. Walford (eds), *Horizons in Human Geography.* London: Macmillian. pp. 102–17

Gärling, T. and Golledge, R.G. (eds) (1993) *Behaviour and Environment: Psychological and Geographical Approaches.* London: North Holland.

Gleeson, B.J. (1996) 'A geography for disabled people?', *Transactions of the Institute of British Geographers,* 21: 387–96.

Gold, J.R. (1980) *An Introduction to Behavioural Geography.* Oxford: Blackwell.

Gold, J.R. (1992) 'Image and environment: the decline of cognitive-behaviouralism in human geography and grounds for regeneration', *Geoforum,* 23: 239–47.

Golledge, R.G. (1981) 'Misconceptions, misinterpretations, and misrepresentations of behavioural approaches in human geography', *Environment and Planning A,* 13: 1315–44.

Cox, K.R. and Golledge, R.G. (eds) (1981) *Behavioural Problems in Geography. Revisited.* Evanston, IL: Northwestern University Press.

Couclelis, H. and Golledge, R.G. (1983) 'Analytical research, positivism and behavioural geography', *Annals of the Association of American Geographers,* 73: 95–113.

Golledge, R.G. (1996) 'A response to Gleeson and Imrie', *Transactions of the Institute of British Geographers,* 21: 404–10.

Golledge, R.G. (1997) 'On reassembling one's life: overcoming disability in the academic environment', *Environment and Planning D: Society and Space,* 15: 391–409.

Golledge, R.G. (ed.) (1999) *Wayfinding Behaviour: Cognitive Mapping and Other Spatial Processes.* Baltimore: Johns Hopkins University Press.

Greenburg, D. (1984) 'Whodunit? Structure and subjectivity in behavioural geography', in T.F. Saarinen, D. Seamon and J.L. Sell (eds), *Environmental Perception and Behaviour: An Inventory and Prospect.* Research paper 209, Department of Geography, University of Chicago. pp. 68–79.

Imrie, R.F. (1996) 'Ableist geographies, disablist spaces: towards a reconstruction of Golledge's geography and the disabled', *Transactions of the Institute of British Geographers,* 21: 397–403.

King, L. and Golledge, R.G. (1978) *Cities, Space and Behaviour.* Englewood Cliffs, NJ: Prentice Hall.

Kitchin, R.M. and Blades, M. (2001) *The Cognition of Geographic Space.* London: IB Taurus.

Kitchin, R.M. and Freundschuh, S. (eds) (2000) *Cognitive Mapping: Past, Present and Future.* London: Routledge.

Ley, D. (1981) 'Behavioural geography and the philosophies of meaning', in K.R. Cox and R.G. Golledge (eds), *Behavioural Problems in Geography Revisited.* Evanston, IL: Northwestern University Press. pp. 209–30.

Saarinen, T.F., Seamon, D. and Sell, J.L. (eds) (1984) *Environmental Perception and Behavior: An Inventory and Prospect.* Research paper 209, Department of Geography, University of Chicago.

Thrift, N. (1981) 'Behavioural geography', in N. Wrigley and R. Bennett (eds), *Quantitative Geography in Britain.* London: Routledge and Kegan Paul. pp 352–65.

Walmsley, D.J. and Lewis, G. (1993) *People and Environment.* Harlow: Longman.

Rob Kitchin, National University of Ireland, Maynooth

25 Derek Gregory

BIOGRAPHICAL DETAILS AND THEORETICAL CONTEXT

Derek Gregory is one of geography's leading theoreticians. Born in England in 1951, he was raised in Bromley, Kent. He attended a local grammar school and won a scholarship to become a Fellow at Sidney Sussex College, Cambridge, in 1969. He completed his BA, MA, and PhD (1981) at Cambridge University, and worked as a lecturer there from 1981 to 1988. In 1989, he moved to the University of British Columbia in Vancouver, Canada, where he became Distinguished University Scholar and Professor of Geography. He is the recipient of numerous prizes, awards, medals, and honorary degrees. He has also been mentor to a number of highly successful academic geographers, including Felix Driver, Matt Sparke, Alison Blunt, Chris Philo, and Noel Castree.

Since 1976, Gregory has published a series of highly influential and well-received works. His MA thesis, published as *Ideology, Science, and Human Geography* (1978b), has been extensively cited for its elegant critiques of structuralism, positivism, and reflexivity within the discipline. The volume *Recollections of a Revolution* (Billinge et al., 1984) revealed the positivist coup as peopled, i.e., not simply the inevitable triumph of rational logic over empiricism but the product of active human actors embedded in a changing, politicized matrix of academic, personal, and social circumstances. He also offered scathing critiques of traditional location theory (1982b), systems theory (Gregory, 1980), diffusion theory (1985c), and humanistic geography (Gregory, 1981a), the latter of which he criticised as too often preoccupied with the 'casual interrogation of the obvious'.

Simultaneously, Gregory (1989c) played, along with other theorists such as **Nigel Thrift**, an influential role in introducing **Anthony Giddens**' theory of structuration to geographers, a view that resolved the long-standing schism between overly deterministic perspectives that emphasised social structures over individual behaviour on the one hand and idealist views that began, and typically ended, with the consciousness of the mind on the other. Thus, he argued, geographical research, in both historical and contemporary contexts, should seek to recover the thoughts, desires, and meanings of actors, but avoid collapsing its understanding into those same motivations, for social (and spatial) relations forever escape the intentions of their creators. The construction of geographies is thus a 'sensuous swirl of contingency and determination' (Gregory 1982: 246). Structuration theory gradually became a standard part of the core body of theory in human geography and facilitated the rise of more recent schools of post-structuralist thought.

Gregory's early works introduced social theory into historical geography (1976; 1978a), a field then characterised by its stubborn empiricism. Following the footsteps of E.P. Thompson, he was long concerned with class struggle in England during the Industrial Revolution (1978; 1984a). For example, his doctoral dissertation (Gregory, 1982b) applied structuration theory to the Yorkshire woollen industry. Such works led to the unearthing of the origins of modernity, which allowed him to disclose its historically specific nature, despite the claims of Enlightenment science, both positivist and Marxist, to universal applicability. The historicisation of modernity led him to examine its crisis and decline in the contemporary historical era (Gregory, 1991). Although he never self-identified as a postmodernist, Gregory's works nonetheless were instrumental in introducing its primary precepts into the discipline: the distrust of meta-narratives, the sensitivity to difference and multiplicity, and the close relations between knowledge and power.

SPATIAL CONTRIBUTIONS

By the late 1980s, Gregory's contributions had surpassed critiques of existing perspectives to offer important alternatives that viewed geographies not as given but made, i.e., as the products and producers of situated social practices. In 'Solid Geometry' (Gregory 1988a), he took to task structuralist views that hold forth the possibility of considering space, time, and society independently. Spatial structures are much more than the passive manifestations of structural transformations that occur aspatially; rather, Gregory argued, geographies are active participants in the process of social change, and to appreciate their significance the discipline needed a new repertoire of tools ranging from time-geography to the constitutive phenomenology of a reformulated humanism.

Geographical Imaginations (1994a), one of Gregory's most famous works, explored how place and space are theorised across the humanities and social sciences. His argument focused on how seemingly different paradigms reflect particular 'scopic regimes', power/knowledge configurations that appear 'natural' to their subscribers. Western social science, including geography, long subscribed to the notion of a detached, all-knowing, objective observer. Arising during modernity's march to hegemony, this perspective is common to various Marxist and positivist conceptions of space, and confers a particular status, and thus power, to the knower as a rational, presumably male, all-knowing ego. This mythical being, devoid of social context, increasingly questionable in an age of mounting relativism, forms the foundation for the particular epistemological standpoint that Gregory labels the 'world-as-exhibition'. This view was endlessly replicated in various Weberian (both Max and Alfred), empiricist, neo-classical, and instrumentalist conceptions of geographic relations, and denied the inescapable social situatedness of knowledge. Within geography, it was reflected in the triumph of abstract space over lived experience, as manifested in the rigid models of positivism.

However, Gregory maintains, the world-as-exhibition amounts to but one scopic regime among many. Far from being inherently objective, modernity's ocular-centrism is incomplete and situated, and linked to particular power interests. Far from comprising some all-knowing portrait of 'reality as it really is', the world-as-exhibition is thus a quintessentially modern and modernist way of enframing the world, one well suited, not coincidentally, to the historical process of commodifying social life and space. Jettisoning the world-as-exhibition opens the door to new perspectives, including post-colonialism and subalternity, which take seriously marginalised voices and their positionality within the topographies of power. He points to conceptual perspectives that draw upon the experiences of local inhabitants as legitimate sources of meaning. Gregory's work thus helped to pave the way for post-structuralist theorising within geography.

Language for Gregory occupies a pivotal position in the acquisition, interpretation, transmission, and representation of information about peoples, contexts, and places. He became well known for the elegance of his writing, particularly his eloquent phraseology. **Harvey** (1995: 161), for example, notes his 'legendary skills as "phraseur"'. Like the human subjects about whom he writes, and whose moist and pungent worlds he seeks to recover, Gregory's textual strategies are deliberately, self-consciously poetic, and provided a model for other geographers to emulate as they discarded the desiccated and boring language of positivism.

Gregory has also been a co-editor in all five editions of *The Dictionary of Human Geography* (1981; 1986; 1994; 2000; 2009). A series of increasingly voluminous tomes, these works have provided concise but informative summaries of the discipline's essential terminology and concepts, making clear for numerous graduate students (and no doubt faculty) the implications

of words and phrases whose meanings have often been lost in the obscurantist gobbledygook of academics seeking to impress other academics.

KEY ADVANCES AND CONTROVERSIES

Gregory's career has been characterised by a long-standing Foucauldian interest in the mutually constitutive relations between knowledge, power, and space. In the tradition of Western (non-structuralist) Marxism, he portrays social relations and geographies as the contingent (if largely unintended) outcomes of human actors whose networks are structured, but not predetermined, by shifting regimes of power and knowledge.

In the wake of the enormously influential perspective launched by **Edward Said** (1978), Gregory focused on Orientalism as a discourse intimately intertwined with the European conquest of non-Western spaces (Gregory, 1999b). Geography as a way of knowing space – the active 'geo-graphing' of various parts of the globe – was part and parcel of the Western power/knowledge regimes that became hegemonic throughout most of the world during the heyday of colonialism. The colonial world-as-exhibition thus naturalised Western domination and asserted a parallel implication of non-Western inferiority. Western notions of space were vital parts of the colonial imaginary: the ways in which space was demarcated and brought into Western frames of understanding drew critical boundaries between identities, self and other. Colonialism was thus as much a cultural and ideological project as an economic and political one, and Geography has been deeply Eurocentric in ways that continue to shape it today.

Empirically, Gregory focused on European and American representations of Egypt in the late nineteenth and early twentieth centuries (Gregory 1995a, 2002a). In the nineteenth century, with the Rosetta Stone deciphered and Egyptology all the rage in Europe, Egypt occupied an important geographical and ideological position in the evolving self-conception of the West: the ancient, stagnant, senile culture, simultaneously proximate and distant, which could be rendered sensible only through the application of Western rationality. Drawing upon the observations of travellers and administrators, Gregory unpacks the 'imaginative geographies' that their writings revealed, tracing them to the patriarchical, sexualised, and often racist imagery that pervaded Western views of the Arabic 'Other'. The opening of Verdi's opera *Aida* to a British audience in Cairo in the mid-nineteenth century, for example, revealed the 'microphysics of imperialism' with contemporary newspaper accounts recalling how the audience was made to feel 'as if they were in Egypt', i.e., the idealised land of their fantasies rather than the sordid, dirty, and impoverished reality that their own policies had helped to construct. Space, power, and identity were thus inseparably fused as Egypt was 'geo-graphed' by a panopticonic foreign authority. Grounding Orientalism spatially reveals, then, how textual and discursive practices can have profound material consequences, allowing as they do the appropriation of space by rendering it meaningful to those capable of exerting control: the world-as-exhibition is always an exhibition for *someone*. Duncan and Gregory's (1999) edited collection *Writes of Passage* emerged as an important statement on

the ties between Western misunderstanding of the exotic other and the real geographies of difference produced by voyages beyond the familiar.

Gregory's post-colonial turn led him to facilitate a creative engagement between Orientalism and the social construction of nature (Gregory, 2001). During the Western conquest of the Other, for example, he noted how the developing world was enframed within Eurocentric ways of knowing that depicted 'the tropics' as either fecund Gardens of Eden inhabited by child-like innocents or disease-ridden swamps populated by savages. In Egypt, the desert sand dunes – utterly foreign to conquerors from Britain – were first portrayed as irrational ('like a pack of wolves') before being subjected to the process of rational scientific dissection, i.e., aeolian geomorphology.

Since the millennium, Gregory's post-colonial turn has led him to explore contemporary issues of war, peace, and justice, particularly American interventions in the Middle East initiated as part of the post-9/11 'war on terror', a set of topics that comprises the core of his current research agenda. This body of work has focused on the cultural dimensions of war, the ways in which global geopolitics are intimately bound up with the biopolitics of everyday life (Gregory 2008a; 2008b). Central to this concern was the widespread use of bombing against defenceless civilians, a strategy that collapses urban space into an abstract set of coordinates and masks the devastation and suffering beneath (Gregory, 2006b). *The Colonial Present: Afghanistan, Palestine, Iraq* (2004) charted the neo-liberal Orientalist nature of recent US, British, and Israeli policies in three nations, uncovering how the discursive politics of how diverse Arab and Muslim peoples were represented (e.g., as inherently irrational and blood-thirsty) were folded into imperialist ambitions. Such manoeuvres aid in humanising a vast swath of humanity that has been systematically dehumanised through right-wing nationalist, racist, and triumphalist discourses. Post-colonial thought is thus a means of giving voice to geographical imaginations rendered voiceless by the hegemony of conservative politics of the mainstream media.

This line of thought also led Gregory to explore the spatiality of law in the form of US human rights abuses, particularly as they were reflected in the military base and prison at Guantánamo, Cuba; in delving into this matter, he drew upon the insights of the Italian philosopher Giorgio Agamben (Gregory, 2006). In all of these instances, American policies are portrayed as necessary and therapeutic, as correctives to the unjustified actions of counter-insurgents. *Violent Geographies* (2007), co-edited with the late **Allan Pred**, offered a comprehensive series of essays on how political terror, daily life, and space were intertwined in a variety of different contexts, including Muslim and Hindu fundamentalism, state-sponsored terrorism, the Pentagon's actions unleashed as part of the terrifying war on terror, and the discursive sanitisation of extreme violence. Always attuned to biopolitics, Gregory and Pred (2007: 6) note in the introduction to *Violent Geographies* that 'political violence compresses the sometimes forbiddingly abstract space of geopolitics and geo-economics into the intimacies of everyday life and the innermost recesses of the human body.'

For three decades, Derek Gregory introduced one novel perspective after another into the discipline of geography: structuration theory, postmodernism, Orientalism, in particular, have been among his major imports. Throughout, he has remained steadfast in his insistence on the need for a deeply historical perspective in which time and space are produced and reproduced by ordinary people in everyday life. His works have firmly established in geography the need to take the intentions and context of actors seriously in the explanation of spatial relations, suturing spatial scales ranging from the global to the body. Moreover, in no small part thanks to his efforts, human geography has become irrevocably *critical* in nature, i.e., self-reflective of its social position and epistemological underpinnings, one that puts power at the forefront of its agenda, is sensitive to issues of justice and inequality, and armed with a progressive morality designed to enhance emancipatory projects.

Gregory's works decisively demonstrated the need to understand colonialism and capitalism in discursive terms, and he has been an astute observer of the roles played by language in the process of representation. In so doing, he has helped geographers wrench the exercise of language from its perch as a passive exercise in interpretation and recast it as an active process of constructing meaning. Gregory has remained sensitive throughout his career to the politics of representation, the ways in which all forms of understanding are inescapably entwined with regimes of power/knowledge: discourses simultaneously reflect and constitute the relations they depict and that give rise to them. He thus was a significant contributor to the contemporary fusion of power, knowledge, and space.

Finally, Gregory played a pivotal role introducing geographers and theories of post-colonialism to one another, helping to awaken the discipline to the profound but often invisible ways in which geography as discourse was, and often still is, complicit in the systematic othering of non-Western peoples. As arguably geography's leading practitioner of post-colonialism, his works constitute much more than passive academic reflection, but serve as political interventions to destabilise conventional, taken-for-granted assumptions about contemporary geopolitical events and processes. His research agenda on the Arab and Muslim worlds reveals that Orientalism is far from some dusty doctrine of a bygone age, but very much still alive in the policies pursued by the US as it seeks to reassert its hegemony in the Middle East. As a model of the activist academic, his writings serve to bridge the chasm between theory and practice.

GREGORY'S KEY WORKS

Duncan, J. and Gregory, D. (eds) (1999) *Writes of Passage: Reading Travel Writing*. London: Routledge.

Gregory, D. (1978b) *Ideology, Science and Human Geography*. London: Hutchinson.

Gregory, D. (1989a) 'Areal differentiation and post-modern human geography', in D. Gregory and R. Walford (eds), *Horizons in Human Geography*. London: Macmillan. pp. 67–97.

Gregory, D. (1989b) 'The crisis of modernity? Human geography and critical social theory', in R. Peet and N. Thrift (eds), *New Models in Geography*. London: Unwin Hyman. pp. 348–85.

Gregory, D. (1994a) *Geographical Imaginations*. Cambridge, MA: Blackwell.

Gregory, D. (1995d) 'Imaginative geographies', *Progress in Human Geography*. 19: 447–85.

Gregory, D. (2004) *The Colonial Present: Afghanistan, Palestine, Iraq*. New York: Wiley-Blackwell.

Gregory, D. (2006a) 'The black flag: Guantánamo Bay and the space of exception', *Geografiska Annaler B*, 89: 405–27.

Gregory, D. (2008b) 'The biopolitics of Baghdad: counterinsurgency and the counter city', *Human Geography*, 1: 6–27.

Gregory, D. and Castree, N. (eds) (2006) *David Harvey: A Critical Reader*. New York: Wiley-Blackwell.

Gregory, D. and Pred, A. (eds) (2007) *Violent Geographies: Fear, Terror, and Political Violence*. New York: Routledge.

Gregory, D. and Urry, J. (eds) (1985) *Social Relations and Spatial Structures*. New York: St Martin's.

Secondary Sources and References

Barnes, T. and Gregory, D. (eds) (1997) *Reading Human Geography: The Poetics and Politics of Inquiry*. London: Arnold.

Billinge, M., Gregory, D. and Martin, R. (eds) (1984) *Recollections of a Revolution: Geography as Spatial Science*. London: Macmillan.

Deutsche, R. (1995) 'Surprising geography', *Annals of the Association of American Geographers*, 85: 168–75.

Gregory, D. (1976) 'Rethinking historical geography', *Area*, 8: 295–9.

Gregory, D. (1978a) 'The discourse of the past: phenomenology, structuralism and historical geography', *Journal of Historical Geography*, 4: 16–73.

Gregory, D. (1980) 'The ideology of control: systems theory and geography', *Tijdschrift voor Economische en Sociale Geographie*, 71: 327–42.

Gregory, D. (1981a) 'Human agency and human geography', *Transactions of the Institute of British Geographers*, 6: 1–18.

Gregory, D. (1982b) *Regional Transformation and Industrial Revolution: A Geography of the Yorkshire Woollen Industry, 1780–1840*. Minneapolis: University of Minneapolis Press.

Gregory, D. (1984a) 'Contours of crisis? Sketches for a geography of class struggle in the early Industrial Revolution in England', in A. Baker and D. Gregory (eds), *Explorations in Historical Geography*. Cambridge: Cambridge University Press. pp. 68–117.

Gregory, D. (1985a) 'Suspended animation: The stasis of diffusion theory', in D. Gregory and J. Urry (eds), *Social Relations and Spatial Structures*. New York: St Martin's. pp. 296–336.

Gregory, D. (1985c) 'Suspended animation: the stasis of diffusion theory', in D. Gregory and J. Urry (eds) *Social Relations and Spatial Structures*. New York: St Martin's. pp. 296–336.

Gregory, D. (1988a) 'Solid geometry: notes on the recovery of spatial structure', in R. Golledge, H. Couclelis and P. Gould (eds), *A Ground for Common Search*. Santa Barbara: Santa Barbara Geographical Press.

Gregory, D. (1989c) 'Presences and absences: time-space relations and structuration theory', in D. Held and J. Thompson (eds), *Critical Theory of Modern Societies.* Cambridge: Cambridge University Press. pp. 185–214.

Gregory, D. (1991) 'Interventions in the historical geography of modernity: social theory, spatiality and the politics of representation', *Geografiska Annaler,* 73B: 17–44.

Gregory, D. (1995a) 'Lefebvre, Lacan and the production of space', in G. Benko and U. Strohmayer (eds), *Geography, History and Social Science.* Dordrecht: Kluwer.

Gregory, D. (1995b) 'Between the book and the lamp: imaginative geographies of Egypt, 1849–50', *Transactions of the Institute of British Geographers,* 20: 29–57.

Gregory, D. (1995c) 'Commitments: the work of theory in Human Geography', *Economic Geography,* 72: 73–80.

Gregory, D. (1995d) 'A geographical unconscious: spaces for dialogue and difference', *Annals of the Association of American Geographers,* 85: 175–86.

Gregory, D. (1999b) 'Scripting Egypt: orientalism and the cultures of travel', in J. Duncan and D. Gregory (eds), *Writes of Passage: Reading Travel Writing.* London: Routledge. pp. 115–50.

Gregory, D. (2001) '(Post) colonialism and the production of nature', in N. Castree and B. Braun (eds), *Social Nature: Theory, Practice, and Politics.* Oxford: Blackwell. pp. 84–111.

Gregory, D. (2002a) 'Emperors of the gaze: photographic practices and the captivation of space in Egypt, 1839–1914', in J. Schwartz and J. Ryan (eds), *Picturing Place: Photography and Imaginative Geographies.* New York: I.B. Tauris. pp. 195–225.

Gregory, D. (2006b) 'In another time', *Arab World Geographer,* 9 (2): 88–111.

Gregory, D. (2008a) 'The rush to the intimate: counterinsurgency and the cultural turn in late modern war', *Radical Philosophy,* 150: 8–23.

Gregory, D. and Baker, A. (eds) (1984a) *Explorations in Historical Geography: Some Interpretative Essays.* Cambridge: Cambridge University Press.

Gregory, D., Johnston, R., Haggett, P., Smith, D. and Stoddart, D. (eds) (1981b) *The Dictionary of Human Geography.* Oxford: Blackwell.

Gregory, D., Martin, R. and Smith, G. (eds) (1994) *Human Geography: Society, Space and Social Science.* London: Macmillan, and Minneapolis: University of Minnesota Press.

Gregory, D. and Walford, R. (eds) (1989) *New Horizons in Human Geography.* London: Macmillan.

Harvey, D. (1995) 'Geographical knowledge in the eye of power: reflections on Derek Gregory's *Geographical Imaginations*', *Annals of the Association of American Geographers,* 85: 160–4.

Johnston, R.J., Gregory, D. and Smith, D. (eds) (2000) *The Dictionary of Human Geography* (4th edition). Cambridge: Blackwell.

Katz, C. (1995) 'Major/minor: theory, nature, and politics', *Annals of the Association of American Geographers,* 85: 164–8.

Said, E. (1978) *Orientalism.* New York: Vintage.

Soja, E. (1980) 'The socio-spatial dialectic', *Annals of the Association of American Geographers,* 70: 207–25.

Barney Warf, University of Kansas

26 Torsten Hägerstrand

BIOGRAPHICAL DETAILS AND THEORETICAL CONTEXT

Stig Torsten Erik Hägerstrand was born in 1916 and grew up in rural Sweden. He studied at Lund University, Sweden, obtaining his BA in 1944 and his PhD in 1953. His initial impressions of geography were negative: 'lectures in regional geography were abominably boring ... Geography appeared not as a realm of ideas or a perspective on the world but as an endless array of encyclopedic data' (Hagerstrand, 1983: 244). Matters improved when he undertook a regional study around Asby in Southern Sweden, based on the biographies of every inhabitant from 1840 to 1940. He later realised that this large set of unique information showed stability over time and could be described in quantitative terms. At Lund he was also introduced to the location theories of von Thunen and Christaller by Edgar Kant (see Hägerstrand, 1983). This introduction was to spark off a realisation that probability theory could be used to study settlement patterns. It was this interest in the 'science of locations' that was to culminate in his renowned models of spatial diffusion.

Most of Hägerstrand's career was spent in Lund's Department of Social and Economic Geography, where he was appointed as associate professor in 1953, taking over as chair in 1957 (see **Pred**, 1967, for an account of Hägerstrand's academic progression). In addition to academic research and teaching, Hägerstrand also played a major role in planning for the Swedish national government. His work included the redivision of Sweden into new local government units, the reorganisation of the provincial government, the national land- and water-use plan, and the formulation of a national settlement strategy. He died in May 2004 in Lund. In an obituary, **Peter Haggett** (2004: 17) discusses his career in depth, concluding that his was 'a life which ignored boundaries and rejoiced in the joy of bringing both ideas and people together, of seeing pattern and order where others saw only chaos and randomness'.

Hagerstrand's publications on innovation diffusion led to his taking on a leading role in the 'quantitative' revolution in the 1950s and 1960s and his later development of time geography made him a leader in the behavioural geography that came to prominence in the 1970s. At a time when many Anglophone geographers paid little attention to scholars outside Britain and North America, Hagerstrand's impact did much to ensure that geography in Sweden became and remained visible at a time when French and German geography was (no doubt unjustly) widely ignored. This contribution was celebrated through the publication of a *Festschrift* for Hägerstrand in 1981 (edited by Allan Pred), which includes a bibliography of his published writings.

SPATIAL CONTRIBUTIONS

Hägerstrand was responsible for introducing several important ideas into human geography, many of these contributions coming from his thesis and early publications. His early study of migration in Sweden (1957) included some interesting generalisations about the inverse relationship of migration to distance and how it changed over time, based on detailed and painstaking individual biographies of residents of the small town of Asby. His work on the decline of migration with distance proved a starting point of the important tradition of quantitative research on distance and human interaction (e.g., Olsson, 1965). He also identified the historical decline in the importance of distance. The impact of the analysis was strengthened considerably by his innovative use of map projections, notably his depiction of the space relevant to migration decisions in terms of an azimuthal logarithmic distance map centred on Asby.

Empirically, he introduced the simulation of diffusion to Geography, particularly the concept of wave or contagious diffusion which he originally applied to agricultural innovation but was extended by others to encompass many other geographical phenomena, including the spread of the ghetto (Morrill, 1965) and the settlement of Polynesia (Levison et al., 1973). The concept of 'mean information field' was an important concept at the heart of Hägerstrand's conceptualisation

of diffusion; this was a matrix of probabilities arranged around a central location. A person located at the centre was regarded as receiving messages from one of the surrounding places with probability given by the mean information field. In the context of the diffusion of agricultural innovations, this could be regarded as generating the probability at each time period of a farmer being aware of a particular innovation (such as a new agricultural technology or form of cultivation). Another important introduction into geography associated with this work is the use of simulation to shed light on what would have happened if a simple contagious process had determined the uptake of an innovation. The use of random numbers to model how the process of innovation diffusion unfolded was new to geography but proved popular subsequently in a wide range of fields, especially as it became clear that simulation remained an option when mathematical characterisation of a process was too difficult. Simulations of a spatial process could be mapped and compared to reality, giving at least an intuitive idea of whether the observed pattern could have resulted from the process simulated.

Hägerstrand was also one of a number of quantitative geographers who moved on to emphasise the importance of individual behaviour in geography. This developed into the idea of time geography (Hägerstrand, 1973), which attracted a large number of geographers in Sweden and elsewhere (Carlstein et al., 1978; Parkes and Thrift, 1980). **Gregory** (2000b) explains Hägerstrand's basic framework in terms of four basic propositions. First, space and time are finite resources on which individuals have to draw in order to realise projects. Second, realisation of any project is subject to constraints of three types: capability constraints, which limit what is physically possible for people to do given their location and time resources; coupling constraints, which determine where, when and for how long individuals can meet; and authority constraints, which impose conditions of access to particular time-space domains. Third, these constraints delineate what is possible for individuals to fulfil particular projects. Fourth, the 'central problem for analysis' is usually competition between projects for 'open space-times'.

Practising time geography involves the detailed dissection of individuals' movements over very short time periods, looking at the paths in space which people traverse over time, including daily or weekly space-time paths. There may be trade-offs between expenditures of time and other resources. Interesting perspectives about people's activities can be appreciated, for example, by looking at people who meet at a particular time but who may have made very different types of journey to get there. It may also be interesting to look at household members who may all be together at the beginning and end of the day but may have followed very different space-time paths in the mean time. Developments of these ideas, often expressed in diagrammatic form, incorporate concepts like space-time prisms, which describe the set of times and locations which can be reached by somebody who has to be at particular places at times before and after.

KEY ADVANCES AND CONTROVERSIES

Like **Peter Haggett** and others involved in the spread of the new ideas known as the 'quantitative revolution', Hägerstrand was more concerned with theory and generalised models than empirical description. He was also interested in processes operating in space and over time, perhaps in contrast to the more purely geometric (and static) approaches characteristic of much location theory. One such process was diffusion. In contrast to earlier work on diffusion conducted in the tradition of Berkeley School and Carl Sauer, which tended to view diffusion as a phenomenon at the level of a society or culture, his perspective focused on individuals located at specific points in space making decisions to adopt (or not to adopt) an innovation. When he moved into behavioural geography (Hägerstrand, 1970) these individuals could be regarded not just as 'economic man' but as decision-makers operating with incomplete knowledge and imperfect ability to calculate the benefits of alternative actions. He also acknowledged that decisions were usually made in conditions of uncertainty.

Geographical diffusion theory developed from Hägerstrand's work, partly through the application of his diffusion models to other phenomena, such as fashions or rumours. There was also work separating out different forms of diffusion. Hudson's work (1969) on diffusion within a central place hierarchy was certainly important here, but the field developed in terms of increasingly realistic models of diffusion in a range of different concepts. At the same time, there was also a convergence of interest between geographical and sociological work on diffusion.

The other difference between Hägerstrand's studies and earlier work on diffusion was the concern with general models, expressable in quantitative terms, rather than the specific times and places where particular innovations could be assumed to have occurred.

Indeed, Hägerstrand's models of diffusion were explicitly probabilistic. The simulation methodology meant that an array of different outcomes was presented, rather than one 'true' deterministic outcome. This resulted in a view of the world, shared by other quantitative geographers like Curry (1964) and Dacey (1966), where what happened was one of a (large) number of possible eventualities. Geographers were encouraged to adopt a deductive approach to inference, where the issue was to test whether a given state of affairs could have been generated by the assumptions of a simple model. This approach could be (and was) criticised when the assumptions of the model were totally unrealistic (for example, in classical central place theory). Hägerstrand's work, however, was grounded in detailed collection of data, preceding the development of general theory.

Gregory (2000a) gives a succinct account of Hägerstrand's work on diffusion and some of the reactions to it. An important development has been the derivation of more complex models of spatial diffusion, especially through the work by Cliff, Haggett and others on the modelling of epidemics (see Haggett et al., 1977, chapter seven). Blaikie (1978) criticised diffusion research for its preoccupation with spatial form and space-time sequence, while Gregory (1985) criticised the unwillingness of diffusion theory to engage with social theory which clarifies the conditions under which diffusion occurs and the consequences of the diffusion.

Hägerstrand's ideas about time geography were followed up by several other authors, in Sweden and elsewhere. The study of time constraints emphasised differences in resources which confirmed other aspects of social class and difference. In particular, time geography has drawn attention to gender differences in the availability of time resources,

especially to the time-related problems of mothers with young children. Other studies have picked up on other aspects of the role of time in geography, such as **Thrift**'s study (1977) of the spread of standardised time in nineteenth-century England through the influence of the railways, and the development of factorial ecology to incorporate time as well as space (Parkes and Thrift, 1980, chapter eight). In addition to geographers, the concept of time geography attracted the attention of sociologists in the 1980s (**Giddens**, 1989) and, as such, was influential in increasing the status of geography among sociologists. Many of the terms and concepts associated with time geography have accordingly remained an important part of human geography's theoretical landscape up to the present (see May and Thrift, 2001; Miller, 2005).

Nonetheless, a common criticism of time geography has been its 'physicalism' – the emphasis on people's locations in space/time and the constraints affecting which projects are possible for them to undertake. Some critics, like Rose (1977), suggest that this downplays the role of attitudes, motives and choices (some of which may of course be irrational or unconscious in derivation). Rose's criticisms are addressed by Parkes and Thrift (1980: 275–7), who argue that they arise either from misconceptions of what time geography is, or from the fact that the approach has not been able to explain all aspects of the social use and allocation of time and space. From a feminist perspective, **Rose** (1993) likewise criticises time geography for its conception of the person as a basic 'elementary particle' for time-geographic studies from which all social and cultural identities, such as race, gender and sexuality, have been erased. Hoppe and Langton (1988) have made the point that time geography has tended to confine itself to the micro-scale and short-term, with little regard for the changing structures and contexts in which they operate. Accordingly, they have tried to develop time geography to cast light on macro-scale processes operating over longer time spans.

Hägerstrand himself (1983: 254) reported and acknowledged criticisms of his time-geography work on the grounds that it 'neglected and ran over the more important part of human existence: the internal realms of experience and meaning'. For example, he admits the truth of criticisms from **Anne Buttimer** (in Hägerstrand 1983: 254) to the effect that his time-geography diagrams seemed to omit crucial dimensions of human temporality – images and perceptions of

time, and bio-ecological rhythms. As this last point implies, Hägerstrand's perspective does not exclude humanistic insight into the human condition. Indeed, van Paassen (1981) presents a humanistic analysis of Hägerstrand's thinking, relating it to the ideas of Vidal de la Blache. This often overlooked humanistic element to Hägerstrand's work is perhaps best encapsulated in the title of his (1970) paper 'What about people in regional science?' Unlike other quantitative geographers, Hägerstrand's ideas have therefore been of interest to geographers of different persuasions (including humanistic geographers such as Buttimer) and remain an important component of social and cultural geography's conceptual toolkit.

HÄGERSTRAND'S KEY WORKS

Hägerstrand, T. (1952) 'The propagation of innovation waves', *Lund Studies in Geography, Series B*, 4: 3–19.
Hägerstrand, T. (1953)' *Innovationsforloppet ur Korologisk Synpunkt'*, PhD thesis, Lund.
Hägerstrand, T. (1957) 'Migration and area', in D. Hannerberg, T. Hägerstrand and B. Odeving (eds), *Migration in Sweden: A Symposium*, Lund Studies in Geography, Series B, No. 13.
Hägerstrand, T (1967a) *Innovation Diffusion as a Spatial Process.* Chicago: University of Chicago Press.
Hägerstrand, T. (1967b) 'On Monte Carlo simulation of diffusion' in W.L. Garrison and D.F. Marble (eds), *Quantitative Geography: Part I. Economic and Cultural Topics.* Northwestern University Studies in Geography 13: 1–32.
Hägerstrand, T. (1970) 'What about people in regional science?', *Papers of the Regional Science Association*, 24: 7–21.
Hägerstrand, T. (1973) 'The domain of human geography', in R.J. Chorley (ed.), *Directions in Geography.* London: Methuen. pp. 67–87.
Hägerstrand, T. (1982) 'Diorama, path and project', *Tijdschrift voor Economische en Sociale Geographie*, 73: 323–39.

Secondary Sources and References

Blaikie, P.M. (1978) 'The theory of the spatial diffusion of innovations: a spacious cul-de-sac', *Progress in Human Geography*, 2: 268–95
Carlstein, T., Parkes, D.N. and Thrift, N.J. (eds) (1978) *Making Sense of Time* (3 volumes). Chichester: Wiley.
Curry, L. (1964) 'The random spatial economy: an exploration in settlement theory', *Annals of the Association of American Geographers*, 54: 138–46
Dacey, M.F. (1966) 'A compound probability law for a pattern more dispersed than random and with areal inhomogeneity', *Economic Geography*, 42: 172–9.
Giddens, A. (1989) *Sociology.* Cambridge: Polity Press.

Gregory, D. (1985) 'Suspended animation: the stasis of diffusion theory', in D. Gregory and J. Urry (eds), *Social Relations and Spatial Structures*. London: Macmillan. pp. 296–336.

Gregory, D. (2000a) 'Diffusion', in R.J. Johnston, D. Gregory, G. Pratt and M. Watts (eds), *The Dictionary of Human Geography*. Oxford: Blackwell. pp. 175–7.

Gregory, D. (2000b) 'Time-geography', in R.J. Johnston, D. Gregory, G. Pratt and M. Watts (eds), *The Dictionary of Human Geography*. Oxford: Blackwell. pp. 830–3.

Hägerstrand, T. (1975) 'Space, time and human conditions', in A. Karlqvist, L. Lundqvist and F. Snickars (eds), *Dynamic Allocation of Urban Space*. Farnborough: Saxon House. pp. 3–14.

Hägerstrand, T. (1976) 'Geography and the study of interaction between society and nature', *Geoforum*, 7: 329–34

Hägerstrand, T. (1978a) 'A note on the quality of life-times', in T. Carlstein, D.N. Parkes and N.J. Thrift (eds), *Making Sense of Time, Volume 2: Human Activity and Time Geography*. Chichester: Wiley. pp. 214–24.

Hägerstrand, T. (1978b) 'Survival and arena: on the life-history of individuals in relation to their geographical environment', in T. Carlstein, D.N. Parkes and N. Thrift (eds), *Making Sense of Time, Volume 2: Human Activity and Time Geography*. Chichester: Wiley. pp. 122–45.

Hägerstrand, T. (1983) 'In search for the sources of concepts', in A. Buttimer (ed.), *The Practice of Geography*. Harlow: Longman. pp. 238–56.

Hägerstrand, T. (1984) 'Presence and absence: a look at conceptual choices and bodily necessities', *Regional Studies*, 18: 373–80.

Haggett, P. (2004) 'Obituary: Torsten Hägerstrand', *The Independent*, 24 May: 17.

Haggett, P., Cliff, A.D. and Frey, A. (1977) *Locational Analysis in Human Geography* (2nd edititon). London: Arnold.

Hoppe, G. and Langton, J. (1988) 'Time-geography and economic development: the changing structure of livelihood positions on farms in nineteenth-century Sweden', *Geografiska Annaler B*, 68: 115–37

Hudson, J.C. (1969) 'Diffusion in a central place system', *Geographical Analysis*, 1: 45–58.

Levison, M., Ward, G.R. and Webb, J.W. (1973) *The Settlement of Polynesia: A Computer Simulation*. Minneapolis: University of Minnesota Press.

May, J. and Thrift, N. (eds) (2001) *Timespace: Geographies of Temporality*. London: Routledge.

Miller, H.J. (2005) 'A measurement theory for time geography', *Geographical Analysis* 37 (1): 17–45.

Morrill, R.L. (1965) 'The negro ghetto: problems and alternatives', *Geographical Review*, 55: 339–61.

Olsson, G. (1965) 'Distance and human interaction: a migration study', *Geografiska Annaler B*, 47: 3–43.

van Paassen, C. (1981) 'The philosophy of geography: from Vidal to Hägerstrand', in A. Pred (ed.), (1981) *Space and Time in Geography: Essays Dedicated to Torsten Hägerstrand*. Lund: Lund Studies in Geography, Series B, No. 48: 17–29.

Parkes, D.N. and Thrift, N.J. (1980) *Times, Spaces and Places: A Chronogeographic Perspective*. Chichester: Wiley.

Pred, A. (1967) 'Postscript', in Hägerstrand, T. (1967) *Innovation Diffusion as a Spatial Process*. Chicago: University of Chicago Press. pp. 299–324.

Pred, A. (ed.) (1981) *Space and Time in Geography: Essays Dedicated to Torsten Hägerstrand*. Lund: Lund Studies in Geography, Series B, No. 48.

Rose, C. (1977) 'Reflections on the notion of time incorporated in Hägerstrand's time-geographic model of society', *Tijdschrift voor Economische en Sociale Geografie*, 68: 43–50.

Rose, G. (1993) *Feminism and Geography: The Limits of Geographical Knowledge*. Cambridge: Polity.

Thrift, N.J. (1977) 'The diffusion of Greenwich Mean Time: an essay in social and economic history', *Working Paper* 192, School of Geography, University of Leeds.

Robin Flowerdew, University of St Andrews

27 Peter Haggett

BIOGRAPHICAL DETAILS AND THEORETICAL CONTEXT

Peter Haggett was born in 1933 and grew up in rural Somerset. He later attributed his interest in geography to his experience of touring his home area on foot and by bicycle – for the geographer, he argued, 'locomotion should be slow; the slower the better' (Haggett, 1965). He studied at St Catherine's College, Cambridge, where his contemporaries included Peter Hall, Michael Chisholm, Ken Warren and Gerald Manners. He received his BA from Cambridge in 1954 (a First), and his PhD in 1960. In his doctoral research, concerned with forestry in Brazil, he began to think about locational analysis and to develop an interest in quantitative approaches and modelling. After a short period at University College London (1955–57), he moved to Cambridge, first as University Demonstrator in Geography and from 1962 as University Lecturer in Geography. He moved to Bristol as Professor of Urban and Regional Geography in 1966 where he spent the rest of his career. At Bristol, he played an important role in university administration, where he was Pro-Vice-Chancellor from 1979 to 1982 and Acting Vice-Chancellor from 1984 to 1985. He

was awarded a CBE in 1993. Since retirement, he has maintained his activity in geographical research and publication.

Haggett's career can be seen as mirroring a wider series of transformations in how geography is studied. At the start of his career, human geography was clearly defined as a descriptive 'art'. Hartshorne's discussions on the nature of geography (1939; 1959) were the major statements attempting to define the discipline. Human geography was mainly taught on a region-by-region basis, with each region described in a standard form implicitly or explicitly showing how the human geography arose from the natural environment. It was an atheoretical discipline concentrating on description with little serious attempt to measure the patterns observed and even less attempt to explain them. Haggett was one of the geographers most responsible for changing the nature of geography, its methods, its theories, and (to a degree) its subject matter. Nevertheless, he maintained interests in many traditional branches of the subject; indeed, Chorley (1995) describes him as 'a quantitative, regional, historical, and economic geographer with biogeographical interests'.

A short essay like this can do little more than scratch the surface of Haggett's contributions to human geography; fortunately two books have appeared which give far more information about his biography and geographical concerns. Haggett himself produced a memoir, *The Geographer's Art* (1990), intended to convey his approach to, and passion for, the subject. A few years later, Cliff et al. (1995) produced a *Festschrift*, which includes papers by leading geographers on most of Haggett's major interests, and more personal memoirs by Chorley (1995) and **Thrift** (1995).

SPATIAL CONTRIBUTIONS

It is hard to overestimate Peter Haggett's contribution to human geography from the 1960s onwards. With the physical geographer Richard Chorley, he organised a series of symposia at Madingley Hall, outside Cambridge, resulting in the very influential *Frontiers in Geographical Teaching* (Chorley and Haggett, 1965) and the even more influential *Models in Geography* (Chorley and Haggett, 1967). Both books consisted of a series of chapters discussing new approaches in the different branches of geography, many of them written by the editors' Cambridge colleagues. Not all the chapters in these books represented major departures from the established ways of studying the subject, but most, especially Haggett's own (Haggett and Chorley, 1967; Haggett, 1967), were influenced by a new and powerful set of ideas that became pivotal in human geography's putative 'quantitative revolution'.

The term 'quantitative revolution', however, does not do justice to the changes Haggett and his colleagues tried to bring about (and largely succeeded) in the way geography was studied. Certainly geographers made increasing use of numbers, measurements and computers (Haggett, 1969) rather than relying on verbal descriptions, but the changes went way beyond this. The use of statistical analysis, largely unknown in geography beforehand, became more and more important. Geographers began to think in terms of hypotheses and how to test them, many adopting the hypothetico-deductive approach regarded as typifying the scientific method (**Harvey**, 1969; Amedeo and **Golledge**, 1975). Geographers also developed the idea of constructing theory, sometimes based on working out the consequences of a set of assumptions.

One of the most important aspects of Haggett's work was to align human geography with the social sciences rather than the arts, and to increase its respectability as an intellectual discipline. Most fundamentally of all, he introduced ideas, concepts and readings from a wide range of other disciplines, starting the outward-looking tradition that is arguably one of geography's greatest strengths today. For instance, Haggett did much to popularise the locational theories of von Thünen (1826) and Christaller (1933), little known previously in geography but highly relevant to Haggett's concepts of spatial analysis as applied to agricultural land use and urban location respectively. The hugely influential *Locational Analysis in Human Geography* (1965) thus laid the foundations for a completely new approach to human geography, organised not by region or by systematic subfield, but by geometric form. As manifest in the chapter headings – Movement, Nodes, Networks, Hierarchies, Surfaces – this book introduced to geography a whole new language of spatial science. Simultaneously, it showcased new concerns and exemplars, including a few hitherto little-known geographers, like **Torsten Hägerstrand**, and many economists, like Weber, Losch and Isard, together with engineers, systems theorists and philosophers of science. An expanded second edition was produced in 1977 (Haggett et al., 1977), while another joint publication with Chorley appeared in 1969, in which methods for studying networks in both human and physical geography were discussed (ranging from transport networks to fluvial systems). With Cliff et al. (1975), Haggett also studied space-time diffusion in economic systems, such as spatio-temporal changes in unemployment. His work also stressed the practical uses of such models, in particular through the development and application of spatial forecasting (Chisholm et al., 1970; Haggett, 1973). In all these books, Haggett adopted an abstract but elegant approach, using mathematical and statistical methods to tackle a wide range of examples from all over the world.

A contribution of a different kind was made by his influential textbook *Geography: A Modern Synthesis* (first edition 1972; subsequent editions 1975, 1979, 1983; rewritten as *Geography: A Global Synthesis*, published 2001). Widely adopted as a student text in Britain and elsewhere, it was important in upholding the unity of geography at a time when many human geographers were turning their backs on physical geography (and vice versa). Many of Haggett's ideas filtered through to school geography, especially in Britain. His use of the beach as a focus for explaining many of what he regarded as basic geographical concepts gave the book an appealing and innovative start, although the attempt to introduce the 'G-scale' as a way of expressing a variety of spatial scales proved unsuccessful in the longer term.

Starting from a largely accidental linkage with a group of epidemiologists in Geneva (see Haggett, 2000: 9–10), Haggett's later career became increasingly concerned with medical geography, in particular the diffusion of infectious diseases (see Cliff and Haggett, 1989; Cliff et al., 1981, 1986; Cliff et al., 2008). By

careful choice of disease and study area (measles in Iceland was a particularly successful choice), he was able to find out a great deal about the spread of such diseases, including the ability to predict the return time and proportion of population likely to be infected. Haggett (2000) provides an excellent and (as with all his work) well-written discussion of the major themes of his work in the field, much of which takes diffusion studies (Hägerstrand, 1969) as a starting point. Considerable conceptual and mathematical development was needed, however, to apply the ideas to disease diffusion, adapting the structure of the model to fit in with the characteristics of the specific disease and the way in which it spread. Although much of his work has established the spatio-temporal characteristics of epidemics in small and relatively closed geographical areas, he has developed an interest in processes operating at a global scale over a longer time period. He has also studied ways in which the spread of epidemics can be controlled. With collaborators, he produced an *Atlas of Disease Distributions* (Cliff and Haggett, 1988) – in fact far more than an atlas – and *The International Atlas of AIDS* (Smallman-Raynor et al., 1992). He has also acted as a consultant to many scientific and medical bodies, including the World Health Organisation.

KEY ADVANCES AND CONTROVERSIES

As stated above, Haggett was a great innovator in British human geography. His work was one of the main foundations of the definition of geography as spatial science. His adoption of the scientific method, later pilloried as positivism, was also seminal for a generation of British geographers. Both notions were poorly received by establishment Geography at the time (for example, see David Stoddart's account of the reception of a 1964 Royal Geographical Society lecture presenting a statistical model for the distribution of forest cover in Brazil, cited in Thrift, 1995: 381–2). However, they achieved greater acceptance among the younger generation of scholars (an unusually numerous group because the British university system was expanding rapidly at the time). Taylor (1976) provides an interesting perspective on these debates. He argued that a shift of paradigm was aided by the use of language which was difficult for an older generation to come to terms with (certainly true of statistical arguments) but not too difficult for the younger ones to master.

Positivism and spatial science held sway for much of the 1970s, but criticisms of positivism and quantification began to emerge before too long (Mercer, 1984; **Gregory**, 1978). Such criticisms came from two main quarters. First, an increasingly vocal group of Marxist geographers, augmented by some of Haggett's earlier followers, like **David Harvey** and **Peter Taylor**, gained impetus from the wider critique of capitalism, the military-industrial complex and the Vietnam War. Their commitments to unobservable structures as the basis of social formations, and to dialectic rather than scientific method as a guide to reasoning, were opposed to the positivist tradition that Haggett had brought into Geography. A second group of geographers reacted against the abstract models Haggett had made fashionable in geography, stressing the importance of artistic and humanistic insights and the limitations of idealised models of the individual like 'economic man' in adequately representing thinking, feeling people (see **David Ley** and **Yi-Fu Tuan**).

The idea of Geography as spatial science also came under attack at the same period. One element of this attack was from geographers whose interests did not lie in this area. These included people interested in the traditional geographical concern of the relationships between people and environment, and others interested in development studies grounded in specific places and their experiences. More philosophically grounded objections appeared, such as Sack's (1974) rejection of the idea that space could be a subject of study in itself. Both Marxists and humanists, not to mention feminists and postmodernists, tended to reject or at least play down the spatial perspective, either because it was unimportant in their view to the major social trends or because abstract models of spatial structure did not apply to the real people and events they were interested in.

Haggett's ideas are, however, far from dead. Despite the unfashionability of modelling, quantification and positivism for the last two decades, work of this kind continues to flourish, arguably being returned to prominence by the growth of geographical information science (GIS) in the 1990s. Similarly, spatial analysis remains as an important if minority interest in contemporary human geography, if only because there are many applications to commercial and public location problems. The importance of space as a key concept in geography has also revived in recent years, with increased attention being devoted to the social construction of space and the role of space in mediating social relations and processes. Haggett himself, while unfailingly polite and respectful of work done under new paradigms, remains consistent in his interests and approaches, and continues to be an enthusiastic and effective advocate of his own ideas.

HAGGETT'S KEY WORKS

Chorley, R.J. and Haggett, P. (eds) (1965) *Frontiers in Geographical Teaching.* London: Methuen.
Haggett, P. (1965) *Locational Analysis in Human Geography.* London: Arnold.
Chorley, R.J. and Haggett, P. (eds) (1967) *Models in Geography.* London: Methuen.
Haggett, P. and Chorley, R.J. (1969) *Network Analysis in Geography.* London: Arnold.
Cliff, A.D., Haggett, P., Ord, J.K., Bassett, K.A. and Davies, R.B. (1975) *Elements of Spatial Structure: A Quantitative Approach.* Cambridge: Cambridge University Press.
Cliff, A.D., Haggett, P. and Ord, J.K. (1986) *Spatial Aspects of Influenza Epidemics.* London: Pion.
Haggett, P. (1990) *The Geographer's Art.* Oxford: Blackwell.
Haggett, P. (2000) *The Geographical Structure of Epidemics.* Oxford: Oxford University Press.
Haggett, P. (2001) *Geography: A Global Synthesis.* Harlow: Prentice Hall.

Secondary Sources and References

Amedeo, D. and Golledge, R.G. (1975) *An Introduction to Scientific Reasoning in Geography.* Chichester: Wiley.
Chisholm, M.D.I., Frey, A.E. and Haggett, P. (eds) (1970) *Regional Forecasting.* London: Butterworth.
Chorley, R.J. (1995) 'Haggett's Cambridge: 1957–1966', in A.D. Cliff, P.R. Gould, A.G. Hoare and N.J. Thrift (eds), *Diffusing Geography: Essays for Peter Haggett.* Oxford: Blackwell. pp. 355–74.
Christaller, W. (1933) *Die zentralen Orte in Suddeutschland.* Jena : Fischer.
Cliff, A.D., Gould, P.R., Hoare, A.G. and Thrift, N.J. (eds) (1995) *Diffusing Geography: Essays for Peter Haggett.* Oxford: Blackwell.
Cliff, A.D. and Haggett, P. (1988) *Atlas of Disease Distributions.* Oxford: Blackwell.
Cliff, A.D. and Haggett, P. (1989) 'Spatial aspects of epidemic control', *Progress in Human Geography,* 13: 315–47.
Cliff, A.D., Haggett, P., Ord, J.K. and Versey, G.R. (1981) *Spatial Diffusion: An Historical Geography of Epidemics in an Island Community.* Cambridge: Cambridge University Press.
Cliff, A.D. and Haggett, P. (2004) 'Time, travel and infection', *British Medical Bulletin,* 69 (1): 87–99.
Cliff A.D., Haggett, P. and Smallman-Raynor, M. (2008) 'An exploratory method for estimating the changing speed of epidemic waves from historical data', *International Journal of Epidemiology,* 37 (1): 106–12.
Gregory, D. (1978) *Ideology, Science and Human Geography.* London: Hutchinson.
Hägerstrand, T. (1969) *Innovation Diffusion as a Spatial Process.* Chicago: University of Chicago Press.
Haggett, P. (1967) 'Network models in geography', in R.J. Chorley and P. Haggett (eds), *Models in Geography.* London: Methuen. pp. 609–68.
Haggett, P. (1969) 'Geographical research in a computer environment', *Geographical Journal,* 135: 500–9.
Haggett, P. (1972) *Geography: A Modern Synthesis.* London: Harper and Row.
Haggett, P. (1973) 'Forecasting alternative spatial, ecological and regional futures: problems and possibilities', in R.J. Chorley (ed.) *Directions in Geography.* London: Methuen. pp. 219–35.
Haggett, P. and Chorley, R.J. (1967) 'Models, paradigms and the new geography', in R.J. Chorley and P. Haggett (eds), *Models in Geography.* London: Methuen. pp.19–41.
Haggett, P., Cliff, A.D. and Frey, A.E. (1977) *Locational Analysis in Human Geography* (2nd edition). London: Arnold.
Hartshorne, R. (1939) *The Nature of Geography.* Washington: Association of American Geographers.
Hartshorne, R. (1959) *Perspective on the Nature of Geography.* New York: Rand McNally.
Harvey, D. (1969) *Explanation in Geography.* London: Arnold.
Mercer, D.C. (1984) 'Unmasking technocratic geography', in M. Billinge, D. Gregory, and R. Martin (eds), *Recollections of a Revolution: Geography as Spatial Science.* London: Macmillan. pp. 153–99.
Sack, R.D. (1974) 'The spatial separatist theme in geography', *Economic Geography,* 50: 1–19.
Smallman-Raynor, M., Cliff, A.D. and Haggett, P. (1992) *International Atlas of AIDS.* Oxford: Blackwell.

Taylor, P.J. (1976) 'An interpretation of the quantification debate in British geography', *Transactions of the Institute of British Geographers NS*, 1: 129–42.

Thrift, N.J. (1995) 'Peter Haggett's life in geography', in A.D. Cliff, P.R. Gould, A.G. Hoare and N.J. Thrift (eds), *Diffusing Geography: Essays for Peter Haggett*. Oxford: Blackwell. pp. 375–95.

von Thünen, J.H. (1826) *Der isolierte Staat in Beziehung auf Landwirtschaft und Nationalökonomie*. Hamburg.

Robin Flowerdew, University of St Andrews

28 Stuart Hall

BIOGRAPHICAL DETAILS AND THEORETICAL CONTEXT

A prolific essayist and editor, founding and prominent member of the British New Left, guiding influence in the development of the Birmingham Centre for Contemporary Cultural Studies (CCCS) during the 1970s, prominent teacher at the Open University in the 1980s and 1990s, and globally sought-after speaker on questions of culture, identity and race Stuart Hall has shaped the multinational project of Cultural Studies in decisive ways. He has also been described as the leading Black theorist of Black Britain, influencing public debate about the politics of race and class through his continuing (post-retirement) media and lecture appearances, as well as through numerous contributions to committees charged with exploring issues of ethnic disadvantage and community cohesion in the UK. Awarded a Fellowship of the British Academy for his academic contributions, in geography his influence is evidenced primarily through the adoption of CCCS interests – subcultures, hegemony, and resistance – by the 'new cultural geography' that emerged in the 1990s, and in the subsequent disciplinary turn to questions of identity, post-coloniality, and diaspora.

Hall was born in Kingston, Jamaica in 1932 to middle-class parents. In terms of class and (mixed) colour, Hall's family 'played out ... culturally ... the conflict between the local and the imperial in the colonised context' (Chen, 1996: 484–5). Hall says he was 'the blackest member of the family' and so 'always had the identity [of] being the one from outside, the one who didn't fit, and the one who was blacker than the others' (Chen 1996: 484–5). This sense of marginality was crucial to the development of Hall's theoretical and political interventions.

Hall went to Oxford University in 1951 as a Rhodes Scholar. Despite his sense of outsider-ness in England, Hall was a chief architect of the British New Left. In response to the Soviet invasion of Hungary and the British invasion of Suez in 1956, and with the support of the Socialist Society (which 'had always opposed stalinism [sic] and imperialism' (Chen, 1996: 493)), Hall and others started the *Universities and Left Review* (*ULR*) as a forum for the political and intellectual debates unleashed by the events of 1956. The 1956 invasions had other decisive impacts on Hall, leading him, to reconsider his decision to write a PhD dissertation on Henry James. and turn to the study of Marx (Hall, 1996b); He moved to London, to supply teach during the day and edit the *ULR* at night. Simultaneously, he began a serious study of film (Whannel and Hall,1964). In 1960, the *ULR* merged with the *New Reasoner* to form the *New Left Review* (*NLR*) with Hall as its first editor. The *NLR*, like its parent journals, was closely affiliated with the Campaign for Nuclear Disarmament (CND). When the decline of CND as a social movement (in 1961) suggested that a new editorial direction was necessary, Hall left to take a post teaching media studies and popular culture at Chelsea College, University of London, probably the first ever post of its kind in Britain (Chen 1996: 497).

In 1964, Richard Hoggart invited Hall to the University of Birmingham to manage Hoggart's new Centre for Contemporary Cultural Studies (CCCS). When Hoggart left the CCCS in 1968, Hall became its director remaining so until he left the CCCS in 1979. The years under Hall's direction were CCCS's most productive and most innovative. Staff and students engaged in wide-ranging theoretical exploration while also developing innova-tive empirical studies of the socialisation of working-class youth, the importance of 'style' in subcultural formation and prac-tices of resistance, the ideological role of the mass media, and the policing of race and unrest. Hall organised many of these efforts as editor of the studies that resulted, but he was also highly prolific in his own right, producing some 60 aca-demic and popular essays over the course of his career at CCCS.

The highly collaborative, and deeply political, nature of the work at CCCS led to innumerable ideological and practi-cal battles. In particular, 'the question of feminism' (Chen,1996: 500; Brunsdon, 1996; Women's Study Group, 1978) led to what Hall (1996b: 268) irritably describes as an 'interruption' in the work of the Centre as women members of the Cen-tre struggled to promote their theoretical and political concerns (Brunsdon 1996, 278–9). Of the feminist 'interruptions' Hall says:

I was checkmated by feminists; I couldn't come to terms with it, in the Centre's work. It wasn't a personal thing ... It was a structural thing. I couldn't any longer do any useful work, from that position. It was time to go.

(Chen, 1996: 500)

Hall left CCCS in 1979 to become Pro-fessor in the Sociology Department of the Open University (OU) where he remained until his retirement in 1999. While the OU provided new teaching opportunities, it also meant that Hall was no longer engaged in the type of collaborative work typical of CCCS. In particular there was less opportunity for the sort of strongly empirical work that had grounded the Centre's theoretical endeavours. Concurrent with this move, Hall aligned himself with the magazine *Marxism Today*. In regular contributions to the magazine, Hall explored the rise of Thatcherism as a hegemonic project, seeking to learn political and strategic les-sons from its success. Hall's theorisation of Thatcherism and the 'New Times' it augured owed much to the ideas of Gram-sci, but also to Althusserian theories of ideology, overdetermination, and the con-stitution of identity (Hall, 1988a; 1988b) Much of this Althusser-inspired work is highly technical, highly abstract, and dif-ficult in language, being indicative of a more general move in Hall's work, which subtly moved from focusing on questions of culture as systems of meaning and pol-itics related to social formations, to one of understanding the complex cultural processes central to the construction of *identity* (Hall and du Gay, 1996). This was particularly apparent in Hall's work on the identities produced as a *condition* of neo-liberal globalisation, and his continu-ing contributions to debates on ethnicity, diversity and community cohesion in the UK.

SPATIAL CONTRIBUTIONS

In order to understand Hall's impact in geography, it is essential to first understand his impact in British cultural studies and politics. Hall's work at CCCS sought to construct cultural theory that moved beyond traditional literary studies, yet which did not succumb to the 'structuralist-functionalist methodology' of classical sociology (Hall, 1980a). In particular he showed how 'meaning' was constructed (through the media and otherwise) and how it shaped people's lives.

In an influential essay called 'Encoding/Decoding', Hall (1980b) argued that any media 'text' circulated through several linked 'moments'. Besides the moment of production, when dominant meanings were encoded in the text, there were also the moments of circulation, distribution, consumption, and reproduction, when meanings were decoded and when *new* meanings were encoded. In the process of circulation and distribution, critics not only decode the intended meanings, but add layers of meaning to the text itself; likewise 'readers' (or listeners or viewers) both decode the text and transform its meaning based on their own frames of reference. Sometimes readings will be in accordance with the intended reading; other times new meanings will be 'negotiated' between readers and texts; and still other times, resistant, counter-hegemonic readings will arise. The process of decoding and re-encoding is strongly influenced by class or other social positions, since these create both differential access to (discursive or other) resources for decoding, and differential desires and needs when reading. This implies the need for both a sociological and a geographical analysis of the construction and transformation of meaning. Such analyses, Hall argued, could uncover the 'maps of meaning' that constitute culture as lived experience. Such 'maps of meaning' were the means by which people made sense of the world, constituting a site of social contestation.

One of the primary arguments of Hall (and the CCCS) was that these *modes* of contestation through which maps of meaning are highly varied. Resistance can appear, for example, in the development of a new subcultural *style* that takes the products and practices of the dominant culture and reshapes them into something new that gives a subcultural group an *identity*. In a landmark study (Hall and Jefferson, 1976), Hall and his collaborators at CCCS argued that subcultural style and resistance was always formed in relation to hegemony, that is, in dialectical relation to dominant society's need to gain the consent, or coerce the acquiescence, of subordinate classes. The negotiation of these relations of domination is always contentious (even if conflict is sometimes sublimated). But perhaps most importantly, the negotiation of subcultural identity within a hegemonic order requires that subcultural groups '*win space* ... to mark out and appropriate "territory"' (Hall and Jefferson, 1976: 45). The negotiation of hegemony hence requires the production of space.

In the 1980s, Hall elaborated the theory of hegemony within the context of Thatcherism (the right-wing conservative politics espoused by the British Prime Minister of the time, Margaret Thatcher) Hall argued that the 'authoritarian populism' (Hall, 1989) of Thatcherism worked in dialectical relationship to a capitalism 'increasingly characterised by diversity, differentiation and fragmentation' (Hall and Jacques, 1989: 11). 'Populism' in this context referred to a new populism of the flexible marketplace and the new opportunities it seemed to open up; 'authoritarianism' referred to the new social conservativism that Thatcher harnessed to the rise of a punitive state. 'Authoritarian populism' thus named the conjuncture of forces that shaped British social and cultural life in the 1980s. It also indicated the way that Thatcher won the consent of large portions of the working class to her administration's project of political and social restructuring (Hall, 1988a). To make this argument, Hall drew on Althusser's (1969) idea of 'interpellation' which refers to a subject being 'hailed' into a particular subject position through the working of ideology. Subjects were 'interpellated' through the 'over-determined' political, social, and economic restructuring that gave rise to new ideologies, new maps of meaning that structured the moments of encoding and decoding possible at any particular time and place.

Hall thus became more animated by questions of subjectivity and identity than with understanding social and political transformations *per se*. In particular, he deepened his commitment to understanding the *experience* of race, ethnicity, and subjectivity. Hall argued that *diaspora* provided a window on what Hall called the 'articulation' of the subject in postmodern and post-colonial global circumstances. During the 1980s and into the 1990s, the concept of 'articulation' rather than 'interpellation' came to be Hall's predominant metaphor for understanding subjectivity:

> [A] theory of articulation is both a way of understanding how ideological elements come, under certain conditions, to cohere within a discourse, and a way of asking how they do or do not become articulated, at specific conjunctures ... [T]he theory of articulation asks how an ideology discovers its subject rather than how a

subject thinks the necessary and inevitable thoughts which belongs to it.

(Hall, cited in Grossberg, 1996: 141–2)

The legacy of Althusser's idealist, hyper-antihumanism is still obvious, but Hall, unlike Althusser, does at least suggest some room for a 'subject' to do the 'articulating'. Indeed, Hall argued that the theory of 'articulation' allowed for an understanding how 'ideology empowers people, enabling them to make some sense ... of their historical situation, without reducing that [sense] to their socio-economic or class location or social position' (Hall, 1996a: 142).

'Making sense' was a function of cultural politics. In 'New Ethnicities', Hall (1996a: 442–3) argued that 'black cultural politics' (and by extension other identity-based politics) underwent a shift in the 1980s 'from a struggle over the relations of representation to a politics of representation itself'. This is important because:

> How things are represented and the 'machineries' and regimes of representation in culture do play a *constitutive*, and not merely a reflexive, after-the-event role. This gives questions of culture and the scenarios of representation – subjectivity, identity, politics – a formative, not merely an expressive, place in the constitution of social and political life.

(Hall, 1996a: 443)

This politics of representation, Hall argued, was – or had to be – inflected through a further politics of heterogeneity (Hall, 1996a: 444). To make this argument, Hall returned to one of his primary tropes, arguing that black cultural politics as a politics of representation required an 'awareness of the black experience as a *diasporic* experience' and thus an understanding of 'the consequences this carries for the process of unsettling, recombination, hybridization, and "cut-and-mix" – in short, the process of cultural *diaspora-ization* (to coin an ugly term) which it implies' (Hall, 1996a: 447). In other words, Hall remained interested in 'maps of meaning,' but now at a much higher level of abstraction.

Perhaps the earliest sustained engagement with Stuart Hall's (and CCCS's) work in Geography was by **Peter Jackson** both in his work on the geographies of racism, and especially in his book *Maps of Meaning* (1989). The title is taken, of course, from one of Hall's signature phrases and the book itself is a sustained engagement with, and geographical development of, the issues and theoretical approaches that animated the CCCS. The work of the CCCS was also central to such key works of the 1990s as Cresswell's (1996) *In Place/Out of Place*, which established the importance of geographical research on resistance. But interestingly, work by the CCCS and Hall barely figure at all in the 1997 volume *Geographies of Resistance* (Pile and Keith, 1997). Such a volume, however, was simply unthinkable without the decisive impact that Cultural Studies made in geography in the 1990s; the study of resistance in its myriad forms (popular culture, style, out-and-out opposition, etc.) no longer required an elaborate justification, either through recourse to the foundational work of the Centre or through the explicit development of theories that establish 'culture' as a prime ground for 'resistance'. This can be taken as some evidence of the very success of the CCCS's projects: to study subcultural resistance is now just part of the regular intellectual agenda in geography.

So too is studying geographies of subjectivity and identity. In *Mapping the Subject* Pile and **Thrift** (1995: 10) draw extensively on Hall's theories of diaspora as decisive in the structuring of subjectivity. For Pile and Thrift (1995: 10), quoting Hall (1995: 207), diasporic subjects 'represent new kinds of identities – new

ways of "being someone" in the late modern world' that entail people learning 'to think of themselves, of their identities and their relationship to culture and to place in ... more open ways.' Understanding subjectivity in this way, Pile and Thrift (1995: 11–12) cleverly argue, challenges us 'to consider the subject anew' and to make a commitment to:

> map the subject; a subject which is in some ways detachable, reversible and changeable; in other ways fixed, solid and dependable; located in, with and by power, knowledge and social relations. This map, this subject, this book are not the same: they seek new paths, new performances, new politics.
>
> (Pile and Thrift, 1995: 11–12)

The source for Pile and Thrift's argument is an essay Hall (1995) wrote for an Open University geography textbook called *A Place in the World* (Massey and Jess, 1995). This essay is perhaps Hall's most frequently cited work in the field, bringing together many of his arguments about the ways that a focus on diaspora helps us to see how cultures must always be understood as 'complex combination[s] of *continuities and breaks, similarities and differences*: what Gilroy ... calls a conception of tradition as the "changing same"' (Hall, 1995: 208). Hall is speaking here specifically of the black diaspora but he intends his point to be more encompassing than that. Or more accurately it is the black diaspora (and others like it) that is the model: it is a truer representation of culture and identity (and their formation) than static concepts of culture and identity. Geography is critical. Hall argues that what we need to understand is that it is routes rather than roots that are determinant:

> From the *diaspora* perspective, identity has many imagined 'homes' (and therefore no

one single homeland); it has many different ways of 'being at home' – since
it conceives of individuals as capable of
drawing on different maps of meaning
and locating them in different geographies at one and the same time – but it
is not tied to one, particular place.

(Hall, 1995: 207)

Doreen Massey (1994) concurs, and
argues that one of the key political tasks
ahead of us (as citizens of a diasporic
world and as geographers) is to forge a
'global sense of place', a map of meaning that takes interconnectedness rather
than separatism, routes rather than roots,
as its foundation. For Hall, as for Massey,
this means that we need to understand
the way that 'culture' entails a politics
of emplacement and displacement. Hall
draws directly on Massey and other
geographers to argue that culture, identity, and maps of meaning must always
be understood in relation to geography,
even, or perhaps especially, when trying to understand the current 'revival
of ethnicity' and other 'more "closed"
definitions of culture, in the face of what
they see as the threats to cultural identity
which globalization in its late-twentieth-
century forms represents' (Hall, 1995:
200–1).

KEY ADVANCES AND CONTROVERSIES

What is evident here is a confluence of
concerns between the work of many
geographers and Hall's arguments about
culture and identity, as each opens
up new avenues of inquiry for the
other. This is clear in Hall's (1991b) and

Massey's (1994) concurrent interest in
geographies of the home. But it is also
clear in the interest in post-structuralism
and post-coloniality in geography. Hall's
post-structuralist theory of articulation
requires theories of space and spatiality –
the very metaphor of 'joining up' makes
that clear – even as his encounter with the
metaphor of language requires attention
to the different spatialities of different
kinds of texts (see Barnes and Duncan,
1992). And geography's focus on the
geographies of the body also owes a considerable amount to Hall's (e.g., 1991a;
1991b) theories of identity (Teather,
1999: 11). But current theories of identity
and subjectivity, and of the globalisation process that give these their shape,
indebted as is Hall's to a post-structuralism
borne of Althusser's condescending anti-
humanism that understands the sort of
subjectivity that allows us to act and to
think and to be political as only 'a fiction,
an inevitable failure' (Chambers, 1994:
26), are arguably an inadequate response
to the political and intellectual demands
that face the discipline, and, more importantly, the geopolitical world.

As Hall would be the first to argue, the
development of his own work, and hence
its relationship to our various projects in
Geography, is over-determined. His work
and his concerns have arisen from particular 'conjunctural' moments, and have
become 'articulated' in specific, but not
at all necessary, ways. The identities of
both Hall and of the geographies influenced by him have as much to do with
their routes through a set of historical
and political debates and projects (over
the nature of globalisation, the formation of subjectivity, the nature of determination, or the rise of popular culture)
as their roots in specific disciplinary
formations. But what remains unclear
is whether these routes will take geographers working with and through Hall's

ideas away from the Althusserian ideal-ism and hyper-antihumanism that has come to animate Hall's own project of uncovering the determinations of iden-tity and subjectivity, and return it, in new and more productive ways, to its roots in the much more thoroughly materialist politic of culture that Hall advocates, but which his own theories of diasporic 'New Times' tend to ignore (see Hall, 1996a).

HALL'S KEY WORKS

CCCS (1982) *The Empire Strikes Back: Race and Racism in 70s Britain*. London: Hutchison.

Hall, S. (1975) *Television as a Medium in Relation to its Culture*. Birmingham : CCCS.

Hall, S. (1988a) *The Hard Road to Renewal: Thatcherism and the Crisis of the Left*. London: Verso.

Hall, S. (1997) *Representation: Cultural Representation and Signifying Practices*. Thousand Oaks: Sage.

Hall, S., Critcher, C., Jefferson, T., Clarke, C. and Roberts, B. (1978) *Policing the Crisis: Mugging, the State and Law and Order*. London: Macmillan.

Hall, S., Hobson, D., Lowe, A., and Willis, P. (eds) (1980) *Culture, Media, Language: Working Papers in Cultural Studies (1972–1979)*. London: Hutchinson.

Hall, S. and Jacques, M. (eds) (1983) *The Politics of Thatcherism*. London: Lawrence and Wishart.

Hall, S. and Jacques, M. (eds) (1989) *New Times: The Changing Face of Politics in the 1990s*. London: Lawrence and Wishart.

Hall, S. and Jefferson, T. (eds) (1976*) Resistance Through Rituals: Youth Subcultures in Post-War Britain*. London: Hutchison.

Secondary Sources and References

Althusser, L. (1969) *For Marx*. London: Allen Lane.

Barnes, T. and Duncan, J. (eds) (1992) *Writing Worlds: Discourse, Text, and Metaphor in the Representation of Landscapes*. London: Routledge.

Brundson, C. 1996. 'A thief in the night: stories of feminism in the 1970s at the CCCS', in D. Morley and K-H. Chen (eds), *Stuart Hall: Critical Dialogues in Cultural Studies*. London: Routledge. pp. 276–86.

Chambers, I. (1994) *Migrancy, Culture, Identity*. London: Routledge.

Chen, K-H. (1996) 'The formation of a diasporic intellectual: an interview with Stuart Hall', in D. Morley and K-H. Chen (eds) *Stuart Hall: Critical Dialogues in Cultural Studies*. London: Routledge. pp. 484–503.

Cresswell, T. (1996) *In Place/Out of Place: Geography, Ideology, and Transgression*. Minneapolis: University of Minnesota Press.

Gilroy, P., Grossberg, L. and McRobbie, A. (eds) (2000) *Without Guarantees: In Honour of Stuart Hall*. London: Verso.

Grossberg, L. (1996 [1986]) 'On postmodernism and articulation: an interview with Stuart Hall', in D. Morley and K-H. Chen (eds) *Stuart Hall: Critical Dialogues in Cultural Studies*. London: Routledge. pp. 131–50; first published in *Journal of Communication Inquiry*, 10: 45–60.

Hall, S. (1980a) 'Cultural studies and the centre: some problematics and problems', in S. Hall, D. Hobson, A. Lowe, and P. Willis (eds), *Culture, Media, Language: Working Papers in Cultural Studies (1972–1979)*. London: Hutchinson. pp. 15–47.

Hall, S. (1980b [1973]) 'Encoding/decoding', in S. Hall, D. Hobson, A. Lowe, and P. Willis (eds), *Culture, Media, Language: Working Papers in Cultural Studies (1972–1979)*. London: Hutchinson. pp. 128–38; first published as 'Encoding and decoding in the media discourse', Stencilled Paper 7. Birmingham: CCCS.

Hall, S. (1988b) 'The toad in the garden: Thatcherism among the theorists', in C. Nelson and L. Grossberg (eds), *Marxism and the Interpretation of Culture*. Champaign: University of Illinois Press. pp. 35–57.

Hall, S. (1989) 'Authoritarian populism', in B. Jessop et al. (eds), *Thatcherism*. Cambridge: Polity Press. pp. 99–107.

Hall, S. (1991a) 'Old and new identities, old and new ethnicities', in A. King (ed.), *Culture, Globalization and the World System*. London: Macmillan. pp. 41–68.

Hall, S. (1991b) 'The local and the global: globalization and ethnicity', in A. King (ed.), *Culture, Globalization and the World System*. London: Macmillan. pp. 19–39.

Hall, S. (1995) 'New cultures for old', in D. Massey and P. Jess (eds), *A Place in the World? Places, Cultures and Globalization*. Oxford: Oxford University Press. pp. 175–213.

Hall S. (1996a [1989]) 'New ethnicities', in D. Morley and K-H. Chen (eds), *Stuart Hall: Critical Dialogues in Cultural Studies*. London: Routledge. pp. 441–64; first published in *ICA Documents 7: Black Film, British Cinema*.

Hall, S. (1996b [1992]) 'Cultural studies and its theoretical legacies', in D. Morley and K-H. Chen (eds), *Stuart Hall: Critical Dialogues in Cultural Studies*. London: Routledge. pp. 262–75; first published in L. Grossberg et al. (eds.), *Cultural Studies*. London: Routledge. pp. 277–86.

Hall, S. and du Gay, P. (eds) (1996) *Questions of Cultural Identity*. Thousand Oaks: Sage.

Hall, S., Maharaj, S., Campbell, S. and Tawadros, G. (2001) *Modernity and Difference*. London: Institute of Visual Arts.

Jackson, P. (1989) *Maps of Meaning*. London : Routledge.

Massey, D. (1994) *Space, Place, and Gender*. Minneapolis: University of Minnesota Press.

Massey, D. and Jess, P. (eds) (1995) *A Place in the World? Places, Cultures and Globalization*. Oxford: Oxford University Press.

Morley, D. and Chen, K-H. (eds) (1996) *Stuart Hall: Critical Dialogues in Cultural Studies*. London: Routledge.

Pile, S. and Keith, M. (eds) (1997) *Geographies of Resistance*. London: Routledge.

Pile, S. and Thrift, N. (1995) 'Introduction', in S. Pile and N. Thrift (eds) *Mapping the Subject: Geographies of Cultural Transformation*. London: Routledge. pp. 1–12.

Teather, E. (ed.) (1999) *Embodied Geographies: Spaces, Bodies and Rites of Passage*. London: Routledge.

Whannel, P. and Hall, S. (eds) (1964) *Studies in the Teaching of Film Within Formal Education*. London: BFI.

Women's Study Group (1978) *Women Take Issue*. London: Hutchinson.

Don Mitchell, Syracuse University

29　Donna Haraway

BIOGRAPHICAL DETAILS AND THEORETICAL CONTEXT

As a thinker and writer whose extensive and wide-ranging work combines theoretical innovation with political commitment, Donna Haraway has been a key figure in debates surrounding knowledge, science, technology, nature and culture throughout the social sciences. Haraway was born in 1944 in Denver, Colorado, attending Colorado College where her undergraduate studies combined zoology, English and philosophy. Following her graduation in 1966, she spent a year in France where she developed an existing interest in political activism, and on her return to the US, participated in anti-Vietnam war protests and the civil rights movement. Simultaneously, she began a PhD in Biology at Yale University. A switch in direction from experimental biology to the study of the history and philosophy of biology was pivotal in the emergence of Haraway's philosophy, allowing her to expose the social production of scientific knowledge. Contrasting conventional ideas of science as objective knowledge of an external reality with the idea that science is simultaneously material and discursive, Haraway began to develop a powerful critique of science as a masculinist

endeavour, concerned with the mastery of nature.

After working at the University of Hawaii, where she completed her thesis, and at Johns Hopkins University, Haraway moved to the University of California, Santa Cruz in 1979. Here, she joined the new Program in the History of Consciousness, teaching and writing in the areas of feminist studies and science studies, and becoming Professor and more recently Chair of the History of Consciousness Program. Throughout, her work has continued to transcend conventional academic disciplinary boundaries, bringing biology into dialogue with primatology, post-structural and postmodern theory, feminist and science and technology studies, cultural theory, and more, in a series of influential and innovative papers and books. The titles of two particularly influential essays (revised and reprinted in Haraway's 1991 book *Simians, Cyborgs and Women: The Reinvention of Nature*) give an indication of her interests – 'Manifesto for cyborgs: science, technology and socialist feminism in the 1980s' (1985) and 'Situated knowledges: the science question in feminism as a site of discourse on the privilege of partial perspective' (1988). Other key works include *Primate Visions: Gender, Race and Nature in the World of Modern Science* (1989), a deconstruction of dualistic categories of, for example, nature/culture; *Modest_Witness@Second_Millennium*.

FemaleMan©_Meets_OncoMouse™. *Femi-nism and Technoscience* (1997), an analysis of the hybrid status of cybertechnologi-cal and biotechnological entities and of the rhetoric and mythology surrounding their existence; *How Like a Leaf* (2000), an interview in which Haraway discusses the influences on her intellectual devel-opment; and *When Species Meet* (2008), in large part a manifesto for co-emergent 'companion species' sharing particular spaces and intersecting lives (see also Haraway, 2003).

SPATIAL CONTRIBUTIONS

Haraway's academic career, her eclectic interests and experience of working in scientific as well as social scientific dis-ciplinary areas, have made her an impor-tant contributor to inter-disciplinary or post-disciplinary debates on space and place. Of particular importance is her questioning of the conventional distinc-tions drawn between those things which are considered 'natural' and those seen as 'cultural', arguing instead for recognition of the 'hybridity' of things and develop-ing metaphorical terminologies for refer-ring to entities which are simultaneously natural and cultural, natural and techno-logical, human and non-human, material and semiotic.

Within human geography, Haraway's critique of scientific objectivity has been especially influential. She argues that modern science attempts to perform what she calls the 'god trick' (Haraway, 1991) of displacing the (necessarily subjective) human observer of the world in favour of supposedly objective observational technologies which claim to produce a

truthful account of the world. Here, the metaphorical use of scientific 'vision' is significant (see **Gregory**, 1994; Barnes and Gregory, 1997), with Haraway argu-ing that science attempts to create a 'view from nowhere', a mythical objectivity external to social conditions. Visual tech-nologies designed to observe the world at the largest scale (e.g. satellite-mounted earth observation systems) and smallest scale (e.g., electron microscopes) serve to illustrate attempts to 'see' everything, and to present nature as a set of observ-able, factual, manageable phenomena:

> Vision in this technological feast becomes unregulated gluttony; all perspective gives way to infinitely mobile vision, which no longer seems just mythically about the god-trick of seeing everything from nowhere, but to have put the myth into ordinary practice.

(Haraway, 1991: 189)

For Haraway, however, such a god trick perpetuates a distinctively masculinist and exploitative understanding of the world. For example, 'feminine' nature becomes something to be observed, rationally explained, and mastered. Thus, the 'view from nowhere' dissimulates the way in which science is actually a cultural, power-laden process: it is not value-free:

> [A]ccording to the 'Modern Constitution' of scientific practice, a standard trick has been to generate representational systems of meaning that hide or obscure the sub-jectivity of the physical body. Objectivity has been socio-materially constructed by placing the situated and embodied char-acter of all knowledge-and-practice, including the Observer, in the background.

(Gren, 2001: 212)

Two related themes in Haraway's writ-ing emerge from this understanding of scientific enquiry: first, an emphasis on overcoming the scientific separation of the natural and the cultural (leading to a conceptualisation of things as hybrid, 'material-semiotic' or 'cyborg'); and second, a concept of 'situated knowledge' which is positioned against the supposedly objective knowledge of modern science.

In relation to the former, Haraway has explored how science reproduces a dualism of nature and culture: science, and the objective nature it purports to study, is seen as other to a socio-cultural realm of subjectivity and meaning. Along with others working on the sociology of science, she has instead described the ways in which science is a social and cultural process, so that the nature known through science is a cultural artefact, constituted through both the practices and technologies of scientific research and the language used to describe and explain scientific findings. But only in part. Opposing forms of social constructivism which suggest the world is simply a cultural or linguistic construct, Haraway has also been concerned to maintain a sense of the materiality or corporeality of nature (including humans, who are embodied subjects). Thus, things are never simply either natural or cultural. Neither are they simply either material or linguistic (see Demeritt, 1994). Entities such as genes, living organisms, disease microbes, cancer cells or electrons are ineluctably all of these things; they have a 'real' or material presence, which, significantly, produces agency (i.e. the ability to do things) within the complex and heterogeneous systems in which they exist, and are simultaneously conceptualised within linguistic or semiotic systems which constitute them as known entities within cultural systems. The term 'material-semiotic entity' is employed by Haraway to encompass this sense of simultaneity in describing such objects; material-semiotic entities are hybrids of what are conventionally considered as nature and culture.

While science is theorised as a socio-cultural process, for Haraway society and culture have, particularly in the post-Second World War period, become increasingly scientific and technological. In this context, she deploys a further metaphor – that of the cyborg – to overcome dualistic thinking. The idea of the cyborg, drawing upon the imaginaries of science fiction, is that of the biological body as supplemented or conjoined with technological apparatus to extend its capabilities. For instance, biotechnology, genetic engineering, cloning and so on, point to the ways that technoscience increasingly works with biological materials in ways which erode conventionally-held distinctions between the human and the non-human, between the biological and the technical and again, between nature and culture. The figure of the cyborg is key in Haraway's writing, both an attempt to describe the complex ways in which humans and other organisms are increasingly caught up in machine-like assemblages of material, biological and communications technologies, and a metaphor used to describe alternative forms of political and social identity which do not conform to conventional models of identification (by questioning, for example, prevailing categorisations of gender, race or sexuality).

For Haraway, there are negative and positive aspects to the emergence of cyborgs in the contemporary world. While she associates them with capitalist exploitation of the planet and oppression of some human and non-human beings, she also sees in them a liberatory potential to undermine conventional dualisms and categories. Here, Haraway wishes to deconstruct the categories associated with race, gender, age, sexuality, etc. which become seen as 'natural' and given, and are associated with specific social roles and cultural representations. Such a deconstruction has possibilities for liberation from assigned roles through the emergence of new, hybrid identities and new understandings of embodiment and subjectivity as dynamic, fluid products, rather than pre-given and fixed. Hence, a 'cyborg politics' which brings into question dualisms associated with gender, race and so on might be of value to those seeking to work towards the emancipation of subjugated groups, and has, for example, been adopted by geographers such as **Gillian Rose** as part of projects exploring how women are socially and spatially marginalised and oppressed. The figure of the cyborg is thus used by Haraway to signify a seditious political identity, an identity continually being reforged in processes of subverting totalising and dualistic theory and practice.

The concept of 'situated knowledge' again makes use of the metaphor of vision, and works with the notion of cyborg identity to suggest an alternative to the myth of scientific objective knowledge. For Haraway, situated knowledges are those of embodied, located subjects (using Haraway's geographical terminology, they are views from somewhere, rather than views from nowhere). They are necessarily partial perspectives, are geographically- and historically-specific, and are continually structuring, and being structured by, social conditions. While situated knowledges cannot simply be added together to produce totalising worldviews, 'shared conversations' (Haraway, 1991) are possible within the complex networks of connection binding people together, producing meeting points of shared solidarity around which layers of difference nevertheless persist. Such shared conversations are political and ethical, potentially affecting our ways of being in the world through the meeting, but not the resolution, of differently situated knowledges. As Haraway writes (1991: 195), 'I am

arguing for politics and epistemologies of location, positioning and situating, where partiality and not universality is the condition of being heard to make rational knowledge claims.'

In contrast to the association of objective scientific vision with male, white, Western domination, situated knowledges can include the knowledge perspectives of subjugated, marginalised groups – women, people of colour, and so on. Again, there is an association here with wider feminist theory, and also with (for example) post-colonial theory. For different people, then, understandings of nature, technology, and society can vary, and this multiplicity of situated knowledges must be recognised. Here, for example, Haraway has been instrumental in the emergence of ecofeminist perspectives in the sociology of science and technology and in relation to environmental issues (e.g., Instone, 1998). However, she cautions against simply romanticising the perspectives and knowledges of 'other' groups; they incorporate other biases and power relations, and hence are never 'innocent'. In addition, they may be difficult to access:

> 'Subjugated' standpoints are preferred because they seem to promise more adequate, sustained, objective, transforming accounts of the world. But *how* to see from below is a problem requiring at least as much skill with bodies and language, with the mediations of vision, as the 'highest' techno-scientific visualisations.
>
> (Haraway, 1991: 191)

Yet, Haraway does not adopt an anti-science position. Instead, she argues that we must create *better* accounts of the world: since science is a social activity, alternative scientific praxis can be undertaken which does not reproduce the regimes of domination, and illusion of objectivity, of conventional science.

Situated knowledges, including hypothetical situated *scientific* knowledges, differ from conventional scientific knowledge in reflexively recognising how the conditions of their production affect their conceptualisation of particular objects of study. They might thus also be described as 'objective' knowledges, dealing with the 'facts' of a situation, whilst recognising that from other somewheres the facts might be rather different. For Haraway, situated knowledges are bound into the notion of taking responsibility for what we 'see', for how we have learned to see, for the associated ethical positions we take towards the world, and for our actions. While she ascribes agency to non-human entities, Haraway nevertheless emphasises that 'it is people who are ethical, not these non-human entities' (Haraway, 2000: 134).

KEY ADVANCES AND CONTROVERSIES

The 'implosion' or collapse of dualistic and ontological categories in Haraway's writing has, as part of geographers' more general engagement with what **Nigel Thrift** (1996) calls 'non-representational theory', stimulated reconceptualisations of nature, culture, agency and ethical community. In her later work, Haraway (1997, 2008) goes beyond her writing on cyborgs (hybrids of human and technology) to insist on the agency of a much wider range of non-human actors. Here, there are similarities to the Actor-Network Theory associated with writers like Michel Callon, **Bruno Latour** and John Law, which disrupts realist accounts of the world in favour of understandings of the complex material-semiotic

relationships existing between things in heterogeneous networks or assemblages. For example, 'companion species' are 'webbed bio-social-technical apparatuses of humans, animals, artifacts, and institutions in which particular ways of being emerge and are sustained' (Haraway, 2008: 134). For Haraway, non-human (and human) technoscientific material-semiotic entities must be understood in ways which transcend conventional categories of analysis, and which juxtapose categories, spaces and entities such that the 'cleanliness' and orderliness associated with the technical is dissolved in a proliferation of interpenetrated 'sticky threads'. As she argues:

> Any interesting being in technoscience, such as a textbook, molecule, equation, mouse, pipette, bomb, fungus, technician, agitator, or scientist, can – and often should – be teased open to show the sticky economic, technical, political, organic, historical, mythic, and textual threads that make up its tissues. 'Implosion' does not imply that technoscience is 'socially constructed', as if the 'social' were ontologically real and separate, 'implosion' *is* a claim for heterogeneous and continual construction through historically located practice, where the actors are not all human.
>
> (Haraway, 1997: 68)

Extrapolating away from the realm of technoscience, such 'teasing open' might also be applied to other complex objects and representations, such as the global financial systems which draw simultaneously on discourses of transnationalism and technoscience (see Chernaik, 1999). Such discourses, importantly, 'are not just "words", they are material-semiotic practices through which objects of attention and knowing subjects are constituted' (Haraway, 1997: 218). Similarly, in relation to environmental systems, ecofeminist politics based on partial, positioned knowledge, might reformulate approaches to issues like environmental degradation, with environments imagined in terms of specific conjunctions of 'nature' and 'culture' (Instone, 1998). At smaller geographical scales, the situated agency of non-human actors is being drawn upon by geographers interested in rethinking the active and semiotic contributions of, for example, trees (Cloke and Jones, 2002) and animals (Whatmore, 2002; Wolch, 1998) to networks which also include human actors.

Haraway's work has also had implications for understandings of ethics in Geography. Contrasting with ethical models that ascribe rights to autonomous individuals, Haraway's dissolution of centred human subjectivity in favour of a focus on 'proliferations of naturalsocial relationalities in companion-species worlds linking humans and animals in myriad ways in the regime of lively capital' (Haraway, 2008: 62) – encourages an understanding of heterogeneous ethical communities (Whatmore, 1997). As Haraway (2008: 45) puts it, 'Trans-species encounter value is about relationships among a motley array of living beings, in which commerce and consciousness, evolution and bioengineering, and ethics and utilities are all in play.' The ethical entanglement of species is, she argues, a 'never settled biopolitics' (2008: 295), always an ethical encounter in progress and not something which can be settled by recourse to moral absolutes.

Here, then, relationships between entities are implicated in situated moral understandings (Lynn, 1998) and a conceptualisation emerges of ethics as situated praxis, rather than as an aspatial moral framework (Whatmore, 2002). As with Haraway's notion of shared conversations, this idea of ethical community implies a continuous process of negotiating partial understanding and solidarity.

It also suggests ways that ethical community might extend over space in different ways to conventional understandings that have often relied on the close proximity of autonomous ethical subjects. Instead, ethical community can be understood as connecting and enfolding different spaces within networks of ethical connection (e.g. through the material-semiotic exchange of money, goods, people and information on a global scale).

While it is clear that geographers have worked sympathetically with Haraway's theorisation in relation to a wide range of topics, criticisms have nevertheless arisen. Key among these has been a sense that, where her analytical strategy has involved the juxtaposition of different categories of thought in order to deconstruct and make problematic the status of technoscientific and other human and non-human entities, it is unclear exactly how such entities move or exist simultaneously across such categories. For example, in relation to possibilities for new understandings of ethical community,

> although Haraway's account of hybridity successfully disrupts the purification of nature and society and the relegation of 'nonhumans' to a world of objects, it is less helpful in trying to 'flesh out' the 'material' dimensions of the practices and technologies of connectivity that make the communicability of experience across difference, and hence the constitution of ethical community, possible. These dimensions require a closer scrutiny of overlapping life-practices and corporeal processes, for example those mediated by food, energy, disease, birth and death, than Haraway has so far admitted.
>
> (Whatmore, 1997: 47)

As such, 'Haraway does not consider as fully as she might do the transformation of actors, from the social to the non-social, the human to the nonhuman, the micro to the macro, and back again' (Michael,

1996: 42). Similarly, Haraway's accounts of hybridity and the cyborg are criticised as apparently reliant on the combination of pre-existing entities into a new entity. Such accounts raise the problem of who or what conducts this combination (see Whatmore, 2002), an issue recognised by Haraway in writing of the ambiguities inherent in, and essential to, her understanding of such entities. Cyborgs and hybrid actors make 'thoroughly ambiguous the difference between natural and artificial, mind and body, *self-developing and externally-designed...*' (Haraway, 1991: 152, emphasis added). Even so, for Doel (1999), notions of hybridity and situatedness are 'unbecoming' and 'sedentary', relying on the addition of units and embedded (even if only temporary) locatedness, rather than fully submitting to a world of ephemera, dislocation, promiscuity and becoming. For others, the notion of hybridity retains a privileging of the human, with arguments being

made that the concept should be extended to acknowledge those situations of co-production and hybridisation between entities where humans are not involved (Lulka, 2009).

Despite such criticism, Donna Haraway's influence on current human geographical theory has been significant, challenging conventional understandings of human subjectivity and ideas about nature through accounts of the emancipatory potential of cyborg, hybrid and multiple political identities (e.g., Hinchliffe, 2007; Whatmore, 2002) while maintaining the analytical and political value of concepts of class, race, gender and so on. At the same time, her work opens up ways of approaching space which emphasise material-semiotic connectivity, and present possibilities for making sense of micro- and macro-scale entities in ways which do not simply reduce them to the usual categories of nature or culture, human or non-human, subject or object.

HARAWAY'S KEY WORKS

Haraway, D. J. (1976) *Crystals, Fabrics and Fields: Metaphors of Organicism in 20th Century Developmental Biology.* New Haven, CT: Yale University Press.

Haraway, D. J. (1989) *Primate Visions: Gender, Race and Nature in the World of Modern Science.* London: Routledge.

Haraway, D. J. (1991) *Simians, Cyborgs and Women: The Reinvention of Nature.* London: Free Association Books.

Haraway, D. J. (1997) *Modest_Witness@Second_Millennium. FemaleMan©_Meets_OncoMouse™. Feminism and Technoscience.* London: Routledge.

Haraway, D. J. (2000) *How Like a Leaf: An Interview with Thyrza Nichols Goodeve.* London: Routledge.

Haraway, D. J. (2003) *The Companion Species Manifesto: Dogs, People and Significant Otherness.* Chicago, IL: Prickly Paradigm Press.

Haraway, D. J. (2008) *When Species Meet.* Minneapolis, MN: University of Minnesota Press.

Secondary Sources and References

Barnes, T. and Gregory, D. (1997) *Reading Human Geography: The Poetics and Politics of Inquiry.* London: Arnold.

Chernaik, L. (1999) 'Transnationalism, technoscience and difference: the analysis of material-semiotic practices', in M. Crang, P. Crang and J. May (eds), *Virtual Geographies: Bodies, Space and Relations.* London: Routledge. pp.79–91.

Cloke, P. and Jones, O. (2002) *Tree Cultures: The Place of Trees and Trees in Their Place.* Oxford: Berg.

Demeritt, D. (1994) 'The nature of metaphors in cultural geography and environmental history', *Progress in Human Geography*, 18 (2) 163–85.

Doel, M. (1999) *Poststructuralist Geographies: The Diabolical Art of Spatial Science.* Edinburgh: University of Edinburgh Press.

Gregory, D. (1994) *Geographical Imaginations.* Oxford: Blackwell.

Gren, M. (2001) 'Time-geography matters', in J. May and N. Thrift, (eds), *Timespace: Geographies of Temporality.* London: Routledge. pp. 208–25.

Haraway, D. J. (1985) 'Mainfesto for cyborgs: science, technology and socialist feminism in the 1980s', *Socialist Review*, 80: 65–108.

Haraway, D. J. (1988) 'Situated knowledges: the science question in feminism as a site of discourse on the privilege of partial perspective', *Feminist Studies*, 14(3) : 575–99.

Haraway, D.J.(1997) *Modest_Witness@Second_Millennium. FemaleMan©_Meets_OncoMouse™. Feminism and Techno-science.* London: Routledge.

Hinchliffe, S. (2007) *Geographies of Nature: Societies, Environments, Ecologies.* Sage: London.

Instone, L. (1998) 'The coyote's at the door: revisioning human-environment relations in the Australian context', *Ecumene*, 5 (4): 452–67.

Lulka, D. (2009) 'The residual humanism of hybridity: retaining a sense of the earth', *Transactions of the Institute of British Geographers*, 34: 378–93.

Lynn, W. (1998) 'Contested moralities: animals and moral value in the Dear/Symanski debate', *Ethics, Place and Environment*, 1, 223–42.

Michael, M. (1996) *Constructing Identities: The Social, the Nonhuman and Change.* London: Sage.

Thrift, N. (1996) *Spatial Formations.* London: Sage.

Whatmore, S. (1997) 'Dissecting the autonomous self: hybrid cartographies for a relational ethics', *Environment and Planning D: Society and Space*, 15: 37–53.

Whatmore, S. (1999) 'Hybrid geographies: rethinking the 'human' in human geography', in D. Massey, J. Allen and P. Sarre (eds), *Human Geography Today.* Cambridge: Polity Press. pp. 22–39.

Whatmore, S. (2002) *Hybrid Geographies: Natures Cultures Spaces.* London: Sage.

Wolch, J. (1998) 'Zoöpolis', in J. Wolch and J. Emel (eds), *Animal Geographies: Place, Politics and Identity in the Nature–Culture Borderlands.* London: Verso. pp. 119–38.

Lewis Holloway, University of Hull

30 J. Brian Harley

BIOGRAPHICAL DETAILS AND THEORETICAL CONTEXT

It may be that some might think it odd to see J. B. Harley appearing here as a 'key thinker' on space and place. For some Harley will be thought of mainly as an eminent and highly prolific cartographic historian with a strong empirical approach to the history of mapping and map-making. For others, however, this aspect of Harley's work will be less well known, particularly perhaps to undergraduate students of Geography whose encounter with Harley may be just through his later, more theoretically-informed approach to maps and mapping, his attempts to 'deconstruct the map' of the late 1980s and early 1990s (Harley, 1988a; 1988b; 1989a; 1989b). So Harley's contribution to geographical thinking and knowledge is twofold – partly empirical and partly theoretical, depending on whether Harley's academic work is being examined in its early or later phases. As an historical geographer whose academic career spanned more than 30 years (he died in 1991), Harley witnessed many changes in how geographers go about their work, particularly the change in approach referred to as 'the cultural turn', a move within human geography from a broadly

positivist approach to a more critical philosophy and epistemology (see Philo, 2000). While some historical geographers of his age and tradition did not themselves make this 'turn', Harley not only embraced it, and the new currents in geographical thinking that were so characteristic of the late 1980s, but also played a key role in steering human geography through this 'cultural turn'. In this sense, Harley quite rightly appears in a volume of key thinkers on space and place, for he changed the way geographers and cartographers view maps and map-making.

Harley's later papers have been brought together in a posthumous edited volume with introductory pieces by Laxton and Andrews which offer very useful overviews of his life, his work and his scholarly contributions (Harley, 2001; see also Daston, 2001; Edney, 2001). In his preface, Laxton remarks on the enduring impact of Harley's latter work, what he calls Harley's 'philosophy of cartographic history', a way of approaching maps and mapping that 'has been influential beyond the confines of map history' and which continues 'to excite students from a variety of disciplines', not just students of geography (Laxton, 2001: ix). Yet it is worth looking back, too, to Harley's earlier career and the very important part he played in shaping geographical discourse as an historical geographer working in a tradition that owed much to H. C. Darby's work on 'Domesday geographies'. Indeed,

Harley's PhD thesis undertaken at the University of Birmingham under Harry Thorpe's supervision was a study of the demographic and agricultural development of medieval Warwickshire (Harley, 1960), a study that might at first appear to be a long way from the work he later did on the philosophy of cartographic history, showcasing Harley as a cartographer, mapping out from taxation accounts the spatial patterns of population and economy of medieval Warwickshire. Far from being simply a commentator on mapping, therefore, Harley had practical experience of making maps. While his interest in medieval settlement and landscape continued during the 1960s (Harley, 1961; 1964a), it was to be his developing work on early-modern and modern British maps and map-making that positioned J. B. Harley as a respected academic cartographic historian, with contributions to numerous articles and papers on cartographers and surveyors, including those of the British Ordnance Survey.

Harley's engagement with Ordnance Survey maps and mapping took up most of his academic career, from the later 1960s through into the 1980s. This is the material by which some would define the significance of Harley's contribution to geography, with his detailed historical analyses of the Ordnance Survey's surveyors and cartographers of the early nineteenth century (e.g., Harley, 1982), his numerous bibliographical notes on reprints of First Edition One-Inch Ordnance Survey maps (e.g., Harley, 1986), as well as his advice 'manuals' on how to use early Ordnance Survey maps in local history and topographical study (Harley, 1964b; 1972; 1975). For those concerned with a broadly empirical historical geography and cartographic history, these contributions were invaluable. It was during the 1980s though, at the same time as Harley was co-editing the magnificent *History*

of Cartography volumes for the University of Chicago Press, that he began to deal more with the meanings of maps and mapping as a language of power. This was of course a time when other historical geographers were looking more critically at other kinds of geographical knowledge, and the complicity of past geographers in, say, colonialism and imperialism, where geographical knowledges – including maps – were being used to meet political ends. As UK and US historical geographers generally began to engage more with critical theory, particularly under the influence of French post-structuralists such as **Michel Foucault** and Jacques Derrida, uncertainty rose over the nature of Geography – its philosophical and epistemological assumptions – and questions began to be raised about those aspects of Geography that had, under positivism, always seemed somehow so secure, like landscapes and maps. This growing unease was to fuel Human Geography's 'cultural turn', as social, cultural and historical geographers (in particular) started to take more critical, theorised views of the world around them. Harley was one of them.

SPATIAL CONTRIBUTIONS

Harley was not alone in the later 1980s in beginning to look more critically at maps and map-making (Wood, 1992). But what makes Harley's 'philosophy of cartographic history' particularly important in geographical thinking is the way that he adopted the new currents of critical theory and used them to make sense of the maps he had long been studying empirically. By so doing, Harley put cartography and cartographic history firmly back on geography's curriculum. Through his critical engagement with the 'science' of cartography, and his querying of the map's authority, Harley made maps and mapping a fashionable subject again in academic geography. His approach was to draw upon those same theoretical arguments that were being used by human geographers during the 1980s in order to 'argue that we need to regard ... maps as text rather than as "objective" technical representations which can be considered apart from the social implications of our discourse' (Harley, 1989a: 80). For Harley (1989b), this meant 'deconstructing the map' – the title of one of his most cited papers – dealing not only with the ways in which maps are constructed but also how maps and mapping have agency in the world – the purposes they serve. The phrase 'politics in maps, maps in politics', coined by **Taylor** (1992) in his posthumous tribute to Harley, sums up nicely the approach that Harley was developing in his 'philosophy of cartographic history'.

It was really only in four key papers that Harley set out his new and critical philosophy of cartographic history, though just before his death he had drafted plans for 'a book of his own published or forthcoming essays to be called *The New Nature of Maps*' (Harley, 1988a; 1988b; 1989a; 1989b; Laxton, 2001: ix). These papers more or less dealt with the same issue, that 'cartography is seldom what cartographers say it is' (Harley, 1989b: 1). To deal with this Harley (1992: 232) was seeking 'to show how cartography also belongs to the terrain of the social world in which it is produced', and in this sense the arguments he was developing about cartography were cognate to those that Cosgrove and Daniels (1988) were developing at around the same time about landscape (see **Denis Cosgrove**). Indeed one of Harley's key

papers was a contribution to their *Iconography of Landscape* (Harley, 1988a). In these papers Harley tackled cartography on a number of different fronts. These are perhaps most clearly elucidated in 'Deconstructing the map', a paper that has been reprinted three times since it was first published, one of which Harley himself modified slightly (Harley, 1992; see also Harley, 2001: 149–68).

In trying to 'deconstruct' the map, one tactic Harley used was to expose the 'rules of cartography' (Harley, 1992: 233). Here he was primarily drawing upon Foucault's notion of 'discourse', as other historical geographers were likewise doing at the time (Driver, 1993; Philo, 1992). One of the 'rules of cartography' Harley drew geographers' attention to was the 'positivistic epistemology' of map-making – a belief upheld by cartographers that their approach was 'scientific' and 'untainted by social factors' (Harley, 1992: 234). This Harley argued against, saying 'we have to read between the lines of technical procedures or of the map's topographical content' and that when we do what becomes clear is that the 'rules of cartography' are seen to be influenced by the rules 'governing the cultural production of the map', that is, they are 'related to values, such as those of ethnicity, politics, religion or social class, and they are also embedded in the map-producing society at large' (Harley, 1992: 236). The rules of cartography and 'the rules of society' are thus 'mutually reinforcing the same image' of the world (Harley, 1992: 237). The 'ideology' of the map was not just in its image, therefore, but in the very modes of its production, in its 'mask of a seemingly neutral science' (Harley, 1992: 238).

Having established this, another of Harley's tactics was to then bring in the arguments of Derrida to deconstruct the map, to look for the slippages and contradictions within maps and map-making that actually undermines their authority and reason, and exposes their ideologies further. To this end, Harley (1992: 238) suggests that 'maps are a cultural text: not one code but a collection of codes', a text that is rhetoric, that silences, as well as informs (see also Harley, 1988b). As he put it, 'all maps state an argument about the world, and they are propositional in nature', and that includes even those topographical maps – such as the British Ordnance Survey – which on first sight might not appear to be 'ideological', and not just the maps traditionally thought of as 'distorted' or 'propaganda'. As Harley states, it is 'all maps', not just some, that 'are rhetorical' (Harley, 1992: 242). Harley thus saw maps as documents that deceive and dupe, that cartographers in their work tried to cover their tracks by projecting their maps as ever more scientific and true. He also tried other tactics to expose maps and map-making.

Again following **Foucault**, Harley dealt with the 'agency' of maps, how 'the map works in society as a form of power-knowledge' (Harley, 1992: 243). With this tactic, Harley was making the point that maps convey particular geographical knowledges to meet the needs and requirements of those who are doing the mapping or having the maps made. Maps are a key aspect of geography's history as a discipline, like fieldwork, and during the late 1980s and early 1990s, historical and cultural geographers increasingly drew attention to the relationship between geography and capitalism, and geography and imperialism (Livingstone, 1992; **Gregory**, 1994; Driver, 2001). Maps were a part of this complicity of Geography, for in their explorations of the eighteenth, nineteenth and twentieth century world(s) geographers drawing maps were not only charting territories but, by mapping them, were bringing distant lands under the control, scrutiny and

'gaze' of colonial powers such as Britain and France, aiding their governments' colonisation of the world and its peoples.

This 'agency' of the map is what Harley saw as an 'exercise of power', where 'cartographers manufacture power: they create a spatial panopticon' through which the land and its people can be watched over, controlled, subjugated (Harley, 1992: 244). Not only that, these maps circulated around the globe, and in so doing conveyed geographical knowledge that was itself crucial in projecting a particular view of the world. Thus, as Harley (1992: 245) put it, 'the power of the map maker was generally exercised not only over individuals but over the knowledge of the world made available to people in general'. Hence late Victorian maps of the British empire not only showed where territorial dominions lay, but also, in schools and government departments, these maps communicated 'to people in general' Britain's imperial might, a knowledge of British imperialism. Harley dealt with this topic of 'maps, knowledge and power' in his paper in Cosgrove and Daniel's (1988) *Iconography of Landscape*, where he considers some examples of 'the specific functions of maps in the exercise of power', maps which fused 'polity and territory', at different scales, 'ranging from global empire building, to the preservation of the nation state, to the local assertion of individual property rights' – maps meant power to those who had them (Harley, 1988a: 281–2).

In all then, Harley showed how the map and mapping were open to suspicion, that neither geographers or anyone else could, or should, take them at face value. Instead, he argued that maps are ideological, and always have been, that they are embedded with cultural and social values and beliefs that say as much about the mapper as the mapped. This was the work Harley was undertaking in the latter years of his academic life, opening up new ways of looking at maps and map-making. He saw no difference between, for example, the overtly political 'propaganda' maps of, say, Nazi Europe and the apparently 'neutral' topographical maps of the US Geological Survey, or between maps of the British Empire and maps produced by using modern technologies of Geographic Information Systems – to Harley all were open to same critical interpretation, to which he sought the advice of particularly those cultural theorists who in the 1980s were having such a hold on geographical enquiry, those such as Foucault and Derrida.

KEY ADVANCES AND CONTROVERSIES

Harley's work on maps and mapping has long influenced geographical thought, from his earlier historical studies of cartographers and early maps, to the more recent work he did from a more theoretically-informed position on the ideology of maps and map-making. So it is not unusual to see geographers and others still making reference to Harley's empirical studies of the Ordnance Survey of Great Britain, as well as to his later probing into the 'science' of cartography. In terms of his contribution as a key thinker on space and place, it is, however, his more theorised work that singles Harley out as a 'thinker', for he engaged with the conceptual changes that were characterising geographical thinking more broadly in the 1980s, developing positions from critical theory and drawing upon postmodern and post-colonial literatures to

raise geographers' and cartographers' awareness of maps and mapping in the themes that were becoming more significant, such as geography's history, imperialism, modernity, nationalism, identity, landscape, power, and so forth (see Cosgrove and Daniels, 1988; Daniels, 1993; Graham and Nash, 2000). So when it comes to discussing these issues, it becomes necessary to study maps too. Maps are implicated in the making of the geographical world. To ignore them was perilous at best and naive at worst. In this sense, in the 1980s and 1990s Harley helped to put maps back on the 'map' of geographical thinking, and in so doing he helped 'to make cartography exciting again' (Harley, 1989a: 88).

As a key thinker, then, Harley made a significant contribution to how geographers understand the world. But there are those who have suggested his arguments were over-stated and that his theorising hindered more than it helped in supporting his views (Belyea, 1992; Andrews, 2001). Indeed, Harley did not delve too deeply into the theoretical insights of Foucault and Derrida. Instead he called upon them to help him open up arguments and see things differently. In this context, it may be said that Harley did not himself make much of a conceptual contribution to Geography through his work – he did not seek to advance the theoretical arguments in themselves as part of his work. No, what he was doing was engaging with theoretical debates, and in so doing looking differently at his subject of cartography where others had not, while at the same time talking about maps and map-making in a language that was concurrently being used by other geographers to discuss the world around them. This was Harley's contribution, then. He was able to challenge orthodoxy in cartographic history, and able to show geographers that they could not afford to leave maps and map-making behind in their theorising and writing.

Harley himself recognised the difficulties – and perhaps risks – of his use of theoretical work. With Foucault and Derrida in particular, he acknowledged that their 'theoretical positions ... are sometimes incompatible', and yet he sees these philosophies as ways in which he could begin to 'search for the social forces that have structured cartography and to locate the presence of power – and its effects – in all map knowledge' (Harley, 1992: 232). So he proceeds by calling upon theoretical arguments even though he rarely cited their authors first-hand, and even though he did not see his work as theoretical in and of itself. Harley's contributions, though theorised, therefore remained largely empirical. Indeed it has been suggested that in his last works, those written shortly before his death, Harley was deliberately downplaying the theoretical arguments and literatures he had been citing, and reflecting more fully on what he meant by an 'ideology' of maps and mapping (see Andrews, 2001). Nevertheless, Harley's more theoretically-informed work certainly changed the way geographers think about maps and map-making, and also helped to steer human geographers through the 'cultural turn' of the 1980s and 1990s.

As Laxton (2001: x) has said, there is a risk that Harley's work – particularly his later 'philosophy of maps' – might simply be reduced to 'an unquestioned orthodoxy or, worse, a catechism'. This risk is perhaps heightened because of Harley's immediate writing style, 'fluent, zestful, and compulsively readable', and his ability to capture in just a few words, in a memorable passage, something inherently complex and uncertain, as he did with 'deconstructing the map' (Andrews, 2001: 2; Harley, 1992). Whatever the criticisms levelled at him and his approach since his death, there is no doubt that 'Harley's work continues to excite great interest among geographers, historians, and the substantial number of cultural and literary historians currently exploring the relationship between maps, literature, and the visual arts' (Laxton, 2001: xiv). That this influence is still palpable ten years after Harley's death is testament to his contribution as a key thinker on space.

HARLEY'S KEY WORKS

Harley, J.B. (1988a) 'Maps, knowledge, and power', in D.E. Cosgrove and S. Daniels (eds), *Iconography of Landscape: Essays on the Symbolic Representation, Design and Use of Past Environments*. Cambridge: Cambridge University Press. pp. 277–312.
Harley, J.B. (1988b) 'Silences and secrecy: the hidden agenda of cartography in early modern Europe', *Imago Mundi*, 40: 57–76.
Harley, J.B. (1989a) 'Historical geography and the cartographic illusion', *Journal of Historical Geography*, 15: 80–91.
Harley, J.B. (1989b) 'Deconstructing the map', *Cartographica*, 26: 1–20.
Harley, J.B. (2001) *The New Nature of Maps: Essays in the History of Cartography*. Baltimore: Johns Hopkins University Press.

Secondary Sources and References

Andrews, J.H. (2001) 'Meaning, knowledge, and power in the map philosophy of J.B. Harley', in J.B. Harley (ed.), *The New Nature of Maps: Essays in the History of Cartography*. Baltimore: Johns Hopkins University Press. pp. 1–32.
Belyea, B. (1992) 'Images of power: Derrida/Foucault/Harley', *Cartographica*, 29: 1–9.

Cosgrove, D.E. and Daniels, S. (eds) (1988) *Iconography of Landscape: Essays on the Symbolic Representation, Design and Use of Past Environments.* Cambridge: Cambridge University Press.

Daniels, S. (1993) *Fields of Vision: Landscape Imagery and National Identity in England and the United States.* Cambridge: Polity.

Daston, S. (2001) 'Language of power', *London Review of Books,* 1 November: 3–6.

Edney, M.E. (2001) 'Works by J.B. Harley', in J.B. Harley (ed.), *The New Nature of Maps: Essays in the History of Cartography.* Baltimore: Johns Hopkins University Press. pp. 281–96.

Driver, F. (1993) *Power and Pauperism: The Workhouse System, 1834–1884.* Cambridge: Cambridge University Press.

Driver, F. (2001) *Geography Militant: Cultures of Exploration and Empire.* Oxford: Blackwell.

Graham, B. and Nash, C. (eds) (2000) *Modern Historical Geographies.* Harlow: Pearson.

Gregory, D. (1994) *Geographical Imaginations.* Oxford: Blackwell.

Harley, J.B. (1960) 'Population and land-utilisation in the Warwickshire Hundreds of Stoneleigh and Kineton, 1086–1300'. Unpublished PhD thesis, University of Birmingham.

Harley, J.B. (1961) 'The Hundred Rolls of 1279', *Amateur Historian,* 5 (Autumn): 9–16.

Harley, J.B. (1964a) 'The settlement geography of early medieval Warwickshire', *Transactions of Institute of British Geographers,* 34: 115–30.

Harley, J.B. (1964b) *The Historian's Guide to Ordnance Survey Maps.* London: National Council of Social Service for the Standing Conference for Local History.

Harley, J.B. (1972) *Maps for the Local Historian: A Guide to the British Sources.* London: National Council of Social Service for the Standing Conference for Local History.

Harley, J.B. (1975) *Ordnance Survey Maps: A Descriptive Manual.* Southampton: Ordnance Survey.

Harley, J.B. (1982) 'The Ordnance Survey 1:528 Board of Health town plans in Warwickshire', in T.R. Slater and P.J. Jarvis (eds), *Field and Forest: An Historical Geography of Warwickshire and Worcestershire.* Norwich: Geobooks. pp. 347–84.

Harley, J.B. (1986) 'Introductory essay' in *Central England, Volume Four – The Old Series Ordnance Survey Maps of England and Wales.* Lympne Castle, Kent: Harry Margary. pp. vii– xxxv.

Harley, J.B. (1992) 'Deconstructing the map', in T.J. Barnes and J.S. Duncan (eds), *Writing Worlds: Discourse, Text and Metaphor.* London: Routledge. pp. 231–47.

Laxton, P. (2001) 'Preface' in J.B. Harley, *The New Nature of Maps: Essays in the History of Cartography.* Baltimore: Johns Hopkins University Press. pp. ix–xv.

Livingstone, D. (1992) *The Geographical Tradition.* Oxford: Blackwell.

Philo, C. (1992) 'Foucault's geography', *Environment and Planning D: Society and Space,* 10: 137–61.

Philo, C. (2000) 'More words, more worlds', in I. Cook, D. Crouch, S. Naylor and J. Ryan (eds), *Cultural Turns/Geographical Turns.* Harlow: Pearson. pp. 26–53.

Taylor, P. (1992) 'Politics in maps, maps in politics: a tribute to Brian Harley', *Political Geography,* 11: 127–9.

Wood, D. (1992) *The Power of Maps.* London: Routledge.

Keith Lilley, Queen's University, Belfast

31   David Harvey

BIOGRAPHICAL DETAILS AND THEORETICAL CONTEXT

David Harvey was born in England in 1935, and raised in Gillingham, Kent. He completed his BA and PhD at Cambridge University in the Department of Geography, leaving in 1960. During the 1950s, as was common in British geography departments, Cambridge stressed the importance of regional study – that is, the analysis of geographical particularity and difference – in its degree programmes. The Cambridge Geography Department was also known for its historical geography research. Accordingly, Harvey's doctoral thesis focused on the changing location of hop production in nineteenth-century Kent. However, no sooner had the results of this research been published (Harvey, 1963) – than Harvey started to move in an altogether different intellectual direction. Following a post-doctoral year at the University of Uppsala (where he encountered Gunnar Olsson), Harvey spent the 1960s working as Lecturer in Geography at Bristol University.

It was during his time at Bristol – which was punctuated by study leave at Pennsylvania State University, a major centre for scientific and quantitative geography – that Harvey made his name as a philosopher and theorist of positivism. His landmark book *Explanation in Geography* (1969) gave the profusion of statistical methods and techniques in 1960s human geography a robust and consistent intellectual foundation. In the book, Harvey explored systematically the nature of scientific explanation in general; the role of theories, hypotheses, laws and models; the use of mathematics, geometry and probability as languages of explanation; the nature of observation, data classification and data representation; and different forms of scientific explanation. *Explanation in Geography* served two purposes. First, it gave Harvey's generation of geographers – the so-called 'spatial scientists' who rose to prominence during the 1960s – a heavyweight justification and manifesto for their project of identifying spatial patterns, departing from an earlier generation (the generation that had educated Harvey and his cohort at Cambridge and elsewhere) concerned with what Fredric Schaefer (1953) had called 'exceptionalism'. Secondly, *Explanation in Geography* served to align the discipline with the so-called 'real' sciences like physics and, for some geographers, boosted the discipline's self-image. This was achieved by Harvey drawing upon the ideas of philosophers of science like Karl Popper.

Explanation in Geography, ironically, marked both the high-point and the end-point of Harvey's desire to fashion the foundations of a properly scientific geography. Almost immediately after the book's publication, Harvey took up an Associate Professorship in the Department of

Geography and Environmental Engineering at the Johns Hopkins University, Baltimore. This was triply significant. First, though a port city like Bristol, Baltimore was far poorer and had suffered major economic decline throughout the post-war years. Second, Harvey's new department was less narrowly disciplinary than Bristol had been and this, arguably, gave him licence to roam intellectually. Thirdly, at Hopkins, Harvey encountered a group of graduate students and academics that wanted to understand the radical ideas of the nineteenth-century political economist Karl Marx. It was in this context that Harvey wrote *Social Justice and the City* (1973), a book of equal – if very different – significance to its predecessor. As its title suggests, Harvey's second book focused on how to alleviate urban ills like poverty. Where *Explanation in Geography* was strangely detached from its wider sociopolitical context – namely, the attempts of the Labour government to make Britain a fairer society, and the more distant civil rights and anti-Vietnam protests in the US – *Social Justice* was thoroughly immersed in it. The book charts Harvey's rapidly changing intellectual and political trajectory. Part One, titled 'Liberal formulations', focuses on how existing mechanisms of urban planning could bring about a more just urban society in Western countries. But Part Two, called 'Socialist formulations', moves beyond the reformism of Part One and proposes a revolution in urban affairs predicated on the ideas of political economists like Marx. One of the book's key essays, 'Revolutionary and counter-revolutionary theory in geography and the problem of ghetto formation', proposed nothing less than a wholesale rejection of the way human geographers both studied cities and thought about solving urban social problems.

Social Justice established Harvey as a major dissenting voice in urban studies and caused quite a stir. It did so for three reasons. First, because it chronicled Harvey's reinvention as a 'radical geographer', it took many spatial scientists by surprise. Like Gunnar Olsson's (1975) *Birds in Egg/Eggs in Bird*, *Social Justice* was deliberately schizophrenic, literally a book of two halves. Second, *Social Justice* challenged the prevailing view in scientific geography that 'facts' and 'values' can be kept separate. Harvey called for a geography that could study the world in order to *change it* along more socially just lines. Finally, *Social Justice* was the first major example of a left-wing style of geography. Specifically, it opened the door for the subsequent development of Marxist geography, of which Harvey was to be a pioneer along with some of his graduate students (see **Neil Smith**).

Harvey's turn to Marxism meant that he became preoccupied with *capitalism* and its workings. Yet he did not entirely abandon earlier themes. In *Explanation in Geography*, Harvey was interested in how social processes produce spatial forms, and he ended the book with the declaration that 'without theory we cannot hope for ... consistent, and rational, explanation of events' (Harvey, 1969: 486). These two themes animate his 1970s writings, which are an attempt to fashion a Marxian theory of how geography is both produced by, and alters, the workings of the capitalist economy. By 'geography', Harvey did not mean the discipline of that name, but the material landscape of towns, cities and transport networks that act as the 'arteries' of capitalism. To fashion this 'historical-geographical materialism' Harvey spent the mid-to-late 1970s reading Marx's later works like *Capital* and *Grundrisse*. This effort culminated in Harvey's most sophisticated book *The Limits to Capital* (1982). This book is nothing less than a reconstruction and extension of Marx's theory of capitalism;

the extensions are primarily geographical because Marx paid little attention to
how geography influences capitalism's
operation.

In the mid-1980s, with his reputation as
the leading Marxist (and, indeed, human)
geographer established, Harvey returned
to the urban issues that were the focus of
Social Justice. Inquiring into the specific
nature and problems of capitalist cities,
his two 'Studies in the History and Consciousness of Urbanisation' essentially
took the perspectives of 'structure' and
'agency' respectively. *The Urbanization of
Capital* (1985a) unfolds a Marxian theory
of how capitalism produces cities with
characteristic material properties and contradictions; *Consciousness and the Urban
Experience* (1985b) theorises how people
respond to having to live in capitalist cities, especially those who lack economic
and political power (see also *The Urban
Experience*, 1989a).

Shortly after publishing these two
books, Harvey returned to England as Halford Mackinder Professor of Geography
at Oxford University. Leaving Reagan's
America for Thatcher's Britain, Harvey
felt himself confronted with an increasingly conservative, anti-Marxist British
Left and said so in an outspoken critique
of UK urban studies (Harvey, 1987a).
While at Oxford, Harvey also wrote his
best-selling book *The Condition of Postmodernity* (1989b), a critical analysis of the
rise of postmodernism in several walks
of contemporary cultural life (including
urban consumption, architecture and
even academia). Returning to Hopkins in
1993 for academic and personal reasons,
he then revisited the theme of social justice and linked it to environmental issues
in his *Justice, Nature and the Geography of
Difference* (1996). Latterly, Harvey moved
to City University New York to become
Professor of Anthropology, publishing
two collections of essays, one a 'greatest

hits' volume (*Spaces of Capital*, 2001), the
other about the continued relevance of
Marxism to the wider project of creating a
better socio-environmental future (*Spaces
of Hope*, 2000).

As the latter book recounts, Harvey's
designation as a 'Marxist' represents
something very different today in the
Anglophone world compared with the
early 1970s. Today Marxism is seen as
rather 'old-hat' among radicals, which
makes Harvey's continued commitment
to it all the more remarkable given the
number of post- and ex-Marxists that litter the intellectual landscape (such as
Manuel Castells and **Doreen Massey**).
This said, Marx's work enjoyed a minor
revival in light of the sub-prime lending
crisis in the US in 2007. Harvey played a
role in this revival by authoring two books
on contemporary global affairs, namely
The New Imperialism (2003) and *A Brief
History of Neoliberalism* (2005). The first
analyses America's recent overseas ventures in Iraq and Afghanistan, the latter
the spread of neo-liberal ideas and policies since the early 1970s. Both texts use
Marx's basic insights about the dynamics
of capital accumulation to explain global
trends. At the same time, *The Limits to
Capital* has been reissued twice (in 1999
and 2006) – a reflection of its fundamental insights into the economic turbulence
of the last 20 years.

SPATIAL CONTRIBUTIONS

Harvey was among the first geographers
to insist that space is not given and absolute or a 'container' into which intrinsically 'non-spatial' things are stuffed. As
he put it in *Social Justice* (1973: 14) 'The

question "What is space?" [must] ... be replaced by the question "how is it that distinctive human practices create and make use of distinctive ... space[s]?'" For Harvey, social practices and process create spaces and these spaces, in turn, constrain, enable and alter those practices and process – what **Ed Soja** (1989: 78) called a 'socio-spatial dialectic'. This means that Harvey has long rejected the polar belief that space has no social effects (common among twentieth-century critical theorists) or that it has effects 'in itself' – what Sack (1974) called 'spatial separatism'. This latter belief sometimes crept into the work of Anglophone geography's spatial scientists, who now and then fixated on spatial pattern over social process. Harvey's mid-way position entails arguing that space – the material form that processes assume 'on the ground' as buildings, infrastructure, consumption sites and so on – is *both* cause and effect in/of social life – what he once called an 'active moment' (Harvey, 1985a: 3) in human affairs (see also Harvey, 1997).

Harvey's general belief that space is relative and constructed, leads us to his reading of capitalist space. For Marx, capitalism is a contradictory economic system based on three 'logics': accumulation for accumulation's sake (i.e., the quest for profit as an end in itself); competition between rival producers fighting for market share; and technological innovation in production processes and products. This trinity leads to internal contradictions in the capitalist system, as Marx's *magnum opus Capital* explains. Periodically, these erupt in major 'crises of overaccumulation' in which pools of unutilised workers and commodities can find no productive use. One reason for these crises is that it is 'rational' in a capitalist system for businesses to replace workers with machinery in order to make production cheaper or more efficient. The paradox is that if

many or most businesses do this then a collective problem for all businesses arises: since workers are also consumers then laying-off workers removes a major market for commodities, thus precipitating an economic crisis.

What has any of this to do with space? In *The Limits to Capital* Harvey shows how splurges of investment in buildings, roads and other infrastructure can provide capitalism with a mechanism for crisis displacement. Two of the unique features of built environments is that they are exceedingly expensive to build and the return on investment from this expenditure is strung out over a number of years. Thus a new convention centre might cost $80 million, the returns on which will trickle back to investors in the form of repeat conference fees over many years. What this means, according to Harvey, is that at times of incipient economic crisis, the capitalist system tends to 'switch' investment from current production into long-term fixed capital investments in the geographical landscape. These investments stave off economic crisis by tying up excess capital and amount to what Harvey has famously called a 'spatial fix' for capitalism's contradictions. However, at a later date, these physical investments can become barriers to further accumulation because they are so hard to replace once made. Thus, when automobiles challenged railways in the early twentieth century as a principal way of moving people and commodities, the enormous investments in rail networks acted as temporary hindrance to new rounds of fixed capital investment. In sum, for Harvey space is *produced* within capitalism and expresses the system's inner contradictions. Harvey is among the few Marxists to insert space into Marx's theory of capitalism by way of these ideas (others include **Neil Smith**).

Another important theme in Harvey's writings relates to the particular–general or space–place relationship. By 'place' Harvey means the unique conjunction of built environments, cultures, peoples, etc. that distinguish one locality from another. However, unlike the regional geographers of the pre-1960s era, Harvey does not think that places are *singular* – that is, absolutely different – because in a capitalist world economy *different* places are linked within a *common* economic framework. For geographers, one of the major intellectual challenges is thus how to understand the persistence of place distinctiveness amidst heightened place-interdependence (that is, heightened ties across a wider space). Harvey's answer to this challenge is disarmingly simple. In *The Urbanization of Capital* he argues that we can view capitalism as a circulation process where money is advanced by businesses to purchase labour, inputs and means of production to produce commodities that are sold for the amount of their production cost plus an increment (profit). This process involves commodity production in different places becoming subject to a logic that is indifferent to the qualitative specificities of these places. Thus a rug made in Calcutta is a means of making money just as much as a microchip made in Silicon Valley, indeed, the two different places are united when a chip designer in the latter place buys a rug from the former. Hence, because capitalism practically brings different places within the same economic universe it becomes possible 'to make universal generalisations about the evident unique particularities of [pl]ace' (Harvey, 1985a: 45; see also Merrifield, 1993).

Beyond the 'objective' or material side of the particular–general/place–space relationship there is its 'subjective' side: the way it is perceived and acted on by people living in real places. To be aware of how lives in one place are affected by the unseen actions of distant strangers

elsewhere is to possess what Harvey (1990) terms a 'geographical imagination'. To lack such awareness is to fall into the trap of inter-place competition and rivalry that is part of the geographical logic of capitalism (Harvey, 1985c; 1988). In *Justice, Nature and the Geography of Difference*, Harvey highlights the dilemmas that beset all attempts to make progressive anti-capitalist links among oppressed peoples in different places. One of these relates to 'militant particularism', which is the elemental fact that any wider movement against global capitalism will necessarily be composed of lots of actions by locally-based people. The problem, Harvey argues, is that what makes sense at the local scale may not make sense at a broader geographical scale. Harvey has illustrated this key problem in a book co-edited during his time at Oxford, called *The Factory and the City* (Harvey and Hayter, 1993). This book is about the fight by Rover car workers near Oxford to keep their jobs in the late 1980s. Therein, Harvey argues that while keeping car jobs creates much needed local employment, at a broader scale it is hardly a worthy socialist objective to make polluting automobiles for middle-class consumers. The question then becomes at which scale – the local or the global – should political objectives be set?

Ultimately the key contribution Harvey has made to contemporary conceptions of space and place is to insist that the two can be theorised. This is not as trite a statement as it at first sight seems. **Andrew Sayer** (1985) famously argued that space and place cannot be meaningfully theorised because the difference they make to social practices and processes is contingent. In other words, for Sayer the material importance of place and space cannot be specified at the level of theory but only at the level of detailed, empirical research. This risks relegating geography as a discipline (and geographical matters more generally) to largely factual concerns. Harvey disagrees with this view showing it is possible to make substantive theoretical statements about the role of space in modern life (see Castree, 2001). More particularly, he has been an exponent of what is called 'grand' or 'meta-theory'. This is a form of theory that presumes there to be broad logics at work in the world that it is the task of the theoretician to identify conceptually and produce a mental map of. For Harvey, capitalism possesses fundamental logics of this sort, even when it appears otherwise, and space is *internal* to these logics. In *The Condition of Postmodernity* Harvey argues that the idea that we are now in a 'postmodern era' where difference, complexity and plurality have replaced similarity is a fiction. Underlying various forms of postmodern expression – in architecture and consumption, for example – Harvey sees the same old logics of capitalism using the production of difference (real and symbolic) in the form of commodities as a means of making money.

KEY ADVANCES AND CONTROVERSIES

While Harvey's work over the last 30 years is very consistent – intellectually and politically – it is wrong to assume that there have been no cognitive or normative shifts in his thinking (Castree, 2007). However, Harvey is justly celebrated as a Marxist thinker, and has arguably achieved three things. First, he gave Marxist geography the intellectual

foundation it needed through the 1970s and 80s, along with other emerging Marxists like Neil Smith, Erik Swyngedouw and Richard Walker (three of Harvey's graduate students at Hopkins). Second, he set a precedent for radical geography more generally, emboldening younger human geographers to take up the cause of women, gays and lesbians, people of colour and so on. Finally, Harvey's writings have persuaded many Marxists at large that space and place matter to capitalism and are thus integral to any project to overthrow it.

Examples of how Harvey's ideas have been developed abound. Two key trajectories in contemporary human geography illustrate this. First, in economic geography, several writers have applied ideas of the spatial (and temporal) fix to specific research issues – like the way farmers use credit to finance long-term investments in capitalist agriculture (Henderson, 2001). Secondly, in urban geography, Harvey's idea of how inter-place competition is a necessary feature of the capitalist mode of production has inspired detailed studies of the so-called 'growth coalitions' that vie for jobs and inward investment (e.g., Cox and Mair, 1989). Indeed, the literature on urban entrepreneurialism and place promotion draws substantially on Harvey's theoretical imagination in its attempt to make sense of the lengths that cities will go to entice capital to 'come to town'.

However, Harvey's work has been subject to increasing criticism since *The Condition of Postmodernity* was published, especially from human geographers. In part this is because the intellectual Zeitgeist has changed, with Marxism now being seen as a rather out-dated critical theory by a younger generation of radical academics (despite signs of a renewed interest in Marxism by some social scientists and many political activists). Three criticisms of Harvey's work loom large. First, he has been upbraided for the 'muscular' nature of his theoretical ideas. Feminists such as Deutsche (1991) and Morris (1992) criticised Harvey's apparent belief that his Marxism offers a privileged perspective on the 'truth' of the world. They maintained that his confidence in his theoretical claims bespeaks a distinctively masculine desire for cognitive mastery and control, one that excludes other ways of knowing the world. The result, they maintained, is that Harvey is blind to all manner of important real world processes and events that do not fit with his Marxist worldview.

This links, secondly, with the criticism that Harvey's Marxism cannot accommodate 'difference'. Over the last decade those on the academic left have accentuated social 'difference' as a way of escaping the Marxist obsession with class as the primary axis of oppression and resistance in modern societies. The differences celebrated include those within and between women, gay men and lesbians and people of colour. Harvey (1996) has responded by clarifying his position, arguing that non-class differences between people must be linked to, but are not reducible to, any project to overthrow capitalism.

Thirdly, some (e.g., Dennis, 1987) have worried that Harvey's grand theoretical abstractions are insufficiently grounded in the messy complexities of the real world. Harvey (1987b; 1989a) has responded with the argument that theory is not intended to exhaustively explain any given situation but rather to open a window onto the key processes at work. Because of these (and some other) criticism, many geographers have developed new arguments in direct reaction or opposition to Harvey's – using them as a 'negative launchpad' if you like. Examples include Herod's (2001) work on how wage labourers fight back against business in place and across space (whereas Harvey tends to be preoccupied with the power of capital) and **Peter Jackson's** (1999) work on the consumption of commodities, which gives consumers a more active role than Harvey is seemingly prepared to.

This given, Harvey's later works have continued to be influential, but not because they break fresh intellectual ground or respond to such critiques. *The New Imperialism* (2003) and *A Brief History of Neoliberalism* (2005), for example, revisit Marx's basic theory of capital accumulation to explain current global affairs. Though not theoretically original, their insights appear fresh to a younger generation of readers unfamiliar with Marxist ideas. Moreover, Harvey's knack of coining neologisms – such as 'accumulation by dispossession' – has continued to make his work eminently citable.

HARVEY'S KEY WORKS

Harvey, D. (1969) *Explanation in Geography.* London: Edward Arnold.
Harvey, D. (1973) *Social Justice and the City.* London: Arnold.
Harvey, D. (1982/1999/2006) *The Limits to Capital.* Oxford: Blackwell; London: Verso (twice).
Harvey, D. (1985a) *The Urbanization of Capital.* Oxford: Blackwell.
Harvey, D. (1985b) *Consciousness and the Urban Experience.* Oxford: Blackwell.
Harvey, D. (1989a) *The Urban Experience.* Oxford: Blackwell.
Harvey, D. (1989b) *The Condition of Postmodernity.* Oxford: Blackwell.
Harvey, D. (1996) *Justice, Nature and the Geography of Difference.* Oxford: Blackwell.

Harvey, D. (2000) *Spaces of Hope*. Edinburgh: Edinburgh University Press.
Harvey, D. (2003) *The New Imperialism*. Oxford: Oxford University Press.
Harvey, D. (2005) *A Brief History of Neoliberalism*. Oxford: Oxford University Press.
Harvey has his own website, where his seminar on Marx's *Capital*, Volume 1, can be viewed (davidharvey.org/).

Secondary Sources and References

Castree, N. (2001) 'From spaces of antagonism to spaces of engagement', in A. Brown., S. Fleetwood and J. M. Roberts (eds), *Marxism and Critical Realism*. Routledge: London and New York. pp. 187–214.
Castree, N. (2007) 'David Harvey: Marxism, capitalism and the geographical imagination', *New Political Economy*, 12(1): 97–115.
Cox, K. and Mair, A. (1989) 'Locality and community in the politics of local economic development', *Annals of the Association of American Geographers*, 78: 307–25.
Dennis, R. (1987) 'Faith in the city', *Journal of Historical Geography*, 13: 310–16.
Deutsche, R. (1991) 'Boy's town', *Environment and Planning D: Society and Space*, 9: 5–30.
Harvey, D. (1963) 'Locational change in the Kentish hop industry and the analysis of land use patterns', *Transactions of the Institute of British Geographers*, 33: 123–40.
Harvey, D. (1981) 'The spatial fix', *Antipode* 13 (3): 1–12.
Harvey, D. (1985c) 'The geopolitics of capitalism', in D. Gregory and J. Urry (eds), *Social Relations and Spatial Structures*. London: Macmillan. pp. 128–63.
Harvey, D. (1987a) 'Three myths in search of a reality in urban studies', *Environment and Planning D: Society and Space*, 5: 367–76.
Harvey, D. (1987b) 'The representation of urban life', *Journal of Historical Geography*, 13: 317–21.
Harvey, D. (1988) 'The geographical and geopolitical consequences of the transition from Fordism to flexible accumulation', in G. Sternlieb and J. Hughes (eds), *America's New Market Geography*. New Brunswick: Rutgers University Press. pp. 101–35.
Harvey, D. (1990) 'Between space and time: reflections on the geographical imagination', *Annals of the Association of American Geographers*, 80: 418–34.
Harvey, D. (1997) 'Contested cities: social process and spatial form', in N. Jewson and S. MacGregor (eds), *Transforming Cities*. London: Routledge. pp. 19–27.
Harvey, D. (1999) 'Foreword' to *The Limits to Capital* (2nd edition). London: Verso.
Harvey, D. (2001) *Spaces of Capital*. Edinburgh: Edinburgh University Press.
Harvey, D. and Scott, A. (1987) 'The practice of human geography: theory and empirical specificity in the transition from Fordism to flexible accumulation', in B. Macmillan (ed.) *Remodelling Geography*. Oxford: Blackwell. pp. 217–29.
Harvey, D. and Hayter, T. (1993) *The Factory and the City*. London: Mansell.
Henderson, G. (2001) *California and the Fictions of Capital*. Oxford: Oxford University Press.
Herod, A. (2001) *Labor Geographies*. New York: Guilford.
Jackson, P. (1999) 'Commodity cultures: the traffic in things', *Transactions of the Institute of British Geographers*, 24: 95–108.
Merrifield, A. (1993) 'Space and place: a Lefebvrian reconciliation', *Transactions of the Institute of British Geographers*, 18: 516–31.
Morris, M. (1992) 'The man in the mirror', *Theory, Culture and Society*, 9: 253–79.
Olsson, G. (1975) *Birds in Egg/Eggs in Bird*. London: Pion.
Sack, R. (1974) 'The spatial separatist theme in geography', *Economic Geography*, 50: 1–19.
Sayer, A. (1985) 'The difference that space makes', in D. Gregory and J. Urry (eds), *Social Relations and Spatial Structures*. London: Macmillan. pp. 49–66.
Schaefer, F. (1953) 'Exceptionalism in geography', *Annals of the Association of American Geographers*, 43: 226–9.
Soja, E. (1989) *Postmodern Geographies*. London: Verso.

Noel Castree, University of Manchester

32 bell hooks

BIOGRAPHICAL DETAILS AND THEORETICAL CONTEXT

Having published over 20 books of theory, poetry, fiction and autobiography, bell hooks is one of the most prominent and influential feminist philosophers of recent years. Her devotion to black activism, intellectual life, and cultural politics in the US has shaped her commitment to dismantling what she terms 'white supremacist capitalist patriarchy' via an emphasis on the liberatory politics inherent in blackness, community, and healing. It is from the margins – specifically the experiences of subaltern and disenfranchised communities – that she offers progressive ways of working through the difficulties of race, class, gender, and sexual domination(s).

bell hooks/Gloria Watkins was born in Hopkinsville, Kentucky, in 1952. She has argued that her familial and household politics forced her, as a young child, to theorise the problems of black patriarchy, sexism, and gender subordination (hooks, 1994b: 59–76). hooks received her BA from Stanford University, and her MA from the University of Wisconsin. She received her PhD from the University of California at Santa Cruz, writing her dissertation on the US novelist and academic Toni Morrison. hooks

subsequently taught at Yale, Oberlin, the City College of New York, and Berea College, Kentucky.

Her experiences as an undergraduate and graduate student advanced her earlier feminist thinking and her contributions to black feminist thought. First, hooks recognised the lack of historical and contemporary writings by and about black women; secondly, she noticed that second-wave feminism – although not formally named as 'white' or 'white supremacist' – unjustly marginalised, and in some cases explicitly dismissed, non-white women. This discursive and experiential racism and sexism led her to produce two texts that 'spoke back' to these interconnected forms of black marginalisation. Prior to receiving her PhD, hooks (1981) completed *Ain't I A Woman? Black Women and Feminism*, a text she had been preparing for several years. Contributing to the long tradition of North American black feminist history and black feminist thought – such as the work produced by Michele Wallace, Audre Lorde, Angela Davis and Zora Neale Hurston, among others – *Ain't I A Woman?* maps out US black women's contemporary and historical experiences. In addition to this, as the title suggests, *Ain't I A Woman?* calls into question the white-racialised meaning of womanhood, asking the reader to consider alternative ways of conceptualising gender, feminism, and political unity vis-à-vis black women's struggles and histories.

hooks' (1984) *Feminist Theory: From Margin to Center* focuses specifically on feminist politics and progressive struggles within and outside black communities. Drawing on her activist and feminist experiences, as well as black and white feminism, *From Margin to Center* outlines a series of feminist issues – such as parenting, sexual oppression, paid and unpaid labour, and political allegiances. The text suggests that black women's 'special vantage point' (hooks, 1984: 15) necessarily enriches feminist theory and praxis. In addition to this, *From Margin to Center* also suggests that racism, sexism, and exclusion have not prevented black women from feminist theorising in the academy and the everyday.

Following these two texts, hooks produced a series of theoretical texts which sought to strengthen her commentary on exclusion, black feminist thought, and cultural politics. Slowly moving away from explicit critiques of white feminism, but not abandoning her fundamental political commitments, hooks' later texts address pedagogy, representational politics, popular culture, desire, internalised racism, black femininity, stereotypes, and visual art. Her many texts, the most cited being *Talking Back: Thinking Feminist, Thinking Black* (1989), *Yearning: Race, Gender, and Cultural Politics* (1990), *Black Looks: Race and Representation* (1992), *Outlaw Culture: Resisting Representations* (1994a), and *Teaching to Transgress: Education as the Practice of Freedom* (1994b) consider black experiences and knowledges in relation to the disabling processes of racial, sexual, and economic domination. Drawing on thinkers such as Frantz Fanon, Toni Morrison, Paulo Freire, Cornel West, Audre Lorde, Zora Neale Hurston, and Kobena Mercer, among others, hooks outlines how pervasive processes of domination are evident in national and local politics, education, employment, mass media, and the self.

For hooks, the existence of pervasive forms of racial, economic and sexual domination suggests that black politics, and activism in general, must be radically open and oppositional. In addition to this, she suggests the self must be repaired by being radically open and oppositional (hence, 'talking back' to, and looking back at, the intricacies and practitioners of oppression). The underlying messages in many of her texts, most notably *Salvation: Black People and Love* (2001), are that processes of self-renewal and resistance, and associated practices of love and desire, must be produced in a landscape which has systematically discouraged loving blackness and social differences. This incites 'the deepest revolution, the turning away from the world as we know it, toward the world we must make if we are to be one with the planet' (hooks, 2001: 225; see also hooks, 1992: 9–20). These arguments, concerning healing and ethical-love-politics, while not taken up extensively by other academics, interestingly weave together most of her key ideas by infusing her political agenda with questions of psychic decolonisation, critical thinking, black feminist subjectivity, and the combination of care, knowledge, responsibility, respect, trust and commitment (hooks, 2001).

SPATIAL CONTRIBUTIONS

Like many feminist and critical race theorists, hooks has contributed to the ways 'identity' is understood in social theory. Identity, for hooks, is formed according to white supremacist capitalist patriarchy. This means that the black sense of self is constructed according to broader ideo-logical and material patterns that inscribe 'difference' or 'otherness' on the black psy-che, the black body and the black commu-nity. Identity, then, is shaped by processes of marginalisation and *it is within* this mar-ginal space that diverse black identities are produced. What hooks gives a sense of is the doubleness of black identities – identi-ties that are produced according to crude forms of race/racism *and* identities that are diversely challenging the meaning of these forms of race/racism. This understand-ing of identity, also explored by several other non-white theorists, is nuanced by hooks' commitment to oppositional strate-gies. Thus, the black subject (re)produces identity and black politics by implicitly or explicitly 'coming to voice ... where one moves from being object to being subject' (hooks, 1989: 12). hooks' conceptualisa-tion of black identities contributes to the geographical shift away from stable, white Euro-American, and androcentric iden-tity formations (cf. Kobayashi and Peake, 1994). By positing the possibility of, for example, diverse black feminine subjec-tivities that are actively producing their identities vis-à-vis domination, resistance, and the margin, hooks suggests that the production of space is simultaneously con-textual and hegemonic.

In 'Choosing the Margin as a Space of Radical Openness' (in *Yearning*, hooks, 1990: 145–53), hooks builds on her work in *From Margin to Center* (1984). She argues that the margin and the centre are neither antitheti-cal nor an indication of a white-non-white disconnection. Instead, she suggests that racial, sexual, economic and social differ-ences shape a response to, and therefore a connection with, existing cultural norms. This connection, as it is understood from the margins, is significantly oppositional:

marginality [*is*] much more than a site of deprivation ... it is also the site of radical

possibility, a space of resistance. It was this marginality that I was naming [in *From Margin to Center*] as a central location for the production of counter-hegemonic discourse that is not just found in works but in habits of being and the way one lives. As such, I was not speaking of a marginality which one wants to lose – to give up or surrender as part of moving to the center – but rather a site one stays in ... It offers to one the possibility of radical perspective from which to see and create, to imagine alternatives, new worlds. (hooks, 1990: 149–50)

hooks thus stresses the interplay between margin–centre relations, suggesting that the black subject's positionality informs political alternatives. Furthermore, she suggests the margin is a legitimate loca-tion from which to produce knowl-edge and confront pain. Spatialising black identities and knowledges, hooks' work on space, place and the margin, is advanced by work on 'the politics of location' (hooks, 1990: 145; see also Rich 1986) and **Stuart Hall's** 'politics of artic-ulation' (hooks, 1990: 146; Hall, 1986: 45–60). While the politics of location attaches social identity to a distinct spa-tial location (e.g. how race, class, gender, or sexuality inform one's environment and choices), the politics of articula-tion, while differing slightly from Stuart Hall's (1986) position, suggests that one's social and spatial identity is also shaped by the ways ideological forces do, or do not, offer openings for alternative voices. Together, location and articulation – how one verbally and non-verbally negotiates one's political self – produce a space of radical openness: a space 'which affirms and sustains our subjectivity, which gives us a new location from which to articu-late our sense of the world' (hooks, 1990: 149, 153).

In *Yearning* (1990), hooks reconsiders white feminist approaches to home, the family, and community. Second-wave feminists critiqued the home, suggesting that it can be a feminised space where patriarchal norms are reproduced, violence is enacted, and women's unpaid work is de-valued. Thus, the home was not a 'safe' or liberating space for those (white) women who performed paid and unpaid labour in that it institutionalised female subordination through gender socialisation, and entrenched the material base of patriarchy (cf. Hartmann, 1981). Implicitly opposing the ways black women have been constructed in relation to the home – in which their roles as wives, mothers, sisters, domestic workers, and paid and unpaid labourers are undermined by stereotypes of overpowering matriarchs, 'natural' house-servants, and nurturers of whiteness – homeplace, for bell hooks is a subversive and feminist space.

hooks' re-conceptualisation of home begins with her childhood journeys through unfamiliar white neighbourhoods. These travels disclosed different forms of white supremacy, danger and fear which were diminished upon arriving 'home': 'the feeling of safety, of arrival, of homecoming ... the warmth and comfort of shelter, the feeding of our bodies, the nurturing of our souls' (hooks, 1990: 41). By positing that the homeplace was, and is, a potential (but often unrecognised) site of resistance for black women and black communities, hooks overturns the oppressive nature of domestic space. Rather than suggesting that black communities neatly replicate white feminist theories, hooks revisits the history of black homeplaces: spaces that were most often created by black women in order to provide an environment in which the black community can learn to love and respect blackness and heal from the wounds inflicted by white supremacy. Although sexist norms are certainly evident in black homes, hooks

calls for the reclamation of the kind of place where resistance is possible and these norms are discouraged.

The concepts that lie at the heart of hooks' work – identity, the margin, and homeplace – are necessarily linked to space and place, with the spatialisation of difference being a key motif in hooks' writing. Feminist and human geographers have thus used hooks' writing to clarify the ways space and place not only adversely shape black choices and subjectivities, but also to explore the complexities inherent in spatial production. There are three ways this is done. First, geographers turn to hooks' understandings of the ways 'whiteness' and racism shape identity formation. hooks' work, primarily in *Black Looks* (1992) and *Yearning* (1990), describes the historical and everyday terrors black people encounter in a white, capitalist, patriarchal world. Spatial power and domination therefore produce the outer world, while black subjects are forced to negotiate a world that offers few opportunities for an 'open-minded public space' (Ruddick, 1996: 136). Geographers argue that this lack of public open-mindedness and the legacy of race, racism and (in)formal segregation, spatialise difference, thus repeating and renewing the ways in which non-white racial bodies can, or cannot, occupy space. In addition to this, the non-white racialised body exposes how landscape, space, place, infrastructure, mapping, and knowledge (in the academy and the everyday) can, or cannot, be open to blackness or difference (Jackson, 1992; Gregory, 1994).

Secondly, feminist and human geographers have turned to hooks' politicisation of location. hooks' discussion of black homeplace(s) and the margin as a site of resistance have been taken up by feminists and other geographers to underscore 'a different sense of place [one which is] no longer passive, no longer fixed, no longer undialectical' (Keith and Pile, 1993: 5). Homeplace(s) and the margins have contributed to how some geographers theorise the mutual flexibility of identity and place. Feminist geographers such as Nancy Duncan (1996), **Doreen Massey** (1994) and **Linda McDowell** (1999) have briefly touched on hooks' analysis of home in order to clarify the contradictory nature of femininity, race, and domestic/private spaces. Duncan, furthermore, suggests that hooks' analysis can speak to other female/feminist spaces – specifically the spaces produced by, and in relation to, abused women and sexual minorities. These spaces, although sites of deep sexualisation and gendering, also hold in them the possibility of politicised resistance (Duncan, 1996: 142–3). Both **Derek Gregory** (1994) and **Ed Soja** (Soja and Hooper, 1993; Soja, 1996) have also used hooks to identify how social differences challenge geographical theory and the production of space. Soja, in particular, unpacks hooks' textual and experiential geographies and suggests that they are indicative of a 'postmodern' way of understanding space and difference. Her positionality emphasises the complex political possibilities that coincide with contemporary, or 'postmodern,' time-space patterns. Soja and Hooper thus write hooks into a 'spatial turn,' arguing that her geographical contributions 'move beyond modernist binary oppositions of race, gender and class into the multiplicity of *other* spaces that difference makes; into a re-visioned spatiality that creates from difference new sites for struggle and for the construction of interconnected communities of resistance' (Soja and Hooper, 1993: 189; emphasis in the original).

Finally, some feminist and human geographers bring together hooks' *subjective experiences* in, and descriptions of *her* spaces and places, with her more conceptual/

metaphorical advances – such as the margin. This underscores the ways geography and hooks herself are, together, 'multiple and intersecting, provisional and shifting' (Rose, 1993: 155). hooks' experiential and oppositional spaces are therefore simultaneously real and metaphorical. By bringing together the margins, spaces of resistance, blackness and experience, **Gillian Rose** identifies the complex potential of hooks' black feminist spaces:

> her argument develops from her experience of growing up in a Southern black community, segregated from the white centre of the town by the railway tracks. Its segregation on the margin of the town belies its importance to the town's economy, however, for many of its service workers – without which the town would cease to function – live there ... its poverty is structured by those social relations. But hooks refuses to comprehend its geography by seeing it mapped only in these terms, a margin defined only by its relation to the centre ... [instead] hooks describes this as a place of transgression.

(Rose, 1993: 56)

KEY ADVANCES AND CONTROVERSIES

In their introduction to *Place and the Politics of Identity*, Keith and Pile (1993: 5) open up the possibility for mapping the politics of identity 'by turning to bell hooks, who is fast becoming a shibboleth for white academic men – including us – who want to prove beyond a shadow of a doubt their radical credentials' (Keith and Pile, 1993: 5). Despite their self-depreciation, and their positioning of bell hooks as an object-subject catchword who necessarily provokes radical (and arguably racially 'safe') theorising, Keith and Pile accurately spatialise hooks herself (and inadvertently 'eat the other,' to coin hooks' memorable description of racial-sexual objectification) (hooks 1992: 61–77). hooks' extensive and accessible production of theory and texts about blackness and black femininity, her additional writings in *Vibe*, *The Village Voice*, and *Z Magazine*, her canonisation within introductory women's studies classes, and the breadth of her subject matter – from slavery to the films of Spike Lee – have made her one of the most cited, and often the only cited, black female academics. Unfortunately, this disregards the work of other non-US black feminists, the work of hooks' US black colleagues, her forefathers and foremothers, other black geographical investigations, and the work of black geographers in general (cf. Gilmore, 2002; Woods, 1998; Sanders, 1990; Wilson, 2002). What this does, then, is reduce hooks/black womanhood to an authentic embodiment of blackness who is cited to lend texture to theory. As Valerie Smith (1989) argues, this use of black womanhood risks re-colonising blackness and homogenising all black women's experiences and identities.

Although hooks is occasionally cited alongside Frantz Fanon, **Edward Said**, Gloria Anzuldúa, **Gayatri Spivak**, and Chandra Talpade Mohanty, it is also important to think about how hooks herself (as a site, theory, and subject for geographic investigation) has effectively undermined other black feminist geographies because she is seemingly the only authentic black female voice available. Although there are exceptions to this (see Rose, 1993), critical engagements with hooks often only *describe* her experiences and work; many theorists resist confronting her deeper concerns, such as the struggles and meanings inherent in loving blackness, and often fail to rigorously critique her positionality or framework (an exception is Pratt and Hanson's (1994: 9) somewhat hasty critique of 'the margin'). Geographies of difference, and in particular those geographies incited by hooks herself, not only call for a working through of how the production of space is simultaneously material, subjective, empowering and unjust, but also how multiple subaltern geographical knowledges open up new and diverse spaces for consideration.

In her most recent book, *Belonging: A Culture of Place* (2008), hooks addresses geographic knowledge by attending to questions of landownership, territory, race, gender, economy, and home. Here, she poses a challenge to geographers and social theorists alike by delineating the ways in which social injustices are expressed spatially – clarifying how her intellectual contributions are firmly rooted in place. Indeed, in this text hooks not only uncovers the ongoing geographies of racial segregation, labour, and migration, she brings into focus how the black community's sense of the environment has opened up a politics of belonging that is not structured by interlocking workings of profit and commonsensical racial disavowal. This is to say in trusting hooks' sense of belonging in this work – and relating it to her earlier writings – she discloses an important philosophical task: to disclose the spatial and ontological limitations of geographic determinism by honouring the political strategies engendered by subaltern communities. Indeed, to collectively recover our environment and to ethically practise belonging, involves a refusal to profit from longstanding, commonsense, uneven geographies.

HOOKS' KEY WORKS

hooks, b. (1981) *Ain't I A Woman? Black Women and Feminism*. Boston: South End Press.
hooks, b. (1984) *Feminist Theory: From Margin to Center*. Boston: South End Press.
hooks, b. (1989) *Talking Back: Thinking Feminist, Thinking Black*. Toronto: Between the Lines Press.
hooks, b. (1990) *Yearning: Race, Gender and Cultural Politics*. Toronto: Between the Lines Press.
hooks, b. (1992) *Black Looks: Race and Representation*. Toronto: Between the Lines Press.
hooks, b. (1994a) *Outlaw Culture: Resisting Representations*. New York: Routledge.
hooks, b. (1994b) *Teaching to Transgress: Education as the Practice of Freedom*. New York: Routledge.
hooks, b. (2001) *Salvation: Black People and Love*. New York: HarperCollins.
hooks, b. (2008) *Belonging: A Culture of Place*. New York: Routledge.
hooks, b. and Gilroy, P. (1993) 'A dialogue with bell hooks', in P. Gilroy (ed.), *Small Acts*. London: Serpent's Tail. pp. 39–45.

Secondary Sources and References

Duncan, N. (1996) 'Renegotiating gender and sexuality in public and private spaces', in N. Duncan (ed.) *BodySpace: Destabilizing Geographies of Gender and Sexuality*. New York and London: Routledge. pp. 127–45.
Gilmore, R. W. (2002) 'Fatal couplings of power and difference: notes on racism and geography', *The Professional Geographer*, 54: 15–24.
Gregory, D. (1994) *Geographical Imaginations*. Cambridge and Harvard: Blackwell.
Hall, S. (1986) 'On postmodernism and articulation: an interview with Stuart Hall', *Journal of Communication Inquiry*, 10: 45–60.
Hartmann, H. (1981) 'The unhappy marriage of Marxism and feminism: towards a more progressive union', in L. Sargent (ed.) *The Unhappy Marriage of Marxism and Feminism: A Debate on Class and Patriarchy*. London: Pluto. pp. 1–41.
Jackson, P. (1992) 'The politics of the streets: a geography of Caribana', *Political Geography*, 11: 130–51.
Keith, M. and Pile S. (1993) 'Introduction: The politics of place', in M. Keith and S. Pile (eds), *Place and the Politics of Identity*. London and New York: Routledge. pp. 1–21.
Kobayashi, A. and Peake. L. (1994) 'Unnatural discourse: 'race' and gender in geography', *Gender, Place and Culture*, 1: 225–43.
Massey, D. (1994) *Space, Place and Gender*. Minneapolis: University of Minnesota Press.
McDowell, L. (1999) *Gender, Identity and Place: Understanding Feminist Geographies*. Minneapolis: University of Minnesota Press.
Pratt, G. and S. Hanson (1994) 'Geography and the construction of difference', *Gender, Place and Culture*, 1: 5–29.
Rich, A. (1986) *Blood, Bread and Poetry: Selected Prose, 1979–1985*. New York: W.W. Norton.
Rose, G. (1993) *Feminism and Geography: The Limits of Geographical Knowledge*. Cambridge and Oxford: Polity Press.
Ruddick, S. (1996) 'Constructing difference in public spaces: race, class and gender as interlocking systems', *Urban Geography*, 17: 132–51.
Sanders, R. (1990) 'Integrating race and ethnicity into geographic gender studies', *The Professional Geographer*, 42: 228–31.
Smith, V. (1989) 'Black feminist theory and the representation of the "Other"' in C. A. Wall (ed.) *Changing Our Words*. New Brunswick and London: Rutgers University Press. pp. 38–57.
Soja, E. and Hooper, B. (1993) 'The space that difference makes: some notes on the geographical margins of the new cultural politics', in M. Keith and S. Pile, (eds), *Place and the Politics of Identity*. London and New York: Routledge. pp. 183–205.
Soja, E. (1996) *Thirdspace: Journeys to Los Angeles and Other Real-and-Imagined Places*. Cambridge: Blackwell.
Wilson, B. M. (2002) 'Critically understanding race-connected practices: a reading of W.E.B. Du Bois and Richard Wright', *The Professional Geographer*, 54: 31–41.
Woods, C. (1998) *Development Arrested: The Blues and Plantation Power in the Mississippi Delta*. New York and London: Verso.

Katherine McKittrick, Queen's University, Kingston, Canada

33 Tim Ingold

BIOGRAPHICAL DETAILS AND THEORETICAL CONTEXT

Tim Ingold is a social anthropologist who has developed a particular and individual vision for a discipline that he defined (during a BBC radio interview) as 'a science of engagement'. With anthropology shaped as his academic home, Ingold's thinking and writing is increasingly directed outwards, generating dialogue with neighbouring practitioners, specifically in archaeology, architecture and art. If by dint of its unhelpful first letter, geography does not find an easy fit in this first-order of 'A-class' subjects, Ingold's writing has, however, significantly shaped human geographers' understanding of ecological processes of place-making and inhabitation as well as the ways social relations encompass, and are constituted by, more-than-human forms of life.

Born in 1948, Ingold grew up in Kent and studied at the University of Cambridge. Having initially intended to read natural science, he became quickly disillusioned with the institutional structures, professional hierarchies and military-industrial patronage upon which the modern scientific establishment was organised and dependent. A switch of studies to social anthropology carried different appeal and promise: a freer academic community; a subject which did not as yet know itself fully; and, precious opportunity to forge experimental links between the arts and humanities on the one hand, and the natural sciences on the other. He graduated with a BA in 1970. The award of a PhD followed in 1976. Ingold's doctoral research was based on the findings of ethnographic fieldwork undertaken among the Skolt Saami of northeastern Finland. Published in 1976, this study positioned traditional and adaptive practices of reindeer herding centrally in the livelihoods of a re-settled minority community.

Following a year spent at the University of Helsinki, Ingold was appointed to a Lectureship in Social Anthropology at the University of Manchester in 1974. He was promoted to a Chair in 1990, and five years later became Max Gluckman Professor of Social Anthropology. At Manchester, research interests in northern circumpolar reindeer hunting and herding cultures continued. Here also began an interest in the comparative analysis of hunter-gatherer and pastoral societies, and a more general, long-standing concern with human–animal relations, exemplified by the edited volume *What Is An Animal?* (1988). In parallel, he pursued work on anthropological theory which sought to establish explanations of human distinctiveness according to a critical reconsideration of tool-making, extending to an interest in the connections between technology, language and art across the span of human evolution.

By the 1990s, this expansive intellectual project had crystalised around the concept of 'skilled practice'. Herein, existed an effort to turn anthropological studies of material culture away from the idea of objects as the primary locus of creative expression, and instead to favour the embodied processes of enskillment necessary for the making of any thing; be that the building of a wall, the tying of a knot, or the throwing of a pot.

An appreciation of skilled practice is also pivotal to Ingold's anthropology of environmental perception, or put more simply, his ongoing inquiries into how environments are perceived, shaped and understood by humans. Dissatisfied with traditional models of genetic and genealogical transmission, founded upon an alliance of neo-Darwinian biology and cognitive science that sustained the theory of cultural transmission accepted by his anthropological forebears, he sought out a more satisfactory alternative for understanding human life. The ecological approach offers nothing less than a replacement paradigm, reflecting his preference for the idea of growth embodied in skills of perception and action, existing within particular social and environmental contexts of development. As solutions are sometimes wont to do, this one appeared in a flash, following several long years of puzzling:

> I vividly remember one Saturday morning in April 1988 – an entirely ordinary one for Manchester at that time of year, with grey skies and a little rain – when, on my way to catch a bus, it suddenly dawned on me that the organism and the person could be one and the same. Instead of trying to reconstruct the complete human being from two separate but complementary components, respectively biophysical and sociocultural, held together with a film of psychological cement, it struck me that we should be trying to find a way of talking about human life that eliminates

> the need to splice it up into these different layers. Everything I have written since has been driven by this agenda.
>
> (Ingold, 2000: 3)

His realisation had catalytic effect, resulting in *The Perception of the Environment* (2000), a major work comprising 23 essays on matters of livelihood, dwelling and skill, each of which might be read as a stand-alone piece, but which unite to form a phenomenological appreciation of different designs for life, existing *between* the biological and the cultural.

Since 1999, when he left Manchester to take up a newly appointed Chair of Social Anthropology at the University of Aberdeen, Ingold has been instrumental in re-establishing the subject as a department and a taught degree. Theorising in ecological anthropology has continued through a comparative exploration of various kinds of skilled practice – walking (see also Ingold, 2004; Ingold and Lee Vergunst, 2008), writing, drawing and storytelling – as exercises in 'line making'. *Lines: A Brief History* (2007a) is the result. A work of intellectual and historical synthesis, it defies easy categorisation, and advances a philosophy of line-making as a creative, generative, sustaining and enriching process in a relational world. Here, earliest experiences from ethnographic fieldwork still have their say. Among the Sammi in Lapland, people and other living beings are understood to live lives along paths. These paths are formed and come to be known and remembered as a result of physical movement through the landscape. Stories might be told according to these pathways, allowing associations to be made between person and place. Such life-lines of existence have significant implication for the formulation of personhood. For Ingold, persons should be thought of not as self-contained objects, or as sovereign things, on the move between point A and point B; rather, a person is something, or someone, who is immanent: a trajectory that exists as it goes along. Lines are the paths of its own movement, and its relationships, through a world always in formation (Ingold, 2006c; 2007a).

Ingold's efforts to re-fashion theories of life according to an ecological approach can be traced according to a history of theoretical ideas. These influences are widely constellated, encompassing keystone contributions to: existential phenomenology (Maurice Merleau-Ponty, Gaston Bachelard and Martin Heidegger); process philosophy (Alfred North Whitehead and **Gilles Deleuze**); labour and value theory (Karl Marx and E.P. Thompson); and, non-conformist thinkers in ecological psychology (James Gibson), anthropology (Gregory Bateson) and ethology (Jakob von Uexküll). From Geography, it is the ideas of those who first featured in the discipline's humanistic episode that feature most prominently (**Denis Cosgrove** and Stephen Daniels, **Yi-Fu Tuan** and David Lowenthal); though sometimes only as counterpoints allowing for the advancement of a distinctive anthropological perspective. Such intellectual debts acknowledged, Ingold's writing is noticeable for being less studded with the names of other theorists (or doctrinal quotations from their works) than might ordinarily be expected in academic literature. In part, this reflects personal style and taste, a favouring of the long-form essay where observation and argument can exist unfettered by encyclopedic lists of citations. But it represents a political statement and ethical commitment too. For Ingold, philosophical lessons are to be sourced *in life*, that is, in the skills and practices by which people perceive and understand their immediate surroundings and so make themselves at home as they go about making the world.

When advancing or substantiating argument, his habit is to turn first to anthropologists' ethnographic observations of non-Western, indigenous lifestyles, and the cosmologies of which these day-to-day practicalities are an informing part. In any detailed description of a task's careful undertaking – such as, say, basket-weaving, animal-naming, wayfinding or tool-making – cross-references with social theory might be footnoted, sometimes surfacing briefly in the main text, but true wisdom is found first in the realities of the lived world, and in places where social practice is organic, embodied and emergent. His ontological claims therefore hold true to the axiom that 'to be is to know, and to know is to be'. So, too, do his preferences for teaching practice. Learning the embodied skills of practice, both by its rudiments and the intricacies of technique, is a scholastic tradition observed through experimental, participative workshops, enlisting the tutelage of skilled practitioners, and with fellow apprentices comprising colleagues and students.

SPATIAL CONTRIBUTIONS

Care is necessary in any assessment of Ingold's spatial contribution since he is no advocate of space. Assessing the concept's potential as analytical tool he declares himself a 'flat-earther', harbouring objections which are visceral in nature: 'I just cannot get out of my head the idea of space as a void, as non-world, as absence rather than co-presence' (2006b: 892). It seems reasonable to assume, therefore, that he would determine 'Spatial Contributions' as a theoretical formulation that – whilst reflecting accurately the spatial turn taken in much social sciences research of late – is ultimately unhelpful, both in its reasoning and usage (Ingold, 2006b). Though antagonistic, the stance he takes *against* space is a principled one, stemming from a strong dislike for theoretical discourse judged to be detached from the lived world. By his account, space is unhelpful since it cannot but connote lifelessness, fixity, finitude and enclosure. Philosophically speaking, his foundational preference is for time, or more specifically *life*-times, and for inquiries into the rhythms and temporal textures of existence. Thus, where geographers find time-space everywhere abounding (and submit to lengthy debate concerning nuances of position and interpretation), Ingold observes the life-worlds and life-lines of living beings. He is at pains to point out that this is not simply a case of semantics but one also of styles of language. Finding virtue in clarity of expression and a precision of argument that speaks directly to worldly experience, his prickliest comment is saved for academic expression that in its operating logic can have an alienating effect, holding thinkers apart from possible readers. This social theory of defective social theory is explained thus:

> [It]...could be called the reification of hyperabstraction: start with an abstraction, turn this into a quality of something yet more abstract, and then imagine that this meta-abstraction is concretely and plurally present in the world, instantiated in the very things from which the whole process of abstraction started in the first place. For philosophers the attraction of this strategy lies in its circularity: at no point in the cycle is one actually required to observe or engage directly with the world itself.

(Ingold, 2006b: 892)

Abstract riffing on space ('Space-Spatial-Spatiality-Spatialities') is cited as a prime example of the habit, and the effect of comparable proliferations around 'materialities', 'temporalities' and 'multiplicities' judged equally problematic. Criticism in this vein might conceivably align Ingold with traditional, conservative voices in geography, given to occasional, jaundiced prognostications about the future and the fate of the discipline. This would be an accidental effect, and a rogue alliance. Candour and a sharp eye for post-structuralist pretension noted, intellectually Ingold has much in common with a generation of cultural geographers who enjoy a newly enlarged palette of interests.

Across contemporary geographical thought and current research practice, three identifiable fields of study show up Ingold's influence. All are informed by work published in the middle phase of his academic career, since it was in the mid-1990s that he was first brought to the general notice of the geographical community primarily through original published versions of material (Ingold, 1993; 1995a) that would later appear in amended form in *The Perception of the Environment* (2000). In the same historiographical vein, it is noteworthy that one primary point of diffusion (and also arguably of 'spatialised translation') for his ideas can be charted on a map of modern geographical thought. Academic staff and graduate students based at the time in the School of Geographical Sciences, University of Bristol, can be credited with introducing Ingold's writing to a wider geographical readership.

The first key area of influence might usefully be labelled the push for practice. Ingold's theory of skilled practice bolstered a forceful argument, voiced variously within human geography, that the prevailing understanding of cultural expression and subjectivity was too narrowly focused on a search for interpretable meaning in textual representations, significations and discursive forms of identity formation (**Thrift**, 1996). Embodiments, enactments and performances constituted complex worlds of spatial practice, everywhere apparent and yet, paradoxically, left largely untouched during the discipline's 'cultural turn'. The effect of this blindness was a deadening of each geographer's sensorium and their collective sensibilities (Thrift and Dewsbury, 2000). As a novel means to breathe life back into geographers' encounters with the world, as something apprehensible and experiential, strong advocacy for the concept of skilled practice can therefore be read as an act of strategic conscription. However, here Ingold was but one among a slew of theoretical reference points spread across phenomenology, post-structuralist thought and science-and-technology studies (Thrift, 1999). This turn to practice had significant impact, and the alternative approach posited has gained real ground. Non-representational theory is today well established in the Anglo-American geographical tradition (Thrift, 2007; Lorimer, 2008) where it is recognised as having re-cast disciplinary approaches after the cultural turn (see entry on **Nigel Thrift**). Ingold did not offer direct comment on what was, in largest part, an inwardly directed debate, but his work clearly placed an imperative on practice, powering a shift towards ethnographic studies of the ordinary activities, social relations and day-to-day phenomena by which the world continuously takes place.

Ingold's second signature contribution to geographical thought centres on the 'dwelling perspective' informing approaches to the study of landscape, and of place–concepts long cherished by geographers, and frequently deployed as synonyms for one another, though each possessing a distinctive intellectual history (Wylie, 2007).

Ingold introduced the dwelling perspective in two essays (Ingold, 1993; 1995b; see also Ingold, 2000). The latter begins by directly engaging with the iconographic view of landscape presented by **Denis Cosgrove** and Stephen Daniels (1988), originating in geography's humanities tradition. Ingold did not take their view that landscape exists as 'a cultural image, a pictorial way of representing or symbolizing surroundings' (Cosgrove and Daniels, 1988: 1). To accept such a premise, he argued, was to ignore the material existence of the places where people dwell, and to render nature as something existing apart. The favouring of landscape's iconography thereby cemented a flawed division between the inner and outer worlds of human experience, making distinctions between mind and matter, meaning and substance, where none actually exist (Ingold, 2000: 203).

By the terms of Ingold's well-mannered provocation, landscape needed defending from its defenders. While accommodating cultural meaning and symbolism, his orientation is fundamentally different, conceiving of landscape as a lived phenomenon in which people form themselves as active participants, rather than being figured as peripheral spectators. Colour and character are brought to this argument in a memorable description of the sixteenth-century painting by Pieter Bruegel the Elder, *The Harvesters*. Readers are invited to imagine themselves present in the midst of the framed scene, and become familiar with its local topography shaped through materially inscriptive worlds of work, the round of seasonal tasks being undertaken (tending, tilling, picking, pruning), and the movements that these demand. The case he makes is for a phenomenological appreciation of dwelling. Tellingly, a re-production of *The Harvesters* is to be found in the entrance lobby of Ingold's family home, hung above the shoe-rack, behind the coat and hat stand. Gathered up and bundled together, he terms these rhythms and intimacies of encounter, the 'taskscape'. The influence of these concepts in Geography was seen first in research on the place of trees where observations of arboriculture entangle the natural and the cultural to a point where it is difficult to discern difference (Cloke and Jones, 1999; 2001; Jones and Cloke, 2002). Subsequent studies have carried the twin concepts of dwelling and taskscape elsewhere, seeking to produce narratives about landscapes made meaningful by the meshed lives of animals, humans and other agents in their living surrounds (Lorimer, 2003; 2006). In a certain light, Ingold's feeling for processes of dwelling has unexpected effects, giving cause to revisit earlier geographical traditions of studying folk cultures, and observing the customs and habits by which people leave marks of their presence in place.

Ingold's third and final contribution is, in part, anticipated in the closing remarks offered about the second: namely, his work has aided geographers' understanding of the placing of the lives of non-human animals in human geographies, and the placing of the lives of humans in animal geographies. A revivified literature on 'animal geographies' (Philo and Wilbert, 2000) and the more recently emergent field of 'hybrid geographies' (Whatmore, 2002) or 'more than human geographies' (Braun, 2008) have, to different degrees, struggled to grapple with questions concerning the extent to which it is ever possible to know animality. On the one hand, ontological concerns are raised about anthropomorphism, and on the other, anxieties remain about the ultimately unknowable beastly qualities and capacities of being animal. For Johnston (2008) the impasse created is overcome by Ingold's treatment of animality and

humanity as relational expressions of personhood, and is presently being advanced by research where interspecies relations producing properties of togetherness are embedded in daily operations.

KEY ADVANCES AND CONTROVERSIES

Ingold is not shy of engaging in critical academic debate and has proven himself a formidable foe in print (Ingold, 2005a; 2007a; 2007b); though this fierce streak is always belied in person. His treatment of faulty structures of knowledge or lazy argument can be totalising, clearing the ground for fresh thinking or radical re-interpretation. By way of recent example, witness his analytical deconstruction of 'soundscape' (Ingold, 2008b), a concept in widespread use and hitherto largely unquestioned. Equally so, he willingly highlights errors in his own work, and makes plain the reasons for revisions in thinking; recent criticism that the dwelling perspective might imply too great an emphasis on cultural stasis and earthy settlement (Hinchliffe, 2003) leading to his proposition that processes of 'inhabiting' present a preferable alternative (Ingold, 2008a). Another feature of Ingold's thought worthy of comment is the relation he envisages between theory and method. Readers will search his corpus in vain for direct statements on methodology, or for that matter, the operations of ethnographic fieldwork. What then is Ingold's relation to method? By his version of events, a simple and transferable motif suffices, demanding little elaboration: all lessons are learned by participating.

For some, there will be aspects to Ingold's relational ecology that are problematic given their quiet espousal of a more rustic, idealistic, even neo-romantic existence. Certainly his writings exhibit an obvious personal preference for textures and rhythms of place-making which are elemental, organic, borne of the open air and habits of clean-living and self-sufficiency (Ingold, 2008a). This makes for a thoroughly wholesome and democratic worldview, but one generally untroubled by the raw disputes of environmental politics or indigenous rights. Ingold would counter such argument strongly (see Ingold, 2005b), pointing to detailed explanations of the wisdoms inherent in non-Western ontologies. These are, in many respects, exemplary lifeworlds that demand more widespread, and deeper, attention.

To the geographer, Ingold's work speaks compellingly of how place is perceived by persons, human or otherwise, and made real through different modes of living. If this 'take-home' message seems already familiar, then his body of thought offers geographers salutary reminders of the benefits to be gained by dealing with the world as it is experienced through first-hand encounter and movement (Ingold, 2006a), and how an understanding of different sorts of environment is formed most thoroughly through the practicalities of living. The same enquiring spirit impels published essays (Ingold, 2005c; 2006c; 2007d; 2008a) where his attentions tilt upwards to the skies, and turn 360 degrees. Here Ingold explores the visual and non-visual perception of phenomena such as light, sound and wind. These 'weather-worlds', he argues, are as much constitutive of landscape as the earth on which our feet are grounded. It is through these kinds of planetary attunement – to atmospheric, terrestrial and aquatic environments – that he reckons the world can remain a live-able and sustainable place in future, when, as seems likely, adaptive designs for life will be required in response to anthropogenic climate change.

INGOLD'S KEY WORKS

Ingold, T. (1976) *The Skolt Lapps Today*. Cambridge: Cambridge University Press.

Ingold, T. (1988) (ed.) *What Is An Animal?* London: Unwin Hyman.

Ingold, T. (1993) 'The temporality of the landscape', *World Archaeology*, 25: 152–74.

Ingold, T. (1995b) 'Building, dwelling, living: how animals and people make themselves at home in the world', in M. Strathern, (ed.) *Shifting Contexts*. London: Routledge. pp 57–80.

Ingold, T. (2000) *The Perception of the Environment: Essays on Livelihood, Dwelling and Skill*. London: Routledge.

Ingold, T. (2006a) 'Up, across and along', *Place and Location: Studies in Environmental Aesthetics and Semiotics*, 5: 21–36.

Ingold, T. (2007a) *Lines: A Brief History*. London: Routledge.

Ingold, T. (2008a) 'Bindings against boundaries: entanglements of life in an open world', *Environment and Planning A*, 40 (8): 1796–810.

Secondary Sources and References

Braun, B. (2008) 'Environmental issues: inventive life', *Progress in Human Geography*, 32: 667–79.

Cloke P. and Jones O. (1999) 'From wasteland to woodland to "Little Switzerland": environmental and recreational management in place, culture and time', in J. Tribe and X. Font (eds), *Tourism and Recreation: Case Studies in Environmental Management*. Oxford: CABI Publishing. pp. 161–82.

Cloke, P. and Jones, O. (2001) 'Dwelling, place, and landscape: an orchard in Somerset', *Environment and Planning A,* 33: 649–66.

Cosgrove D. and Daniels. S. (1988) (eds), *The Iconography of Landscape.* Cambridge: Cambridge University Press.

Hinchliffe, S. (2003) 'Inhabiting: landscapes and natures', in K. Anderson, M. Domosh, S. Pile and N. Thrift (eds), *Handbook of Cultural Geography.* London: Sage. pp. 207–25.

Ingold, T. (1995a) 'Work, time and industry', *Time and Society,* 4: 5–28.

Ingold, T. (2004) 'Culture on the ground: the world perceived through the feet', *Journal of Material Culture,* 9 (3): 315–40.

Ingold, T. (2005a) 'Comments on Christopher Tilley: *The Materiality of Stone: Explorations in Landscape Phenomenology* (Oxford: Berg)', *Norwegian Archaeological Review,* 38 (2): 122–9.

Ingold, T. (2005b) 'Epilogue: towards a politics of dwelling', *Conservation and Society,* 3: 501–8.

Ingold, T. (2005c) 'The eye of the storm: visual perception and the weather', *Visual Studies,* 20: 97–104.

Ingold, T. (2006b) 'Book review of: D. Massey, *For Space* (London: Sage)', *Journal of Historical Geography* 32: 891–3.

Ingold, T. (2006c) 'Rethinking the animate, re-animating thought', *Ethnos,* 71: 9–20.

Ingold, T. (2007b) 'Materials against materiality', *Archaeological Dialogues,* 14: 1–16.

Ingold, T. (2007c) 'Writing texts, reading materials: a response to my critics', *Archaeological Dialogues,* 14: 31–8.

Ingold, T. (2007d) 'Earth, sky, wind and weather', *Journal of the Royal Anthropological Institute N.S.,* 13: 19–38.

Ingold, T. (2008b) 'Against soundscape', in A. Carlyle (ed.), *Autumn Leaves: Sound and the environment in Artistic Practice.* Paris: Double Entendre. pp. 10–13.

Ingold, T. and Lee Vergunst, J. (2008) (eds), *Ways Of Walking: Ethnography and Practice on Foot.* Aldershot: Ashgate.

Jones, O. and Cloke, P. (2002) *Tree Cultures: The Place of Trees and Trees in Their Place.* Berg: Oxford.

Johnston, E. (2008) 'Beyond the clearing: towards a dwelt animal geography', *Progress in Human Geography,* 32: 633–49.

Lorimer, H. (2003) 'The geographical fieldcourse as active archive', *Cultural Geographies,* 10: 278–308.

Lorimer, H. (2006) 'Herding memories of humans and animals', *Environment and Planning D: Society and Space,* 24: 497–518.

Lorimer, H. (2008) 'Cultural geography: nonrepresentational conditions and concerns', *Progress in Human Geography,* 32: 551–9.

Philo, C. and Wilbert, C. (2000) *Animal Spaces, Beastly Places: New Geographies of Human–Animal Relations.* London: Routledge.

Thrift, N. (1996) *Spatial Formations.* London: Sage.

Thrift, N. (1999) 'Steps to an ecology of place', in D. Massey, J. Allen and P. Sarre (eds), *Human Geography Today.* Cambridge: Polity Press. pp. 295–323.

Thrift, N. (2007) *Non-representational Theory: Space, Politics, Affect.* London: Routledge.

Thrift, N. and Dewsbury, J.D. (2000) 'Dead geographies – and how to make them live', *Environment and Planning D: Society and Space,* 18: 411–32.

Whatmore, S. (2002) *Hybrid Geographies.* London: Sage.

Wylie, J. (2007) *Landscape.* London: Routledge.

Hayden Lorimer, University of Glasgow

34 Peter Jackson

BIOGRAPHICAL DETAILS AND THEORETICAL CONTEXT

Peter Jackson is a leading voice in Anglophone social and cultural geography, having been central in the formulation of a 'new cultural geography' via his work on the social construction of race, masculinity and the geographies of consumption.

Jackson was born in 1955 in Stoneleigh, Surrey, England. After grammar school in nearby Epsom, he went to Keble College, Oxford, where he earned a First Class BA Honours degree in 1976. A year later he received a diploma in Social Anthropology and left for a Fulbright scholarship year in the Department of Geography at Columbia University in New York. He returned to Oxford in 1979 and earned a DPhil in geography a year later. His thesis was entitled, 'A Social Geography of Puerto Ricans in New York,' a good indication of his early orientation and interests in geography. Finishing his degree, Jackson took a job as lecturer in geography at University College, London. He was promoted to Senior Lecturer in 1992. In 1993 he became Professor of Geography at the University of Sheffield. He has served as visiting lecturer at universities in the US, Canada, Finland, New Zealand, Greece, and the UK.

Jackson has written, co-written, or edited eight books and published well over 70 articles and book chapters. In addition to his prolific writing, Jackson has served on numerous editorial boards (including *Environment and Planning A* and *Geography*) and has been an influential supervisor of postgraduate students. Among these have been scholars who have gone on to play central roles in the development of queer geographies, postcolonial geographies, and studies of the geography of consumption.

SPATIAL CONTRIBUTIONS

Jackson's work has been influential in four main, overlapping areas of human geography: social geographies of race and racism; new cultural geographies; geographies of masculinity; and geographies of consumption. In all of these there is an overriding interest in issues of identity, especially its social and geographical construction.

The evolution of Jackson's interest in social geography and issues of race and racism can be traced through three prominent edited collections. *Social Interaction and Ethnic Segregation* (1981) and *Exploring Social Geography* (1984), both co-edited with Susan Smith, examine patterns of social interaction and segregation, the social processes at work in ghettoisation, and in the promotion of inequality. The first book is framed in part as an assessment of the legacy of the Chicago School of sociology in geography. Jackson and Smith (1981a: 6) argued that a social geography concerned with segregation and integration required 'a clear conception of social *structure*', and thus required a move away from the 'natural orders' sociology of the Chicago School of the pre-war years and an encounter with Marxian theories of racism as 'an institutionalized ideology' (Jackson and Smith, 1981a: 11). Therefore, Jackson and Smith (1981a: 12) argued that ethnicity had to be understood as a 'negotiated variable' and not a biological given.

The second collection of essays explored the dynamics behind such social structures and negotiated variables, suggesting that ethnicity had to be understood as contingent rather than essential (Jackson and Smith, 1984). Ethnicity was hence viewed as a product of social relations and contextual variables. This was evident to Jackson (1985) resulting from the context of the riots in Brixton, and in the official report that examined the riots. Such events, together with the Greater London Council's 1984 'London Against Racism' initiative, induced a 'quite remarkable' volume of research on the sociology and geography of race and racism (Jackson, 1985: 99, 102). Indeed, around this time the discourse in social geography shifted clearly from one about ethnicity and segregation to one about race, racism, and ideology. Jackson was a leader of this move (though he acknowledges that school teachers were also pivotal in challenging racism, see Jackson, 1995), codifying arguments about the geography of racist ideology in his introduction to the third edited collection, *'Race' and Racism: Essays in Social Geography* (1987).

Simultaneously with completing his DPhil, Jackson began to question why cultural theory had been so underemphasised in British human geography (Jackson, 1980). In part Jackson concluded that this was due to the way that cultural geography had been reduced to the study of the visible landscape (especially in American cultural geography). He argued that 'cultural geography can finally only be of interest to the British Geographical profession if it can successfully accomplish a rapprochement with social geography, in a joint commitment to study the spatial aspects of social organization and human culture – not just those aspects which are directly observable in the landscape' (Jackson, 1980: 113). Such a rapprochement required a focus on social interaction and social relations (see also Duncan, 1980). Jackson went beyond the dominant interactionism of the time to also suggest that cultural geography required a much more direct focus on, and analysis of, the social construction of *cultural identity*.

Jackson thus turned to the work of **Stuart Hall** and the Birmingham Centre for Contemporary Cultural Studies (CCCS). In doing so, he argued that social and cultural geography needed to focus on 'popular subcultural forms, interpreting their specific contemporary meanings in relation to their specific materials context' (Cosgrove and Jackson, 1987: 98). The CCCS had shown that subcultures should 'not be seen as an autonomous cultural domain, but as involving the *appropriation* of certain artifacts and significations from the dominant ... culture, and their *transformation* into symbolic forms which take on new meanings and significance for those who adopt these styles' (ibid.: 99, original emphasis). The inference here was that subcultural groups fashion identity through appropriation and transformation. Jackson thus advocated a Gramscian-style analysis of hegemony that showed how subcultures are structured – given form and direction – through power. Jackson (1989: 2, original emphasis) argued that cultural geography had to shift its emphasis from 'culture itself to the domain of *cultural politics*' and to understanding how '*the cultural is political*'.

Jackson first made these arguments in an article with **Denis Cosgrove** outlining the development of a *new* cultural geography, and then in a major book, *Maps of Meaning* (1989) that established a new 'agenda for cultural geography'. *Maps of Meaning* drew on the work of **Raymond Williams** as well as that of the CCCS to develop a *cultural materialism* appropriate for geography. In this book, Jackson brilliantly exemplified this turn to cultural studies and cultural materialism, while also developing the need for a geography of identity *per se*. 'Maps of meaning' is a term borrowed from Hall, who used it to describe how people make sense of the work they are thrown into: 'cultures are *maps of meaning* through which the world is made intelligible' (Jackson, 1989: 2, original emphasis). Jackson traced out these maps of meaning first by establishing the need for a geographical cultural materialism, and then by exploring the use of cultural materialism in the understanding of ideology, popular culture and class (a classic CCCS topic), gender and sexuality, race and racism, and the politics of language. In each of these there is a close focus on the *discourses* or *languages* of social and cultural categorisation. Discourses, Jackson (1989) argues, are vitally central to cultural materialism, even if, as he makes clear, they are not all of it. Jackson argues (by example) that social constructionism, which during the 1980s and 1990s became closely wed to

discourse theory, had to be at the heart of cultural geography. Even so, Jackson was perfectly clear in his warning that:

> There are serious problems with the social constructionist approach. In challenging the naturalness of categories like 'race' and gender, we run the political danger of evacuating the very concepts around which people's struggles against oppression are being organized.

(Jackson, 1991a: 193, original emphasis)

That is why cultural geography's focus had to be on cultural politics, and not just culture as such.

Maps of Meaning was a truly important book. It was published during a remarkable year, rocked politically in ways that have transformed the sorts of meanings through which we structure our identities. It spoke directly to many of the cultural issues that arose out of that turmoil. Within the discipline it was part of a rash of books published that year (**Harvey**, 1989; Peet and **Thrift**, 1989; **Soja**, 1989; **Storper** and Walker, 1989) that contributed to multidisciplinary debates about how to best understand the rapid social, political, and cultural restructuring brought on by the massive transformation of the global capitalist political economy over the preceding two decades and the consequent rise of postmodernism in art, philosophy, and culture more widely. They were all also prescient interventions into the scalar politics of geopolitical and cultural realignment attendant upon the Tiananmen uprising in China and the collapse of state socialism in Eastern Europe. Jackson (1989: 5) locates the development of his own focus on cultural politics in a reaction to the 'current politics of fiscal retrenchment, privatization, and economic recession in Thatcher's Britain [and] Bush's America', and in tandem with other, now classic works of the 'new cultural geography' (e.g. Cosgrove,

1984; Daniels, 1989; Duncan, 1990; Philo, 1991; *Society and Space,* 1988), *Maps of Meaning* served to transform cultural geography into a politically and socially relevant field. As such, it helped to name and shape the much broader 'cultural turn' that reoriented human geography and the wider social sciences.

Significantly, a chapter of *Maps of Meaning* was devoted to gender and sexuality. In it Jackson (1989: 128–9) presented a reminder that today merely sounds like commonsense, but at the time, in geography at least, seemed revolutionary: 'gender relations are embedded in a matrix of social relations involving *both men and women*, while the study of sexuality cannot be confined to the study of gay men.' Feminism's entry into geography had come as part of a socialist feminist movement to understand the structural relations of inequality under patriarchal capitalism, and from there explored the domination of women in public and private spheres. Only during the late 1980s did it begin to focus on questions of identity, drawing heavily from feminist psychoanalytic approaches. Much of this work was focused on *women* as the bearers of gender, while men remained something of an unmarked category. Missing, he argued, was a focus on the construction of masculinity as a contested, gendered identity. Similarly, studies of sexuality moved from examinations of gay ghettos, to, by the late 1980s, studies of gay male identity. Only in the 1990s did focus in geography shift to sexual identities, and broaden to include the social construction of heterosexuality (rather than seeing it only as the norm against which homosexuality was fashioned) (Hubbard, 2008).

Making good his own critique in *Maps of Meaning* Jackson (1991b), launched a programme designed to analyse the geographical construction of masculinity that eventually culminated in a book

that, firmly entrenched in standard practices of cultural studies, showed how men's magazines were a central location for the negotiation of gendered identities (Jackson et al., 2001). As with his work on 'race', Jackson remained concerned in his studies on masculinity to show how gender is socially and ideologically constructed, and how, at the same time, it becomes incorporated into affective identity and thus a means by which people fashion themselves. Gender is not just an imposition: it is a negotiation.

Jackson hence focused on the role of advertising in establishing the contours of the cultural politics of masculinity. Jackson's interests in advertising and identity have also come together and been broadened within subsequent research programmes on the geographies and cultural politics of consumption. With a number of colleagues, Jackson has explored how shopping has become a central practice in fashioning identity and the production of cultural meaning. This research effort sought to 'transcend the cultural and economic' (Jackson, 2002b), and thus was both a part of his theories of geographical cultural materialism and a negation of them. As part of the cultural turn in human geography, which understands the economy to be a cultural production and culture to be a central explanatory force in economics, Jackson's studies of consumption and identity use ethnographies of the sites of consumption to show how both local cultures and economies are formed and reproduced through acts of consumption (Holbrook and Jackson, 1996; Jackson, 1999a).

However, as with the forms of racialisation he earlier studied, Jackson (2004) notes that the local cultural identities formed through consumption are never only local. How can they be when identity is fashioned through commodities produced around the world, and often by transnational corporations? In projects on fashion (Jackson et al., 2007) and food (Jackson et al., 2009), this argument was developed through examples which carefully traced the commodity chains that link the global scale of international markets to the domestic scale of individual households and families. Identity, as constructed through consumption is, in this sense, viewed as a local constellation of multiscalar forces and processes of consumption. Or, to connect this argument to his earlier development of subcultural theories, Jackson remains concerned with the appropriation and transformation, by different groups, of the materials of everyday life into something meaningful (Jackson, 1995; Jackson and Holbrook, 1995; Jackson, 1999b).

Jackson's work in the cultural politics of consumption, though always attendant to geographies of power, is nonetheless highly affirmative. It is concerned with the positive making, more than the negative imposition, of meaning and identity. He is, nonetheless, also concerned with the ways in which identities are exclusionary, and often the product of powerful impositions. This comes out especially in his studies of race and the racialisation process, and in an edited collection of essays on *Constructions of Race, Place, and Nation* (Jackson and Penrose, 1993). But it also serves as a foil to some of his later recent work on the production of transnational spaces and identities. Along with Phil Crang and Clare Dwyer, Jackson has completed an edited book on *Transnational Spaces* (Jackson et al. 2002) which is the result of a project examining 'commodity culture and South Asian transnationality'. In common with his other studies on consumption, the focus here is on the construction of identity through consumption, but it also explores the processes of exclusion and inclusion that constitute the 'transnational'.

KEY ADVANCES AND CONTROVERSIES

Over his career Jackson has been instrumental in introducing into critical human geography a range of arguments that are now central in cultural and social geography. He helped introduce the field both to sociological and anthropological work on the social construction of race and the materialist politics of racist ideology, and to cultural studies as it was practised by the CCCS. He established an agenda for cultural geography that was materialist in theoretical orientation, topically focused on cultural politics, and integral to the development of the study of geographies of identity. He pushed the frontiers of identity study to include the analysis of masculinity. And, most recently, he helped shift human geography's orientation from the study of geographies of production to the study of geographies of consumption through his focus on advertising and the worlds of fashion and food.

None of these moves are without certain costs, as Jackson (e.g., 1996; 2002a) himself freely admits. Focus on the racialisation process can too easily sidestep the social agency of those subject to it, even as it can fail to recognise the (positive) importance of racial categorisation to those who are racially marginalised. Examinations of subcultures often degenerate into celebrations of ingenuity rather than critical analyses of power-laden processes; and the focus on consumption might bend the stick back too far in its obsession with the agency of shoppers, failing to register the perhaps even more powerful agency of the social and geographical relations of production (something Jackson has to some extent recognised in his work on commodity chains which situate consumption within wider networks of production and translation).

Direct criticism of Jackson's work has been aimed at his development of the 'maps of meaning' metaphor for culture. Jackson argues that culture can best be understood:

> As the medium or idiom through which meanings are expressed. If one accepts ... arguments for a plurality of cultures, then 'culture' is the domain in which these meanings are contested.
>
> (Jackson, 1989: 180)

This way of framing culture has been condemned as being neither political nor materialist enough (Mitchell, 1995). The notion that culture is plural, it can be argued, elides the power relations that are always ongoing in the formation of culture as ideology (which is Jackson's starting point). Moreover, the metaphors of medium, sphere, domain and maps all reify what is always an ongoing struggle: or, more accurately, these metaphors turn attention away from the question of *who* reifies, by not asking directly why the map is of this and not that, why the domain exists here and not there, or why the limits of the sphere are drawn at this circumference and not that one. These are preeminently social questions. They are also economic, and economic in a certain way. They require less an analysis of consumption than of the geographies of production. Jackson's (1996, 2002b) response to this criticism has been to agree with the problematic nature of the metaphors he used, to restate his commitment that cultural *politics* needs to be at the forefront

of analysis, and most importantly, to argue for a deeper and ongoing commitment to the ethnographic study of these cultural politics. His commitment to ethnography derives from exactly the argument that he made in *Maps of Meaning*: namely, that it is the appropriation and transformation of the materials of social and cultural life that matter.

And yet such a defence, correct as it may be, also points to a weakness in the conceptual categories of cultural studies-inspired geography. This weakness is a relative disinterest in the language of expropriation, fetishisation, and especially alienation that is also part of **Raymond Williams**'s and other Marxist approaches to the politics of culture. Studies of geographies of consumption – whether ethnographic or otherwise – that do not consider alienation and fetishisation as integral to the commodity form, threaten to miss exactly the political power and importance of the cultural materialist theoretical framework that Williams helped to establish (and Jackson promotes). As importantly, it turns attention too far from the role of culture-as-ideology. In particular, even as focus turns to issues like transnationalism as a context for geographies of consumption and identity, it reduces the *scale* of appropriation and transformation to the individual and local, which undermines the role that critical, materialist cultural geography could play in explaining and contesting the global-scale cultural politics of capitalist globalisation, the 'war on terrorism', and the geopolitical/ geocultural/ geoeconomic imperialism that links them.

JACKSON'S KEY WORKS

Jackson, P. and Smith, S. (eds) (1981b) *Social Interaction and Ethnic Segregation*. London: Academic Press.
Jackson, P. and Smith, S. (eds) (1984) *Exploring Social Geography*. London: Allen and Unwin.

Jackson, P. (ed.) (1987) *Race and Racism: Essays in Social Geography.* London: Allen and Unwin.
Jackson, P. (1989) *Maps of Meaning.* London: Unwin Hyman.
Jackson, P. (2004) 'Local consumption cultures in a globalizing world', *Transactions of the Institute of British Geographers,* 29 (2): 165–78.
Jackson, P. and Penrose, J. (eds) (1993) *Constructions of Race, Place and Nation.* London: UCL Press.
Miller, D., Jackson, P., Thrift, N., Holbrook, B. and Rowlands, M. (1998) *Shopping, Place, and Identity.* London: Routledge.
Jackson, P., Lowe, M., Miller, D. and Mort, F. (eds) (2000) *Commercial Cultures.* Oxford: Berg.
Jackson, P., Stevenson, N. and Brooks, K. (2001) *Making Sense of Men's Magazines.* Cambridge: Polity.
Jackson, P., Crang, P. and Dwyer, C. (eds) (2002) *Transnational Spaces.* London: Routledge.
Jackson, P., Thomas, N. and Dwyer, C. (2007) 'Consuming transnational fashion in London and Mumbai', *Geoforum,* 38 (5): 908–24.
Jackson, P., Ward, N. and Russell, P. (2009) 'Moral economies of food and geographies of responsibility', *Transactions of the Institute of British Geographers,* 34 (1): 908–24.

Secondary Sources and References

Cosgrove, D. (1984) *Social Formation and Symbolic Landscape.* London: Croom Helm.
Cosgrove, D. and Jackson, P. (1987) 'New directions in cultural geography', *Area,* 19: 95–101.
Daniels, S. (1989) 'Marxism, culture and the duplicity of landscape', in R. Peet and N. Thrift (eds), *New Models in Geography,* Volume 2. London: Unwin Hyman. pp. 196–220.
Duncan, J. (1980) 'The superorganic in American cultural geography'. *Annals of the Association of American Geographers,* 70: 181–98.
Duncan, J. (1990) *The City as Text: The Politics of Landscape Interpretation in the Kandyan Kingdom.* Cambridge: Cambridge University Press.
Harvey, D. (1989) *The Condition of Postmodernity.* Oxford: Blackwell.
Holbrook, B. and Jackson, P. (1996) 'The social milieux of two North London shopping centres,' *Geoforum,* 27: 193–204.
Hubbard, P. (2008) 'Here, there, everywhere: the ubiquitous geographies of heteronormativity', *Geography Compass,* 2(3): 640–58.
Jackson, P. (1980) 'A plea for cultural geography', *Area,* 12: 110–13.
Jackson, P. (1985) 'Social geography: race and racism', *Progress in Human Geography,* 10: 118–24.
Jackson, P. (1991a) 'Repositioning social and cultural geography', in C. Philo (ed.), *New Words, New Worlds.* Aberystwyth: Cambrian Printers.
Jackson, P. (1991b) 'The cultural politics of masculinity: towards a social geography', *Transactions of the Institute of British Geographers,* 16: 199–213.
Jackson, P. (1995) 'Manufacturing meaning: culture, capital and urban change,' in A. Rogers and S. Vertovex (eds), *The Urban Context: Ethnicity, Situational Analysis and Social Networks.* Oxford: Berg.
Jackson, P. (1996) 'The idea of culture: a reply to Don Mitchell', *Transactions of the Institute of British Geographers,* 21: 572–3.
Jackson, P. (1999a) 'Commodity cultures: the traffic in things', *Transactions of the Institute of British Geographers,* 24: 95–108.
Jackson, P. (1999b) 'Consumption and identity: a cultural politics of shopping', *European Planning Studies,* 7: 25–39.
Jackson, P. (2002a) 'Ambiguous spaces and cultures of resistance', *Antipode.* 34: 326–9.
Jackson, P. (2002b) 'Commercial cultures: transcending the cultural and the economic', *Progress in Human Geography.* 26: 3–18.
Jackson, P. and Holbrook, B. (1995) 'Multiple meanings: shopping and the cultural politics of identity,' *Environment and Planning A.* 27: 1913–30.
Jackson, P. and Smith, S. (1981a) 'Introduction', in P. Jackson and S. Smith (eds), *Social Interaction and Ethnic Segregation.* London: Academic Press, 1–17.
Mitchell, D. (1995) 'There's no such thing as culture: towards a reconceptualization of the idea of culture in geography', *Transactions of the Institute of British Geographers,* 20: 102–16.
Peet, R. and Thrift, N. (eds) (1989) *New Models in Geography* (2 volumes). London: Unwin Hyman.
Philo, C. (ed.) (1991) *New Words, New Worlds.* Aberystwyth: Cambrian Printers.
Society and Space (1988) Special Issue on New Cultural Geographies, 6 (2).
Soja, E. (1989) *Postmodern Geographies.* Oxford: Blackwell.
Storper, M. and Walker, R. (1989) *The Capitalist Imperative: Territory, Technology, and Industrial Growth.* Oxford: Blackwell.

Don Mitchell, Syracuse University

35   Cindi Katz

BIOGRAPHICAL DETAILS AND THEORETICAL CONTEXT

Cindi Katz was born in the Bronx, New York, US. This was home throughout her early childhood until her family relocated north to Westchester County and the suburb of Larchmont on Long Island Sound. In her last years of secondary school she was an active member of the New York Women's Health and Abortion Project in New York City, which among other things provided low cost abortion on demand when New York State was one of only five states where abortion was legal in the US. In 1971, aged 17, she left home to attend Clark University in Worcester, Massachusetts, where she was initially an English major studying to be a medical doctor. She discovered geography in her third year of university, and graduated with a BA in geography in 1975. While an undergraduate at Clark, Katz was a founding member of the Worcester Rape Crisis Center. She remained at Clark for her postgraduate studies receiving her MA in 1979 and her PhD in 1986. After her masters she took up a visiting lectureship at Khartoum University in Sudan for the Fall term of 1979. From late 1980 through 1981 Katz conducted critical ethnographic fieldwork in rural Sudan and specifically in a village with the fictitious name, Howa. This field research formed the basis of her PhD and has been an extremely important foundation for Katz's contribution to spatial and social theorisation, much of which has focused on social reproduction.

Returning to her beloved New York, Katz began her long-established career with the Graduate School and University Center, City University of New York in 1987. She was promoted to Associate Professor in 1994 and five years later conferred with a Professorship. Throughout her career Katz has received many scholarships, fellowships and awards. In 2003–4 she was a fellow at the Radcliffe Institute for Advanced Study at Harvard and there began a fruitful strand of research on the shifting geographies of US children, childhoods and parenting from the 1990s to the present (2005, 2007b, 2008a and 2008b). More recently in 2007 she held the Janice Monk Distinguished Visiting Professor in Feminist Geography award at the University of Arizona and presented the *Gender, Place and Culture* Janice Monk Distinguished Lecture at the Royal Geographical Society with the Institute of British Geographers, UK (2008c). Katz's journal editorial service has maintained a multidisciplinary approach, specifically related to feminist studies and human geography, and has included *Children's Environments Quarterly*, *Social and Cultural Geography* and *WSQ (Women's Studies Quarterly)*, combined with editorial board posts on 13 international scholarly journals.

Katz is an eloquent, witty and engaging speaker and writer. She has articulated her theorisations in many arenas on a range of topics which can be broadly framed as: social reproduction and the production of space, place and nature; social theory and the politics of knowledge, with specific attention to feminist theory; children, childhood and environments; and the consequences of global restructuring for everyday life. She has presented more than 170 keynote and plenary addresses, conference papers and invited lectures since the mid-1970s, many of them beyond the borders of the US; and has published several theoretical contributions to human geography that have had a wide-ranging influence within and beyond geography's borders. This is evidenced by the fact that her work, in particular her monograph, *Growing up Global: Economic Restructuring and Children's Everyday Lives* (2004), has been widely cited and many of her articles are reprinted in textbooks. Katz has been involved in projects concerning children's spaces for play in New York City, although she acknowledges the tensions and exhaustions of being both an academic and trying to effectively participate in community activities, in particular the frustration of having to fight with corrupt and/or uncaring city institutions (Del Casino et al., 1997: 44–6).

SPATIAL CONTRIBUTIONS

Katz has made a range of theoretical and empirical interventions within geographical debates. She has had an important influence in discourses of ethnography, fieldwork and the production of knowledge (1992, 1994, 1996a, 2001c) and her

work has been important to feminist geographers (Nelson and Seager 2005, Wright 2009). Katz's scholarship on the life course (1993) was specifically influential in feminist geography and more recently has been an important starting point for emerging contemporary work on geographies of age (Hopkins and Pain, 2007) and intergenerationality (Vanderbeck 2007). Katz has also questioned the very essence of constructions of theory and knowledge within geography through her work on minor and major theory (1995 and 1996b see below). However, what Katz is probably best known for theoretically, is her longitudinal engagement with the conceptualisation of social reproduction: its practices, spaces, places and materialities. Much of this work has centred around children and childhood and hence Katz is an exceptionally important influence in the emerging subdiscipline of children's and young people's geographies, evidenced through the widespread citations of her work in the journal *Children's Geographies*.

Katz's work in Howa, rural Sudan, and later in Harlem, urban New York, sparked a long-term commitment to an intellectual and political project of making the processes and spatialities of social reproduction visible and recognised as integral to effective critical geographical debates about political-economic theory, globalisation and development (Katz, 2004 and Mitchell et al., 2004). Social reproduction happens *somewhere* and takes place at different *scales*. Its very spatialisation as *private* is extremely significant in terms of what it *means*, *who* does it and *how* it is theorised (or not). Katz's work has brought social reproduction, and in particular the social reproductive work of children, into the mainstream of geopolitical and social theoretical debate (2001d, 2007b, 2008a and 2008c) where it rightfully belongs. No economy, nation, city or community would survive without social reproduction. It is the messy, 'fleshy, open-ended stuff of everyday life' (2002: 250), and yet it is hidden (2001a), frequently taken for granted or ignored both in theory, empirical work and by actors in the everyday social relations that would not even survive without this 'life's work'. However, Katz does not only call for social reproduction to be taken seriously because of its profound impact on everyone's lives and its integration with every facet of globalised capitalist production, but also because it holds the possibility of profound structural, material and relational change:

> Everyday life is significant as a critical concept, not as a descriptive notion for the mundane and unspectacular practices by which we construct ourselves and reproduce society, but because inherent in these is the potential for rupture, breakdown and transformation.

(Katz, 1991a: 262)

Katz determinedly positions children, important social and spatial actors, as central to understanding the practices of the globalisation of capitalist production. Such practices are formed and touch down in spaces and places where there are always children. Their impacts on children are profound whether through: war, state violence and displacement; resource extraction; the diversion of funds away from social welfare; the retreat of state support for health, education and housing; collapses in food security; or environmental pollution and destruction. However, so many of the consequences of globalised capitalist production are hidden, especially in urban space; geographical analysis of such globalising processes also serves to hide the material social practices of social reproduction because of an excessive focus on finance, the economy and production (2001a).

Katz calls upon radical geographers to examine what it means for space to hide such consequences and to recognise the complexities of scale through which globalised capitalist production acts; to examine how local, neighbourhood and domestic spaces are central to forming opposing processes of confrontation with, and reworking of, these consequences.

While the negative consequences of capital's remorseless effects might be hidden, capital itself seems to be everywhere. Katz metaphorically describes capital as the placeless 'vagabond' (2001d) that stalks the world without responsibility for its actions, especially neglecting the much more placed/in place activities of social reproduction. The spatial disconnect between capitalist production and social reproduction, the deliberate withdrawal and reduction of the social wage, impoverishes people's lives and intensifies insecurity and vulnerability for the vast majority. Katz argues that akin to, and integrated within, globalisation, social reproduction has political-economic, cultural and environmental *aspects*; consequently analysis of globalisation and capitalist production cannot be effective unless social reproduction is considered, and vice versa.

Katz's theorisations include an attention to the significance of place and the emplacement of globalisation. The above mentioned three *aspects* are expertly woven together by Katz in her complex and illuminating analysis of the aftermath of Hurricane Katrina in New Orleans (2008c). Without diminishing the powerful natural impact of Katrina, Katz demonstrates that decades of evisceration, neglect and obliteration of the social reproductive necessities of environment and relief infrastructure, health care, education, housing and social justice in New Orleans exposed everyone to the inevitable disastrous impacts of the natural hazard. However, the destructive effects of the hurricane and flooding, the shockingly inadequate rescue programme and debilitating neglect of the 'so-called' recovery and re-development programme exposed:

> all that is wrong with neo-liberal capitalism as it works over a landscape of racialised and gendered class inequality, injustice, and enduring cronyism and corruption.

(Katz, 2008c: 16)

The full complexities of the New Orleans and Katrina affair can *only* be theoretically and analytically understood and 'unhidden' through paying attention to the geo-political, econo-cultural, environmental and *social reproductive* elements of everyday life in that city.

Through her detailed attention to place, global capital, and social reproductive practices and materialities in sites such as rural Sudan, Harlem, New York and New Orleans, Katz has developed spatial metaphors that combine to serve as an organising foundation for resistive political responses, conceptual frameworks and methodological tools. These are topographies, countertopographies and contour lines (2001b, 2001d, 2004, 2008c). Topographies are detailed descriptions of 'a particular location and the totality of the features that comprise the place itself' (2001d: 720) they are produced and utilised by those in power and hence play a role in maintaining and advancing uneven development. Consequently, they can be used as tools by the powerless. Topographies allow an examination of processes at play in certain places and specifically the effects of their encounters with social relations of reproduction and production; they illustrate the landscapes of social life. The common effects of capitalism can thence be examined as

they are experienced in different places in different ways, but the connections can be made, and through the use of countertopographies, a geographical and political response to contemporary processes of globalisation can be built. Contour lines mark places where particular processes, such as the deskilling of workers and young people, are happening and provide an analytical connection between these places, but importantly allow the visibility of the distinctive characters of the particular places. Katz states:

> The political, theoretical and methodological project I want to advance is one that constructs countertopographies linking different places analytically in order to both develop the contours of common struggles and imagine a different kind of practical response to the problems confronting them.

(Katz, 2001d: 722)

Reflexively, Katz has produced her own topographies and analytical contours between Howa, Harlem, New York City and New Orleans to enunciate the denudation of social reproductive resources and practices, but also the countertopographies that are developed through people's, including children's, reworking, resilience and resistive practices that can provide groundings for political and material organising and geographies of hope (1998 and 2004).

Having established the centrality of social reproduction as a theoretical, conceptual, analytical and methodological construction through which to explore, examine and understand globalised capitalist production and its effect on everyday life, Katz has recently focused on state, city and household surveillance, security/insecurity, banal terrorism and fear (2001d, 2001e, 2007a, 2007b, 2008a, 2008b). Hence she weaves together social reproduction and geo-political analysis to provide a holistic interpretation of what is happening in New York in particular, but throughout US cities and homes in general. Through her examination of developments in the US of an ontological and material insecurity which spatially fetishises urban processes of camouflage, citadelisation, fortressification, manifest through technologies sold generically by a rapidly growing 'security' industry, Katz demonstrates the ways in which the intensification of 'protection' of children and the home effectively closes down scrutiny of the state's erosion of political and civil rights and neglect of social reproduction resources. She ponders what effective and long-term protection and security can be offered to children by surveillance technologies in a world where education, health care, infrastructure, secure employment, environmental safety and play spaces are increasingly neglected and eroded. The hypervigilance afforded some children through the purchasing power for watching technologies ironically fails to see the vulnerability of other children in neighbouring areas of the same city who face the consequences of city and state withdrawal of the social wage and responsibility of social reproduction.

KEY ADVANCES AND CONTROVERSIES

As stated above Katz's feminist work and her focus on children have both had very widespread influence within geography and beyond. Recently a range of authors has advanced her conceptualisations of topographies, countertopographies and contours to examine a diversity of theoretical, geographical and other social complexities. Pratt and Yeoh (2003) provide an argument for the importance of a gender analysis of transnational migration. They stress the importance of performing 'research on transnational subjects "transnationally" – tracing pathways, crossing space, encountering borders, negotiating scales and difference, forging connections' (2003: 164) in order to formulate countertopographies which elucidate the specificities and struggles of place which are produced differently according to the transnationalisms that touch down in those sites. Similarly in her analysis of geography, development and gender, Radcliffe (2006) shows that the concepts of topographies and countertopographies provide a multiscalar approach for examining elements such as gendered and racialised nationalism, neo-liberal globalisation and the complex intersectionalities of difference between men and women in a range of geographies.

Authors analysing processes of justice and injustice, and people's struggles to change the exploitative situations they face through global capitalist production practices, have utilised topographies. Rossiter and Wood (2005) show the importance of mapping the situated and grounded experiences of colonialism, neo-liberal economic logic and capitalist production in the complexities of land and citizenship claims by indigenous peoples in Canada. Martin's 'analytical lens of a topography' (2005: 203) is used to examine the ways in which neo-liberalism is materialised in differentiated, segmented and uneven ways in two Mexican localities and what political-economic processes produce such distinctions. Nelson (2004) links paradoxical and transnational productions of citizenship with indigenous, rural Mexican women through a topographical analysis in order to examine how local changes, such as gendered political transformations, articulate with global dynamics around citizenship. Beyond geography, combining liberation psychology and transnational feminism, Chaudhry and Bertram (2009) analyse women's responses to violence in Karachi, Pakistan. They use feminist countertopographies as in-depth markers of specific sites which are grounded in translocal politics to enable them to show the collusion between global capitalism, imperialism, nation-building, regional politics and patriarchy which creates women's experiences of, and responses to, trauma.

In many ways, although Katz's work radically challenges many forms of spatial knowledge it paradoxically seems to lack controversy. As noted, Katz has written about the production of geographical knowledge. I wish to close with a brief focus on two specific interventions (1995; 1996b), and discussion in an interview (Del Casino et al., 1997) which posed a challenge to so-called 'Big Boy' theory to encourage it to reflect upon the ways in which it plays a particular role in the production of geographical theory and knowledge. Such major theoretical approaches privilege certain forms of abstract grand theories that are relatively disengaged from real, lived, social relations. Such a practice serves to continually marginalise those who work at scales, in places and with social relations that are not categorised within grand theories.

Using **Deleuze** and Guattari's work on minor literature where an author uses a major language that is not their own in ways that subvert the major language from within, Katz devised the concept of 'minor theory'. She argues that minor theory is not a theory of the margins and it is not in binary opposition to 'major' theory but rather it works *with* and *within* major theory; minor theory is interstitial. Minor

theory works to change both theory and practice simultaneously and Katz links it to the critical concerns of feminism, Marxism, anti-racism and queer theory. However, based on her own experience of Marxism and feminism, the former was often constructed as major theory and the latter minor (minor could also include post-colonial or queer theories). Minor and major are not embattled theories but rather woven together in a process of tension, becoming and change. Minor theory is about subversion and transformation, about rupture, deterritorialization and new forms of expression, but as it works on major theory from within, minor theory is itself transformed. Katz's notion of minor theory and its interstitial engagement with major theory aimed to reconfigure the production of geographical knowledge in order to develop a political academic project. Such a project would (and as she practises it, it does) allow the movement between abstract grand theory and global political processes through to the small-scale local everyday life experiences examined through ethnography.

What is surprising is the lack of correspondence between those producing 'Big Boy' theory and Katz. It seems that her development of minor theory is effectively a controversy that didn't happen. In a personal communication Katz reflected that while several theorists noted her critique privately they did not engage her challenge publicly. Silence or actively ignoring is a powerful way to dismiss challenges and refuse to re-think the limits to one's approach. However, many scholars who consider themselves marginalised within the academy because of their subject matter or their approach, corresponded with Katz to express agreement and enthusiasm (Del Casino et al., 1997: 51). Katz herself has said that she avoided using the word 'children' in titles of her early work because she felt people would dismiss it and her arguments. That was in 1991. Thankfully geography has changed and there appears to have been an effective intersectionality between *minor* and *major* theory and theorists (even if such terms are not used). Katz's work has been, and continues to be, published in top geographical journals, influential edited collections and is orated at major international academic meetings.

Her recent work that tackles global political processes and the lived realities of social reproduction in combination, often boldly carries the word 'children'. This is testament to a theorist's political commitment to render visible, central and placed those who feel most keenly the negative consequences of global capitalist vagabondage but who, at the same time, force us to have hope for the future.

KATZ'S KEY WORKS

Katz, C. (1991a) 'Sow what you know: the struggle for social reproduction in rural Sudan', *Annals of the Association of American Geographers*, 81 (3): 488–514.

Katz, C. (1992) 'All the world is staged: intellectuals and the projects of ethnography', *Environment and Planning D: Society and Space*, 10 (5): 495–510.

Katz, C. (1994) 'Playing the field: questions of fieldwork in geography', *Professional Geographer*, 46 (1): 67–72.

Katz, C. (1995) 'Major/minor theory: theory, nature and politics', *Annals of the Association of American Geographers*, 85 (1): 164–8.

Katz, C. (1996a) 'The expeditions of conjurors: ethnography, power and pretence', in D. L. Wolf (ed.), *Feminist Dilemmas in Field Research*. Colorado: Westview Press, pp. 170–84.

Katz, C. (1996b) 'Towards minor theory', *Environment and Planning D: Society and Space*, 14: 487–99.

Katz, C. (2001a) 'Hiding the target: social reproduction in the privatised urban environment', in C. Minca (ed.), *Postmodern Geography: Theory and Praxis*. Oxford: Blackwell. pp. 93–110.

Katz, C. (2001b) 'On the grounds of globalization: a topography for feminist political engagement', *SIGNS: Journal of Women in Culture and Society*, 26 (4): 1231–4.

Katz, C. (2001d) 'Vagabond capitalism and the necessity of social reproduction', *Antipode*, 33 (4): 708–27.

Katz, C. (2001e) 'The state goes home: local hypervigilance and the global retreat from social reproduction', *Social Justice*, 28 (3).

Katz, C. (2004) *Growing up Global: Economic Restructuring and Children's Everyday Lives*. Minnesota: University of Minnesota Press.

Katz, C. (2005) 'The terrors of hypervigilance: security and the compromised spaces of contemporary childhood', in J. Qvortrup (ed.), *Studies in Modern Childhood: Society, Agency, Culture*. London: Palgrave. pp. 99–114.

Katz, C. (2007a) 'Banal terrorism: spatial fetishism and everyday insecurity', in D. Gregory and A. Pred (eds), *Violent Geographies: Fear, Terror and Political Violence*. New York: Routledge, pp. 349–61.

Katz, C. (2007b) 'Me and my monkey: what's hiding in the security state', in M. Sorkin (ed.), *Indefensible Space: The Architecture of the National Insecurity State*. New York: Routledge. pp. 305–23.

Katz, C. (2008a) 'The death wish of modernity and the politics of mimesis', *Public Culture*, 20 (3): 551–60.

Katz, C. (2008b) 'Childhood as spectacle: relays of anxiety and the reconfiguration of the child', *Cultural Geographies*, 15 (1): 5–17.

Katz, C. (2008c) 'Bad elements: Katrina and the scoured landscape of social reproduction', *Gender, Place and Culture*, 15 (1): 15–29.

Secondary Sources and References

Chaudhry, L. N. and Bertram, C. (2009) 'Narrating trauma and reconstruction in in the margins', *Feminism and Psychology*, 19 (3): 298–312.

Del Casino, V., Dorn, M. and Gallaher, C. (1997) 'Interview: Cindi Katz: creating safe space and the materiality of the margins', *disClosure: A Journal of Social Theory*, 6: 36–55.

Hopkins, P.E. and Pain, R. (2007)' Geographies of Age: Thinking Relationally; *Area*, 29 (3) : 287–294.

Katz, C. (1986) 'Children and the environment: work, play and learning in rural Sudan', *Children's Environments Quarterly*, 3 (4): 43–51.

Katz, C. (1998) 'Disintegrating developments: global economic restructuring and the eroding ecologies of youth', in T. Skelton and G. Valentine (eds), *Cool Places: Geographies of Youth Cultures*. London: Routledge. pp. 130–44.

Katz, C. (2001c) 'Disciplining interdisciplinarity', *Feminist Studies*, 27 (3): 519–23.

Katz, C. (2002) 'Stuck in place: children and the globalization of social reproduction', in R. J. Johnston, P. J. Taylor and M. J. Watts (eds), *Geographies of Global Change: Remapping the World* (2nd edition). Oxford: Blackwell. pp. 248–59.

Katz, C. and Monk, J. (1993) (eds) *Full Circles: Geographies of Women over the Life Course*. London: Routledge.

Mitchell, K., Marston, S.A. and Katz, C. (2004) (eds) *Life's Work: Geographies of Social Reproduction*. Oxford: Blackwell.

Martin, P. M. (2005) 'Comparative topographies of neoliberalism in Mexico', *Environment and Planning A*, 37: 203–20.

Nelson, L. (2004) 'Topographies of citizenship: Purhépechan Mexican women claiming political subjectivities', *Gender, Place and Culture*, 11 (2): 163–87.

Nelson, L. and Seager, J. (2005) (eds) *A Companion to Feminist Geography*. Malden, MA: Blackwell.

Pratt, G. and Yeoh, B. (2003) 'Transnational (counter)topographies', *Gender, Place and Culture*, 10 (2): 159–66.

Radcliffe, S. (2006) 'Development and geography: gendered subjects in development processes and interventions', *Progress in Human Geography*, 30 (4): 524–32.

Rossiter, D. and Wood, P. K. (2005) 'Fantastic topographies: neo-liberal responses to Aboriginal land claims in British Colombia', *Canadian Geographer Le Géographe canadien*, 49 (4): 352–66.

Vanderbeck, R. (2007) 'Intergenerational geographies: age relations, segregation and re-engagements', *Geography Compass*, 1/2: 200–21.

Wright, M. (2009) 'Gender and geography: knowledge and activism across the intimately global', *Progress in Human Geography*, 33 (3): 379–86.

Tracey Skelton, National University of Singapore

36 Bruno Latour

BIOGRAPHICAL DETAILS AND THEORETICAL CONTEXT

Born in 1947, Bruno Latour comes from a well-established wine growing family in Burgundy (*not* Bordeaux, home of 'Chateau Latour'). One of his more unusual ambitions, for an academic, is 'that people would say "I read a Latour 1992" with the same pleasure as they would say "I drank a Latour 1992"' (cited in an interview with Hugh Crawford, 1993: 248). From the outset he took the less travelled path in French intellectual life. He was educated in the provinces of Dijon rather than Paris, and after starting training in the philosophy of religion, in a typical Latourian reversal, acquired his belief in social science and switched to anthropology. His initial anthropological fieldwork was in the Ivory Coast, followed up by what has become recognised as an iconoclastic study of a laboratory in California. For the larger part of his career since then he has, instead of living the lone life of French intellectual, been based in a collective 'laboratory' at the École Nationale Supérieure des Mines, collaborated widely with other researchers, policy-makers, managers, philosophers and curated two international exhibitions 'Iconoclash' and 'Makings Things Public'. He is most widely recognised for the part he has played alongside Michel Callon and John Law in the initiation and remarkable spread of Actor–Network Theory (ANT). Though firmly based in science studies, he and his work have travelled very widely; passing through sociology, art history, law, ecology, public transportation, fiction, geography and primatology amongst other disciplines.

Frequently mistaken for a social constructivist, Latour *is* a constructivist, not a *social* constructivist. This unexpected disavowal of the social is rooted in a reaction to the influential 'strong programme' in the sociology of scientific knowledge which sought to *symmetrically* explain successes *and* failure in scientific progress in terms of social factors (Bloor, 1976). The strong programme accordingly suggested that when certain scientific fields (phrenology versus neuroscience) or certain phenomena (such as X-rays versus N-rays) came to be taken as fact, or conversely, were discredited, this was not a purely scientific victory but was also a victory associated with social and cultural forces. Histories of scientific discoveries and technological breakthroughs had, until Bloor's initiative, tended to act as if scientific disciplines, facts, proofs, the number 'zero', statistics and various technologies existed independently of cultural norms, departmental struggles over funding, state armaments programmes, the cost of equipment, project cancellations, educational institutions, professional regulations and the influence of charismatic figures. Conventionally, each of these was acknowledged as external biases that might delay or disrupt scientific progress. Truth though was internal to science, and thus guaranteed to come out and vanquish falsity. In contrast, the so-called symmetrical programme conceived of society as of one of the internal forces that gives science the shape that it has, rather than a force that bent true science or technology out of shape from the outside. Latour took this already remarkable programme a step further. Rather than allowing the social sciences a privileged vantage point he used scientific activity to *symmetrically* explain failures and successes in *society*. In fact, Latour often shows that science is a far better analyser of society than social science; he shows scientists making facts, objects and networks to be, in effect, practical sociologists.

SPATIAL CONTRIBUTIONS

There are good reasons why Latour has been enthusiastically received in geography, not least that his work straddles the divide between science and society, a division echoed in the split between physical and human geography. At first taken up for his studies of science in action (Hinchliffe, 1996; Latour, 1987; Whatmore, 1997), Latour gained renown and his widest audience in geography by way of his most polemic book: *We Have Never Been Modern* (Latour, 1993) which argued not just against the existence of postmodernity but against modernity itself as any kind of separate age from the pre-modern (or non-modern).

In Latour's work geographers have been pleased to find an abiding attention to the connecting up, assembling, centring and distributing of all manner of things in space (Bingham, 1996; Murdoch, 1998). In describing how actor–networks are gradually extended, stabilised and sometimes collapsed, Latour radically shifts away from a Euclidean concept of space and time as universal abstract axes which contain and constrain events (Latour, 1997b). For him, as for other researchers in ANT, space and time come about as consequences of the ways in which particular heterogenous elements are related to one another. The term 'topological' is therefore used to capture this sense of space as being made out of relations between its parts.

There are many controversial arguments in Latour's delightful books, not least his attribution of social agency to 'actants' which can as easily be nonhuman as human. This democratisation of who can act, away from the anthropocentrism of the social sciences, has raised an awareness of the 'agency of things' previously restricted to debates over animal rights and the nature of artificial intelligence. It is characteristic of the flattening out of subjectivity found elsewhere in poststructural thought which has critiqued the Enlightenment's position of 'man' at a privileged level above all other life forms (or in Latour's case, 'things'). Geographers have been equally inspired and perplexed by Latour's extension of social agency, rights and obligations to automatic door closers, sleeping policemen (Latour, 1992), bacteria (Latour, 1988[1984]), public transport systems (Latour, 1997a), sheep dogs and fences (Latour, 1996). Referring to diverse objects and life forms that make up the world as 'the missing masses', Latour argues that they have been ignored socially, politically and philosophically, even as we clearly attend to, care for and depend on them in our everyday lives. Moreover it is, once again, scientists and engineers who pay special attention to the things of the world, providing extraordinary devices whereby we can listen, look or feel their wants, their characteristics and their actions.

A proverb often recited by historians is that 'there is nothing new under the sun'; for Latour 'there are many things new under the sun' since every once in a while something special happens: new things come to exist in the world. Their existence is in no way *inevitable*, they may perish as quickly as they came to gain a foothold on the earth (Latour, 1997a). Without this historically assembled support of a multitude of perishable things, Latour suggests, we would live in a socially *unstable* world akin to that of baboons where trials of strength have to be resettled daily. In the endless busy proliferation of things as mediators, delegates, boundaries, 'immutable mobiles' we achieve the *complicated* places we live in. Geographers inspired by this attention to lowly devices and the emergence of new socio-technical-scientific agents have investigated the BSE crisis (Hinchliffe, 2001), histories of taxation (Ogborn, 1998), financial systems in the city of London (Thrift, 1996), geographical scale (Collinge, 2006; Marston et al., 2005), GM crops (Bingham, 2006), climate change (Demeritt, 2006), political movements (Featherstone, 2007; Routledge, 2008), urban ecologies (Hinchliffe et al., 2007) and high-rise buildings (Jacobs et al., 2007).

Latour is an unusual figure in that cultural geographers of a highly theoretical bent have embraced his work, as have those whose inquiries are based primarily in field studies. It would be hard to imagine this kind of dual popularity for say either Jacques Derrida or Bronislaw Malinowski. Although critical of the reflexive strategies of postmodern anthropologists and textual experimenters like Steve Woolgar (1999) or Malcolm Ashmore (1989), he is nevertheless similarly creative, humorous and stylised in the construction of his texts. In *Aramis or the Love of Technology* (Latour, 1997a) he writes polyphonically – mixing together a murder mystery, an ethnographic case study, philosophical reflections and the imagined voices of machines. Hence, just as he crosses the theorist/fieldworker divide, Latour also crosses the conventional/avant garde writing divide in the social sciences and humanities.

KEY ADVANCES AND CONTROVERSIES

The longstanding problem of *structure-agency* is one to which Latour offers a novel solution. Where many social theorists, and political philosophers, from Hobbes onwards, set up a binary opposition between social structure and individual agency, Latour pursues impure entities that have characteristics of structure *and* agency. They are, in other words, actors *and* networks or actor-networks. Latour suggests that those who employ an empty gulf between agency and structure do so by ignoring the dark matter of material objects that articulate, embody, co-ordinate and, even, author actions.

Just as Latour uses the 'actor-network' to fill the gap between agency and structure, so he uses 'hybrids' to refer to the proliferating entities that are made and re-made as mixes of culture *and* nature. In doing so he responds to the endless controversies based in culture *versus* nature that have been at their most symptomatic in the 'science wars'. Rather than accepting culture or nature as explanations at face value, Latour, like many others in science and technology studies, turns them over from being explanations to being topics for his inquiries. Where the argument, at its starkest, uses, say 'bacteria' as a source of explanation, Latour makes 'bacteria becoming an explanation for X happening' the topic of his inquiry (Latour, 1988[1984]). From his studies what we then find are the connections which associate specific explanations and ensuing courses of action (i.e., building the networks of pasteurisation, practice of sterilisation in hospitals, changes in food production, etc.) with specific kinds of bacteria. His studies convincingly describe a world where there is no pure nature nor pure culture. There are only fibrous webs gradually extending and contracting, erasing one another, copying one another and producing the shape of space and time in doing so. It is in this concern with how different assemblies of actants can connect up that Latourian spaces are often called 'topological'.

As was noted at the outset, Latour's extension of the symmetry principle deprived society from being the explanation of successes and failures in science. A priori favourites of the social sciences like class, race, gender and politics cannot be assumed as relevant in scientific and technological events, nor can everyday unexplicated terms like 'hard facts', 'geniuses' nor 'bias', be brought in to explain how the world moves or what moves the world. So what does Latour offer us, having denied the traditional explanatory terms for how the pure will of the subject or the blind force of the object gets bent out of shape by other effects? In typically elegant prose Latour delivers his credo of *irreductions*:

> Nothing can be reduced to anything else, nothing can be deduced from anything else, everything may be allied to everything else.
>
> (Latour, 1988: 163)

To make anything similar to or different from anything else requires translation, deformation, reformation or other forms of alteration. To make one thing identical to another, to make one place the same as another place requires building relations between them 'out of bits and pieces with much toil and sweat' (Latour, 1988: 162). With this leap away from the various reductions of various theories, Latour sets the 'things' free to do what they do, to ally with what they ally. As analysts we can follow their movements as they grow and shrink, associate, locate one another, become aligned, produce insides and outsides, subjectify and objectify. All of which sounds rather abstract but Latour is never far from perspicuous examples:

> We neither think nor reason. Rather, we work on fragile materials – texts, inscriptions, traces, or paints – with other people ... The butcher's trade extends as far as the practice of butchers, their stalls, their cold storage, their pastures, and their slaughterhouses. Next door to the butcher – at the grocer's, for example – there is not butchery. It is the same with psychoanalysis, theoretical physics, philosophy, social security, in short all trades. However, certain trades claim that they are able to extend themselves potentially or 'in theory'beyond the networks in which they practice. The butcher would never entertain the idea of reducing theoretical physics to the art of butchery, but the psychoanalyst claims to be able to reduce butchery to the murder of the father and epistemologists happily talk of the 'foundations of physics'. Though all networks are the same size, arrogance is not equally distributed.
>
> (Latour, 1998: 187)

He is showing us here an example of the actor-network of butchering to remind us that all actors only gain agency by being part of particular networks made of more or less durable materials. If we take the butcher out of the assembly of farmers, delivery companies, freezers, trucks, sharp knives and saws, cash registers and banking then we have a weak actor able to do very little for his trade. Latour in his studies of scientists brings them down from their privileged position to place them on a level with butchers and grocers. Whilst retaining the greatest respect for the toil of science, he dispels its fairy tale and miraculous existence in favour of taking seriously its rootedness and routedness in practices and things.

Through an experimental 'virtual book' (Latour, 2003) on Paris which involved a collaboration with a photographer and web designer and is a fine example of his textual inventiveness, Latour put forth an important critique of panopticism. This is a concept originally from **Foucault**'s (Foucault, 1977) *Discipline and Punish* which gained theoretical dominance over the ensuing two decades. In this book he examines how Paris was planned, how it is currently monitored through a number of control rooms in which 'very little can be seen at any time, but everything appears with great precision' (1977: 35) and how equally what seem to be small-scale intimate moments such as having a cup of coffee are linked to a swarm of tokens in circulation. It is a remarkable series of sketches of how Paris holds together as city, how numerous entities within it circulate and how as soon as you try to zoom out for a macro-view or zoom-in for a micro-view quite what the connections are that constitute the city's very fabric begin to disappear.

Latour is, it should always be born in mind, anti-theory. A good reason, as he notes (Latour, 1999a) for ditching the term 'actor-network *theory*' since it has led many to believe it is yet another Theory to add to the social sciences' extensive and perhaps excessive collection:

> There is no metalanguage, only infralanguages. In other words there are only languages. We can no more reduce one language to another than build the tower of Babel.
>
> (Latour, 1988: 179)

An *infralanguage* for Latour holds the promise of being able to write and reveal things about science, engineering and society without claiming that he is laying foundations, nor knows better than those he is studying what it is that they do, nor is socially critiquing their community. Yet, he does not wish to simply describe scientific practice in detail, and this is where he differentiates himself from ethnomethodological studies of science (Lynch, 1985; Lynch, 1993). Akin to Latour, ethnomethodology describes the practical activities of scientists (e.g. utilising equipment in laboratories) whilst also being critical of blanket social constructivist explanation. However, Latour parts way with ethnomethodology since he wishes to map out his infralanguage of paths, connections, displacements, associations, topologies and networks, strands of ordering which are otherwise invisible since they are hidden behind terms like 'science', 'genius' and 'society'.

LATOUR'S KEY WORKS

Latour, B. (1987) *Science in Action: How to Follow Scientists and Engineers through Society.* Milton Keynes: Open University Press.

Latour, B. (1988) [1984] *The Pasteurization of France*. London: Harvard University Press.
Latour, B. (1992) 'Where are the missing masses? The sociology of a few mundane artefacts', in W. L. J. Bijker, (ed.), *Shaping Technology/Building Society*. London: MIT Press. pp. 225–58.
Latour, B. (1993) *We Have Never Been Modern*. London: Harvester Wheatsheaf.
Latour, B. (1996) 'On interobjectivity', *Mind, Culture and Activity*, 3: 228–45.
Latour, B. (1997a) *Aramis, or the Love of Technology*. London: Routledge.
Latour, B. (1997b) 'Trains of thought: Piaget, formalism and the fifth dimension', *Common Knowledge*, 6: 170–91.
Latour, B. (1999a) 'On recalling ANT', in J. Law, and J. Hassard (eds), *Actor Network and After*. Oxford: Blackwell with the Sociological Review, pp. 15–25.
Latour, B. (1999b) *Pandora's Hope, Essays on the Reality of Science Studies*. London: Harvard University Press.
Latour, B. (2003) *Paris, Invisible City*, virtual book available from Bruno Latour's website, photographs Natalie Hermant and web design by Patricia Reed.
Latour, B. (2005) *Re-assembling the Social: An Introduction to Actor-Network Theory*. Oxford: Oxford Unversity Press.
Latour, B (2009) *The Making of Law: An Ethnography of the Conseil D'Etat*. Oxford: Oxford University Press.

Secondary Sources and References

Ashmore, M. (1989) *The Reflexive Thesis: Wrighting the Sociology of Scientific Knowledge*. Chicago: University of Chicago Press.
Bingham, N. (1996) 'Object-ions: from technological determinism towards geographies of relations', *Environment and Planning D: Society and Space*, 14: 635–57.
Bingham, N. (2006) 'Bees, butterflies, and bacteria: biotechnology and the politics of nonhuman friendship', *Environment and Planning A*. 38, 483–98.
Bloor, D. (1976). *Knowledge and Social Imagery*. London: Routledge and Kegan Paul.
Collinge, C. (2006) 'Flat ontology and the deconstruction of scale: a response to Marston, Jones and Woodward', *Transactions of the Institute of British Geographers*, NS, 31, 244–51.
Crawford, T. H. (1993) 'An Interview with Bruno Latour', *Configurations*, 3(2) : 247–68.
Demeritt, D. (2006) 'Science studies, climate change and the prospects for constructivist critique', *Economy and Society*, 35 (3): 453–79.
Featherstone, D. (2007) 'Skills for heterogeneous associations: the Whiteboys, collective experimentation, and subaltern political ecologies', *Environment and Planning D: Society and Space*. 25: 284–306.
Foucault, M. (1977) *Discipline and Punish: The Birth of the Prison*. Trans. A. Sheridan. London: Allen Lane.
Hinchliffe, S. (1996) 'Technology, power and space – the means and ends of geographies of technology', *Environment and Planning D: Society and Space*, 14: 659–82.
Hinchliffe, S. (2001) 'Indeterminacy in decisions: science, policy and politics in the BSE crisis', *Transactions of the Institute of British Geographers*. NS 26 (2), 182–204.
Hinchliffe, S., Kearnes, M., Degen, M. and Whatmore, S. (2007) 'Ecologies and economies of action – sustainability, calculations, and other things', *Environment and Planning A*, 39: 260–82.
Jacobs, J. M., Cairns, S. and Strebel, I. (2007). '"A tall storey ... but, a fact just the same": The Red Road highrise as a black box', *Urban Studies*. 44 (3): 609–29.
Lynch, M. (1985). *Art and Artifact in Laboratory Science, A Study of Shop Work and Shop Talk in a Research Laboratory*. London: Routledge.
Lynch, M. (1993) *Scientific Practice and Ordinary Action: Ethnomethodology and Social Studies of Science*. Cambridge: Cambridge University Press.
Marston, S. A., Jones III, J. P. and Woodward, K. (2005). 'Human geography without scale', *Transactions of the Institute of British Geographers*, NS 30: 416–32.
Murdoch, J. (1998) 'The spaces of actor-network theory', *Geoforum*, 29: 357–74.
Ogborn, M. (1998) *Spaces of Modernity: London's Geographies 1680–1780*. New York: Guilford Press.
Routledge, P. (2008) 'Acting in the network: ANT and the politics of generating associations', *Environment and Planning D: Society and Space*, 26: 199–217.
Thrift, N. (1996). *Spatial Formations*. London: Sage.

Whatmore, S. (1997) 'Dissecting the autonomous self', *Environment and Planning D: Society and Space*, 15, 37–45.
Woolgar, S., and Cooper, G. (1999). 'Do artefacts have ambivalence? Moses' bridges, Winner's bridges and other urban legends in S&TS', *Social Studies of Science*, 29 (3): 433–49.

Eric Laurier, University of Edinburgh

37 Henri Lefebvre

BIOGRAPHICAL DETAILS AND THEORETICAL CONTEXT

Henri Lefebvre was a Neo-Marxist and Existentialist philosopher (1901–1991), a sociologist of urban and rural life and a theorist of the State, of international flows of capital and of social space. He was a witness to the modernisation of everyday life, the industrialisation of the economy, and suburbanisation of cities in France, noting the way they combined to destroy the life of the traditional peasant. One indicator of his influence is the widespread appearance of some of his signature-concepts in left-intellectual discourse. Although not exclusively 'his' of course, Lefebvre contributed so much to certain lines of inquiry that it is difficult to discuss notions such as 'everyday life', 'modernity', 'mystification', 'the social production of space', 'humanistic Marxism', or even 'alienation' without retracing some of his arguments. Lefebvre's relevance and impact on late twentieth-century Anglo-American human geography cannot be overstated, but he cannot be fitted into a geographical straightjacket. Indeed, he was a critic of disciplinary overspecialisation in economics, geography and sociology, which he argued 'parcelled-up' the study of space.

After his initial schooling on the West coast of France at St. Brieuc, in Aix-en-Provence and in Paris, he was profoundly affected by the post-First World War malaise of the French populace who felt alienated from the new industrialised forms of work and the bureaucratic institutions of civil society. This spurred him to focus on alienation and led him to the social criticism of Marx and Hegel. Although he published a number of groundbreaking translations of Marx, Hegel and texts on Nietzsche and on Dialectical Materialism in the 1930s, his career was disrupted by the Second World War. Because of this, his doctoral thesis focusing on rural sociology was not successfully defended until the early 1950s.

He obtained a permanent university professorship in Strasbourg in the mid-1950s, identifying with the political avant garde and applying the critiques of an earlier generation of surrealists and communists to the counter-culture of the 1960s. He moved to the new university of Nanterre in suburban Paris where he was an influential figure in the May 1968 student occupation of the Sorbonne and Left Bank. Nanterre provided an environment in which he developed his critique of alienation being obscured by the mystifications of consumerism, suburban sprawl and Paris's heritage and tourism industries. These critiques of the city were the basis for Lefebvre's investigation of the cultural construction of stereotypical notions of cities, of nature and of regions. During his international travels from the early 1970s he developed one of the first theories of what came to be referred to as 'globalisation'. Although retired he continued to write and to lecture internationally until his death in mid-1991, participating in the lively debates of the 'Groupe de Hagetmau' published in the magazine *M-Marxismes, Mensuels, Mensonges.*

Before discovering the work of Hegel and Marx, Lefebvre was influenced by Schopenhauer to develop a romantic humanism which glorified 'adventure', spontaneity and self-expression. Lefebvre was part of the group 'Philosophes' (including also Nisan, Friedman, and Mandelbrot) who were loosely connected with André Gide, Surrealists (such as Breton) and Dada-ists such as (Tristan Tzara). In turn, the 'Philosophes' rejection of metaphysical solutions in favour of action influenced Sartre and his circle (Short, 1966, 1979). Lefebvre's Marxist primer on the theory of *Dialectical Materialism* (1939; English translation 1968) made him one of the most translated French authors. He collaborated with Norbert Guterman to publish the first European translations of the work of the young Marx (1934) and one of the first introductions to Hegel (1938).

SPATIAL CONTRIBUTIONS

Lefebvre's collaboration with the *Situationniste International* (SI) group, led by Guy Debord, was crucial in directing his attention to urban environments as contexts for everyday life and the expression of social relations of production. Lefebvre subsequently extended his critique of the domestic life of the household to neighbourhoods and urban life, posing the question as to what constitutes 'the urban'? His answer was that the urban is not a certain population, a geographic size, or a collection of buildings; nor is it a node, a transhipment point or a centre of production. It is all of these together, and thus any definition must search for the essential quality of all of these aspects. Lefebvre understands the urban from this phenomenological basis as a Hegelian *form*. The urban *is* social centrality, where the many elements and aspects of capitalism intersect in space despite often merely being part of the place for a short time, as is the case with goods or people in transit. This position can be contrasted with **Manuel Castells'** dichotomy of place and the space of flows. 'City-ness' is the simultaneous gathering and dispersing of goods, information and people. Some cities achieve this more fully than others – and hence our own perceptions of some as 'great cities' *per se.*

Every person has a *Right to the City* (excerpted in Lefebvre 1996) which is to insist that the city is understood as the pre-eminent site of social interaction and exchange, which Lefebvre refers to as 'social centrality'. Conceiving the citizen's 'right to the city' as a universalising principle, Lefebvre develops Marx's analysis of the citizen as a universalising Enlightenment moment. Marx conceives the citizen as a Hegelian synthesis which holds the promise of resolving the thesis–antithesis opposition of Christian and Jew (Marx, 1844) but criticises Rousseau for reducing the citizen to a legal abstraction separate from the passions and beliefs of live persons. Lefebvre spatialises this, making a seminal link between the city as a technology of citizenship, transcending the differences of communities and individuals, but criticises the manner in which citizens are seen as means, rather than ends as truly free and authentic political actors (Ostrowetsky, 2008).

This wonderfully illustrates Lefebvre's method of spatialising Marxist theory and his championing of the humanistic tradition's authentically 'real' persons as opposed to legally 'correct' or politically 'true' individuals.

The Production of Space (1991b, first published 1974) forms the keystone of the all-important 'second phase' of Lefebvre's analysis of the urban and the rural. This later phase deals with social space itself as a national and 'planetary' expression of modes of production. Lefebvre gives his term *l'espace* the broad sense of active creation: 'spatialisation' is a strong translation of this sense into English (Shields, 1989). In *De l'Etat* (Vol 4, 1978b) Lefebvre moved his analysis of 'space' from the old synchronic order of discourses 'on' space (archetypically, that of 'social space' as found in sociological texts on 'territoriality' and social ecology) to the manner in which understandings of geographical space, landscape, and property are cultural and therefore have a history of change. Rather than discussing a particular theory of social space, he examined struggles over the meaning of space and considered how relations across territories were given cultural meaning. In the process, Lefebvre attempted to establish the importance of 'lived' grassroots experiences and argued that geographical space is fundamentally social. This is proposed as a critique of theories of space promulgated by disciplines such as planning or geography or the everyday attitude that took spatiality for granted. To avoid typecasting spatialisations, Lefebvre insists on *not* finalising his analysis, presenting instead three forays into the topic. This disorderly and 'open text' resists what he detects as capitalism's method of control, which is to fix identities in a static manner and to flatten differences (Lefebvre, 1991b: 23; 423; Soja, 1996: 8–9; Snart, 2001). Lefebvre's multidimensional thesis

is in direct contrast to the more customary reduction of space to part of one of production, exchange or accumulation (as in Castells, 1977). In addition to these, Lefebvre argues that space is a fourth and determining realm of social relations – one in which the production, exchange and accumulation of wealth and surplus value takes place. Space is not a given, nor is the city an object – hence the difficulties with defining them. Rather space and the urban are both intangible but constitutive aspects of society: its virtual image, so to speak (Lefebvre, 2003: 45).

Historical spatialisations are analysed by Lefebvre on three axes which are dialectically related to each other in a shifting balance. These three aspects are explained in different ways by Lefebvre – simplified for the purpose of introducing them, we might say that the 'perceived space' (*le perçu*) of everyday social life and commonsensical perception blends popular action and outlook but is often ignored in the professional and theoretical 'conceived space' (*le conçu*) of cartographers, urban planners, or property speculators. Nonetheless, the person who is fully human (*l'homme totale*) also dwells in a 'lived space' (*le vécu*) of the imagination which has been kept alive and accessible by the arts and literature. This 'third' space not only transcends but has the power to refigure the balance of popular 'perceived space' and official 'conceived space' (Shields, 1989, 1990). Gottdiener (1985) takes up Lefebvre's argument that this sphere offers lived space at its richest and most symbolic. Although suppressed in the abstract space of capitalist societies, it remains in art, literature and fantasy. Lefebvre cites Dada, the work of the surrealists, and particularly the works of René Magritte as examples challenging taken-for-granted understandings and practices of space. Also included in this aspect are clandestine and underground spatial practices which suggest and prompt

revolutionary restructurings of institutionalised discourses of space and new modes
of spatial praxis, such as that of squatters,
illegal aliens, and Third World slum dwellers, who fashion a spatial presence and
practice outside of the norms of the prevailing (enforced) social spatialisation.

Edward Soja tentatively envisions this
three-part dialectic (*dialectique de triplic-
ité*) as not 'an additive combination of its
binary antecedents but rather ... a disordering, deconstruction, and tentative
reconstitution of their presumed totalisa-
tion producing an open alternative that is
both similar and strikingly different.' The
'triplicity' that he derives from Lefebvre's position as 'Thirding', 'decomposes
the dialectic through an intrusive disrup-
tion that explicitly spatializes dialectical
reasoning.... [and] produces what might
best be called a cumulative *trialectics* that
is radically open to additional othern-
esses, to a continued expansion of spatial
knowledge' (Soja, 1996: 61). **Neil Smith**
and others who note the links between
increasing homelessness and the pri-
vatisation of public space have drawn
on the many sections of *Production of
Space* which was devoted to developing
a radical phenomenology of space as the
humanistic basis from which to launch a
critique of the denial of individuals' and
communities' 'rights to space'. In capitalist societies, for example, geographical space is 'spatialised' as lots – always
owned by someone. Hence a privatised
notion of space anchors the understanding of property which is a central feature
of all capitalist societies.

In his analysis, Lefebvre broadened
the concept of production to 'social production' (unaware of social constructivist theories that had been developed by
non-Francophone writers such as Berger
and Luckman or by Garfinkel). Contem-
poraneously with Poulanzas in the mid-
1970s he later refined his analysis via an

assessment of the role of the State. This
included his interest in the changing history of capitalism and the globalisation
of socio-economic relations. This was
also a turn to rhythm and to space-time
(Lefebvre and Régulier, 2003). A history
of 'modes of production of space' or spatialisations emerged which completed
Marx's vision in urban, environmental
and attitudinal terms. A true Communist
revolution, Lefebvre suggested, must not
only change the relationship of labourers to the means of production, but also
create a new spatialisation – shifting the
balance away from the 'conceived space'
of which private property, city lots and
the surveyor's grid are prime examples.
Embracing the 'lived space' of avant
gardes is a device for harnessing its
potential and redirecting the 'perceived
space' of everyday practice. This theory
provides an early bridge from Marxist
thought to the formative positions of the
German Green Party, not to mention the
punk countercultures of the 1970s and
anti-globalisation protests of the new
millennium.

KEY ADVANCES AND CONTROVERSIES

The core of Lefebvre's humanism is his
critique of the alienating conditions of
everyday life. The greatness of *The Production of Space* is that as an open text it
transposes Marx into a method inviting
readers to make their own critical synthesis of the book and of their world.
Lefebvre originally developed this stance
together with Guterman as a critique of
the alienation and false consciousness,

or 'mythification' in 1930s popular and consumer culture (1936). In 1947 he published the first of what were to be three volumes of *Critique of Everyday Life*. In this series, Lefebvre presented a Marxist materialist critique of 'Everydayness' (*quotidienneté, Alltäglichkeit* or 'banality') as a soul-destroying feature of modernity culture, social interaction and the material environment. Against 'mystification', against the banality of the *'métro-boulot-dodo'* ('subway-work-sleep') life of the suburban commuter, Lefebvre proposed that we seize and act on all 'Moments' of revelation, emotional clarity and self-presence as the basis for becoming more self-fulfilled (*l'homme totale* – see 1959). This concept of 'Moments' reappears throughout his work as a theory of presence and the foundation of a practice of emancipation. Experiences of revelation, déjà vu sensations, but especially love and committed struggle are examples of 'Moments'. By definition, 'Moments' have no duration, but can be relived. Lefebvre argues that these cannot easily be reappropriated by consumer capitalism and commodified; they cannot be codified. **David Harvey** has taken up Lefebvre's thinking about urban social life in both its economic and symbolic dimensions. This work is imbued with a keen awareness of the temporality of urban life both in the sense of long term accumulation in the cycles of finance, industry and infrastructure and in the shorter term of memory and meaning at the scale of individuals and communities.

After the failure of the student occupations of May 1968, Lefebvre's oeuvre was eclipsed by Louis Althusser's 'Scientific Marxism' in which the base-superstructure division was a privileged element of a structural analysis of the repressive forces and institutions of capitalist states (Zimmerman, 1975). Ironically, Lefebvre first became well known to English-speaking theorists through the critiques of his work by Althusserians, such as Manuel Castells, who, in *The Urban Question* (1977), criticized Lefebvre's urban works for their anti-structuralist bias. Lefebvre's patriarchal approach to the household, his gender-blindness and celebration of heterosexuality limit the usefulness of his theories for theorists of the body and sexualities. He remained within the patriarchal tradition dividing bodies and spaces heterosexually into male and female. These are conceived on the basis of a simple negation (A/not-A; that is, male/not-male) and Lefebvre, like most French theorists, was untouched by Commonwealth and American writers' theories of gay and lesbian identities as a 'third' alternative (A/not-A/ neither) outside a heterosexual dualism (Blum and Nast, 1996). Late twentieth-century post-colonial writers developed alternative theories of ethnic and race identity without citing Lefebvre's work (with some exceptions see **Gregory**, 1994; Soja suggests links between **bell hooks** and Lefebvre). Maria Lugones (2003) proposes the figure of the 'street-walker theorist' as a critique of Lefebvre's own spatialisation which disembeds theoretical representation from the tissue of everyday urban life.

Reliance on the dialectic has been surpassed by theories of alterity as complexity rather than contradiction or negation, and although he championed global underclasses of the landless poor Lefebvre did not foresee the emerging politics of multiculturalism and ethnicity. Lefebvre has little to say on the question of discrimination, or on 'insiders and outsiders' and the ethics of their relationships. He tends to conceive of the state as a once-authentic instrument of a single people which has been seized by the capitalist class for itself.

Nonetheless, Lefebvre goes beyond twentieth-century philosophical debates on the nature of space which considered people and things merely as being 'in' space to present a coherent theory of the development of systems of spatiality in different historical periods. These 'spatialisations' are not just physical arrangements of things, but spatial patterns of social action and embodied routine, as well as historical conceptions of space and the world (such as a fear of falling off the edge of a flat world). These regimes operate at all scales. At the most personal, we think of ourselves in spatialised terms, imagining ourselves as an ego contained within an objectified body. People extend themselves – mentally and physically – out into space much as a spider extends its limbs in the form of a web. We become as much a part of these extensions, as they are of us. Arrangements of objects, work teams, landscapes and architecture are the concrete instances of this spatialisation. Equally, ideas about regions, media images of cities and perceptions of 'good neighbourhoods' are other aspects of this space which is necessarily produced by each society as it makes its mark on the Earth.

What is the use of such an 'unpacking' of the production of the spatial? Lefebvre uses the changing types of historical space to explain why capitalistic accumulation did not occur earlier, even in those ancient economies which were commodity and money-based, which were committed to reason and science, and which were based in cities (see Merrifield, 1993). One well-known explanation is that slavery stunted the development of wage-labour. Lefebvre found this unconvincing. Instead he postulated that a secular space, itself commodified as lots and private property, quantified by surveyors and stripped of the old local gods and spirits of place, was a necessary precondition for the separation of people from the means to their own subsistence other than by work in return for wages.

As well as being a *product*, Lefebvre reminds us space is a *medium*. Changes in the way we understand and live spatially provide clues to how our capitalist world of nation-states is giving way to a unanticipated geo-politics at all scales – a new sense of our relation to our own bodies, own world and the planets as a changing space of distance and difference.

LEFEBVRE'S KEY WORKS

Lefebvre, H. and Guterman, N. (1934) *Morceaux choisis de Karl Marx*. Paris: NRF.
Lefebvre, H. and Guterman, N. (1936) *La Conscience Mystifiée*. Paris: Gallimard.
Lefebvre, H. and Guterman, N. (1938) *Morceaux choisis de Hegel*. Paris: Gallimard.
Lefebvre, H. (1947) *Critique de la vie quotidienne, I: Introduction*. Paris: Grasset.
Lefebvre, H.(1959) *La Somme et le reste*. Paris: La Nef de Paris.
Lefebvre, H. (1968a) *Sociology of Marx*. Trans. N. Guterman. New York: Pantheon.
Lefebvre, H. (1968b) *Dialectical Materialism*. Trans. J. Sturrock, London: Cape.
Lefebvre, H. (1969) *The Explosion: From Nanterre to the Summit*. Paris: Monthly Review Press (orig. published 1968).
Lefebvre, H. (1978) 'Les Contradiction de L'Etat', *De L'Etat*, Vol. 4. Paris: UGE.
Lefebvre, H. (1991a) *The Critique of Everyday Life, Volume 1*. Trans. J. Moore, London: Verso (orig. published 1947).
Lefebvre, H. (1991b) *The Production of Space*. Trans. N. Donaldson-Smith, Oxford: Basil Blackwell (orig. published 1974).
Lefebvre, H. (1996) *Writings on Cities*. Trans. and eds. E. Kofman and E. Lebas, Oxford: Basil Blackwell.
Lefebvre, H. (2002) *Critique of Everyday Life II*. London: Verso (orig. published 1961).
Lefebvre, H.and Régulier, C. (2003) *Henri Lefebvre: Key Writings*. Trans. and eds. S. Elden, E. Lebas and E. Kofman, London: Continuum.
Lefebvre, H. (2003) *The Urban Revolution*. Trans. R. Bononno, Minneapolis: University of Minnesota Press.

Secondary Sources and References

Blum, V. and Nast, H. (1996) 'Where's the difference? The heterosexualization of alterity in Henri Lefebvre and Jacques Lacan', *Environment and Planning D: Society and Space* 14: 559–80.

Castells, M. (1977) *The Urban Question: A Marxist approach.* London: Edward Arnold.

Gottdiener, M. (1985) *Social Production of Urban Space.* Austin: University of Texas.

Gregory, D. (1994) *Geographical Imaginations.* Oxford: Blackwell.

Hess, R. (1988) *Henri Lefebvre et l'aventure du siècle.* Paris: Editions A. M. Métailié.

Home, S. (1988) *The Assault on Culture: Utopian Currents from Lettrisme to Class War.* London: Aporia Press and Unpopular Books.

Jameson, F. (1991) *Postmodernism or, the Cultural Logic of Late Capitalism.* London: Verso.

Lugones, M. (2003) *Pilgrimages/Peregrinajes: Theorizing Coalition against Multiple Oppressions.* Lanham, MD: Rowman & Littlefield.

Marcus, G. (1989) *Lipstick Traces.* Cambridge, MA: Harvard.

Martins, M. (1983) 'The theory of social space in the work of Henri Lefebvre', in R. Forrest, J. Henderson and P. Williams (eds), *Urban Political Economy and Social Theory: Critical Essays in Urban Studies.* London: Gower. pp.160–85.

Marx, K. (1844) 'The Jewish question', H.J. Stenning (trans.), *Selected Essays*, Leonard Parsons 1926. pp. 40-97. Originally published 1844. Revised translation online: www.marxists.org/archive/marx/works/1844/jewish-question/ Accessed July 15 2009.

Merrifield, A. (1993) 'Space and place: a Lefebvrian reconciliation', *Transactions of the Institute of British Geographers*, 18: 516–31.

Ostrowetsky, S. (2008) 'L'Identité des droits'. Paper presented to Colloque de la pensée d'Henri Lefebvre, Vienna 2000, *La Somme et le Reste: Etudes Lefebvriennes* 13, pp.2–14. Online: cep.cl/Cenda/Cen_Documentos/Varios/S&R-13.pdf Accessed 1 July 2009.

Poster, M. (1975) *Existential Marxism in Postwar France: From Sartre to Althusser.* Princeton, NJ: Princeton University Press.

Ross, K. (1988) *The Emergence of Social Space: Rimbaud and the Paris Commune.* New York: Macmillan.

Sartre, J.-P. (1958) *Being and Nothingness.* Trans H.E. Barnes, New York: Methuen/Philosophical Library (origi published as *L'Etre et le Néant*, Gallimard 1943).

Shields, R. (1989) 'Social Spatialisation and the Built Environment : The Case of the West Edmonton Mall', *Environment and planning D : Society and Space*, 7.2 (Summer). pp. 147–64.

Shields, R. (1990) *Places on the Margin: Alternate Geographies of Modernity.* London: Routledge.

Shields, R. (1999) *Lefebvre: Love and Struggle: Spatial Dialectics.* London: Routledge.

Short, R.S. (1966) 'The politics of surrealism 1920–1936', *Journal of Contemporary History,* 1: 3–26.

Short, R.S. (1979) 'Paris Dada and surrealism', *Journal of European Studies* 9: 1–2 (March/June).

Smith, N. (1984) *Uneven Development; Nature, Capital and the Production of Space.* Oxford: Blackwell.

Snart, J. (2001) 'Disorder and entropy in Pynchon's *Entropy* and Lefebvre's *The Production of Space'. CLCWeb: Comparative Literature and Culture* 3.4 (December). Online: clcwebjournal.lib.purdue.edu/clcweb01-4/snart01.html Accessed Sept 1 2006.

Soja, E. (1989) *Postmodern Geographies, the Reassertion of Space in Critical Social Theory.* London: Verso.

Soja, E. (1996) *Third Space.* Oxford: Blackwell.

Zimmerman, M. (1975) 'Polarities and contradictions: theorectical bases of the Marxist-Structuralist encounter', *New German Critique*, 3: 1(Winter). pp. 69–90.

Rob Shields, University of Alberta

38   David Ley

BACKGROUND DETAILS AND THEORETICAL CONTEXT

An urban geographer noted for research on Canadian cities, David Ley completed his BA in geography at Oxford University in 1968 and his PhD at Pennsylvania State University in 1972. These formative years coincided with significant controversy and change in Anglo-American geography, as the 'paradigm' of spatial science was rejected by a new generation drawn to the alternative perspectives of critical social theory and humanistic philosophies. At the time when William Bunge (1969), the positivist spatial theorist, was returning to research 'on the streets' in Detroit, and **David Harvey** (1973) was opening up the question of Social Justice in the City with a move towards Marxist social theory, David Ley was exploring in empirical detail a Philadelphia neighbourhood for his postgraduate research. Later published as *The Black Inner City as Frontier Outpost: Images and Behaviour of a Philadelphia Neighbourhood* (Ley, 1974), this innovative study was to quickly establish his reputation. In many ways this 'classic' study (see Jackson et al., 1998) is not only indicative of the focus of his future career – urban social geography – but also illustrates his distinctive research strategy, one which draws upon diverse quantitative and qualitative sources, and critically combines and synthesises different theoretical perspectives.

David Ley has devoted over 35 years to detailed empirical research and creative theorising on the contemporary issues of urban transformation. For many years based at the University of British Columbia, Vancouver, he has extensively researched and published on issues of urban transformation. His interest has included inner-city subcultures, housing and other community land-uses (e.g., Ley, 1974), the emergence of the 'new middle class' and related issues of gentrification (e.g., Ley, 1987; Ley and Olds, 1988, 1996; Ley and Dobson, 2008), immigration, ethnicity and globalisation (e.g., Ley, 1995, 1999, 2007; Ley and Smith, 2000), as well as occasional reflective essays on the wider development of social geography, postmodernism and the city (e.g., Duncan and Ley, 1993; Ley, 1985, 1993a, 1994, 2003, 2006). Latterly, he has developed interests in wealthy migrants to Canada from East Asia, immigrant poverty in Canadian cities (particularly Toronto and Vancouver), multiculturalism and the governance of diversity, the immigrant church as an urban service hub, housing markets in a globalised era, and stopping gentrification (Ley, 2009). A recent co-edited collection for the journal *Urban Studies* – 'Gentrification and public policy' (Lees and Ley, 2008) – is particularly illustrative of Ley's extended, local and international, engagement and indicative of the continued standing he has in the field of urban social geography.

There are four particular characteristics of his contribution worthy of note. First, he has demonstrated a continued commitment to detailed empirical research combining critical development of theory conditioned by sensitivity to local circumstance and its particular historical, geographical and political context (e.g., Ley, 1996; Ley and Tutchener, 2001). Second, he has continued an interest in issues-based research and a commitment to policy relevance. Third, he has employed an eclectic, critical and synthetic approach to theoretical perspectives, sources and methods, drawing on both qualitative and quantitative evidence: as he puts it, 'I am not persuaded by the view that "interpretation" and "measurement" are in some manner incompatible' (Ley, 1998: 79). Fourth, throughout his career he has demonstrated a strong commitment to collaboration, as manifest in a large number of co-authored articles and several co-edited collections of essays. In 2003, David Ley received a Trudeau Foundation Award, one of only four given in the first year of this Canadian award. The Foundation was set up to promote outstanding research in the social sciences and humanities, with particular emphasis on 'democratic values and human rights, citizenship and social equity, and human interaction with the environment' (UBC, 2009: np).

In broad theoretical terms, Ley has critically and cumulatively engaged with three key approaches in human geography: humanistic perspectives, and in particular a phenomenological informed interest in the social (inter-subjective life world) (e.g. Ley, 1977; Ley and Samuels, 1978), a critique of Marxism and structuralism (e.g., Ley and Duncan, 1982) and post-structural and postmodern ideas (e.g. Ley, 1993a, 1993b, 2003).

SPATIAL CONTRIBUTIONS

Ley's career coincided with a period of considerable critical debate and pluralism in theoretical frameworks for explanation of urban social phenomena. By the 1970s, positivist models of urban structure with their basis in 'general laws' and reliance on quantitative measures, devoid of any real interest in the people who lived there or the specifics of locale, were largely rejected by a new generation of geographers who sought understanding of the 'real' problems of contemporary cities in all their variety and vibrancy. For some, critical social theory – and in particular that inspired by Marxism – was to provide the framework for a deeper level of analysis of the social geography of cities situated within an understanding of social structures (class), the flows of capital (and in particular globalisation), and mechanisms of urban politics (or power). Other urban geographers took a more empirical turn, and drew upon earlier more humanistic traditions in the study of the social geography of cities. Here, the unique historical and cultural experience of individual cities was seen as of critical importance, together with attention to how local communities perceived and behaved in these spaces – though local particularity was set within broader international contexts and explanatory frameworks.

Ley adopted this more humanistic approach in his initial work on Philadelphia (Ley, 1974) drawing upon the diverse but not unrelated French tradition of *geographie humaine,* the Chicago School of urban ecology, behavioural science and environmental psychology, and the emerging geographical interest in phenomenology.

Rather than using a theoretical framework as a kind of lens through which to view the city, Ley started with direct knowledge of Philadelphia neighbourhoods and the experiences of its residents, 'triangulating' a range of sources and methods of analysis, drawing upon a plurality of theoretical frameworks. He juxtaposed the personal and the reflective, with the more abstract and theoretical language of urban analysis. **Peter Jackson** (Jackson et al., 1998: 75) notes that 'the reason for our enthusiasm when the book was first published is clear. It has a directness born of experience and spoke to readers with the voice of authority. The author had been there and was telling it like it is. Only later did we learn to be more sceptical about such claims to "ethnographical authority". Then as now, the book signalled a turning point in the development of social geography.'

Continuing throughout his career to engage critically with current theoretical frameworks, Ley has nevertheless maintained a consistent interest in the humanistic perspective and the urban experience as a socio-cultural one. This is facilitated in large part by his continued commitment to combining both qualitative and quantitative methodologies, including the use of participant observation and in-depth interviews in combination with statistical records, official documents and even urban and regional novels. For Ley, space has history as well as a location and, above all, space has a range of meanings for the communities who live there. His own explanations therefore draw upon multiple factors – economic, political, social, personal, historical and cultural – to explain urban transformation, both generically and within specific cities and neighbourhoods.

Interestingly, when completing a review for *Progress in Human Geography* in 1985, he chose to title it 'Cultural/

humanistic geography', perhaps in recognition of both relationships and also tensions between the emerging 'new' cultural geography and the earlier humanistic geography (Ley, 1985). This also reflects the development of his ideas, as he has absorbed the progressive theoretical developments in the discipline, whilst maintaining a humanistic and liberal thread through his work. He has shown a scepticism of the efficacy of theory *per se* but has contributed to its critical development through a keen eye for the empirical, the actual geography as experienced by communities. It is in this sense Ley is essentially an exponent of 'grounded theory' (Hamnett, 1998).

The frequency of citations of his publications, the extensive range of his collaborations, and his senior position in learned societies, suggests that Ley continues to have a significant impact upon the discipline of geography, both within urban social geography and beyond. His contribution is first as an urban geographer who has conducted extensive empirical studies and drawn on a plurality of contemporary theories to develop a synthetic and distinctive explanation of the restructuring of cities in the last half of the twentieth century, and second as a social and cultural geographer with an applied interest in the relevance of research to public policy, and respect for the complex interplay between socio-economic space, communities and cultures, local governance, and wider (national and international) economic and political processes. Ley has also made important contributions to the philosophical and theoretical development of geography. Amongst these are his critique of positivism and the related promotion of a more phenomenological perspective in social (and cultural) geography (Ley, 1977), his critique of structuralist/Marxist approaches (Ley and Duncan, 1982), and contributions to debates about the 'post-modern city' (Ley, 1989, 2003; Duncan and Ley, 1993).

Throughout his career, he has also had much influence on the emerging generation of planners, policy-makers and researchers through his commitment to teaching and postgraduate supervision. In *A Social Geography of the City* (1983) Ley provided a popular undergraduate text which illustrated the scope and critical synthesis of his conception of social (and cultural) urban geography – an interest in everyday life, the social basis of urban life, the city as home and as a human experience.

KEY ADVANCES AND CONTROVERSIES

There is a continuity and critical development in Ley's contribution from the early 1970s to the present through his interest in urban transformation as a social and cultural experience. He has made a distinctive and sometimes contested contribution to current debates. This is reflected in his work on the restructuring in contemporary Canadian cities, and in particular the process of gentrification and more recently the impact of immigration through his role in the Canadian Metropolis Project (Ley, 1995; Ley and Tutchener, 2001). Ley has developed an explanation which brings together both economic and cultural factors, as well as the global and the local. This synthesis is a significant achievement born of detailed empirical research and a critical stance on the scope, contribution and potential integration of different theoretical perspectives.

For instance, in *The New Middle Class and the Remaking of the Central City* (Ley, 1996) he draws upon the theories of the transition to post-industrialisation to develop a convincing explanation of the differential development of gentrification in contemporary cities. Although the study is based on detailed analysis of six Canadian cities, his explanation can be applied to develop understanding of urban change in other national contexts. Ley argues that gentrification is the result of changes in the local labour market, in particular the development of the financial and service sector. This sector is concentrated in the central areas of cities and has a disproportionate share of professional and managerial employees. His argument combines both local and cultural factors with wider economic and global forces. He notes in particular that cities that develop districts of gentrification are also those places that are most culturally vibrant and creative (presaging some of Richard Florida's later arguments about the creative class). He argues that hippies and artists are the 'storm-troopers of the new middle class' (Ley, 1996: 194), moving into run-down inner city districts, renovating and revitalising them. This is followed by a transition in which the new middle classes – the professional and managerial groups – start to move in, perhaps initially frequenting the new cafés and cultural venues, and then in due course impacting on the local housing market.

Ley, in humanistic vein, thus describes the gentrifiers as responding to the 'structure of feeling', that is the emerging cultural identity of these changing inner city districts. Gentrification therefore results from the coming together of both wider economic and political forces (the development of the financial and business services, which is itself dependent on innovation) and the development of local cultural identity and creativity grounded in the specifics of a given locality (now commodified and marketed to the incoming new middle-class residents). While some commentators – notably **Neil Smith** (1996) – remain sceptical of the importance that Ley places on the agency of the new middle class in promoting gentrification, his focus on the cultures of consumption implicated in the making of the postmodern city centre has proved widely influential in urban geography (see Hamnett, 1998).

In approaching the concept of the 'postmodern city', Ley avoids the excessive theorising and linguistic gymnastics of 'postmodern geographers' (e.g., **Ed Soja**), and explores the postmodern through an empirical study of the cultural politics of the everyday urban environment. For instance, in exploring co-operative housing in Vancouver, Ley argues that 'post-modern landscapes, like others, also need to be seen as duplicitous, or better, ambivalent, not simply showcases for a new bourgeoisie but also capable of supporting humane, indeed moral, public values' (Ley, 1993b:

130). He subsequently goes on to refer to a 'postmodernism of resistance' and to the opportunity for 'sensitive urban place-making'. Here, he compares his own empirical analysis with the 'highly partisan discourse over architectural post-modernism, which frequently avoids careful definition of its concepts and engages in a façadism offering the thinnest of landscape interpretations' (Ley, 1993b: 145). In conclusion, he thus argues for an 'oppositional post-modernism in the built environment in terms of an ontology of difference, a multi-vocal epistemology and a politics of participation'. Justifying this stance on postmodernism, Ley argues that to apply the term merely as a generic descriptor of contemporary culture and urbanism is to fall into the very trap of formulating it as a totalising and uncontested entity. Rather, he argues that if we see landscape as a process, we recognise the contingent geographical and historical contexts that enable particular urban landscape forms to emerge (cf. Harvey, 1989).

LEY'S KEY WORKS

Ley, D. (1974) *The Black Inner City as Frontier Outpost: Images and Behaviour of a Philadelphia Neighbourhood.* Washington DC: Association of American Geographers.

Ley, D. and Samuels, M. (ed.) (1978) *Humanistic Geography: Problems and Prospects.* London: Croom Helm.

Ley, D. and Duncan, J. (1982) 'Structural Marxism and human geography: a critical assessment', *Annals of the Association of American Geographers*, 72: 30–59

Ley, D. (1983) *A Social Geography of the City.* New York: Harper and Row.

Ley, D. (1985) 'Cultural/humanist geography', *Progress in Human Geography*, 9: 415–23.

Ley, D. (1998) 'Revisiting the black inner city', *Progress in Human Geography*, 21: 78–80.

Duncan, J. and Ley, D. (eds) (1993) *Place/Culture /Representation.* London: Routledge.

Ley, D. and Hasson, S. (1994) *Neighbourhood Organisation and the Welfare State.* Toronto: Toronto University Press.

Ley, D. (1996) *The New Middle Class and the Remaking of the Central City.* Oxford: Oxford University Press.

Ley, D. (1999) 'Myths and meanings of immigration and the metropolis', *Canadian Geographer*, 43: 2–19.

Secondary Sources and References

Bunge, W. (1969) 'The first years of the Detroit Geographical Expedition: a personal report', Field Notes 1: 1–9. Reprinted in R. Peet (ed.) *Radical Geography* (1977). London: Methuen. pp. 31–9.

Hamnett, C. (1998) '*The New Urban Frontier: Gentrification and the Revanchist City* (Neil Smith), *The New Middle Class and the Remaking of the Central City* (David Ley), *Gentrification and the Middle Class* (Tim Butler): Book Review Essay', *Transactions of the Institute of British Geography*, 23: 412–16.

Harvey, D. (1973) *Social Justice and the City.* Oxford: Blackwell.

Hayvey, D. (1990) *Condition of Postmodernity.* Cambridge: Blackwell.

Jackson, P., Palm, R. and Ley, D. (1998) 'Classics in human geography re-visited: David Ley (1974) *The Black Inner City as Frontier Outpost* – Commentaries 1 and 2, and Response from David Ley', *Progress in Human Geography*, 22: 75–80.

Lees, L. and Ley, D. (2008) 'Gentrification and public policy', *Urban Studies*, 45 (12): 2379–648

Ley, D. (1977) 'Social geography and the taken for granted world', *Transactions of the Institute of British Geographers*, 2: 498–512.

Ley, D. (1987) 'Styles of the times: liberal and neo-conservative landscapes of inner Vancouver 1968–1996', *Journal of Historical Geography*, 113: 40–56.

Ley, D. (1989) 'Modernism, postmodernism and the struggles for place', in J. Agnew and J. Duncan (eds), *The Power of Place.* London: Unwin Hyman pp. 44–55.

Ley, D (1993a) 'Postmodernism, or the cultural logic of advanced intellectual capital', *Tijdschrift voor Economische en Sociale Geografie*, 84: 171–4.

Ley, D. (1993b) 'Co-operative housing as a moral landscape: re-examining "the post-modern city"', in D. Ley and L. Bourne (eds), *The Changing Social Geography of Canadian Cities.* Montreal: McGill University Press. pp. 128–48.

Ley, D (1994) 'Theoretical pluralism in Anglo-American human geography', *Annals of the Japan Association of Economic Geographers*, 40: 63–74.

Ley, D. (1995) 'Between Europe and Asia: the case of the missing sequoias', *Ecumene*, 2: 187–210.

Ley, D (2003) 'Forgetting postmodernism? Recuperating a social history of local knowledge', *Progress in Human Geography*, 26: 537–60.

Ley, D (2006) 'Places and contexts in the making of a geographer', in S. Aiken and G. Valentine (eds), *Philosophies, People and Practices: An Introduction to Approaches in Human Geography.* London: Sage. pp. 173–83.

Ley, D (2007) 'Countervailing immigration and domestic immigration in gateway cities: Australian and Canadian variations on an American theme', *Economic Geography*, 83 (3): 231–54.

Ley, D (2009) www.geog.ubc.ca/~dley/homepage.html – David Ley's University of British Columbia web pages which include his list of publications and postgraduate students supervised since 1983. Accessed June 2009.

Ley, D. and Dobson, C. (2008) 'Are there limits to gentrification? The contexts of impeded gentrification in Vancouver', *Urban Studies*, 45(12): 2471–98.

Ley, D. and Olds, K. (1988) 'Landscape as spectacle: world fairs and the culture of heroic consumption', *Environment and Planning D: Society and Space*, 6: 191–212.

Ley, D. and Smith, H. (2000) 'Relations between deprivation and immigrant groups in large Canadian cities', *Urban Studies*, 37: 37–62.

Ley, D. and Tutchener, J. (2001) 'Immigration, globalisation and house prices in Canada's gateway cities', *Housing Studies*, 16: 199–223.

Smith, N. (1996) *New Urban Frontier: Gentrification and the Revanchist City.* New York: Routledge.

UBC (2009) University of British Columbia, Geography Department www.geog.ubc.ca/department/news.html Accessed June 2009.

Paul Rodaway, Lancaster University

BIOGRAPHICAL DETAILS AND THEORETICAL CONTEXT

Like many of America's leading urbanists, Kevin Andrew Lynch had close links with Chicago – the crucible of urban studies – although his associations concerned his childhood rather than professional career. Born in 1918 as the third and youngest child of a family of Irish descent, he grew up in an ethnically-mixed and modestly affluent area on the city's north side. Educated first by private tutors and then at the neighbourhood Catholic primary school, Kevin followed his two brothers to Francis W. Parker – a secular high school with a progressive curriculum that encouraged students to think about the world around them. Significantly at a time of economic depression, this included thinking about social issues. In later life, he credited his school experience as instrumental in interesting him in architecture and philosophy and in stimulating his lifelong interest in human environments and social justice (Banerjee and Southworth, 1990: 11).

By contrast, his higher education and professional training followed an uncertain path – albeit one that serendipitously allowed him to blend an architect's three-dimensional and visual design sensitivities with a planner's understanding of urban form and structure. A year's architectural study at Yale (1935–6) was followed by 18 months spent with the Fellowship of trainee architects run by the veteran modern architect Frank Lloyd Wright, and then by a move to the Rensselaer Polytechnic Institute to study structural engineering and then biology (1939–40). After briefly being employed by a private architectural practice, he was drafted into the US Army Corps of Engineers for the duration of the Second World War, returning to higher education under a demobilisation scheme in 1946. He earned a Bachelor of City Planning from the Massachusetts Institute of Technology (MIT) in 1947. This would prove to be his only degree, since he never undertook postgraduate study.

These repeated changes in direction contrasted markedly with the trajectory of the remainder of his career. After a year spent employed as a town planner in Greensboro (North Carolina, US), Lynch was invited to return to MIT in 1948 as an instructor in town planning, largely on the strength of his undergraduate dissertation – an enthusiastic treatise on urban renewal with case-study material from Cambridge, Massachusetts (Lynch, 1947). He worked his way up to full Professor by 1963, remaining at MIT until retirement in 1978. Subsequently devoting himself to consultancy through the firm that he founded with his colleague Stephen Carr (Carr, Lynch and Associates), he nevertheless retained his research and teaching links with MIT until his sudden death in July 1984.

This stability of employment at MIT perhaps contributed to the consistency shown in his approach to research, since themes that he developed in his work during the 1950s were continually revisited throughout his career. For example, he had pondered the question of how people navigated the streets of big cities as early as 1952, when he linked this issue to broader questions of aesthetics in a seminar at MIT (Lynch, 1984: 152). A year abroad funded by a Ford Foundation grant and largely spent in Florence allowed him to develop a deep appreciation of the significance of place within a city, to devise principles of notation through which to record his observations, and to reflect on the nature of urban form. This abiding fascination with urban form (see also Lynch, 1954) led to a five-year research programme, funded by the Rockefeller Foundation, which Lynch co-directed with Gyorgy Kepes, the founder and head of MIT's Centre for Advanced Visual Studies. As initiated in 1954, the aim was to undertake an 'investigation directed toward development of a theoretical concept of city form ... and to supply the fundamental criteria and techniques for conceiving, expressing and controlling our perceptual environment' (MIT, 2009: np). The emphasis inverted, however, as the project matured. By 1958–9, it had become 'an investigation of the individual's perception of the urban landscape ... the inhabitant's and the highway traveller's image of the city, and the use of the signs and symbols in the cityscape'. The objective of this work was 'the development of new design possibilities and principles for the city' (ibid.).

The principal results of this programme appeared in *The Image of the City* (Lynch, 1960), easily the most cited of his seven books (Pearce and Fagence, 1996: 584) and the one that effectively laid down the guidelines for his research in future years. An ensuing textbook entitled *Site Planning* (Lynch, 1962) developed the planning implications of the perceptual analyses offered by *The Image of the City*, with the jointly-authored *A View from the Road* (Appleyard et al., 1964) considering the role played by road travel in constructing urban imagery. After a fallow period of critical contemplation (Carr et al., 1984: 523), Lynch published a further sequence of four books. *What Time is This Place?* (Lynch, 1972) reflected on the temporal meaning of places within the city. Its strong support for the notion of conservation tied in with his next volume, the ambitious *Managing the Sense of a Region* (Lynch, 1976). Here, Lynch addressed the question of managing the sensory meaning of the environment, considering: 'what one can see, how it feels underfoot, the smell of the air, the sounds of bells and motorcycles, how patterns of these sensations make up the quality of places, and how that quality affects our immediate well-being, our actions, and our understandings' (Lynch, 1976: 8). *Growing up in Cities* (Lynch, 1977) drew on a participatory multinational programme funded by UNESCO to investigate children's perceptions of the city. Finally, *A Theory of Good City Form* (Lynch, 1981) considered the relationship between fundamental human values and the city, examining how such values should guide the performance dimensions necessary for good spatial and physical design.

SPATIAL CONTRIBUTIONS

Broadly speaking, Lynch made four major contributions towards developing a more profound understanding of urban spatial cognition. First, he provided insight into citizens' differential knowledge of the urban environment and supplied an accessible methodology by which it might be studied. Lynch argued that spatial knowledge centres on environmental 'images' – mental representations of the world that people develop through their experience and which act as the basis for their behaviour. This concept, which mirrored a similar idea developed earlier by Kenneth Boulding (1956), was made relevant to an urban context through the concept of 'legibility', or the ease with which individuals can organise the various elements of urban form into coherent 'images'. Lynch (1960) suggested that cities varied in the extent that they evoked a strong image – a quality that he called 'imageability' – arguing it was most likely that 'imageable' cities were ones that could be apprehended as patterns of high continuity with interconnected parts. In other words, if a city was 'imageable', it was also likely to be 'legible'.

The Image of the City reported on how Lynch and his team tested this idea in three American cities: Boston, Los Angeles, and Jersey City (New Jersey). In brief outline, they interviewed small samples of predominantly middle-class people in each city to investigate residents' perceptions of the central city, using such techniques as sketch maps, verbal lists of distinctive features, directions for making specific trips in the city, and informal questions about orientation. Findings for individual respondents were aggregated and compared with visual surveys carried out by trained observers. The assessments were made on the basis of a five-fold typology of urban elements, namely: 'paths' (channels along which people moved through the city), 'edges' (boundaries), 'districts', 'landmarks' (such as familiar stores, public buildings, statues or physical features),

and 'nodes' (strategic places where navigational decisions have to be made). The results suggested that urban space was perceived in terms of well-known clusters of points linked together by clearly defined paths that traverse less familiar areas. Perception of districts waned as residents became more familiar with the city, presumably through gaining more detailed knowledge, whereas landmarks assumed greater prominence with familiarity, seemingly because of their role in navigation.

Lynch's second contribution concerned way-finding and the importance of the street in structuring urban experience. Juxtaposed against the prevailing ideology that saw the significance of streets primarily in terms of how well they handled flows, Lynch argued that paths – which primarily meant streets – were the main structural element in images of the city and that the sensory experience gained from travelling through urban space was qualitatively important in image formation. Lynch and Rivkin (1959) studied the diverse and sometimes unexpected features that subjects recalled after a walk around a block in central Boston. As noted above, *The View from the Road* (Appleyard et al., 1964) extended the analysis to road travel, which was accomplished by studying the conscious, aesthetic and largely visual experience of motorists travelling along freeways into four American cities (Boston, Hartford, New York and Philadelphia). This was supplemented with a more detailed study carried out on a seven-mile section of the Northeast Expressway into Boston. The explanatory results suggested that experience gained from car travel could shape urban imagery beyond the realm currently in focus. For example, the vista of the distant city skyline, the changing impressions of land and water, and a series of notable landmarks all served to give clues about the nature of

Boston itself, which the individual could use to make inference.

Thirdly, Lynch stressed the importance of time in the meaning of place. In part, this was a corrective to earlier emphases. The 1950s research programme was concerned with the identity and structure of city images, which effectively separated meaning from form. Yet he always regarded 'the image of the spatial environment ... as a scaffold to which we attach meanings' (Lynch, 1972: 241) – a subject that he partly addressed through his multifaceted research on the temporal dimension of the individual's experience of the city. Most notably, *What Time is This Place?* (Lynch, 1972) maintained that people's innate sense of time was a vital part of the meaning allotted to place and an important ingredient in individual well-being. The feelings of attachment and identity so engendered needed to be respected both in policies for environmental change and when dealing with issues involving conservation.

Finally, Lynch played an important part in reassessing the value of neighbourhood life in children's development. One of his first articles dealt with the elements of the city's physical environment that left the deepest impression, concluding that 'knowledge of how people react to their physical environment, and how they invest it with emotional qualities, is quite as important as knowing the technical or economic or sociological resultants of a given form' (Lukashok and Lynch, 1956: 152). Two decades later, *Growing up in Cities* (Lynch, 1977) reported on the ways in which small groups of adolescents from four countries (Argentina, Australia, Mexico and Poland) used and valued the urban environment. In each case, the evidence stressed the role of the home neighbourhood as an anchor point in the child's experience of the city, recognising too the close relationship between place and the formation of community identity.

KEY ADVANCES AND CONTROVERSIES

As an academic always seeking to be actively involved in practice, Lynch's work needs to be viewed through a dual lens. In terms of practice, he ranks alongside Jane Jacobs, Mark Fried, Ian Nairn and a handful of others who looked beyond the consensual Modernist approaches guiding urban policy in the years after the Second World War and resensitised our appreciation of the intricacies of the urban mosaic. Although some have argued that the publication of *The Image of the City* in 1960 was in tune with the increasing abstraction of the city by heralding 'the transformation of the city into mere signs' (e.g. Maki, 2009: 91), Lynch's work undoubtedly contributed to a new agenda that paid attention to the human scale. As such, it recognised the realities of individual experience at a time when urban renewal policies threatened to brush such niceties aside in the Olympian pursuit of bringing planned order to perceived urban chaos. Yet, as Lynch himself (1984: 159) later recognised, the impact of his original studies on policy for city design was rather less than he had hoped, which he self-deprecatingly argued was because 'they have proved so difficult to apply'. Certainly, interest in direct application of his techniques to practical planning issues proved at best short-lived.

By contrast his writings, and most notably his books, left a potent legacy for research in a variety of fields. *A Theory of Good City Form* (Lynch, 1981), a book which straddled the interstices of urban, environmental and utopian discourse, has retained an enduring appeal for researchers interested in the ideas of cities as expressions of core human values. *The View from the Road* (Appleyard et al. 1964) with its focus on visual perception and highway travel, was an early study of driving landscapes (Merriman, 2007: 2) and among the first of a 'long-running ... collection of ethnographies of the 'road' (Laurier et al., 2008: 3). For its part, *Growing up in Cities* (Lynch, 1977) was the forerunner of further international collaborative projects on the development of children in cities (Malone, 1999), as well as contributing to the fields of developmental psychology and children's geographies.

The influence of these writings, however, is dwarfed by the lasting impact of *The Image of the City* (Lynch, 1960), which, even after half a century, can still be found firmly lodged in the bestseller lists of books about the urban environment. Its success came from a combination of innovative thinking, timeliness, accessibility and apparent policy relevance. Geographers in particular were looking for new insights into the relationships between spatial cognition and behaviour. In such circumstances, Lynch's work offered an inclusive package that blended conceptual clarity (based on the concepts of 'legibility' and 'imageability') with ready-made methods of data collection and analysis that apparently revealed the cognitive (or mental) maps held by city residents. Not surprisingly, it quickly became one of the mainstays of the cognitive-behavioural movement that flourished within geography in the 1960s and early 1970s, with the basic concepts and methods soon adopted and replicated by others. Within 15 years, there were substantive studies consolidating his

findings in, *inter alia*, other cities of the US, the Netherlands, Lebanon, the Federal Republic of Germany, Venezuela, the UK, and Italy (e.g., Jonge, 1962; Gulick, 1963; Klein, 1967; Appleyard, 1969; Goodey et al., 1971; Francescato and Mebane, 1973; and Orleans, 1973). His former colleague Donald Appleyard (1976) applied Lynch's ideas to the development of a new town (Ciudad Guayana, Venezuela) and gave credence – at least in the minds of social science researchers – to the belief that cognitive-behavioural research might provide direct input into urban policy.

These replications quickly suggested extensions and the need for modification (Gold, 1980: 97–106). Use of freehand sketch-maps was criticised as possibly indicating more about cartographic abilities rather than about cognitive representations of the city (Spencer, 1973). There were criticisms of the emphasis upon vision as opposed to non-visual components of sensory experience (Southworth, 1969) and of the lack of attention to the functional and symbolic meanings of urban space (Steinitz, 1968). Researchers attempting to use the five-fold typology of spatial cognitive elements quickly realised that the classification system was often difficult to apply and had no specific basis in psychological theory (Goodey et al., 1971).

In Lynch's defence, answers can be offered for most of these criticisms. The original studies were avowedly tentative and invited extension or modification. There was no ready-made body of theory or methodology that could be pressed into service for studies of urban spatial cognition. Psychologists, the most likely sources of such insights, were then strongly influenced by Skinnerian behaviourism and preferred strict laboratory control to the vagaries of environmental settings. Both the conceptual frameworks and methods, therefore, were derived on an ad hoc basis from a mixture of intuition, observation and applied commonsense – a potent amalgam that has maintained the appeal of Lynch's approaches despite the reservations expressed by researchers. Hence, while many recent citations of *The Image of the City* are contextual and essentially reflect the book's special status as the progenitor of an important discourse about urbanism, a substantial number of studies still employ the original research techniques or conceptual frameworks as an integral part of their research design regardless of the existing weight of criticism (e.g., see Everitt et al., 2008; Huynh et al., 2008; Vertesi, 2008).

To some extent, these conclusions are tempered by recognition that the long-term legacy of Lynch's writings varies from discipline to discipline. For instance, while his oeuvre remains a source of inspiration for researchers within planning and architecture (e.g. Appleyard, 1978; Ellin, 1996: 34–6ff; Bridge and Watson, 2002: 6), it has declined as an active influence upon the research agenda of human geography. This stems primarily from the close association between Lynch-inspired studies of urban imagery and behavioural geography, which atrophied markedly from 1980 onwards (see entry on **Reg Golledge**). Yet, notwithstanding the changing directions and priorities of geographical research, it is important even here not to underestimate Lynch's pervasive contribution. Certainly, there is no denying the role that his work played in the recent past as a cornerstone of an impressive corpus of humanely-informed research or its continuing status as a genuine contribution towards building a deeper understanding of the experiential qualities of urban space and place.

LYNCH'S KEY WORKS

Appleyard, D. Lynch, K. and Myer, J.R. (1964) *The View from the Road.* Cambridge, MA: MIT Press.
Lynch, K. (1960) *The Image of the City.* Cambridge, MA: MIT Press.
Lynch, K. (1962) *Site Planning.* Cambridge, MA: MIT Press.
Lynch, K. (1972) *What Time is This Place?* Cambridge, MA: MIT Press.
Lynch, K. (1976) *Managing the Sense of a Region.* Cambridge, MA: MIT Press.
Lynch, K. (ed.) (1977) *Growing up in Cities: Studies of the Spatial Environment of Adolescence in Crakow, Melbourne, Mexico City, Salta, Toluca and Warsaw.* Cambridge, MA: MIT Press.
Lynch, K. (1981) *A Theory of Good City Form.* Cambridge, MA: MIT Press.

Secondary Sources and References

Appleyard, D. (1969) 'City designers and the pluralistic city', in L. Rodwin and Associates (eds), *Planning, Urban Growth and Regional Development: The Experience of the Guayana Programme of Venezuela.* Cambridge, MA: MIT Press. pp. 422–52.
Appleyard, D. (1976) *Planning a Pluralist City: Conflicting Realities in Ciudad Guayana.* Cambridge, MA: MIT Press.
Appleyard, D. (1978) 'The major published works of Kevin Lynch: an appraisal', *Town Planning Review*, 49: 551–7.
Banerjee, T. and Southworth, M. (1990) 'Kevin Lynch: his life and work', in T. Banerjee and M. Southworth (eds), *City Sense and City Design: Writings and Projects of Kevin Lynch.* Cambridge, MA: MIT Press. pp. 1–29.
Boulding, K.E. (1956) *The Image: Knowledge in Life and Society.* Ann Arbor: University of Michigan Press.

Bridge, G. and Watson, S. (2002) 'Introduction: reading city imaginations', in G. Bridge and S. Watson (eds), *The Blackwell City Reader*. Oxford: Blackwell. pp. 3–10.

Carr, S., Rodwin, L. and Hack, G. (1984) 'Kevin Lynch: designing the image of the city', *American Planning Association Journal*, 59: 523–5.

Ellin, N. (1996) *Postmodern Urbanism*. Oxford: Blackwell.

Everitt, J., Massam, B.H., Chávez-Dagostino, R.M., Sánchez, R.E. and Romo, E.A. (2008) 'The imprints of tourism on Puerto Vallarta, Jalisco, Mexico', *Canadian Geographer*, 52, 83–104.

Francescato, D, and Mebane, W. (1973) 'How citizens view two great cities: Milan and Rome' in R.M. Downs and D. Stea (eds), *Image and Environment*. Chicago: Aldine. pp. 131–47.

Gold, J.R. (1980) *An Introduction to Behavioural Geography*. Oxford: Oxford University Press.

Goodey, B., Duffett, A.W., Gold, J.R. and Spencer, D. (1971) *'The city scene: an exploration into the image of central Birmingham as seen by area residents'*, Research Memorandum 10. Birmingham: Centre for Urban and Regional Studies, University of Birmingham.

Gulick, J. (1963) 'Images of an Arab city', *Journal of the American Institute of Planners*, 29: 179–97.

Huynh, N., Hall, G.B., Doherty, S. and Smith, W. (2008) 'Interpreting urban space through cognitive map sketching and sequence analysis', *Canadian Geographer*, 52: 222–40.

Jonge, D. de (1962) 'Images of urban areas: their structure and psychological foundations', *Journal of the American Institute of Planners*, 28: 266–76.

Klein, H.J. (1967) 'The delineation of the town centre in the image of its citizens: a report of methods and preliminary results of a town-sociological study', in Sociological Department, University of Amsterdam (eds), *Urban Core and Inner City*. Leiden: E.J. Brill. pp. 286–306.

Laurier, E., Lorimer, H., Brown, B., Jones, O., Juhlin, O., Noble, A., Perry, M., Pica, D., Sormani, P., Strebel, I., Swan, L., Taylor, A.S., Watts, L. and Weilenmann, A. (2008) 'Driving and "passengering": notes on the ordinary organization of car travel', *Mobilities*, 3: 1–23.

Lukashok, A. and Lynch, K. (1956) 'Some childhood memories of the city', *Journal of the American Institute of Planners*, 22: 142–152.

Lynch, K. (1947) *'Controlling the flow of rebuilding and replanning in residential areas'*, Unpublished Bachelor of City Planning thesis, Department of City and Regional Planning, Massachusetts Institute of Technology, available at: hdl.handle.net/1721.1/12525 Accessed 28 August 2009.

Lynch, K. (1954) 'The form of cities', *Scientific American*, 190 (4): 54–63.

Lynch, K. (1984) 'Reconsidering *The Image of the City*', in L. Rodwin and R. Hollister (eds), *Cities of the Mind*. New York: Plenum. pp. 151–62.

Lynch, K. and Rivkin, M. (1959) 'A walk around the block', *Landscape*, 8: 24–34.

Maki, F. (2009) 'Fragmentation and friction as urban threats in the post-1956 city', in A. Krieger and W.S. Saunders (eds), *Urban Design*. Minneapolis: University of Minnesota Press. pp. 88–109.

Malone, K.E. (1999) 'Growing up in cities as a model of participatory planning and "place-making" with young people', *Youth Studies Australia*, 18 (2): 17–23.

Merriman, P. (2007) *Driving Spaces*. Oxford: Blackwell.

MIT (Institute Archives and Special Collections, Massachusetts Institute of Technology) (2009) 'Perceptual form of the city 1951–1960: historical note', libraries.mit.edu/archives/research/collections/collections-mc/mc208.html#toc Accessed 17 August 2009.

Orleans, P. (1973) 'Differential cognition of urban residents: effects of social scale on mapping' in R.M. Downs and D. Stea (eds), *Image and Environment*, Chicago: Aldine. pp 115–30.

Pearce, P.L. and Fagence, M. (1996) 'The legacy of Kevin Lynch: research implications', *Annals of Tourism Research*, 23: 576–98.

Southworth, M. (1969) 'The sonic environment of cities', *Environment and Behaviour*, 1: 49–70.

Spencer, D. (1973) *'An evaluation of cognitive mapping in neighbourhood perception'*, Research Memorandum 23. Birmingham: Centre for Urban and Regional Studies, University of Birmingham.

Steinitz, C. (1968) 'Meaning and the congruence of urban form and activity', *Journal of the American Institute of Planners*, 34: 233–48.

Vertesi, J. (2008) 'Mind the gap: the London Underground map and users' representations of urban space', *Social Studies of Science*, 38: 7–33.

John R. Gold, Oxford Brookes University

40 Doreen Massey

BIOGRAPHICAL DETAILS AND THEORETICAL CONTEXT

Born in Manchester in 1944, Doreen Massey has proved to be one of geography's most enduring and influential writers. She gained her MA in Regional Science from the University of Pennsylvania in 1972, and, from 1968 to 1980, worked at the Centre for Environmental Studies in London (a research institute, now closed, that was established by Harold Wilson to focus on urban and regional questions). She followed this with a two-year stint as a Social Science Research Council (SSRC) Industrial Location Research Fellow. Massey has been a Professor of Geography in the Faculty of Social Sciences at the Open University (United Kingdom) since 1982, and in 2002 was made a Fellow of the British Academy. Increasingly lauded as one of British geography's most important voices, she has assumed a role as one of the discipline's few 'public intellectuals', regularly contributing to media debates. In 2009, the first Annual Doreen Massey Lecture was held at the Royal Geographical Society, London, in her honour, providing a platform for prominent geographers (including Ash Amin, **Nigel Thrift**, Jane Wills and Jamie Peck), sociologists (**Stuart Hall** and Chantal Mouffe) and politicians (notably former London mayor, Ken Livingston) to debate the links between space, place and politics (a theme that has animated much of her work)

Massey's numerous publications stretching back to the early 1970s have greatly affected the directions that human geography and those disciplines close to it (particularly sociology and cultural studies) have taken. To put it simply, Massey's work has been central in transforming human geography into a disciplinary domain dedicated to the project of social theory, while encouraging the social sciences to take on board the complexity of space and place within their formulations. The significance of Massey's work arises, in other words, not simply from its content and methodology, but, more fundamentally, from its insistence on the importance of *conceptualising* space and place. For Massey is adamant that *how* one formulates an object of study is crucial for the theoretical and empirical claims one makes about that object of study. *How*, in other words, one formulates the concept of space or place radically shapes one's understanding of the social world and how to effect transformation in and of it. In the course of three decades of writing, Massey's reconceptualisations of a suite of key terms – space, place, region, locality – have helped revolutionise geographical thinking within the social sciences as a whole. Massey, in working through the implications of the rallying call 'geography matters', has produced a powerful and nuanced set of theories, frameworks and empirically-based studies with which to understand spatial differentiation, uneven development, and historical and geographical change.

Massey shot to academic prominence by virtue of several path-breaking articles that displaced the dominant orthodoxies framing discussions of industrial location and of British regional 'problems' in the 1970s. She showed how a-spatial, neo-classical accounts of industrial location were fundamentally disrupted when the spatial dimension was addressed (Massey, 1973); she also launched a powerful attack on the reliance within urban and regional studies on statistical techniques and hence on the field's implicit endorsement of a naive empiricism. Asking '[i]n what sense ... are "regional" problems *regional* problems' (1979: 241), Massey disputed the usual logic whereby inner cities and more peripheral regions were somehow themselves responsible for their declining fates. Instead she suggested that '[d]ifferent modes of response by industry, implying different spatial divisions of labour within its overall process of production, may ... generate different forms of "regional problem"' (Massey, 1979: 234). Massey demonstrated that since the development of these new divisions of labour 'will be overlaid on, and combined with, the pattern produced in previous periods by different forms of spatial division', this will result in a series of geographically differentiated economic 'layers' that will reshape patterns of inequality and affect ensuing rounds of investment (1978: 115–16).

In 1984, *Spatial Divisions of Labour* was published. The book transformed economic geography, and would become Massey's most highly cited monograph. It aimed to reconceptualise how the very sphere of 'the economic' was understood, and was an extension and refinement of Massey's earlier arguments. Massey argued that economic geography had to address the spatial organisation of the relations of production rather than simply describe and render visible geographical distributions. For her, addressing spatial organisation entailed paying adequate attention to the constitution of particular, regionally differentiated places rather than focusing exclusively on the general tendencies of capitalist accumulation:

> behind major shifts between dominant spatial divisions of labour within a country lie changes in the spatial organization of capitalist relations of production, the development and reorganization of what we shall call spatial structures of production. Such shifts in spatial structures are a response to changes in class relations, economic and political, national and international.
>
> (Massey, 1984: 7)

Massey developed her general claims about 'layers of investment' and 'spatial structures of production' by setting out three examples of spatial structures that she put to work in an analysis of how the British economic landscape was transformed in the 1960s and 1970s:

1. *Single region* (where the whole process of production is confined within a single geographical area).
2. *Cloning* (one branch is the headquarters, but the production process itself is geographically undifferentiated such that the whole process takes place at each branch).
3. *Part-process* (multi-locational, with a managerial hierarchy and a complex production process that is spatially stretched out across different plants).

Of critical importance here was Massey's insistence that spatial structures of production could not be determined a priori, but rather that they were solidified, combated and transformed by various political and economic strategies and actors working at differing scales.

Important too, was Massey's acknowledgement of how ideologies of gender and race complicated her analysis of the labour process. For although her analysis worked around the axis of class, she made clear how changes in spatial divisions of labour were both affected by, and in part brought about by, social definitions of skill categorising certain jobs as characteristic of certain types of people. But of perhaps greatest importance, and hence subject to greatest debate, was Massey's conviction that the existence of spatial variety must not be seen as a deviation from inexorable laws of capitalist accumulation. '[W]hat lies behind the whole notion of uneven development is the fact of highly differentiated and unique outcomes,' Massey insisted (1984: 49): the book thus argued for and offered a rejuvenated and radically transformed regional geography.

It is invidious to represent a smooth lineage linking an author's early and later work. Nonetheless, it is perhaps helpful to see Massey's work after *Spatial Divisions of Labour* as extending some of the central claims of that book concerning specificity, transformation and spatial connectedness. Massey's research since the mid-1980s might, then, be collected under three broad headings. The first relates to gender in economic and social processes. Massey has been keen to analyse how the construction of gender relations is central to the spatial organisation of social relations (Massey, 1994). Her writings in this area include further elaborations of how industries make strategic use of regional differences in systems of gender relations; relational accounts of identity formation; and analyses of how conceptualisations of time and space

have often been problematically mapped on to the dualism masculinity–femininity. Her accounts of the high-technology industry around Cambridge (United Kingdom) have argued, in this regard, that the masculinisation of the work of scientists and engineers is buttressed by the temporal and spatial flexibility of that work – a flexibility in which the masculinised workplace trumps the feminised home, and 'transcendent' mental labour trumps domestic labour and the social sphere (Massey, 1995a).

The second important trajectory relates to theorisations of 'place'. Massey has produced a rich body of writings that refuses the easy association of place with nostalgia, inertia and, by implication, regressive politics. These writings include further elaborations of the concept of the region (Allen et al., 1998), and interventions into the debate over 'time–space compression'. All these writings show how places might be understood as 'porous networks of social relations' (Massey, 1994: 121), and Massey has developed the term 'power geometry' to emphasise how groups and individuals are differently positioned within these porous networks.

A third key trope of Massey's work is the concept 'space–time'. Massey has demonstrated how the cemented divide between time and space is problematic in its flawed association of change with the temporal, and stasis with the spatial. She has therefore developed an alternative view of space – as 'space–time' – in which space and time are seen as inseparable (Massey, 1992). The term aims to reinforce her conviction that 'the spatial is integral to the production of history, and thus to the possibility of politics, just as the temporal is to geography' (1994: 269).

These three tropes or themes arguably come together in her book *For Space* (Massey, 2005), which revisits some of the key questions she has posed about the

regional question, globalisation and identity via a mainly theoretical exposition
inspired by a disparate range of structural and post-structural thinkers, including Laclau, Derrida and Bergson (see
Anderson, 2008). Becoming something
of a touchstone in debates concerning
relational geographies, *For Space* makes
a powerful argument for considering the
connectedness of space, its always heterogeneous constitution and its unfinished
nature: in other words, its relationality, its
multiplicity and its openness. The book is,
hence, described by Massey (2005: 13) as
comprising 'an essay on the challenge of
space, the multiple ruses through which
that challenge has been so persistently
evaded, and the political implications of
practising it differently'. The latter hints
at the fact that Massey is at pains to
consider how we might engage with the
world more ethically and openly, respect-
ing both difference and alterity whilst
recognising the manifold nature of space.

For Space underlines that Massey is
passionate about communicating across
disciplinary divides and beyond the academy. She was, for example, a regular contributor to *Marxism Today* (a key locus for
British New Left thought in the 1980s),
and has long taken an active role in policy discussions concerning British urban
and regional questions (for example, in
relation to the regeneration of the London Docklands). Her 2007 book *World
City* can be read as perhaps the clearest
manifestation of this, being an accessible
and urgent volume on the challenges facing the governors of London in a global
era, informed by her ideas of relational
space and the necessity of a politics of
mutuality that stretches well beyond the
city limits. The fact that the book makes
frequent and sometimes extremely positive references to the work of Labour
mayor of London Ken Livingston underlines that Massey remains unequivocally

for the left. In 1995, she, together with
Stuart Hall and Michael Rustin, founded
Soundings: A Journal of Politics and Culture,
a journal dedicated to thinking the 'radical democratic project'. That a significant
number of Massey's publications have
either been co-authored (Richard Meegan
and John Allen are particularly important
in this regard), or have emerged from
joint research projects further demonstrates Massey's commitment to intellectual collaboration and exchange. One
should note here the institutional role of
Massey's academic home, the Open University: the distance teaching that that
university conducts is dependent on its
faculty publishing co-authored course
books, and these have provided an important conduit for the dissemination of
Massey's ideas.

SPATIAL CONTRIBUTIONS

Massey (1995b: 317) stated that *Spatial Divisions of Labour* was committed
to 'reinterpreting "objects in space" as
products of the spatial organization of
relations'. This phrase elegantly captures
what is characteristic of Massey's oeuvre
as a whole: its dedication to understanding 'things' *relationally* – whether those
'things' be places, identities or socio-spatial formations such as the nation state.
Massey's most fundamental contribution
to thinking space and place is arguably
her conviction that the social and the spatial need to be conceptualized *together*.
But this does not imply the mechanical
insertion of 'space' as a motivating or
explanatory factor: '[i]t is not spatial form
in itself (nor distance, nor movement)

that has effects, but the spatial form of particular and specified social processes and social relationships' (Massey and Allen, 1984: 5).

Massey's intricate analyses both of the 'spatial' and, later, of 'space–time', have been inspirational for countless geographers. Massey can therefore be characterised as part of a cohort of geographers – that might include **David Harvey**, **Derek Gregory**, **Nigel Thrift** and **Gillian Rose** – who have refused to imagine space and time as neutral, a priori categories and instead have developed rich accounts of space and time as sutured within and productive of the formations and deformations making up the 'natural' and the 'social' world.

Many of the concepts and frameworks elaborated in *Spatial Divisions of Labour* are now central to the fields of economic, industrial and labour geography. The book broke with the models of economic change provided both by empiricist neo-classical economics and by overly rigid structuralist Marxist accounts, and presented an elastic and powerful analytic framework that was taken up by numerous academics and regional specialists. The book was undoubtedly a catalyst for an intensified cross-disciplinary dialogue between urban/social/economic geographers and sociologists (see **Andrew Sayer**) vis-à-vis how spatial structure might be understood as a structuring medium through which social relations unfold (see for example Gregory and **Urry**, 1985). The book's theoretical terrain prefigured what would in the late 1980s and early 1990s become key discussions within geography and social theory: the role of local uniqueness, the usefulness of the terms 'flexibility' and post-Fordism, and critiques of universal and universalising explanations and theories.

Massey's neologisms 'power geometry' and 'space–time' have also been enormously influential within human geography – both in their theoretical impact, and for their ability to provide structuring frameworks for those keen to understand how fights over space and place might be understood as fights about spatialised power. Massey herself has recently directed her interrogations of spatiality towards debates on the role of World Cities and governance in a global era to mount a powerful critique of the dominant, commonsense, '*aspatial* view of globalization' (1999: 34). In arguing that such an account turns 'real spatial difference into the homogeny of temporal sequence (we'll all be globalized in this way eventually)', she shows how such modes of thinking render impossible the thinking of 'difference' (1999: 40).

KEY ADVANCES AND CONTROVERSIES

Massey's ideas have, on occasion, been both subject to, and developed out of, vigorous contestation. The frequency and willingness with which Massey has made specific responses to her interlocutors' concerns and criticisms indicates her belief in the productivity of exchange. Alongside the huge excitement generated by the publication of *Spatial Divisions of Labour* came several refutations and criticisms of Massey's framework. Cochrane (1987) argued that her desire to create a 'new regional geography' was hampered by the book's tendency towards a 'microstructuralism' that ended up reneging on the project of tackling capitalism at national and international levels. David Harvey also disagreed with Massey's reworking of Marxism – excoriating the book's 'rhetoric of contingency, place, and the specificity of history' which, he claimed, reduced 'the whole guiding thread of Marxian argument ... to a set of echoes and reverberations of inert Marxian categories' (Harvey, 1987: 373). Others accused Massey of overemphasising the national framework of industrial transformation at the expense of the global. Massey's deliberate decision to focus her analysis on the workplace (and the book's concomitant underemphasis on the reproductive realm) came in for criticism by several feminist geographers (though Gillian Rose, 1993, helpfully shows how Massey's framework acted as a catalyst for further feminist-geographical research on how home and community, as well as the workplace, are key sites for the consolidation and contestation of capitalist and patriarchal social relations).

Spatial Divisions of Labour also became enmeshed in the heated 'locality debate' of the 1980s. The British Economic and Social Research Council (ESRC) set up three large 'locality' research programmes in the mid-1980s to explore the wide-ranging social and economic changes affecting Britain in the 1970s and 1980s by focusing attention on various small-scale localities. Of these, the Changing Urban and Regional System in the UK (CURS) programme received by far the most academic attention. Massey herself had initiated the original proposal and drawn up the original research outline, though was not directly involved in the undertaking of research herself. The CURS programme was seen by many as an abdication of 'theory' (usually meaning Marxist theories of capital accumulation) in favour of empiricism. Massey's book was often seen as a prime mover in this abdication, and participants in the debate frequently failed to distinguish 'locality' as a concept used by Massey from its use as a descriptor of the research programmes.

The locality debate circled around the problematic of 'contingency' and how it should be understood in relation to the concepts of specificity, the local, the general and the abstract. The debate was also very much a political and institutional one: what kinds of research projects should geographers be developing and what theoretical frameworks should they use to guide them? Massey, reflecting on the locality studies debate, has argued that the couplet 'specific–general' was frequently and mistakenly elided with that of 'concrete–abstract', such that it was generally assumed that only localities are 'concrete'. She has, in contrast, argued that 'the current world economy ... is no less concrete than a local one' (Massey, 1991c: 270). Arguing that the study of local areas need not entail a return to individual, descriptive portraits of geographical regions, she has averred that studying localities does not necessitate fetishising the local. Massey has reflected at length on the locality debate, and other criticisms relating to *Spatial Divisions of Labour*, in the second edition of that book (1995b).

Massey's long-held interest in understanding regional particularity received new impetus by virtue of the debates over 'time-space compression' and postmodernism following the publication of David Harvey's *The Condition of Postmodernity* (1989). Massey profoundly disagreed with several of the overarching formulations in that book, and her famous essay 'Flexible sexism' (1991b) was an extended critique of both Harvey's and **Ed Soja**'s conceptualisations of postmodernity and the postmodern. Massey argued that while neither author 'would want to be thought of as anti-feminist', both books, she claimed, 'are in fact quite fundamentally so' (1991b: 32). Massey was particularly exercised by what she saw as Harvey's relegation of feminism to the position of a 'local' struggle in comparison with the 'general' struggle of class. She cautioned that Harvey, in desiring to construct unity by subsuming all struggles within the umbrella of class politics, was urging 'a unity enforced through the tutelage of one group over others' (1991b: 55).

Massey's difficulties with Harvey's account of 'time-space compression' provided the driving force for another of her famous essays 'A global sense of place' (Massey, 1991a). Massey countered the claim that thinking in terms of place was necessarily reactionary – a claim implied by Harvey – and argued that a sense of place 'adequate to this era of time-space compression' demanded developing an account that was not wedded to the lure of introversion, but that understood a place's specificity as 'constructed out of a particular constellation of social relations, meeting and weaving together at a particular locus' (1991a: 28). Massey's use of the term 'power-geometry' to understand this 'meeting and weaving' in terms of differential mobilities, and her famous call for 'a global sense of the local, a global sense of place' (1991a: 29) were brought to life in a vignette of her own London neighbourhood, Kilburn. Massey's several interventions concerning 'place' and the 'local' register the continuing and unresolved debates within geography over the relations between the 'general' and the 'particular' and the terms space and place – debates that are, it should be noted, far more wide-ranging than the specific differences separating Massey and Harvey.

Massey's emphasis on mobility, openness, flow and differential power relations has contributed to those terms becoming guiding principles in human geography. Yet it is worth considering whether the ready assimilation of 'relationality' within geography is in the process of establishing an orthodoxy of the contingent and the open. We might ask what an (over-)emphasis on the contingent and open might occlude, and whether particular spaces and places are valorised at the expense of others (a question that lingers after reading the obdurately London-centric view of the UK economy offered in *World City*). McGuinness, for example, has interrogated Massey's reliance on a particular representation of 'difference' in 'A global sense of place', suggesting that her vignette of the Kilburn High Road 'could easily be seen as a very particular white Western construction of a world of difference' (McGuinness, 2000: 228). Precisely because 'difference' – in the sense of visibly marked difference – is so easy to notice in a multiethnic area such as Kilburn, McGuinness wonders whether 'for the normalizing white eye' hybridity becomes fundamentally associated with blackness. Massey herself would doubtless agree with McGuinness that the concept of hybridity must not function to sideline consideration of postcolonial 'white' identity formations, since much of her own oeuvre has been dedicated to unsettling, rather than reinforcing, 'normalising' frames of geographical thinking.

MASSEY'S KEY WORKS

Allen, J., Massey, D. and Cochrane, A. (1998) *Rethinking the Region*. London and New York: Routledge.

Massey, D. (1973) 'Towards a critique of industrial location theory', *Antipode*, 5: 33–9.

Massey, D. (1984) *Spatial Divisions of Labour: Social Structures and the Geography of Production*. London and Basingstoke: Macmillan.

Massey, D. (1991a) 'A global sense of place', *Marxism Today*, June: 24–9.

Massey, D. (1991b) 'Flexible sexism', *Environment and Planning D: Society and Space*, 9: 31–57.

Massey, D. (1994) *Space, Place, and Gender*. Cambridge: Polity Press.

Massey, D. (1995a) 'Masculinity, dualisms and high technology', *Transactions of the Institute of British Geographers*, 20: 487–99.

Massey, D. (1995b) *Spatial Divisions of Labour: Social Structures and the Geography of Production* (2nd edition). Basingstoke: Macmillan.

Massey, D, (1999) 'Imagining globalization: power-geometries of time-space', in A. Brah, M.J. Hickman and M. Mac an Ghaill (eds), *Global Futures: Migration, Environment and Globalisation*. Basingstoke: Macmillan. pp. 27–44.

Massey, D. (2005) *For Space*. London: Sage.

Massey, D. (2007) *World City*. Cambridge: Polity Press.

Massey D, Quintas, P. and Wield, D. (1992) *High-tech Fantasies: Science Parks in Society, Science and Space*. London: Routledge.

Secondary Sources and References

Anderson, B. (2008) 'Doreen Massey's *For Space*', in P. Hubbard, R. Kitchin and G. Valentine (eds), *Key Texts in Human Geography*. London: Sage.

Cochrane, A. (1987) 'What a difference the place makes: the new structuralism of locality', *Antipode*, 19: 354–63.

Environment and Planning A (1989) Special issue – 'Spatial divisions of labour in practice', 21: 655–700.

Environment and Planning A (1991) Special issue – 'New perspectives on the locality debate', 23 (2).

Gregory, D. and Urry, J. (eds) (1985) *Social Relations and Spatial Structures*. Basingstoke: Macmillan.

Harvey, D. (1987) 'Three myths in search of a reality in urban studies', *Environment and Planning D: Society and Space*, 5: 367–76.

Harvey, D. (1989) *The Condition of Postmodernity*. Oxford: Blackwell.

Martin, R., Markusen, A. and Massey, D. (1993) 'Classics in human geography revisited: Massey D (1984) "Spatial divisions of labour"', *Progress in Human Geography*, 17: 69–72.

Massey, D. (1978) 'Regionalism: some current issues', *Capital and Class*, 6: 106–25.

Massey, D. (1979) 'In what sense a regional problem?', *Regional Studies*, 13: 233–43.

Massey D (1991c) 'The political place of locality studies', *Environment and Planning A*, 23: 267–81.

Massey, D. (1992) 'Politics and space/time', *New Left Review*, 196: 65–84.

Massey, D. and Allen, J. (eds) (1984) *Geography Matters! A Reader*. Cambridge: Cambridge University Press in association with the Open University.

Massey, D. and Allen, J. (eds) (1988) *The Economy in Question*. London: Sage in association with the Open University.

McGuinness, M. (2000) 'Geography matters? Whiteness and contemporary geography', *Area*, 32: 225–30.

Rose, G. (1993) 'Spatial divisions and other spaces: production, reproduction and beyond', in *Feminism and Geography*. Minneapolis: University of Minnesota Press. pp. 113–36.

Felicity Callard, Queen Mary, University of London

41 Linda McDowell

BIOGRAPHICAL DETAILS AND THEORETICAL CONTEXT

Over the course of her career, Linda McDowell has played a leading role in developing feminist theoretical and methodological approaches within human geography. Grounded in rigorous empirical research, her most significant research monographs, journal papers and edited collections have focused on processes of social and economic restructuring in Britain. In so doing, she has contributed significantly to conceptual understandings of labour market dynamics and the changing nature of work in advanced capitalist economies. In addition to her own research, she has mentored a considerable number of graduate students, many of whom have gone on to develop successful academic careers of their own. More broadly, she has played an important role in documenting the gendered nature of the academy and the social practice of geography as a discipline. These research interests are heavily influenced by her own biography of growing up and being educated in the UK in the second half of the twentieth century, something that she has reflected on in a number of publications (McDowell, 2003, 2007).

Linda McDowell was born in Stockport, just south of Manchester. After attending a girl's grammar school, she studied at a women's college at the University of Cambridge and was awarded a BA (Hons) degree in Geography in 1971. Here, her early interest in the ways individuals experience economic restructuring was already evident in her undergraduate dissertation. In this piece of work she conducted interviews with male workers from a number of Eastern European countries who were employed in the steel industry in the English Midlands. These men had come to Britain following the end of the Second World War as EVWs (European Volunteer Workers) and were employed as labourers in heavy industries such as steel-making in order to contribute to the rebuilding of Britain's industrial base at the time. Reflecting her commitment to studying the gendered nature of the economy, she subsequently returned to the subject of post-Second World War European migration through a study of the lives of Latvian women who had migrated to Britain at the same time as the men who were the focus of her undergraduate dissertation and who were also part of the EVW scheme established by the British Government (McDowell, 2005).

Following her undergraduate career, McDowell was awarded an MPhil degree in Town Planning at University College London in 1973. She then held research positions at the Centre for Research in the Social Sciences, University of Kent at

Canterbury and the Institute of Communities Studies in London. In 1978, McDowell moved to a Lectureship in Urban Studies and Geography at the Open University, during which time she had a son (1981) and a daughter (1983). In 1986 she was promoted to Senior Lecturer at The Open University and was also awarded her PhD from University College London. The disjuncture between these early experiences of working in the academy and her formative familial and educational experiences in which 'if you were prepared to work hard, then, it seemed nothing was impossible' (McDowell, 2007: 60) proved to be an important stimulus for her work both as a feminist scholar and her concern about the social practice of geography as a discipline. As she wrote:

> When I became a university teacher in the 1970s, I found an academy dominated by men. My earlier life, before entering the labour market, however, had not totally resonated with my practical knowledge of men's superiority

(McDowell, 2003: ix).

These experiences gave rise to several papers exploring the gendered power relations within the academy (McDowell, 1990a, 1990b). McDowell also extended her interests in this area beyond academic writing by founding, with a number of other feminists, the Women in Geography Working Party (subsequently the Women in Geography Study Group) of the Institute of British Geographers in 1979, a group that she went on to Chair.

In 1992, she moved to the University of Cambridge. In addition to her duties in the Department of Geography, she played a significant role in the management of Newnham College, becoming Vice-Principal between 1997 and 1999. It was during her time at Cambridge that she completed her hugely influential study of the gendered identities at work in the

rapidly changing merchant banking industry in the City of London. In addition to a number of papers (McDowell, 1994a, 1994b), this study was also published as the monograph *Capital Culture: Gender at Work in the City* (1997a). This book clearly demonstrates the significance of her work across a number of geographical subdisciplines in addition to the social sciences more widely. At one level, her analysis reveals the persistence of gendered occupational segregation within financial services while, at another, the research makes a significant contribution to conceptual understandings of the embodied nature and performative qualities of gender identities in the workplace, developing the work of **Judith Butler** (1990). In so doing, this research was one of the earliest and most detailed demonstrations of the need to take issues of culture seriously within economic geography following the 'cultural turn', a research agenda that has subsequently expanded substantially (McDowell, 1997b; see also Amin and **Thrift**, 2004; Pryke and Du Gay, 2007).

Since leaving Cambridge in 1999, McDowell has held Chairs at the London School of Economics, University College London and most recently at the University of Oxford. In common with the earlier stages of her career, the importance of her own biography in shaping her research interests remains evident. The most notable example is her research into the labour market experiences of young white males in Britain who had been identified as 'underachieving' at school. This research extends McDowell's interest in the embodied nature of gendered identities to include the construction of multiple masculinities as young men negotiate low-skilled labour markets that have become increasingly dominated by low-paid, short-term service sector jobs. Part of the inspiration for this research stemmed from McDowell's observations of her (then) teenage son's classmates as they left education to enter the world of paid work. As she writes, 'while many of the young women in his peer group achieved good results in school-leaving exams, too many of his male friends lost their commitment to academic success and left school to look for work in a local labour market increasingly dominated by low-paid service-sector jobs' (McDowell, 2003: x). This research, and the methodological issues associated with it, has been published in a number of journal papers (McDowell, 2001a, 2001b, 2001c) and in the monograph *Redundant Masculinities: Employment Change and White Working Class Youth* (2003).

By conducting research into the labour market experiences of young men, this research brings together McDowell's twin interests in the processes and consequences of economic restructuring in Britain, on the one hand, and the embodied and gendered nature of work and workplace identities, on the other. She has continued to combine these research interests in her most recent work on the experiences of minority workers employed in the service sector in London (McDowell et al., 2007; Batzinsky et al., 2008).

SPATIAL CONTRIBUTIONS

McDowell's research is characterised by an interdisciplinary theoretical approach that is grounded in rigorous, largely qualitative, research. The contribution her work has made to advancing feminist scholarship within human geography (McDowell, 1993, 1999) and developing conceptual and empirical understandings

of the gendered nature and geographical specificities of both labour markets and workplace identities is considerable. These contributions can be summarised around three main themes.

First, McDowell has been at the forefront of work in geography that theorises the relationships between the embodied nature of gendered identities and the changing nature of service work. In so doing, she has moved beyond her earlier work that adopted a materialist approach to analyse gendered occupational segregation (see, for example, McDowell and **Massey**, 1984). This shift reflects broader changes in the nature of feminist scholarship that:

> Turned from the measurement and explanation of sex segregation in the labour market towards approaches emphasising 'doing' gender, the construction of embodied performances in the labour market, and the fluidity and mutability of gendered identities in different sectors, places and occupations where everyday interactions as well as institutional rules and regulations are part of the construction of workplace-based identifies.
>
> (McDowell, 2004: 46)

By adopting such a perspective McDowell's later work has been important in challenging enduring discourses concerning the gendered nature of the workplace. For example, her research into the gendered identities performed by merchant bankers in London's financial district was conducted in the wake of significant deregulatory changes collectively known as Big Bang. These changes facilitated greater foreign, particularly US, ownership of financial firms in the City. Such firms were seen to be more meritocratic in terms of their organisational cultures compared to the hitherto dominant merchant banks where trust-based relations based on shared education and social backgrounds dominated (Thrift, 1994).

The widespread arrival of US investment banking working practices, coupled with the growing emphasis placed on customer service (frequently stereotyped as a feminine quality) within investment banking were seen as having the potential to significantly increase the participation and power of women within financial services in London, thereby eroding the established power of 'gentlemanly capitalism' (Augar, 2001).

However, McDowell demonstrates how men by and large retained their established positions of power within the City. She achieves this by documenting how:

> Widespread social attitudes about women's work, the changing circumstances of the City of London in the 1980s and early 1990s, popular images and representations of investment banking, and cultures of British banks combine to construct and regulate a restricted range of gender performances at work [in London's financial services industry].
>
> (McDowell, 1997a: 205)

In so doing, her work provides a powerful reminder of the unequal opportunities that still exist within finance, in common with other business services. Similarly in her more recent work on the experiences of male school leavers with few or no qualifications, she sought to counter popular understandings of such young men in Britain as irresponsible 'yobs'. Through interview-based research conducted in Sheffield and Cambridge, she has explored the commitment often demonstrated by such men to 'acquire and hold down a job and to construct lives imbued with the value of domestic respectability, while negotiating the complex and often contradictory expectations associated with working class masculinity' (McDowell, 2003: 2).

The significance of this work is not limited to demonstrating the analytical purchase afforded by an approach focused on their embodied and performative qualities of gender. McDowell's work also reveals the co-constitutive relationship between the structures within economies that serve to reproduce occupational segregation for men and women and the dynamic performance of gendered identities. Consequently, the second theme that has characterised her work and geographical contribution to date is a commitment to combine both structuralist and post-structuralist perspectives to understand identity formation and its reproduction in the workplace. She has written a number of predominantly theoretical pieces that explore this issue through an examination of the relationship between identity, inequality and labour market change (see, for example, McDowell, 2001d, 2004). In particular, she has developed these theoretical interests through a focus on the intersections between gendered identities and class relations (McDowell, 2006, 2008).

In this respect, she has played a leading role in challenging 'conventional assumptions made by geographers and other theorists ... about the nature and location of class struggles' (McDowell, 2006: 826). In particular, she has problematised the binary separation in which class relations are understood to be a function of the public sphere whilst gender relations are limited to the preserve of the private sphere, particularly the home. Here she has critiqued post-structuralist approaches that focus on (gendered) difference in and of itself and drawn attention to the continued importance of the intersection between structural inequalities and gender through a focus on class divisions *between* women. This work takes as its starting point the relatively familiar statistics on the increasing participation of women in the paid labour market in the UK, in common with other advanced capitalist economies, through-out the second half of the twentieth century. However, McDowell focuses on the uneven class differences that are emerging amongst women working in different geographical and sectoral labour markets associated, most notably, with the consumption by middle-class women, particularly mothers, of domestic services provided by working-class women. For McDowell, these developments raise important theoretical questions. As she writes:

> Just as women's entry into the labour market raises questions about the overall structure of the class hierarchy and the degree of polarisation between classes, the growing importance of commodified domestic labour – especially childcare in which middle class women buy services from typically working class women to facilitate their own labour market participation – also raises new questions about class divisions and class contacts between women ... both within and outside the space of the home.

(McDowell, 2006: 840)

In making these arguments, she has contributed to the renewed interest in class relations in geography by developing a relational understanding of class that takes issues of gender seriously in its analysis.

The third theme that runs through McDowell's work is a commitment to advancing feminist methodological approaches within geographical research and reflecting on the gendered way in which this research is undertaken within the academy (McDowell, 1992a). Methodologically, her work predominantly uses detailed qualititative research typified by interviews and oral histories. These methodological choices reflect the fact that her work is firmly grounded in feminist critiques of 'scientific' method and an appreciation of the need for researchers to be reflexive about the situated

nature of knowledge produced through academic research (McDowell, 1992b). This commitment is reflected in the detailed methodological appendices that are included in all her monographs and her openness in terms of acknowledging possible weaknesses in her own research approach (McDowell, 2003).

In so doing, her work has been particularly important in highlighting the methodological possibilities within economic geography as interviews, participatory and ethnographic methods have become increasingly widely used in the wake of the 'cultural turn'. However, McDowell has not only played an important role in developing the research practices of contemporary human geography; she has also been an influential commentator on the practice of geography as an academic discipline and the nature of work in the academy more generally (McDowell, 1990b), something that continues to be important given the disproportionately small number of women working in geography departments in higher education institutes (particularly at higher levels) when compared to the popularity of geography amongst undergraduate women.

KEY ADVANCES AND CONTROVERSIES

McDowell's commitment to ensuring that feminist perspectives and methodologies are placed more centrally within geographical scholarship has not always been easy. As she writes:

> It has been tough, especially initially, when feminist work was derided as 'political' and 'biased' ... I became used to

criticism from referees who saw feminist theories and methods as an anathema, to sexism and hostility from audiences, to colleagues who thought married women had no need of promotion as their husband should be the main breadwinner, to being the only woman on all-male committees.

(McDowell, 2007: 61)

However, by working through such challenges, McDowell's work has been developed and extended through several contemporary research agendas and debates in both geography and the wider social sciences. First, her work on the embodied and performative qualities of identities, provided an early example of work at the interface of economic, social and cultural geography. This area of research developed subsequently as economic geographers have sought to theorise the entangled nature of economy and culture. Whilst McDowell's empirical focus in this regard is primarily on labour market change and the workplace, recent work has extended this agenda to include issues ranging from individual experiences of transnationalism to a growing attention to consumption practices within the economy (see **Ley**, 2004; **Jackson**, 2002 respectively). Moreover, theoretically, McDowell's work on performativity has been extended through recent inter-disciplinary debates in cultural economy. This latter work privileges understandings of performativity that follow philosophical work on performative speech acts and is significantly influenced by insights from science and technology studies, rather than McDowell's approach, which draws heavily on the work of Judith Butler (see for example MacKenzie, 2006). However, cultural economy research in geography and beyond is beginning to examine the possibilities for a rapprochement between these different approaches to performativity (Berndt and Boeckler, 2009).

Second, McDowell's work on the complex and place specific nature of identity construction and (re)production from a feminist perspective has been debated and developed by both geographers and social scientists more generally. In particular, McDowell has noted the possibilities for developing this work further by focusing on issues of intersectionality. For instance, she suggests that her work on working-class masculinities points to the importance of interrogating questions of race in studies of working-class identities, a research agenda that has begun to be advanced within social geography (see Hopkins, 2007). Meanwhile, whilst McDowell remains committed to combining structural and post-structural approaches to identity formation, recent work in geography has been more heavily influenced by post-structural thought. This has given rise to feminist scholarship within and beyond geography that privileges detailed, ethnographic research methods to focus on issues of meaning and representation (see for example Pratt, 2004). In response, McDowell (2006) has argued strongly that structural inequalities must not be erased from social scientific analysis, particular the intersections between class and gender, echoing debates in feminist scholarship beyond geography (Adkins, 2002).

Finally, McDowell's research agenda and the way in which she 'practises' geography have played an important role in the academy beyond geography. Intellectually, she is one of a relatively small number of geographers whose research not only draws on debates beyond geography but importantly contributes to work in the broader social sciences, most notably by emphasising the critical role played by space and place in shaping the gendered nature of workplace identities and labour market change. Meanwhile, in terms of the contemporary academy, in addition to drawing attention to the gendered nature of its own labour markets, her own research practices are also likely to be important in the future. In particular, throughout her career, research monographs have been central to the ways in which she has written up and disseminated her research. Indeed, her latest research that develops further her interest in the performative qualities of service work is published in her fifth sole-authored monograph, *Working Bodies* (2009). This dissemination strategy is significant given the concerns regarding this form of publication in an academy increasingly driven by metrics (see *Progress in Human Geography,* 2009). Taken together, these elements of McDowell's research and writing provide considerable stimulus for future research into the gendered nature of workplace identity formation and their geographies as well as the ways in which geography is practised and organised as an academic discipline.

MCDOWELL'S KEY WORKS

McDowell, L. (1991) 'Life without Father and Ford: the new gender order of post-Fordism', *Transactions of the Institute of British Geographers,* 16: 400–19.

McDowell, L. (1992a) 'Doing gender: feminism, feminists and research methods in human geography', *Transactions of the Institute of British Geographers,* 17: 399–416.

McDowell, L. (1993) 'Space, place and gender relations: identity, difference, feminist geometries and geographies', *Progress in Human Geography,* 17: 305–18.

McDowell, L. (1997a) *Capital Culture: Gender at Work in the City.* Oxford: Blackwell.

McDowell, L. (1999) *Gender, Identity and Place.* Cambridge: Polity.

McDowell, L. (2003) *Redundant Masculinities? Employment Change and White Working Class Youth.* Oxford: Blackwell.

McDowell, L. (2005) *Hard Labour: The Forgotten Voices of Latvian Migrant 'Volunteer' Workers.* London: UCL Press.

Secondary Sources and References

Adkins, L. (2002) *Revisions: Gender and Sexuality in Late Modernity.* Buckingham: Open University Press.

Amin, A. and Thrift, N. (2004) *The Blackwell Cultural Economy Reader.* Oxford: Blackwell.

Augar, P. (2001) *The Death of Gentlemanly Capitalism.* London: Penguin.

Batzinsky, A., McDowell, L. and Dyer, S. (2008) 'A middle class global mobility: the working lives of Indian men in a west London hotel', *Global Networks,* 8: 51–70.

Berndt, C. and Boeckler, M. (2009) 'Geographies of circulation and exchange: constructions of markets', *Progress in Human Geography,* 33: 535–51.

Butler, J. (1990) *Gender Trouble: Feminism and the Subversion of Identity.* London: Routledge.

Hopkins, P. (2007) 'Young people, masculinity, religion and race: new social geographies', *Progress in Human Geography,* 31: 163–77.

Jackson, P. (2002) 'Commercial cultures: transcending the cultural and the economic', *Progress in Human Geography,* 26: 3–18.

Ley, D. (2004) 'Transnational spaces and everyday lives', *Transactions of the Institute of British Geographers,* 29: 151–64.

MacKenzie, D. (2006) *An Engine not a Camera: How Financial Models Shape Markets.* Cambridge, MA: MIT Press.

McDowell, L. (1990a) 'Women in British geography revisited', *Journal of Geography in Higher Education,* 14: 19–32.

McDowell, L. (1990b) 'Sex and power in academia', *Area,* 22: 323–32.

McDowell, L. (1992b) 'Multiple voices: speaking from inside and outside the project', *Antipode,* 24: 6–72.

McDowell, L. (1994a) 'Gender divisions of labour in the post-Fordist economy: the maintenance of occupational sex segregation in the financial services sector', *Environment and Planning A,* 26: 1397–418.

McDowell, L. (1994b) 'Performing work: bodily representations in merchant banks', *Environment and Planning D: Society and Space,* 12: 727–50.

McDowell, L. (1997b) 'A tale of two cities? Embedded organisations and embodied workers in the City of London', in R. Lee, and J. Wills (eds), *Geographies of Economies.* London: Arnold. pp. 118–29.

McDowell, L. (2001a) 'It's that Linda again: ethical and practical issues in research with young men', *Ethics, Place and Environment,* 4: 88–100.

McDowell, L. (2001b) 'Father and Ford revisited: gender, class and employment change in the new millennium', *Transactions of the Institute of British Geographers,* 24: 448–64.

McDowell, L. (2001c) 'Masculine discourses and dissonances: Strutting "lads", protest masculinity and domestic respectability', *Environment and Planning D: Society and Space,* 20: 97–119.

McDowell, L. (2001d) 'Rethinking scale: some reflections on the significance of research on gender and organisations for economic geography', *Journal of Economic Geography* 1: 227–50.

McDowell, L. (2004) 'Masculinity, identity and labour market change: some reflections on the implications of thinking relationally about difference and the politics of inclusion', *Geografiska Annaler, B,* 86: 45–56.

McDowell, L. (2006) 'Reconfigurations of gender and class relations: class differences, class condescension and the changing place of class relations', *Antipode,* 25: 825–50.

McDowell, L. (2007) 'Sexing the economy, theorizing bodies', in A. Tickell, E. Sheppard, J. Peck, and T. Barnes (eds), *Politics and Practice in Economic Geography.* London: Sage. pp. 60–70.

McDowell, L. (2008) 'Thinking through class and gender in the context of working class studies', *Antipode,* 40: 20–24.

McDowell, L. (2009) *Working Bodies: Interactive Service Employment and Workplace Identities.* London: Wiley Blackwell.

McDowell, L., Batnitzky, A. and Dyer, S. (2007) 'Division, segmentation and interpellation: the embodied labours of migrant workers in a Greater London hotel', *Economic Geography,* 82: 1–26.

McDowell, L. and Massey, D. (1984) 'A woman's place?', in D. Massey and J. Allen (eds), *Geography Matters.* Cambridge: Cambridge University Press. pp. 128–47.

Pratt, G. (2004) *Working Feminism.* Edinburgh: Edinburgh University Press.

Pryke, M. and Du Gay, P. (2007) 'Take an issue: cultural economy and finance', *Economy and Society,* 36: 339–54.

Progress in Human Geography (2009) 'Forum: The future of research monographs: an international set of perspectives', 33: 102–26.

Thrift, N. (1994) 'On the social and cultural determinants of international financial centres: the case of the City of London', in S. Corbridge, R. Martin and N. Thrift (eds), *Money, Power and Space.* Oxford: Blackwell. pp. 327–55.

Sarah Hall, University of Nottingham

42 Anssi Paasi

BIOGRAPHICAL DETAILS AND THEORETICAL CONTEXT

Anssi Paasi is one of the world's foremost political geographers and has contributed in extensive and innovative ways to geographers' understanding of critical spatial concepts, most especially in relation to the region and the nation and the way in which these spatial concepts are defined by territories/boundaries. To date, he has published over 150 papers, reviews and chapters, as well as 19 books and monographs in both Finnish and English on these themes. While the empirical focus of Paasi's research throughout his career has been on Finland and its relationship with a broader Baltic region, the theoretical import of his work has ensured that it has travelled well beyond the shores of the Baltic Sea.

Paasi began his university education at the University of Joensuu in Eastern Finland in 1979 and remained there until 1986, gaining Masters, Licentiate and Doctoral degrees in the process. Following his doctorate, he was appointed to the post of Docent in the University of Joensuu and was subsequently promoted to a Chair in Geography in the University of Oulu in 1990, later becoming the recipient of a four-year Research Professorship sponsored by the Academy of Finland.

His status within – and indeed beyond– Finland is demonstrated by the fact that he is the first geographer to receive such an award. As well as being recognised for his research skills within Finland, Anssi Paasi has also gained external recognition for his contribution to geographical knowledge. He was elected as an Honorary Professor of Human Geography in the University of Wales, Aberystwyth in 2006. He has, additionally, held visiting positions in the University of Nijmegen, Loughborough University and UCLA and served as editor of the prestigious journal *Progress in Human Geography*.

It has been argued that an understanding of individual biographies is enriched if one considers the way in which they are also embedded in particular places and spaces. A focus on Anssi Paasi's 'life-path' or spatialised biography illustrates the significance of such ideas. To begin with, the fact that Anssi Paasi is a *Finnish* geographer has had a profound effect on his career. In a prosaic sense, Anssi Paasi's nationality has meant that he has focused the vast majority of his empirical research on Finland as a country and on particular regions within it, most notably Karelia. Additionally, this has meant that he has published a large proportion of his work in Finnish-language publications, especially during the early periods of his career. At the same time, Anssi Paasi's Finnish identity has influenced his research career in more subtle ways. His status as a Finnish geographer, for instance, has meant that he has had to strive against a human and political geography that is dominated, to a large extent, by geographers living and working within an Anglo-American academy. Working as such in the relative spatial 'margins' of an Anglo-American academy, Paasi is to be commended for leading academic debates on key spatial concepts, such as region, nation, territory and boundary. It could be argued, nonetheless, that some of Paasi's potential impact on understandings of these concepts in an international context may well have been lessened as a result of being a voice speaking from the 'margin' (Paasi, 2005a). The fact that a large amount of Paasi's research has been published through the medium of Finnish – and has not, therefore, become part of an international academic debate conducted largely in English – is the clearest indication of this relative loss of academic impact.

In addition to this international context, one must also focus on the trajectory of Paasi's career within Finland. Addressing the state of the discipline of geography within Finland, Paasi (2005b) noted that the character of human geography within Finland has historically been influenced by two factors. First, human geography has traditionally been affiliated to faculties of science within the vast majority of Finnish universities. Second, and especially during the 1970s and early 1980s, human geography in Finland was dominated by an older generation of human geographers who were proponents of quantitative and positivist approaches. These two factors posed difficulties for an emerging group of critical human geographers, such as Paasi, who struggled to gain academic recognition. For instance, Paasi's early work on regions (1986a; 1986b; 1991) was viewed by more traditional Finnish human geographers as something that was peripheral to Finnish human geography. Significantly, Paasi was labelled by these individuals as a 'spatial sociologist' rather than a human geographer. Paasi, in his own words, considered himself to be a geographer who was in the 'wrong place'. It is also perhaps as a result of this relative antipathy to his work in Finland, at least during the 1980s, that he increasingly sought to publish his research through the medium of English.

Second, the geographical specificities of Anssi Paasi's higher education influenced his engagement with spatial concepts. As noted above, he received his formal geographic education in the University of Joensuu and this had two important implications for his career. Firstly he has noted that the department of geography in the University of Joensuu acted as a significant location for the emergence of a more critical form of geography within Finland (2005b: 608). 'Close connections with fields such as history, economics, sociology and social policy', according to Paasi (ibid.), enabled human geographers within this department to engage with the important philosophical currents that were affecting human geographers elsewhere from the 1970s onwards in a more sustained manner. In the second place, one also needs to remember the location of the University of Joensuu within Finland. The University of Joensuu, significantly, lies in Finnish North Karelia and it can be argued that Paasi's experience of living and working here helped fuel his enagagement with some of the key concepts that have underpinned his academic career.

SPATIAL CONTRIBUTIONS

Paasi's contributions to understanding of regions, nations, territories and borders are manifold. Critical is his work on the institutionalisation of regions; the socio-spatial processes that help to reproduce nationalism; the broader significance of borders and territories as a way of articulating a socio-spatial consciousness. Arguably, the most important strand has been his work on the institutionalisation of regions. The inspiration for this work derived in large part from emerging academic debates about social constructionism and, in particular, the way in which these were articulated in the specific contributions made by geographers such as **Allan Pred** (1984) and **Nigel Thrift** (1983). While some of this work was beginning to focus on the meaning of regions in more sophisticated ways than had hitherto been the case, Paasi (pers. comm.) maintained that this research failed to explain how 'regions became what they were'. His aim at the beginning of his career, therefore, was to provide a new theoretical and methodological way of understanding regions (1991). A region was conceived by Paasi as a socio-spatial unit and 'a representation of "higher-scale" history into which inhabitants are socialised as part of the reproduction of ... society'. His main contribution to understanding of regions, therefore, is that regions do not merely exist but are rather institutionalised over time.

Four stages are said to be critical to this institutionalisation (Paasi, 1986b: 119–30; 1991: 243–47). While each is distinct to a degree, they are also mutually constitutive and should not be considered as incremental or developmental in character. The first stage relates to the 'territorial shape' of a region or, in effect, the extent to which the territorial make-up of a region becomes understood and appreciated within the individual or collective consciousness. Second, Paasi notes the importance of the 'symbolic shape' of a region, which equates to the degree to which symbols help to represent the region in question; in the form of languages, flags and so forth. Third, a region may gain 'institutional shape' from a variety of institutions, which give some formal and quasi-permanent structure to socio-spatial life within the region. Finally, Paasi (1991: 247) notes that regions may become 'established' within the socio-spatial consciousness and may assume 'the material expression of the ends to which state power is applied'. Attention is drawn here to the degree to which regions help to shape the material decisions made by the state concerning the allocation of resources. When viewed as a whole, Paasi's work on regions is concerned with explaining how regions are in a constant process of 'becoming' in a variety of different contexts. Regions may emerge and become consolidated or 'institutionalised' within society. Conversely, they may become marginal to people's lives and, indeed, they may even disappear. It is significant, in this respect, that Paasi's conceptualisation of regions has remained relatively constant throughout his career.

As well as developing a conceptual and methodological framework for understanding the institutionalisation of regions, Paasi has been concerned with demonstrating the empirical validity of his claims. In the mid-1980s, for instance, he conducted an in-depth empirical study of the institutionalisation of four Finnish regions: Lapland, Southern Ostro-Bothnia, Northern Karelia and Uusimaa. The project's empirical basis comprised archival material – including administrative documents, maps and atlases, regional newspapers, school textbooks – and 2,600 questionnaires. Paasi used this material in order to examine the degree to which the regions in question had become institutionalised within the socio-spatial consciousness of the inhabitants of the four regions (Paasi, 1986a; 1986b). Latterly, he has sought to examine how the process of institution-alisation has unfolded in a range of 'new' and 'old' regions within Europe.

Even though Paasi's main contribution to geographical knowledge has centred on understanding the region as a socio-spatial concept, he has also developed an interest in two other related spatial cat-egories: nations and national territories. He has thought of these as spaces that can also experience processes of institu-tionalisation – specifically in the context of Finland (Paasi, 1996a; 1996b; 2002c). In general terms, Passi's work in this area has attempted to show how nations, national territories and their bounda-ries are produced through a mixture of a socio-spatial consciousness – based on the practices of the state's agents at the national scale – and a social representa-tion – which is centred on the lives of more ordinary people within localities (Paasi, 1996a: 11). The empirical focus for this research has been the Finnish nation, specifically with regard to the role played by the border region of Karelia in reflecting and shaping the Finnish nation's socio-spatial consciousness and social representation. Significantly, his research has shown how the Finnish nation and national territory has been formed as a result of a combination of formal state-building projects and the more mundane and day-to-day practices of ordinary people.

Paasi's interest in the role played by the Finnish-Russian border in defining the Finnish nation has also encouraged him to pursue a second new area of research in recent years, namely, his effort to study the broader impact of globalisation on borders and boundaries in the contem-porary world (Newman and Paasi, 1998; Paasi, 1994a; 1999a; 1999c; 2002a; 2003b;

2005c). This research has been part of a broader academic project to deliver a more conceptually-attuned understanding of borders and boundaries (Newman and Paasi, 1998: 189). Echoing his work on regions and nations/national territories, the main thrust of this research has been to demonstrate how borders and bound-aries should be viewed as spatial concepts that are produced, rather than being pre-given or static in character, using insights from social and cultural theory to suggest boundaries should be viewed as contin-gent processes in motion. Furthermore, borders and boundaries are geographical entities that are continuously emerging as a result of a mixture of processes; some of these are state driven but other actors within civil society are also associated with the process of 'narrating boundar-ies' (Paasi, 2002b). Neither is the impact of globalisation on the character of con-temporary globalisation on borders and boundaries as straightforward as some assume. Rather than undermining the significance of boundaries, globalisation has merely made more complicated and contingent the processes that reproduce or narrate contemporary borders.

KEY ADVANCES AND CONTROVERSIES

Paasi's work, when viewed as a whole, has formed a remarkably coherent aca-demic project over a number of years. He has drawn inspiration from social and cultural theory in order to re-think the significance of key spatial concepts, most notably those relating to regions, nations/ territories and boundaries. His major contribution in each of these instances has been to demonstrate that these spatial concepts are not pre-given or static in character but are rather socially produced as a result of the practices of, and discourses emanating from, a range of actors. In this regard, Paasi has been able to use ideas about the becoming of place, which were becoming increasingly significant during the early 1980s (Pred, 1984; Thrift, 1983) and to use the tenor of these arguments as a way of informing similar ideas about the becoming of regions, territories and borders.

Three key issues emerge from Paasi's stress on the becoming of such spatial categories. First, Paasi's work testifies to the contingency of some of the major spatial categories with which we are familiar. Regions, nations and borders have not remained stable over the long term but have varied in terms of their significance. In certain instances, some regions have assumed greater significance and others may well have lost their socio-spatial significance as they have become 'de-institutionalised'. Second, Paasi has been able to show how recent challenges to borders and national territories have not been novel in any real way but have been part of an ongoing process whereby spatial categories are 'narrated'. In this way, Paasi has been able to counter some of the more excitable contributions made by the so-called 'hyper-globalisers' about the far-reaching impact of the processes of globalisation on different kinds of boundaries in the contemporary world. Third, Paasi's work has the potential to show how different individuals and groups

within society may well have varying conceptions of the significance of regions, nations and borders. In other words, the institutionalisation of spatial categories such as regions, nations and borders is not a homogeneous and uncontested process. Rather, there may be conflicting interpretations of the importance and even the geographical location of these spaces.

Evidence of the significance and value ascribed to Paasi's work lies in the fact that it has inspired other geographers to examine regions, nations and borders as continuously-emerging spatial features. Empirical examinations of the institutionalisation of the region have occurred across Europe and in a variety of economic and cultural contexts (e.g., Bialasiewicz, 2002; Cumbers et al., 2003; Giordano, 2000; Häkli, 1998; Jones and MacLeod, 2004). Studies of nations and borders within an era of globalisation have also been informed by the insights emerging from Paasi's work (Berg and Oras, 2000; Jones and Fowler, 2007; O'Dowd, 2002; Sparke, 2006). While many academics, predominantly geographers, have drawn inspiration from Paasi's work, there is no real evidence that his research has generated many controversies either within or beyond the discipline's boundaries. There is a real sense in which his insights into the emerging character of regions, nations and borders have become accepted conceptualisations of the nature of these spatial categories. In this respect, it is clear that the impact of Paasi's work has been widespread in geography and further afield and is highly likely to remain so in future years.

PAASI'S KEY WORKS

Paasi, A. (1986a) 'The institutionalization of regions: a theoretical framework for understanding the emergence of regions and the constitution of regional identity', *Fennia*, 164: 105–46.

Paasi, A. (1991) 'Deconstructing regions: notes on the scales of human life', *Environment and Planning A*, 23: 239–56.

Paasi, A. (1996a) *Territories, Boundaries and Consciousness.* Chichester: John Wiley.

Paasi, A. (1999a) 'Boundaries as social processes: territoriality in the world of flows', in D. Newman (ed.), *Boundaries, Territory and Postmodernity.* London: Frank Cass. pp. 69–88.

Paasi, A. (2002a) 'Bounded spaces in the mobile world: deconstructing "regional identity"', *Tijdschrift voor Economische en Sociale Geografie,* 93: 137–48.

Paasi, A. (2004) 'Place and region: looking through the prism of scale', *Progress in Human Geography,* 28: 536–46.

Paasi, A. (2005a) 'Globalization, academic capitalism and the uneven geographies of international journal publishing spaces', *Environment and Planning A,* 37: 769–89.

Paasi, A. (2005b) 'Between national and international pressures: contextualizing the progress of Finnish social and cultural geography', *Social and Cultural Geography,* 6: 607–15.

Secondary Sources and References

Berg, E. and Oras, S. (2000) 'Writing post-Soviet Estonia on to the world map', *Political Geography,* 19: 601–25.

Bialasiewicz, L. (2002) 'Upper Silesia: rebirth of a regional identity in Poland', *Regional and Federal Studies,* 12: 111–32.

Cumbers, A., McKinnon, D. and McMaster, R. (2003) 'Institutions, power and space: assessing the limits to institutionalism in economic geography', *European Urban and Regional Studies,* 4: 325–42.

Giordano, B. (2000) 'Italian regionalism or 'Padanian' nationalism – the political project of the Lega Nord in Italian politics', *Political Geography,* 19: 445–71.

Häkli, J. (1998) 'Discourse in the production of political space: decolonizing the symbolism of provinces in Finland', *Political Geography,* 17: 331–63.

Jones, M. and MacLeod, G. (2004) 'Regional spaces, spaces of regionalism: territory, insurgent politics and the English question', *Transactions of the Institute of British Geographers,* 29: 433–52.

Jones, R. and Fowler, C. (2007) '"Where is Wales?" Narrating the territories and borders of the Welsh nation', *Regional Studies,* 41: 89–101.

Newman, D. and Paasi, A. (1998) 'Fences and neighbours in a postmodern world: boundary narratives in political geography', *Progress in Human Geography,* 22: 186–207.

O'Dowd, L. (2002) 'The changing significance of European borders', *Regional and Federal Studies,* 12: 13–36.

Paasi, A. (1986b) 'Neljä maakuntaa [Four provinces in Finland: a geographical study on the development of regional conscious-ness]', University of Joensuu, Joensuu. Published in Social Sciences no. 8.

Paasi, A. (1994a) 'The changing representations of the Finnish-Russian boundary', in W.A. Galluser, M. Bürgin and W. Leimgruber (eds), *Political Boundaries and Coexistence.* Bern/Paris/New York: Peter Lang. pp. 103–111.

Paasi, A. (1999b) 'The changing pedagogies of space: the representation of the Other in Finnish school geography textbooks', in S.D. Brunn, A. Buttimer and U. Wardenga (eds), *Text and Image: Social Construction of Regional Knowledges.* Leipzig: Institut für Länderkunde, pp. 226–37.

Paasi, A. (1999c) 'The political geography of boundaries at the end of the millennium: the challenges of the de-territorializing world', in H. Eskelinen, I. Liikanen and J. Oksa (eds), *Curtains of Iron and Gold: Reconstructing Borders and Scales of Interaction.* London: Ashgate Publishers, pp. 9–24.

Paasi, A. (2002b) 'Place and region: regional worlds and word', *Progress in Human Geography,* 28: 802–811.

Paasi, A. (2002c) 'Place, boundaries, and the construction of Finnish territory', in D. Kaplan and J. Häkli (eds), *Boundaries and Place: European Borderlands in Geographical Context.* Lanham, Boulder: Rowman & Littlefield. pp. 178–99.

Paasi, A. (2003a) 'Region and place: regional identity in question', *Progress in Human Geography,* 28: 475–85.

Paasi, A. (2003b) 'Boundaries in a globalizing world', in K. Anderson, M. Domosh, S. Pile and N. Thrift (eds), *Handbook of Cultural Geography.* London: Sage. pp. 462–72.

Paasi, A. (2005c) 'The changing discourses on political boundaries: mapping the backgrounds, contexts and contents', in H. van Houtum, O. Kramsch and W. Zierhofer (eds), *B/ordering the World.* London: Ashgate. pp. 17–31.

Pred, A. (1984) 'Place as historically contingent process: structuration and the time-geography of becoming places', *Annals of the Association of American Geographers,* 74: 279–97.

Sparke, M. (2006) 'A neoliberal nexus: economy, security and the biopolitics of citizenship on the border', *Political Geography,* 25: 151–80.

Thrift, N. (1983) 'On the determination of social action in space and time', *Environment and Planning D: Society and Space,* 1: 23–57.

Rhys Jones, Aberystwyth University

43 Allan Pred

BIOGRAPHICAL DETAILS AND THEORETICAL CONTEXT

Allan Pred was initially most influential for his work on the spatial dynamics of urban development. Later he received widespread notice for his inventive, textually challenging, studies of the everyday spatialities of capitalist societies. Pred's writing is defined by a commitment to explicate the relationship between contemporary spatial structures and the historical legacies that have shaped the emergence of these structures. In the first half of his career, these historical legacies are framed almost entirely in terms of complex but nonetheless map-able economic relationships. From the 1980s onwards, Pred's writings were increasingly concerned with the complexities of temporality itself. His writing came to focus on the ways the present is shot through with all sorts of remnants of past times and spaces. The trajectory of Pred's work hence mirrors that of much of human geography over the past four decades. It is marked by a movement away from the idea of the spatial as a distinct element of social life, towards a concept of the social as being inherently spatialised. Pred's work also came to be defined by an engagement with a range of heterodox intellectual traditions that located Pred's writing as in much within the domain of critical social theory, as within the discipline of human geography.

Born in New York City in 1936, Pred gained degrees from Antioch College – where he began reading for his degree aged just 16 – and Pennsylvania State University, before moving to the University of Chicago to undertake doctoral research. By the late 1950s, when Pred arrived, the University of Chicago was a key centre in the emerging subdisciplines of quantitative geography and regional science. Rejecting the idea that geography was defined by a concern for the unique particularities of regions and places, quantitative geography and regional science recast human geography as a science of the spatial. Graduating with a PhD from Chicago in 1962, Pred was thus at the vanguard of what was later to become known as the quantitative revolution (see entries on **Brian Berry**, **Peter Haggett**, **Waldo Tobler** and **Alan Wilson**).

From Chicago, Pred joined the geography department of the University of California, Berkeley. A precocious talent, Pred obtained tenure at Berkeley within five years, and a full professorship by the age of 34. These professional achievements were driven by the publication of a remarkable series of books and articles that helped define the possibilities of geography's turn towards the spatial. These included a trilogy of books exploring the emergence of the American urban system: *The Spatial Dynamics of*

US Urban-Industrial Growth, 1800–1914 (1966); *Urban Growth and the Circulation of Information* (1973); and *Urban Growth and the City: Systems in the United States, 1840–1860* (1980); along with a highly regarded textbook that summarised his ideas, *City-Systems in Advanced Economies* (1977).

The 1980s and the 1990s saw a sharp shift in Pred's intellectual focus as his work shifted away from quantitative geography and away from North America as he split his time between Berkeley and Sweden (his wife being of Swedish descent). However, there was no diminishing of his productivity. In another trilogy of books (*Practice, Place and Structure: Social and Spatial Transformation in Southern Sweden, 1750–1850* (1986); *Lost Words, Lost Worlds: Modernity and the Language of Everyday Life in Late Nineteenth Century Stockholm*, and *Making Histories and Constructing Human Geographies: The Local Transformation of Practice, Power Relations and Consciousness* (both 1990)) Pred explored the making of everyday consciousness in eighteeth and nineteeth-century Sweden. In a final trilogy (*Recognising European Modernities: A Montage of the Present* (1995); *Even in Sweden: Racisms, Racialized Spaces, and the Popular Geographical Imagination* (2000); and *The Past Is Not Dead* (2004)) Pred's attention was focused on contemporary Sweden. Pred died in 2007.

SPATIAL CONTRIBUTIONS

Perhaps the easiest way to characterise Pred's intellectual trajectory would be to divide it into an early positivist, quantitative period, and a latter post-positivist non-quantitative phase. Certainly, a quick look at the title of Pred's major publications does suggest such a split. However, to focus on this division would misrepresent the subtlety and originally of Pred's writing. It would also, as **Trevor Barnes** (2001; 2003; 2004) has highlighted in a series of articles analysing the recent history of human geography, underplay the importance played by the quantitative revolution of the 1960s and 1970s in establishing an intellectual climate whereby the *theoretical* arguments developed by non- or anti-positive geographers could be taken seriously.

In fact, from the beginning of his career Pred's writing was characterised by its eclecticism and openness to a variety of intellectual sources. Much of his writing from the 1960s and 1970s is best read as an ongoing critique of the more rigid and dogmatic strands of positivistic quantitative geography. Whereas, the mainstream of quantitative geography, and certainly all of regional science, stressed the primacy of that which is measurable, and that which was economically rational, in the introduction to his first book, *The Spatial Dynamics of US Urban-Industrial Growth*, Pred argued that the goal of urban geographers should be to:

> embellish existing ... location theory by taking into account irrational behaviour, imperfect knowledge, other psychological variables, socially dictated constraints, and the impact of existing patterns.

(Pred, 1966: 5)

He went on to argue for the importance of understanding spatial forms as sets of evolving historical-geographic processes. These are themes – re-framed, re-theorised, and re-contextualised – that Pred returned to repeatedly over 45 years of writing. Thus, rather than slicing Pred's oeuvre into a simple pre-positivism and post-positivism divide, it is more productive to approach Pred's work in terms of its major empirical foci. Tracking his empirical concerns allows us to gain a better sense of how Pred's writing is marked by a series of subtle intellectual shifts, rather than sharp breaks. It also allows a better sense of how each major period of his writings represents an evolution and extension of his spatial imagination. As such, Pred's work can be divided into three major empirical periods: firstly, 1960–1980, when he focused on the spatial dynamics of urban growth in nineteenth century US; secondly, 1980–1992, examining the making of everyday places and spaces in eighteenth and nineteenth century Sweden; and, finally, from 1992–2006 a critical montage of Sweden's present.

Pred's writing in the 1960s and 1970s was defined by a series of attempts to develop an urban geography capable of accounting for the enduring patterns of urban development apparent in the North American urban system. While it was clear that the organisation of US cities did indeed form a kind of unified system, the dynamics of this system did not neatly fit the models used by quantitative geographers and regional scientists. It was possible, for example, to describe the establishment of the eastern manufacturing belt using Alfred Weber's location theory. Weber's theory could not explain why some cities once they had become established centres for a particular product, subsequently became centres of manufacturing in a range of cognate industries; nor did it explain the fact that once cities had obtained a dominant position in an inter-urban hierarchy they were remarkably robust in maintaining their position. As the US urban system grew so do did the largest cities. The more established cities were not growing simply because of their initial locational advantage. So, why were they growing? And, indeed,

why did it seem that the more ties a large city had to other similar cities, the more dynamic was its economic development? The importance of such non-hierarchical connections seemed to turn the central place theory of Walter Christaller (1966) and August Lösch (1954) on its head.

One answer to the question of the persistent success of already large cities was to focus on the initial advantages early growth gave to a city. Drawing both on the economist Gunnar Olsson's concept of cumulative causation and the innovation diffusion models of the Swedish geographer **Torsten Hägerstrand** ([[1953] 1967), Pred argued that a series of positive feedback loops reinforced the initial advantages that propelled a city's growth in the first instance. Eventually, the networks produced by these feedback loops become the principle source of a city's economic dynamism, even if the original source of a city's locational advantage becomes eroded or is superseded.

Internal urban dynamics, however, are not sufficient to explain *in toto* the persistent success of large cities. Pred's second answer to the puzzle of the enduring stability of the American urban system was to explore the ways in which large cities within America had indeed come to form an interdependent urban system, and how this system functioned to secure the locational position of those cities already at the top of the urban hierarchy. In *Urban Growth and the Circulation of Information* (1973) Pred mapped the historical evolution of information flows such as newspaper distribution, postal volumes, and telegraphic messages within the urban system. Through so doing, he showed how large cities not only dominated the movement of information, but that a significant proportion of the information moving between cities was focused on communication between large cities. And it was this concentration of information flows, and the resultant privileging of large cities in the diffusion of key technological and organisation innovations, that largely explains the stability of the rank ordering of the American urban system.

Pred christened the model he developed from this historical data The Large City Rank Stability Model. He went on to argue for the wider relevance of The Large City Rank Stability Model and the diffusion model that underpinned it (see Pred, 1975a; 1975b; 1976; 1977a). In hindsight, however, what is most interesting about these models is not their general validity or invalidity. It is the way that through these and other models (see Pred, 1967; 1969) Pred's thinking brought into relief the connection between patterns of technological innovation, the formation of historically contingent clusterings of economic activity, and the persistent unevenness of geographic development. Indeed, in his concern for the spatial dynamics of economic innovation Pred's work prefigured – and in many ways defined – the intellectual terrain for economic geography's intense concern for innovation clusters, Marshallian industrial districts, and so on through the 1980s and 1990s.

If Pred's many publications on the dynamics of urban growth were at the cutting edge of human geography, and in many ways defined an ongoing research field within economic and urban geography, by the end of the 1970s his intellectual interests were nonetheless shifting. Where he had primarily focused on the economic activities and economic institutions that led (or did not lead) to economic growth, Pred was increasingly drawn to the question of understanding how capitalism as a whole social system transformed the ways of life of those caught within it. Pred's initial formulations (see Pred, 1977b; 1978; 1981a; 1981b) of this question were organised through the

language of Hägerstrand's time-geography. Pred, however, came to realise that he needed more than just time-geography to frame the relationship between individual agency and social structure. Where time-geography counterpoised individual action to existing institutional structures and conventions, Pred sought to develop a conceptual language that highlighted the dialectical interplay between 'the structural condition of practice and the effects of practice on structure' (Pred, 1986: 6).

In trying to puzzle out this dialectic of structure and agency, Pred cast his intellectual net wide. He drew on **Anthony Giddens'** structuration theory, Vidal de la Blache's concept of the *genre de vie*, **Raymond Williams'** writing on structures of feeling, and **Michel Foucault's** work on power/knowledge, amongst a diverse array of other influences. He also began to question the forms of writing and representation appropriate to address the multiple becomings enfolded within the historically contingent formation of places. In part, this was an extension of the representation experimentation that defined both time-geography with its new grammar of daily life-paths, time-space prisms, time-space aquariums, and so on, and quantitative geography more generally: quantitative geography had, after all, defined itself not just by its commitment to numbers but also to constructing new ways of diagramming spatial relationships. However, Pred's experiments were driven by an ethos that was both more pluralistic and more avant garde than either time-geography or quantitative geography. To explore the multiple spatialities, the multiple consciousness, the multiple materialities that defined the making of place required the fashioning of different styles of writing and different representational techniques. It required an engagement not just with social science, but with poetry, photography, ethnography, creative writing, and a host of other (re) presentational techniques for which mainstream human geography generally had little time.

Pred's writing during this period addressed a range of detailed empirical cases. *Place, Practice, and Structure* published in 1986 was a study of agricultural enclosures in late eigtheenth century southern Sweden, while both *Lost Words and Lost Worlds* (1990a) and *Making Histories and Constructing Human Geographies* (1990b) explored the emerging capitalist relations shaping nineteenth and early twentieth century Stockholm. Nonetheless, it was Pred's experimentations with different styles of academic writing that gained most attention. With its interest in experimentation, poly-vocality, and willingness to entertain a certain textual playfulness, Pred's writing can be seen as a kind of postmodern geography. Certainly, that is how many of his critics read his work. However, Pred's various textual strategies were organised around a very clear intellectual goal. Pred wanted to show his readers how ordinary people, caught up in the routines of their day-to-day lives, were in all sorts of often forgotten ways involved in the making of historical geographies. And in this sense, his ethos was anything but postmodern. As he wrote at the end of *Lost Words and Lost Worlds*:

> Lost languages of production, distribution, and consumption,
>
> lost languages of spatial orientation,
>
> lost languages of social reference and address,
>
> lost languages of practical engagement in the world,
>
> lost wor(l)ds,
>
> are not to be studied as ends in themselves,
>
> but as part of larger agenda,

> as part of an effort to understand,
>
> the DNA of human, social, and cultural phenomena,
>
> the double helix of individual and society,
>
> the simultaneous constitution of subject and society in place,
>
> the context bound, context producing interplay,
>
> between practice, power, and forms of consciousness.
>
> A vast terrain of inquiry. A new area of confluence between human geography,
>
> historical ethnography, political economy, and (critical) semiotics,
>
> trampled upon by few,
>
> lies open for new forms of exploration.
>
> (Pred, 1990a: 246)

Pieces of writing like this represented a remarkable break from the norms of writing within human geography. Nonetheless, it is easy to exaggerate the textual dissonance of Pred's work during this period of the 1980s and early 1990s. Certainly, on their publication they did feel like strange and exotic impostors on the sensible world of human geographic publishing. But, for their textual flourishes, books like *Place, Practice, and Structure* and *Lost Words and Lost Worlds* were in fact characterised more by the normal paraphernalia of historical geography than by Pred's flights of experimentation, dominated as they were by tightly argued essays, and a wealth of carefully referenced maps and tables. It took the discovery of the work of the mid-twentieth century German Jewish writer Walter Benjamin for Pred's textual experiments to really take flight.

For Benjamin questions of style, form, and presentation were essential. Benjamin (1999) believed capitalist commodity culture had numbed our ability for critical thought. Thus, the role of the critic had to be to shock readers out of their collective slumber; to bring them to wakefulness through the shock of a momentary flash of illumination. Benjamin was convinced that the development of a sophisticated style of historical montage was necessary to engineer the illuminations he was seeking. And Pred, reading Benjamin, sensed in montage the possibility to reconfigure the historical-geographical weight of his work on nineteenth and early twentieth century Sweden. Pred's writing in the 1980s and early 1990s provided moving examples of a series of worlds that had been lost in the emergence, first of a capitalist agriculture, and then an emerging industrial modernity. But they did not provide much sense of how these lost worlds might have a presence or afterlife within contemporary Swedish society.

Place, Practice, and Structure, Lost Words and Lost Worlds, and *Making Histories and Constructing Human Geographies* were about a recovery of the agency and dignity of Swedish working people from what the English historian E. P. Thompson (1968: 12) called 'the enormous condescension of posterity'. Montage suggested a more radical and a more active place for the historical, or rather the historical-geographical. Montage involved the splicing together of diverse often apparently unconnected materials, quotes, images, diagrams, aphorisms, so arranged that they produced not a neat linear story but flashes of insight, recognition of verisimilitude, resonances across centuries. As Benjamin (in Pred, 1995: 5) wrote, 'It isn't that the past casts its light on what is present or that what is present casts its light on what is past; rather, an image is that in which the Then [and There] and the [Here and] Now come together into a constellation like a flash of lightning.'

Each of Pred's last three major works, *Recognising European Modernities* (1995), *Even in Sweden* (2000), and *The Past is Not Dead* (2004) is organised through the logic of montage. Through combining quotations, photographs, cartoons, poetry, and short intellectual asides these books produce complex and often disorientating diagrams of Swedish society. Refusing any kind of simple linear historical-geographical narrative they bring together material across decades, across centuries, and from a heterogeneous world of places. *Recognising European Modernities* illuminates a Sweden that is repeatedly struggling with the sense of its own globalisations and its various modernities, while *Even in Sweden* and *The Past is Not Dead* encounter the complex temporal-spatialities of everyday Swedish racism.

KEY ADVANCES AND CONTROVERSIES

Pred's oeuvre offers a remarkable tour through the evolution of human geography's theoretical engagements with the spatial over the past five decades. It shows the potential and the limitations of a vision of geography as 'spatial science'. It also shows how the geography that came out of the quantitative revolution of the 1950s and 1960s was not uniform in its framing of the problematic of the spatial. Pred's early writings are emblematic of this diversity, just as his subsequent experiments with time-geography, structuration theory, and the work of Benjamin, speak to the growing theoretical cosmopolitanism of work in human geography from the late 1970s through to the early 2000s. But perhaps more than anything, Pred's publications in the last two decades of his career are notable – and worthy of repeated reading – for the invention and consequentiality with which they confronted the question of *how* one should write critical human geography.

PRED'S KEY WORKS

Pred, A. (1966) *The Spatial Dynamics of US Urban-Industrial Growth, 1800–1914: Interpretative and Theoretical Essays.* Cambridge, MA: MIT.

Pred, A. (1967) *Behaviour and Location: Foundations for a Geographic and Dynamic Location Theory*, Part 1. Lund: Gleerup.

Pred, A. (1969) *Behaviour and Location: Foundations for a Geographic and Dynamic Location Theory*, Part 2. Lund: Gleerup.

Pred, A. (1973) *Urban Growth and the Circulation of Information: The United States System of Cities, 1790–1840.* Cambridge, MA: Harvard University Press.

Pred, A. (1977a) *City-Systems in Advanced Economies: Past Growth, Present Processes and Future Development Options.* London: Hutchinson.

Pred, A. (1980) *Urban Growth and City Systems in the United States, 1840–1860.* Cambridge, MA.: Harvard University Press.

Pred, A. (1986) *Practice, Place and Structure: Social and Spatial Transformation in Southern Sweden, 1750–1850.* Cambridge: Polity.

Pred, A. (1990a) *Lost Words, Lost Worlds: Modernity and the Language of Everyday Life in Late Nineteenth Century Stockholm.* Cambridge: Cambridge University.

Pred, A. (1990b) *Making Histories and Constructing Human Geographies: The Local Transformation of Practice, Power Relations and Consciousness.* Boulder, CO: Westview.

Pred, A. and Watts, M. (1992) *Reworking Modernity: Capitalisms and Symbolic Discontent.* New Brunswick: Rutgers University.

Pred, A. (1995) *Recognising European Modernities: A Montage of the Present.* London: Routledge.

Pred, A. (2000) *Even in Sweden: Racisms, Racialized Spaces, and the Popular Geographical Imagination.* Berkeley: University of California.

Pred, A. (2004) *The Past Is Not Dead.* Minneapolis: University of Minnesota.

Secondary Sources and References

Barnes, T. J. (2001) 'Lives lived, and lives told: biographies of geography's quantitative revolution', *Environment and Planning D: Society and Space*, 19: 409–29.

Barnes, T. J. (2003) 'The place of locational analysis: a selective and interpretive history', *Progress in Human Geography*, 27: 69–95.

Barnes, T. J. (2004) 'Placing ideas: genius loci, heterotopia, and geography's quantitative revolution', *Progress in Human Geography*, 29: 565–95.

Benjamin, W. (1999) *The Arcades Project.* Cambridge, MA: Harvard University.

Christaller, W. (1966) *Central Places in Southern Germany.* Englewood Cliffs, NJ : Prentice Hall.

Hägerstrand, T. (1967) *Innovation Diffusion as a Spatial Process.* Chicago: University of Chicago.

Lösch, A.(1954) *The Economics of Location.* New Haven, CT: Yale University Press.

Pred, A. (1975a) 'Diffusion, organisational spatial structure, and city-system development', *Economic Geography*, 51: 252–68.

Pred, A. (1975b) 'On the spatial structure of organisations and the complexity of metropolitan interdependence', *Papers of the Regional Science Association*, 35: 115–42.

Pred, A. (1976) 'The interurban transmission of growth in advanced economies: empirical findings verses regional planning assumptions', *Regional Studies*, 10: 151–71.

Pred, A. (1977b) 'The choreography of existence: comments on Hägerstrand's time-geography and its usefulness', *Economic Geography*, 53: 207–21.

Pred, A. (1978) 'The impact of technological and institutional innovations on life content: some time-geographic observations', *Geographical Analysis*, 10: 345–72.

Pred, A. (1981a) 'Production, family and free-time projects: a time-geographic perspective on the individual and social change in nineteenth century United States cities', *Journal of Historical Geography*, 7: 3–36.

Pred, A. (1981b) 'Social reproduction and the time-geography of everyday life', *Geografiska Annaler*, 63B 5–22.

Thompson, E.P. (1968) *The Making of the English Working Class*. London: Penguin.

Alan Latham, University College London

44 Gillian Rose

BIOGRAPHICAL DETAILS AND THEORETICAL CONTEXT

Gillian Rose was born in 1963 in England. She completed her BA in Geography from the University of Cambridge in 1985, and went on to complete a PhD in 1989, entitled 'Locality, Politics and Culture: Poplar in the 1920s' also at Cambridge. Her first teaching post was at the University of London at Queen Mary College. She then became a Lecturer in Geography at the University of Edinburgh for six years before moving to the Open University in 1999. Throughout, Rose's contributions to geography have encouraged geographers to consider the gendered constructions of geographical knowledge, and to take seriously the importance of visual culture. Her disciplinary history in geography has very much shaped her perspective. In writing about her academic trajectory and her relationship with feminism within and outside geography, she states:

> The only thing I was successful at apparently was academic work. I was bright at school, I won a place to Cambridge University, my initial stumblings around feminist historians' accounts of public and private space were encouraged by my Director of Studies … I've had it relatively easy in the academy, helped by my Cambridge connections, [and] the recent fashionableness of a certain kind of feminism.
>
> (WGSG, 1997: 35)

Drawing from 'a feminism that [felt] intensely personal' (WGSG, 1997: 35), Rose's research spans many subject areas from the cultural politics of landscape to notions of the performative, including empirical accounts of community arts projects to critiques of visual methodological approaches. She has collaborated with a variety of geographers, including Steve Pile (Rose and Pile, 1992), Nicky Gregson (Gregson and Rose, 2000) and **Doreen Massey**.

Rose is perhaps best known for her book *Feminism and Geography*, published in 1993. The scope of the book has been seen as both courageous and ambitious. Through an explicit critique of geography's intrinsic masculinist approach to the discipline, Rose revealed the ways in which geographers have constructed a geography which legitimates masculine forms of geographical knowledge, effectively isolating women's ways of knowing. Connected to this privileging of masculine over feminine knowledge is the construction of a culture–nature dualism. Rose demonstrates the pervasive nature of the nature–culture binary through her discussion of two strands of thought: the social scientific, which lays claims to rational and objective truths; and the aesthetic, which feminises places and landscapes. By addressing the ways in which cultural geographers' work on landscape embodies masculinist perspectives, Rose (1993a) effectively demonstrates how understandings and experiences in places have been marginalized in the discipline. As well as challenging the masculinist nature of the discipline, Rose has also intervened in feminist methodological debates. For example, drawing on insights from Judith Butler's (1990) work on performativity, Rose (1997b) has critiqued some of the assumptions in feminists' use of reflexivity as a strategy for situating geographical knowledges. Additionally, her work on visual methods has provided the basis of *Visual Methodologies* (2001), a remarkably lucid text written for a cross-disciplinary audience which considers questions of meaning and representation across a variety of sites and through different modalities.

This interest in visual culture has informed Rose's later work in a variety of strong ways. Informed in part by her own experiences as a young mother, one notable project (Rose, 2004) involved interviews with female parents and carers to explore the ways in which they displayed photos of their own children. Focusing on the domestic realm, an extension of this work then considered the emotional geographies associated with the display of photos of victims of violence (Rose, 2009). An engaging exploration of necro-politics, this work connect notions of care and visuality to offer a distinctive take on the connections of bodies, looks and spaces. In a rather different, though related, vein, a project with Monica Degan explored the aesthetics and visualities associated with post-war urban landscapes in the UK, utilising innovative methods to register the ways that people engage with seemingly mundane landscapes in multisensory and complex ways.

SPATIAL CONTRIBUTIONS

Rose's treatise on geography's overarching masculinist approach, *Feminism and Geography*, provided the first cohesive and comprehensive analysis of human geography's resistance to work on and by women. Citing geography's deep reluctance to listen to feminism and its focus on women, Rose (1993a: 4) explored the idea that 'it is the specific notion of knowledge through which geographers think that marginalizes women in the discipline.' Rose's book was met with an uneasy mixture of criticism and praise when it was initially published, especially from feminist geographers, despite its decidedly pro-feminist stance. While many agreed that the book finally 'br[ought] academic geography up to date with ... feminist theory, something geography badly needed' (Morin, 1995: 415), others insisted that '[Rose] does not interrogate the categories ... of gender, class, ethnicity, nationality or sexual preference, nor is there much idea of change or struggle' (Hyndman, 1995: 197). Yet others still challenged its seemingly dry, academic tone in what would become a recurring critique of the book (Burgess, 1996). Even Rose herself admits that she has concerns with the narrative style of the book in an early chapter: 'I have tried to make my prose sound differently from the unmarked tone of so much geographical writing, but, as you have probably noticed, I have found it extraordinarily difficult to break away' (see also Penrose et al., 1992).

Rose's last chapter of the book, evocatively titled 'A Politics of Paradoxical Space', has sparked ongoing debate among feminist geographers about the meaning and value of the metaphor. Rose never provides a precise definition of paradoxical space (Desbiens, 1999), nor does she 'specify how the [concept can] displace the master subject' (Hyndman, 1995: 201). As such some commentators have criticised the concept of paradoxical space for being 'elusive and multiple in meaning', claiming that it represents an overzealous attempt by Rose to end her book on a high note (Desbiens, 1999). Yet, at the same time, it has also been suggested that it is a 'tantalizing' concept which has the potential to provide a radical framework for feminist geography (Katz, 1997; Desbiens, 1999). Mahtani (2001) for example has used the concept of paradoxical space to provide a useful theoretical underpinning for her own research on 'mixed race women' in Canada, highlighting the subversive potential of such a position. Mahtani (2001) further insists that it is precisely the fluid nature of paradoxical space that serves to provide feminist geographers with a nuanced theoretical model for understanding complex forms of oppression (vis-à-vis race and class) in the academy. Despite its mixed reviews, *Feminism and Geography* remains an essential reference for the amplification of a feminist geographical perspective (Desbiens, 1999) and is considered required reading for human geographers. It opened up new forms of engagement about the varied forms of patriarchy within the discipline (see WGSG, 1997) and also outside geography in the area of cultural studies and literary theory (see Friedman, 1998 and George, 1996).

Perhaps unwittingly responding to concerns about her lack of engagement with race and class in *Feminism and Geography*, Rose's second book, *Writing Women and Space: Colonial and Postcolonial Geographies,* co-edited with Alison Blunt, explicitly articulated the complicit

and complicated relations between gender, race, class and sexuality through an edited collection about women's multiple, contested, and shifting senses of subjectivities as experienced through written representations of spatial differentiation. The 1994 collection complemented Rose's first book by effectively providing grounded empirical examples of feminist geographical research, addressing the paucity of woman-centred knowledges in the discipline.

Rose continued to elaborate on the themes of patriarchy inside and outside of geography well into 1995, notably through a paper, 'Tradition and Paternity: Same Difference?' in the *Transactions of the Institute of British Geographers.* This article explored issues of sameness and difference (versus her discussion of the same and other in *Feminism and Geography*). Paying particular attention to the ways that gendered sameness and difference is constituted through geographical traditions, Rose explained that 'given th[e] persistent erasure of women, the construction of geographical traditions might ... be described as the construction of geography's paternal lines of descent' (Rose, 1995e: 414). Asking 'how can feminists place women in relation to this paternal geographical tradition?' (Rose, 1995e: 415), Rose emphasised that 'feminists ... need to critique the transparent territorialization of tradition ... we need to focus on the boundaries at which difference is constituted ... this project ... entails thinking about geography through a different spatiality: a multiple space' (Rose, 1995e: 416).

In *Writing Women and Space* Rose provided a feminist geographical critique of the work of the critical 'race' theorist **Homi Bhabha**, cautioning geographers that his theory was often dressed up in an enigmatic and masculinist vocabulary, couched in language that makes it more inaccessible than it need be. She noted, 'the optimism of Bhabha's brave new hybrid world ... is perhaps gendered in both its practice and its writing' (Rose, 1995b: 372). Rose argued that Bhabha tended to over-accentuate hyperfluency in favour of a negation of the social. She writes: '[Bhabha's] spatialities remain analytical, not lived ... he remains resolutely disembodied, unbloodied if not bowed ... his violence remains epistemic and not bloody' (Rose, 1995b: 372). Reminding us of the importance of the grounded material realities, Rose's critique of Bhabha's theory effectively demonstrated that she had not forgotten about the lived day-to-day, as some had suspected with the publication of her first book (see also McDowell, 1999).

That same year, Rose contemplated the 'spatial subversions' of Jenny Holzer, Barbara Kruger and Cindy Sherman in her chapter entitled 'Making Space for The Female Subject of Feminism' in the edited collection *Mapping the Subject* (Pile and Keith, 1995). Rose suggests that the 'process of representation is central to everyday space and to the en-gendering of subjects in that space' (Rose, 1995f: 348) and points out that:

> to think about the geography of the female subject of feminism is not to be able to name a specific kind of spatiality which she would produce; rather, it is to be vigilant about the consequences of different kinds of spatiality, and to keep dreaming of a space and a subject which we cannot yet imagine.
>
> (Rose, 1995f: 354)

Hence, a recurring theme in much of Rose's writing is her concern with voice and authority in the narrative of the text. In her 1996 article, 'As if the Mirrors Had Bled: Masculine Dwelling, Masculinist Theory and Feminist Masquerade', Rose experiments with style and voice, adopting several personas in the piece. Rose literally 'performed' the piece at Syracuse University's symposium on 'Place, Space and Gender.' Providing one of geography's first engagements with the work of Judith Butler and her notion of performance, and enthusiastically drawing from the work of Luce Irigaray, Rose self-consciously articulated different identities to explore the spaces of movement and fluidity that are possible through a displacement of the opposition between real and imagined space, emphasising that this distinction reflects a performance of masculinist power. Geographers were particularly motivated by Rose's attempts not to prioritise the 'real' over 'metaphorical' space (Brown, 2000).

Rose (1993a; 1993b) makes politically strategic use of feminist discourses on the maternal body, or woman as mother, in order to subvert masculinist structures of knowledge in geography. Her work has been strongly influenced by psychoanalysis and this has largely shaped her understanding and theorisation of space. The sophistication of Rose's arguments, especially her continual questioning of the epistemology and ontology of the discipline, suggests that the notion of an 'explicit sexualisation of knowledges' (Grosz, 1993: 188) must be taken seriously by geographers.

Rose's 1997 article, 'Situating knowledges: positionality, reflexivities, and other tactics' served as a critique of feminist geography's engagement with reflexivity. In a poignant example of Rose's intimate style, the article begins with the statement: 'This is an article written from a sense of failure' (Rose, 1997b: 305). Through a case-study of her own challenges in completing fieldwork, Rose suggests that the notion of self-reflexivity as understood among feminist geographers relies on an assertion of transparency – a 'knowable agent whose motivations can be fully known' (Rose, 1997b: 309). She ends by suggesting that we 'inscribe into our research practices some absences and fallibilities while recognizing that the significance of this does not rest entirely in our own hands' (Rose, 1997b: 319). Lise Nelson (1999) challenged this view, suggesting that Rose cannot conceive of a self or subject that is constituted by both discursive processes and at the same time being potentially aware of them (Nelson, 1999: 350). According to Nelson, Rose is 'haunted by humanist idealizations, arrested by an ability to conceptualize self-reflexivity as anything but transparent ... [and is] condemned to a cycle of critique without exit' (Nelson, 1999: 350).

Rose returned to examine the notion of the performative in the late 1990s, explaining how space could be seen as performative. Her chapter 'Performing Space' in *Human Geography Today* considers space as a discursive practice – as not only fantasised but also corporealised, thus making the spatial contradictory, complex and multitextured (Rose, 1999). By focusing on the spatial articulations of sexual difference, Rose again acts out a performance reminiscent to the one performed in her chapter in *Body Space*, this time critically engaging with the work of Butler, Irigaray and de Lauretis. She ends by emphasising that bodily performances produce space. A year later, Rose would offer a collaborative and grounded discussion of these themes with feminist geographer Nicky Gregson. Their article, 'Taking Butler elsewhere: performativities, spatialities, and subjectivities' unveils two case-studies of car-boot sales and community arts programmes. Suggesting that we should consider spaces as performative of power relations, Gregson and Rose insist upon the importance of contemplating subjectivities produced through specific performances of knowledge production, focusing on the rich complexity and 'messiness' of performances and performed spaces (Gregson and Rose, 2000). In a case-study analysis of interviews with community arts workers, Rose bravely acknowledges that she found the 'practice' of doing interviews difficult, noting that she continually questioned her own role in the acquisition of narratives and explained she did not plan any more interview-based research anytime soon (Gregson and Rose, 2000).

Her 2001 book, *Visual Methodologies: An Introduction to the Interpretation of Visual Material* gave Rose an opportunity to consider the analysis of images rather than interviews. Rose puts forward a comprehensive study in methods to examine visual culture, from discourse analysis techniques to the study of audiences. This book offered geographers a way to understand culture through visual representations. Examining how we interpret images and how these processes are laden with power and cultural meaning, Rose provides a critical visual methodology where she examines the visual in terms of cultural significance, social practices and complex power relations. Drawing again on her understanding of psychoanalytical theory, Rose persuasively discusses the ways that sexual difference is articulated through visual practice (Rose, 2001). Rose's argument about critical visual methodologies has already been effectively extended into the arena of GIS imaging (Kwan, 2002) and has proven an important contribution in geography and representation (Hubbard et al., 2002). Panning between questions of visual culture and gender, her later work on photographs of children and victims of violence opens up new perspectives on the connections between gender, space and vision and suggests that geography is an inherently visual discipline in many senses.

KEY ADVANCES AND CONTROVERSIES

It can be argued that the greatest appeal in Rose's work lies in her efforts to remain transparent about her own power, positionality, and knowledge within, and outside, the academy in her writing. Her research in the last decade in the arenas of performance and visual culture has demonstrated a recurring interest in understanding the theoretical and methodological possibilities for comprehending power and knowledge production, while indicating all the while how her own role as a researcher influences the structure of geographical knowledge. Although it has been said that her musings are often open-ended, and offer more questions than answers through her continual focus on fissures (Rose, 1997b) paradoxes (Rose, 1993a) and contradictions (Rose, 1995e). It is a criticism that Rose herself acknowledges. In her 1997 article 'Situating knowledges: positionality, reflexivities and other tactics' she writes: 'I've tried to produce a gap in my own interpretative project ... I'm not sure I succeeded, and I don't think I can or should be sure' (Rose, 1997b: 305). It is precisely this kind of transparency and honesty that many geographers find both courageous and attractive

(Desbiens, 1999; Mahtani, 2001). Her research always focuses on the possibilities for more thoughtful discussions in feminist geography. Her final words in *Feminism and Geography* sum this up well:

> Space itself – and landscape and place likewise – far from being firm foundations for disciplinary expertise and power, are insecure, precarious and fluctuating. They are destabilized both by the internal contradictions of the geographical desire to know and by the resistance of the marginalized victims of that desire. And other possibilities, other sorts of geographies, with different compulsions, desires and effects, complement and contest one another. This chapter has tried to describe just one of them. There are many more.
>
> (Rose, 1993a: 160)

Rose's words inspired feminist geographers to consider other ways of telling stories about women and space outside masculinist narratives, and has thus served to see those contemplations as legitimate within the discipline. Feminist geographers have responded by mapping their own complex understandings of space through a diverse array of feminist geographies that pay particular attention to the masculinist nature of geographies rife with power relations. Gillian Rose's research has self-consciously articulated the challenges, as well as the risks, of unveiling the masculinism of the discipline and has thus created productive spaces for new cartographies of diversity and difference in geography.

ROSE'S KEY WORKS

Rose, G. (1993a) *Feminism and Geography.* Minneapolis: University of Minnesota Press.

Rose, G. (1995a) 'Geography and gender: cartographies and corporealities', *Progress in Human Geography,* 19: 544–8.

Rose, G. (1995d) 'Distance, surface, elsewhere: a feminist critique of the space of phallocentric self/knowledge', *Environment and Planning D: Society and Space,* 13: 761–81.

Rose, G. (1996) 'As if the mirrors had bled: masculine dwelling, masculinist theory and feminist masquerade', in N. Duncan (ed.), *Bodyspace.* London: Routledge. pp. 56–74.

Rose, G. (1997b) 'Situating knowledges: positionality, reflexivities and other tactics', *Progress in Human Geography,* 21: 305–20.

Rose, G. (1997c) 'Performing inoperative community: the space and the resistance of some community arts projects', in S. Pile and M. Keith (eds), *Geographies of Resistance.* London: Routledge. 184–203.

Rose, G. (1999) 'Performing space', in D. Massey, J. Allen and P. Sarre (eds), *Human Geography Today.* Cambridge: Polity. pp. 247–59.

Rose, G. (2001*) Visual Methodologies:* London: Sage (2nd edition, 2007).

Rose, G. (2004) '"Everyone's cuddled up and it just looks really nice": the emotional geography of some mums and their family photos', *Social and Cultural Geography,* 5: 549–64.

Rose, G. (2003b) 'Domestic spacings and family photography: a case study', *Transactions of the Institute of British Geographers,* 28: 5–18.

Rose, G. (2009) 'Who cares for which dead and how: British newspaper reporting of the bombs in London, July 2005', *Geoforum,* 40: 46–54.

Dorrian, M. and Rose, G. (eds) (2003) *Deterritoralisations: Revisioning Landscape and Politics.* London: Black Dog Press.

Secondary sources and references

Brown, M. (2000) *Closet Space.* London: Routledge.

Blunt, A. and Rose, G. (eds) (1994) *Writing Women and Space: Colonial and Postcolonial Geographies.* New York: Guilford.

Butler, J. (1990) *Gender Trouble.* London: Routledge.

Burgess, J. (1994) 'Review of *Feminism and Geography*', *Geographical Journal,* 160: 225–26.

Desbiens, C. (1999) 'Feminism 'in' geography: elsewhere beyond and the politics of paradoxical space', *Gender, Place and Culture,* 6: 179–85.

Friedman, B. (1998) *Mappings.* London: Routledge.

George, R.M. (1996) *The Politics of Home.* Cambridge: Cambridge University Press.

Gregson, N. and Rose, G. (2000) 'Taking Butler elsewhere: performativities, spatialities and subjectivities', *Environment and Planning D: Society and Space,* 18: 422–52.

Grosz, E. (1993) 'Bodies and knowledges: feminism and the crisis of reason', in L. Alcoff and E. Potter (eds), *Feminist Epistemologies.* New York: Routledge. pp. 187–216.

Hubbard, P., Kitchin, R., Bartley, B. and Fuller, D. (2002) *Thinking Geographically.* London: Continuum.

Hyndman, J. (1995) 'Solo feminist geography: a lesson in space', *Antipode,* 27: 197–207.

Katz, C. (1997) 'Review of *Feminism and Geography: the Limits of Geographical Knowledge*', *Ecumen,* 4: 227–30.

Kwan, M. (2002) 'Is GIS for women? Reflections on the critical discourse in the 1990s', *Gender, Place and Culture,* 9: 271–9.

Mahtani, M. (2001) 'Racial reMappings: the potential of paradoxical space', *Gender, Place and Culture: A Journal of Feminist Geography,* 8: 299–305.

McDowell, L. (1999) *Gender, Identity and Place: Understanding Feminist Geography.* Minneapolis: University of Minnesota Press.

Morin, K. (1995) 'Review of *Feminism and Geography: The Limits of Geographical Knowledge*', *Postmodern Culture,* 5: 78–9.

Nelson, L. (1999) 'Bodies and spaces do matter,' *Gender, Place and Culture,* 6: 331–53.

Penrose, J., Bondi L., McDowell L., Kofman, E., Rose, G. and Whatmore, S. (1992) 'Feminists and feminism in the academy', *Antipode,* 24: 218–37.

Pile, S. and Keith, M. (eds)(1995) *Geographies of Resistance.* London: Routledge.

Pile, S. and Rose, G. (1992) 'All or nothing? Politics and critique in modernism and postmodernism', *Environment and Planning D: Society and Space,* 10(1): 123–36.

Rose, G. (1990) 'The struggle for political democracy: emancipation, gender, and geography', *Environment and Planning D: Society and Space,* 8: 395–408.

Rose, G. (1993b) 'Speculations on what the future holds in store', *Environment and Planning A,* 25: 26–9.

Rose, G. (1994) 'The cultural politics of place: local representation and oppositional discourse in two films', *Transactions of the Institute of British Geographers,* 19: 46–60.

Rose, G. (1995b) 'The interstitial perspective: a review essay on Homi Bhabha's *The Location of Culture*', *Environment and Planning D: Society and Space,* 13: 365–73.

Rose, G. (1995c) 'Review of "The man question: visions of subjectivity in feminist theory" and "Sexing the self: gendered positions in cultural studies"', *Environment and Planning D: Society and Space*, 13: 241–3.

Rose, G. (1995e) 'Tradition and paternity: same difference?' *Transactions of the Institute of British Geographers*, 20: 414–16.

Rose, G. (1995f) 'Making space for the female subject of feminism', in S. Pile and M. Keith (eds), *Mapping the Subject*. London: Routledge. pp. 332–54.

Rose, G. (1997a) 'Review of *Evictions: Art and Spatial Politics'*, *Environment and Planning D: Society and Space*, 15: 627–32.

Rose, G. (2003a) 'Just how, exactly, is geography visual?', *Antipode*, 35: 12–21.

Rose, G. (2005) '"You just have to make a conscious effort to keep snapping away, I think": a case study of family photos, mothering and familial space', in S. Hardy, and C. Wiedmer, (eds), *Motherhood and Space: Configurations of the Maternal Through Politics, Home, and the Body*. London: Palgrave Macmillan. pp.221–40.

Women and Geography Study Group (1997) *Feminist Geographies: Explorations in Diversity and Difference*. London: Longman.

Minelle Mahtani, University of Toronto

45 Edward W. Said

BIOGRAPHICAL DETAILS AND THEORETICAL CONTEXT

Edward Said was one of the most brilliant and prominent public intellectuals of the second half of the twentieth century. Said was known for his ground-breaking works on the relationship between culture and imperialism – which were foundational to the field of Post-colonial Studies – and he also fought unrelentingly for Palestinian self-determination. During his prolific career Said published more than 20 books; was translated into 37 languages; and was regularly interviewed in print and on television, including in several documentaries. Said, whose last academic position was as University Professor of English and Comparative Literature at Columbia University, New York, received numerous distinguished awards and honours, including Harvard's Bowdoin Prize in 1963; a Guggenheim Fellowship in 1972; and Columbia's Lionel Trilling Award in 1976 and again in 1994.

Said served as President of the Modern Language Association in 1999, and was a member of the American Academy of Arts and Letters, American Academy of Sciences, American Philosophical Society and the Royal Society of Literature. He received approximately 20 honorary doctoral degrees. His book *Orientalism* (1978) was a runner-up for the National Book Critics Circle Award, and his autobiography, *Out of Place* (1999), won the New Yorker Book Award for non-fiction. Said's articles regularly appeared internationally – in the US in *The Nation, The New York Times*, and the *Wall Street Journal*; in London's *The Times, The Observer*, and *The Guardian*; the French *Le Monde Diplomatique*; in the Arabic *al-Hayat;* and in Madrid's *El Pais*.

When Said was born in 1935 to a privileged Christian-Arab family in Jerusalem, Palestine had been under British administration for 15 years. Said was baptised at an Anglican mission school in Jerusalem, and following his family's exile to Cairo during the 1947 partition and war, Said attended British schools. During his youth Said read avidly, listened to classical music, learned several languages (being fluent in English, Arabic, and French, and literate in several others), and played the piano. He finished his secondary education at Mount Hermon Preparatory School in Massachusetts, attended Julliard School of Music, and went on to receive his BA from Princeton University in 1957, and an MA (1960) and PhD (1964) from Harvard University. His doctoral dissertation in comparative literature focused on the interplay between Joseph Conrad's fiction and his correspondence. While travelling widely and serving many visiting positions and fellowships at other institutions, Said remained at New York's Columbia University from 1963 onwards. He died of leukemia in 2003.

The themes of exile and displacement, and especially his advocacy for Palestinian rights, grew out of both his personal experiences and a broader concern for the Palestinian people. While Said's work prior to 1967 primarily focused on 'high' European canonical literature, the Arab–Israeli war that broke out that year marked a radicalising moment in Said's life when his own identity as a Palestinian became inseparable from his scholarly pursuits. He lived and worked in a pro-Israeli environment hostile to Arabs, leading Said to shift attention to the West's distorted view of the Middle East and Arab world. As an academic but also a major voice in the mass media, Said contested the caricature of Arab people as terrorists and barbarians. He was a major dissenting voice during the Persian Gulf War, and was perhaps the most frequently cited and interviewed critic of American foreign policy in the Middle East for the several decades preceding his death. Said was a member of the Palestinian National Council and supporter of the Palestinian Liberation Organisation (PLO), as well as its critic. He turned down an invitation to attend the White House signing of the Oslo agreements in 1993, arguing that they ignored the majority of Palestinians residing outside of Gaza and the West Bank. Not surprisingly, Said received harsh criticism and even death threats for his support for Palestine.

Said's self-construction as an exiled Palestinian was central to his scholarly arguments, and it was the apparent contradiction between his personal location and his scholarly works that some critics focused on. He was born into a Christian-Arab, not Islamic, family (though he was secular in orientation); he lived in the Middle East only during his youth and was educated in the West's most elite institutions; he was a political exile but a wealthy, privileged, 'cosmopolitan' one; and he was a scholar who advocated concern for 'narratives of the forgotten' but who himself devoted attention throughout his life to the West's high canonical literature, music, and culture (Ahmad, 1993; Ashcroft and Ahluwalia, 1999). Though not to be dismissed, the politics of his own paradoxical location do little to undermine Said's extraordinary contributions to cultural studies and cultural and social geography.

SPATIAL CONTRIBUTIONS

Edward Said's intellectual contributions are difficult to categorise in disciplinary terms. He wrote on subjects as diverse as the role of the intellectual, music criticism (he was *The Nation*'s music critic), Palestinian politics, the experience of exile, as well as on culture and imperialism. His work initiated debates across the humanities and social sciences, from literature to music to anthropology to political science to geography. Much, if not all, of Said's work was explicitly geographical, although it would be highly un-Saidian to attempt to separate his geographical contributions and sensitivity from the rest of his literary and social theory. While much of Said's work can be classified as literary criticism, he strongly advocated against disciplinary boundaries and the excessive specialisation they encourage. To him, all texts, literary or otherwise, are political, and must be 'worlded' – located in the world and exposed for the geographical imaginations from which they arise. Much of Said's work was devoted to analysis of literary, political, and journalistic texts; and he was at his most geographic in such attempts to emplace texts, writers, audiences, and, indeed, himself: 'geography ... is the only way that I can coherently express my history' he noted (Katz and Smith, 2003: 643).

Said's influence in human geography, particularly his theory of Orientalism, was so compelling that one might describe it as almost transparent to practitioners today. Said not only initiated a spatial turn in post-colonial and cultural studies, but within the field of geography itself his work transformed the terms around which the histories of geography, critical historical geographies, geographies of empire, and analyses of territory and land dispossession are discussed today. While geographers have long-understood that imperialism and colonialism ought to be conceptualised geographically, Said theorised the cultural processes and discursive formations that aid colonial or imperial control over people and place. The complex cultural, ideological, and intellectual processes involved in domination and control that accompany the political, economic, and territorial, hence, become standard in geographical studies, thanks in part to Said's ground-breaking works. Said's notion of the 'imaginative geographies' embedded in colonial discourse formed the basis of two of his books, Orientalism (1978) and Culture and Imperialism (1983a). This concept has done much to invigorate post-colonial and cultural studies with a spatial sensitivity. Imaginative geography to Said refers to the invention and construction of geographical space beyond a physical territory, which constructs boundaries around our very consciousness and attitudes, often by inattention to or the obscuring of local realities (Said, 2000b: 181). Said arguably laid the foundation for post-colonial

studies with the publication of Orientalism, and it was this book that launched his international reputation and established some of the main terms of debate that other post-colonial critics, such as **Gayatri Spivak** and **Homi Bhabha**, have engaged. (For their personal reflections on Said following his death, as well as that of others of his close associates, see Bhabha and Mitchell, 2004).

Orientalism moved the concepts of colony and empire to centre stage in the American academy in the 1970s, in addition to infusing it with the critical methods of French post-structuralism. Orientalism as a field of study predated Said, taking in two millennia of studies of Eastern culture by the West. What distinguished Said's work was his attention to the totalising essentialism, ethnocentrism, and racism embedded in studies of the Orient. Said examined the works of an array of eighteenth-and nineteenth-century British and French novelists, poets, journalists, politicians, historians, travellers, and colonial administrators (applying the same type of analysis to twentieth century American discourses and hegemony in later works). He argued that through a series of oppositions, these works systematically represented the Orient/East as irrational, despotic, static, and backward, while the Occident/West was rational, democratic, dynamic and progressive. Importantly, it did not matter to Said whether the stereotype was positive or negative (and many were in fact positive), since either is equally essentialising. In a Foucauldian move Said showed how such stereotyped representations stood for 'knowledge' itself and were deeply implicated in the exercise of authoritarian power. Where the focus of Said's work becomes cultural imperialism is in showing how the political or economic or administrative fact of dominance relies on this legitimating discourse.

Orientalism formed the first part of a trilogy that subsequently included *The Question of Palestine* (1980) and *Covering Islam* (1981). Together these books demonstrated how European colonialism, Zionism, and American geo-politics all worked together to dispossess Palestinians of their homeland, and even a past. In the latter two works, Said moved away from literary scholarship to a more political and historical investigation of Palestinian dispossession. Probably the most powerful argument in *The Question of Palestine* is that Israeli Zionism is itself an Orientalist (i.e., racist) discourse, with critiques of Israeli politics being too easily dismissed as anti-Semitic. *Covering Islam* showed how the US media and foreign policy worked in an Orientalist fashion in the late twentieth century. In this book Said took his ideas about cultural representation into the arena of practical politics. At the time (1979) the US was engaged with the Iranian 'hostage crisis' when students seized the American embassy in Teheran. Said asserted that journalists' uninformed reports seemed devoid of any historical contextualisation (such as previous US involvement in Iran, including helping train their secret police), and simply reinforced images of Islamic barbarism and terrorism and, in contrast, American innocence and heroism. Said followed up on Palestine's unique position as the 'victim of victims' in several later books. No other contemporary academic had so passionately attempted to tell a counter-narrative of Palestine. Other books, including *The End of the Peace Process* (2000a), document Said's political position on the Israel–Palestine conflict. He consistently argued against partition and for a bi-national state in Israel, insisting that the terms of citizenship must be made inclusive and democratic and not based on principles of racial or religious difference.

The World, the Text, and the Critic (1983) followed Said's trilogy on cultural imperialism. This book, a collection of essays written between 1968 and 1983, received much notoriety for two pieces in particular, 'Secular Criticism' and 'Travelling Theory'. In the former Said lamented what he saw as an apolitical cult of professionalism that had saturated intellectual life and argued for a more politically charged oppositional literary criticism and role for the intellectual. In 'Travelling Theory' Said developed a geographical model of how ideas or theories 'travel' from place to place, and what happens to them when they do. He argued that because theories develop within particular socio-historical contexts, they lose their oppositional weight when moved and 'domesticated' into other spatio-temporal contexts. He later revised this position, conceding that possibilities exist for theories to be effectively reconstituted in new political situations (Said, 2000b).

Said described his next major work, *Culture and Imperialism* (1993a), as the sequel to *Orientalism*. In this series of essays he addressed some of the intellectual conundrums to which *Orientalism* had given rise. Here, he adopted a musical term for literary criticism, offering a strategy of 'contrapuntal' reading of texts. To read a text contrapuntally 'is to read with a simultaneous awareness of both the metropolitan history that it narrates and of those other histories against which (and together with which) the dominating discourses act' (1993a: 51). These essays were more attuned than was *Orientalism* to 'dialogues' between colony and empire – intertwined histories and spaces of resistance to European metropolitan cultural products that produced not exactly hybrid outcomes, but 'harmonisations' of a sort. Said's controversial essay on *Mansfield Park*, for example, fundamentally shifted the terms of discussion about Jane Austen's novel by politicising and grounding it in the colonial geography of the Caribbean.

In some of his later works, Said continued to reflect on his own personal experience of exile and on relationships between memory and place. He considered the pain of exile in several of his works, including most profoundly in his autobiography, *Out of Place* (1999). While he struggled with his own displacement and the experience of never feeling completely at home anywhere, Said also recognised the empowering potential in remaining distanced from partisan politics and the habitual order. In 'Invention, memory and place' (2000b) Said further reflected on the importance of narratives to collective memories and senses of place, and on new constellations of power and identity around which 'invented' memories in place take shape. Using Palestine as a case-study, Said showed the overlapping and competing place memories that arise there for Christians, Jews, and Muslims, based as they are on historical narratives, landscape features and physical structures. Part of Palestine's problem, according to Said, is that its leaders have failed to articulate an effective, collective, national narrative as part of its independence struggle: a debatable position (Gerber, 2003).

KEY ADVANCES AND CONTROVERSIES

The full force of Said's scholarship, the numerous studies, books, theses, conferences, and discussions that it inspired, can be barely hinted at via the selected secondary source list below. Much of the criticism of Said's work can be thought of as *extensions* of his thinking rather than attacks on it. Nonetheless, there have been a number of debates and controversies to which it has given rise, again attesting to its provocative power more than anything else. Such arguments have flourished principally around Orientalism; on Said's own subjectivity in relation to his published work; and on some basic tensions at play with respect to Said's humanism, Marxism, and post-structuralism.

A number of Islamic and Arabic specialists criticised *Orientalism* as unnecessarily politicising scholarship on the Orient. Such critics unconvincingly claimed that knowledge of the Orient produced by Western scholars over the last couple of millennia was well-intentioned and 'disinterested' politically, refusing the notion that all knowledge is situated and produced to serve particular purposes, whether consciously intended or not. Conversely, in-depth, fruitful debates of *Orientalism* emerged from scholars examining the cultural aspects of empire and theories of representation (e.g., Clifford, 1988; Hussein, 2002). One of its most contested aspects was Said's inclination to commit 'Orientalism in reverse' – that is, he failed to recognise vast differences within Orientalist discourses about the Orient and Middle East. Critics asserted that Said himself produced a (counter-) stereotype of a homogenised, racist and ethnocentric Westerner. Texts, discourses and representations about the Orient are considerably more ambivalent, heterogeneous, and dynamic than Said at first allowed, especially if looking across Western academic discourses and disciplines (literature versus social science, for example) and across national cultures (Britain, France, and the US), which Said had tended to downplay in his attempt to prove resonances among them. Critics, especially those outside the West, were also quick to point out Said's failure to consider resistance and opposition to Orientalist stereotypes, which itself reinforced an (Orientalist) image of an Eastern subject as passive, inarticulate and lacking self-determination. Said corrected this silence in later works, including in *Culture and Imperialism* (1993a).

Other social axes of difference were likewise ignored by Said in his attempt to construct a coherent Orientalism. He, for the most part, neglected gender as an analytical framework, and feminists in particular made some key advances on *Orientalism*, especially those focusing on colonial women travellers, missionaries, educators, and so on (albeit going beyond the spaces of the 'Orient' to which Said had limited his own discussions). Said's work was brought to bear widely on the role of travel writing in the creation of imaginative, popular geographies of empire (e.g., Duncan and Gregory, 1999; Kennedy, 2000). In fact it is arguable that the proliferation of scholarship on travel writing as a genre of colonialist discourse is attributable to Said's theories of representation and cultural imperialism. Much of the feminist work within this subfield demonstrates the contradictory, heterogeneous, and sometimes counter-hegemonic positions women occupied with respect to colonial and imperial discourses and structures of power (e.g., Mills, 1991).

Although most would dismiss such divisions today, the notion that Said's literary theories and 'aberrant textualism' should be better grounded in material practices initially found popular backing in geography (**Smith**, 1994), an argument that mirrored Marxist and neo-Marxist debates in other fields (**Gregory**, 1995). Ahmed (1993) submitted one of the most infamous critical assessments of Said's writing, though other, more discerning critiques came from Lazarus (1999) and Hussein (2002). Working from a materialist

standpoint, Ahmed challenged Said on the relationships between texts and representations and their associated social and material practices. Ahmed criticised Said's excessive 'textualism', arguing that we come to know the world through the effects of global capitalism, not through texts and representations. This is a false dichotomy, since representations are materially located in the world, and, as Said noted, maintain 'a web of affiliations' in the world. Among other complaints, Ahmed also noted that Said failed to 'world' himself in his particular historical, cultural, and institutional frameworks that are, just as are the subjects Said studied, governed by dominant ideologies and political imperatives. Said's own privileged class position and his affiliation with elite American schools (which, as Ahmed points out, reproduce the international division of labour), as well as his position as part of the metropolitan elite more generally (even if an exiled one), arguably limited Said's ability to challenge the status quo.

Numerous critics also maintained that Said's methodological and theoretical framework was at best eclectic and justifiably impatient with received dogmas; at worst inconsistent, arbitrary and sometimes at odds with itself. Some critics see strength in Said's ability to bring together diverse theoretical orientations, as situated provocatively between 'the West Bank and the Left Bank' (Gregory, 1995: 448). Hussein (2002: 4) in particular stresses the positive aspects of Said's methodology – his 'technique of trouble' – which he argues allowed Said to subject received wisdom to 'theoretical and historical insight and to what might be called the controlled anarchism of critical consciousness'. However, Said's eclecticism raises thorny, not easily resolvable issues for others. Said has been criticised, for example, for his ambivalence about whether a 'real' Orient exists beyond its representation. On one hand, Said argued that Orientalism is a misrepresentation of the 'real' Orient, in which case Orientalism is a type of ideological knowledge in a Marxian sense. On the other, Said followed the logic of discourse theory in implying that no 'real' Orient exists, and is solely a Western construct, an imaginative geography (see Clifford, 1988: 255–76 for an extended discussion). For Said, the issue was not so much 'a dominant representation hiding a reality, but of the struggle between different and contesting representations' (Ashcroft and Ahluwalia, 1999: 4).

Said's frequent recourse to his own lived experience and thus traditional humanist arguments about human agency also raised questions about his alliance with discourse theory. Though parting with **Michel Foucault** in the notion of authorless texts, Said followed him in privileging discourse and language as prime determinants of social reality, and knowledge as a type of power or force that works impersonally through a multiplicity of sites and channels. Yet Said adopted a more conventional realist approach when discussing American foreign policy in Israel and Palestinian rights. In addition, Said can be considered Marxian in orientation, particularly in his development of Gramsci's theories of cultural hegemony, the dynamics of domination, and possibilities for resistance. Yet here too, he aligned with other post-colonial critics in pointing out the limits of (an ethnocentric) Marxist theory in confronting the needs and experiences of the colonized world. As such, Said's work consistently implied that a non-dominating, non-coercive mode of knowledge is possible and desirable, and he oftentimes cited the role of the courageous intellectual in creating it, including in his final book, *Humanism and Democratic Criticism* (2003), published posthumously. Among other things, in this work Said admonished the intellectual to protect against and forestall the disappearance of the past, and to construct fields of co-existence – rather than battle – as the ultimate outcome of our intellectual labour.

SAID'S KEY WORKS

Said, E. (1966) *Joseph Conrad and the Fiction of Autobiography.* Cambridge, MA: Harvard University Press.

Said, E. (1975) *Beginnings: Intention and Method.* New York: Basic Books.

Said, E. (1978) *Orientalism: Western Conceptions of the Orient.* London: Kegan Paul.

Said, E. (1980) *The Question of Palestine.* New York: Routledge.

Said, E. (1981) *Covering Islam: How the Media and the Experts Determine How We See the Rest of the World.* New York: Pantheon Books.

Said, E. (1983) *The World, The Text, and the Critic.* Cambridge: Harvard University Press.

Said, E. (1986) *After the Last Sky: Palestinian Lives* (photographs by Jean Mohr). New York: Pantheon.

Said, E. (1990) *Nationalism, Colonialism, and Literature.* Minneapolis: University of Minnesota Press.

Said, E. (1991) *Musical Elaborations.* New York: Columbia University Press.

Said, E. (1993a) *Culture and Imperialism.* New York: Alfred A. Knopf.

Said, E. (1993b) *Peace in the Middle East.* New York: New Press.

Said, E. (1994a) *Representations of the Intellectual.* New York: Pantheon.

Said, E. (1994b) *The Politics of Dispossession: The Struggle for Palestinian Self-Determination, 1969–1994.* New York: Pantheon.

Said, E. (1995) *Peace and Its Discontents: Essays on Palestine in the Middle East Peace Process.* New York: Vintage.

Said, E. (1999) *Out of Place: A Memoir.* New York: Alfred A. Knopf.

Said, E. (2000a) *The End of the Peace Process: Oslo and After.* New York: Pantheon Books.
Said, E. (2000b) 'Invention, memory, and place', *Critical Inquiry,* 26: 175–92.
Said, E. (2000c) *Reflections on Exile and Other Essays.* Cambridge: Harvard University Press.
Said, E. (2001) *Power, Politics and Culture.* New York: Pantheon.
Said, E. (2003) *Humanism and Democratic Criticism.* New York: Columbia University Press.

Secondary Sources and References

Ahmed, A. (1993) *In Theory: Classes, Nations, Literatures.* London: Verso.
Ashcroft, B. and Ahluwalia, P. (1999) *Edward Said: The Paradox of Identity.* London: Routledge.
Bhabha, H. and Mitchell, W.J.T. (eds), (2004) *Edward Said: Continuing the Conversation.* Chicago: The University of Chicago Press.
Clifford, J. (1988) *The Predicament of Culture: Twentieth-Century Ethnography, Literature, and Art.* Cambridge, MA: Harvard University Press.
Contemporary Literary Criticism (2000) 'Edward Said' Volume 123, Detroit Gale Group.
Duncan, J. and Gregory, D. (eds) (1999) *Writes of Passage: Reading Travel Writing.* London: Routledge.
Gerber. H. (2003) 'Zionism, orientalism, and the Palestinians', *Journal of Palestine Studies,* 23: 23–14.
Gregory, D. (1995) 'Imaginative geographies', *Progress in Human Geography,* 19: 447–85.
Hussein, A.A. (2002) *Edward Said: Criticism and Society.* London: Verso.
Kasbarian, J.A. (1996) 'Mapping Edward Said: geography, identity, and the politics of location', *Environment and Planning D: Society and Space,* 14: 529–57.
Katz, C. and Smith, N. (2003) 'An interview with Edward Said', *Environment and Planning D: Society and Space,* 21: 635–51.
Kennedy, V. (2000) *Edward Said: A Critical Introduction.* Cambridge: Polity Press.
Kucich, J. (1988) 'Edward Said', *Dictionary of Literary Biography,* 67: 249–59.
Lazarus, N. (1999) *Nationalism and Cultural Practice in the Postcolonial World.* Cambridge: Cambridge University Press.
Mills, S. (1991) *Discourses of Difference: An Analysis of Women's Travel Writing and Colonialism.* New York: Routledge.
Moore-Gilbert, B. (1997) *Postcolonial Theory: Contexts, Practices, Politics.* London: Verso.
Smith, N. (1994) 'Geography, empire and social theory', *Progress in Human Geography,* 18: 491–500.

Karen M. Morin, Bucknell University

46 Saskia Sassen

BIOGRAPHICAL DETAILS AND THEORETICAL CONTEXT

Saskia Sassen was born in The Hague, in the Netherlands, in 1949 but moved with her parents to Buenos Aires within a few years. This move from the Netherlands to Argentina was to be one of many international relocations experienced by Sassen, with time spent in Italy, the US and France during her early years, studying at the Università degli Studi di Roma, the University of Notre Dame in Indiana and the Université de Poitiers. As she points out, this constant mobility made her somebody who is 'always a foreigner, always at home' (Sassen, 2005) and this transnational perspective continues to influence her work.

One way that mobility has influenced Sassen's work relates to her use of language. Growing up competent in five languages gave her an awareness of particular 'gaps' in a given language compared to another, and vice versa. This awareness projected itself on the larger stage of research and explanation because, for Sassen, it made theorising important and meaningful as part of an attempt to compensate for existing language's deficiencies. Another influence of mobility was the experience of acting in ways that were 'out of place' due to a lack of situated knowledge. Sassen found that small actions, particularly when 'out of place', could have an effect on even the most powerful events or processes. This led her eventually to develop the proposition that, under certain conditions, powerlessness can be complex and thereby be a factor in the making of a history and a politics (see Sassen, 2007a, and Gane, 2004 for a more detailed discussion of these points). In addition, Sassen's time at universities in different countries facilitated encounters with a range of philosophies and theoretical perspectives as diverse as Marxist political economy, the work of Berger, Luckman, Kuhn, **Deleuze**-Guattari, **Foucault** and Althusser. This would influence her in a variety of ways and most importantly would encourage her to develop an approach to research that focuses on what she sees as strategic empirical domains – that is, conditions that are heuristic in that they produce knowledge about more than themselves: cities, immigration, and nation-states are three such subjects.

In the context of her nomadic early years, it is perhaps unsurprising that migration acted as the focus for the research which led to Sassen's first major publication – *The Mobility of Labor and Capital* (1988 and continuously reprinted since then). In this book her original contribution is to contest the notion that foreign direct investment will actually develop countries and keep them from becoming labour-exporters; her research suggests quite the opposite. In *Guests and Aliens* (2000) Sassen follows up on this work and uses 200 years of intra-European migrations to explore two commonly-held beliefs about migration: firstly, if richer countries do not control their borders, they will be invaded by poor migrants; and, secondly, when the outsider is from the same religion and race, discrimination does not occur. She concludes that Europe's history shows that both of these commonly-held notions are wrong.

Sassen is also a prolific writer on the sociology of globalisation, developing her arguments through several key books. In *Globalization and its Discontents* (1999) she covers a number of key issues associated with globalisation: immigration, cities, the feminisation of survival, the nation-state, and networked technologies. In doing this she highlights the negative consequence of processes of globalisation for many. Most recently, in *A Sociology of Globalization* (2007b) Sassen examines a vast scholarship in the social sciences that has never engaged with the question of globalisation and shows that such work provides significant resources – empirical, methodological and theoretical – for studying the mix of current processes, conditions, and subjectivities that are commonly grouped under the term globalisation.

Territory, Authority, Rights (published originally in 2006 and in an updated form in 2008) examines the making of global spaces and is particularly focused on the global spaces that inhabit national institutional and territorial framings. Sassen finds that much of the transformation we call global is actually better described as a *denationalising* of what was historically constructed as national. It is, however, the books *The Global City* (first published in 1991 and revised in 2001) and *Cities in*

a World Economy (first published in 1994 and revised in 2000 and 2006) that have gained Sassen most acclaim. The books, which set out Sassen's understanding of the role of global cities such as London and New York in the global economy of the late twentieth and early twenty-first centuries, have gained Sassen worldwide recognition in academic and public policy circles. Both books offer a complete rethinking of the processes that make cities and define their role in globalisation.

The above only begins to summarise Sassen's impressive list of publications. In addition, she has also authored numerous journal and newspaper articles and has published interviews, book chapters and edited books. Her publications have been translated into 19 different languages in total. This has all been achieved whilst working at numerous institutions, including at Harvard University where she had her first appointment in the form of a postdoctoral fellowship, and the University of Chicago, Columbia University and the London School of Economics and Political Science. In addition Sassen has held various positions on editorial boards, has been awarded numerous honorary degrees and has secured herself the position as one of, if not the leading figure, in the study of the sociology of globalisation.

SPATIAL CONTRIBUTIONS

It is difficult to capture here all of Sassen's contributions to spatial theory but three do stand out as being especially important. First, Sassen has provided inspired analysis of the nature, role, causes and consequences of migration in the global economy in the late twentieth and early twenty-first-century, challenging many early assumptions about the process. Her work has helped place migration at the centre of debates about globalisation and has shown the impossibility of explaining contemporary geographies of migration without reference to geographies of the global economy. The importance of this theme in Sassen's work is unsurprising considering her biography: in addition to mobility during the early years of her life, Sassen now constantly commutes between London and New York and has homes in both cities which she shares with her husband, the esteemed writer Richard Sennett.

Initially through *The Mobility of Labor and Capital,* a piece of work inspired both by the experience of living in multiple countries, witnessing a range of social, economic and political tensions, and being involved with Chavez's efforts to get a child-care centre established for the children of Mexican farm workers (see Sassen, 2007a), Sassen redirected thinking about labour migration and revealed it to be a phenomenon encouraged by and an integral part of economic globalisation. Developing this idea more recently, *Globalization and its Discontents* and *Guests and Aliens* both highlight how contemporary economic migration, especially to the US in the latter part of the twentieth century, mirrored processes that had been experienced worldwide and, as such, was not a new phenomenon but a particular manifestation of the United States' leading role in the global economy. Sassen also uses this work on migration to highlight the inequality and hardship associated with many forms of migration. Those fulfilling demand for maids, nannies and cleaners, entering the informal economy such as in clothing sweatshops or becoming part of the underground economy such as the sex

industry in major cities have been shown to be the 'losers' of global capitalism, being exploited and suffering inequality, particularly in the context of migration to global cities (see below). Her participation in the accompanying documentary to the film *Children of Men*, directed by Alfonso Guaron is just one example of how Sassen has conveyed these arguments to the general public using the world of the media.

Secondly, in relation to the theorisation of globalisation, Sassen's work comprehensively documents the value of studying not the outcomes of globalisation (e.g., transnational corporations) but the underlying infrastructures and practices that make up the global economy. As she puts it:

> A key proposition that has long guided my research is that we cannot understand the x – in this case globalization – by confining our study to the characteristics of x – i.e. global processes and institutions. This type of confinement is a kind of endogeneity trap, one all too common in the social sciences and spectacularly so in the globalization literature ... There are consequences to a type of analytics that posits that an explanation of x needs to be configured in terms of non-x. For one, it demands a focus on the work that produced the new condition – in this case, globalization.
>
> (Sassen, 2006b: 4)

By focusing on the non-x – i.e., the institutions, technologies and infrastructures that evolved during the twentieth century to produce globalisation – Sassen has been able to engage both in debates about the distinctiveness of globalisation in the late twentieth and early twenty-first century (see Held et al. (1999) on such debates) and about the spatial architecture of the global economy (see **Castells** (2000) in particular). Most recently this has led her to highlight the way that the global and national are interdependent and, therefore, that globalisation as a set of processes interacts with the national scale in more ways than many have recognised.

Sassen's third major contribution has been to develop ideas about the importance of place and local and national scales in globalisation through theorisation of the role of cities in globalisation. Through careful analysis of cities including London, New York and Tokyo, the books *Cities in a World Economy* and *The Global City* show that cities – as particular types of place – have actually become more important in recent global times. In particular Sassen argues that cities are strategic places for the making of the organisational instruments needed to redeploy economic activities across the globe. As she puts it:

> Since the 1980s, major transformations in the composition of the world economy, including the sharp growth of specialized services for firms and finance, have renewed the importance of major cities as sites for producing strategic global inputs.

(Sassen, 2006a: 7)

The inputs produced in cities are both informational and directly related to global finance but are also political and infrastructural, ranging from technologies to regulations. In particular, Sassen reveals through her work on global cities that the deep economic history of complex cities have produced the key components of the so-called knowledge economy. This also explains why as corporate economic globalisation expanded in the 1990s and onwards, the number of major and minor global cities continued to grow. Sassen's work on cities has, therefore, provided the foundations for further investigations of the uneven geographies of the global service economy in the same way that **Doreen Massey** and others had earlier laid the foundations for work on the geography of global manufacturing (see

Massey, 1995). In addition, her work has made her a leading member of public policy groups such as the Mastercard Worldwide Centres of Commerce programme.

KEY ADVANCES AND CONTROVERSIES

Sassen's aim in all of her work has been to unsettle existing modes of thinking and theorising. As a result, each of the three major contributions discussed above have advanced theory and understanding of globalisation and set new agendas for research. In particular her theorisation of the sociology of globalisation has redirected thinking by highlighting the importance of a range of *practices* that constitute the global – ranging from the construction of monetary and fiscal policies to the exercising of political imaginaries and production of international law. As a result she has been able to highlight the folly of the way:

> When the social sciences focus on globalization – still rare enough deep in the academy – it is typically not on these types of practices and dynamics but rather on the self-evidently global scale. And although the social sciences have made important contributions to the study of this self-evidently global scale ... there is much work left. At least some of this work entails distinguishing (a) the various scales that global processes constitute, ranging from supra-national and global to sub-national, and (b) the specific contents and institutional locations of the multiscalar globalization.

(Sassen, 2007a: 91)

Through her work, and especially through her book *Territory, Authority, Rights*, she has, therefore, forced scholars of globalisation to take seriously the ways in which the global is constructed through multiple institutions, technologies and infrastructures rather than existing as an independent, singular process. In doing this Sassen has argued that the national scale is far more important in globalisation than many have realised, in particular because globalisation is actually a process of denationalisation in which the apparatus constructed to support the role of the nation-state in the past is reconfigured to support global institutions and frameworks in the present.

In addition to advancing theoretical debates about the process of globalisation, Sassen has also forced a rethinking of the way migration and its role in the global economy is theorised. *The Mobility of Labor and Capital* countered claims that growing levels of foreign direct investment into developing countries would prevent worker migration and showed that investment actually drives emigration rather than encouraging citizens to stay and work in the newly established branch plants. By highlighting what at the time was a relatively novel concept – *transnational space* as created by foreign direct investment – Sassen showed how the US had become connected to developing countries in new ways, not least because of the presence of US firms overseas and the growing awareness of the ideologies and supposed ideals of US life this created. When coupled with increasing demand for low paid labour in the US, this spurred flows of migrant workers. By developing these points in her subsequent work, Sassen has shown how migration is intimately tied to processes of globalisation, not just in the form of the transnational elites conceptualised by Castells (2000) and Sklair (2001), but also in the form of poorly paid labourers who flock to global cities. She has shown

that these workers are an integral part of the global economy (what Sassen, 2006a, calls the 'other workers of the advanced corporate economy') and, as a result, it has become clear that low-skilled as well as high-skilled migration has to be central in any theorisation of the 'human side' of the global economy.

Finally, Sassen's work on global cities has emphasised the fact that the information economy is *made*, that it has a production process, and hence needs a range of specific places and diverse types of workers, from experts to cleaners. This suggestion that the informational economy is produced, contextually, is in line with her suggestion that the national and global are not mutually exclusive and allows her to highlight how production and innovation in global cities produce the technologies, infrastructures and regulations that constitute globalisation. As a result, Sassen has shown that cities need to be conceptualised as sites of global economic productivity as well as sites of struggle, thus making them a crucible for economic, social and political processes in the context of contemporary globalisation.

As a leading light in the study of globalisation, Sassen has both laid the groundwork for and developed work by a range of other leading scholars of space and place, including Manuel Castells, **Immanuel Wallerstein** and in particular **Peter Taylor** and his work on globalisation and World Cities (as manifest in the GaWC network and project). At times she has disagreed with some of her fellow theorists. For example, Rantanen (2006) notes that for a long time Castells disagreed with one of her first published articles where she argued that low paid migrants are an integral part of the global economy. Likewise, Sassen prefers to use the term global city when referring to the production capitals of the global economy, in line with her belief that a fundamental reconstitution of the economy has occurred as part of globalisation in the late twentieth and early twenty-first centuries, while others (e.g., Taylor, 2003) prefer the term World City to reflect a subtly different conceptualisation based on world systems analyses. Nonetheless, such differences are overshadowed by Sassen's achievement in gaining widespread recognition for the idea that globalisation is a socio-technical achievement, with the socio rather than the technical being emphasised. As a result, she has been at the heart of successful attempts to counter hyperbolic assertions of globalisation as the 'end of geography' (O'Brien, 1992) and the emergence of a 'borderless world' (Ohmae, 1992) and has promoted a social analysis of technology and globalisation which parallels the work of Karin Knorr-Cetina (see, for example, Knorr-Cetina and Bruegger, 2002) but which is distinctive because of its emphasis on the importance of social place in the production of globally networked economic space.

SASSEN'S KEY WORKS

Sassen, S. (1988) *The Mobility of Labor and Capital: A Study in International Investment and Labor Flow.* Cambridge: Cambridge University Press.

Sassen, S. (1991) *The Global City: New York, London, Tokyo.* Princeton: Princeton University Press (2nd updated edition in 2001).

Sassen, S. (1996) *Losing Control? Sovereignty in an Age of Globalization.* New York: Columbia University Press.

Sassen, S. (1999) *Globalization and its Discontents.* New York: The New Press.

Sassen, S. (2000) *Guests and Aliens.* New York: The New Press.

Sassen, S. (2005) 'Always a foreigner, always at home', in A. Sica and S. Turner (eds), *The Disobedient Generation: Social Theorists in the Sixties.* Chicago: University of Chicago Press. pp. 221–51.

Sassen, S. (2006a) *Cities in a World Economy* (3rd edition). London: Sage.

Sassen, S. (2006b) *Territory, Authority, Rights: From Medieval to Global Assemblages.* Princeton and Oxford: Princeton University Press (2nd updated edition in 2008).

Sassen, S. (2007a) 'Going digging in the shadow of master categories', in M. Deflem (ed.), *Sociologists in a Global Age: Biographical Perspectives.* Aldershot: Ashgate. pp. 85–98.

Sassen, S. (2007b) *A Sociology of Globalization.* New York: W. W. Norton & Co.

Secondary Sources and References

Castells, M. (2000) *The Rise of the Network Society.* Malden, MA: Blackwell.

Friedman, J. (1986) 'The world city hypothesis', *Development and Change,* 17 (1) 69–83.

Gane, N. (2004) 'Saskia Sassen: space and power', in *The Future of Social Theory.* London: Continuum International Publishing Group. pp. 125–42.

Held, D., McGrew, A., Goldblatt, D. and Perraton, J. (1999) *Global Transformations. Politics, Economics and Culture.* Cambridge: Polity Press.

Knorr-Cetina, K. and Bruegger, U. (2002) 'Global microstructures: the virtual societies of financial markets', *American Journal of Sociology,* 107 (4): 905–50.

Massey, D. (1995) *Spatial Divisions of Labour: Social Structures and the Geography of Production.* Basingstoke: Macmillan.

O'Brien, R. (1992) *Global Financial Integration: The End of Geography.* London: Royal Institute of International Affairs.

Ohmae, K. (1992) *The Borderless World: Power and Strategy in the Interlinked Economy.* New York: Harper Business.

Rantanen, T. (2006) 'Digging the global mine: an interview with Saskia Sassen', *Global Media and Communication,* 2 (2): 142–59.

Sklair, L. (2001) *The Transnational Capitalist Class.* Oxford: Blackwell.

Taylor, P. J. (2003) *World City Network: A Global Urban Analysis.* London: Routledge.

James Faulconbridge, Lancaster University

47 Andrew Sayer

Andrew Sayer completed his undergraduate honours degree (BA Geography) at Cambridgeshire College of Arts and Technology (later Anglia Ruskin University) in the late 1960s, completing an MA and DPhil in Urban and Regional Studies at Sussex University in the early 1970s. He was subsequently appointed to a lecturing post at the same university. In 1993, he moved to the Department of Sociology at Lancaster University where he was to become Professor of Social Theory and Political Economy. Sayer's scholarly work is wide ranging but has two major themes: on the one hand the relationship between social theory and political economy, and the relations of philosophy and methodology in the social sciences on the other. The first strand is illustrated by empirical work on topics in economic geography– for example, *Microcircuits of Capital* (Morgan and Sayer, 1988), and *The New Social Economy: Reworking the Division of Labour* (Sayer and Walker, 1992) – as well as in more theoretical discussions that have discussed the restructuring of the political economy (Sayer, 1995) and the ensuing relationships between political and moral economies (Ray and Sayer, 1999). The second strand is clearly indicated by

Method in Social Science (Sayer, 1984, with a second edition published in 1992) and *Realism and Social Science* (Sayer, 2000).

Andrew Sayer's best-known contribution to the field of human geography, and subsequently to the social sciences, has been his explication and development of critical realism. His arguments about space are not his central point, but they flow directly from this project. It is important here to appreciate the context in which the debate about critical realism was played out if we are to understand the appropriations of, and reactions to, Sayer's position by those exploring the constitutive role of space (and time) in contemporary life. In the late 1980s Critical Realism became, in the Anglo-American context, a major touchstone for geographers struggling with two issues: first, the waning of interest in Marxist structuralism (and/or the perceived lack of analytical rigour in structuralist accounts of economic restructuring); second, the perceived lack of explanatory power accorded to positivist descriptions of economic restructuring. Critical realism seemed to address these lacunae and offer a new way of approaching economic geography; accordingly, critical realism briefly shifted into a hegemonic position in the discipline of geography, and particularly the subdiscipline of economic geography, only to be quickly displaced by postmodern and post-structural critiques in the 1990s. Even so, it is a moot point whether the popular support for critical realism was translated into practice and understanding, or whether it simply acted as a flag of convenience for 'business as usual'. Sayer (2000) has subsequently argued that not only was/is critical realism unfairly painted as oppositional to post-structuralism, but also that the popularly assumed critical realist position that 'space matters' is a misinterpretation of its key tenets. Critical realists argue that the central point is *how* space matters. However, an answer to this question can only be reached via a re-theorisation of space.

Sayer's intellectual trajectory is significant. He began as a geographer, and then was a student, lecturer and researcher in a multidisciplinary setting; he is currently located in a sociology department where he defines himself as 'post-disciplinary'. Sussex University, whose organisational structure is characterised by broad overarching schools, such as Social and Community Studies, rather than traditional disciplines and faculties, presented Sayer an opportunity to develop and test his ideas in a broader social science context than that afforded most geographers. Moreover, teaching in the Graduate Division of Urban and Regional Studies brought together a diverse range of staff in what turned out to be a productive and challenging environment (his colleagues included, among others, Peter Saunders, Kevin Morgan, Simon Duncan, Mike Savage, Susan Halford, James Barlow, Peter Dicken, Peter Ambrose and Tony Fielding). Sayer's rigorous attention to social theory and methodology while at Sussex led him to question a range of issues surrounding the formation of knowledge and how we both acquire and apply it. The attention to internal relationships and causality led him to work against what he described as the disciplinary parochialism that is prone to 'reductionism, blinkered interpretation and misattribution of

causality' (Sayer, 2000: 7). As we will note below, this position has not tended to court easy support for his ideas amongst those more wedded to disciplinary norms, or among those who have sought to mobilise notions of 'space' to strengthen the discipline of geography. Nonethless, Sayer's commentary on critical realism and the relations between theory and empirical work in the context of the social sciences has been particularly influential within the discipline of geography. His ideas have also found their way directly into sociology, and, to a lesser extent, economics; furthermore, methodologically, they have had an impact across the whole of the social sciences by popularising and demonstrating the application of critical realism.

SPATIAL CONTRIBUTIONS

Sayer's position on 'space' is inextricably woven with his exposition of critical realism, and the critique of positivism. Sayer's 'turn to realism' was prompted by an attempt to resolve questions in his doctoral thesis about 'urban modelling'. Urban modelling was, at the time, a dominant mode of conceptualising social and economic, and spatial, interaction in the form of systemic modelling that could be operationalised with quantitative measures often through the application of 'social physics' models such as the gravity model (in passing, we might note that such approaches experienced something of a revival in the late 1990s). Sayer's (1976) reaction against closed systems and the search for causality in regularity that these models assumed led him to explore critiques of positivism upon which such approaches were based (albeit unacknowledged). Sayer looked to the newly-minted literature on critical realism (for example, Bhaskar, 1975; **Harré**, 1972; Keat and **Urry**, 1975) for insight. Simultaneously, this philosophical framework provided him with a means of distancing himself from the limitations of the 'grand narratives' and 'over-determination' that characterised the dominant structural Marxism of the time.

Sayer's point of entry was via a discussion of 'abstraction'. The 1981 paper of that title, the 1982 paper 'Explanation in economic geography', and finally the 1984 book, *Method in Social Science*, clearly laid out the case for critical realism for a social science audience. Critical realism places central importance on the notion of a 'depth ontology' that admits the possibility of a debate about the 'necessary', or 'internal' relations that constitute the 'causal powers' of things which then can be seen to have the potential to be mobilised in particular settings (i.e., they are contingent relations). Critically, this ontologically-rich account of social reality implies a generative, as opposed to a successionist, view of causality. In contrast, positivist approaches have an atomistic (as opposed to relational) view of interaction; they have no ontological depth (i.e., what you see is what you get); and causality is inferred from regularity: the whole is based upon the idea of closed, rather than open, systems.

This philosophical grounding allows Sayer to make some significant points about 'space'; the main one being that there is very little that one can say about space *in the abstract*. Therefore, there is no recourse to a theory of space that might, *pace* **David Harvey** (1985), create a bedrock, and a justification, for geography. Thus, contrary also to **Ed Soja** (1985), Sayer argued there was no magic spatial insight that geographers might

claim knowledge of, which if applied to other social theories (which are notably *aspatial*), would revolutionise them.

This does not mean that Sayer had nothing positive to say about 'space'. His point about abstract space, particularly the tendency of geographers to 'rake over' sociology and to accuse it of aspatiality, is that the degree of 'violence of abstraction' is variable. For example, the injury done by ignoring space in an abstract debate about social stratification may be negligible. However, the discussion of particular instances of stratification will require the consideration of 'physical space'. It is this notion of 'physical space' that Sayer stresses: the manifestation of a 'space-time-matter' combination. Sayer argues that abstraction tends to 'scramble' our understanding of causality. We can point to two types of examples: on one hand, empiricist accounts that look for regularity in relation to an abstract model; and, on the other hand, abstract theories of space that seek to selectively abstract concrete situations (substance and space) and recombine them in inappropriate ways. Both instances are akin to taking apart a machine and putting it back together incorrectly; metaphorically speaking, causality is disrupted: the machine doesn't work. By way of explication, we can point to the common tendency in geography to recombine processes in discrete spatial units (global, nation, region and locale); spatial or analytical units that may not be the relevant ones to the processes under investigation. It should be pointed out that geographers have been less culpable than those working in other disciplines who commonly uncritically recombine processes at the national scale. Thus, Sayer contends, it is crucial for empirical work to be carried out attending to the specificity of concrete processes and their temporal ordering lest one falls into the trap of spatial fetishism and reductionism.

Into the 1990s, Sayer turned his attention to the analysis of the culture–economy relationship (Sayer, 1999). Here, Sayer echoed the concern of many geographers – social, cultural and economic – about what the social embeddedness of the economic might mean (stemming from a disregard of the non-economic in political economic and neo-classical approaches); moreover, he wanted to ask what value might mean. However, Sayer gives short shrift to a relativist position; one that has celebrated the subjective experience. Sayer argues that modern social theory has sidelined normative statements in favour of positive statements. In simple terms: it has shifted from how the world ought to be, to how the world is. He argues that this stress on a positive social science has gained an apparent cloak of objectivity, but at the same time limited the possibility of critique (as positive accounts are deficient in their definition of how the world 'is': they exhibit an ontological shallowness).

However, his approach goes a step further by bringing back the notion of moral economy, a term that he rescues from writers of the Scottish Enlightenment such as Adam Smith; an approach which in the hands of Sayer, drawing upon the writings of Habermas and Bourdieu, is styled 'critical moral economy'. In this way Sayer seeks to bring back centre stage questions of value: questions that have been, on one hand, marginalised as subjective in positive and scientific analyses; or, on the other hand, emptied of meaning in relativist, or strong social constructivist, formulations. Philosophically, he challenges the dualism of subjectivity and objectivity that have become the norm in the last 50 years in the social sciences, he also challenges the value judgements that commentators within the social sciences have laid upon these terms. He argues for the reintroduction of normative moral judgements; for Sayer this does not mean a reverse into subjectivity, but a *conditional* subjectivity: one that acknowledges competing discourses but also considers the objective impacts of such subjective judgements/ beliefs. How else, he asks, are we to evaluate views that may be different, but some of which have (objective) material effects: for example, the range of beliefs about cures to illness. Consequentially, he argues that we need to examine the relationship between beliefs that are subjective, exploring their objectivity (or truth status) and their material effects.

Sayer's position here is a qualified one, specifically qualified by the object: in this case humans. As in his earlier discussions of critical realism, Sayer draws upon notions of naturalism and ontology to stress the ontological, or 'thing-ness' of objects. Here one can see Sayer's work offering a parallel, but critical, concern with embodiment as those writing about performativity. Sayer's point is that ultimately a strong social constructivist position (such as those offered within analyses of performativity) makes it impossible to ague for the fallibility of beliefs. He has used this approach to develop a book-length critique of 'class' in the social sciences in which he locates questions of value at the centre of analyses (Sayer, 2005).

KEY ADVANCES AND CONTROVERSIES

The reactions to Sayer's ideas have been varied. At one level his interventions have been widely cited; the notion of critical realism, and the need for a particular kind of theoretically informed concrete research certainly struck a chord. Notable development of realist work was carried out by John Allen and **Linda McDowell**; as well as **Doreen Massey** at the Open University (Massey, Allen and Sayer met as an informal group 'the Brighton Pier Space and Social Theory Group'). Duncan and his collaborators (Savage and Goodwin) based at Sussex/London also were key propagandists. Finally, the 'Lancaster Regionalism' group (amongst them, John Urry, as well as Paul Bagguley, Jane Mark-Lawson, Dan Shapiro, Sophie Walby, and Alan Warde) also adapted both the ideas and terminology of critical realism although most of this group would not see themselves as realists. Yet one has to be more sceptical as to whether geographers, or social scientists, do social science any differently as a result of Sayer's espousal of critical realism. One of the infuriating points for many has been that critical realism requires some basic philosophical rethinking on behalf of users, and that there is no 'off the shelf' 'toolkit' (see Pratt, 1995). But, it may well be argued, this is the point: to re-think the way we do research rather than follow 'business as usual'.

It is here that we should note that Sayer's critical comments on space were of interest to sociologists in the wake of sociology's 'turn to space' – a 'turn' partly prompted most notably by **Anthony Giddens'** (1984) structuration project which was given significant momentum by Urry (himself a realist sociologist, although he moved away from realism in the late 1980s). The edited book, *Social Relations and Spatial Structures* (Gregory and Urry, 1985), pulled together a number of key writers to debate the role of space in the constitution of social life (namely: Cooke, Giddens, **Gregory**, **Harvey**, **Massey**, Saunders, Sayer, **Soja**, and Urry). Interestingly, we can perhaps

date the arrival of human geography as a 'new kid on the block' of social science to this time. As noted above, Soja (1985) was seeking to radically overhaul the social sciences by 're-thinking them spatially'; Harvey (1985) continued to aspire to a geo-historical materialism; Giddens' (1985) pointed the way to mid-range theories. The tenor of the times was almost an inoculation metaphor; to inject some geography into sociology in particular, and the social sciences in general. The whole debate was given an extra spin by the growing awareness of space by postmodernist writers, especially urban theorists (including members of the so-called LA School – **Mike Davis, Michael Dear**, Allen Scott, **Michael Storper** and **Ed Soja**). Due to the configuration of the debate, it was not long before cultural studies began to look to geography for some spatial concepts. In this context, the geography cupboard was not exactly full of ideas, so some frantic writing followed. However, Sayer's (1985) response was a let-down for the incipient geographical colonisers: as we noted above, there is no 'bolt on' spatial theory, and abstract spatial concepts will not help us either.

The application of critical realism to practice, and to physical space, should have been the key moment in the debate. It turned out to be so, but in a rather complex manner that reminds us that ideas never simply pass through the world as their makers may have imagined. The key debate to focus on here is that of 'localities'. This debate has its roots in a UK Economic and Social Research Council research project that was to examine the differential economic and social restructuring on place (see Cooke, 1989). The study was based on five case studies: the 'localities'. Cooke, the project director, had drawn upon Massey's (1984) *Spatial Division of Labour* for both an empirical focus and a broad conceptual steer.

However, at the first airing of the debate at an Institute of British Geographers conference (before concrete research actually began), Cooke drew withering attacks, notably from **Neil Smith** (1987). The main charge was one of empiricism, and that this represented a return of geography to its idiographic roots. This attack re-doubled the theoretical debates about space (does it matter, how and why?), as well as increasing the tension between theoretical and empirical work. The debate ran through economic (and, to a lesser degree, social and political) geography for much of the next decade although the localities project lasted just two years: Duncan's (1991) special edited issue of *Environment and Planning A* sought to have the last word on the topic.

The 'Localities' project thus became a lightning conductor for a number of debates. Smith's (1984) castigation of the project was allied to an attempt to defend a mode of theorising that did not admit the possibility of contingency, and was exclusively concerned with internal relations yet at the same time wanted to include every diverse event. It is not surprising that Smith (1987) not only criticised Cooke, but also along with Archer (1987) and Harvey (1985; 1987), sought to demolish the case for critical realism too (with Harvey aspiring to construct a theory of the concrete and particular in the context of the universal and abstract determinations of Marx's theory of capital accumulation). Cooke's pragmatism (practical, and later philosophical) led him to propose local labour markets as the key template for the locality studies. This view was heavily criticised by Duncan (1989), from a position close to Sayer's, arguing that local labour markets were not always the relevant causal structure for the examination of phenomena. Interestingly, Sayer's early work had

been spurred on not only by an attempt to distance himself from positivist urban modelling, but also the structuralism of **Manuel Castells** (1977). In *The Urban Question,* Castells rejects the notion of the urban, accusing it as being an example of spatial fetishism, arguing that spatial effects should be considered social effects. Sayer (1983) agrees with part of this critique of spatial fetishism, but still argues that space matters. Space only has effects via the particular objects, with causal powers, that constitute it.

Sayer (2000) has also sought to consider further another theme raised in the localities debate; the tension between analysis and narrative, or between law-seeking and contextual approaches. Here he notes that the 'old' debate of regional geography was characterised by these problems, and that the same charge was laid at the door of critical realists analysing localities. Specifically he accuses positivists of focusing upon temporal succession but neglecting synchronic relations. This neglect leads to positivists making a fallacious link between the unique and the independent, and assuming that regularity between events equals interdependence. Sayer argues instead for a notion of causality that recognises variety and interdependence, whilst at the same time cautioning that many interdependencies tend to be unique and not transferable. Sayer's argument is that just because spatial relations are constituted by social and natural objects it does not follow that spatial relations can be reduced to their constituents. We have to examine *how* space makes a difference: this requires attention not only to the abstract theory and the specification of necessary relations, but also to the particularity of the contingent conditions that may or may not combine to produce a spatial 'effect'.

SAYER'S KEY WORKS

Sayer, A. (1981) 'Abstraction: a realist interpretation', *Radical Philosophy*, 28: 6–15.

Sayer, A. (1982) 'Explanation in economic geography', *Progress in Human Geography*, 6: 68–88.

Sayer, A. (1983) 'Defining the urban', *GeoJournal*, 9: 279–85.

Sayer, A. (1985) 'The difference that space makes', in D. Gregory and J. Urry (eds), *Social Relations and Spatial Structures*. London: Macmillan. pp. 49–66.

Sayer, A. (1991) 'Behind the locality debate: deconstructing geography's dualisms', *Environment and Planning A*, 23: 283–308.

Sayer, A. (2000) *Realism and Social Science*. London: Sage.

Sayer, A. (2001) 'For a critical cultural political economy', *Antipode*, 33: 687–708.

Secondary Sources and References

Archer, K. (1987) 'Mythology and the problem of reading in urban and regional research', *Environment and Planning D: Society and Space*, 5: 384–93.

Bhaskar, R. (1975) *A Realist Theory of Science*. Leeds: Leeds Books.

Castells, M. (1977) *The Urban Question*. Oxford: Blackwell.

Cooke, P. (1989) (ed.) *Localities: The Changing Face of Urban Britain*. London: Unwin.

Duncan, S. (1989) 'Uneven development and the difference that space makes', *Geoforum*, 20: 131–9.

Duncan, S. (1991) Special issue on 'Localities', *Environment and Planning A*, 23.

Giddens, A. (1984) *The Constitution of Society*. Cambridge: Polity.

Giddens, A. (1985) 'Time, space and regionalisation', in D. Gregory and J. Urry (eds), *Social Relations and Spatial Structures*. London: Macmillan. pp. 265–95.

Gregory, D. and Urry, J. (eds) (1985) *Social Relations and Spatial Structures*. London: Macmillan.

Harré, R. (1972) *The Philosophies of Science*. Oxford: Oxford University Press.

Harvey, D. (1985) 'The geopolitics of capitalism', in D. Gregory and J. Urry (eds), *Social Relations and Spatial Structures*. London: Macmillan. pp. 128–63.

Harvey, D. (1987) 'Three myths in search of reality in urban studies', *Environment and Planning D: Society and Space*, 5: 367–76.

Keat, R. and Urry, J. (1975) *Social Theory as Science*. London: Routledge.

Massey, D. (1984) *Spatial Divisions of Labour*. London: Hutchinson.

Morgan, K. and Sayer, A. (1988) *Microcircuits of Capital*. Cambridge: Polity.

Pratt, A.C. (1995) 'Putting critical realism to work: the practical implications for geographical research', *Progress in Human Geography*, 19: 61–74.

Ray, L. and Sayer, A. (eds) (1999) *Culture and Economy after the Cultural Turn*. London, Sage.

Sayer, A. (1976) 'A critique of urban modelling', *Progress in Planning* 6: 187–254.

Sayer, A. (1984) *Method in Social Science* (2nd edition 1992). London: Hutchinson.

Sayer, A. (1995) *Radical Political Economy: A Critique*. Oxford: Blackwell.

Sayer, A. (1999) 'Valuing culture and economy', in L.J. Ray and A. Sayer (eds), *Culture and Economy after the Cultural Turn*. London: Sage. pp. 53–75.

Sayer, A. (2005) *The Moral Significance of Class*. Cambridge: Cambridge University Press,

Sayer, A. and Walker, R. (1992) *The New Social Economy*. Oxford: Blackwell.

Smith, N. (1984) *Uneven Development: Nature, Capital and the Production of Space*. Oxford: Blackwell.

Smith, N. (1987) 'The dangers of the empirical turn: some comments on the CURS initiative', *Antipode*, 19: 59–68.

Soja, E. (1985) 'The spatiality of social life: towards a transformative retheorisation', in D. Gregory and J. Urry (eds), *Social Relations and Spatial Structures*. London: Macmillan. pp. 90–127.

Andy C. Pratt, King's College London

48 Amartya Sen

BIOGRAPHICAL DETAILS AND THEORETICAL CONTEXT

Amartya Kumar Sen is an intellectual of global stature, and highly influential in international public debate. He was born in 1933 and grew up in Dhaka (then India, now Bangladesh) in a middle-class academic family. Sen was partly educated at Santiniketan (in present-day West Bengal) at a school founded by the towering Bengali literary figure, Tagore. He attended the elite Presidency College in Calcutta, graduating rapidly with a degree in economics (during which time he also survived throat cancer), and moved to England in 1953 to read economics at Trinity College, University of Cambridge. After more undergraduate work he then completed a PhD in one year, studying with Joan Robinson (Sen, 1960), before returning to India to a Chair at Jadavpur University, Calcutta. Remarkably, therefore, he has been a Professor since his twenties. He then became Professor of Economics at the University of Delhi from 1963 to 1971, at the London School of Economics from 1971 to 1977, at Oxford from 1977, before leaving for Harvard in 1987 as Lamont Professor of Economics and Philosophy. He then served a spell as Master of Trinity College, Cambridge, from 1998–2003 (the first Asian to Chair an Oxbridge College) before returning to his old job at Harvard in 2004. Among his many accolades, Sen was awarded the Senator Giovanni Agnelli International Prize in Ethics, the Bharat Ratna (the President of India's highest honour), and in 1998 The Nobel Prize for Economics. The Nobel was widely perceived to be long overdue. Its tardiness may be linked to the fact that Sen has 'not been captured by economics imperialism and, unlike its practitioners, he opens and is open to debate across key issues' (Fine, 2001:13). Indeed, while never forsaking his discipline, he has repeatedly criticized some of its core neo-classical assumptions.

Sen's interests are diverse, and have led him to intellectual engagements that have spread well beyond his early classical and neo-classical training. Over the years he has contributed to social choice theory (a technical field in economics) and welfare economics, the understanding and measurement of poverty, explanations of famine and hunger, agrarian change and rural development issues, as well as engaging with ethics and political philosophy. His empirical investigations involve wide-ranging international comparisons, but with a primary focus on South Asia. Perhaps the central theme that links his writings – which span 55 years and include almost 30 books – has been his passionate concern to redress economic and social inequality and to improve human wellbeing.

In his early years Sen was preoccupied with welfare economics, and first made important contributions to the formalistic (mathematical) expression of social choices (Sen, 1970). His early technical work resulted in significant challenges to Kenneth Arrow's 'impossibility theorem', specifically the notion that individuals act *purely* according to self-interest or utilitarian criteria when making welfare or income decisions (Sen, 1977). Insisting that non-utility concerns like equity, class position, and family influence matter, Sen argued that the technique of 'revealed preferences' did not distinguish what drives decisions and choices. Sen argued that an interpersonal comparison of utility (the value of a commodity achieved in consumption) is vital. Sen's points were challenging and controverisal to neo-classical utilitarianism, although commonsensical to many political economists. Social choice theory still figures in Sen's work since he is interested in how aggregative judgements may be arrived at, given the 'diversity of preferences, concerns, and predicaments of the different individuals within society' (Sen, 1998: no pagination).

Since the 1960s Sen has moved from the development of formalistic models in economics, to theorising the ethical foundations of justice and development. An important bridge-builder in his intellectual journey has been the concept of human 'capability'. By the late 1980s Sen was defining capability as 'a set of functioning bundles representing the various alternative 'beings and doings' that a person can achieve with his or her economic, social, and personal characteristics' (Drèze and Sen, 1989: 18; Sen, 1985). Capability is 'tantamount to the freedom of a person to lead one kind of life rather than another', in an Aristotelian sense (Nussbaum and Sen, 1993: 2). It follows, therefore, that an individual's

capability can be *repressed* (for example, by denying a person access to basic services including food, education, land, freedom of expression, or health care), or *enabled* (for example, through supportive actions by other individuals and institutions including local communities, or even a 'developmentalist' state). The core of development itself is, therefore, the enjoyment of freedom – not just freedom of speech in a narrow sense, but freedom (positive and negative) for individuals to lead valuable lives.

Development as Freedom (Sen, 1999) is consistent with his earlier work on comparisons of individual preferences and values (Sen, 1992a; 1992b). Herein, Sen defines human wellbeing as the enhancement of capabilities, suggesting 'development consists of the removal of various types of unfreedoms that leave people with little choice and little opportunity of exercising their reasoned agency' (Sen, 1999: xii). For Sen, freedom is not just important in and of itself; it is also *instrumental* since it enables people to attain desired ends, and *constitutive* in the making of collective moral decisions through dialogue (Gasper, 2000). Since it is consistent with these three roles, democracy is viewed as the system of governance with the greatest capacity to expand basic freedoms. Achieving development, then, requires the expansion and improvement of capabilities and entitlements for the poor and underprivileged. The purpose of the expansion of capabilities ought to be the enhancement of freedom itself, because the purpose of development is ultimately, freedom. In addition to expanding capability to achieve 'functionings' (the 'beings and doings' constitutive of wellbeing), Sen also argues for the importance of recognising cultural values in this process (Sen, 2004, 2009).

At another stage on his intellectual journey, Sen received widespread acclaim for his efforts to improve the indicators used to measure poverty rates and human development (Sen, 1992b; 1997). The Human Development Index (HDI) and its expression in the United Nations Development Programme's *Human Development Report* thus provided an alternative to the neo-liberal 'Washington Consensus' on income-related poverty measures. He and researchers at the UNDP argued that development priorities should be geared towards improving human development (capabilities) – assessed through wide-ranging multivariate indices – rather than through growth-centred economic policy. Sen has also argued strongly for the extension of freedom and independence to women and children in developing countries, which he says has demonstrable effects on wellbeing, poverty alleviation, and mortality (Agarwal et al., 2005). He regards the neglect of women's nutrition and health (not least among poor African-Americans in the US), and sex-selective abortion in developing countries, as criminal (Sen, 1990; 1999).

Despite these applications of his work, Sen has largely abstained from collective protest or activism (Corbridge, 2002), although he was involved in left-wing Bengali politics as a student (Sen, 2001). He is cautious about giving policy advice and has not done so directly to governments, but he has used funds from his Nobel to set up the Pratichi Trust concerned with literacy and schooling in India and Bangladesh (issues explored in Drèze and Sen, 2002). In Indian affairs he labels himself somewhat left of centre, certainly opposed to the excesses of Hindu nationalism and nuclear proliferation, and remains a strong supporter of gender equality, pluralism, and pro-poor policies. *The Argumentative Indian* (2005) brings together his work on these and other components of heterodox Indian identity. Sen has publicly distanced

himself from some more radical positions on development, particularly in relation to Gandhi's belief in local self-sufficiency and technological scepticism, and he sees an 'ugly side' to many forms of localist, communitarian, and sectarian politics.

Sen is a qualified supporter of economic globalisation for its potential to tackle poverty and inequality, even though it 'doesn't always work' (Sen, 2001: no pagination) and should not be reduced to the unfettered expansion of trade and markets. His point here is that globalisation is nothing new, and that the poor should be able to share in its gains. His qualified support for civil society movements comes with a caveat: 'One's concern for equity and justice in the world must not carry one into the alien territory of unreasoned belief' (Sen, 2001: no pagination).

Equality and justice, and the rights of the poor not to suffer 'unfreedoms', figure centrally in almost all his work (Sen, 2001: no pagination). *The Idea of Justice* (2009) cross-references most of the major arguments. It is a major work of political philosophy, which controversially dismisses a search for instrumental social justice delivered through strong institutions, in favour of pluralist and comparative conceptions of what is 'right', focusing on delivering acceptable outcomes. The reader is taken full circle back to his early work on social choice; justice is a function of its definition and expression, and simple criteria and rules can never define it.

SPATIAL CONTRIBUTIONS

In his attempt to insert the theoretical space for a dialogue on equality into the rather introverted world of mainstream economics, and to be specific about equality and justice and how to realise these, Sen has made some insights that have been debated and applied by geographers and in development studies. Much of his work involves inter-regional and inter-state comparisons (e.g., Drèze and Sen, 2002) and makes detailed reference to places and historical events, but he has never contributed directly to the discipline. Yet Sen holds to a cosmopolitan view of territoriality, and thus in accordance with his belief in universal rights, he argues that culture transcends place, rather than, as **Arturo Escobar** argues, that culture 'resides in places'. As Sen puts it, 'culture' is not impermeable to rational consideration and choice (Sen, 2004). *The Argumentative Indian* (2005) makes this point strongly.

The greatest attention paid to Sen by geographers has been to his work on poverty and famine. Sen has not been alone in identifying insidious, quotidian hunger as a major concern, but his explanation of widespread famine has certainly seized the public interest. When Sen was a small boy he witnessed the direct effects of the 1943–5 famine in Bengal. The central argument of his acclaimed *Poverty and Famines* (Sen, 1981; see also Devereux, 2001) is that famine is not caused by a negative Malthusian relationship between population and food supply, but by the inability of famine-prone individuals to *access* food in times of great need, even when food supplies are adequate and the rich are still eating well. Although this is not phrased as a normative statement, the implication is that famine can be construed as a food *demand* problem, not a *supply* problem. Food is obtained only when one has entitlement to access it, and 'Famine results where access to food is reduced because of processes denying or lessening entitlement to food' (Sen,

1981). 'Endowments' are the assets and resources that people may theoretically access. 'Entitlements' are those that are available, and are therefore cognate with 'acquisition power'. Survivors of serious famines have the power to acquire food – to grow it (production-based entitlements), to buy it (trade-based entitlements), by selling their labour for cash or food (own labour entitlement), by being given food by others (inheritance and transfer entitlement), or through what Sen terms 'extended entitlements' (including looting – Drèze and Sen, 1989).

Poverty and Famines was highly influential, and his 'food entitlement decline' (FED) explanation was further elaborated with the gifted economist Jean Drèze, in several volumes, using extended empirical cases (Drèze and Sen, 1989, 1990/1991). India, as Sen noted, has not suffered a major famine since 1947 (but has come close) because its leaders have been held to account through voting and a free press, which has influenced a more proactive stance on addressing demand-side constraints through food distribution and work programmes. His ideas have been influential to the work of geographers and anthropologists including Piers Blaikie (see Blaikie et al., 1994), Neil Adger, Susanna Davies, Robert Kates, Ken Hewitt, Hans Bohle (1993), and **Michael Watts** (1983). They have been taken up in famine relief management, encouraging agencies to focus more on access to food as well as basic food relief. Sen's theories have also informed famine early-warning systems that scrutinise price signals in markets for signs of impending food stress.

A fascinating offshoot of entitlement theory is 'environmental entitlements' (Leach et al., 1999). Here entitlements and endowments thinking was re-oriented to refer to natural resources, not food availability, with a specific focus on the role of institutions in mediating differentiated resource access and entitlements. Tony Bebbington, Gordon Conway, Robert Chambers and Ian Scoones have also been instrumental in unpacking the dynamic and flexible ways in which rural people manage their endowments and risks in ways that echo some of Sen's core insights (Bebbington, 1999). 'Livelihoods thinking' shows how different entitlements are juggled by individuals and households, and it has guided work in several international development agencies for over a decade. Williams and Windebank (2003) have now applied livelihood and capability analysis to alternative economic geographies and poverty in the UK.

KEY ADVANCES AND CONTROVERSIES

Sen's work is particularly challenging to critical scholars because much of it is highly original and cuts across disciplines and schools of thought, making it difficult to stereotype. The radical implications that may be drawn from his support for human emancipation, equality, justice and poverty alleviation have largely been taken up by others. Sen himself practices 'cautious boldness', raising issues dear to the critical left, but retaining a faith in market economics. Calls to extend his frameworks are thus more common than pleas to reject them (Fine, 2001; Alkire, 2002). For example, Ben Fine (a former student) finds an 'unresolved tension between micro-foundations of entitlement analytic and the broader recognition of famine as irreducibly macro, not least

because famine is more than the sum of its individual parts' (Fine, 2001: 8). Sen is aware of political-economic forces, pointing out that 'famine is dependent upon 'the exercise of power and authority ... alienation of the rulers from those who ruled . . . the social and political distance between the governors and the governed' (Sen, 1999: 170) but Fine suggests Sen's understanding of power and structures is 'superimposed, not built, upon the micro-foundations'.

Development geographers have likewise taken up the challenge of explaining famines. Blaikie et al. (1994) develop heuristic models that make multilevel causation of famine, and processes of vulnerability, more explicit. **Michael Watts**, who provided the most detailed Marxist argument for the colonial origins of famine (1983), is broadly sympathetic to Sen. He argues that if poverty (and famine) is a result of 'capability failure' and a lack of entitlements, the prime response must be to overcome vulnerability and to address demand for food. But processes of oppression can lie at famine's roots, the development of 'critical autonomy' and a strong 'sense of society' is needed to enhance freedoms (Watts, 2000: 57). Following Marx, Watts suggests entitlements are '...both constituted and reproduced through conflict, negotiation and struggle' (Watts, 2000: 62).

Others have taken on this argument about the social and political embeddedness of entitlement failures. Armed conflict and violence in famine situations serves certain elite interests, and famine can be used as a political weapon (Keen, 1994; De Waal, 1989; Middleton and O'Keefe, 1998). Other important criticisms include the fact that many famine deaths occur through ill health, not starvation (De Waal, 1989), and that endowments – like communal livestock herds, or common property – lack clear property rights, making them 'fuzzy' and thus hard to catalogue (Devereux, 2001:253).

The instrumentality of 'complex emergencies' and 'war famines', where 'freedom to choose' is clearly constrained by the powerful, is not always recognised by Sen. In *Identity and Violence* (Sen, 2006), however, he does explore the causes of violence, choosing to reject simplistic explanations like Samuel Huntingdon's *Clash of Civilizations*, or the equally reductionist idea that inequality and poverty always generate violent conflict. Much more complex, multifaceted explanations of violence are called for. Here, Sen's neo-liberal economic training has been extended but perhaps not overturned (Fine 2001). **Stuart Corbridge** argued that 'Sen's liberalism leaves him poorly equipped to deal with questions of entrenched power and the politics of conflict and social mobilization' (2002: 203), and hence his failure (or refusal) to elaborate a strong political economy of capitalism.

This is surprising given the political and ethically charged issues that Sen has addressed, and the fact that he is clearly aware of the debates (Fine, 2001: 12; Sen, 2001, 2003, 2006). In Sen's work there are few links made between the production of 'opulence' resulting from growth and from wealth, and the reduction of entitlement for the poor (Cameron and Gasper, 2000: 986). Other critics call for a richer conception of 'self' that sees human agents as much more than beings seeking to attain capabilities (Giri, 2000: 1018). Unlike **Anthony Giddens'** conception of the *autotelic self* – a reflective dimension of self with world views and responsibility – selfhood is not always a full part of Sen's analysis despite his call

to insert value into welfare analysis and in his accounts of social conflict (Alkire, 2002; Sen, 2006).

Lastly, there is a certain level of ambiguity in Sen's notion of 'development as freedom'. Freedom is, more often than not, accompanied by its foreclosure. Sen is less than clear about tackling the conflicts that result from people's pursuit of freedom: development seems to be about opportunity and 'choice', to which there must surely be limitations (Gasper, 2000: 999). But how exactly are freedoms achieved? By what political means? How may the poor marshal power to challenge vested interests other than through votes? Does Sen support protest? Critics see difficulties here, and a failure to recognise the vitality of 'concerted struggles against the powers of vested interests, at all spatial scales' (Corbridge, 2002: 209). In *The Idea of Justice* (2009) it becomes clearer that for Sen it is the *quality* of governance, and the opportunities it affords for rational debate, that is most important for equitable development and human wellbeing.

Amartya Sen is a beacon of commonsense in the inter-disciplinary terrain he occupies. Entitlements and capability stress human agency, not constraint, and they carry 'some sense of worth and of real people's lives' (Gasper, 2000: 996). His insistence on understanding and resolving inequality, tackling justice and expanding basic freedoms has placed many mainstream economists and utilitarians in a heavily compromised position. Social scientists in general should be grateful that this important ambassador for 'humane economics' (Desai, 2001) has reached the ears of policy-makers worldwide with his beguiling ideas.

SEN'S KEY WORKS

Drèze, J. and Sen, A.K. (1989) *Hunger and Public Action.* Oxford: Clarendon Press.

Nussbaum, M. and Sen, A.K. (1993) *The Quality of Life.* Oxford: Clarendon Press.

Sen, A.K. (1970) *Collective Choice and Social Welfare.* San Francisco: Holden-Day.

Sen, A.K (1981) *Poverty and Famines: An Essay on Entitlements and Deprivation.* Oxford: Clarendon Press.

Sen A.K. (1997) *On Economic Inequality. An Expanded Edition with a Substantial Annexe by James Foster and Amartya Sen.* Oxford: Clarendon Press (1st edition 1973)

Sen, A.K. (1999) *Development as Freedom.* Oxford: Oxford University Press.

Sen A.K. (2005) *The Argumentative Indian.* London: Penguin Books.

Sen A.K. (2006) *Identity and Violence: The Illusion of Destiny.* London and Delhi: Penguin.

Sen, A.K. (2009) *The Idea of Justice.* Boston: Harvard University Press.

Secondary Sources and References

Agarwal, B. Humphries J. and Robeyns I. (eds) (2005) *Amartya Sen's Work and Ideas: A Gender Prespective.* London: Routledge.

Alkire, S. (2002) *Valuing Freedoms. Sen's Capability Approach and Poverty Reduction.* Oxford: Oxford University Press.

Bebbington, A.J. (1999) 'Capitals and capabilities: a framework for analyzing peasant viability, rural livelihoods and poverty', *World Development,* 27: 2021–44.

Blaikie P., Cannon, T., Davis I. and Wisner B. (eds) (1994) *At Risk: Natural Hazards, People's Vulnerability and Disasters.* London: Routledge (2nd edition 2003).

Bohle, H-G (ed.) (1993) *Worlds of Pain and Hunger: Geographical Perspectives on Disaster Vulnerability and Food Security.* Saarbrucken/Fort Lauderdale, FL: Verlag Breitenbach Publishers.

Cameron. J. and Gasper, D. (2000) 'Amartya Sen on inequality, human well-being, and development as freedom', *Journal of International Development,* 12 (7): 985–8.

Corbridge S.E. (2002) 'Development as freedom: the spaces of Amartya Sen,' *Progress in Development Studies,* 2: 183–217.

Desai, M. (2001) 'Amartya Sen's contribution to development economics', *Oxford Development Studies,* 29 (3): 213–23.

Drèze, J. and Sen, A.K. (eds) (1990/1991) *The Political Economy of Hunger* (3 volumes). Oxford: Clarendon Press.

Drèze, J. and Sen, A.K. (2002) *India: Development and Participation.* Oxford: Oxford University Press.

Devereux, S. (2001) 'Sen's entitlement approach: critiques and counter-critiques', *Oxford Development Studies,* 29 (3): 244–63.

Fine, B. (2001) 'Amartya Sen: A Partial and Personal Appreciation'. CDPR Discussion Paper 1601. Centre for Development and Policy Research. SOAS www.soas.ac.uk/cdpr/publications/papers/file24315.pdf

Giri, A.K. (2000) 'Rethinking human well-being: a dialogue with Amartya Sen', *Journal of International Development,* 12: 1003–18

Gasper, D. (2000) 'Development as freedom: taking economics beyond commodities – the cautious boldness of Amartya Sen', *Journal of International Development,* 12: 989–1001.

Huntington, S. P. (1996) *The Clash of Civilizations and the Remaking of World Order.* New York: Simon and Schuster.

Keen, D. (1994) *The Benefits of Famine. A Political Economy of Famine and Relief in Southwestern Sudan, 1983–1989.* Princeton: Princeton University Press.

Leach, M., Mearns, R. and Scoones, I. (1999) 'Environmental entitlements: dynamics and institutions in community-based natural resource management', *World Development,* 27: 225–47.

Middleton, N. and O'Keefe, P. (1998) *Disaster and Development: The Politics of Humanitarian Aid.* London: Pluto.

Sen, A.K. (1960) *Choice of Techniques.* Oxford: Blackwell.

Sen, A.K. (1977) 'Rational fools: a critique of the behavioral foundations of economic theory', *Philosophy and Public Affairs,* 6 (4): 317–44.

Sen, A.K. (1985) *Commodities and Capabilities.* Amsterdam: North-Holland.

Sen, A.K. (1990) 'More than 100 million women are missing', *New York Review of Books,* 20 December: 61–6.

Sen, A.K. (1992a) *Choice, Welfare and Measurement.* Oxford: Blackwell.

Sen, A.K. (1992b) *Inequality Re-examined.* Oxford: Oxford University Press.

Sen, A.K. (1995) 'Rationality and social choice', *American Economic Review,* 85 (1): 1–24.

Sen, A.K. (1998) Autobiography. Swedish Academy of Sciences Nobel Prize website. www.nobel.se/economics/laureates/1998/sen-autobio.html (Published in *Les Prix Nobel,* 1999.)

Sen, A.K. (2001) 'Interview with Sen by David Barsamian'. Alternative Radio, Colorado. www.indiatogether.org/interviews/sen.htm

Sen, A.K. (2003) *Rationality and Freedom.* Cambridge, MA: Harvard University Press.

Sen, A.K. (2004) 'How does culture matter?', in V. Rao and M. Walton (eds), *Culture and Public Action.* Stanford: Stanford University Press. pp. 38–50.

de Waal, A. (1989) *Famine That Kills: Darfur, Sudan, 1984–1985.* Oxford: Clarendon Press.

Watts, M.J. (1983) *Silent Violence: Food, Famine and Peasantry in Northern Nigeria.* Berkeley, CA: University of California Press.

Watts, M.J. (2000) 'Struggles over geography: violence, freedom and development at the millennium', Hettner Lectures No. 3. Heidelberg: Department of Geography, University of Heidelberg.

Williams, C.C. and Windebank, J. (2003) *Poverty and the Third Way.* Routledge: London.

Simon Batterbury, University of Melbourne and Jude L. Fernando, Clark University

BIOGRAPHICAL DETAILS AND THEORETICAL CONTEXT

David Sibley's research on socio-spatial exclusionary processes has enhanced geographers' understanding of exclusion, marginalisation and difference. Born in 1940, Sibley completed his first degree in geography at Liverpool University in 1962, and then travelled to the US, where he was awarded an MA at Southern Illinois University. Sibley then returned to the UK to take up a planning job in Durham for two years before returning to the US in 1966 to teach at Temple University. While at Temple, Sibley read **Peter Haggett's** *Locational Analysis in Human Geography*, and this book influenced his decision to return to England to start a PhD in geographical modelling at Cambridge. His thesis analysed the mathematical modelling of gradients, surfaces and point patterns (see Sibley, 1970; 1972; 1973). Reflecting on this, Sibley recalls, 'I was rather taken by the beauty of curves and impressed by my own ability to do maths, having been bottom of the class most of the time during high school!' (personal correspondence, 2002).

Sibley's research took on a dramatically different focus after his Cambridge days. He spent several years working outside the academy with English gypsies, together with his partner who started a school for gypsy children in the Hull area. This collaborative work, written while he was at University of Hull, was to provide the basis of his first book, *Outsiders in an Urban Society* (1981). Drawing from theory in educational sociology (especially that of Basil Bernstein) and social anthropology (in particular, the work of Mary Douglas) *Outsiders in an Urban Society* began to develop a distinctive take on the social construction of space. Sibley's engagement with Douglas' ideas on purity and danger was particularly noteworthy, having been introduced to her work through a radio interview with Judith Okely (author of *The Traveller Gypsies*).

Sibley would spend much of the next 20 years developing his ideas about 'outsiders' and the production of space, extending his research beyond gypsies to include children and family dynamics, with a particular focus on domestic space. In the process he continued to cross further disciplinary boundaries. This work and thinking culminated in 1995 in the publication of *Geographies of Exclusion*, a book which has provided a key contribution to the geographic literature on identity and marginalisation (see Hubbard, 2008). Herein, Sibley drew from not just social anthropology, but also feminist theory, human geography and (especially) psychoanalysis to showcase the tendency of powerful groups to 'purify' space and to see minority groups as dirty and polluting.

Drawing particularly on psychoanalytical ideas about the importance of maintaining self-identity (literally, maintaining the boundaries of the Self), Sibley argued that the urge to exclude threatening Others from one's proximity is connected to deeply engrained and often subconscious desires to maintain cleanliness and purity, many of which may be inculcated in early infancy:

> Experience of the world in childhood also involves the confirmation of the boundaries of the self and situating the self in the social world through the sorting of people and things into 'good' and 'bad' categories. 'Good' and 'bad' enter the unconscious and, in the process of socialisation, they are projected onto others who become the objects of fears and desires.
>
> (Sibley, 2001: 244)

Following Douglas' (1966: 41) argument that dirt is 'matter out of place', *Geographies of Exclusion* explored the ways in which this abject fear of the self being defiled or polluted is mapped onto those individuals and groups depicted by hegemonic society as deviant or dangerous. This engagement with psychoanalytical 'object relations' theory offered new ways for thinking about processes of marginalisation, implying that the way people seek to exclude Other groups can only be understood with reference to the manner in which people identify with or against particular stereotypes on a psychic level. These ideas have been developed in his subsequent writing that considers the notion of psychogeographies and applying spatialised object relations theory in other fields outside geography, in relation to animal geographies (Griffiths et al., 2000), perspectives on the lifecourse (Sibley, 2001) and the effects on incarceration on prison inmates (van Hoven and Sibley, 2008), the latter having been his principal research focus whilst based at the University

of Leeds, which he joined in 2006 after a three-year Visiting Professorship.

SPATIAL CONTRIBUTIONS

Sibley's research has shown that varied forms of spatial exclusion reinforce and maintain social boundaries in society. He has effectively demonstrated that individuals attempt to distance themselves from 'bad' objects/subjects because of their desire to maintain purity and cleanliness. Such understandings, Sibley argues, are circulated within the larger culture through cultural representations of marginalised groups as deviant, different and dangerous. Yet, Sibley's understandings of identity, marginalisation and exclusion have shifted since he first considered these concepts in the early 1980s, perhaps as a result of his growing interest in psychoanalysis and the work of Melanie Klein and Julia Kristeva. In his first book, *Outsiders in Urban Societies,* he insisted that a nuanced analysis of gypsies and indigenous minorities in society can only be accomplished through a comparative framework that takes into account 'changes in the economy and social structure of the outsider group as they are affected by processes operating in the dominant social system' (Sibley, 1981: vii). *Geographies of Exclusion* extended this perspective on the insider/outsider binary by drawing from psychoanalytical theory to understand the relation of Self and Other (Hubbard, 2008).

Exploring how social and spatial boundary processes separate some groups and individuals from the mainstream, *Geographies of Exclusion* provided an elegant conceptualisation of social and spatial exclusion, demonstrating that 'who is felt to belong and not to belong contributes in an important way to the shaping of social space' (Sibley, 1995a: 3). Further, it provided one of the first attempts by a geographer to explore the role of the psyche in socio-spatial process. The merits of such an approach are summarised by Sibley thus:

> Psychoanalysis provides one way of thinking about social relationships and relationships with the material world. It brings the unconscious into social theory, connecting the unconscious with the phenomenal and experiential aspects of life ... it constitutes a way of articulating anxieties and desires which are elements of the spatiality of human experience.

(Sibley, 2001: 243)

Highlighting the fears and insecurities that we carry around with us as a result of the often traumatic separation of (pre-Oedipal) Infant and Mother, Sibley's use of psychoanalytical theory thus relates the search for spatial order to the personal search for certainty and security. In discussing the merits of psychoanalysis for understanding socio-spatial process, Sibley notes that psychoanalytical theory 'has considerable value because it can help us to understand better not only the representation of others but also our own feelings about the abject, our own insecurities about difference which affect our academic practice' (Sibley, 1995a: 185).

Sibley has also accordingly written about social exclusion within the discipline of geography itself, underscoring how geography as a whole tends to marginalise particular groups, especially women and people of colour. Extending his concerns on the exclusionary nature of academic practice, Sibley developed notions around power and the ways it is conceptualised in academe. Sibley admits that his interest in the sociology of knowledge was

in part inspired by an array of rejection letters he received in regard to his article on the purification of space that was eventually published in *Society and Space* (Sibley, 1988; 1999). He suggests that local boundary disputes in academia are symptomatic of wider processes of gender and racial oppression. Noting the exclusions that impinge on the production of geographic knowledge, he argues for a more inclusive discipline:

> If critical ideas come from the oppressed, for example, from women or black authors in certain contexts ... they may be considered dangerous because they challenge white, heterosexual male domination of the western knowledge industry.

(Sibley, 1995a: 116)

Sibley maps the exclusionary nature of geography by taking urban studies to task for neglecting the research of W.E.B. Dubois, and suggesting that gender, politics and epistemology worked to marginalise women researchers examining the city between 1910–1930. Cautioning geographers that academic postmodern writing that celebrates diversity may not necessarily signal a significant break with the masculine and racist nature of geography, Sibley shows how the failure or success of particular ideas in geography are profoundly affected by the contexts in which they are produced.

Within the framework of his interest on social exclusion and space, Sibley has made a significant contribution to work in social geography on family dynamics and the production of domestic space. Although geographical work on the home had identified it as a 'locus of power relations' (Sibley, 1995a: 92), this research predominantly focused on gender relations between adult household members. Sibley (1995a; 1995b) addressed the implicit adultist nature of this research by highlighting the role of the home as an important site for the negotiation of child–adult relations. In a collaborative project with psychologists Geoff Lowe and David Foxcroft, from the University of Hull (Sibley and Lowe, 1992; Lowe et al., 1993) Sibley studied the psychosocial dynamics of the home life of drinkers as a means through which to understand the patterns that contribute to adult drinking behaviour.

In doing so Sibley (and colleagues) drew once again on the work of Basil Bernstein. In categorising families Bernstein distinguishes between, what he terms *positional* and *personalising* families. In *positional* families power is vested in positions, for example in that of 'the father', in *personalising* families power is more equally distributed between members. Sibley and colleagues (Sibley and Lowe, 1992; Lowe et al., 1993) used this distinction to reflect on the boundaries of acceptable behaviour in different households, including limits on the use of time and space. They argued that children's use of space and time in positional families is strongly bounded by a set of rigid rules; in contrast *personalising* families are less constrained by arbitrary rules, and children are given a greater voice in negotiating domestic spatial and temporal boundaries.

In subsequent solo work Sibley (1995b) further developed his interest in the bounding of domestic space. Here, he drew on data about middle-class childhoods in the UK from a Mass Observation archive to show how children, when given their own bedrooms, appropriate, transform and secure the boundaries of this space to make it their own. He compared these accounts with descriptions of other spaces within the home where children are subject to more parental control. Notably he highlighted that whether a living room is a child space or an adult space can change with the time of day, and he showed how the timing of activities and the division of space can create liminal zones within the home. Reflecting on domestic tensions between adults and children about the use of different rooms within the home, Sibley (1995b) concluded that they represent a clash between adults' desire to establish order, regularity and strong boundaries, and children's preferences for disorder and weak boundaries. This focus on boundaries and segregation resurfaced in later work, with Bettina van Hoven, on the prison system in the US (van Hoven and Sibley, 2008), which explores the ways that the relationships between officer and inmates are shaped by the material geographies of the prison. Noting that the weak boundaries can result in anxieties about personal space, they conclude that power relations within the prison are shaped as much – if not more so – by interpersonal relations between inmates as by the technologies of 'panoptic' surveillance (see **Michel Foucault** on institutional surveillance).

KEY ADVANCES AND CONTROVERSIES

Sibley's work has proven pivotal and inspirational for geographers who are concerned with the role of the unconscious in everyday life (see Vol. 4 (3) of *Social and Cultural Geography*) as well as those seeking to construct anti-essentialist and relational theories of identity and space (Dwyer and Jones, 2000). In particular, Sibley's (1995a) *Geographies of Exclusion* has provided an important template for geographers who wished to understand how psychologically-rooted fears of the Other are reproduced in various societies (e.g., Takahashi, 1997; Hubbard, 1998). However, Sibley's psychoanalytic geographies are primarily focused around understanding boundary-making and spatial transgression through the work of 'object-relations' theory (especially the work of Julia Kristeva and Melanie Klein). Others have extended this engagement by exploring the exclusionary geographies implied in the work of Freud and Lacan; for example, Wilton (1998) has utilised Freud's concept of *unheimlich* (the uncanny) to explore processes of exclusion in his research on community opposition to human service facilities.

Other geographers have used Freud and/ or Lacan to re-theorise other aspects of the relationship between subjectivity and spatiality. For example, Steve Pile (1996) has brought the work of Freud and Lacan into dialogue with the work of **Henri Lefebvre** to think through the relationship of the body and the city, while Stuart Aitken (2001) has used both Freud and the object relations theorist Derek Winnicott to analyse the contested spaces of childhood. Moreover, given the emphasis placed on the production and repression of sexuality in many psychoanalytical theories, it is perhaps unsurprising that this geographic engagement with psychoanalysis has been particularly pronounced in feminist geography. Liz Bondi (1999), for example, has drawn on a number of psychoanalytic theories to think through the relationship between psychotherapeutic practice and an empathic human geography, while Heidi Nast (1998; 2000) has examined the spatialisation of Oedipalisation on a variety of different scales. Furthermore, Rose (1995; 1996) and Bondi (1997) have engaged with the ideas of Luce Irigaray to critique the epistemology of geographical enquiry itself. As such, while Sibley, along with Steve Pile and **Gillian Rose**, have been hugely important for initiating a 'psychoanalytic turn' in geography,

others have quickly forged new paths, adopting alternative theories and frameworks to examine a multitude of different issues.

Sibley's work has also been influential in the development of the subdisciplinary area of children's and young people's geographies. In a 1990 article published in the journal *Area*, James asked the question: 'Is there a place for children in geography?' (James, 1990). Sibley wrote a response to this in which he highlighted work on children within the discipline that had been largely overlooked, and made a case for the importance of understanding children's use of space. This debate did much to spark new interest in this field. The subsequent decade saw work on children's and young people's geographies begin to reach a critical mass (Skelton and Valentine, 1998; Holloway and Valentine, 2000). Sibley, along with Chris Philo, played an important role in this development, not only through his own work about adult–child relations and the bounding of space, but also through the support and encouragement he provided to young academics who were beginning to publish and organise conference sessions in this area.

Beyond his own work on adult–child relations, Sibley's theorisation of exclusion has been mobilised by others to explore young people's experiences of space. For example, Sibley's insistence that '[the] child/adult illustrates a contested boundary ... [and that] adolescence is an ambiguous zone within which the child/adult boundary can be variously located according to who is doing the categorizing' (Sibley, 1995a: 34–5) has been invoked by cultural geographers seeking to understand the fluid and shifting ways that 'youth' has been identified and constructed as a transitional category between childhood and adulthood (Skelton and Valentine, 1998). **Doreen Massey**, in her research on the spatial identities of youth cultures, also draws from Sibley's research on the territorialisation of space to demonstrate that strategies of spatial organisation are always embedded within the social production of identities (Massey, 1998). Drawing from case studies in Mexico and the UK, Massey argues that youth carve out their own spaces for interaction. Tim Lucas (1998) also finds Sibley's research useful in his own analysis of panic, anxiety and fear that is incited through local concerns with gang violence in Santa Cruz, California. Employing Sibley's insights on images of difference and the ways stereotypes collude to create landscapes of exclusion (Sibley, 1995a), Lucas points out that the social and spatial distancing of the city's Beach Flats area has been successfully invoked through oppressive representations of the community as 'an eyesore, dirty and unhealthy' (Lucas, 1998:148). Sibley's 'language of defilement' (Sibley 1995a: 55) serves to illuminate the ways the neighbourhood is framed and defined, thus creating geographies of representation that serve to exclude residents of the Beach Flats.

Though some geographers remain indif-ferent or even hostile to the language and methods of psychoanalysis (see Philo and Parr, 2003), there is little doubt that Sibley's development of psychoanalytical theory has thus greatly contributed to geographical understandings of Othering and segregation. Furthermore, his work on exclusion within the discipline, notably the ways that minority and women's voices are marginalised within geography have informed other geographer's critiques of the masculine and racist nature of the discipline. Overall, Sibley's insights on exclusion continue to play a formative role in creating space for new geographies to emerge that are open to different kinds of knowledges about how Self and Other are conceptualised.

SIBLEY'S KEY WORKS

Sibley, D. (1981) *Outsiders in Urban Societies*. New York: St Martin's Press.
Sibley, D. (1986) 'Persistence or change? Conflicting interpretations of peripheral minorities', *Environment and Planning D: Society and Space*, 4: 57–70.
Sibley, D. (1988) 'Survey 13: purification of space', *Environment and Planning D: Society and Space*, 6: 409–21.
Sibley, D. (1990) 'Invisible women? The contribution of the Chicago School of Social Service Administration to urban analysis', *Environment and Planning A*, 22: 733–45.
Sibley, D. (1991) 'Children's geographies: some problems of representation', *Area*, 3: 269–70.
Sibley, D. and Lowe, G. (1991) 'Boundary enforcement in the home environment and adolescent alcohol abuse', *Family Dynamics of Addiction Quarterly*, 1: 52–8.
Sibley, D. (1995a) *Geographies of Exclusion*. London: Routledge.
Sibley, D. (1995b) 'Families and domestic routines: constructing the boundaries of childhood', in S. Pile and N. Thrift (eds), *Mapping the Subject*. London: Routledge. pp. 123–37.
Sibley. D. (2001) 'The binary city', *Urban Studies*, 38: 239–50.
Sibley, D. (2003) 'Reflections on geography and psychoanalysis', *Social and Cultural Geography*, 4: 391–99.
Atkinson, D., Jackson, P., Sibley, D. and Washbourne, N. (eds) (2005) *Cultural Geography: A Critical Dictionary*. London: I.B. Tauris.
van Hoven, B. and Sibley, D. (2008) '"Just duck": the role of vision in the production of prison spaces', *Environment and Planning D: Society and Space*, 26 (6): 1001–17.

Secondary Sources and References

Aitken, S. (2001) *Geographies of Young People*. London: Routledge.
Bondi, L. (1997) 'In whose words? On gender identities, knowledge and writing practices', *Transactions of the Institute of British Geographers*, NS 22: 245–58.

Bondi, L. (1999) 'Stages on journeys: some remarks about human geography and psychotherapeutic practice', *Professional Geographer*, 51: 11–24.

Callard, F. (2003) 'The taming of psychoanalysis in geography', *Social and Cultural Geography*, 4 (3) : 295–312.

Douglas, M. (1966) *Purity and Danger*. Harmondsworth: Penguin.

Dwyer, O. and Jones, J.P. (2000) 'White socio-spatial epistemology', *Journal of Social and Cultural Geography*, 1: 209–22.

Griffiths, H., Poulter, I. and Sibley, D. (2000) 'Feral cats in the city', in C. Philo and C . Wilbert (eds), *Animal Spaces, Beastly Places: New Geographies of Human–animal Relations*. London: Routledge. pp. 56–70.

Holloway, S.L. and Valentine, G. (eds) (2000) *Children's Geographies: Playing, Living, Learning*. London: Routledge.

Hubbard, P. (1998) 'Community action and the displacement of street prostitution: evidence from British cities', *Geoforum*, 29: 269–86.

Hubbard, P. (2008) 'David Sibley's *Geographies of Exclusion*', in P. Hubbard, R. Kitchin and G. Valentine (eds), *Key Texts in Human Geography*. London: Sage. pp. 250–77.

James, S. (1990) 'Is there a place for children in geography?' *Area*, 22: 278–83.

Longhurst, R. (2001) 'Geography and gender: looking back, looking forward', *Progress in Human Geography*, 25: 641–8.

Lowe, G., Foxcroft, D. and Sibley, D. (1993) *Adolescent Drinking and Family Life*. London: Harwood.

Lucas, T. (1998) 'Youth gangs and moral panics in Santa Cruz, California', in T. Skelton and G. Valentine (eds), *Cool Places: Geographies of Youth Culture*. London: Routledge. pp. 145–60.

Massey, D. (1998) 'The spatial construction of youth cultures', in T. Skelton and G. Valentine (eds), *Cool Places: Geographies of Youth Cultures*. New York: Routledge. pp. 121–9.

Nast, H. (1998) 'Unsexy geographies', *Gender, Place and Culture*, 5: 191–206.

Nast, H. (2000) 'Mapping the "'unconscious": racism and the Oedipal family', *Annals of the Association of American Geographers*, 90: 215–55.

Okely, J. (1983) *The Traveller-gypsies*. Cambridge: Cambridge University Press.

Parr, H. and Philo, C. (2003) 'Psychoanalytic geographies: an introduction', *Social and Cultural Geography*, 4 (3): 283–93.

Philo, C. (1986) *The Same and The Other: On Geography, Madness and Outsiders*, Loughborough University of Technology, Department of Geography, Occasional Paper 11.

Philo, C. (1997) 'Of other rurals?', in P. Cloke and J. Little, (eds), *Contested Countryside Cultures: Otherness, Marginalisation and Rurality*. London: Routledge. pp.19–50.

Philo, C. and Parr, H. (2003) 'Psychoanalytical Geographies: An Introduction', *Social and Cultural Geography*, 4(3) : 283–93.

Pile, S. (1996) *The Body and the City: Psychoanalysis, Space and Subjectivity*. London: Routledge.

Rose, G. (1995) 'Distance, surface, elsewhere: a feminist critique of the space of phallocentric self/knowledge', *Environment and Planning D: Society and Space*, 13: 761–81.

Rose, G. (1996) 'As if the mirror had bled: masculine dwelling, masculinist theory and feminist masquerade', in N. Duncan (ed.), *BodySpace*. London: Routledge. pp. 56–74.

Sibley, D. (1970) 'Density gradients and urban growth', *Urban Studies*, 7: 294–7.

Sibley, D. (1972) 'Strategy and tactics in the selection of shop locations', *Area*, 4: 151–7.

Sibley, D. (1973) 'The density gradients of small shops in cities', *Environment and Planning*, 5: 233–40.

Sibley, D. (1978) 'Classification and control in local government', *Town Planning Review*, 49: 319–28.

Sibley, D. (1990) 'Urban change and the exclusion of minority groups in British cities', *Geoforum*, 21: 483–88.

Sibley, D. and Lowe, G. (1991) 'Boundary enforcement in the home environment and adolesent alcohol abuse', *Family Dynamics of Addiction Quarterly*, 1: 52–8.

Sibley, D. (1994) 'The sin of transgression', *Area*, 26: 300–3.

Sibley, D. (1998) 'Sensations and spatial science: gratification and anxiety in the production of ordered landscapes', *Environment and Planning A*, 30: 235–46.

Sibley, D. (1999) 'Comments on "Stages on Journeys" by Liz Bondi', *The Professional Geographer*, 51: 451–2.

Skelton, T. and Valentine, G. (eds.) (1998) *Cool Places: Geographies of Youth Cultures*. London: Routledge.

Takahashi, L. (1997) 'The socio-spatial stigmatisation of homelessness and HIV/AIDS: towards an explanation of the NIMBY syndrome', *Social Science and Medicine*, 45: 903–14.

Wilton R. (1998) 'The constitution of difference: space and psyche in landscapes of exclusion', *Geoforum*, 29: 173–85.

Minelle Mahtani, University of Toronto

50 Neil Smith

BIOGRAPHICAL DETAILS AND THEORETICAL CONTEXT

Neil Smith was born in Scotland in 1954 and completed a BA in Geography at the University of St Andrews. In 1977 he left Scotland for Baltimore, where he began PhD research into gentrification under the supervision of **David Harvey** at Johns Hopkins University (graduating in 1982). Though younger than Harvey, Smith underwent a similar academic and political transformation to that of his supervisor. This entailed a rejection of the kind of geography taught to him as an undergraduate – a so-called 'spatial science' that Harvey's late-1960s writings embodied – and an embrace of the Marxist approach that Harvey pioneered in his 1973 book *Social Justice and the City*.

At Johns Hopkins, Smith engaged deeply with the later works of nineteenth-century political economist Karl Marx. This engagement was, initially, focused on the issue of the gentrification of inner city neighbourhoods in Western cities. From the late 1960s a number of so-called 'ghettos' (or inner city blight areas) underwent redevelopment in cities like New York. This redevelopment had a physical and social dimension, wherein the removal and renovation of older buildings was accompanied by an influx of urban

professionals. Smith's principal concern, in his doctoral thesis, was to explain why gentrification occurs. The result was the concept of the 'rent gap' which Smith outlined and popularised in some of his early publications (e.g., Smith, 1979).

However, Smith's engagement with Marxism saw his interests spiral out from the issue of gentrification. This issue, Smith came to realise, was just one instance of a wider phenomena of uneven geographical development. Though a number of non-geographers had written insightfully about the causes of uneven development during the 1960s and 70s (e.g., Amin, 1977), few had done so with an eye for how space was what Harvey (1985a: 4) called 'an active moment' in the process. What is more, few of these authors had drawn-out the largely implicit theory of uneven development to be found in Marx's later writings about the operations of the capitalist economic system – a system that, by the late 1970s, was increasingly global in reach. The result was Smith's landmark book *Uneven Development* (1984) published while Smith was an Assistant Professor of Geography at Columbia University, New York. Like Harvey's magisterial *The Limits to Capital*, published two years earlier, *Uneven Development* was a major attempt to show how and why space matters to capitalism and capitalism to space. The book thereby served two principal purposes: it provided a theoretical basis for future work among an emergent Marxist community in the discipline of geography; and it was among the first books published within the wider, inter-disciplinary community of Marxists that inserted space into the core of Marx's theory of capitalism – Harvey and **Henri Lefebvre** being the two other main proponents of a spatialised Marxism at that time.

Uneven Development contained highly fertile ideas that subsequently inspired both Smith and a generation of radical geographers (it has been reissued twice, 1991 and 2008). Aside from uneven development, these ideas included 'the production of nature', the 'production of space' and the production of 'geographical scale' – the first and last of which will be explored below. Shortly after *Uneven Development* was published Smith moved to the Geography department at Rutgers University, New Jersey where he remained until 2000. There, he extended his earlier researches and embarked upon new ones. On the one side, he continued his theoretical and empirical inquiries into gentrification in New York and elsewhere, resulting in *The New Urban Frontier* (1996) and subsequent refinements and applications of the rent gap thesis (e.g., Hackworth and Smith, 2001). This was accompanied by a development of Smith's interest in geographical scale in the direction of what he called a 'spatialized politics' (Smith, 1992; 1993). This is a politics that recognises the importance of space in everyday life and shows struggles over the control of space to be flashpoints for power and resistance.

On the other side, Smith developed an interest in the role of professional geographers and geography as a discipline in their wider societies (e.g., Smith, 1986a; Smith and Godlewska, 1994). Specifically, he focused on the life of American political geographer Isaiah Bowman (1878–1950) and his role in America's rise to geo-political dominance before, during and after the Second World War. This resulted in *American Empire: Roosevelt's Geographer and the Prelude to Globalization* (2003) which sets Bowman in his academic and political context and shows the links between his intellectual work and US geo-political strategy (see also Smith, 1986a). This book is one of an emerging set of 'critical histories' of the production, circulation and use of geographical knowledge. These histories show that geographical ideas are political and material, altering the very realities they purport simply to describe. Smith's enduring interest in America's geo-political and geo-economic manoeuvrings on the world-stage, also produced *Endgame of Globalization* (2005). This book, echoing David Harvey's (2003) *The New Imperialism*, argued that America's global hegemony is on the wane – even as the country tries, not for the first time, to disguise its global ambitions in a rhetoric of liberal internationalism.

Latterly Professor in Anthropology at New York University (and a former Director of the Interdisciplinary Center for Place, Culture and Politics at the same institution), Smith's project has been to insert geographical concepts like space and nature into the heart of critical thinking whilst showing that geography is too important to be left to geographers alone. Within the discipline of geography he has been, alongside his former supervisor, a leading voice of the Left, having been a co-founder of the International Critical Geography Group, which aims through conferences and other means to create a transnational community of scholars and activists with interests in geography, power and resistance (Desbiens and Smith, 1999). Outside geography, he is recognised as an important voice, along with Harvey and Lefebvre, in the development and defence of a spatialised Marxism. Reflecting his strong desire to make academic inquiry relevant to real world struggles, virtually all Smith's writings are animated by political passion. Along with David Harvey and **Doreen Massey** he is arguably the closest thing the discipline of geography has to a 'public intellectual', having had opinion pieces published in *The New York Times, Newsday, The Philadelphia Inquirer, The Guardian*, and the *LA Times*.

SPATIAL CONTRIBUTIONS

As noted above, Smith's main intellectual contributions are theoretical ones (which is not to say that his empirical research has lacked significance) and include concepts crucial to debates on space and place such as the 'rent gap', 'the production of space', 'uneven geographical development', and the 'production of scale'. The first of these relates specifically to the issues of gentrification in Western cities. Smith observed in his doctoral research that many inner-city neighbourhoods spiral into decline until they reach a threshold point, after which a wave of capital investment leads to relatively rapid physical and social regeneration. This regeneration, he suggested, did not simply reflect the cultural preferences of certain groups for city-centre living. Nor, he argued, is regeneration straightforwardly 'good' because it entails the control of inner-city space by wealthy professional classes at the expense of existing low income residents – a process facilitated by property developments, local planners, and credit institutions (like banks). Why, Smith asked, does this 'flip' from decline to reinvestment occur? His answer was disarmingly simple (Smith, 1979). He observed that the economic

returns (or rent) to be made from land and buildings in any part of a city is only partly related to their physical properties and use value. Once a neighbourhood enters a decline – because, say the businesses that exist in it are no longer competitive compared to rival businesses elsewhere – then the actual rent starts to diverge from the 'potential ground rent' that could be earned from a different use of the land there. Over time a 'valley' of low rent appears between city centre and outer city areas until it becomes economical for investors to reinvest in the inner area with new residences and businesses. Of all the possible types of reinvestment, expensive private property investment is typically favoured because of the high profit margins to be had. The idea of the rent gap has received empirical confirmation in several Western cities since Smith first proposed it back in the late 1970s. Gentrification thus emerges as a class-based project in the built environment, driven by land and property developers intent on making money.

Smith's work on gentrification also connects to ideas on the social production of space. Like David Harvey, Smith has long argued that space is a product of social relations and processes rather than an empty matrix to be filled. In *Uneven Development* he formalised this idea with an extended presentation of the difference between 'absolute' and 'relative' space. Conventionally, space is viewed as absolute: that is, an empty grid within which things and process are located. This absolute view of space was, until relatively recently, dominant in academic geography – especially among 'spatial scientists' who sought to identify the geographical patterning of things *in and across space* (e.g., migration patterns, disease diffusion patterns, and so on). In *Uneven Development*, Smith expounded an alternative conception of relative space. Relative space contrasts with absolute space in at least two ways. First, it is *both an effect and cause of socio-economic processes*; that is, different socio-economic processes produce different spaces which, in turn, may reproduce or alter those processes. Second, relative space thus does not pre-exist its construction and its form cannot be determined a priori. Smith's conception of relative space helped open the way for a generation of critical human geographers to do research on how spaces are part and parcel of diverse forms of power and resistance in the contemporary world.

Of course, social researchers have long observed that economic and social development is geographically uneven. However, prior to Smith's *Uneven Development* it was often assumed that uneven development was a random or accidental outcome of economic growth and industrialisation. What Smith argued, by contrast, is that uneven development is a *systematic* and *necessary* aspect of modern capitalism. Thus, when agglomeration of industry and people occurs in one place and region it can, over time, lead to dis-economies (traffic congestion, increased land prices, etc.). Meanwhile, non-industrialised areas might become prime candidates for investment because of cheap land, unexploited resources, etc. Equally, over time technical innovations that allowed one area to gain a competitive advantage are copied in other places, leading to an equalisation in profit rates. This dialectic of geographical differentiation and equalisation, according to Smith, is ongoing, leading to the constant fall and decline of cities, regions and countries within contemporary capitalism. Though it once occurred through capitalism expanding 'outwards' into new territories, today it is increasing 'internal' to capitalism because few geographical pastures remain untouched by it.

As well as problematising the production of space, Smith has explored the production of scale. Like space, geographical scale is often thought to be fixed and given, as with the cartographic scale on a map. However, in a number of publications, Smith has elaborated a theory of geographical scale that shows scale to be actively constructed by societies (Smith, 1993). Thus scales like 'local', 'national' and 'global' are not given in nature but contingent and historically variable outcomes of various social processes. Thus, the European Union has come to overlay the borders and regulations of individual member states since its foundation, materially altering the objective and subjective meaning of 'Europe'. For Smith, the importance of scale is that it materially 'contains' actions and events with ambivalent consequences. Thus the powerful can seek to further their agendas by limiting the scale of action of those who oppose them. For example, in the West, many national governments have assisted big business by diluting the power of national trades unions so that worker–firm negotiations now take place primarily at the local scale. On the other side, those who lack power can attempt to 'upscale' their resistance activities to larger scales in order to be more effective. For instance, many trades unions have now constructed new global networks in order to combat the power of transnational firms (see Herod, 1995).

KEY ADVANCES AND CONTROVERSIES

Smith's writings have been very influential, primarily in the discipline of geography but increasingly beyond it too. First, his rent gap thesis remains a key idea in gentrification studies and has also ensured a Marxist voice has loomed large in these debates. Second, his notions of the production of space and uneven development helped, during the 1980s and 90s, to bolster the growing Marxist geography movement. Finally, his notion of the production of scale has inspired Marxist geographers and non-Marxists alike. A minor cottage industry researching geographical scale now exists and is in large part inspired by Smith's germinal thinking in this area (along with that of British geographer **Peter Taylor**). Key theorists in this new work on geographical scale are the geographer Kevin Cox (1998) and sociologist Neil Brenner (2001).

Unlike David Harvey, Smith's work has not been the subject of too much criticism by other geographers – though he, conversely, has often been a fierce critic of others' work. Specifically, he has been involved in three debates. First, in the early 1980s, he engaged with the work of the critical geographers Richard Peet (1981) and John Browett (1984) over the issues of space and uneven development respectively. The former, he argued, wrongly saw space as having effects 'in itself' and thus took Marxist geography down the wrong intellectual path (Smith, 1981). Browett accused Smith of misconstruing uneven development as a systematic and necessary dimension of capitalism, to which Smith responded uncompromisingly. Contra Browett, he showed that uneven geographical development is not merely a *contingent* outcome of ostensibly

'non-spatial' processes of economic growth and decline (Smith, 1986b). Second, during the mid-1980s, Smith chastised several British geographers for fixating on place at the expense of broader translocal processes that, today, make places what they are (Smith, 1987a; 1987b). Like **Doreen Massey**, Smith argued that the global is now *in* the local, not separate from it. This, he argued, means that a purely localist politics is inappropriate as well as reactionary. Finally, Smith's work on geographical scale has provoked implicit critiques. Where Smith sees scales as relatively hierarchical and enduring once they are socially produced, others think the metaphor of nested scales is inappropriate. For instance, Whatmore and Thorne (1997) prefer to talk of *networks* of greater or shorter length – networks of trade, production, finance, etc. This network metaphor does away with labels like 'local' and 'global' or 'place' and 'space'. It encourages a less rigid view of how the powerful and the less powerful construct geographical landscapes to suit their purposes.

Since the late 1980s, Smith's Marxism has broadened out intellectually and politically. He is recognised as a critical geographer seeking to build bridges among diverse radical causes and, arguably, has courted less disciplinary controversy than someone like Harvey for this reason. This said, he pulls no punches when he detects any challenge to fundamental Left-wing precepts of equality and justice (see Smith, 2005). His research and teaching remains thoroughly Marxist, even as he acknowledges the insufficiency of an exclusively Marxist outlook.

SMITH'S KEY WORKS

Smith, N. (1979) 'Toward a theory of gentrification: a back to the city movement by capital, not people', *Journal of the American Planning Association*, 45: 4: 538–48.

Smith, N. (1986b) 'On the necessity of uneven development', *International Journal of Urban and Regional Research*, 9: 87–104.

Smith, N. (1991/2008) *Uneven Development: Nature, Capital and the Production of Space*. Oxford: Basil Blackwell (2nd edition); Athens: University of Georgia Press (3rd edition).
Smith, N. (1993) 'Homeless/global: scaling places', in J. Bird, B. Curtis, T. Putnam, G. Robertson and L. Tickner (eds), *Mapping the Futures: Local Cultures, Global Change*. London: Routledge. pp. 87–119.
Smith, N. and Godlewska, A. (1994) (eds) *Geography and Empire: Critical Studies in the History of Geography*. Oxford: Basil Blackwell.
Smith, N. (1996) *New Urban Frontier: Gentrification and the Revanchist City*. New York: Routledge.
Smith, N. (2003) *American Empire*. Berkeley: University of California Press.
Smith, N. (2005) *Endgame of Globalization*. New York: Routledge.

Secondary Sources and References

Amin, S. (1977) *Imperialism and Unequal Development*. New York: Monthly Review Press.
Brenner, N. (2001) 'The limits to scale? Methodological reflections on scalar structuration', *Progress in Human Geography*, 25 (4): 591–614.
Browett, J. (1984) 'On the necessity and inevitability of uneven spatial development under capitalism', *International Journal of Urban and Regional Research*, 8: 155–76.
Cox, K.R. (1998) 'Spaces of dependence, spaces of engagement and the politics of scale, or: looking for local politics', *Political Geography*, 17(1): 1–24.
Desbiens, C. and Smith, N. (1999) 'The International Critical Geography Group: forbidden optimism?', *Environment and Planning D: Society and Space*, 18: 379–82.
Hackworth, J. and Smith, N. (2001) 'The changing state of gentrification', *Tijdschrift voor Economische en Sociale Geografie*, 92: 464–77.
Harvey, D. (1973) *Social Justice and The City*. London: Edward Arnold.
Harvey, D. (1982) *The Limits to Capital*. Oxford: Blackwell.
Harvey, D. (1985a) *The Urbanisation of Capital*. Oxford: Blackwell.
Harvey, D. (2003) *The New Imperialism*. Oxford: Oxford University. Press.
Herod, A. (1995) 'The practice of international labor solidarity', *Economic Geography*, 71 (4): 341–63.
Peet, R. (1981) 'Spatial dialectics and Marxist geography', *Progress in Human Geography*, 5 (1): 105–10.
Smith, N. (1981) 'Degeneracy in theory and practice: spatial interactionism and radical eclecticism', *Progress in Human Geography* 55, 111–18.
Smith, N. (1986a) 'Bowman's new world and the Council on Foreign Relations', *Geographical Review*, 76: 438–60.
Smith, N. (1987a) 'Rascal concepts, minimalizing discourse and the politics of geography', *Environment and Planning D: Society and Space*, 5: 377–83.
Smith, N. (1987b) 'Dangers of the empirical turn: some comments on the CURS initiative', *Antipode*, 19: 59–68.
Smith, N. (1992) 'Contours of a spatialized politics: homeless vehicles and the production of geographical scale', *Social Text*, 33: 54–81.
Smith, N. (2005) 'Neo-critical geography', *Antipode*, 37 (5): 887–99.
Whatmore, S. and Thorne, L. (1997) 'Nourishing networks', in D. Goodman and M. Watts (eds), *Globalising Food*. London: Routledge. pp. 287–304.

Noel Castree, University of Manchester

51   Edward W. Soja

BIOGRAPHICAL DETAILS AND THEORETICAL CONTEXT

American urban geographer, social theorist, and key member of the Los Angeles School of Urban Studies, Soja was born and raised in the Bronx. From the mid-1960s he undertook graduate research at Syracuse University, New York State. This formed the basis of his first book, *The Geography of Modernization in Kenya: A Spatial Analysis of Social, Economic, and Political Change* (1968). Although firmly located within the then dominant paradigm of spatial analysis, a tradition that Soja (1989: 51) was later to dismiss as little more than 'mathematized ... description', *The Geography of Modernization* was, nonetheless, organised around a leitmotiv that was to become central to all his subsequent work – the centrality of space in the constitution of society. As he wrote in the preface, *The Geography of Modernization* was underpinned 'by a strong feeling that the geographer's spatial perspective could contribute significantly to the rapidly expanding research cluster involved with the problems of social and economic change in developing areas' (Soja, 1968: v).

Teaching first at Northwestern University and then from 1972 at the Graduate School of Architecture and Urban Planning at the University of California, Los Angeles, Soja continued to explore the geography of Third World economic and social development through much of the 1970s (see Soja and Tobin, 1974; Soja and Weaver, 1976). However, mirroring developments elsewhere in human geography, his work gradually moved away from a wholehearted embrace of modernisation theory towards a radical scepticism of mainstream social science (Soja, 1979; Soja and Hadjimichalis, 1979). This scepticism was rooted in the belief that mainstream, positivistic, approaches failed to describe the underlying mechanisms behind persistent geographies of uneven development. This new scepticism not only signalled the development of a self-consciously critical edge to Soja's writing. It was also to produce a major shift in the focus of Soja's intellectual project. Throughout the next two decades Soja devoted his energies to an ambitious attempt to place spatiality at the centre of radical social theoretical thinking. This search for a thoroughly spatialised, postmodern, social theory produced three major books, *Postmodern Geographies: The Reassertion of Space in Critical Social Theory* (1989), *Thirdspace: Journeys to Los Angeles and Other Real-And-Imagined Places* (1996), and *Postmetropolis: Critical Studies in Cities and Regions* (2000), as well as more than a dozen major articles.

SPATIAL CONTRIBUTIONS

The primary elements of Soja's argument for a spatiality-oriented, postmodern social theory have remained basically unchanged over the course of the past quarter of a century, and can be summarised relatively straightforwardly. Indeed, each of his three postmodern books essentially offers refinements and repetitions of three central propositions:

1   that the capitalist order is being reorganised in ways that profoundly privilege the spatial over the temporal;
2   that spatiality is fundamentally constitutive of social life; and
3   that critical social theory needs to take space seriously if it is to make sense of society.

Here Soja's work echoes that of Marxist human geographers like **David Harvey**, Richard Peet, **Neil Smith**, and **Doreen Massey** – as well as a related group of more theoretically-eclectic writers such as **Anthony Giddens, Derek Gregory, Nigel Thrift, Allan Pred, Manuel Castells** and **John Urry** – who have sought to highlight the profound spatiality of social life. All these writers stress that in contrast to the fundamental emphasis placed on history and temporality in traditional social theory, spatiality has been profoundly under-acknowledged and unexplored. For Soja, however, this is not enough. Spatiality does not just need to be taken into account by social theorists; it must be placed firmly back at the centre of every element of social theory.

Establishing the basis of this claim is the central narrative obsession driving

Soja's (1989) *Postmodern Geographies*. In this influential and forcefully-argued case for the re-spatialisation of social theory, Soja asserts that critical social theory had not simply ignored space, it had actively repressed and denied spatiality. Space had been 'treated as fixed, the undialectical, the immobile. Time on the contrary was richness, fecundity, life, dialectic' (**Foucault** cited in Soja, 1989: 10). What Soja seeks to map out in *Postmodern Geographies* is an emerging counter-current within social theory that repudiates this dominant tradition of 'historicism' and instead reaches towards a spatialised mode of thinking based on 'a triple dialectic of space, time, and social being: a transformative re-theorization of the relations between history, geography and modernity' (Soja, 1989: 12). While this argument built upon the work of Marxist human geographers, *Postmodern Geographies* also sought to situate a number of more disparate writers within this counter-current. These included the Belgian economic historian Ernst Mandel (who was praised for his recognition of the spatiality central to the recurring cyclical crises of capitalist accumulation), as well as cultural commentators including John Berger, Marshall Berman and Fredric Jameson (who were seen as offering incisive accounts of how the experience of lived space was being profoundly reworked under conditions of contemporary capitalism). More purely theoretical sustenance was offered by Michel Foucault, John Paul Sartre, Martin Heidegger, and Anthony Giddens, each of whom had in some way sought to place spatiality at the centre of their theoretical projects.

Rising above all these thinkers is the figure of **Henri Lefebvre**. An idiosyncratic French Marxist whose intellectual energies were focused principally on exploring everyday life and the process of urbanisation, Lefebvre had since the 1960s been arguing that the production of spatiality, rather than history, had become the central armature of capitalist development and contradiction. As he wrote in his short book *The Survival of Capitalism*:

> The dialectic is back on the agenda. But it is no longer Marx's dialectic, just as Marx's was no longer Hegel's ... The dialectic today no longer clings to historicity and historical time, or to a temporal mechanism such as 'thesis-antithesis-synthesis' or 'affirmation-negation-negation of the negation' ... To recognise space, recognise what 'takes place' there and what it is used for, is to resume the dialectic: analysis will reveal the contradictions of space.
>
> (Lefebvre, 1976, cited in Soja, 1989: 43)

Lefebvre's thesis provides the central logical framework of *Postmodern Geographies*, and Soja's wider postmodern project. It is through the filter of Lefebvre's claims for the centrality of spatiality in social life that Soja interprets the theoretical materials discussed in *Postmodern Geographies*. And it is through the use of this Lefebvrian filter that Soja can make the argument that the diverse collection of writers brought together in his writing do indeed offer an outline of a new kind of postmodern human geography.

For those familiar with conventional accounts of postmodernism, Soja's postmodernism is idiosyncratic. Indeed, more than one reviewer of *Postmodern Geographies* suggested that Soja was 'a postmodernist with an identity crisis' (Resch, 1992: 146). Given that a common thread of the self-consciously postmodern philosophical project that emerged in the 1970s and 1980s was an 'incredulity towards metanarratives' (Lyotard, 1984: xxiv), particularly those of Marxism, Soja's attempt to tie postmodernism to a Marxian-inflected

historical materialism appears problematic. Soja, however, views his postmodern geographies as postmodern because they recognise the salience of Lefebvre's claim that 'it is now space more than time that hides things from us' and, following on from this, 'that the demystification of spatiality and its veiled instrumentality of power is the key to making practical, political, and theoretical sense of the contemporary era' (Soja, 1989: 61). He consequently argues that the postmodern epoch should be read as the latest manifestation of a series of waves of capitalist development, and that the aim of postmodern social theory is to make sense of the capitalist restructuring that has brought this epoch into being.

Defining postmodernism in this unusual and idiosyncratic way, Soja sought to capture the idea of the postmodern for the politically-progressive traditions of the radical, socialist left. He also sought to compel leftist researchers to grasp the fundamental originality of the contemporary geo-historical moment. So while the bulk of *Postmodern Geographies* is devoted to establishing the conceptual ground for a spatialised, postmodern social theory rooted within the broad traditions of historical materialism, it concludes with two chapters that illustrate what an empirically-informed postmodern account might look like. Both chapters focus on Los Angeles, which Soja argues offers a privileged window on the ferocious restructuring processes that shape the postmodern world:

> Ignored for so long as aberrant, idiosyncratic, or bizarrely exceptional, Los Angeles, in another paradoxical twist, has more than any other place, become the paradigmatic window through which to see the last half of the twentieth century.
>
> (Soja, 1989: 221)

These empirical investigations present an overview of the fundamental geo-economic imperatives that had been reshaping the social space of the Los Angeles metropolitan area. Yet, within Soja's view of 'an emerging post-Fordist urban landscape filled with more flexible systems of production, consumption, exploitation, spatialisation and social control' (Soja, 1989: 221) something seemed to be missing. For all the rhetorical flourishes and complex narrative structure, Soja's postmodern account did not seem in essence much different to that presented by more conventional urban political economists. This raises the obvious question: if it is not that different why expend so much trying to stake a claim for it?

KEY ADVANCES AND CONTROVERSIES

Postmodern Geographies was a hugely influential book. It brought together in a lucid form a key collection of articles by an author at the forefront of the attempt to place human geography within the mainstream of social theory. It also presented one of the first responses by a human geographer to the challenge of postmodernism (see Graham, 2006; Wharf, 2006; Soja, 2006). But while the breadth and erudition of Soja's scholarship was widely acknowledged both within human geography and the wider social science community, the vision of a postmodern geography set out in *Postmodern Geographies* met with widespread and frequently vociferous criticism.

Three central criticisms were aimed at *Postmodern Geographies*. The first criticism was that the basic premise of *Postmodern Geographies* was simply unfounded. The world might be changing in rapid and

unexpected ways but this was no reason to ditch established modes of analysis in favour of some kind of postmodernism (see Short, 1993; de Pater, 1993). A second set of criticisms more sympathetic to the idea of postmodernism was perhaps more telling. A key attraction of postmodernism was its democratic, eclectic, and inclusive ethos. Yet, in some ways Soja appeared to be suspicious of this pluralistic spirit, or – in the case of feminism's engagement with postmodern thinking – strangely unaware of its significance (see Gregory, 1994; Massey, 1994; **Rose**, 1991). For all its positive attributes, *Postmodern Geographies* was therefore criticised by some commentators for offering a limiting and emaciated reading of the postmodern: as **Dear** (1991: 653) wrote in a generally sympathetic commentary on *Postmodern Geographies*, the 'brilliant potential [of postmodernism] has been tempered by the discipline of Marxist thought.' A third set of criticisms centred on the way *Postmodern Geographies*, despite its claims to be profoundly concerned with everyday spatialities, constantly reduced the everyday to little more than an epiphenomenon of underlying economic processes. This is most obvious in the final chapters on Los Angeles where Soja, while stating his intention to show how the experience of space and time in the metropolis was being transformed, offers the reader what is very much a god's-eye view of the city. Rather than a living spatiality Soja offers 'a morphology of landscape that ... is rarely disturbed by human forms' (Gregory, 1994: 301).

In *Thirdspace: Journeys to Los Angeles and Other Real-And-Imagined Places* (1996) and *Postmetropolis: Critical Studies of Cities and Regions* (2000), Soja sought to respond to these critiques by further elaborating his vision of a radically spatialised, postmodern analysis. As such, Soja introduces a number of new concepts to clarify and crystallise the key co-ordinates of his project. The 'socio-spatial dialectic' (see Soja, 1980) is refined into the notion of a *trialectics of being* – the insight that the ontology of being can only be interpreted by examining the interlocking of spatiality, historicality, and sociality. In a similar way, *thirdspace* comes to absorb the idea of a postmodern analysis, referring both to a style of analysis that places a spatialised trialectics at its centre and the particular texture of everyday lived spaces that exceeds the compartmentalised knowledges of the conventional social sciences. Furthermore, Soja is keen to demonstrate the openness of his postmodern/thirdspace project; **Henri Lefebvre** retains his privileged position, but a new range of postcolonial and feminist writers like **bell hooks**, **Homi Bhabha**, **Edward Said**, **Gayatri Spivak**, Gloria Anzaldúa, and **Gillian Rose** become part of Soja's project. Yet, for all this, huge swathes of the social sciences are simply dismissed for their narrow focus on what is dubbed firstspace (i.e., 'the 'real' material world') or secondspace (i.e., 'imagined' representations of spatiality' – Soja, 1996: 6). For Soja, thirdspace is *the* privileged space of analysis, despite the fact for all the hundreds of pages of *Thirdspace* and *Postmetropolis* it remains a slippery term:

> *Everything* comes together in Thirdspace: subjectivity and objectivity, the abstract and the concrete, the real and the imagined, the knowable and the unimaginable, the repetitive and the differential, structure and agency, mind and body, consciousness and unconsciousness, the disciplined and the transdisciplinary, everyday life and unending history.
>
> (Soja, 1996: 56–7, original emphasis)

Thirdspace is claimed to encompass everything there is to say about anything (and perhaps, as a result, nothing at all?). Indeed, one reviewer (Barnett,

1997: 529) was moved to wonder, after quoting the above passage, 'Is Elvis still alive in Thirdspace?'

Facetious though this comment sounds it does point to an on-going problem within *Thirdspace* and *Postmetropolis*. In his keenness to stress just how new his 'radical postmodernism' (Soja 1996: 3) is, Soja seems to completely de-anchor himself from any established intellectual tradition. This compels him to work at a level of abstraction that undermines some of the most productive and interesting elements of his argument. As Barnett – the unsympathetic reviewer quoted above– wrote of *Thirdspace*, throughout the book, terms like the trialectics of being and thirdspace 'are discussed at a very high level of "ontological" generality, which tends to obscure the fact that all Soja seems to be saying is that time, space and society are mutually constitutive' (Barnett, 1997: 528; see also Merrifield, 1999; Price, 1999; Soja, 1999).

Indeed, while much of the critical reception of both *Thirdspace* and *Postmetropolis* focused on Soja's theoretical arguments, the most compelling sections of both books are where Soja turns to describing the contemporary metropolitan condition. In these sections, the majority of which like *Postmodern Geographies* focus on Los Angeles, Soja presents a series of routes through what he calls the contemporary postmetropolis: the new spaces of industrialisation and economic exploitation ('the postfordist industrial metropolis'); the city turned inside out ('the exopolis'); the city reshaped by globalisation ('the cosmopolis'); the city of multiple and divided sociality ('the fractal city'); the privatised and sanitised city ('the carceral archipelago'); and spaces of urban simulation ('simcities'). Taken together, and combined with Soja's attempt in the opening chapters of *Postmetropolis* to outline a geo-historical account of the importance of urban agglomeration (what he calls 'synekism') to all social development, these accounts offer some of the most comprehensive and daring attempts to summarise and interpret what is happening to the Western cityscape over the past two decades.

As one of a small number of human geographers whose writing has been taken up and read by cultural theorists and the wider social science community, Soja's contribution to contemporary debates around the spatiality of social life are substantial. *Postmodern Geographies* – and to a lesser extent *Thirdspace* and *Postmetropolis* – are notable achievements. They offer a remarkable attempt to re-imagine the human geographic project. Indeed, perhaps the greatest legacy of Soja's work is not the idea of a postmodern geography *per se*; rather it is how his writing has widened the theoretical and conceptual horizons of both human geography and the social sciences in general. Soja's work has not only made a compelling case for the profound importance of spatiality, it has helped generate an enormously fecund dialogue between human geography and critical social theory, whilst at the same time demonstrating the productiveness of experimenting with innovative forms and styles of presentation and argumentation.

SOJA'S KEY WORKS

Soja, E. W. (1968) *The Geography of Modernization in Kenya: A Spatial Analysis of Social, Economic and Political Change.* Syracuse, NY: Syracuse University.

Soja, E. W. (1989) *Postmodern Geographies: The Reassertion of Space in Critical Social Theory.* London: Verso.

Soja, E. W. (1996) *Thirdspace: Journeys to Los Angeles and Other Real-And-Imagined-Places.* Oxford: Blackwell.

Soja, E. W. (2000) *Postmetropolis: Critical Studies of Cities and Regions.* Oxford: Blackwell.

Soja, E.W. (2010) *Seeking Spatial Justice.* Minneapolis: University of Minnesota Press.

Secondary Sources and References

Barnett, C. (1997) 'Review of *Thirdspace*', *Transactions of the Institute of British Geographers,* NS 22 (3): 529–30.

De Pater, B. (1993) 'The quest for disorder: on the dogma of a contingent, chaotic world', *Tidschrift voor Economische en Sociale Geografie,* 84 (3): 175–7.

Dear, M. (1991) 'Review of Edward Soja *Postmodern Geographies: The Reassertion of Space in Critical Social Theory*', *Annals of the Association of American Geographers,* 80 (4): 649–54.

Graham, E. (2006) '*Postmodern Geographies* – Commentary 1', *Progress in Human Geography,* 30 (6): 812–14.

Gregory, D. (1994) *Geographical Imaginations.* Oxford: Blackwell.

Lefebvre, H. (1976) *The Survival of Capitalism.* London: Allen and Busby.

Lyotard, J-F. (1986) *The Postmodern Condition: A Report on Knowledge.* Manchester: Manchester University Press.

Massey, D. (1994) *Space, Place, and Gender.* Cambridge: Polity.

Merrifield, A. (1999) 'The extraordinary voyages of Ed Soja: inside the 'trialectics of spatiality', *Annals of the Association of American Geographers,* 89 (2): 345–8.

Philo, C. (1992) 'Foucault's geography', *Environment and Planning D: Society and Space,* 10: 137–61.

Price, P. (1999) 'Longing for less of the same', *Annals of the Association of American Geographers,* 89 (2): 342–4.

Resch, R. (1992) 'Review of Edward Soja – *Postmodern Geographies: The Reassertion of Space in Critical Social Theory*', *Theory and Society,* 21 (1): 145–54.

Rose, G. (1991) 'Review of Edward Soja – *Postmodern Geographies: The Reassertion of Space in Critical Social Theory* and David Harvey – *The Condition of Postmodernity: An Enquiry into the Origins of Cultural Change*', *Journal of Historical Geography*, 17 (1): 118–121.

Short, J. (1993) 'The "myth" of postmodernism', *Tijdschrift voor Economische en Sociale Geografie*, 84 (3): 169–71.

Soja, E. W. (1979) 'The geography of modernisation: a radical reappraisal', in R. A. Obudho and F. Taylor (eds), *The Spatial Structure of Development*. Boulder: Westview. pp. 28–45.

Soja, E. W. (1980) 'The socio-spatial dialectic', *Annals of the Association of American Geographers*, 70: 207–25.

Soja, E. W. (1999) 'Keeping space open', *Annals of the Association of American Geographers*, 89 (2): 348–53.

Soja, E. W. (2006) 'Writing geography differently', *Progress in Human Geography*, 30 (6): 817–20.

Soja, E. W. and Hadjimichalis, C. (1980) 'Between historical materialism and spatial fetishism: some observations of the development of Marxist spatial analysis', *Antipode*, 11 (3): 3–11.

Soja, E. W. and Tobin, R. (1974) 'The geography of modernization: paths, patterns, and processes of spatial change in developing countries', in G. Brewer and R. D. Brunner (eds), *Political Development and Change: A Policy Approach*. New York: Free Press. pp. 197–243.

Soja, E. W. and Weaver, C. (1976) 'Urbanization and underdevelopment in east Africa', in B. Berry (ed.), *Urbanization and Counterurbanization*. Beverly Hills: Sage. pp. 233–66.

Warf, B. (2006) '*Postmodern Geographies* – Commentary 2', *Progress in Human Geography*, 30 (6): 814–17.

Alan Latham, University College London

52 Gayatri Chakravorty Spivak

BIOGRAPHICAL DETAILS AND THEORETICAL CONTEXT

Gayatri Chakravorty Spivak was born in Calcutta, in colonial India, in 1942 to a middle-class family. The experiences of colonisation, the struggle for independence and 'post-colonialism' have been central to her work. She graduated from the Presidency College of the University of Calcutta in 1959 with first-class honours in English having received gold medals for English and Bengali literature. Spivak was highly conscious that the teaching of English Literature in colonial India was a central part of the 'civilising mission' of imperialism. In 'Three women's texts and a critique of imperialism' she argues that 'it should not be possible to read nineteenth-century British literature without remembering that imperialism, understood as England's social mission, was a crucial part of the cultural representation of England to the English' (Spivak, 1985: 243).

Spivak continued her education in the US where she pursued a Masters degree (1962) in English at Cornell University. She also spent a year in Britain at Cambridge University as a fellow at Girton College before returning to the US to take up an instructors' post at the University of Iowa. At the same time she worked on a PhD (awarded in 1967). Her doctoral dissertation was on the work of Irish poet W.B. Yeats, undertaken again at Cornell University, supervised by Paul de Man (1919–1983). Spivak was appointed Avalon Foundation Professor in the Humanities at the Department of English and Comparative Literature at Columbia University (New York) in 1992, alongside **Edward Said** (1935–2003). A frequent traveller and engaging guest speaker, Spivak is often invited to speak across many disciplines as well as outside the academy in activist circles and at literary events.

A useful guide to her work begins by noting that:

> Gayatri Chakravorty Spivak is best known for her overtly political use of contemporary cultural and critical theories to challenge the legacy of colonialism on the way we read and think about literature and culture. What is more, Spivak's critical interventions encompass a range of theoretical interests, including Marxism, feminism, deconstruction, postcolonial theory and cutting-edge work on globalization.
>
> (Morton, 2003: 1)

Thus for many geographers and other scholars, the name of Gayatri Chakravorty Spivak is synonymous with deconstruction and post-colonial feminism. It is no secret, however, that Spivak's work with its dense style sometimes promotes elitism or invokes dismissal. It certainly defies easy summary. Perhaps too there is sometimes an impression that those who are able to extract meaning from her works have gained access to a select circle of intellectuals who have demonstrated their intellectual capacity 'to know' by referencing Spivak (we will return to this issue of style later). Amongst her vast range of book-length published work is a translation into English and critical introduction to Jacques Derrida's *De la Grammatologie* (1976); other works include *In Other Worlds: Essays in Cultural Politics* (1987); *Outside in the Teaching Machine* (1993); *A Critique of Post-Colonial Reason* (1999); and *Other Asias* (2005). Most of these books comprise sets of essays, sometimes retaining the tone of the original spoken delivery (though supported with extensive footnotes and references). She has also authored dozens of articles, some of the most influential being: 'Three women's texts and a critique of imperialism' (1985); 'Poststructuralism, marginality, postcoloniality and value' (1990a); 'Can the subaltern speak?' (1988a) and 'Who claims alterity?' (1989). Throughout, Spivak's work draws on and is informed by the key conceptual frameworks of Marxism, feminism and deconstruction.

Spivak's introduction to deconstruction was via Paul de Man who was its most prominent advocate in the US at a time when Derrida was making similar arguments in Europe. Both de Man and Derrida questioned the stability and transparency of textual meaning. Deconstruction developed as a critique of 'logocentrism', wary of the privileging of an authoritative presence held to be characteristic of much Western thought. It is, in part, an approach to reading. Yet it is not so much a method as a strategy for de-linking, destabilising and undermining these oppositions by revealing their mutual constitution. Barbara Johnson (1980: 5) thus notes 'the deconstruction of a text does not proceed by random doubt or arbitrary subversion, but the careful

teasing out of warring forces of signification within the text.' For Spivak:

> Deconstruction does not say there is no subject, there is no truth. It simply questions the privileging of identity so that someone is believed to have the truth. It is not the exposure of error. It is constantly and persistently looking into how truths are produced. That's why deconstruction doesn't say logocentrism is a pathology, or metaphysical enclosures are something you can escape. Deconstruction, if one wants a formula, is among other things, a persistent critique of what one cannot not want.
>
> (Spivak, 1994: 280)

SPATIAL CONTRIBUTIONS

The sheer density of Spivak's prose means that the geographical applications of her work are not necessarily immediately obvious. Moreover, it is difficult to entirely separate her from Derrida's impacts (recall that she translated *De la Grammatologie*). Anglophone geographers have also cited Derrida frequently since the 1990s. However, one contribution to geography relates to the so-called 'crisis of representation' and the vexed issue of 'positionality' (see **Gregory** 1994; England, 1994; Radcliffe, 1994; Robinson, 1994; Barnett, 1995; **Rose**, 1997; Sidaway 1992). In this context, Spivak's work has been drawn on to highlight the ethnocentricity of hegemonic knowledges and problematise Western, modernist epistemologies. Spivak's (1990a: 224) concern with 'the imbrication of techniques of knowledge with strategies of power' is that representations do not just describe reality but are constitutive of it. Spivak

(1988a) elaborates on this when she defines representation as both 'a speaking of' that describes or depicts a perceived reality, through language and communication and a 'speaking for' which is the same as the representation of a particular constituency (Spivak, 1988a).

In her essay 'Can the subaltern speak?', she deals directly with such questions, and takes issue with the radical claims by intellectuals to speak for the disempowered, placing them alongside the benevolent colonialists who saved Hindu women from widow sacrifice in the nineteenth century. In doing so, Spivak argues that such interlocutors (even as they claim to represent and speak for the disempowered) have silenced subordinated subalterns (where the latter are distinguished in their class, gender and 'caste'). The subaltern may speak, but she is misheard, ignored or her words and actions are misinterpreted by a dominant culture whose terms of meaning, truth and understanding exclude subalterns by positioning them and interpreting their actions through dominant frames of reference. She examines how, in Morton's (2003: 57) terms; 'the historical and structural conditions of political representations do not guarantee that the interests of particular subaltern groups will be recognised or that their voices will be heard.'

At the same time, she argues that Western feminisms have sometimes propagated the 'lie of a global sisterhood', failing to recognise the differences between women (Spivak, 1986: 226). In response to such critiques, the questions of differences *between* women have occupied feminist geographers particularly in terms of the implications for the production of geographical knowledge (**McDowell**, 1993). This has seen feminist geographers at the forefront of debates on the implications of the politics of representation for the production of geography both in terms

of fieldwork and writing (**Barnes** and Duncan, 1992; Duncan and Sharp, 1993; **Gregory**, 1994; **Katz**, 1992; Katz, 1996; Mohammed, 2001; Nast, 1994) leading to ongoing debates about ways out of this dilemma.

For Spivak, an 'insider' can simultaneously be an 'outsider'. She argues that authorial claims based on one-dimensional experience of marginality serve to negate multiple differences which distinguish and mark the distance of those being represented from the researcher/writer. Thus 'Other' or 'Third World' intellectuals may be regarded by some as the 'authentic inhabitants of the margin' (Spivak, 1990a: 224), positioned to legitimately speak on behalf of their group, constituting and adjudicating both the 'limits of knowledge about the Other and the graphematic space the latter occupies/inscribes' (Spivak, 1990b: 175). But it is precisely the Third World intellectual's distance from the wholly Other – produced by the uneven experience of oppression – that positions some 'Others' closer to the 'Same', from which they derive the power to speak for the subaltern.

Another way in which questions of representation have been registered in geography is in the history of the discipline. Spivak offers inspiration to those who would seek alternative histories and lineages of geographical writing in the age of formal European imperialism. To McEwan, therefore, Spivak offers some pathways to the recovery of subaltern agency and presence in the critical re-examination of colonial geography and exploration:

> Deconstructing the colonial archive also allows for a more subtle analysis of the production of geographical knowledge, and the possibility of decentring a putatively western tradition by viewing the production of those knowledges as a complex process of cultural exchange and

negotiation, in which colonized populations played an active part.

(McEwan, 1998: 374)

Similarly, Spivak offers some departures for re-thinking geographies of development by reconceptualising development as a project whose origins and trajectory are imbued with both the potential for liberation and the reality of enduring forms of imperial, class and gender inequality (Radcliffe, 1994, Wainwright, 2008). Likewise, when Spivak (as in her 1998 essay on 'Revisiting the "Global Village"') interprets the former as a mode of 'cultural talk' that recodes disjuncture and difference but whose parameters derive from capitalism and imperialism, geographers have seized the deconstructive impulse in Spivak and others to problematise the discourse of 'globalisation' and the assumptions about its pervasiveness and putative power (Gibson-Graham, 1996).

KEY ADVANCES AND CONTROVERSIES

For some, Spivak's density of writing and her mode of deconstruction may be off-putting – or worse. Terry Eagleton (1999) for example, called Spivak's *A Critique of Post-Colonial Reason* 'obscurantist'. Edward Said (1983) had earlier criticised the style of some literary theory that 'alienates' rather than communicates with the reader, something that for many is confirmed by Spivak's work. For Said, the dense jargon [of literary theory] 'obscures' social reality and 'encourage[s] a scholarship of "modes of excellence" very far from daily life' (Said, 1983: 4).

Moreover, Spivak's avowed political aim is to understand the oppressed, the marginalised, the excluded, the subaltern. How can this be pursued through the act of reading, of deconstruction? How can Spivak reconcile such political aims with the charges of textual idealism that have sometimes been levelled at deconstruction, apparently confirmed in the contention that 'there is nothing outside of the text' (Derrida, 1976: 158)?

Yet Spivak (1988a) deploys deconstruction to contend with such problematic and limited understanding of texts. Instead, her deconstruction follows Derrida's understanding of the text:

> The text is not the book; it is not confined in a volume, itself confined to the library. It does not suspend reference – to history, to the world, to reality.

(Derrida, 1988: 137)

Rather it is:

> differential network, a fabric of traces referring endlessly to something other than itself, to other differential traces. Thus the text over runs all the limits assigned to it so far (not submerging or drowning them in an undifferentiated homogeneity, but rather making them more complex, dividing and multiplying strokes and lines) – all the limits, everything that was set up in opposition to writing (speech, life, the world, the real, history, ... every field of reference – to body or mind, to conscious or unconscious, politics, economics, and so forth).

(Derrida, 1979: 84–5)

'There is nothing outside the text' might therefore mean texts contain multiple traces of the wider world, and/or that the world is rendered through a series of 'texts'; not simply literary texts and codes, but perhaps other inscriptions of difference and meaning (such as accounts and systems of value like money). Following

Derrida, Spivak's work aims to make visible the constitution of the world in and through the fabric and fabrication of texts; for example those that elaborate government policies or produce legal apparatus. Thus Spivak utilises the strategy of deconstruction, of reading texts, to pursue political goals that are also very much informed by Marxism, feminism and anti-imperialism.

Two key areas of Spivak's contribution have therefore been on post-colonial issues relating to class and gender. In relation to the former, Spivak reads Marx creatively. Her deconstructive approach to texts (including that of *Das Kapital* itself) in sympathy with Marx's determination to expose the categories of value, economy and class to critical scrutiny (Castree, 1997). And in her essay on 'Supplementing Marxism', Spivak rethinks the meaning and definition of socialism, which becomes a project that:

> is not in opposition to the form of the capitalist mode of production. It is rather a constant pushing away – a differing and a deferral – of the *capital*-ist harnessing of the social mobility of capital.

(Spivak, 1995: 119)

In specific terms, Spivak (1989) illuminates the continued disempowerment of the 'Subaltern' in post-colonial India. With reference to internal colonisation, transnational capitalism and new forms of imperial power, she explains how the national independence movement left the existing highly polarised class structure in South Asia more or less intact. The Subaltern Studies group of radical historians of India (see Chari, 2009) have sought to rewrite a history from below, but Spivak engages with some of the limits to this. She has drawn on the work of Subaltern Studies to argue that Western Marxism has proven unable to represent the complexity of subaltern histories of insurgency and resistance. Spivak thus questions the ability of both conventional nationalist histories or of Western Marxism (even as developed by the Subaltern Studies group) to recover and represent the historical roles of disenfranchised Indians (see Morton, 2003).

For Spivak, Marxism and feminism are vital political projects, but she argues these should be supplemented with deconstruction to provide those conceptual tools or vocabulary that would do justice to the everyday lives of marginalised (subaltern) women – both historically and in the present day – for such lives are complex, contradictory, and frequently obscured from view. They are written out of history, or invoked as passive masses or victims without their subjectivity intact and therefore represented minus their capacity to make history and geography. Moreover, the geo-political category of the 'Third World' is, for Spivak, to be questioned in terms that regard it as not simply as a place or space that is a mere supplement to the Western history of capitalism. Instead Spivak sees it as a necessary (but neglected) constituent of that wider history; without which Western hegemony and capitalism could not have taken its exploitative course.

Rather than attempting to represent 'Third World' women Spivak has thus sought to disrupt the codes and conventions of Western knowledges that have sought to represent the Third World. In 'Literary representation of the subaltern' (1988b) Spivak provides a critical reading of the work of Mahasweti Devi, the 'Breast Giver' (1995). The 'Breast Giver' follows the life of the protagonist Jashoda who is employed as a wet nurse in an upper-class, high-caste Bengali household. Spivak highlights the limits of the bourgeois 'Mother India' ideal, marking the failure of Indian nationalist projects to eliminate gendered-classed oppressions. She also draws on this work to point out to Western feminists that women's reproductive labour is not always unwaged and domestic. In 'Three women's texts and imperialism' (1985) Spivak reads Bronte's (1847) *Jane Eyre* against the hegemonic Western feminist readings which she argues point to the complicity of Western feminism and imperialism. Such readings celebrate *Jane Eyre* as a text that privileges the narrative of its female protagonist who is read as a liberated Western female individual. Spivak's reading finds Jane's liberation as an individual rests on the representation of Bertha Mason (the Jamaican Creole, who is the 'mad' first wife of Jane's fiancé Rochester), as 'Other' as 'not yet human' (Spivak, 1985: 247).

Spivak's (2003) *Death of a Discipline* returns to the issue of the production of disciplinary knowledge in the context of translation, globalisation and diversity. In particular she draws attention to the ways in which the business (flows of money, bottom lines and profits) of knowledge production shapes fields such as comparative literature. The US becomes a centre of publication and academic authority which then travel back to influence the sites where 'foreign' literatures originate. A similar interrogation of categories is sustained in *Other Asias* (2008): an eclectic set of essays about comparative area studies, disciplinary knowledges and what is signified by the term 'Asia' in the context of geo-political and economic shifts. Throughout these and her extensive breadth of writings and interviews, Spivak's attention to the 'margins' and the occlusion of difference will continue to be instructive for those who take the time and trouble to engage carefully with her works and to tease out their mappings of enduring colonial legacies and indictments of neo-colonial complicities.

SPIVAK'S KEY WORKS

Spivak, G. C. (1985) 'Three women's texts and a critique of imperialism', *Critical Inquiry*, 12: 243–61.

Spivak, G. C. (1987) *In Other Worlds: Essays in Cultural Politics*. New York: Methuen.

Spivak, G. C. (1988a) 'Can the subaltern speak? Speculations on widow sacrifice', in C. Nelson and L. Grossberg (eds), *Marxism and the Interpretation of Culture*. London: Macmillan. pp. 271–313.

Spivak, G. C. (1988b) 'Literary representations of the subaltern', in R. Guha (ed.), *Subaltern Studies*. New Delhi: Oxford University Press. pp. 86–111.

Spivak, G. C. (1989) 'Who claims alterity', in B. Kruger and P. Mariani (eds), *Remaking History*. Dia Art Foundation Discussions in Contemporary Culture No. 4. Seattle: Bay Press. pp. 269–92.

Spivak, G. C. (1990a) 'Poststructuralism, marginality, postcoloniality and value', in P. Collier and H. Geyer-Ryan (eds), *Literary Theory Today*. Cambridge: Polity Press. pp. 219–44.

Spivak, G. C. (1993) *Outside in the Teaching Machine*. New York: Routledge.

Spivak, G. C. (1994) 'Bonding in difference', in A. Arteaga (ed.), *An Other Tongue: Nation and Ethnicity in the Linguistic Borderlands*. Durham: Duke University Press. pp. 273–83.

Spivak, G. C. (1995) 'Supplementing Marxism', in C. Cullenberg and B. Magbus (eds), *Whither Marxism: Global Crises in International Perspective*. New York: Routledge. pp. 109–19.

Spivak, G. C. (1999) *A Critique of Post-Colonial Reason: Toward a History of the Vanishing Present*. Cambridge, MA: Harvard University Press.

Spivak, G. C. (2003) *Death of a Discipline*. New York: Columbia University Press.

Spivak, G. C. (2008) *Other Asias*. Malden, MA: Blackwell.

Secondary Sources and References

Barnes, T. and Duncan, J. (eds) (1992) *Writing Worlds: Discourse, Text and Metaphor in the Representation of Landscape.* London: Routledge.

Barnett, C. (1995) 'Why theory?', *Economic Geography*, 71: 427–35.

Castree, N. (1997) 'Invisible leviathan: speculations on Marx, Spivak and the question of value', *Rethinking Marxism*, 9: 45–78.

Chari, S. (2009) 'Subaltern studies', in D. Gregory, R.J. Johnston, G. Pratt, M. Watts and S. Whatmore (eds), *The Dictionary of Human Geography* (5th edition). Oxford: Blackwell-Wiley. pp. 727–8.

Derrida, J. (1976) *Of Grammatology.* Trans. G. C. Spivak. Baltimore: Johns Hopkins University Press.

Derrida, J. (1979) *Spurs: Nietzsche's Styles/Eperons: Les Styles de Nietzsche.* Trans. Barbara Harlow. Chicago: University of Chicago Press.

Derrida, J. (1988) *Limited Inc.* Trans. S. Weber. Editor's Foreword G. Graff. Evanston IL: Northwestern University Press.

Devi, M. (1995) 'Breast-giver', in S. Thames and M. Gazzaniga (eds), *The Breast: An Anthology.* New York: Global City Press. pp. 86–111.

Duncan, N. and Sharp, J. P. (1993) 'Confronting representation(s)', *Environment and Planning D: Society and Space*, 11: 373–486.

Eagleton, T. (1999) 'In the gaudy supermarket', *London Review of Books*, 21: 10.

England, K.V.L. (1994) 'Getting personal: reflexivity, positionality, and feminist research', *Professional Geographer*, 46: 80–9.

Gibson-Graham (1996) *The End of Capitalism (As We Knew It): A Feminist Critique of Political Economy.* Oxford: Blackwell.

Gregory, D. (1994) *Geographical Imaginations.* Oxford: Blackwell.

Johnson, B. (1980) *The Critical Difference.* Baltimore: Johns Hopkins University Press.

Katz, C. (1992) 'All the world is staged: intellectuals and the projects of ethnography', *Environment and Planning D: Society and Space*, 10: 495–510.

Katz, C. (1996) 'The expeditions of conjurors: ethnography, power and pretense', in D.L. Wolf (ed.), *Feminist Dilemmas in Field Research.* Boulder, CO: Westview Press. pp. 170–84.

McDowell, L. (1993) 'Space, place and gender relations, part II: identity, difference, feminist geometries and geographies', *Progress in Human Geography*, 17: 305–18.

McEwan, C. (1998) 'Cutting power lines within the palace? Countering paternity and Eurocentrism in the "geographical tradition"', *Transactions of the Institute of British Geographers*, 23: 371–84.

Mohammad, R. (2001) '"Insiders" and/or "Outsiders": positionality theory and praxis', in M. Limb and C. Dwyer (eds), *Qualitative Methodologies for Geographers.* London: Arnold. pp. 101–17.

Morton, S. (2003) *Gayatri Chakravorty Spivak.* London and New York: Routledge.

Nast, H. J. (1994) 'Women in the field: critical feminist methodologies and theoretical perspectives', *Professional Geographer*, 46: 54–60.

Radcliffe, S. A. (1994) '(Representing) post-colonial women: authority, difference and feminisms', *Area*, 26: 25–32.

Robinson, J. (1994) 'White women representing/researching "others": from anti-apartheid to Post-colonialism?', in A. Blunt and G. Rose (eds), *Writing Women and Space Colonial and Postcolonial Geographies.* Guildford Press: New York. pp. 197–226.

Rose, G. (1997) 'Situating knowledges: positionality, reflexivities and other tactics', *Progress in Human Geography*, 21 (3): 305–20.

Said, E. (1983) *The World, The Text, The Critic.* Cambridge, MA: Harvard University Press.

Sidaway, J. D. (1992) 'In other worlds: on the politics of research by "First World" geographers in the "Third World"', *Area*, 24: 403–08.

Spivak, G. C. (1986) 'Imperialism and sexual difference', *Oxford Literary Review*, 7 (1–2): 225–40.

Spivak, G. C. (1990b) 'Versions of the margin: Coetzee's foe reading Defoe's Crusoe/Roxana', in J. Arac and B. Johnson (eds), *Consequences of Theory.* Baltimore: Johns Hopkins University Press. pp. 154–80.

Spivak, G. C. (1998) 'Cultural talks in the hot peace: revisiting the "Global Village"', in P. Cheah and B. Robbins (eds), *Cosmopolitics: Thinking and Feeling beyond the Nation.* Minneapolis: University of Minnesota Press. pp. 329–50.

Wainwright, J. (2008) *Decolonizing Development: Colonial Power and the Maya.* London: Wiley-Blackwell.

Robina Mohammad, University of Reading and James D. Sidaway, University of Amsterdam

53   Michael Storper

BIOGRAPHICAL DETAILS AND THEORETICAL CONTEXT

Michael Storper was born in New York City in 1954. He was awarded a BA in sociology and history by the University of California, Berkeley in 1975 and an MA in geography in 1979. Storper completed his PhD in Geography at the University of California, Berkeley in 1982, supervised by Richard Walker (who was, in turn, a graduate student of **David Harvey**). Storper began working in the Graduate School of Architecture and Urban Planning, University of California, Los Angeles (UCLA) in 1982, being appointed as Professor of Regional and International Development in the Department of Urban Planning at UCLA in 1992. He became a Visiting Centennial Professor of Economic Geography at the London School of Economics in 2000. At the time of writing, Storper holds posts across three countries: Professor of Regional and International Development, UCLA; Professor of Economic Sociology, Institut d'Études Politiques de Paris, and Centennial Professor of Economic Geography, London School of Economics.

Storper's writing has addressed the changing spatial dynamics of production and work; the development of territorial production complexes; and more recently the importance of regional 'worlds of production' within advanced capitalist economies. Much of his work on regional development theory has sought to critically engage with debates beyond the disciplinary boundaries of geography, most notably those occurring in institutional economics (e.g., Storper and Salais, 1997; Storper, 1997). Storper also has sought cross-disciplinary audiences through publication in journals as diverse as *Futures* (Storper and Scott, 1995) and *Public Culture* (Storper, 2000). In many ways, the trajectory of Storper's work has moved broadly in tandem with broader shifts in the subdiscipline of economic geography, from an interest in the ever-changing landscapes of capital created through an incessant search for profit (Storper and Walker, 1989) and more specific concerns about the nature of flexibility and flexible specialisation (Storper, 1989; Christopherson and Storper, 1989) through to later preoccupations with the nature of regional development in a globalising world economy.

Yet, Storper has been more than a follower of these trends, playing a crucial role in shaping the trajectory of economic geography. For example, the mid-1980s volume *Production, Work, Territory: The Geographical Anatomy of Industrialised Capitalism* (Scott and Storper, 1986) quickly became *de rigueur* reading for researchers in economic geography. Edited with Allen Scott, the book presented a Marxist-inflected counter to existing conceptualisations of 'post-industrial' cities (Scott and Storper, 1986: vii), albeit at the same time representing a critique of some of the more 'abstract structural imperative[s]' (Scott and Storper, 1986: 4) presented in classical Marxist accounts. *Production, Work, Territory* developed ideas about the 'spatially-specific circumstances' (Scott and Storper, 1986: 13) of commodity production which shaped and were shaped by the new 'realities' of late twentieth-century capitalism.

The book had a particularly strong impact given that for many English-speaking readers it represented one of the first introductions to the writings of the French Regulation School, which examined the institutional forms evolving to secure particular modes of production under capitalism (Lipietz, 1987). French Regulationist influences upon the so-called 'California School' of economic geography – represented by the work of Storper, Walker and Scott – included an examination of the transition from an era dominated by a rigid, Fordist regime of accumulation to a more flexible 'post-Fordism'. Arguing that particular regimes of accumulation and their associated modes of production favoured particular production locations, Storper and colleagues began to expose the 'inconsistent' geographies of capitalism by documenting the emergence of new flexible production complexes in California.

The importance of meso-level theorising to economic geography continued to be emphasised in Storper's work (with Susan Christopherson) on flexible specialisation in the film industry in Los Angeles. By the later 1990s, Storper had become more centrally interested in the regional dimensions of territorial development, largely within the context of debates about globalisation. Perhaps unsurprisingly given his institutional base in Los Angeles, Storper's work occasionally has been viewed as part of a so-called

'LA School' (including **Michael Dear** and **Ed Soja**) that holds up Los Angeles as the archetypal urban formation of the twenty-first century (e.g., Curry and Kenney, 1999; see also the response in Storper, 1999). However, the scope of Storper's investigations has extended much further than this: his arguments about the formation of 'regional growth complexes' being based upon consideration of a range of case-studies (e.g., Northeast Central Italy and Paris, France). Furthermore, he became increasingly interested in more wide-ranging debates such as the relationship between economic globalisation and the rise of consumerist identities (Storper, 2000). With Allen Scott, he latterly intervened in debates surrounding the 'creative class', reinterpreting existing understandings of skill, creativity and urban dynamism (Storper and Scott, 2009).

SPATIAL CONTRIBUTIONS

Extending the themes of *Production, Work, Territory*, Storper and Walker's (1989) co-authored volume on territorial production complexes (*The Capitalist Imperative*) represented an extensive elaboration of the uneven landscapes of production created by advanced capitalism. Read alongside **Massey**'s (1984) *Spatial Divisions of Labour*, the book contributed significantly to the theorisation of the spatiality of 1980s restructuring. Primarily, *The Capitalist Imperative* was concerned to investigate the relationships between changing geographies of production and transformations in divisions of labour. In particular, Storper and Walker (1989) stressed that divisions of labour

were not the simple outcomes of decisions made by individual capitalists but
rather represented part of broader social
processes (see Warf, 1991: 223). Like
*Production, Work, Territory, The Capital-
ist Imperative* sought to combine Marxist
economic ideas together with 'conventional but heterodox theories of technology, external economies and industrial
organisation' (Storper, 2001: 159, n. 18).
Storper and Walker thus sought to view
'the capitalist process in broad terms'
whilst admitting 'that Marxism had little
to say about concrete issues such as technological change and industrial organisation' (Storper, 2001: 159).

Insights into the changing geographies
of production which had begun to characterise the broad transition from mass
production to 'post-Fordist' forms led to
more specific investigations of the Los
Angeles film industry. Storper and Christopherson were particularly interested
in the ways in which an entire industry
had shifted from mass production to flexible specialisation, involving the significant vertical disintegration of large firms
and the rise of small specialist production units (Storper, 1991; Storper, 1989;
Christopherson and Storper, 1989). Not
only did the LA film industry represent
a very early example of the abandonment
of routinised batch production, but also it
stood as a key American industry of the
twentieth century, 'lacking the artisanal
and regional traditions of Europe, and
without the nineteenth century antecedents of other industries' (Storper, 1991:
200). As such, this consideration of the
film industry enabled a close and detailed
historico-geographical study of flexible
specialisation.

Alongside many other analysts at the
fin-de-siècle, Storper became caught up
with a wide-ranging set of debates about
the broad contours of processes of 'globalisation' and emergent relationships

between the local, regional and global
bases of economic development. Specifically, Storper's contribution was to suggest that the global system can best be
viewed as networks of local and regional
economies – or regional 'worlds of production' (Storper and Salais, 1997). Such
'worlds' are defined by a set of *conventions* consisting of 'practices, institutions and material objects/tools [as well
as] specific forms of cognition, theories,
doctrines, institutions and rules' (Storper,
1997: 136). Individuals, markets, governments, households and firms shape these
'conventionally-based and regionalised
frameworks of action', encouraging distinctive worlds of production to emerge
(Storper, 1997: 137). Significant emphasis
is placed on the 'learning economy' of
regions, which consist of 'an ensemble
of competitive possibilities, reflexive in
nature, engendered by capitalism's new
metacapacities, as well as the risks or
constraints manufactured by the reflexive learning of others' (Storper, 1997: 31).

By spatially locating this purposive
learning in spaces where physical proximity allows for the social organisation of
production, Storper argues that innovation primarily relies upon agglomeration.
While he is concerned with documenting
the way that new technologies are changing the importance of face-to-face contacts,
Storper nonetheless argues it is the *city-re-
gion* that potentially plays the greatest role
in nurturing economic development:

> The most striking forms of agglomeration
> in evidence today are the super-agglom-
> erations or city-regions that have come
> into being all over the world in the last
> few decades, with their complex inter-
> nal structures comprising multiple urban
> cores, extended suburban appendages,
> and widely-ranging hinterland areas,
> themselves often sites of scattered urban
> settlements ... These city-regions are loco-
> motives of the national economies within
> which they are situated, in that they are

the sites of dense masses of interrelated economic activities that also typically have high levels of productivity by reason of their jointly-generated agglomeration economies and their innovative potentials.

(Scott and Storper, 2003: 6)

Acknowledging the dialectic dynamic of 'globalization and territorialization' at work in the construction of urban-regional economies, Storper (1997: 248) demonstrates that the resurgence of the regional economy in a global era can only be understood if we explore the meso-level (regional) resolution of macro-and micro-economic forces. Dispensing with traditional distinctions between the categorisations of urban and regional (and for that matter, global and local: see especially Storper, 2009), he critically syn-thesises ideas about learning, reflexivity and place in order to contribute to the ongoing theorisation of the production of space under capitalism.

KEY ADVANCES AND CONTROVERSIES

It is interesting to reflect upon the movement in Storper's work from an earlier 'trinity' of production/work/territory to that of technologies/organisations/territories. His theoretical emphases now relate more distantly to transformations in the nature of work and employment and connect more closely with the broader dynamics of, for example, knowledge formation within regional economies. The landscapes of capitalism (in the form of territory/territories) are still with us, to be sure. However, as a number of critics have suggested, Storper's more recent

focus on the creation of 'relational assets' or considerations of the ways in which groups of 'reflexive human actors' shape economic development in regions poten-tially can overshadow unequal power relations between specific actors (Pike, 1999; Sunley, 1999). Pike has argued, for example, that 'throughout [The Regional World] questions of ownership, power and control are skirted around with often only passing recognition that some inter-ests shape the agenda and basis for (re) creating "relational assets" more than oth-ers' (Pike, 1999: 2). In other words, frame-works of action in particular regions may appear homogenous, but a conceptualisa-tion of the collective institutionalisation of rules and norms may mask a diversity of ability to participate in such frameworks (Berndt, 2000: 797).

Additionally, a number of critics have expressed concerns about Storper's rela-tively generalised theorisation of con-ventions. How do conventions 'work' in practice? Gertler, for example, has suggested that 'Storper is more specific about the effects that conventions have on economic interaction in product-based technological learning (PBTL)-based tech-nology districts than he is about their sources or origins' (Gertler, 1997: 49, ital-ics in original). Or as Sunley notes:

> At times it is hard to see where conven-tions actually start and stop. As all eco-nomic activity, including regional econo-mies, involves relational conventions of some sort, further research needs to ex-plain why certain mixes of regional con-vention are successful and others not.
>
> (Sunley, 1999: 493)

Storper's interest in notions of 'reflexiv-ity' and the 'untraded interdependencies', or 'soft', non-exchange-based aspects of relationships between economic actors has been seen by one commentator as reflecting 'the ongoing socio-cultural ('reflexive') turn in economic geography' (Oinas, 2001: 381). Certainly, an emphasis on the shared conventions and cultural attributes which are created and recreated within regions does suggest sympathy with more 'culturalist' approaches to the study of economic activity. In a consideration of the transformations of consumer society, Storper has indicated that the conceptualisation of conventions is important because they co-ordinate consumption as well as production (Storper, 2000: 392). Further, he has argued that economic actors can take on multiple positionalities: they 'are not only wage earners, but also consumers, not to mention citizens' (Storper, 2000: 404). In a recent extension of 'the earlier notion of a world' (Storper, 2009: 13); he proposes that economic geographers be attentive to the *context* in which actors are situated; within which choices and decisions are made; and which conditions motivation.

Somewhat ironically, however, Storper (2001) has in fact vehemently attacked the notion of a so-called 'cultural turn' within the social sciences and humanities. His particular objection has been to what he sees as the 'celebratory relativism' which characterises 'postmodernist and cultural-turn radicals' (Storper, 2001: 167 and 170). Geographical work characteristic of such thinking is seen to include that of **Edward Soja, Trevor Barnes** (particularly Barnes, 1996) and **Gibson-Graham** (1996). Like many other critics of postmodernism, Storper feels that

movements which have their origins in identity- or community-based politics are insufficient to achieve societal change; and that they are in danger of being co-opted by an individualistic 'right wing' political agenda. He exhorts scholars to 'reaffirm their engagement with questions of political economy (issues of wide spatio-temporal extent)' (Storper, 2001: 173). However, the singularity with which Storper defines 'the cultural turn' is of note:

> It is seen as theory-and research-based on the overall notion that the keys to understanding contemporary society and to transforming it lie in the ways that culture orients our behaviours and shapes what we are able to know about the world ... *the* cultural turn variously blends postmodernist philosophy, cultural theories of society and poststructuralist philosophy.
>
> (Storper, 2001: 161, emphasis added)

Yet as Crang has observed 'the precise forms of [cultural] turns have been multiple and contested. There is no single cultural turn (1997: 3). Storper's (2001: 273) characterisation of 'cultural turn radicals' thus at times appears to verge on caricature. Ultimately, however, Storper (2001: 173) does acknowledge that any form of radical theorising and action should be attentive to 'sensitivities ... which have been sharpened by the cultural turn; questions of difference as well as a need to engage with more complex notions of human actors and actions.'

STORPER'S KEY WORKS

Scott, A.J. and Storper, M. (1986) *Production, Work, Territory: The Geographical Anatomy of Industrial Capitalism.* London: Unwin Hyman.
Storper, M. and Walker, R. (1989) *The Capitalist Imperative: Territory, Technology and Industrial Growth.* Oxford: Blackwell.
Storper, M. and Scott, A. (1992) *Pathways to Industrialisation and Regional Development.* London: Routledge.

Storper, M. and Salais, R. (1997) *Worlds of Production: The Action Frameworks of the Economy.* Cambridge, MA Harvard University Press

Storper, M. (1997) *The Regional World: Territorial Development in a Global Economy.* New York: Guilford.

Storper, M., Tsipouri, L. and Thomadakis, S. (1998) *Latecomers in the Global Economy.* London: Routledge.

Storper, M (2004) *Institutions, Incentives and Communication in Economic Geography.* Stuttgart: Franz Steiner Verlag. Publication of The Hettner Lectures, Heidelberg, June 2003.

Secondary Sources and References

Barnes, T.J. (1996) *The Logics of Dislocation: Models, Metaphors and Meanings of Economic Space.* New York: Guilford.

Berndt, C. (2000) 'Review of *Worlds of Production*', *Annals of the Association of American Geographers*, 90: 796–7.

Christopherson, S. and Storper, M. (1989) 'The effects of flexible specialisation on industrial politics and the labour market: the motion picture industry', *Industrial and Labor Relations Review*, 42: 331–47.

Crang, P. (1997) 'Cultural turns and the (re)constitution of economic geography', in R. Lee and J. Wills (eds), *Geographies of Economies.* London: Arnold. pp. 3–15.

Curry, J. and Kenney, M. (1999) 'The paradigmatic city: postindustrial illusion and the Los Angeles school', *Antipode*, 31: 1–28.

Gertler, M. (1997) 'The invention of regional culture', in R. Lee and J. Wills (eds), *Geographies of Economies.* London: Arnold. pp. 47–58.

Gibson-Graham, J.K. (1996) *The End of Capitalism (As We Knew It): A Feminist Critique of Political Economy.* Oxford: Blackwell.

Lipietz, A. (1987) *Mirages and Miracles: The Crisis of Global Fordism.* London: Verso.

Massey, D. (1984) *Spatial Divisions of Labour.* London: Macmillan.

Oinas, P. (2001) 'Review of The Regional World', *Tijdschrift Voor Economische en Social Geografie*, 92: 381–4.

Pike, A. (1999) 'Review of *The Regional World*', Economic Geography Research Group Book Reviews, available at www.egrg.org.uk/pdfs/storper.pdf' Accessed September 2009.

Scott, A. and Storper, M. (2003) 'Regions, globalization, development', *Regional Studies*, 37: 579–93.

Storper, M. (1991) 'The transition to flexible specialisation in the US film industry: external economies, the division of labour and the crossing of industrial divides', in A. Amin (ed.) *Post-Fordism: A Reader.* Oxford: Blackwell. pp. 195–226.

Storper, M. (1989) 'The transition to flexible specialisation in the US film industry: external economies, the division of labour and the crossing of industrial divides', *Cambridge Journal of Economics*, 13: 273–305.

Storper, M. (1997b) 'Regional economies as relational assets', in R. Lee and J. Wills (eds), *Geographies of Economies.* London: Arnold. pp. 248–58.

Storper, M. (1999) 'The poverty of paleo-leftism: a response to Curry and Kenney', *Antipode*, 31: 37–44.

Storper, M. (2000) 'Lived effects of the contemporary economy: globalisation, inequality and consumer society', *Public Culture*, 12: 375–409.

Storper, M. (2001) 'The poverty of radical theory today: from the false promises of Marxism to the mirage of the cultural turn', *International Journal of Urban and Regional Research*, 25: 155–79.

Storper, M. (2009) 'Regional context and global trade', Roepke Lecture in Economic Geography, *Economic Geography*, 85: 1–21.

Storper, M. and Scott, A.J. (1989) 'The geographical foundations and social regulation of flexible production systems', in M. Dear and J. Wolch (eds), *The Power of Geography.* London: Unwin Hyman. pp. 21–40.

Storper, M. and Scott, A.J. (1995) 'The wealth of regions: market forces and policy imperatives in local and global context', *Futures*, 27: 505–26.

Storper, M. and Scott, A.J. (2009) 'Rethinking human capital, creativity and urban growth', *Journal of Economic Geography*, 9: 147–67.

Sunley, P. (1999) 'Review of *The Regional World*', *Regional Studies*, 33: 493.

Warf, B. (1991) 'Review of *The Capitalist Imperative*', *Journal of Regional Science*, 31: 222–4.

Suzanne Reimer, Southampton University

54   Peter Taylor

BIOGRAPHICAL DETAILS AND THEORETICAL CONTEXT

Peter James Taylor was born in 1944 and grew up in Calverton, near Nottingham, England. He received his BA in Geography from Liverpool University in 1966 and his PhD in Geography from Liverpool in 1970. From 1968 to 1995, he taught at Newcastle University, and after 1995 lectured at Loughborough University. During 1990 Taylor was a research associate for a MacArthur Foundation research project on comparative hegemonies at the Fernand Braudel Center of the State University of New York, Binghamton. Significantly, Taylor was invited to participate in this project by **Immanuel Wallerstein**, head of the Braudel Centre and acknowledged founder of world-systems analysis. Since 1998, Taylor has served as founder and director of the Globalization and World Cities (GaWC) Research Network. In 2004 he was named a Fellow of the British Academy.

Though his work spans quantitative analyses of elections through to studies of financial services, Taylor is perhaps best known within geography for bringing a world-systems perspective to bear on issues within political geography. In context, this must be seen as a significant contribution given that political geography was widely regarded as a moribund subdiscipline in the 1960s. Taylor's work was one of the stimuli that informed the development of a more theoretically-inclined approach that revived the field in the 1980s and 1990s. At the same time, his work has contributed an analysis of states and political power to the world-systems perspective. Given that the original formulations of a world-systems perspective in the 1970s and early 1980s were widely seen as providing a very limited understanding of the working of states within the global economy, Taylor's writings since the early 1980s have helped to redress significant lacunae in political theory. In addition, and latterly, his work on World Cities under conditions of contemporary globalisation has sought to challenge state-centric understandings of geo-politics, creating a lively dialogue between urban and political geographers.

SPATIAL CONTRIBUTIONS

Much of Taylor's earliest scholarship focused on theoretical and methodological concerns within electoral geography (Johnston and Taylor, 1979). Yet his introduction of world-systems analysis to political geography (1981, 1982) not only demanded a reconceptualisation of electoral politics, but wider notions of territory and governance. Taylor starts with the world-systems' division of states into core, semi-periphery, and periphery. This tripartite division refers to the kinds of economic processes that predominate within the boundaries of states. *Core* economic processes are relatively technologically advanced and pay high wages; *peripheral* economic processes are by contrast less technologically advanced and based on the employment of low wage labour. A small number of states, whose territories house most of the high wage/advanced technology processes at a given time, are referred to as 'core states'. A much larger group of states whose territories predominantly house low wage/basic technology processes are referred to as 'peripheral states'. Between these, at any given time, there exists a small but politically important group of states that combine a substantial amount of both core-like and periphery-like processes, and these are referred to as '*semi-peripheral* states'.

Taylor's application of this tripartite division of the world-system to electoral geography (1986) suggests the need to reconsider the significance of different kinds of political-electoral processes in relation to the position of states within the hierarchical global structure. Specifically, Taylor argues that the prevalence of liberal, multi-party democracies within particular states, and the absence of this political form in others, is best explained by the position of states in the global hierarchy, rather than by attributes internal to these states such as their economic ideologies or cultural histories. Multi-party, liberal democratic systems thrive within the core countries of the global economy – forming what Taylor refers to as 'liberal democratic states' – because the high level of wealth within these states allows a redistributive politics. Broad participation in elections reflects

the ability of parties within core states to satisfy certain demands of the broader populace, even while they serve to reproduce capitalist class power. In the periphery, by contrast, the absence of a large surplus to redistribute encourages elites to limit or prevent broad-based popular participation that might lead to democratic demands for redistribution. Thus, in contrast to the core, the periphery is marked by higher prevalence of military dictatorship and other political forms that limit democratic demands. Moreover, such undemocratic forms are especially prevalent in semi-peripheral states, which utilise political repression as a tool for intensifying the exploitation of labour in order to maximise capital accumulation in the attempt to 'catch up' economically with core states (Taylor, 1986; Taylor and Flint, 2000: 38, 235–85).

The significance of this argument is that it challenges the 'developmentalism' prominent in orthodox development theory, where it was often assumed that peripheral countries with undemocratic governments were simply at an earlier stage of development than the already developed liberal democracies and would eventually 'catch up'. Taylor's argument, by contrast, suggests that the socio-spatial inequalities inherent in global capitalism are likely to prevent any simultaneous process of 'catching up' by all states. From a world-systems perspective, the global capitalist economy is systematically and inevitably hierarchical, in both a social and a spatial sense. Such a hierarchy will always lead to different sets of political possibilities at the top and the bottom of the system, because of the difference in possibilities for redistribution. Thus, even where there have been recent, formally democratic developments in the periphery and semi-periphery of the global economy, Taylor suggests that these are likely to be highly unstable and subject to reversal (Taylor and Flint, 2000: 281–5).

Beyond theorising electoral politics from a world-systems perspective, one of Taylor's significant contributions to world-systems analysis has been to theorise the development of the modern territorial state and its relationship to the global economy. For world-systems analysts, the capitalist world-system comprises two structural features that are very different in their spatiality:

1   a capitalist market economy, based on global commodity chains, these having developed in Europe by the sixteenth century and expanded to become fully global in the twenty-first century; and

2   a system of bounded territorial states that have more limited geographical range but nonetheless perform crucial functions in facilitating the global process of capitalist accumulation.

While Wallerstein had theorised the necessity of the territorial state as a facilitator of capitalist accumulation, he did not in his early work provide extended discussions of the nature of the international system of sovereign territorial states. Taylor's work, along with that of several other world-systems theorists (e.g., Chase-Dunn, 1989; Arrighi, 1990) has helped fill in this lacuna. In particular, Taylor has theorised the way modern states came into existence in relation to the political-territorial development of a state *system*. Taylor emphasises that while most state theories – including Marxist theories of the capitalist state – have focused on the *internal* political economic conditions for development of territorial states (such as domestic class structures), one cannot fully understand modern states without understanding the *external* conditions necessary for their

existence. In particular, the modern territorial state that developed with the rise of capitalism came to have exclusive control, or sovereignty, over the entirety of its internal territory, a condition that is only meaningful insofar as it implies the recognition of that sovereignty by other states. The condition of mutual recognition is what Taylor refers to as 'interstateness', and his work has not only theorised this process but discussed its evolution, emphasising that it is a historical social construct (Taylor, 1994, 1995a).

In developing a historical account of modern territorial states, Taylor has extensively addressed one particular feature of the capitalist interstate system – namely, that there have been three periods in which the system was dominated by one particular state that can be referred to as 'hegemonic'. Hegemony, following the ideas of the Italian theorist Antonio Gramsci, is taken to mean that the states in question can lead others as much through the consent they are able to generate for their leadership as through the coercive force they are able to exercise. Taylor posits that there have been three hegemonic states in specific periods of historical capitalism, each identified with specific forms of capitalism and leading technologies of the era: firstly, the United Provinces (Netherlands) in the seventeenth-century era of mercantile capitalism, based on dominance in technologies associated with shipping and ship-building; secondly, the UK, in the nineteenth-century era of industrial capitalism, based on dominance in technologies associated with industrial machinery and production processes; and thirdly the US, in the twentieth-century era of consumer capitalism, based on dominance in technologies associated with mass production and communications (Taylor, 1996).

For Taylor, the periods of hegemonic leadership by each of these states are also associated with particular conceptions of what it is to be modern, defined by the practices of the hegemonic power as they are presented to the rest of the world. Thus, seventeenth-century followers attempted to be like the Dutch in their commercial prosperity, while nineteenth-century followers attempted to be like the British in developing industrial prowess, and twentieth-century followers attempted to be like the Americans through participation in consumerism (Taylor, 1999; Slater and Taylor, 1999). These 'prime modernities', as Taylor calls them, illustrate that from a world-systems perspective culture, just like economics and politics, has to be understood through a lens that highlights interconnections at a global scale.

The social construction of the international system of sovereign territorial states and its movement through a series of hegemonies and 'prime modernities' is crucial to a final set of themes Taylor has developed. In world-systems analysis, the state is neither an insignificant player in capitalism nor an all-powerful controller of social processes. Contemporary studies of globalisation that do not take a world-systems view sometimes portray globalisation as representing the outstripping of state power by transnational economic forces. Taylor, like other world-systems analysts, rejects this 'death of the nation-state' thesis as simplistic, but also acknowledges that ongoing changes in the structure of the capitalist world-system are leading to changes in the specific forms of political power and the ways in which they operate.

Utilising a distinction made by **Yi-Fu Tuan** (Tuan, 1977), Taylor argues that there is today a notable tension between *space* – the abstract areal extension across which capital and commodities flow, and *place* – the lived environments in which people create meaning and carry out their day-to-day existence. As an example, Taylor notes increasing ambiguities and

tensions surrounding relationships within two major institutions of the world-system: nation-states and households. Both institutions have been portrayed historically as safe places, as havens from the oppressiveness and callous competitiveness of global capitalism. Yet increasingly, these havens have appeared to their inhabitants as 'cages', being transformed by processes of modernity into spaces rather than places. Thus, nation-states seem tools of the most egregious forms of violence and repression, especially for groups such as racial or ethnic minorities, while households are recognised as spaces of horrendous violence against women (Taylor, 1999, 2000a).

As awareness of the negative possibilities of modern institutions has grown in recent decades, movements have emerged that emphasise localism and local resistance to global capitalism, as well as to the territorial state and the patriarchal household. For Taylor, this manifests an ongoing process of transformation within the world-system. In particular, states are no longer as likely to be seen by progressive social actors as tools of liberation. Instead, social movements increasingly work within local, place-based projects, while also forming transnational linkages, sometimes bypassing the national state in the process. This leads to complex, multiscalar politics. Taylor has argued that in a general sense, the global scale has been produced as an object of human awareness by the reality of world-systems processes, while the national scale has been produced by the dominant ideology of territorial nation-states, and the local has been produced by lived day-to-day experience (Taylor, 1982; Taylor and Flint, 2000: 42–6). But with the ideological power of the national territorial state increasingly contested, the connections between local and global processes ('glocalisation') become more important.

Taylor highlights this transformation in two ways. First, following the 'World Cities' hypothesis developed by John Friedmann in the 1980s (Friedmann, 1986), as well as **Manuel Castells**' ideas of a network society, he shows that economic interactions in the global economy are increasingly constituted by flows of capital, people, and information between a group of globally dominant cities, rather than between states as territorial wholes (Taylor, 1995b, 2000b, 2004). Second, he suggests that the spread of global consumer capitalism under US hegemony is ecologically unsustainable and is destroying liveable places with spaces of constantly expanding global capital flows. Thus, ecological problems constitute the 'ultimate space-place tension' and are bringing forth new responses that challenge the spatial domination exercised by global corporations and territorial states with progressive, place-based yet transnationalised forms of activism (Taylor and Flint, 2000: 366–7).

Taylor has most recently built on these foundations through his World Cities research. Noting that the original formulations of a 'World Cities hypothesis' by Friedmann and others were strong on theory but weak on data, Taylor and other participants in the GaWC research network have developed both analyses and large data sets enabling examination of transnational activities of firms based in major cities – especially advanced producer services (APS) firms in fields such as accounting, advertising, finance, and law. GaWC data, and analyses presented via the GaWC website, have been used by Taylor to advance the argument that the global hierarchy of cities is today somewhat less competitive and somewhat more collaborative than suggested in previously predominant theorisations of urban hierarchies – even though it still features a much greater number of World Cities in the Global North than in the Global South (Taylor, 2004). Developing the ideas of Jane Jacobs on the 'work' of cities, Taylor has thus offered a challenging take on the role of cities in the global economy, emphasising their relationality and the flows that entwine them in a network of World Cities.

KEY ADVANCES AND CONTROVERSIES

Taylor's work has done much to highlight the importance of a holistic, global perspective in the social sciences. Where many geographers had in the past considered entities like regions to have a relatively independent existence (based, for example, on bio-physical features of the area), Taylor's work has been part of the development of 'social constructivist' approaches which suggest that many taken-for-granted geographical concepts – households, localities, regions, states, world regions, and, indeed, the idea of scale itself – are socially and historically produced (Taylor, 1991b). Most importantly, Taylor's work shows how various of these phenomena are produced *in relation to each other*: for Taylor, the only way to fully understand the phenomena in question is to understand them in relationship to the global totality of which they are a part.

Here, however, there is an important controversy surrounding the way Taylor and world-systems analysts approach the constructed character of social reality and the ways this issue has been approached in other leading social constructivist accounts. In recent decades, some of the most important of these other social constructivist accounts have been associated with postmodernist and post-structural philosophies. Many of these 'post-prefixed' approaches have expressed great scepticism about the existence of large-scale, unified wholes (such as global capitalist economies or unified national social formations), and thus they have eschewed attempts to theorise in terms of such wholes. Thus, world-systems analysis and 'post-prefixed' theory represent two very different approaches to social construction and historical contingency.

Taylor explicitly recognises this difference in addressing the revival of political geography through the social theory movement and critical geo-politics. The social theory movement, exemplified by Gordon Clark and **Michael Dear**'s work on state apparatuses and their varied legal and ideological roles (Clark and Dear, 1984), is seen by Taylor as making an important contribution in areas where world-systems theory is weak – i.e., detailed analysis of the internal structures of states – but as missing the importance of states' positions in the interstate system (Taylor, 1991a: 394–7). Critical geo-politics, exemplified by the work of post-structural authors such as **Gearóid Ó Tuathail** (1996) on the relationship between state power and representational practices, is seen by Taylor as making a useful contribution to the understanding of specific dimensions of state power and political contestation, though it is only one part of a broader set of geo-political analyses that need to be brought together in order to provide an adequate analysis (Taylor and Flint, 2000: 50, 102–4). Thus, from Taylor's perspective, the debate between world-systems analysts and 'post-prefixed' theorists generates a 'creative tension' that can push forward critical thinking on politicised space and place.

This 'creative tension' is also present in exchanges between Taylor and critics of his work on World Cities. Jenny Robinson (2006) has criticised Taylor's approach and the project of the GaWC for overstressing the importance of World Cities while ignoring the significance of an array of 'ordinary cities', as well as for overstressing the importance of APS firms while neglecting other kinds of economic activities. In Robinson's view, the 'rosters' of World Cities produced by the GaWC encourage the narrow pursuit of World City status by urban political entrepreneurs while truncating the sense of alternative development possibilities. Taylor has acknowledged the limits of using APS data as the basis for analysing World City formation, seeing it only as a necessary first step, and more recent GaWC projects have attempted to expand the range of activities included in World Cities data sets. While theoretical differences between world-systems approaches and post-colonial theory underpin this debate, both Taylor and Robinson are agreed about the importance of constructing urban futures that are post-colonial and that eschew the attempts of urban political entrepreneurs to outcompete other cities in making themselves successful 'command and control' centres for global capital. The major questions here appear to be tactical, concerning whether or not alternative development possibilities can be produced primarily through local actions or require – as world systems analysis suggests – meeting the power of global capital with a 'globalisation from below', one that links alternative development projects across territories and scales of activity. This is an ongoing issue of great importance both for those within social movements fighting for social justice as well as within the academy.

TAYLOR'S KEY WORKS

Taylor, P. J. (1981) 'Political geography and the world-economy', in A.D. Burnett and P.J. Taylor (eds), *Political Studies from Spatial Perspectives.* New York: Wiley. pp. 157–72.

Taylor, P. J. (1982) 'A materialist framework for political geography', *Transactions of the Institute of British Geographers,* NS 7 (1): 15–34.

Taylor, P. J. (1986) 'An exploration into world-systems analysis of political parties', *Political Geography Quarterly,* 5 (4), supplement: 5–20.

Taylor, P. J. (1991a) 'Political geography within world-systems analysis', *Review,* 14 (3): 387–402.

Taylor, P. J. (1991b) 'A theory and practice of regions: the case of Europes', *Environment and Planning D: Society and Space,* 9 (2): 183–95.

Taylor, P. J. (1994) 'The state as container: territoriality in the modern world-system', *Progress in Human Geography,* 18 (2): 151–62.

Taylor, P.J. (1995a) 'Beyond containers: internationality, interstateness, interterritoriality', *Progress in Human Geography,* 19 (1): 1–15.

Taylor, P.J. (1995b) 'World cities and territorial states: the rise and fall of their mutuality', in P. Knox and P.J. Taylor (eds.) *World Cities in a World-System.* Cambridge: Cambridge University Press. pp. 48–62.

Taylor, P. J. (1996) *The Way The Modern World Works: World Hegemony to World Impasse.* London: Wiley.

Taylor, P.J. (1999) *Modernities: A Geohistorical Interpretation.* Cambridge, UK and Minneapolis: Polity and University of Minnesota Press.

Taylor, P. J. (2000a) 'Havens and cages: reinventing states and households in the modern world-system', *Journal of World-Systems Research,* 6 (2) : 544–62.

Taylor, P. J. (2000b) 'World cities and territorial states under conditions of contemporary globalization', *Political Geography,* 19 (1): 5–32.

Taylor, P. J. and Flint, C. (2000) *Political Geography: World-Economy, Nation-State and Locality* (4th edition). Harlow: Prentice Hall.

Taylor, P.J. (2004). *World City Network: A Global Urban Analysis.* New York and London: Routledge.

Secondary Sources and References

Arrighi, G. (1990) 'The three hegemonies of historical capitalism', *Review,* 13 (3): 365–408.

Chase-Dunn, C. (1989) *Global Formation.* Oxford: Blackwell.

Clark, G. L. and Dear, M. (1984) *State Apparatus.* Boston: Allen and Unwin.

Friedmann, J. (1986) 'The world city hypothesis', *Development and Change,* 17 (1): 69–84.

Globalization and World Cities Research Network (GaWC) (nd). GaWC web site, www.lboro.ac.uk/gawc/

Johnston, R. J. and Taylor, P. J. (1979) *Geography of Elections.* London and New York: Croom Helm and Holmes & Meier.

Ó Tuathail, G. (1996) *Critical Geopolitics.* Minneapolis: University of Minnesota Press.

Robinson, J. (2006). *Ordinary Cities: Between Modernity and Development.* New York and London: Routledge.

Slater, D. and Taylor, P. J. (eds.) (1999) *American Century: Consensus and Coercion in the Projection of American Power.* Oxford: Blackwell.

Tuan, Y.-F. (1977) *Space and Place.* London: Edward Arnold.

Jim Glassman, University of British Columbia

55 Nigel Thrift

BIOGRAPHICAL DETAILS AND THEORETICAL CONTEXT

Working at the intersections of economic, urban, and cultural geography, Nigel Thrift has long been recognised as one of the discipline's most imaginative, articulate, and productive scholars; he is one of geography's five most heavily cited figures. In a lengthy series of papers and books, Thrift has made major contributions to various parts of the field, including: the history of geographical thought; structuration theory; a renewed regional geography; geographies of time; post-Fordism; globalisation; geographies of finance and banking; actor-network theory; and non-representational theory and performativity.

Born in Bath in 1949, Thrift earned his BA in Aberystwyth, Wales, and a PhD from the University of Bristol in 1979. He was stationed briefly in Leeds (1976–1977), spent four years (1979–1983) as a Research Fellow at the Australian National University, and three years (1984–1987) as a Lecturer and Reader at Saint David's University College, Lampeter, Wales. In 1987 he returned to Bristol as Professor in the School of Geographical Sciences. Between 2003 and 2006 he was Pro-Vice-Chancellor for Research at Oxford University. In 2006, he took up the position

of Vice-Chancellor at the University of Warwick. He has taught or carried out research at a number of institutions around the world, is an Academician of the Association of Learned Societies in the Social Sciences, a Fellow of the British Academy, and was awarded the Royal Geographical Society's Heath Award and the Medal of the University of Helsinki. He has supervised numerous doctoral students, obtained considerable research grant funding, and serves on many editorial boards. He serves as managing editor for *Environment and Planning A*, and in 1982 co-founded *Environment and Planning D: Society and Space*. One measure of Thrift's contribution to geography, and to other disciplines, is the sheer volume of his writings: between 1975 and 2009, for example, he authored or co-authored roughly 110 refereed journal articles, 100 book chapters, and wrote, edited, or co-edited 39 books. Of course, mere numbers fail to convey the diversity, depth of insight, and impact of these works.

Thrift rose to prominence as an economic geographer via analyses of industrial linkages and markets and multinational corporations (Taylor and Thrift, 1986), originally focusing on the specific instance of Australia. He also exhibited a sustained interest in geographies of time, including the restructuring of time consciousness in contexts ranging from the medieval to the contemporary, particularly the imperatives of commodity production and capital accumulation

(Thrift, 1988), a notion that closely echoed E.P. Thompson's famous portrayal of the social dynamics of factory time.

It was during the flowering of social theory in the 1980s and 1990s, however, that Thrift came into his own as a leading theoretician of geographies as situated social practices. Throughout Thrift's work runs a Marxist inspiration of the non-structuralist variety, including an abiding concern for class, a position that would later be extended to a variety of non-class based forms of social determination (Thrift and Williams, 1987). Thrift has long insisted that geographies are produced by people in pre-discursive, practical ways. He played a key role in introducing **Anthony Giddens**' notion of structuration into geography (Thrift 1985a; 1993a), with his (1983) paper 'On the determination of social action in space and time' being a landmark piece that both situated structuration theory within the broader intellectual context of 'micro–macro' divisions in the social sciences and pointed toward the emerging reconstruction of regional geography. His works played a key role in forcing geographers to take much more seriously than they had hitherto questions of consciousness, subjectivity, and identity (Pile and Thrift, 1995).

The publication of the two-volume *New Models in Geography* (Peet and Thrift, 1989) heralded the ascendancy of political economy to a central and pivotal status within geography. Extending conventional interpretations concerned mostly with class into new domains, the essays in these books offered comprehensive and insightful interrogations of the production of nature, the state, gender, uneven development, the nation-state, urbanisation, race, culture, and postmodernism.

Throughout his career, Thrift has been fascinated by cities as dense nuclei of economic and social transactions, by the changing possibilities for economic development afforded by globalisation (Thrift, 1987), and by the mutations in urban form and life that such transformations entailed (Pile and Thrift, 2000). Cities, particularly in the knowledge-driven economies of 'soft capitalism' both reflect and constitute the changing dynamics of social life as contingent constellations of meaning (Amin and Thrift, 2002).

Thrift's interest in the differential regional effects of globalisation generated a series of case studies. He has worked extensively on the restructuring of the British space-economy in the face of globalisation and mounting social and regional polarisation, including the rise of the greater London region (Thrift, 1987). He also examined other European regions in various contexts (Amin and Thrift, 1992), including the rising role of dense human networks in leading innovative regions characteristic of advanced post-Fordist production systems. Thrift also worked extensively on Pacific Asia, most notably, Vietnam (Forbes and Thrift, 1987; Thrift and Forbes, 1986). These empirical analyses complemented his insistence that regions mattered not only ontologically (i.e., as units of empirical analysis), but also epistemologically (i.e., that no social process was manifested in the same way in different places).

The latter line of thought would prove to hold wide appeal to the growing legions of geographers who insisted that local uniqueness mattered. Throughout the 1980s, the 'new regional geography' developed linkages between top-down global political economy and 'bottom-up' concerns for living actors and everyday life. Thrift played a key role in articulating this vision of geography, defending it against both positivist and Marxist critics for whom regional analysis could, by definition, scarcely amount to more than reconstituted empiricism. Unlike chorology, however, the reconstituted regionalism was both theoretically informed and paid great attention to the connections among regions, their linkages to the global division of labour, and the sticky issue of the production of spatial scale. The new regionalism made local uniqueness a valid object of scholarly scrutiny, demonstrating that the local *mattered* and that no social process played out exactly in the same way in different time-space contexts. The recovery of regions for social theory obligated the discipline to delve into the intricate dynamics of local actors who populated them and 'made them work': thus the localities school and structuration theory's focus on everyday life were mutually complementary. Yet, this relational materialist perspective maintains that the global 'space of flows' does not float in a disembodied space: rather, global flows and connections are constructed by human beings who are always embedded in networks of power and knowledge that are themselves part of an ever-changing structural context.

This concern with the intersections between the local and global extended into his work on the most abstract and globalised of economic sectors, finance. On this topic, Thrift entered into a fecund relationship with Andrew Leyshon that generated a series of works concerning the international financial system, British financial capital, and banking networks in London (Leyshon and Thrift, 1997; Thrift and Leyshon, 1992; 1994). These works both elucidated the impacts of electronic money and national deregulation and simultaneously demystified money by stressing the key roles played by interpersonal relations predicated on trust and face-to-face contact, including the critical but often overlooked roles played by local milieu, trust, and 'institutional thickness' i.e., the cultural context in which financial transactions are always and everywhere embedded. Money, even in its most rarified electronic form, is thus much more than an abstract economic relation, for its real power lies in its symbolic value and links to national and global distributions of social power (Thrift, 2001). Like all social relations, financial systems are inevitably discursively constituted through particular social-cultural practices in different times and places. Such an approach brought a badly needed human quality to a topic dominated by ethereal understandings devoid of actors, and is vital if the new forms of 'soft' managerial capitalism are to be understood in all their complexity.

More recently, Thrift played an influential role in getting geographers acquainted with various forms of post-structuralism, particularly as it pertains to subjectivity, identity, language, representation, discourse, and performativity (Thrift, 2000; 2007). Although he has never referred to himself as a postmodernist *per se*, his theoretical orientation reveals a common distrust of broad metatheories, an appreciation for local uniqueness, and an emphasis on social structures and change as inherently open-ended and contingent. This line of thought led him to be one of the primary architects of geography's 'cultural turn' which blurred the artificial and often misleading distinctions between the 'economic', the 'cultural', the 'social' and the 'political'(Thrift and Olds, 1996). For example, he maintains that it is increasingly the relations of consumption rather than production that are critical to the negotiation and maintenance of identity.

SPATIAL CONTRIBUTIONS

If there is any theme that permeates Thrift's multitudinous works, perhaps it is his sustained interest in connectivity of one sort or another. His papers have, in different ways and contexts, focused on the diffusion of information (Thrift, 1985b), the reciprocal relations between knowledge and power, and increasingly globalised exchanges of human, symbolic, and financial capital. Thus, he exhibits a consistent concern for the flows of information and knowledge that shape individuals' conceptions of themselves and one another and that play a major role in the routinised reproduction of social relations. Invoking actor-network theory, Thrift extended the insights of **Bruno Latour**, which effectively abandon the distinction between agents and structures altogether. This view focuses on the exercise of power by actors rather than just the embeddedness of power in networks. Throughout his career, Thrift has worked assiduously to portray geographies as embodied, embedded, contingent, and ever-changing, harnessing the fluidity of spatial relations to demonstrate how they are imbricated in changing human relations of power.

Thrift's writings paint a thorough portrait of contemporary, globalised, neoliberal capitalism, dominated by finance and digital information technology. This historically-specific constellation of discourses and practices includes novel forms of production and consumption that reflect, and drive, its pronounced penetration of culture and consciousness. The 'symbolic economy' calls for new forms of performativity for actors in order to function and succeed (Thrift, 2000). In analysing the importance of systems of signification – including discourses, language, texts, and representations – in everyday practice, Thrift argued for an ontological equivalence of subjects and objects, and pioneered a non-representational theory of action that stresses performative, embodied knowledges (Thrift, 1997).

Non-representational theory, which has been widely debated, stresses the preconscious dimensions of life (questions of being and doing) and the worlds of affect and emotion that shape the intentions and behaviours of actors (Thrift, 2004a; 2007).

Thrift's work on contemporary capitalism has emphasised the adoption of information technology and electronic communications, citing these as key indicators of post-Fordist 'soft capitalism' and its attendant digitised, virtual dimensions (Thrift, 1995; 1997). The massive time-space compression unleashed by digital globalisation has thus altered both the field of possibilities of nation-states and of individual actors in everyday life: the renewed regionalism and reconstituted rhythms of daily life are two sides of one coin. Digital capitalism operates, Thrift maintains, in a manner different from its predecessors: it is more mobile, more flexible, more insistently symbolic in nature, and lodges itself into the innermost recesses of the human psyche. At the level of the corporation and everyday life, he has also taken an interest in the possibilities extended by the widespread use of computational technology and mobile telecommunications. In sum, the contingent, simultaneously determinant interactions between culture and technology form a long-standing theme threaded throughout his papers.

KEY ADVANCES AND CONTROVERSIES

Geographers' engagements with Thrift's ideas have taken a variety of forms, of which five are suggested here. First, the popularity of structuration theory in the discipline owed no small part to his writings, which sensitised the discipline to the constructed and contingent nature of space. Thus, human geographers often came to frame their topics, questions, and responses within the terms of intended actions and unintended results, an approach that elevated everyday life from the trivial to the critical.

Second, his repeated calls for an historical geography of time were important both in moving the field toward an emphatically dynamic approach to both theoretical and empirical issues, and hence underscored the social construction of time, which to all outer appearances appears 'natural'. By denaturalising time, Thrift's work pointed towards the broader denaturalisation of other phenomena, including language, power, poverty, representations, and the body.

Third, economic geographers have been motivated by his books and papers to emphasise the role of human actors in varying historical contexts, demystifying even money, the most abstract of social relations. For example, international banking networks were shown to be the very human products of business executives enmeshed in culturally-specific webs of meaning. Such an approach helped geographers decisively to rupture any remaining ties to the comparative statics of neo-classical economics. Yet, Thrift's corpus of writings also advanced the field beyond Marxism, with its frequent teleological social predetermination and reification of class.

Fourth, his sensitivity to regions, not simply as receivers of broader changes but as generators in their own right, has made an appreciation of local uniqueness *de rigueur* within the field. Thrift and others illustrated that no social process unfolds in the same way across different places, raising the significance of context in social explanation to a central position. In this reading, the local was far from simply a handmaiden to the global, and the critical question of spatial scale was problematised across several intellectual perspectives.

Fifth, social and cultural geographers have been much inspired by his turn to non-representation, and Thrift's works have fostered a critical attitude towards discourse and representation within the field, generating marked interest in questions of affect. In large part due to Thrift's efforts, actor-network theory became normalized, and issues of practice, performativity, and non-representation now loom large in discussions of the city (Amin and Thrift, 2002) and economic life (Thrift, 2005). There can be little doubt, therefore, that Thrift's contributions to human geography have left it far more sophisticated, subtle, and nuanced.

THRIFT'S KEY WORKS

Amin, A. and Thrift, N. (2002) *Cities: Reimagining the Urban.* Cambridge: Polity Press.

Corbridge, S., Martin, R. and Thrift, N. (eds), (1997) *Money, Power and Space.* Oxford: Blackwell.

Crang, M. and Thrift, N. (2000) *Thinking Space.* London: Routledge.

Featherstone, M., Thrift, N. and Urry, J. (2005) *Automobilities.* London: Sage.

Leyshon, A. and Thrift, N. (eds) (1997) *Money/Space: Geographies of Monetary Transformation.* London: Routledge.

Peet, R. and Thrift, N. (eds) (1989) *New Models in Geography: The Political-Economy Perspective.* Boston: Unwin-Hyman.

Pile, S. and Thrift, N. (eds) (1995) *Mapping the Subject: Geographies of Cultural Transformation.* New York: Routledge.

Thrift, N. (1981) 'Owners' time and own time: the making of a capitalist time consciousness, 1300–1880', in A. Pred (ed.), *Space and Time in Geography: Essays Dedicated to Torsten Hägerstrand*. Lund: Lund Studies in Geography Series B, No. 48. pp. 56–84.

Thrift, N. (1983) 'On the determination of social action in space and time', *Environment and Planning D: Society and Space*, 1: 23–57.

Thrift, N. (1996b) *Spatial Formations*. Thousand Oaks, CA: Sage.

Thrift, N. (2000) 'Performing cultures in the new economy', *Annals of the Association of American Geographers*, 4: 674–92.

Thrift, N. (2005) *Knowing Capitalism*. London: Sage.

Thrift, N. (2007) *Non-Representational Theory: Space, Politics, Affect*. London: Sage.

Thrift, N. and Olds, K. (1996) 'Refiguring the economic in economic geography', *Progress in Human Geography*, 20: 311–37.

Secondary Sources and References

Anderson, K., Domosh, M., Thrift, N. and Pile, S. (2002) *The Handbook of Cultural Geography*. London: Sage.

Amin, A. and Thrift, N. (1992) 'Neo-marshallian nodes in global networks', *International Journal of Urban and Regional Studies*, 16: 571–87.

Amin, A. and Thrift, N. (eds) (2003) *The Blackwell Cultural Economy Reader*. Oxford: Blackwell.

Amin, A. and Thrift, N. (2005) 'What's Left? Just the future', *Antipode*, 37: 220–338.

Clark, G., Thrift, N. and Tickell, A. (2004) 'Performing finance: the industry, the media and the image', *Review of International Political Economy*, 11: 289–310.

Cloke, P., Doel, M., Matless, D., Phillips, M. and Thrift, N. (1994) *Writing the Rural: Five Cultural Geographies*. London: Paul Chapman.

Forbes, D. and Thrift, N. (eds) (1987) *The Socialist Third World: Urban Development and Territorial Planning*. Oxford: Blackwell.

Lee, R., Leyshon, R., Aldridge, T., Tooke, J., Williams, C. and Thrift, N. (2004) 'Making geographies and histories: constructing local circuits of value', *Environment and Planning D: Society and Space*, 22: 595–618.

Pile, S. and Thrift, N. (eds) (2000) *City A-Z*. New York: Routledge.

Taylor, M. and Thrift, N. (eds) (1986) *Multinationals and the Restructuring of the World Economy*. London: Croom Helm.

Thompson, E.P. (1963) *The Making of the English Working Class*. London: Victor Gollancz.

Thrift, N. (1985a) 'Bear and mouse or bear and tree? Anthony Giddens's reconstitution of social theory', *Sociology* 19: 609–23.

Thrift, N. (1985b) 'Flies and germs: a geography of knowledge', in D. Gregory and J. Urry (eds), *Social Relations and Spatial Structures*. London: Macmillan. pp. 366–402.

Thrift, N. (1987) 'The fixers: the urban geography of international commercial capital', in M. Castells and J. Henderson (eds), *Global Restructuring and Territorial Development*. London: Sage, pp. 203–33.

Thrift, N. (1988) 'Vivos voco: ringing the changes in the historical geography of time consciousness', in T. Schuller, T. and M. Young (eds), *The Rhythms of Society*. London: Routledge. pp. 169–212.

Thrift, N. (1993a) 'Review essay: the arts of the living and the beauty of the dead: anxieties of being in the work of Anthony Giddens', *Progress in Human Geography*, 17: 111–21.

Thrift, N. (1995) 'A hyperactive world', in R.J. Johnston, P. Taylor and M. Watts (eds), *Geographies of Global Change*. Oxford: Blackwell. pp. 82–95.

Thrift, N. (1996a) 'New urban eras and old technological fears: reconfiguring the goodwill of electronic things', *Urban Studies*, 33: 1463–93.

Thrift, N. (1997) 'The rise of soft capitalism', in A. Herod, S. Roberts, and G. Toal (eds), *An Unruly World? Globalisation and Space*. London: Routledge. pp. 25–68.

Thrift, N. (2001) '"It's the romance, not the finance, that makes the business worth pursuing": disclosing a new market culture', *Economy and Society*, 4: 412–32.

Thrift, N. (2004a) 'Intensities of feeling: towards a spatial politics of affect', *Geografiska Annaler*, 86: 57–78.

Thrift, N. (2004b) 'Movement-space: the changing domain of thinking resulting from the development of new kinds of spatial awareness', *Economy and Society*, 33: 582–604.

Thrift, N. (2004c) 'Remembering the technological unconscious by foregrounding knowledges of position', *Environment and Planning D: Society and Space*, 22: 175–90.

Thrift, N. (2005a) 'But malice aforethought: cities and the natural history of hatred', *Transactions of the Institute of British Geographers*, 30: 133–50.

Thrift, N. (2005b) 'From born to made: technology, biology and space', *Transactions of the Institute of British Geographers,* 30: 463–76.

Thrift, N. (2005c) 'Transurbanism', *Urban Geography,* 25: 724–34.

Thrift, N. (2006) 'Re-inventing invention: new tendencies in capitalist commodification', *Economy and Society,* 35: 279–306.

Thrift, N. (2007) 'Immaculate warfare: the spatial practices of extreme violence', in D. Gregory and A. Pred (eds), *Spaces of Terror.* New York: Routledge. pp 273–94.

Thrift, N. (2009) 'Different atmospheres: of Sloterdijk, China, and site', *Environment and Planning D: Society and Space,* 27 (1): 119–38.

Thrift, N. and Forbes, D. (1986) *The Price of War: Urbanization in Vietnam, 1954–1985.* Boston: Allen and Unwin.

Thrift, N. and Leyshon, A. (1992) 'Liberalisation and consolidation: the single European market and the remaking of European financial capital', *Environment and Planning A,* 24: 49–81.

Thrift, N. and Leyshon, A. (1994) 'A phantom state: the de-traditionalization of money, the international financial system and international financial centers', *Political Geography,* 13: 299–327.

Thrift, N. and Williams, P. (1987) *Class and Space: The Making of Urban Society.* New York: Routledge & Kegan Paul.

Barney Warf, University of Kansas

56 Gearóid Ó Tuathail (Gerard Toal)

BIOGRAPHICAL DETAILS AND THEORETICAL CONTEXT

An innovative and prolific political geographer, Gearóid Ó Tuathail (Gerard Toal) was born in the Republic of Ireland in 1962. Growing up in County Monaghan on the border with Northern Ireland was among the influences that pushed Ó Tuathail to study political geography. He graduated with a joint BA in history and geography in 1982 from St. Patrick's College in Maynooth (now the National University of Ireland, Maynooth). Ó Tuathail completed his Master's degree at the University of Illinois at Urbana-Champaign under the direction of John O'Loughlin, and moved to Syracuse University where, supervised by John Agnew and political scientist David Sylvan, he completed his PhD entitled 'Critical geopolitics: the social construction of place and space in the practice of statecraft' (Ó Tuathail, 1989). Ó Tuathail has taught at the University of Liverpool, University of Southern California, University of Minnesota, and Virginia Polytechnic Institute and State University.

His first publication argued for a 'new geopolitics' that was 'much more critical' than traditional evaluations of national interest and policy recommendation (Ó Tuathail, 1986: 73). Defining geo-politics as political discourse structured 'by either explicit reference to geographical location and concepts or by use of certain implicitly geographical policy rationalizations (e.g. *Lebensraum,* domino theory, containment, expansionism)', Ó Tuathail (1986: 73–4) examined US–EL Salvador relations from the 1823 Monroe Doctrine to the 1980s Reagan administration. 'American foreign policy', Ó Tuathail (1986: 83) concluded, 'aims to perpetuate, secure and reaffirm the American way of life. Part of insuring the survival and prosperity of large industrial states such as America involves dominating, controlling and influencing.' His subsequent article assessing US foreign policy, co-authored with John Agnew (1992), 'precipitated a research agenda which conceptualized geopolitics as a form of political discourse rather than simply a descriptive term intended to cover the study of foreign policy and grand statecraft' (Dodds, 2001: 469).

In their paper, Ó Tuathail and Agnew (1992: 192) argued that geo-politics must be studied as 'a discursive practice by which intellectuals of statecraft "spatialize" international politics in such a way as to represent it as a "world" characterized by particular types of places, peoples and dramas'. Focusing on international relations and foreign policy-making, Ó Tuathail and Agnew (1992: 194) maintained that the speeches and writings of politicians, diplomats, policy advisors and the media comprise 'geopolitical reasoning'. These statements can be analysed, not to see whether they are truthful, but rather to critically examine the effects that using certain terms and language have on the practice and impact of international relations. Painter (1995: 146) thus argues that the research agenda initiated by Ó Tuathail's work is 'concerned particularly with the "texts" of international politics', what they mean and how they are used, rather than political events in themselves.

Evaluating geo-politics stimulated a reshaping of political geography in the 1990s, and contrasted with examinations of the geographical facts of politics and state relations. Ó Tuathail and Agnew (1992) argued there was a need to assess how 'geopolitical reasoning' constructs representations of states, territories and political regimes through discourse and how people utilise these discursive understandings to explain events, envision international relations and justify foreign policy actions. This research agenda, therefore, was a departure from existing studies within political geography concerned with state formation, contested national borders and territories, nationalism and secession, voting patterns, geographical impacts of wars and concepts such as world-systems theory, state theory and sovereignty (Painter, 1995; Atkinson and Dodds, 2000; Dodds, 2001).

SPATIAL CONTRIBUTIONS

Ó Tuathail's key contribution to debates on space and place has been his espousal of a critical theory of geo-politics. Traditionally, geo-politics is how state analysts, military or other, interpret the territorial operation of state power and visualise spatial control. In contrast, Ó Tuathail argues for a *critical* geo-politics that recognises and exposes geo-political assertions and makes 'informed critiques of the spatializing practices of power' (Ó Tuathail and Dalby, 1994: 513). Influenced by the end of the Cold War and postmodern, poststructuralist, feminist and psychoanalytic theories, critical geo-politics problematises political discourses, examines their spatial assumptions, questions power relations and challenges the role of the state and how its institutional analysts envision the world. Ó Tuathail draws on **Foucault**'s understanding of governmentality to argue that the articulation of 'geo-power' over both people and territory is a critical function of modern statehood. '[M]y concern', states Ó Tuathail (1996a: 11), 'is the power struggle between different societies over the right to speak sovereignly about geography, space and territory.' Utilising Derrida to assess and deconstruct political discourse, Ó Tuathail (1996a: 66–7) proposes that geo-graphy and geo-politics can be hyphenated to emphasise the process of discourse in writing or 'scripting... global space by state-society intellectuals and institutions'.

Drawing on such diverse theoretical traditions and conversant in contemporary international relations theories, Ó Tuathail productively integrated these approaches to generate analyses that interrogated contemporary international political discourse and stressed the importance to statecraft of geographical representations. Indeed, this is one of Ó Tuathail's most significant geographical contributions. Critical geo-politics made issues of space and political geography pertinent to the discipline of international relations and its practitioners, introducing geographical analyses to intellectual debates and scholars that had largely ignored these perspectives. Critical geo-politics, therefore, is interdisciplinary and Ó Tuathail has been at the forefront of developing this field of study, editing books and special issues of major journals on the topic (e.g., Ó Tuathail and Dalby, 1994; 1998a; Dalby and Ó Tuathail, 1996; Herod et al., 1998; Ó Tuathail et al., 1998).

In his book *Critical Geopolitics*, Ó Tuathail (1996a) deconstructs the canon of late nineteenth- and early twentieth-century geo-political texts by Rudolf Kjellen, Friedrich Ratzel, Karl Haushofer and Halford Mackinder, exposing their assumptions of political power and paying attention to their constructions of space, race and gender. Traditional geo-politics was a science for men who sought to know and control territory and Ó Tuathail (1996a: 82) contends that Mackinder envisioned British East Africa (Kenya) 'as a feminized space to be penetrated, a territory reached by others but not yet conquered'. Further, Ó Tuathail (1996a: 111–29) examines both the fact and fictionalisation of Haushofer and Nazi geo-politics in US magazines *Life* and *Reader's Digest* and the movie *Plan for Destruction* (1943). These examples are contrasted with other geo-political texts produced at the time, such as those by US foreign policy analyst Robert Strausz-Hupé, an Austrian émigré to the US. *Critical Geopolitics* also includes studies of the writings by conservative (post-) Cold War US intellectuals Samuel Huntington and Edward Luttwak (Ó Tuathail, 1996a).

Ó Tuathail has also developed a number of concepts for critically analysing geo-political reasoning, dividing geo-political discourse into 'popular geopolitics' – evident in the mass media, movies and popular culture; 'practical geopolitics' – apparent in foreign policy and state bureaucracy; and 'formal geopolitics' produced in think-tanks and academic venues (Ó Tuathail and Dalby, 1998b). Diagrammatically outlining how this tripartite division intertwines to 'comprise the geopolitical culture of a particular region, state or inter-state alliance',

to produce a 'spatializing of boundaries and dangers' and to construct 'geopolitical representations of self and other', Ó Tuathail and Dalby (1998b: 5) maintain that geo-politics are socio-cultural phenomena evident in everyday life.

Geo-political representations are produced and consumed in myriad ways, from tabloid newspaper headlines and Hollywood films, to presidential speeches advocating military action. Examining the 'geopolitical condition' of contemporary international politics, Ó Tuathail (2000b; 2002b) argues that processes like globalization, telecommunications and the 'world risk society' are challenging extant ways of thinking about state borders, territory, power, defence and security. With world leaders lauding the possibilities of the internet, biotechnology and telecommunications for capital, industry and science, many are simultaneously worried that these advances could get into the 'wrong hands' and generate new threats to state security. Ó Tuathail (e.g., 2002b) expands critical geo-politics beyond discourse analysis, to address the 'geopolitical world order' of state alliances, global relations of production, consumption and the spatial processes of trade or 'geopolitical economy' and world 'techno-territorial complexes' that, through scientific advances, the acceleration of transportation and communications and their utilisations, re-shape power relations within, between and beyond states.

The range of topics across Ó Tuathail's numerous publications suggests that many can find material to resonate with their own interests. Alongside re-evaluations of the discourse of foreign policy debates and interviews with major figures within the geo-political canon (e.g., 1992; 1994; 2000a; 2001; 2005a; 2006; 2008a), Ó Tuathail, often presciently, examines contemporary issues. These include case studies of the intersection of politics and control over territory, such as the 1991 Gulf War (e.g., 1997), the

Balkan Wars of the early 1990s and their aftermath (e.g., 1996a; 1996b; 1999; 2002a; 2006; Ó Tuathail and Dahlman, 2004; 2006; Dahlman and Ó Tuathail, 2005a; 2005b), Russia and crises in the Caucus Mountains in the 2000s (e.g., 2008b; Kolossov and Ó Tuathail, 2007; O'Loughlin et al., 2004; 2006; 2008). One study, centred on reports by Maggie O'Kane in the British daily newspaper *The Guardian,* argues an 'anti-geopolitics' scripted Bosnia as a place of horrors where the West must intervene, but implicitly maintained that Bosnia remains a place that is beyond the Western political sphere (Ó Tuathail, 1996b: 182). Ó Tuathail's initial examinations of Bosnia in US policy discourse were widely applauded; Smith (2000: 365) claimed they comprise 'the most fertile and adventurous critique of a geo-political tradition'. Working with Carl Dahlman, Ó Tuathail advanced his analyses of Bosnia by comparing official political discourse, the language and practical impacts of treaties and legislation, and personal experiences recounted by interviewees. Exploring how the often brutal process of ethnic cleansing established new 'facts on the ground' that shaped subsequent land allocations and created 'new landscape[s] of land plots and housing settlements' (Ó Tuathail and Dahlman, 2006: 305), Ó Tuathail extends critical geo-politics to interrogate both the material and discursive process of state formation.

KEY ADVANCES AND CONTROVERSIES

In the name of heterogeneity and flexibility, Ó Tuathail frequently avoids defining 'critical geopolitics', 'geopolitics', 'territory', 'space' and 'sovereignty'. Some critics question such definitional malleability, claiming that this, coupled with the diverse philosophical sources drawn upon by Ó Tuathail, produce 'theoretically inconstant' assessments (Stephanson, 2000: 381). Others contend that Ó Tuathail's work represents an 'extreme' critical geopolitics and is too dismissive of, and 'disinterest[ed]' in, theorisation (Kelly, 2006: 35, 40). Further, Kelly (2006: 42–3) maintains that although Ó Tuathail and colleagues have taken the understanding of geo-politics beyond current thought and practice in political science, despite their suggestion that a critical approach is a step towards 'emancipation' and 'the ending of hegemonic exploitation,' critical geo-politics offers 'neither a clear characterisation of a better society nor a specific road map for attaining such an improvement.'

Critical Geopolitics (Ó Tuathail, 1996a) was well received. Heffernan (2000: 347) comments that the book is '[i]maginative, intellectually ambitious ... engaging [and] outstanding' and Sharp (2000: 361) claims *Critical Geopolitics* to be 'vital'. The text stimulated a symposium at the annual meeting of the Association of American Geographers in 1997, subsequently published in *Political Geography.* In the ensuing debate, three contentions emerged. Firstly, Ó Tuathail is challenged for over-relying on textual data to the detriment of other empirical materials, such as maps, something that is curious given the importance of visual representation to both the geographical imagination and foreign policy strategy (see Heffernan, 2000; Smith, 2000; Sparke, 2000; Stephanson, 2000). Secondly, issues of embodiment and positionality of both author and subjects were raised; as were, thirdly, contentions that Ó Tuathail's text is inadvertently elitist, focusing on a few 'great men' in the field of geopolitics (Sharp, 2000), some suggesting that Ó Tuathail does not do enough to locate himself outside this canon. Dodds (1998) adds that Ó Tuathail's focus is over-whelmingly Anglo-American.

In sum, critics suggest that Ó Tuathail is guilty of what he accuses in others – an assertion of a transcendental viewpoint from where the world and its political order can be viewed – the difference being that Ó Tuathail takes a counterhegemonic rather than hegemonic perspective. Sharp (2000) maintains that Ó Tuathail elides geo-political discourses in other fields, such as popular culture, and Smith (2000: 367) maintains that although Ó Tuathail is sensitive to '[r]eading race and gender into the texts of geopolitics', this 'is simul-taneously . . . a way of reading class out'. Stephanson (2000: 382) charges that Ó Tuathail's 'attack on totalization' in geo-political discourse and foreign policy itself 'turns out ... to be a totalization', reducing the power of Ó Tuathail's interrogation

to intellectual games of deconstruction rather than empirical assessments of the material impacts of geo-politics on peo-ple's lives. Ó Tuathail (2000c) responded to these challenges, and his subsequent work demonstrates an expansion of critical geo-politics beyond the texts of policy elites to studies detailing the processes of post-war house building and settlement in Bosnia and examining geo-political discourse in popular films such as 2001's *Behind Enemy Lines* (Ó Tuathail, 2005b). Stimulated by Ó Tuathail's influential contribution to 'criti-cal geopolitics' – he magnanimously cred-its **Peter Taylor** with coining this term during discussion at the University of Illinois (Ó Tuathail, 2000) – contemporary analysis of political discourses and their constructions of spatial power relations are hence advancing political geography into significant new arenas.

Ó Tuathail's KEY WORKS

Herod, A., Ó Tuathail, G. and Roberts, S. (eds) (1998) *An Unruly World? Geography, Globalization and Governance.* London: Routledge.
Ó Tuathail, G. (1996a) *Critical Geopolitics: The Politics of Writing Global Space.* Minneapolis: University of Minnesota Press.
Ó Tuathail, G. and Agnew, J. (1992) 'Geopolitics and discourse: practical geopolitical reasoning and American foreign policy', *Political Geography,* 11: 190–204.
Ó Tuathail, G. and Dahlman, C. (2006) '"The West Bank of the Drina": land allocation and ethnic engineering in Republika Srpska', *Transactions of the Institute of British Geographers,* 31: 304–22.
Ó Tuathail, G. and Dalby, S. (eds) (1998a) *Rethinking Geopolitics.* London: Routledge.
Ó Tuathail, G., Dalby, S. and Routledge, P. (eds) (1998) *A Geopolitics Reader.* London: Routledge.

Secondary Sources and References

Atkinson, D. and Dodds, K. (2000) 'Introduction to geopolitical traditions: a century of geopolitical thought', in K. Dodds and D. Atkinson (eds), *Geopolitical Traditions: A Century of Geopolitical Thought.* London: Routledge. pp. 1–24.
Dahlman, C. and Ó Tuathail, G. (2005a) 'Broken Bosnia: the localized geopolitics of displacement and return in two Bosnian places', *Annals of the Association of American Geographers,* 95: 644–62.

Dahlman, C. and Ó Tuathail, G. (2005b) 'The legacy of ethnic cleansing: the returns process in post-Dayton Bosnia', *Political Geography*, 24: 569–99.

Dalby, S. and Ó Tuathail, G. (1996) 'Editorial introduction: the critical geopolitics constellation: problematizing fusions of geographical knowledge and power', *Political Geography*, 15: 451–6.

Dodds, K. (1998) 'Review of *Critical Geopolitics*', *Economic Geography*, 74: 77–9.

Dodds, K. (2001) 'Political geography III: critical geopolitics after ten years', *Progress in Human Geography*, 25: 469–84.

Heffernan, M. (2000) 'Balancing visions: comments on Gearóid Ó Tuathail's critical geopolitics', *Political Geography*, 19: 347–52.

Kelly, P. (2006) 'A critique of critical geopolitics', *Geopolitics*, 11: 24–53.

Kolossov, V. and Ó Tuathail, G. (2007) 'An empire's fraying edge? The North Caucasus instability in Russian geopolitical culture', *Eurasian Geography and Economics*, 48: 202–25.

O'Loughlin, J., Ó Tuathail, G. and Kolossov, V. (2004) 'A "risky westward turn"? Putin's 9–11 script and ordinary Russians', *Europe Asia Studies*, 56: 3–34.

O'Loughlin, J., Ó Tuathail, G. and Kolossov, V. (2006) 'The geopolitical orientations of ordinary Russians: a public opinion analysis', *Eurasian Geography and Economics*, 47: 158–81.

O'Loughlin, J., Ó Tuathail, G. and Kolossov, V. (2008) 'The localized geopolitics of displacement and return in Eastern Prigorodnyy Rayon, North Ossetia', *Eurasian Geography and Economics*, 49: 635–99.

Ó Tuathail, G. (1986) 'The language and nature of the "new" geopolitics: The case of US–El Salvador relations', *Political Geography Quarterly*, 5: 73–85.

Ó Tuathail, G. (1989) 'Critical geopolitics: the social construction of place and space in the practice of statecraft', Unpublished PhD dissertation, Syracuse University, Syracuse.

Ó Tuathail, G. (1992) 'Putting Mackinder in his place: material transformations and myth', *Political Geography*, 11: 100–18.

Ó Tuathail, G. (1994) 'The critical reading/writing of geopolitics: re-reading/writing Wittfogel, Bowman and Lacoste', *Progress in Human Geography*, 18: 313–32.

Ó Tuathail, G. (1996b) 'An anti-geopolitical eye? Maggie O'Kane in Bosnia, 1992–94', *Gender, Place and Culture*, 3: 171–85.

Ó Tuathail, G. (1997 [1993]) 'The effacement of place? US foreign policy and the spatiality of the Gulf Crisis', in J. Agnew (ed.), *Political Geography: A Reader*. London: Edward Arnold. pp. 140–64.

Ó Tuathail, G. (1999) 'A strategic sign: the geopolitical significance of "Bosnia" in US foreign policy', *Environment and Planning D: Society and Space*, 17: 515–33.

Ó Tuathail, G. (2000a) 'Spiritual geopolitics: Father Edmund Walsh and Jesuit anticommunism', in K. Dodds and D. Atkinson (eds), *Geopolitical Traditions: A Century of Geopolitical Thought*. London: Routledge. pp. 187–210.

Ó Tuathail, G. (2000b) 'The postmodern geopolitical condition: states, statecraft, and security into the twenty-first century', *Annals of the Association of American Geographers*, 90: 166–78.

Ó Tuathail, G. (2001) 'A geopolitical discourse with Robert McNamara', *Geopolitics*, 5: 129–44.

Ó Tuathail, G. (2002a) 'Theorizing practical geopolitical reasoning: the case of US Bosnia policy in 1992', *Political Geography*, 21: 601–28.

Ó Tuathail, G. (2002b) 'Post-Cold War geopolitics: contrasting superpowers in a world of global dangers', in R. J. Johnston, P. Taylor and M. Watts (eds), *Geographies of Global Change*. Oxford: Blackwell. pp. 174–89.

Ó Tuathail, G. (2005a) 'Geopolitical discourse: a conversation with Peter Galbraith about Iraq and state building', *Geopolitics*, 10: 167–83.

Ó Tuathail, G. (2005b) 'The frustrations of geopolitics and the pleasures of war: *Behind Enemy Lines* and American geopolitical culture', *Geopolitics*, 10: 356–77.

Ó Tuathail, G. (2006) 'Geopolitical discourse: Paddy Ashdown and the tenth anniversary of the Dayton Peace Accords', *Geopolitics*, 11: 141–58.

Ó Tuathail, G. (2008a) 'The Hamiltonian nationalist: a conversation with Michael Lind', *Geopolitics*, 13: 169–80.

Ó Tuathail, G. (2008b) 'Russia's Kosovo: a critical geopolitics of the August 2008 war over South Ossetia', *Eurasian Geography and Economics*, 49: 670–705.

Ó Tuathail, G. and Dahlman, C. (2004) 'The effort to reverse ethnic cleansing in Bosnia-Herzegovina: the limits of returns', *Eurasian Geography and Economics*, 45: 429–53.

Ó Tuathail, G. and Dalby, S. (1994) 'Editorial: critical geopolitics – unfolding spaces for thought in geography and global politics', *Environment and Planning D: Society and Space*, 12: 513–14.

Ó Tuathail, G. and Dalby, S. (1998b) 'Introduction: rethinking geopolitics – towards a critical geopolitics', in G. Ó Tuathail and S. Dalby (eds), *Rethinking Geopolitics*. London: Routledge. pp. 1–15.

Painter, J. (1995) *Politics, Geography and 'Political Geography': A Critical Perspective*. London: Arnold.

Sharp, J. P. (2000) 'Remasculinising geo-politics? Comments on Gearóid Ó Tuathail's *Critical Geopolitics*', *Political Geography*, 19: 361–4.

Smith, N. (2000) 'Is a critical geopolitics possible? Foucault, class and the vision thing', *Political Geography*, 19: 365–71.

Sparke, M. (2000) 'Graphing the geo in geo-political: *Critical Geopolitics* and the re-visioning of responsibility', *Political Geography*, 19: 373–80.

Stephanson, A. (2000) 'Commentary on Gearóid Ó Tuathail's *Critical Geopolitics*', *Political Geography*, 19: 381–3.

Toal, G/Ó Tuathail, G. (2000c) 'Dis/placing the geo-politics which one cannot not want', *Political Geography*, 19: 385–90.

Euan Hague, DePaul University

BIOGRAPHICAL DETAILS AND THEORETICAL CONTEXT

Waldo Tobler was born in 1930, the son of Swiss parents living in the Pacific Northwest of the US. After schooling in the US and in Switzerland and four years in the American army, he studied at the University of British Columbia, where he took his first cartography course with Ross Mackay. He transferred to the University of Washington, where he received his BA in 1955, his MA in 1957 and his PhD in 1961 for a dissertation entitled 'Map transformations of geographic space'. He was part of the group who studied under John Sherman and William Garrison at Washington in the late 1950s, a group that included Brian Berry, Duane Marble, Richard Morrill, John Nystuen, Michael Dacey and William Bunge. This placed him at the centre of what is often termed geography's 'quantitative revolution'. Tobler (2002) subsequently described this period as 'a most exciting time', noting, however, that his academic concern was for models and theories rather than numbers as such.

Tobler spent 16 years, from 1961 to 1977, at the University of Michigan (with John Nystuen and Gunnar Olsson). Here he developed his interest in computer programming and mathematics, and learnt differential geometry, which proved invaluable for his work on map projections. From 1977, he worked at the University of California, Santa Barbara (with **Golledge**, Smith and Goodchild). At Santa Barbara he was associated with the National Center for Geographic Information and Analysis, taking up the position of Professor Emeritus upon retirement in 1994 and remaining active long into that retirement (e.g., Tobler, 2004). Throughout, Tobler was widely acknowledged with maintaining geography's interest in cartography during the quantitative revolution and acclaimed as a pioneer in the use of computers in cartography. Well-versed in mathematics, Tobler was particularly acclaimed for his development of continuous-space representations of geographical space. He developed interests in other fields too, especially modelling migration flows, and completed innovative methodological work in quantitative geography. He has also worked on spectral analysis and has used vector and tensor analysis, often preferring mathematical methods to the statistical methods favoured by most geographers interested in quantitative modelling.

SPATIAL CONTRIBUTIONS

Tobler's early work was concerned with the development of new perspectives on mapping. He was a leader in the use of computers in cartography (Tobler, 1959; 1967a), especially in the design of new projections. In his PhD thesis, he introduced the concept of maps scaled in travel time or cost, rather than distance. He also developed the idea of employing map transformations in order to represent social or demographic reality rather than just the earth's surface. If a theory, such as those of Christaller or von Thünen, makes unrealistic assumptions about the study area, he suggested that this can be tackled by transforming geographic space to make the assumptions fit. This is done by the use of cartograms, which can be of many types but generally attempt to depict the earth's surface in a way where the size of features reflects not their surface area but their importance (see Tobler, 2004). As he put it, 'In many ways these maps are more realistic than the conventional maps used by geographers ... The important point, of course, is not that the transformations distort area, but that they distribute densities uniformly' (Tobler, 1963). In this and in other contexts, Tobler has consistently been generous in making his software available for other researchers to use.

In addition to cartograms, Tobler developed many new and unusual map projections. He has applied his approach to map projections to examine historical maps and the implicit projections that underlie them (Tobler, 1966). Another interesting historical project was his work with Wineberg (1971) on the location of ancient Hittite settlements. The existence of records of trade links between settlements of the period was exploited to estimate the location (in many cases unknown) of the settlements involved. This was done using an inverse form of the gravity model, in which the number of times two places were mentioned in close proximity was used as an estimate of interaction, and distances were predicted on the basis of

size and interaction. Subsequent archaeological investigation verified the model's predictions.

Much of Tobler's work has been concerned with adopting mathematical methods to new geographical contexts. One example of this is his paper 'Of maps and matrices' (Tobler, 1967b), in which he argues that data for regularly arranged places on the earth's surface can be regarded as forming a matrix, and that matrix multiplication can be performed with such data to yield geographically interesting results. The argument is illustrated using **Torsten Hägerstrand's** simulation of the spread of innovations. Tobler's development of mathematically based but empirically useful techniques is also exemplified by his development of pycnophylactic interpolation (Tobler, 1979) as a solution to the problem of areal interpolation: the problem of comparing geographical distributions (e.g., of population at two dates) when the sets of boundaries are incompatible. His solution is based on the (perhaps questionable) idea that the imposition of a set of areal units on geographical space renders the underlying continuous distribution into a discrete data set. The problem of interpolation becomes one of estimating the continuous surface and then calculating the values of the surface over the new data set. Tobler (1989) has continued to show interest in this issue, and the related 'modifiable areal unit' problem (where fine-grained spatially-referenced data is effectively aggregated 'out of existence' by being published on a broader spatial scale). However, he argues that such problems result from the use of inappropriate statistics like the correlation coefficient instead of the spatial cross-coherence function. For him, geographical distributions should be considered as a two-dimensional spatial series. Not everybody, however, would agree with this, nor his conclusion that the modifiable areal unit problem goes away when geographers use the correct analytical procedures.

Tobler participated in the explosion of interest in geographical information systems associated with the establishment of the National Center for Geographic Information and Analysis at Santa Barbara, particularly with his attempts to conduct geographical analysis which is 'frame independent', that is to say, independent of the areal units used. He proposes that 'all methods of spatial analysis be examined for the invariance of their conclusions under alternative spatial partitionings, and that only those methods be allowed which show such invariance' (Tobler, 1989: 115). He subsequently advocated a new type of geographical information system, like a raster system except that it is not based on regularly located pixels (picture elements) but on irregularly bounded *resels* (resolution elements) such as the administrative areas for which so much geographical information is available. Tobler has also been keen to remind geographers that we live on the surface of a sphere; he finds it 'curious that most spatial analysis done by geographers uses a flat earth' (2002: 315). Thus Tobler and Chen (1986) discussed how the 'quadtree' system of geographical information storage could be adapted to store data for the whole world.

Another innovation in geography to which Tobler has been a major contributor was the use of computer-based simulation, notably his 'computer movie' simulating the population growth of Detroit (Tobler, 1970). Tobler has also contributed to other aspects of quantitative geography, for example in work on geographical variances (Tobler and Moellering, 1972) and on geographical interpolation (Kennedy and Tobler, 1983; Tobler and Kennedy, 1985). He has introduced the concept of bidimensional regression (Tobler, 1994), a procedure for regression analysis in which both the dependent and independent variables are pairs of coordinates (such as latitude and longitude, or eastings and northings). Such a method is particularly relevant to map comparisons, and examples are given from historical cartography and cognitive mapping.

Another long-standing interest of Tobler's has been migration, viewed in aggregate terms (Tobler, 1981; 1987; 1995). Although interested in interaction-based models of interaction his work has been distinctive in viewing migration movements as 'a continuous vector field driven by a partial differential equation representing the attractivity potential' (Tobler, 2002: 315). Migration is regarded as taking place in continuous space, leading to discussion of migration 'winds', 'fields' and 'currents'. Dorigo and Tobler (1983) developed a view of migration defined in terms of pushes and pulls from the origin and destination areas, discounted by a distance deterrence effect. Their model is based on the total numbers of in-migrants and out-migrants for each place, with the total migration flow being the sum of the push effect for the origin and the pull effect for the destination, divided by the distance between. The approach is open to the criticism that such concepts do not give a satisfactory explanation of why observed migration patterns occur, or of exactly what the push and pull factors consist of. It may also seem less intuitively appealing than a gravity model approach where certain entities (cities or states) are easier to relate to economic and other theories.

KEY ADVANCES AND CONTROVERSIES

Tobler's first major achievement was the transformation of geographical cartography from a field basically concerned with visualisation to one where graphical methods could be recast as mathematical operations, and where computers began to be accepted as essential tools for the map-maker. The field of analytical cartography has thus been based to a considerable extent on Tobler's ideas, and given a major boost by the development of geographical information science. Much of the agenda of contemporary geographic information science derives from issues raised or first explored by Tobler. His contribution has not been restricted to the academic world, however, as his cartographic innovations and perspectives have been adopted by government and the software industry.

Tobler's work, especially on map projections, was very relevant to the development in the 1960s of the idea that geography and geometry were closely related, found for example in works by Haggett (1965) and Bunge (1966). Like **Peter Haggett**, Tobler (1963) argued that there were interesting similarities in shape between natural and human phenomena, such as between cities and leaves. Such ideas led **David Harvey** (1969) to argue for geometry as 'the language of spatial form', and to build on Tobler's ideas to explore the relevance of non-Euclidean geometries to reflect social space. This emphasis on geometry was fairly short-lived, with **Cosgrove** (1989: 235), for example seeking alternatives to 'the cold geometries of spatial analysis' and Sack (1972) casting doubt on the ability of geometry to explain geographical reality. Cartograms are still widely used (e.g., Dorling, 1995), as are other aspects of Tobler's work, but quantitative geographers nowadays use these concepts and tools without claiming any special status for geometry as a language for geography.

Tobler's concern with spatial form and with concepts and techniques from geometry lays him open to accusations

that he is more concerned with methods to describe and manipulate geographical reality than he is to explain or understand phenomena. Even on topics such as migration, which have attracted a great deal of behavioural and humanistic study, Tobler's contributions often explicitly avoid such perspectives – not necessarily because he does not think them important, but more because he feels he is best able to contribute in other ways. He also tends to adopt deterministic rather than statistical approaches to modelling geographical phenomena. This may be partly because of his unusual competence (for a geographer) in the relevant branches of mathematics, but is partly because of an approach to modelling in which he is prepared to accept the explanatory limitations of a model if it illuminates an idea that is important.

Another concern of quantitative geographers from the 1960s onwards was the wish to emulate the sciences, and Tobler's use in many of his papers of methods and concepts from the physical sciences and mathematics is an illustration of this. He admits (Tobler, 2002: 322) that these methods yield only crude approximations when applied to human populations, but argues that 'they seem to give definite insight into the processes being studied.' Another attribute of the sciences that has been important in positivist approaches to human geography is the drive to identify 'laws' in the way that has been done in physics (Golledge and Amedeo, 1968). For example, when revisiting Ravenstein's 'laws of migration' (1885), Tobler (1995) suggested they stand up well today, demonstrating (for him) the desirability of identifying such laws. In this context, it is fitting to conclude with what Tobler (1970) called the 'first law of geography', namely: 'everything is related to everything else, but near things are more related than distant things'.

TOBLER'S KEY WORKS

Tobler, W.R. (1959) 'Automation and cartography', *Geographical Review*, 49: 526–34.

Tobler, W.R. (1963) 'Geographic area and map projections', *Geographical Review*, 52: 59–78.

Tobler, W.R. (1966) 'Medieval distortions: the projections of ancient maps', *Annals of the Association of American Geographers*, 56: 351–60.

Tobler, W.R. (1969) 'Geographic filters and their inverses', *Geographical Analysis*, 1: 234–54.

Tobler, W.R. (1970) 'A computer movie simulating urban growth in the Detroit region', *Economic Geography*, 46: 234–40.

Tobler, W.R. and Moellering, H. (1972) 'Geographical variances', *Geographical Analysis*, 4: 34–50.

Tobler, W.R. (1979) 'Smooth pycnophylactic interpolation for geographical regions', *Journal of the American Statistical Association*, 74: 519–36.

Dorigo, G. and Tobler, W.R. (1983) 'Push-pull migration laws', *Annals of the Association of American Geographers*, 73 (1): 1–17.

Tobler, W. (2004) 'Thirty-five years of computer cartograms', *Annals of the Association of American Geographers*, 94 (1): 58–73.

Secondary Sources and References

Bunge, W. (1966) *Theoretical Geography* (2nd edition). Lund: Lund Studies in Geography, Series C, No. 1.

Cosgrove, D.E. (1989) 'Models, description and imagination in geography', in W. Macmillan (ed.), *Remodelling Geography*. Oxford: Blackwell. pp. 230–44.

Dorling, D. (1995) *A New Social Atlas of Britain*. Chichester: Wiley.

Golledge, R.G. and Amedeo, D. (1968) 'On laws in geography', *Annals of the Association of American Geographers*, 58: 760–74.

Haggett, P. (1965) *Locational Analysis in Modern Geography*. London: Arnold.

Harvey, D. (1969) *Explanation in Geography*. London: Arnold.

Kennedy, S. and Tobler, W.R. (1983) 'Geographic interpolation', *Geographical Analysis*, 15: 151–56.

Ravenstein, E.G. (1885) 'The laws of migration,' *Journal of the Royal Statistical Society*, 46: 167–235.

Sack, R.D. (1972) 'Geography, geometry and explanation', *Annals of the Association of American Geographers*, 62: 61–78.

Tobler, W.R. (1963) 'D'Arcy Thompson and the analysis of growth and form', Papers of the Michigan Academy of Science, Arts and Letters, 48: 385–90.

Tobler, W.R. (1964) 'Automation in the preparation of thematic maps', *Cartographic Journal*, 1: 1–7.

Tobler, W.R. (1965) 'Computation of the correspondence of geographical patterns', Papers of the Regional Science Association, 15: 131–9.

Tobler, W.R. (1966) 'Notes on two projections', *Cartographic Journal*, 3: 87–9.

Tobler, W.R. (1967a) 'Computer use in geography', *Behavioral Science*, 12: 57–8.

Tobler, W.R. (1967b) 'Of maps and matrices', *Journal of Regional Science*, 7 (2) (Supplement): 275–80.

Tobler, W.R. (1971) 'Uniform distribution of objects in a homogeneous field: cities on a plain', *Nature*, 233.

Tobler, W.R. (1981) 'A model of geographical movement', *Geographical Analysis*, 13: 1–20.

Tobler, W.R. (1987) 'Experiments in migration mapping by computer', *American Cartographer*, 14: 155–63.

Tobler, W.R. (1989) 'Frame independent spatial analysis', in M. Goodchild and S. Gopal (eds), *Accuracy of Spatial Databases*. London: Taylor & Francis. pp. 115–22.

Tobler, W.R. (1994) 'Bidimensional regression', *Geographical Analysis*, 26: 186–212.

Tobler, W.R. (1995) 'Migration: Ravenstein, Thornthwaite, and beyond', *Urban Geography*, 16: 327–43.

Tobler, W.R. (2002) 'Ma vie', in P. Gould and F.R. Pitts (eds), *Geographical Voices: Fourteen Autobiographical Essays*. Syracuse: Syracuse University Press. pp. 293–322.

Tobler, W.R. and Chen, Z. (1986) 'A quadtree for global information storage', *Geographical Analysis*, 18: 360–71.

Tobler, W.R. and Kennedy, S. (1985) 'Smooth multidimensional interpolation', *Geographical Analysis*, 17: 251–7.

Tobler, W.R. and Wineberg, S. (1971) 'A Cappadocian speculation', *Nature*, 231, 5297: 39–42.

Robin Flowerdew, University of St Andrews

58 Yi-Fu Tuan

BIOGRAPHICAL DETAILS AND THEORETICAL CONTEXT

In *Dear Colleague*, a collection of letters to colleagues which Yi-Fu Tuan describes as 'passages that I have underlined in a book of life', he sums up the human focus of his geographic scholarship: 'to know one person and his world better' (Tuan, 2002: ix–x). Through a long and productive career, Yi-Fu Tuan has challenged us to rethink what it is to be human and questioned our place in the world. He has given us a deeper more metaphysical concept of geography, yet always presents his thought-provoking scholarship in a deceptively simple, reflective style. In a world where cynicism, negativity and nihilism are all too common, Yi-Fu Tuan has continued to find hope and present a message that a respect for and deeper understanding of one another and the world around us can lead us to a better life: hence the title of one of his later works, *Human Goodness* (Tuan, 2008).

Born in Tientsin, China in 1930, Yi-Fu Tuan was educated in China, Australia, the Philippines and England (where he obtained a BA and MA from Oxford University), and moved to the US in 1951 (PhD, University of California, Berkeley). From 1984 to his retirement in 1998, he was based at the University of Wisconsin, Madison. Although Tuan's initial research was in geomorphology – studying pediments in south-western Arizona – his reputation was established as a cultural geographer. Throughout the 1960s, Tuan produced traditional papers on physical phenomena (e.g., Tuan, 1962; 1966) alongside more affective reflections (e.g., 1961; 1964). However, it is from the late 1960s that attitudes to the environment and a more 'humanistic' approach emerged as his primary focus (e.g., Tuan, 1968; 1971). *Topophilia: A Study of Environmental Perception, Attitudes and Values* (Tuan, 1974) quickly became a classic text. The reflective style of writing and the broad range of geographical and literary sources cited became a hallmark of Tuan's scholarship.

Yi-Fu Tuan is author of some 20 books, many of which have become widely recognised for their scholarship and individual voice, and has published numerous refereed articles generally of a reflective and thought-provoking kind. Very much defining 'humanistic geography' for a generation, Tuan pursued the more fundamental questions arising from a search for the meaning of existence based on an understanding of ourselves as 'Being-in-the-World', fundamentally defined by and in relation to the world both physically and emotionally (an interpretation of phenomenology). For Tuan, such research is also about self-discovery, and therefore it is no surprise that one of his later books was entitled *Who am I? An Autobiography Of Emotion, Mind and Spirit*

(1999), in which he reveals much of the motivation behind his work.

Tuan's career corresponded to a momentous period of change and development for the discipline of geography. He worked somewhat outside the more immediate froth of intellectual fashions and has consistently charted his own unique course, more interested in enduring moral and spiritual truths – what he has termed 'the good life' (1986). Tuan drew from a much longer tradition of Western humanism and counter to his contemporaries in the 1960s he was increasingly concerned with the emotional and intimate engagement of people, culture, environment and place. This was not a human geography of statistics and computer simulations, or of models or critical theories, but one of personal encounter, literary reflection, and of humility and wonder and hope.

The 1970s and the reaction to positivist spatial science re-awakened many geographers to the uniqueness of place and the emotional encounter with the environment. Tuan was to quickly become associated with this 'new geography' for which the term 'humanistic geography' gained wide currency. Whilst Tuan has been grouped with practitioners such as David Lowenthal, **Anne Buttimer**, Edward Relph, David Seamon and others, he was never really a leader of any kind of movement, but rather its emergence coincided with his already developing personal perspective. Nevertheless, this period coincided with Tuan's own explorations into the deeper philosophical underpinnings of the 'humanistic' perspective. Seminal papers from this period, much quoted by his contemporaries, were 'Geography, phenomenology and the study of human nature' (1971) and 'Humanistic geography' (1976). Along with books such as *Topophilia* (1974), *Space and Place* (1977) and *Landscapes of Fear* (1979), Tuan established his own

reputation and distinctive contribution to the rebirth of cultural geography.

He absorbed the perspectives of existentialism and phenomenology, and in particular the ideas of Martin Heidegger – concerning 'Being-in-the-World', 'Dwelling' and the four-fold connectivity of Being with the earth, the cosmos, the body and the spirit – were to have a profound impact on his thinking. He did not apply these ideas slavishly, but rather they resonated with his own intuitive understanding of human geography. This more existential, experiential and holistic concept of the intimate connection of people and places, culture and geography, and the relationship to nature or 'geopiety' has been a unifying theme of his work.

Tuan's long-term interest in attitudes to nature parallels the rise of the environmental movement (Tuan, 1974; 1984; 1993). His increasing interest in the nature of human consciousness, the self and society parallel developments in wider social sciences (e.g., Tuan, 1982; 1996). Increasingly, the interest in 'values' (of *Topophilia*) becomes more specifically about meaning, and what it is to be human and the faith in a better life through respect and understanding. *Escapism* (Tuan, 1998b) combines his interests in the meaning of existence, nature and culture with an implicit and somewhat indirect critical counter to the postmodern turn in human geography. His later book, *Human Goodness* (2008) takes a further 'metaphysical step' and reflects on the impact of communal goodness over time through the lens of six very different individuals – Confucius, Socrates, Mozart, Keats, Albert Schweitzer, and Simone Weil. Blending simple and profound observations, Tuan continued to offer challenging accounts of our relationship to the world, one another and ourselves.

Each of his texts explores particular trajectories of the humanistic perspective.

For instance, in *Topophilia* (Tuan, 1974) his interest focuses upon attachments to place, in *Segmented Worlds and Self* (Tuan, 1982) his analysis deepens to a consideration of the link between human consciousness and spatial structures, and in *Dominance and Affection* (Tuan, 1986), his attention moves to the 'aesthetic exploitation' and mistreatment of nature. Throughout his work, there is a consistent exploration, reflection and refinement of his understanding of what it is to be human, that is a 'Being-in-the-World', and human–environment relationships are explicated as not merely objective and material, but are affective and moral.

His achievement has been recognised through numerous prizes. As early as 1968 he was awarded a Guggenheim Fellowship, in 1973 he was given the Association of American Geographer's award for a 'meritous contribution to geography' and again in 1987 he gained from the AAG the Cullum Geographical Medal. He was also elected a fellow of the American Association for the Advancement of Science, and has been a respected member of professional bodies and associations. In 2000, he was named Laureat d'Honneur 2000 of the International Geographical Union. In honour of his contribution to human geography, several collections have been published including *Spirit and Power of Place* (1994), *Textures of Place; Exploring Humanistic Geographies* (2001) and *Progress: Geographical Essays* (2002).

SPATIAL CONTRIBUTIONS

Yi-Fu Tuan sought from his earliest work to expand concepts of geography beyond the physical towards the metaphysical, ethical and aesthetic. He was inspired by von Humboldt, whom he described as a 'hero' figure who, while predominantly known for explaining the physical world, was among the first to use landscape painting and poetry to extend the range of geographical experience – feeling, emotion, and concept (Tuan, 1999). Tuan has also cited the cultural geographers Carl Sauer and J.B. Jackson as important initial influences. In terms of contribution to the discipline he has been both widely quoted by human geographers, and gained a position of respect in learned societies.

He has described himself as 'off-center even in geography ... I now enjoy a modicum of recognition in geography, but it is more a consequence of my longevity ... than of any marked intellectual influence' (Tuan, 1998a). Yet, at a deeper level, his impact has been far more profound, linking with a longer humanistic tradition in geography (when his contemporaries were drawn first by spatial science, and later by critical social theory), and preparing the ground, in many ways, for the resurgence of interest in cultural geography. J. Nicholas Entrikin (in a review of *Cosmos and Hearth*) writes 'without question, Yi-Fu Tuan has been an intellectual force in contemporary cultural geography and environmental thought. His work is cited by authors across a wide range of disciplines, from the more philosophical, such as literary criticism, to the more applied, such as landscape architecture. Surely he is one of the best known geographers outside of his home discipline. As has been the case with other leading humanistic geographers this century ... for example, J.K. Wright, Tuan's contribution to American geography has rarely been given adequate treatment in the histories and surveys of the field' (Entrikin, 1997).

Yi-Fu Tuan has had a paradoxical impact. On the one hand, he has produced a considerable output of books and refereed articles that have been widely read and much valued both within the discipline and beyond. Yet, apart from the surge of interest in 'humanistic geography' in the 1970s, Tuan has always been something of an outsider, following his own highly personal, and sometimes idiosyncratic explorations of cultural values, attitudes to the environment, space and place, the self and the cosmos, emotional and spiritual geographies.

With the rise of critical and postmodern discourses in geography, especially since the 1980s, the humanistic perspective and Tuan's interpretation of it has come under much criticism for its singular authorial voice, tendency to universalise traits across cultures, sometimes essentialist assumptions, and perhaps political naivety. Yet, what is forgotten perhaps is the fundamental humility and wonder within Tuan's discourse. Through his work he re-visits and reworks his themes and examples, testing and fine-tuning his interpretations. Yi-Fu Tuan has held to his underlying search to understand the meaning of 'the good life'. He has not ignored the debates raging in human geography, the social sciences and the humanities at large, but has not been enticed by superficial attractiveness of their 'new language' and concepts. In this respect, it is interesting to compare *Escapism* (Tuan, 1998b) to more recent writing on this theme inspired by postmodern theorists, as it explores the notion of reality and the real from 'systematic humanistic geography' perspective

Monaghan (2001) notes that many of the contemporary interests of geography have an indirect intellectual ancestry in earlier work by Tuan but are never acknowledged as such. Adams et al. (2001: np) argue that 'a lot of people in and out of the discipline consider Yi-Fu as an inspirational figure. But it strikes us that his role has been less to inspire

direct imitation than to inspire people to do things that don't look exactly or much like his work.'

KEY ADVANCES AND CONTROVERSIES

Much of the human geography of the last 50 years has been driven by the desire to explain how specific social, economic and spatial patterns arise, are sustained and ultimately change. The focus has essentially been material and functional, as geographers have sought to describe and explain the world around them in ways that are seen to be useful to policy-makers and society at large.

Yi-Fu Tuan has taken a different journey, fascinated by the more fundamental and difficult question of why – that is, the meaning of existence. In particular, he has focused upon the relationship between human beings (individuals and cultures) and their environment (nature and place), both materially and most especially emotionally and spiritually. Drawing on existential and phenomenological philosophies, Tuan has explored the ways in which we are, or become, Beings-in-the-World, and critical to him has been the establishment of the meaning of this spatial and social existence as it is established at different times and in different cultures. He has sought to uncover more universal characteristics of being human, whilst at the same time not laying claim to discovering any grand theories. In the 1970s, Tuan for a brief time was central to the controversies and debates about 'humanistic geography', but for much of his career he has stood outside such debates. His books of the 1980s and 1990s, whilst making a unique contribution to the discipline, have not generated discipline-wide controversy. In part this is perhaps because they do not directly engage with the contemporary debates of critical social theory, feminism or postmodernism, or with more immediately popular concerns of environmentalism, globalisation or terrorism. Furthermore, the style of analysis and the language of his prose, make his work less suited to the age of sound-bites and quick fixes.

His project has been far more reflective, and less concerned with immediate gain, and its influence has been often less direct. Much closer to his project has been the notion that geographic discovery is also about self-discovery (see also Tuan, 2001). For much of his academic career this was controversial, as many geographers subscribed to notions of scientific objectivity, studying the world (and peoples) as 'objects', de-emphasising the possibility or value of either self-reflection or the potential impact of geographic research upon the researcher. With the rise of humanistic geography in the 1970s, there was a rediscovery of the value of the individual, the subjective and self-reflection. Whilst this 'humanistic' approach has largely been superseded by the ideas of critical social theory, feminism and postmodernism, the importance of the personal, the subjective, the affective and the moral has continued to resonate. Although there is no direct link to Tuan's work, it is interesting that

a number of feminist geographers have asserted the value of personal experience, subjectivity, and self-discovery, as the personal became political.

The Wisconsin Library Association Awards Committee citation notes that: 'when asked "Why are you a geographer?", Yi-Fu Tuan's eloquently simple response was 'I have always wanted to know what it is like to live on earth'. These words provide a key to the man and his writing; he is not only a geographer, but also philosopher and humanist, an unabashed Renaissance man in an age of rigid specialists, as readable as essayist as he is intrepid as scholar' (WLA, 1995). Yi-Fu Tuan summarised his own contribution enigmatically in his Charles Homer Haskins Lecture in 1998:

> I wonder about Socrates'... dictum 'the unexamined life is not worth living'... my own type of work, ostensibly about 'people and environment,' draws so much on the sort of person I am that I have wondered whether I have not written an unconscionably long autobiography. By tiny unmarked steps, examination turns into self-examination. Is it worth doing? Will it lead one to the good life? Or will it, as Saul Bellow believes, make one wish one were dead? I oscillate between the two possibilities. In the end I come down on the side of Socrates, if only because the unexamined life is as prone to despair as the examined one; and if despair – occasional despair – is human, I would prefer to confront it with my eyes open, even convert it into spectacle, than submit to it blindly as though it were implacable fate.

(Tuan, 1998a: np)

TUAN'S KEY WORKS

Tuan, Y-F. (1971) 'Geography, phenomenology and the study of human nature', The Canadian Geographer, 15:181–92.
Tuan, Y-F. (1974) Topophilia: A Study of Environmental Perception, Attitudes and Values. Englewood Cliffs, NJ: Prentice Hall.
Tuan, Y-F. (1976) 'Humanistic geography', Annals of the Association of American Geographers, 66 (2): 266–76.
Tuan, Y-F. (1977) Space and Place: The Perspective of Experience. Minneapolis: University of Minnesota Press.
Tuan, Y-F. (1979) Landscapes of Fear. Oxford: Blackwell.

Tuan, Y-F. (1996) *Cosmos and Hearth: A Cosmopolite's Viewpoint.* Minneapolis: University of Minnesota Press.
Tuan, Y-F. (1998b) *Escapism.* Baltimore: Johns Hopkins University Press.
Tuan, Y-F. (1999) *Who Am I? An Autobiography of Emotion, Mind and Spirit.* Madison: University of Wisconsin Press.
Tuan, Y-F. (2008) *Human Goodness.* Madison: University of Wisconsin Press.

Secondary Sources and References

Adams, P.C., Till, K.E. and Hoelscher, S.D. (eds) (2001) *Textures of Place: Exploring Humanist Geographies.* University of Minnesota Press: Minneapolis.
Entrikin, J.N. (1997) 'Review: *Cosmos and Hearth: Yi-Fu Tuan*', *Annals of the Association of American Geographers,* 87:176–8.
Monaghan, P. (2001) 'Lost in place: Yi-Fu Tuan may be the most influential scholar you've never heard of', chronicle.com/free/v47/i27/27a01401.html
Singh, R.P.B. (ed.) (1994) *Spirit and Power of Place : Essays Dedicated to Yi-Fu Tuan,* Banaras: National Geographic Society of India.
Sack, R.D. (ed.) (2002) 'Progress and anxiety', *Progress: Geographical Essays.* Baltimore: Johns Hopkins University Press.
Tuan, Y-F (1961) 'Topophilia: or a sudden encounter with the landscape', *Landscape,* (61): 29–32. Reprinted in P. English and R. Mayfield (eds), (1972) *Man, Space and Environment.* Oxford: Oxford University Press. pp. 534–8.
Tuan, Y-F (1962) 'Structure, climate and the basin landforms in Arizona and New Mexico', *Annals of the Association of American Geographers* 52: 51–68.
Tuan, Y-F (1964) 'Mountains, ruins and the sentiment of melancholy', *Landscape,* 13: 27–30.
Tuan, Y-F (1966) 'New Mexico's gullies: critical re-examination and new observations', *Annals of the Association of American Geographers,* 56: 573–97.
Tuan, Y-F (1968) 'Discrepancies between environmental attitude and behaviour: examples from Europe and China', *The Canadian Geographer,* 12: 176–91.
Tuan, Y-F. (1982) *Segmented Worlds and Self: A Study of Group Life and Individual Consciousness.* Minneapolis: University of Minnesota Press.
Tuan, Y-F. (1984) *Dominance and Affection: The Making of Pets.* Yale: Yale University Press.
Tuan, Y-F. (1986) *The Good Life.* Madison: University of Wisconsin Press.
Tuan, Y-F. (1989) *Morality and Imagination: Paradoxes of Progress.* Madison: University of Wisconsin Press.
Tuan, Y-F. (1993) *Passing Strange and Wonderful: Aesthetics, Nature and Culture.* Washington, DC: Island Press/Shearwater Books.
Tuan, Y-F. (1998a) 'A life of learning', Charles Homer Haskins Lecture for 1998, at www.worldcat.org/oclc/39893755 Accessed June 2009.
Tuan, Y-F (2001) 'Life as a field trip', *Geographical Review,* 91(1–2): 41–5.
Tuan, Y-F (2002) *Dear Colleague: Common and Uncommon Observations.* Minneapolis: University of Minneapolis Press.
Tuan, Y-F (2009) Official Web Site: http://www.yifutuan.org Accessed June 2009.
Wisconsin Library Association (1995) www.wla.lib.wi.us/readers/WLAC/Notable/Notable1995.html Accessed June 2009.

Paul Rodaway, Lancaster University

59 John Urry

BIOGRAPHICAL DETAILS AND THEORETICAL CONTEXT

John Urry was born in London in 1946. He gained his first degrees from Christ's College, Cambridge in 1967, a 'double first' BA and MA in Economics, before going on to complete his PhD in sociology from the same institution in 1972. He joined Lancaster University as Lecturer in Sociology, becoming Head of Department in 1983. He was made Professor in 1985 and later Dean of Faculty and Distinguished Professor of Sociology.

Urry's research interests extend from his PhD on the emergence of capitalist societies to his more recent examination of mobility, climate change and energy crises in *Beyond the Car* (Urry and Dennis, 2009). A sociologist by trade, Urry has been a dominant force in international sociological debates for more than three decades, but has worked with human geographers and voiced opinion on themes which cross-cut neat disciplinary barriers. Urry has also made significant efforts to build international and inter-disciplinary research spaces such as the Centre for Mobilities Research at Lancaster (CEMORE), the Cosmobilities network – a cross-European Network of mobility researchers – and the editorship of the international journal *Mobilities*.

Writing in the aftermath of May 1968, Urry's doctoral work concerned the sociology of power in Britain and an interest in the philosophy of the social sciences. In the conclusion to his first book *Reference Groups and the Theory of Revolution* (Urry, 1973: 178) he summarised how he had been working 'to provide an explanation of why in some societies at some times there have been a large number of men preparing and organizing both consciously and collectively for the ending of the status quo'. In the manner of his early research topic, Urry has consistently sought to depart from any kind of status quo, seeking new avenues for research focus and innovative conceptual and methodological tools to interrogate them. If one can characterise John Urry's work it is, therefore, best described by its insistence to 'turn': his arguments swerve, change direction and depart from established positions. At the same time, however, they are grounded and fixed; not in the sense that he understands his objects of enquiry as immobile – indeed, this is the exact opposite of his most general points on mobilities. Rather, Urry's investigations of tourism, business interactions, talk, and new forms of economic life, are bound to concrete material contexts and activities – driving apparently superficial actions down into subsurface layers, contexts and structures of economies, labour relations, forms of governance, regions and times. Indeed, it is from such contexts that Urry has been inspired.

In the late 1970s Urry became increasingly interested and influential in the burgeoning study of the region and locality. The Conference of Socialist Economists (CSE) and Lancaster University's own Regionalism Group were to play a particularly significant role. Drawing together research of this type, the groups benefited from an emerging turn within geography towards 'locality studies' or a new kind of 'regional geography'. At that time this research was forefronted by **Doreen Massey**'s (1979) groundbreaking work along with Phillip Cooke and others. In this context, Urry fostered productive intellectual forays into spatial thought and theory as he sought to understand the role of locality upon the social and spatial structures of Britain's emerging service economy, its declining manufacturing industries and the social and material transformations of Thatcherite ideology. Urry was the recipient of one of the seven funded projects in Economic and Social Research Council's programme on *The Changing Urban and Regional System in the UK* (CURS).

Urry's inter-disciplinarity was shaped by processes that influenced many social scientists at work in England and the US in the early 1980s. Along with other social scientists at the time, Urry felt a distinctive need to surpass the disciplines, to make them more 'ill-disciplined' (see Adey et al., 2010). This was reflective of wider economic restructuring in universities, which not only saw departments forced into smaller and more open-looking units, but it also encouraged Urry and his colleagues to embed themselves more tightly into larger networks of international collaborations; and even more so than before, to turn towards the restructuring processes which were altering their working-worlds around them. In 1985 Urry published an influential joint-edited collection with **Derek Gregory**

(1985). Along with several other collections at the time (Allen and Massey, 1988; Thrift and Williams, 1987), it attempted to map out the relations between societal and spatial structures thereby forging new connections between geographers and sociologists coming to terms with the local distinctiveness of state-invoked restructuring.

With Scott Lash, *The End of Organized Capitalism* (Lash and Urry, 1987) and *Economies of Signs and Space* (Lash and Urry, 1994) marked a major development of Urry's study of capitalist economies and societies. Lash and Urry's approach did not, however, follow a traditional political economy path. In their analysis of the restructuring of labour relations, new forms of leisure time and practices of consumption, Lash and Urry helped set in motion a path towards a culturally-nuanced 'postmodern' theory of capitalism (Lovering, 1989: 212). Bubbling away in *The End of Organised Capitalism* we see evidence of the evolution of Urry's thinking – specifically in his conception of mobility – then taken as an albeit interesting by-product of the transition of extensive economic and political processes. This emphasis was soon to change as *The Tourist Gaze* (1990) and *Economies of Signs and Space* were published. For the first time tourism and mobility were taken seriously as a form of social scientific enquiry, reversing the polarity of interest towards consumption from production and to movement from stasis. Now the 'social' was *put into* mobility.

Mobility (or 'new mobilities') is probably Urry's most clear contribution to academic social science to date. Developed in single authored monographs such as *Sociology beyond Societies* (Urry, 2000) and *Mobilities* (Urry, 2007), along with many journal articles and edited collections (see, for example, Axhausen et al., 2006), Urry has gradually sought to re-imagine what we mean by 'the social'. Urry would argue that our societies are far from solid but are fluid and composed of complex mobilities and interactions (Sheller and Urry, 2006). With the influence of Lancaster colleagues such as Mimi Sheller, Anne-Marie Fortier and Sylvia Walby, mobility took on the horizon of both gendered material practices and a metaphorical movement eliciting more supple subject positions than a singular and masculine male point-of-view. Clearly inspired by Actor-Network Theory and its proponents such as John Law and Lucy Suchman, mobility was taken by Urry as encompassing the movements of not only people but things, whose orbits comprised complex socio-material relationships. Urry explains how 'material transformations' are 'remaking the social'. The mobilities of travel, the movements of images and especially information, were reconstructing the 'social as society' into the 'social as mobility' (Urry, 2000: 2; 2007). The mobility agenda has been pushed even further with new international circuits of knowledge from clusters emerging between the Netherlands, Scandinavia and Germany, aligning **Ulrich Beck**'s 'risk society' thesis, 'cosmopolitanism' (see, for example, Canzler et al., 2008; Axhausen et al., 2006), and new understandings of mobility and technology.

SPATIAL CONTRIBUTIONS

The currents of John Urry's research have mixed and flowed along with spatial theory in a manner that has inspired collaborations and new directions within geography and beyond. Urry has been particularly vocal in his articulation of the disciplinary relation between sociology and geography, tracing out the two disciplines' paths in a contribution to *New Models in Geography* (Urry, 1989). Therein, Urry argued that they have not come together simply through a process of convergence whereby, 'sociologists "add" space and geographers "add society" to their respective analyses' (1989: 295). Alternatively, their relatively different disciplinary structures have seen the cross-fertilisation of theories, concepts and methods in quite uneven ways.

Urry's (1981) interventions into the geographies and structures of locality were especially prominent within sociology as the local was given the properties of a powerful social object able to exert forces upon wider processes. The investigations of Lancaster's Regional group into the consumption of specific locations and geographies would prove influential for the spatial analysis of gender, class and region (Murgatroyd et al., 1985; Bagguley et al., 1990), especially in the context of tourism and the consumer industries. Charting changes to the capitalist economy, the growth of the middle classes and increased opportunities to spend travel time, alongside other shifting developments in transportation technology such as the railroad and the aeroplane, Urry sought to examine tourism as 'one of the defining characteristics of being "modern"'. Previously concerned with the structural conditions necessary to produce cultural formations such as tourism, in *Economies of Signs and Space* and *The Tourist Gaze*, the experience of these new forms of mobility were understood as a production in itself, a material condition for new apprehensions of the world and 'the very production of subjectivity' itself (Lash and Urry 1994: 255).

Table 1 Capitalism, tourism and travel	
Stage	Configuration
Pre-capitalism	Organised exploration
Liberal capitalism	Individual travel by the rich
Organised capitalism	Organised mass tourism
Disorganised capitalism	The 'end of tourism'

Source: Lash and Urry, 1994: 259

Urry's turn towards consumption, tourism and mobility departed from accepted 'academic prejudices'. As set out in *The End of Organized Capitalism* and later in *Economies of Signs and Space*, it was a prominent refusal to accept the priority of manufacturing rather than services, 'production rather than consumption, of "work" rather than "leisure", of structure rather than mobility, and of work-related mobility rather than leisure mobility' (Lash and Urry, 1994: 254). Particular kinds of movement, tourism and consumption could be historicised and spaced into *stages* or time-frames of patterns identifiable in capitalist societies (Table 1). This laid the groundwork for important geographical analyses of consumption by geographers such as **Peter Jackson**, Phillip Crang and Ian Cook.

The dichotomy of production and consumption so engrained in social science was befuddled by Urry's illumination of the new economies of images, ideas, data, services and other material objects – all becoming things to be produced and consumed. Geographically speaking, the implication was that any space, terrain and landscape could be commodified and therefore circulated – places could be *consumed*. Representations, images and the gaze of the tourist were central to this expedition into the visual, sensuous and embodied dimensions of new experiences of capitalism. Tourism and travelling, for

instance, could be performed through a host of visual mobile practices. The *gaze* was a 'systemised' and 'socially organised' way of looking. This could mean the images and visions of a tourist destination – stimulated in anticipation through 'daydreaming and fantasy' (Urry, 1990: 3) – or passed on through other mobile media such as tourist brochures and television broadcasts.

Within these frameworks the tendency to see mobility as 'derived' from more substantial processes made it a particularly 'difficult task for social scientists' (Urry, 1990: 7) to grapple with. Mobility appeared fleeting, ephemeral. On the other hand, the implication of these new kinds of movement, illuminated by new ways of theorising mobility, were particularly stark, hard and uneven. Adding up to quite different imaginations of the public realm and civil society, with Mimi Sheller, Kevin Hannam and others, Urry's 'new mobilities paradigm' was to demand the reconceptualisation of processes such as social exclusion. Those unable to move could be excluded from job markets, access to social services such as education, health and other benefits; it could prevent one from voting or evacuating a disaster area (Cresswell, 2006). Mobilities could degrade civil society by eroding public spaces and provide social and economic barriers to upwardly mobile progression. Graham and Marvin's (2001) exploration of networked 'technological mobilities' in *Splintering Urbanism* is perhaps the most comprehensive example of this kind of work, as they explore the unequal relations caught up in infrastructural provision and access. Although mobilities might actually transform political spaces, composing new sites of political engagement and action, in concert with Doreen Massey's (1994) 'politics of mobility', Urry's 'new mobilities' was to inspire a whole landscape of research invested in the inequalities and politics of mobility and movement.

KEY ADVANCES AND CONTROVERSIES

Urry's research has been pivotal for the way geographers have understood mobility. Without mobility there would be no social world. Face-to-face meetings would be impossible. Consumption would fail without the means to get at services or products or have them brought to us. Friendship would be hard without physical proximity or mediated contact by communications like the telephone or email. Leisure activities would be difficult without the means to get to a destination. Work, too, is increasingly done on the move; from the aircraft cabin to driving on the motorway (Laurier, 2004). It is just these sorts of mobilities which Urry argues have remade the social into societies constituted by mobiles – by people, objects and things. Re-imagining the social away from the closed worlds of immobile face-to-face encounters and rigid networks of relationships (Urry, 2004), Urry's 'new mobilities paradigm' has helped to unify a disparate body of research for whom mobility is at their heart.

The impact of these styles of thinking has brought mobilities to the forefront of diverse sets of research interests and disciplinary agendas, and 'mobility' as a concept into the general parlance of social scientific research (Adey, 2009). Scholars of travel and tourism have recently sought to place mobility somewhere at the centre of their understandings of tourism. In criminology (Aas, 2007) the issue of mobility is similarly taken as a fundamental subject to tackle. Indeed, while policy and regulation enables and shapes mobilities, policy itself travels and is shared, copied and 'in motion' (McCann, 2008).

Within geography Urry's influence on mobility is most patently felt within a plethora of research. Developments in transport geography (Knowles et al., 2008) are accommodating the 'new mobilities' paradigm in order to theorise more socially sophisticated concepts of mobility. For cultural geographer Tim Cresswell, Urry's mobilities are invested with significance. Through his humanistic reading Cresswell argues that mobilities are frequently bound up in ideological codings and relations of power, delocating the investiture of fixed points, pauses or places as centres of social significance (Tuan, 1977; Cresswell, 2004) towards the life-worlds of everyday mobilities. Alternatively, for **Nigel Thrift** (1996), mobility captures something more than meaningful experiences but what he determines as the 'structures of feeling' of Western modernity; modernity itself strikes Urry as thoroughly mobile. 'Modern society is a society on the move,' he wrote with Scott Lash (1994: 252). Harnessing the inner and minor worlds of performance, habit and pre-cognition, with some help from phenomenology, mobility has helped establish non-representational-theory as a prominent conceptual and empirical concern which can deal with motion, action and process (Adey, 2009; McCormack, 2002). More considered accounts of technology and movement (Laurier, 2003) have pressed forth the cyborg assemblages of travel from the 'driver-car' (Laurier, 2004; Merriman, 2004; Dant, 2004) to the train (Bissell, 2009b) and the airport.

The apparent priority of the visual in 'new mobilities' and the tourist 'gaze' has come under some criticism. The 'gaze', and the way it is constructed by various practices of seeing, works to secure tourism mobilities as a field apart from other kinds of embodied leisure. Critics contend that it is the whole of the body and not just the eyes that see, experience and compose tourist activity and other styles of mobile practice. Tourism scholar Pau Obrador-Pons (2007) puts this point incredibly simply when he argues that the whole body is involved in tourist dwelling. One could imagine a host of embodiments associated with the tourist experience from smells and touches to excitations, thrills and fears. Others have extended this work towards phenomenological accounts of the feeling and sensation of cycling (Spinney, 2006).

The prioritisation of mobility and action has also had its critics. Post-phenomenological accounts have criticised Urry and others for their vitalism of perpetual action and excitation. For instance, David Bissell (2009a; 2009b; see also Rose and Wylie, 2006) has sought to account for the mobile body as less than active. In his reworking of mobile experience, Bissell explores moments of passivity, boredom, inactivity and silence – a turning-away from the world during very mobile encounters. Harrison (2008) and Kraftl and Horton (2008) similarly address the relation between passivity and productivity arguing for a less excitable account of the everyday but towards more deadened moments of acquiescence and stillness.

Another question has arisen from criticisms levelled at the un-economic character of 'new mobilities' and the failure to ground mobility in economic processes and relations. There is a concern that newer examinations of the mobile are rather light. However, these arguments don't necessarily map that well directly onto Urry's research. Time and again mobility is laden with the signature of the temporal, geographic and the economic. For example, his writings on the automobile understand the technology (Urry and Dennis, 2009; Urry, 2007; 2004; Adey et al., 2010) and the freedom it has provided as a thoroughly twentieth-century phenomenon – its liquidity premised upon the efficient weight-to-power ratio of the oil that powers it. Urry's increasing focus upon the weighty relationships between mobilities and resources seems certain to ground mobility even deeper within the political and economic contexts from which they emerge and transform.

URRY'S KEY WORKS

Urry, J. (1973) *Reference Groups and the Theory of Revolution*. London: Routledge.
Urry, J. (1990) *The Tourist Gaze: Leisure and Travel in Contemporary Societies*. London: Sage.
Urry, J. (1995) *Consuming Places*. London: Routledge.
Urry, J. (2000) *Sociology Beyond Societies: Mobilities for the Twenty-first Century*. London: Routledge.
Urry, J. (2003) *Global Complexities*. Cambridge: Polity.
Urry, J. (2007) *Mobilities*. Cambridge: Polity.
Lash, S. and Urry, J. (1987) *The End of Organized Capitalism*. Cambridge: Polity
Lash, S. and Urry, J. (1994) *Economies of Signs and Space*. London: Sage.

Secondary Sources and References

Aas, K.F. (2007) 'Analysing a world in motion – global flows meet "criminology of the other"', *Theoretical Criminology*, 11 (2): 283–303.

Adey, P., Bissell, D. and Urry, J. (2010) 'Mobilities, meetings and futures: an interview with John Urry', *Environment and Planning D: Society and Space*, 28(1): 1–16.

Adey, P. (2009) *Mobility*. London: Routledge.

Allen, J. and Massey, D. (1988) *The Economy in Question*. London: Sage.

Axhausen, K., Larsen, J., and Urry, J. (2006) *Tracing Mobilities: Towards a Cosmopolitan Perspective*. Aldershot: Ashgate.

Bagguley, P., Lawson, J.M., Shapiro, D., Urry, J., Walby, S. and Warde, A. (1990) *Restructuring: Place, Class and Gender*. London: Sage.

Bissell, D. (2009a) 'Conceptualising differently-mobile passengers: geographies of everyday encumbrance in the railway station', *Social and Cultural Geography*, 10 (2): 173–95.

Bissell, D. (2009b) 'Visualising everyday geographies: practices of vision through travel-time', *Transactions of the Institute of British Geographers*, 34 (1): 42–60.

Canzler, W., Kaufmann, K. and Kesselring, S. (2008) *Tracing Mobilities: Towards a Cosmopolitan Perspective*. Ashgate: Aldershot.

Cresswell, T. (1996) 'Embodiment, power and the politics of mobility: the case of female tramps and hobos', *Transactions of the Institute of British Geographers*, 24 (2): 175–92.

Cresswell, T. (2004) *Place: A Short Introduction*. Oxford: Blackwell.

Cresswell, T. (2006) *On the Move: Mobility in the Modern Western World*. New York: Routledge,

Dant, T. (2004) 'The driver-car', *Theory Culture and Society*, 21 (4–5): 61–75

Graham, S. (2001) *Splintering Urbanism: Networked Infrastructures, Technological Mobilities and the Urban Condition*. London: Routledge.

Gregory, D. and Urry, J. (1985) *Social Relations and Spatial Structures*. London: Macmillan.

Harrison, P. (2008) 'Corporeal remains: vulnerability, proximity, and living on after the end of the world', *Environment and Planning A*, 40 (2): 423–45.

Harvey, D. (1989) *The Condition of Postmodernity*. Oxford: Blackwell.

Knowles, R., Docherty, I. and Shaw, J. (2008) *Transport Geographies: Mobilities, Flows, and Spaces*. Oxford: Blackwell.

Kraftl, P. and Horton, J. (2008) 'Spaces of every-night life: for geographies of sleep, sleeping and sleepiness', *Progress in Human Geography*, 32 (4): 509–24.

Laurier, E. (2003) 'Theme issue: technology and mobility', *Environment and Planning A*, 35 (9): 1521–7.

Laurier, E. (2004) 'Doing office work on the motorway', *Theory Culture and Society*, 21 (4–5): 261–79.

Lovering, J. (1989) 'The restructuring debate', in R. Peet and N. Thrift (eds), *New Models in Geography: The Political-economy Perspective, Vol. 1*. London: Unwin Hyman. pp. 198–223.

Massey, D.B. (1979) 'In what sense a regional problem', *Regional Studies*, 13 (2): 233–43.

Massey, D.B. (1994) *Space, Place and Gender*. Cambridge: Polity.

McCann, E.J. (2008) 'Expertise, truth, and urban policy mobilities: global circuits of knowledge in the development of Vancouver, Canada's "four pillar" drug strategy', *Environment and Planning A*, 40 (4): 885–904.

McCormack, D. P. (2002) 'A paper with an interest in rhythm', *Geoforum*, 33: 469–85.

Merriman, P. (2004) 'Driving places – Marc Augé, non-places, and the geographies of England's M1 motorway', *Theory Culture and Society*, 21 (4–5): 145.

Murgatroyd, L., Savage, M., Shapiro, D., Urry, J., and Walby, S. (1985) *Localities, Class and Gender*. London: Pion.

Obrador-Pons, P. (2007) 'A haptic geography of the beach: naked bodies, vision and touch', *Social and Cultural Geography*, 8 (1): 123–41.

Rose, M. and Wylie, J. (2006) 'Animating landscape', *Environment and Planning D: Society and Space*, 24 (4): 475–9.

Sheller, M. and Urry, J. (2006) 'The new mobilities paradigm', *Environment and Planning A*, 38 (2): 207–26.

Spinney, J. (2006) 'A place of sense: a kinaesthetic ethnography of cyclists on Mont Ventoux', *Environment and Planning D: Society and Space*, 24 (5): 709–32.

Thrift, N.J. (1996) *Spatial Formations*. London: Sage.

Thrift, N. and Williams, P. (1987) *Class and Space: The Making of Urban Society*. London: Routledge and Kegan Paul.

Tuan, Y. (1977) *Space and Place: The Perspective of Experience*. London: Edward Arnold.

Urry, J. (1981) 'Localities, regions and social class', *International Journal of Urban and Regional Research*, 5: 455–73.

Urry, J. (1989) 'Sociology and geography', in R. Peet and N. Thrift (eds), *New Models in Geography: The Political-economy Perspective, Vol 2*. London: Unwin Hyman. pp. 295–317.

Urry, J. (2004) 'The "system" of automobility', *Theory Culture and Society*, 21 (4–5): 25–39.

Urry, J. (2004b) 'Connections', *Environment and Planning D: Society and Space*, 22 (1): 27–37.

Urry, J. (2008) 'Climate change, travel and complex futures', *British Journal of Sociology*, 59 (2): 261–79.

Urry, J. and Dennis, K. (2009) *After the Car*. Cambridge: Polity.

Peter Adey, Keele University

60 Paul Virilio

BIOGRAPHICAL DETAILS AND THEORETICAL CONTEXT

Paul Virilio was born in Paris in 1932, and evacuated to Nantes in 1939, in an attempt to escape the worst of the German *Blitzkrieg*. A self-styled 'urbanist,' he served as a President of the École Spéciale d'Architecture in Paris, where he first gained tenure in 1969, becoming Director General in 1975, and President in 1990. He had previously set up the *Architecture Principe* group with Claude Parent in 1963 (Virilio and Parent, 1996), though a rift between the two developed following Virilio's involvement in *les événements* (the student–worker uprisings) of 1968. Prior to training as an architect and urban planner, Virilio had served an apprenticeship in the craft of *vitrail* (stained-glass window making), working alongside Georges Braque and Henri Matisse. In the late 1950s, he studied philosophy at the Sorbonne, where he was particularly influenced by Maurice Merleau-Ponty's teachings on phenomenology.

Whilst Virilio's twin identity as urbanist and philosopher is sometimes (rather unconvincingly) billed as an incongruous juxtaposition, it is his unrelenting focus on war that gives his work its unique bearing. He has repeatedly claimed that

'War was my university' (Virilio and Lotringer, 1983: 24; Der Derian, 1998: 16), often recounting childhood memories in interviews. He recalls, for instance, hearing news of the German invasion on the radio only minutes before the sound of German tanks rolling into Nantes could be heard outside his window. Later, Virilio was drafted into the French army to fight in the Algerian War (1954–62). Little wonder, therefore, that he should have developed a fascination with the relationship between war and space. His *Bunker Archaeology* project, which began in 1958, and eventually led to an exhibition at the Musée des Arts Décoratifs in Paris in 1975–6, focused on Adolf Hitler's Atlantic Wall – the planned 'impregnable front' running along 2,400 miles of the West European coastline (Virilio, 1994a).

Beginning with *The Insecurity of Territory* (1976a), Virilio's theoretical writings have proceeded to excavate the relationship between military and urban space in terms of perception, technology, and speed. In addition to his many books, Virilio has been actively associated with a variety of journals, including *Architecture Principe, Cahiers du Cinéma, Cause Commune, Critique, Esprit, Le Monde Diplomatique*, and *Traverses*; as well as having initiated, with Georges Perec, Galilée's 'Espace Critique' book series.

As a number of commentators have recently taken pains to emphasise, Virilio's theoretical stance has frequently been misspecified as 'poststructuralist'-cum-'postmodernist' (Armitage, 2000). Although he has had some involvement with the Collège International de Philosophie, Virilio's relation to the likes of Jacques Derrida and Jean-François Lyotard is hardly straightforward. Nor does his work share many philosophical affinities with the work of **Jean Baudrillard**, despite a significant number of resonances. The same can be said of the relation between Virilio and **Michel Foucault**, **Gilles Deleuze**, and Félix Guattari. In fact, Virilio's work inherits the phenomenological mantle of Merleau-Ponty (1962), with an added dose of Gestalt psychology (Guillaume, 1937). Despite many convergences with post-structuralism, therefore, Virilio remains very much a humanist. He is also, moreover, a committed Christian, having been inspired by the example of the Abbé Pierre, the priest who fought for the French Resistance, campaigned for the homeless, and whose dress sense was the subject of an essay by Roland Barthes. Whilst his own work as a campaigner for the homeless and a peace activist is occasionally noted, Virilio is best known for the neologisms and phrases that litter his texts: 'oblique function', 'dromology', 'chronopolitics', the 'aesthetics of disappearance', 'speed pollution', 'infosphere', and so on.

SPATIAL CONTRIBUTIONS

Since Virilio's 'reflections on urbanism are invariably also reflections on politics' (Luke and Ó Tuathail, 2000: 362), there is little sense in attempting to disentangle Virilio's spatial imagination from his social theory. It is appropriate to think of Virilio as a strictly political rather than a social thinker: 'I don't believe in sociology ... I prefer politics and war,' he confesses (Virilio and Lotringer, 1983: 17). Given this emphasis, it is important to recognise that the 'collocation of time and conflict is of the essence of the political for Virilio' (Docherty, 1993: 19). This same conjunction, in Virilio's eyes, lies at the origins of the city – an understanding which provides the launch-pad for a full-blown critique of modern society, science, and technology. The logic that first gave rise to the city finally rebounds in a world 'devoid of spatial dimensions, but inscribed in the singular temporality of an instantaneous diffusion' (Virilio, 1991b: 13).

Virilio begins in the phenomenal realm, with a consideration of appearances and illusion. For Virilio (1991a: 37), the world as we know it is always 'already a kind of dissolving view, reminding us of the reflection of Paul of Tarsus ... [A]ll is calm, and yet: *this world as we see it is passing away.*' One is also reminded of Arthur Schopenhauer, for whom 'the world was its representation' (Virilio, 1999: 6). Virilio similarly adheres to Carl von Clausewitz's (1976) precept that conflict is fundamental to the human species, which relates more closely to his concerns with appearance than is first apparent. Adopting Sun Tzu's (1963) ancient maxim that 'speed is the essence of war', Virilio develops a way of understanding conflict in aesthetic (perceptual) terms: 'a war begins with the planning of its theatre ... the stage on which the scenario should be played out' (Virilio, 1990: 14). The crux of the matter is the sense in which '*war consists in the organization of the field of perception*' (Virilio, 2001b: 185), through a double game of playing off the visible against the invisible, and the perceptible against the imperceptible. War is the orchestrated displacement (i.e., destruction) of the real – as it *appears* (in one's sights), and, more importantly, as it *appears to appear* (as a manifestation of antagonism).

For Virilio this explains the centrality of strategies of deception, dissimulation, and disappearance in creating the 'fog of war', such as camouflage, disinformation, virtualisation, and stealth technologies. This explains Virilio's ambivalent appreciation of the Italian Futurist writer, Filippo Marinetti, whose adulation of the machinery of warfare and celebration of the links between aesthetics and politics became ever more thoroughly imbricated with fascism. More importantly, however, it allows him to construct an account of the urban not in terms of 'the classic opposition of city to country but as that of stasis to circulation' (Virilio, 1986: 5). Such a conception is not without its antecedents. Lewis Mumford (1979: 13), for instance, held that 'Human life swings between two poles: movement and settlement.' For Virilio (1986: 6), however, 'there is only *habitable circulation*' – implying a dialectical and ecumenical resolution of Mumford's opposition against a generalised background of conflict.

According to Virilio (1990: 15), once 'the possibility of pastoral flight disappears, with the advent of agricultural settlements and a change in the nature of wealth (non-transportable goods),' the relationship between humans and their environment profoundly alters. Nomadic existence saw the occasional adoption of elevated vantage-points. Yet taking the high ground was less a defensive manoeuvre than a means of obtaining 'quicker information on the surroundings' (Virilio, 1990: 15), thereby displacing the immediacy of direct encounter. However, rather than simply being *informed* by the environment, a sedentary population actively began to *transform* its surroundings – adopting defensive hilltop positions, constructing observation platforms, building fences and ramparts, etc. This reorganisation of space effects a manipulation of time. Such transformations institute a delay between one's own position and that of potential aggressors. If one has sight of one's enemy before one is in their sights, one can act ahead of time. 'Attack and defense then split on this terrain to form two elements of a single dialectic: the former becomes synonymous with speed, circulation, progression and change; and the latter with opposition to movement, tautological preservation, etc.' (Virilio, 1990: 15–16).

Virilio thus refigures Clausewitz's dialectic of attack and defence as a dialectic of *speed* and *slowness* (the latter of which is routinely missed by those mesmerised by the 'speeding up' of modern life: acceleration is necessarily accompanied by a relative deceleration). This same dialectic governs exchanges other than violent conflict, such as the economic exchanges of commerce and trade. The essence of the city itself thus lies in regulating the passage of others through 'pacemaking', as Parkes and **Thrift**, 1979, once put it in their exposition of time geographies: by creating a position from which the passage of others can be slowed down, one is empowered to act in advance. Hence Virilio's dromological conception of spatial politics (from the Greek, *dromos* – running, course): the *polis* arises in response to the emergence of 'dromomaniacs', whose unpredictable behaviour calls forth a 'dromocratic revolution', resulting in rule by 'dromocrats'. We thus inhabit not a democracy but a 'dromocracy' – a movement bureaucracy or speed (and slowness) technocracy. One thinks of the famous Haussmanisation of Paris in the second half of the nineteenth century, which reconstructed the city with Grand

Boulevards, sewer systems, and central-ised abattoirs in order to expedite the free circulation of some things (goods, con-sumers, capital, traffic, military forces, storm-water, and animals) and impede the circulation of other things (vagrants, the masses, revolutionaries, and miasma).

This dromological perspective is vital to appreciating the attention Virilio lav-ishes on technology. He is far from being the technological fantasist he is some-times held to be. Nor is he a technological determinist; in fact, he is a technological *indeterminist* (cf. **Baudrillard**). He is fas-cinated by the way in which technologies are 'capable of orchestrating the perpet-ual shift of appearances' (Virilio, 1995: 23), thus ensuring an indeterminacy that always opens up the possibility of resist-ance. His prime focus – and here the inevi-table comparison with Marshall McLuhan (1969) is unhelpful – is the way in which the technological 'extensions of man' oper-ate as 'prostheses of speed'. This has to be understood, Virilio maintains, in relation to the forces of destruction (war) rather more than the forces of production (indus-try). In contrast to **David Harvey**'s (1989) account of 'time-space compression', Vir-ilio refuses to regard the political economy of *speed* as subservient to the political economy of *value*, the latter of which is a manifestation of the market and the state. Speed relates to the 'war machine', which is exterior to the state and is its condition of possibility (cf. Clastres, 1977; **Deleuze** and Guattari, 1987).

Virilio argues that the smooth course of life has always been subject to inter-ruption – to acts of God, fate, accidents, and unintended consequences – which give rise to unease, dislocation, and con-flict. War is the exemplary interruption of life. For Virilio, war is the *absolute* acci-dent: its pure form. By a strange dialec-tical twist, however, warfare (*destruction*) has become caught up with the logic of

industry (*production*). The original sense of production was to 'render visible' or to 'make apparent'. While destruction was initially opposed to production, which served to undermine it, this relation has become obscured. Not only do all man-ner of everyday consumer products, from tinned foods to the internet, find their origins in the military-industrial com-plex, Virilio suggests that the industrial mode of production *itself* is the accidental result of the progression of the means of destruction, and has come to serve as a cover for its development towards a state of 'pure war' (Virilio and Lotringer, 1983).

> The *scientific and industrial mode of pro-duction* is perhaps only an avatar or, as they say, fallout, of the development of the means of destruction, of the *absolute accident of war*, of the conflict pursued down through the centuries in every so-ciety, irrespective of its political or eco-nomic status – *the great time war* that never ceases to *unexpectedly befall* us time and again despite the evolution of morals and the means of production, and whose intensity never ceases to grow apace with technological innovations, *to the point where the ultimate energy, nuclear energy, makes its appearance in a weapon that is simultaneously an arm and the absolute accident of History.*
>
> (Virilio, 1993: 212–213)

This is the point at which a process lead-ing unerringly towards *total war* (the nuclear annihilation of life on Earth) mutates into the paradoxical state of *pure war* – a state of 'peace' that is merely the continuation of war by other means. If the 'logic of deterrence' by which pure war reigns was initially a product of the Cold War, Virilio's sense of a society in a perpetual state of preparation for war – and the attendant sense of *apocalypse from now on* – remains all too pertinent in the post-Cold War era (Virilio, 2005, 2007; see Thrift, 2005, for a critique).

Military intelligence continues to pervade society in all manner of pernicious ways, whilst 'the old illusion ... persists that a state of peace means the absence of open warfare, or that the military which no longer fights but "helps" society is peaceful' (Virilio, 1990: 36). The relations between the logistics of perception and the logistics of war point to a decisive but well-camouflaged link between 'civilian' culture and military technology, which only reveals itself incidentally – in the common ancestry of the Gatling gun and the cine-camera, radar and video, and gunpowder and printer's ink, for example. Yet, given that all technologies work as prosthetic devices, simultaneously disabling and enabling the subject, cybernetic extensions of vision inevitably entail the (calculated) loss of other ways of seeing and being in the world. By the 1930s, for instance, 'it was already clear that film was superimposing itself as a geostrategy which for a century or more had inexorably been leading to the direct substitution, and thus sooner or later the disintegration, of things and places' (Virilio, 1989: 47). Virilio (1989, 2002a) consistently conceives of technology in terms of this kind of 'substitution'. New technologies tend to nullify and displace the problems they are meant to solve and overcome, producing new configurations that redefine the direction taken by society as a whole. The world according to Virilio (2002c) is a world in which technological change all too easily follows a trajectory of its own accord, leaving us out of the picture without us even realising the fact. On the brink of pure war, we risk failing to perceive the way in which the 'reality principle' has been usurped by an accelerating series of 'reality effects' (cf. Baudrillard and Deleuze on simulacra).

Perhaps Virilio's lasting legacy will be in terms of his explication of the geographical implications of technology. Today, says Virilio (2001b: 84), 'we live in a world no longer based on geographical expanse but on a temporal distance constantly being decreased by our transportation, transmission and tele-action capacities.' He highlights a broadly chronological transition from *vehicular technologies*, associated with the conquest of space (which create a territorial infrastructure of road and rail networks, ports, airports, and so on – a fixity in space permitting movement over space) to *transmission technologies*, associated with the conquest of time (immaterial, electromagnetic means of communication permitting near-instantaneous contact regardless of physical distance – and retrospectively revealing that physical distances have always been a function of the speed, and cost, with which they could be overcome). Consequently, 'The new space is speed-space; it is no longer a time-space' (Virilio, 2001b: 71). The ultimate limit of these transmission technologies is the speed of light, which would imply a situation of pure telepresence:

> So after the nuclear disintegration of *the space of matter*, which led to the implementation of a global deterrence strategy, the disintegration of *the time of light* is finally upon us. This will most likely involve a new mutation of the war game, with deception finally defeating deterrence.
>
> (Virilio, 1994b: 72)

KEY ADVANCES AND CONTROVERSIES

War at the speed of light, employing technologies of deception, might sound like science fiction. Yet, Virilio insists that this is precisely the point at which we have arrived. The development of techno-science means that, today, 'the battlefield is global' and, in consequence, there is an increasing 'feeling of confinement in the world' (Virilio, in Der Derian, 1998: 17, 21). Such insights into our globalised existence invite frequent accusations that Virilio fails to pay due attention to human corporeality. Yet, nothing could be further from the truth. Virilio's concerns for the body underlie his entire critique. He fears that the internal colonisation of the body by transplant technologies means that our bodies, not merely our cities, territories, and planet, are increasingly the (passive) medium of technological change. 'That which favours the equipping of territories, of cities, in particular, threatens to apply to the human body, as if we had the city in the body and not the city around the body. The city "at home",

in vitro, in vivo' (Virilio, in Der Derian, 1998: 20). In such a situation, we face the development of the 'last vehicle' – a paradoxical 'stationary vehicle' which, like a running machine or flight simulator, induces motion but puts an end to movement by transforming the actor into a tele-actor. 'This tele-actor will no longer throw himself into any means of physical travel, but only into another body, an optical body; and he will go forward without moving, see with other eyes, touch with hands other than his own, to be over there without really being there, a stranger to himself, a deserter from his own body, an exile for evermore' (Virilio, 1999, 85). In the final analysis, then, Virilio might be regarded as having both radicalised and simplified the analysis of speed. Yet he has remained, paradoxically, an optimistic extremist – or, if you prefer, an extreme optimist.

VIRILIO'S KEY WORKS

Virilio, P. (1994a) *Bunker Archaeology.* Trans. G. Collins. New York: Princeton Architectural Press. [1991; first edition 1975]
Virilio, P. (1986) *Speed and Politics: An Essay on Dromology.* Trans. M. Polizotti. New York: Semiotext(e). [1977]
Virilio, P. (1989) *War and Cinema: The Logistics of Perception.* Trans. P. Camiller. London: Verso. [1984]
Virilio, P. (1991a) *The Aesthetics of Disappearance.* Trans. P. Beitchman. New York: Semiotext(e). [1980]
Virilio, P. (1991b) *The Lost Dimension.* Trans. D. Moshenberg. New York: Semiotext(e). [1984]
Virilio, P. (1994b) *The Vision Machine.* Trans. J. Rose. London: British Film Institute. [1988]
Virilio, P. (1995) *The Art of the Motor.* Trans. J. Rose. Minneapolis: University of Minnesota Press. [1993]
Virilio, P (2000) *The Information Bomb.* Trans. C. Turner. London: Verso. [1998]
Virilio, P. (2005) *City of Panic* Trans. J. Rose. Oxford: Berg.
Virilio, P. (2007) *The Original Accident.* Trans. J. Rose. Polity: Cambridge.
Virilio, P. and Lotringer, S. (1983) *Pure War.* Trans. M. Polizotti. New York: Semiotext(e).

Secondary Sources and References

Armitage, J. (ed.) (2000) *Paul Virilio: From Modernism to Hypermodernism and Beyond.* London: Sage. (Also released as *Theory, Culture & Society*, 16 (5–6).)
Clastres, P. (1977) *Society Against the State.* Trans. R. Hurley. Oxford: Blackwell. [1974].
Clausewitz, C. von (1976) *On War.* Trans. M. Howard and P. Paret. Princeton, Guilford: Princeton University Press. [1832]

Deleuze, G. and Guattari, F. (1987) *A Thousand Plateaus: Capitalism and Schizophrenia.* Trans. B. Massumi. Minneapolis: University of Minnesota Press. [1980]

Der Derian, J. (1998) *The Virilio Reader.* Oxford: Blackwell.

Docherty, T. (1993) *Postmodernism: A Reader.* London: Harvester Wheatsheaf.

Guillaume, P. (1937) *La Psychologie de la Forme.* Paris: Flammarion.

Harvey, D. (1989) *The Condition of Postmodernity: An Enquiry into the Origins of Cultural Change.* Oxford: Blackwell.

Lotringer, S. and Virilio, P. (2005) *The Accident of Art.* New York: Semiotext(e).

Luke, T. and Ó Tuathail, G. (2000) 'Thinking geopolitical space: the spatiality of war, speed and vision in the work of Paul Virilio', in N. Thrift and M. Crang (eds), *Thinking Space.* London: Routledge. pp. 360–79.

McLuhan, M. (1969) *Understanding Media: The Extensions of Man.* London: Routledge & Kegan Paul.

Merleau-Ponty, M. (1962) *The Phenomenology of Perception.* Trans. C. Smith. London: Routledge.

Mumford, L. (1979) *The City in History: Its Origins, Its Transformations, and Its Prospects.* Harmondsworth: Penguin.

Parkes, D. and Thrift, N. (1979) 'Time spacemakers and entrainment', *Transactions of the Institute of British Geographers,* 4: 353–72.

Sun Tzu (1963) *The Art of War.* Trans. S. B. Griffith. Oxford: Clarendon Press.

Thrift, N. (2005) 'Panicsville: Paul Virilio and the esthetic of disaster', *Cultural Politics,* 1 (3): 353–63.

Virilio, P. (1976a) *L'Insécurité du territoire.* Paris: Éditions Stock.

Virilio, P. (1976b) *La Dromoscopies ou la lumière de la vitesse.* Paris: Minuit.

Virilio, P. (1984) *L'Espace critique.* Paris: Christian Bourgois.

Virilio, P. (1990) *Popular Defense and Ecological Struggles.* Trans. M. Polizotti. New York: Semiotext(e). [1978]

Virilio, P. (1993) 'The primal accident', in B. Massumi (ed.), *The Politics of Everyday Fear.* Minneapolis: University of Minnesota Press. pp. 211–18.

Virilio, P. (1997) *Open Sky.* Trans. J. Rose. London: Verso. [1995]

Virilio, P. (1999) *Polar Inertia.* Trans. P. Camiller. London: Sage. [1990]

Virilio, P (2000) *The Strategy of Deception.* Trans. C. Turner. London: Verso. [1999]

Virilio, P. (2001a) *A Landscape of Events.* Trans. J. Rose. Cambridge, MA: MIT Press. [1996]

Virilio, P. (2001b) *Virilio Live: Selected Interviews.* Ed. J. Armitage. London: Sage.

Virilio, P. (2002a) *Negative Horizon: Toward a Dromoscopy.* Trans. M. Degener. London: Continuum. [1984]

Virilio, P. (2002b) *Desert Screen: War at the Speed of Light.* Trans. M. Degener. London: Sage. [1991]

Virilio, P. (2002c) *Ground Zero.* Trans. C. Turner. London: Verso. [2002]

Virilio, P. (2003) *Art and Fear.* Trans. J. Rose. London: Continuum.

Virilio, P. (2003) *Unknown Quantity.* New York: Thames & Hudson, Paris: Fondation Cartier pour l'Art Contemporain.

Virilio, P. (2007) *Art as Far as the Eye Can See.* Trans. J. Rose. Oxford: Berg.

Virilio, P. and Lotringer, S. (2002) *Crepuscular Dawn.* Trans. M. Taormina. New York: Semiotext(e).

Virilio, P. and Parent, C. (1996) *Architecture Principe, 1996 et 1966.* Trans. G. Collins. Besançon: L'Imprimeur.

Virilio, P. and Petit, P. (1999) *Politics of the Very Worst.* Trans. M. Cavaliere. Ed. S. Lotringer. New York: Semiotext(e).

Wark, M. (1994) *Virtual Geography: Living with Global Media Events.* Indianapolis: Indiana University Press.

David B. Clarke, Swansea University/Prifysgol Abertawe
and Marcus A. Doel, Swansea University/Prifysgol Abertawe

61 Immanuel Wallerstein

BIOGRAPHICAL DETAILS AND THEORETICAL CONTEXT

Immanuel Wallerstein was born in 1930 in New York, where he attended Columbia College and then Columbia University, receiving his PhD in 1959. He went on to teach in the Sociology department at Columbia, moving to McGill University in Montreal in 1971, and then to the State University of New York at Binghamton in 1976. Wallerstein was based at SUNY-Binghamton after that, serving as Distinguished Professor of Sociology until his retirement in 1999 and as Director of the Fernand Braudel Center for the Study of Economies, Historical Systems, and Civilizations until 2005. The Braudel Center (named in honour of the French historian) has become internationally known for its connection to Wallerstein's work and as an important base for work by a large number of like-minded scholars. Since 2000, Wallerstein has been a Senior Research Scholar in the Department of Sociology at Yale University and in 2003 he received the Career of Distinguished Scholarship Award from the American Sociological Association. He has also been politically active throughout his career. In 1968, he served on a faculty committee that attempted to resolve a student uprising at Columbia University, part of the broader political upheavals of 1968, a process that had significant impact on Wallerstein's thinking. Since the 1990s, he has been a major participant in the World Social Forum (WSF), where many of his ideas have had a favourable reception.

Early in his life, Wallerstein was especially interested in anti-colonial struggle in India, and his academic work from the mid-1950s to the early 1970s focused on African independence, but he has become internationally renowned for works he published in the 1970s and subsequently that addressed broader issues of the global political economy. These works, beginning with a frequently-cited 1974 article on 'The rise and future demise of the world capitalist system' (2000: 71–105) and the first volume of his three volume series *The Modern World-System* (Wallerstein, 1974; 1980; 1989), marked Wallerstein as the founder of world-systems analysis. Wallerstein's development of world-systems analysis originated as part of a broader reaction against modernization theory, exemplified in the work of economic historian Walter W. Rostow (1960). Rostow posited a 'normal' process of development for all countries, in which they moved through 'stages of development', leading from pre-industrial to industrial, as had early industrialising countries like the UK and the US. Wallerstein, like many Latin American structuralist economists and more politically radical dependency theorists, found such a view to be inaccurate and generative of bad political prescriptions. For Wallerstein, as for later collaborators such as Terence Hopkins and the members of his 'Gang of Four' (Andre Gunder Frank, Samir Amin, and Giovanni Arrighi), modernisation theory was based on a perception of the world rooted in the interests of privileged social actors within the most advanced industrial capitalist countries. These actors – primarily economic and political elites and their academic supporters – asserted that it was undesirable for developing country states to either protect domestic industries (the approach championed by the structuralists) or adopt socialist development strategies (the approach championed by the radical dependency theorists). Instead, modernisation theorists encouraged developing country leaders to facilitate foreign investment and trade, and to follow the putatively market-led development path of the already industrialized capitalist countries – an approach that Wallerstein and others saw as insuring continued subordination within the world-system.

World-systems analysis was thus part of the broader development of what came to be called 'core-periphery' theorising, including not just world-systems analysis but also Frank's version of radical dependency theory (1967), Amin's analysis of 'accumulation on a world scale' (1974), and the 'dependent development' approach of Fernando Enrique Cardoso and Enzo Faletto (1979). In spite of significant differences between each of these approaches, they hold in common the view that the development of capitalism cannot be seen as a process that works the same way within the earliest centres of capitalist development as it does in places that were incorporated into the global capitalist economy later under conditions of colonialism and imperialism. Indeed,

it is not accidental that a significant number of such core-periphery theorists have come from countries characterised as part of the periphery and speak from a perspective that they claim represents the interests of the world's most marginalised populations (Porter and Sheppard, 1998: 96–118).

Wallerstein's world-systems approach has one further dimension that transcends these particular core-periphery dimensions. Wallerstein has argued that the political upheavals occurring around the world during 1968 – not only outside the core of the global economy but within it – were representative of a crisis for both global capitalism and the movements that have arisen since the nineteenth century to challenge it (Wallerstein, 2000: 355–73). He calls these the 'anti-systemic movements' and includes among them the social democratic reform movements of Western Europe and North America, the revolutionary movements of the former socialist bloc, and the nationalist movements of the Third World (see Amin et al., 1990). The rebellions of 1968 manifest discontent not only with capitalism but with the anti-systemic movements in power that had claimed to be forwarding viable alternatives to capitalism. World-systems analysis not only countered modernisation theory but presented a framework for analysing this crisis of the anti-systemic movements and their inability to transform the global capitalist economy through their capture of state power (Wallerstein, 2000: xxii).

While the main lines of world-systems analysis were outlined in Wallerstein's work during the 1970s and 1980s, his writing in the 1990s and 2000s has built on this foundation by developing a specific critique of recent US imperialism. Wallerstein has argued that US interventions in the Middle East are an attempt to stave off an overall decline in US power and hegemony, part of a broader, longer-term transformation of the world-system that the US cannot control and which includes the rise of new centres of accumulation in East Asia. In this context, Wallerstein sees the resurgent militarism of US neo-conservative political leaders as reactive, ill-informed, and ultimately destined for failure (Wallerstein, 2003).

SPATIAL CONTRIBUTIONS

Wallerstein (1999: 192) characterised world-systems analysis as helping to 'clear the underbrush' for more useful approaches to the social sciences than then dominant disciplinary approaches. He depicted world-systems analysis as doing this through raising crucial foundational issues. These include issues that he addresses under the headings of 'historicity' and 'globality' (Wallerstein, 1999: 195–6). Historicity is central to Wallerstein's analysis of global capitalism. Following the French historian Fernand Braudel, Wallerstein insists that capitalism is not a development of the last two centuries, a view common among most Marxists. Rather, as he sees it, capitalism had developed in Europe by the middle of the sixteenth century, expanding outward from that period. This makes it necessary to study capitalist development over what Braudel calls the *longue durée*, extended periods of development that encompass economic and political cycles of varying lengths, including Kondratieff cycles of 50–60 years (25–30 years of global economic growth followed by 25–30 years of global economic stagnation).

The geographical dimension of world-systems analysis, what Wallerstein calls its insistence on 'globality', is perhaps its most distinctive feature. Wallerstein's work is 'neo-Marxist' in that it adopts much of Marx's emphasis on class struggle and capital accumulation, along with Marx's critical perspective on capitalism as a social system, but Wallerstein both transforms certain Marxist categories and rejects certain Marxist claims. Like Marx, Wallerstein characterises capitalism as a form of class exploitation reliant on the perpetual accumulation of capital through this process; but unlike many Marxists he does not abstract the capitalist mode of production from its geographical-historical context of development. This means that for Wallerstein the capitalist mode of production existed, from its birth, on a transnational (or world) scale, and integrally involved numerous forms of labour besides the 'free' wage labour Marx focused on in his analysis of capitalism.

Wallerstein's neo-Marxism thus differs from Marxism in the way it approaches class, since the capitalist class structure is seen within world-systems analysis to exist at a world scale right from capitalism's inception – even when capitalists and workers only exhibit a nationalist class consciousness. This difference is important because for Wallerstein capitalism on a world scale involves a complex and geographically expansive class structure that incorporates many more non-proletarians than proletarians, with this non-proletarian labour being indirectly exploited by capitalists. Thus, for Wallerstein, forms of labour such as subsistence and semi-subsistence production, household production, and simple commodity production, are all integral to the actual development of historical capitalism, and one cannot meaningfully abstract from them if one is to understand the functioning of capitalism (Wallerstein, 1979: 119–31).

In this vein, Wallerstein argues that the idealised representation of capitalism as a free market system – which classical and neo-classical economists extolled and which Marx assumed for purposes of critique – has never occurred and could never occur without producing disaster for capitalists. For repeated and expanded capitalist accumulation to occur, capitalists must constantly generate profits, and this is not accomplished solely through direct exploitation of wage labour within a context of market competition but also by the indirect exploitation of non-proletarian labour. Furthermore, profits are generated by the development of monopolies and quasi-monopolies. A truly free and fully competitive market would reduce or eliminate profits and would thus spell the end of capitalism. For this reason, capitalists have always favoured specific forms of state intervention in the market that allow *partial* freedom (especially for investors, less so for workers) while protecting monopolies through various measures. States thus play a crucial and inevitable role in global capitalism.

Wallerstein argues that what is distinctive about capitalism as a historical system is that it involves a social division of labour (and thus class structure) that is *transnational* and built around global commodity chains, along with an interstate system comprising *national* states. These states, moreover, have been brought into the world capitalist system *in relation to one another* and with differing positions in the global capitalist hierarchy. Certain nation states occupy *core* positions within the global capitalist economy, dominating the leading technologies and higher value production processes of the particular era, while others occupy *peripheral* positions within this same economy, having

lesser technological development and typically having to export raw materials or lower value added products to the global core. In between these poles, there are also *semi-peripheral* nation states that contain some mix of core and peripheral production processes. For Wallerstein, this hierarchical structure leads to unequal exchange – i.e., exchange by more peripheral producers of more embodied labour time for less – and such unequal exchange is central to global capitalism, making it inherently polarising in a sociospatial sense.

Within the global process of polarisation, semi-peripheral states are important because they provide outlets for reinvestment of capital from the core during economic downturns in the Kondratieff cycle, and also because they provide some limited prospects for upward mobility within the system, thus potentially undercutting the appeal of anti-capitalist alternatives. What is important to recognise, for Wallerstein, is that the movement of a nation-state up or down the global hierarchy – which has frequently occurred – does not change the overall structure of the system or eliminate its polarising tendencies.

The socio-spatial structure of global capitalism therefore helps account for both of the kinds of phenomena that gave rise to world-systems analysis. First, according to Wallerstein, the failure of modernisation approaches to provide reasonable options for peripheral countries as a whole stems from their failure to address the relational, hierarchical structure and polarising tendencies of capitalism: even when one country successfully and rapidly 'develops' – e.g., moves from periphery to semi-periphery – this does not lift peripheral countries as a whole and in fact makes it more difficult for those that remain because it increases the competition in economic activities that other peripheral countries are attempting to develop. Second, the fact that global capitalism features a transnational economy and a system of national states accounts for the failure of the anti-systemic movements to achieve a reversal of capitalism's polarising tendencies: the anti-systemic movements achieved power only at the level of nation states – social democratic governments, formally 'socialist' governments, and post-colonial nationalist governments – but not within the global capitalist economy as a whole.

Wallerstein's views have done much to explicitly spatialise political theories throughout the social sciences, and they have entered directly into geography through the work of political and economic geographers such as Colin Flint and **Peter J. Taylor** (Taylor and Flint, 2000). Taylor's work has directly utilised a world-systems analysis to approach a range of issues in political geography, including patterns of development of the inter-state system (1996), and the development of global networks of cities (2004). Other geographers have directly employed Wallerstein's tri-partite division of the global economy and his approach to global commodity chains. Most importantly, perhaps, from its inception, world-systems analysis and other core-periphery approaches have directly or indirectly influenced the thinking of geographers concerned with issues of uneven development.

KEY ADVANCES AND CONTROVERSIES

The influence of world-systems analysis on interpretations of the spatiality of

capitalist development has been considerable. Moreover, as the social sciences have increasingly become absorbed in debates about 'globalisation', world-systems analysts' emphasis on interconnections between processes at a global scale has been reinforced by both current events and contemporary discourses of globalisation.

Nonetheless, even as many of its claims have been absorbed by the social sciences, world-systems analysis has been dismissed or criticised by some, in part because of ways in which it challenges established disciplinary boundaries and practices, but also because it raises complex and still unresolved issues regarding how to conceive the spatiality of global capitalism. Where the disciplinary issue is concerned, Wallerstein's efforts are exemplified by his chairing of the Gulbenkian Commission on the Restructuring of the Social Sciences, part of an effort to analyse the historical development of academic disciplines and suggest alternatives for the future – a project that has not been dismissed but has failed to gain great institutional traction. With regard to the spatiality issue, a more dismissive position is reflected in the oft cited criticism of Wallerstein's work raised by Marxist historian Robert Brenner (1977). Brenner critiques Wallerstein, Frank, and Amin as representatives of what he calls 'neo-Smithian' Marxism – a deviant form of Marxism that substitutes Adam Smith's emphasis on market exchange for Marx's emphasis on class relations and exploitation. For Brenner, the global connective tissue of sixteenth-century capitalism emphasised by Wallerstein is nothing more than trade between separate societies. These societies each had different kinds of local or national class structures. The class process by which labour is exploited is thus, for Brenner, fundamentally rooted *within* states, while the processes that lead to unequal exchange are *external* to such class processes. From this perspective, Wallerstein mis-identifies as capitalist exploitation the movement of surplus from periphery to core through trade arrangements that are not in actuality central to the story of capitalist exploitation.

This cuts to precisely the issue of whether or not capitalism should be seen as an abstract mode of production organised at the local or national scale and based on free wage labour, or whether it should be seen as a more inclusive and concrete historical process that involves transnationalised classes and varying types of labour. In contrast to Brenner, Wallerstein sees capitalist exploitation as taking place internationally, integrally involving production in specific locations and trade or exchange with other locations, along with international transfer of surplus value through this trade and exchange. This difference implies a difference in political strategy. For Brenner, the central struggles against exploitation are within nation-states, though nationally-based class struggles may become externally linked through acts of international solidarity. For Wallerstein, on the other hand, struggles against capitalist exploitation exist within an already transnational space and within a complex web of economic relations including non-proletarianised labour

taking place in households and elsewhere (Wallerstein, 2000). Moreover, anti-capitalist struggles may frequently take the form of national liberation movements or struggles in which race or ethnicity come to the foreground. Though this may slow the development of transnational class consciousness and transnational anti-capitalist politics, such struggles cannot be written off as demonstrating false consciousness, since they reflect the real, racialised and ethnicised, socio-spatial polarisation of the global capitalist economy (Wallerstein, 1979; 2000). More recently, on the other hand, Wallerstein's focus has shifted to the ways already transnationalised groups of actors – such as workers subordinated to the same groups of transnational capitalists – can forward their projects through collaboration in forums such as the WSF.

How to understand the spatial structures of global capitalism – as fragmentary or as a unity-in-diversity – is an important and ongoing debate, and it relates directly to practical questions being asked by radical geographers and social scientists about the most appropriate and effective spatial forms for struggles against capitalism. Thus, many in the social sciences are today labouring in fields prepared for them at least in part by the socio-spatial ideas of Wallerstein and other core-periphery thinkers.

WALLERSTEIN'S KEY WORKS

Wallerstein, I. M. (1974) *The Modern World-System I: Capitalist Agriculture and the Origins of the European World-Economy in the Sixteenth Century.* New York: Academic Press.

Wallerstein, I. (1979) *The Capitalist World-Economy.* Cambridge: Cambridge University Press.

Wallerstein, I. M. (1980) *The Modern World-System II: Mercantilism and the Consolidation of the European World Economy, 1600–1750.* New York: Academic Press.

Wallerstein, I. M. (1983) *Historical Capitalism.* London: Verso.

Wallerstein, I. M. (1989) *The Modern World-System III: The Second Era of Great Expansion of the Capitalist World-Economy, 1730–1840s.* San Diego: Academic Press.

Wallerstein, I. M. (1999) 'The rise and future demise of world-systems analysis', in I.M Wallerstein, *The End of the World as We Know It: Social Science for the Twenty-First Century.* Minneapolis: University of Minnesota Press. pp. 192–201.

Wallerstein, I. M. (2000) *The Essential Wallerstein.* New York: The New Press.

Wallerstein, I. M. (2003) *Decline of American Power: the US in a Chaotic World.* New York: Free Press.

Secondary Sources and References

Amin, S. (1974) *Accumulation on a World Scale: A Critique of the Theory of Underdevelopment.* New York and London: Monthly Review Press.

Amin, S., Arrighi, G., Frank, A. G. and Wallerstein, I. M. (1990) *Transforming the Revolution: Social Movements and the World-System.* New York: Monthly Review Press.

Brenner, R. (1977) 'The origins of capitalist development: a critique of neo-Smithian Marxism', *New Left Review,* 104 (July/August): 25–92.

Cardoso, F. H. and Faletto, E. (1979) *Dependency and Development in Latin America.* Berkeley: University of California Press.

Frank, A. G. (1967) *Capitalism and Underdevelopment in Latin America.* New York: Monthly Review Press.

Gulbenkian Commission on the Restructuring of the Social Sciences (1996) *Open the Social Sciences: The Report of the Gulbenkian Commission on the Restructuring of the Social Sciences.* Stanford: Stanford University Press.

Porter, P. W. and Sheppard, E. S. (1998) *A World of Difference: Society, Nature, Development.* New York: Guilford Press.

Rostow, W. W. (1960) *The Stages of Economic Growth: An Anti-communist Manifesto.* New York: Norton.

Taylor, P. J. (1996) *The Way the Modern World Works: World Hegemony to World Impasse.* Chichester: Wiley.

Taylor, P. J. (2004). *World City Network: A Global Urban Analysis.* New York and London: Routledge.

Taylor, P. J. and Flint, C. (2000) *Political Geography: World-Economy, Nation-State and Locality.* Harlow: Prentice Hall.

Jim Glassman, University of British Columbia

BIOGRAPHICAL DETAILS AND THEORETICAL CONTEXT

Michael J. Watts was born in England in 1951. He earned a Bachelor of Science degree in Geography from University College, London, where he graduated with First Class Honours in 1972, going on to pursue graduate studies in Geography in the USA at the University of Michigan, where he earned an MA in 1974, and a PhD in 1979. Watts' geographic education was influenced initially by the various dependency theories of the 1960s, and later by debates within Marxian political economy. His doctoral work at Michigan, under the direction of Bernard Nietschmann, focused initially on the limits of cultural ecology and ecological anthropology as approaches to understanding peasant production systems in semi-arid Africa. During his graduate studies, Watts was taught and advised by a remarkable cast of intellectuals including Gunnar Olsson, Roy Rappaport, Michael Taussig, and Marshall Sahlins, who together left a lasting imprint on his work.

Watts' graduate studies took him to northern Nigeria, where he conducted long-term field research on the effects of capitalist penetration on peasant agricultural systems. This work began as an attempt to understand how farmers perceived their environments in the context of drought and the vulnerability wrought by 'natural' hazards. This initial focus gave way to a study of famine and vulnerability, and led Watts to rethink the fields of human ecology and hazards, with their focus on human adaptation and cybernetic feedback systems. Drawing heavily on the work of E.P. Thompson and Perry Anderson, this research ultimately sought to explain the manner in which the 'moral economy' of the northern Nigerian peasantry was undermined, and made more vulnerable to drought and famine, by colonial capitalism.

After receiving has PhD in 1979, Watts took a position at the University of California, Berkeley, where he became Chancellor's Professor in the Department of Geography, and the Director of the Institute of International Studies. His first major work, *Silent Violence: Food, Famine and Peasantry in Northern Nigeria*, was published in 1983. Based on his doctoral dissertation research, *Silent Violence* was, as Michael Redclift (2001) has noted, 'a big book in every sense'. Its nearly 700 pages sought to explain Nigerian famine in the nineteenth century, examined the implications of British colonialism for peasant economies, and posed a major theoretical challenge to the cultural and human ecology of the 1970s. *Silent Violence* was 'an attempt to ... move beyond the limitations of natural hazards research and cultural ecology, beyond functionalism, the pitfalls of behaviorism, and the reluctance to engage with the political economy of the market' (Watts, 2001). From a personal standpoint, Watts' book collided head on with the cultural ecology of Roy Rappaport, with whom Watts studied anthropology at Michigan, and Barney Nietschmann, his dissertation advisor. Based on extended fieldwork in West Africa, meticulous empirical research, and a rigorous and wide-ranging theoretical engagement with Marxian political economy, *Silent Violence* has influenced two generations of geographers, and helped shape the study of society–environment relations within geography during the 1980s and 1990s. Though to a certain extent overshadowed by Amartya Sen's *Poverty and Famines*, released in the same year, *Silent Violence* remains a landmark work within geography.

Watts' subsequent work has continued to focus on the intersections of political economy, culture, nature, and power. Watts's critical (some might say polemical) contribution to a key volume on hazards research (Hewitt, 1983) argued for a more sophisticated engagement with social theory within the fields of human ecology and natural hazards. Thus Watts, by this time at Berkeley, drew a sharp theoretical distinction between himself and the Berkeley School, though in many respects (such as his concern for historical relationships between society and environment, peasant agricultural systems, and resource use and degradation), his affinity with the legacy of Carl Sauer is clear. Throughout the 1980s and 1990s, he continued to publish on the political economy of agricultural systems, environmental degradation, and the marginalisation of the African peasantry (e.g.,

Watts, 1987; 1989; 1990; Little and Watts, 1994). Watts hence found himself at the centre of debates surrounding the political economy of environmental change and Marxian challenges to cultural and human ecology. He was also to find himself placed in situations of personal danger when exploring the political ecologies and political economies of oil extraction on the Niger Delta, being shot in the hand during a raid on newspaper offices in Port Harcourt in 2007. Nonetheless, his analyses of oil production and extraction, funded in part by a 2003 Guggenheim Fellowship, resulted in an impressive and influential series of papers and books, including the photo essay *Curse of Black Gold* (2008).

Indeed, Watts has arguably been the single most important figure in the formation and development of political ecology as a subfield, both by virtue of his own enormously important work, and for the work of his many students, who as a group have profoundly shaped the examination of the political, economic and cultural contexts of environment–society relations within geography. Watts' own interests have diversified in theme and focus, though he has retained a central commitment to Marxian political economy. In addition to his ongoing work on resource economies in West Africa – especially 'petro-capitalism' on the Niger delta (Watts, 2004) – he has extended his interests to the industrial restructuring of agricultural systems in the US, environmental social movements and the transnational networks of which they are a part, the cultural politics of modernity, and political ecology in general. His work on Third World economic and cultural transformation has earned him a reputation as one of the leading thinkers on development studies within the field of geography.

SPATIAL CONTRIBUTIONS

Monumental as it was, *Silent Violence* was in some respects under-appreciated in geography. Watts later lamented that 'it was a book often cited but rarely read' (Watts, 2001: 626), perhaps because its materialist, and what some might call totalising, narrative attempted to 'reclaim something from Althusser when the rip-tide of social theory was racing in the opposite direction' (ibid.). Indeed, it could be argued that much of the value of this work may be located in its insistence on materialist analysis, and the linking of careful empirical investigation (based largely on long-term fieldwork) with a 'willingness to range widely in the search for ideas and intellectual inspiration' (Redclift, 2001: 622), precisely at a time when much social science research was looking inward, confronted by the 'postmodern turn'. Watts' work serves as a reminder of the value of committed fieldwork, rigorous empiricism, and theoretical breadth.

This is not to say that Watts' own work avoided post-structuralism or cultural theory. By the early 1990s, his writing addressed directly the themes of identity politics, globalisation, and the apparent 'deterritorialisation of culture' about which so much was being written. Retaining his commitment to Marxian analysis, Watts sought to locate culture within a nexus of spatial, political, and economic relations, attempting an interrogation of the 'complex articulations of capitalism, modernity and culture understood as a field of struggle' (Watts, 1991: 7). In this work, Watts was particularly concerned to investigate the questions of identity politics, and the contradictions that certain forms of identity construction have with political mobilisation. Thus, through his work Watts sought to illuminate the spaces of globalisation, not as abstract 'spaces of flows' (**Castells**, 1996) or 'global ethnoscapes' (Appadurai, 1991), but in terms of the territorialisation, de-territorialisation, and re-territorialisation of cultural space. Watts showed particular concern for the interstitial spaces of frontiers, the material and symbolic meeting places of political, economic, and cultural systems:

> Frontiers are, of course, particular sorts of spaces – symbolically, ideologically, and materially ... At the margins of state power, they create their own territorial form of law and (dis)order ... But frontiers are also locally encoded in symbolic terms, and often carry a powerful ideological valence, particularly when national identity itself is seen to derive from 'frontier stock', or, if economic potential ('development') is seen to be wedded to the opening of the frontier.
>
> (Watts, 1992: 116–17)

Watts' concern with the spatiality of cultural difference carries with it a critique of what he saw as the naive celebration of multiculturalism that was increasingly prevalent in academic literature. Concerned by the tone of some debates over hybridity, multiplicity, and contingency, and by the fact that multiple identities (e.g., within a social movement) can erode underlying unity – a fact which is used to the benefit of dominant powers – he notes that, 'Some practices of multiculturalism can, therefore, act to reinforce centralized state power,' and questions 'how identity that rests on difference and splitting can produce a common ground for politics' (Watts, 1991: 125).

These concerns were further examined in *Reworking Modernity*, co-written with **Allan Pred** and published in 1992.

In the co-authored introductory chapter, as well the three chapters of which he is sole author, Watts is concerned with questions of identity and difference within the context of the shifting geographies of capitalism and modernity. Central to this work is a concern for scale: linking processes of globalisation with the transformation of particular places. In this sense, this work may be seen as an ethnography of modernity, with concern for:

> the symbolic discontent that emerges as new forms of capital make their local appearance; as the agents and actions of capital intersect with already existing – more or less deeply sedimented – everyday practices, power relations, and forms of consciousness; as local residents simultaneously experience modernity and hegemony in new guises.
>
> (Pred and Watts, 1992: xiii–xiv)

Watts' longstanding concern with the discourses and practices of international development were further examined in a number of key works during the mid-1990s, including a special double-issue of the journal *Economic Geography* in 1993, co-edited with Richard Peet (see also Watts, 1993; 1996). Many of the contributions to this double issue re-emerged (substantially re-worked) in the 1996 volume *Liberation Ecologies: Environment, Development, Social Movements*, again co-edited with Peet. These collections mark an explicit concern to link political ecology, broadly inspired by Marxian political economy, with a post-structural focus on identity politics, discourse analysis, and 'new social movements'. The volume asserts that 'theories about environment and development – political ecology in its various guises – have been pushed and extended both by the realities of the new social movements themselves, and by intellectual developments associated with discourse theory and poststructuralism' (Peet and Watts, 1996: 2–3). Thus, at the heart of the volume are the practices and discourses by which Third World social movements conceptualise, negotiate and contest development. In particular, Peet and Watts seek to illuminate the liberatory potential of social movements and environmental politics, arguing that contemporary environmental struggles involve not only new social movements, but extend to (and through) various transnational environmental and human rights networks, multilateral institutions, and forms of global governance. Thus, a central concern of the volume is the way in which trans-scalar processes and actors influence (and are in turn influenced by) local-scale environmental struggles. While *Liberation Ecologies* marks a significant contribution to the fields of political ecology and development studies, it nevertheless reproduces some of the weaknesses of that literature by incorporating only studies of rural Third World societies (Neumann, 1998). The extension of the political ecology framework to transnational, First World, and urban contexts would have to await other authors (see, for instance, Bebbington and Batterbury, 2001; McCarthy 2001; Robbins et al., 2001).

KEY ADVANCES AND CONTROVERSIES

Watts' work has been central to the establishment and consolidation of political ecology as a subfield within geography. In part, this is because his own work has been characterised by an emphasis on empirical and theoretical rigour, a dedication to field-based research, and a sensitivity to cultural contingency and global power. The influence of his work is also in part attributable to Watts' own caustic critique of cultural and human ecology, particularly the field of hazards research. His 1983 piece, 'On the poverty of theory,' included as a chapter in an important edited collection on hazards research (Hewitt, 1983), takes head on the functionalist, cybernetic approach to the study of social adaptability (at the heart of much cultural ecological research) and of 'natural' hazards. Drawing on the work of Sahlins, Wadell and others, he criticises what he saw as the mechanistic scientism of these approaches to hazards research, particularly as they were applied to peasant societies in transition, and as they are confronted by global capitalism:

> As is clear in retrospect, these [cross-cultural] field studies were ahistoric, insensitive to culturally varied indigenous adaptive strategies, largely ignorant of the huge body of relevant work on disaster theory in sociology and anthropology, flawed by the absence of any discussion of the political-economic context of hazard occurrence and genesis, and in the final analysis having little credibility in light of the frequent banality and triviality of many of the research findings.

(Watts, 1983)

Watts' call for the incorporation of sophisticated social theoretical analysis into the study of society–environment relations shaped subsequent research on hazards, environmental degradation, struggles over resource access, agricultural production, and environmental conservation. It also helped widen an enduring gulf between various geographical approaches to the study of society–environment relations. Political ecology does not have universal appeal, to say

the least, and itself came under fire by Vayda (whose own work was criticised in Watts' early work): 'Indeed, it may not be an exaggeration to say that overreaction to the "ecology without politics" of three decades ago is resulting now in a "politics without ecology"' (Vayda and Walters, 1999: 168). Ironically, perhaps, Watts himself has called into question the quality of political theory found in much of political ecology, and in particular the 'regional political ecology' of Piers Blaikie and Harold Brookfield's immensely influential volume *Land Degradation and Society*, released in 1987 (see, for example, Watts, 1990; Peet and Watts, 1996). Watts critiqued this work as lacking a coherent political theory and subscribing to a simplistic understanding of power. Nevertheless, *Land Degradation and Society* remains hugely influential, and with Watts' own work helped give rise to the subfield of political ecology.

In addition to his longstanding concern for the highly politicised and violent geographies of oil extraction (e.g. Watts, 1984; 1994; 1997; 2004; 2008), Watts has turned his attention to the alarmist 'environmental security' perspective of resource scarcity and violence, as popularised by journalist Robert Kaplan and scholars Thomas Homer-Dixon and Gunther Baechler. Taken up by the Clinton Administration in the US and argued by international 'strategic experts' in the context of global environmental governance, this body of work is the latest manifestation of the Malthusian nightmare: environmental concerns marshalled in defence of capital accumulation and bourgeois lifestyles, and repackaged as 'national security'. Watts and Nancy Lee Peluso take on these arguments in their edited volume *Violent Environments*, arguing that violence (physical, structural, symbolic) in the context of environmental conflict cannot automatically be attributed to resource 'scarcity'. Again, the arguments are material as well as symbolic, rooted in political economy as well as epistemology: 'scarcity' is socially constructed, and as such must be carefully viewed in the context of power relations, cultural meanings, and the workings of capital:

> Our approach is not intended to merely identify the 'environmental triggers' of violent conflict nor does it start from a presumed 'scarcity'. Rather, *Violent Environments* accounts for ways that specific resource environments (tropical forests or oil reserves) and environmental processes (deforestation, conservation, or resource amelioration) are constituted by, and in part constitute, the political economy of access to and control over resources.

(Peluso and Watts, 2001: 5)

This work has drawn attention to the relationship between environmental conflict and the production of space, and the fact that scarcity and conflict are far from natural phenomena, though they may become 'naturalised' in the highly charged context of resource politics. Spaces of scarcity and the particular places produced through social conflict and violence only exist in relation to other places, spaces, and scales, in a context of uneven capitalist development. In this respect, Watts' work has done much to bridge the gap between the nature/society and space/society traditions in geography which have had remarkably little interaction during the past half century (Hanson, 1999). His call for the careful contextualisation of environmental degradation, peasant marginalisation, and resource conflict has done much to shape the type of work undertaken by contemporary political and cultural ecologists, as well as by those concerned with development studies, peasant studies, and globalisation. The best of this work is attentive to theories of space, place, and scale; incorporates sophisticated theoretical analysis of political economy and culture; and demonstrates a thorough understanding of the complexities of environmental and social processes.

WATTS' KEY WORKS

Watts, M.J. (1983) *Silent Violence: Food, Famine, and Peasantry in Northern Nigeria*. Berkeley: University of California Press.

Watts, M.J. (1999) 'Collective wish images: geographical imaginaries and the crisis of development', in J. Allen and D. Massey (eds), *Human Geography Today*. Cambridge: Polity Press. pp. 85–107.

Watts, M.J. (2000a) '1968 and all that...', *Progress in Human Geography*, 25: 157–88.

Watts, M.J. (2000b) 'Violent geographies: speaking the unspeakable and the politics of space', *City and Society*, XIII(1): 83–115.

Watts, M.J. (2000c) 'Development ethnographies', *Ethnography*, 2: 283–300.

Watts, M.J. (2000d) 'Development at the millennium', *Geographische Zeitschrift*, 88: 67–93.

Watts, M.J. (2004) 'Antinomies of community: some thoughts on geography, resources, empire', *Transactions of the Institute of British Geographers*, NS 29 (2): 195–216.

Watts, M. J. (2006) 'Culture, development and global neoliberalism', in S. Radcliffe (ed.), *Culture and Development in a Globalising World*. London: Routledge. pp. 30–58.

Watts, M.J. (2008) *Curse of Black Gold: 50 Years of Oil on the Niger Delta*. Berkeley: Powerhouse (photos by E. Kashi).

Goodman, D. and Watts, M.J. (eds) (1997) *Globalising Food: Agrarian Questions and Global Restructuring*. London: Routledge.

Peluso, N. and Watts, M.J. (eds) (2001) *Violent Environments*. Ithaca: Cornell University Press.

Peet, R. and Watts, M.J. (eds) (1996) *Liberation Ecologies: Environment, Development, Social Movements*. London: Routledge.

Pred, A. and Watts, M.J. (1992) *Reworking Modernity: Capitalisms and Symbolic Discontent*. New Brunswick: Rutgers University Press.

Secondary Sources and References

Appadurai, A. (1991) 'Global ethnoscapes: notes and queries for a transnational anthropology', in R.G. Fox (ed.), *Recapturing Anthropology: Working in the Present*. Santa Fe, NM: School of American Research Press. pp. 191–210.

Bebbington, A.J. and Batterbury, S.P.J. (2001) 'Transnational livelihoods and landscapes: political ecologies of globalization', *Ecumene*, 8: 369–80.

Blaikie, P. (1985) *The Political Economy of Soil Erosion in Developing Countries*. London: Longman.

Blaikie, P. and Brookfield, H. (1987) *Land Degradation and Society*. London: Methuen.

Castells, M. (1996) *The Information Age: Economy, Society and Culture, Vol 1: The Rise of the Network Society*. Oxford: Blackwell.

Hanson, S. (1999) 'Isms and schisms: healing the rift between the nature-society and space-society traditions in geography', *Annals of the Association of American Geographers*, 89: 133–43.

Hewitt, K. (1983) *Interpretations of Calamity*. Boston: Allen and Unwin.

Little, P.D. and Watts, M.J. (eds) (1994) *Living Under Contract: Contract Farming and Agrarian Transformation in Sub-Saharan Africa*. Madison: University of Wisconsin Press.

McCarthy, J. (2001) 'States of nature and environmental enclosures in the American West', in N.L. Peluso and M.L. Watts (eds), *Violent Environments*. Ithaca: Cornell University Press. pp. 117–45.

Neumann, R (1998) 'Book review of *Liberation Ecologies*', *Economic Geography*, 74: 190–2.

Peet, R. and Watts, M.J. (1996) 'Liberation ecology: development, sustainability, and environment in an age of market triumphalism', in R. Peet and M.J. Watts (eds), *Liberation Ecologies: Environment, Development, Social Movements*. London: Routledge. pp. 1–45.

Peluso, N.L. and Watts, M.J. (2001) 'Violent environments', in N.L. Peluso and M.J. Watts (eds), *Violent Environments*. Ithaca: Cornell University Press. pp. 3–38.

Redclift, M. (2001) 'Classics in human geography revisited: commentary 1', *Progress in Human Geography*, 25: 621–3.

Robbins, P., Polderman, A. and Birkenholtz, T. (2001) 'Lawns and toxins: an ecology of the city', *Cities: The International Journal of Urban Policy and Planning*, 18: 369–80.

Vayda, A. and Walters, B. (1999) 'Against political ecology', *Human Ecology*, 27: 167–79.

Watts, M.J. (1983) 'On the poverty of theory: natural hazards research in context', in K. Hewitt (ed.), *Interpretations of Calamity*. London: Allen and Unwin. pp. 229–62.

Watts, M.J. (1984) 'State, oil, and accumulation: from boom to crisis', *Environment and Planning D: Society and Space*, 2: 403–28.

Watts, M.J. (1987) 'Drought, environment and food security', in M. Glantz (ed.), *Drought and Hunger in Africa*. Cambridge: Cambridge University Press. pp. 171–212.

Watts, M.J. (1989) 'The agrarian question in Africa', *Progress in Human Geography*, 13: 1–41.

Watts, M.J. (1990) 'Is there politics in regional political ecology?', *Capitalism, Nature, Socialism*, 4: 123–31.

Watts, M.J. (1990) 'Visions of excess: African development in an age of market idolatry', *Transition*, 151: 124–41.

Watts, M.J. (1991) 'Mapping meaning, denoting difference, imagining identity: dialectical images and postmodern geographies', *Geografiska Annaler*, 73B: 7–16.

Watts, M.J. (1992) 'Space for everything (a commentary)', *Cultural Anthropology*, 7: 115–29.

Watts, M.J. (1993) 'Development I: power, knowledge, discursive practice', *Progress in Human Geography*, 17: 257–72.

Watts, M.J. (1994) 'The devil's excrement', in S. Corbridge, R. Martin and N. Thrift (eds), *Money, Power and Space*. Oxford: Blackwell. pp. 406–45.

Watts, M.J. (1996) 'Mapping identities: place, space, and community in an African city', in P. Yaeger (ed.), *The Geography of Identity*. Ann Arbor: University of Michigan Press. pp. 59–97.

Watts, M.J. (1997) 'Black gold, white heat', in S. Pile, and M. Keith (eds), *Geographies of Resistance*. London: Routledge. pp. 33–67.

Watts, M.J. (2001) 'Classics in human geography revisited: author's response', *Progress in Human Geography*, 25: 625–8.

Thomas Perreault, Syracuse University

63   Benno Werlen

The Swiss geographer Benno Werlen has been one of the most important innovators in German-speaking geography since the 1980s. He is the founder of an action-based approach in social geography (see Werlen, 1987), which even critics recognise as the most significant German-language contribution to the development of theory in human geography in recent decades. The development of this action theory approach into a practice-centred 'social geography of everyday regionalisations' (Werlen, 1995; 1997) is now a keystone for debating the issues of space and environment in other disciplines as well as geography. Werlen's publications have been published in various languages as well as German and English, including French, Italian, Portuguese, Russian, Spanish and Korean.

Werlen was born in 1952 in the Swiss canton of Valais. He studied geography, ethnology, sociology and economics in Fribourg, Switzerland. After completing his studies he moved to Kiel in the North of Germany where he worked with Dietrich Bartels for some time. Bartels was one of the key figures of post-Second World War Germany geography and published

a meta-theoretical explanation of the *spatial approach* in 1968 that was highly regarded internationally. In 1981 Werlen returned to Fribourg, where he worked as a lecturer and submitted his doctoral thesis in the autumn of 1985. He accepted an Assistant Professorship at the University of Zürich in the following year, a post he occupied until 1995. During this period he also worked at the University of Cambridge (1989–1990) as a visiting researcher, where he began to work with **Anthony Giddens** and embarked on a more intensive study of the English-speaking theoretical debate. After a Visiting Professorship at Salzburg (1995) he was appointed to the Friedrich Schiller University in Jena in 1996, where he has occupied a Chair in Social Geography since 1997.

Werlen's main interest is in the development of foundations and methods for a human geography rooted in the social sciences. He thereby pursues two interconnected aims. The first is to establish *analytical* thought and theory-led research in geography. Here, he opposes a primarily descriptive understanding of the discipline which is expressed both in the view that geography is primarily the art of idiographic (holistic) landscape description and in the theory-free empirical studies partly inspired by the methodological enrichment of the subject in the course of the 'quantitative revolution'. The second is to place human geography on a firm *social*-scientific foundation, rooting it firmly in the context of other social sciences. This second aim is directed against persistent attempts to ascribe social practices to biophysical determinants, explaining the former with the causal procedures of the natural sciences. Thus Werlen rejects determinist or essentialist thinking as well as the spatialisation of socio-cultural phenomena, which was widespread in traditional geography. Instead, Werlen argues in favour of concentrating on the construction of the social world that he conceptualises as an ongoing achievement of social actors in the framework of their everyday social practice. In his view, human geography should rely on the methods of 'interpretative social science' (following Anthony Giddens) in order to describe how geographical reality is created, maintained or changed by meaningful social practices.

Werlen began to grapple with the foundations of this approach in his Master's thesis of 1980. In this early study he describes the methodological and social theoretical implications of functionalist perspectives in the social sciences and human geography in the nineteenth and twentieth centuries (the subjects of his analysis including the approaches developed by Durkheim, Malinowski, Parsons and especially von Thünen, Christaller, Otremba, Schrepfer, Bobek and Bartels – see Werlen, 1984). He continued the discussion of established concepts in Geman-speaking human geography in a highly regarded doctoral thesis entitled *Gesellschaft, Handlung und Raum* ('Society, action and space', Werlen, 1987). In this study Werlen claims that geography cannot be a spatial science which merely describes the localisation and distribution of the different forms of expression of human action in space. Instead, he argues that geography must view space as an element of social practice from the perspective of a spatially-oriented social science, thereby making a contribution to the explanation of human action.

From within this context Werlen takes a fresh look at the German geographical tradition and discovers starting points for a social scientific orientation of human geography in the work of Hans Bobek and Wolfgang Hartke. In the 1950s, Hartke in particular appealed to geographers to study the geography-making of actors capable of action and thereby to contribute to the description of society and the explanation of social processes (Werlen, 2000: 151). Bobek and Hartke did not, however, succeed in living up to their own expectations, as they had neither a detailed background in social theory nor an adequately differentiated conception of social practice. Thus Werlen's aim was to redress this deficit by developing social theoretical foundations for human geography. Via a critical analysis of the classical social science action models (Weber, Pareto, Parsons, Popper and Schütz), he delineated the theoretical and methodological basis for a social geography grounded in action theory (Werlen, 1987).

His central argument was that social practices have different orientations which are emphasised by different action theories. Against such a background, social practices can be primarily normative or significative, depending on their orientation. Since the spatiality of practices varies according to their orientation, the analysis of geography-making must begin with the study of action and its orientation. Based on this assumption, Werlen finally developed a comprehensive outline of a practice-theoretical 'social geography of everyday regionalisations' (published in two volumes in 1995 and 1997), which has since been a central point of reference for theoretical debates in German human geography. The discussion surrounding this approach is documented in a collection of essays (Meusburger, 1999) whilst two recent volumes of collected writing on 'social spatiality' provide an overview of Werlen's oeuvre (Werlen, 2009a; 2010).

SPATIAL CONTRIBUTIONS

With his concept of a social geography of everyday regionalisations Werlen not only makes a significant contribution to human geography research, but the approach also responds critically to structuration theory, which it partly reformulates. With its focus on agency it differs markedly from the reception of structuration theory in the English-speaking debate (see entries on **Alan Pred**, **Derek Gregory** and **Nigel Thrift**). Werlen uses structuration theory to develop his own approach to remedy some of the weaknesses of classical action theory, for example, the issue of power. However, he also demonstrates that structuration theory's concept of space is relatively underdeveloped and subscribes to the model of absolute space (i.e., Newtonian) in some fundamental ways. In contrast, Werlen suggests that as in phenomenology (assocated with Hussserl or Schütz), space should be viewed as a type of grammar for orientation in the physical world (Werlen, 1995: 239). He thereby follows a similar route to John Pickles and Theodore Schatzki but is more social constructivist in his orientation. For Werlen, space as a basic scheme of order makes it possible to relate actions to objects and the activities of other actors. Due to the experience of their own physicality, acting subjects continually create, dissolve

or change spatial relations in their everyday practice. The constitution of space is, like the constitution of society, an either intended or unintended effect of social practices and therefore an integral part of the reproduction of everyday life.

This aspect of geography-making is especially worth studying under what Werlen calls the 'ontological conditions' of late-modern society. In late-modern society, social practice is neither temporarily fixed (in traditions) nor is it embedded in spatial terms. According to Werlen, the meaning of space and time is not yet dissolved, as some globalisation theorists claim, in that neither history nor geography have come to an end. Indeed, spatial and temporal disembeddedness make it both possible and necessary to continuously re-combine the spatial and temporal relations of social practice in everyday life. According to Werlen the entire meaning of space therefore changes; space becomes a formable element and means for the regulation of one's own practice and that of others.

Geography-making in this context involves the exercise of power. It has to do with the regulation of access to (material) resources, the variable organisation of individuals' time-space paths as well as spaces that are individually or collectively occupied or used for communication. Furthermore, it also includes the production of representations of space (spatial semantics) – that is, the production and implementation of interpretative frameworks with which actors make the world comprehensible to themselves and others. In this sense Werlen's social geography of everyday regionalisations confirms the diagnoses made, for example, in critical geography in connection with the work of **Michel Foucault** or **Henri Lefebvre**. In contrast to their work, however, Werlen suggests that geography-making can be studied with regard to three different dimensions of practice. One of these dimensions is *exchange*, the area of economic action. Here, that aspect of studying geography-making which involves the analysis of power is especially concerned with the availability of material goods, production facilities and other types of assets (Werlen 1997; 295ff.). The second dimension of social practice is *legitimation*. This includes prescriptions in the form of territorially-defined inclusions and exclusions, that is, normative definitions ranging from the position of the body in interactions to the division of towns and cities into public and private space. Also included are the nation state and supra- or sub-national units, perhaps the most prominent forms for the control of subjects – a control made possible by the combination of norms, bodies and space (Werlen, 1997: 329ff.). The third dimension of social practice that can be analysed from the point of view of geography-making is *communication*. The main focus here is firstly on the spatiality of information, that is, access to the sources and spatial foci of reporting. A second focus is on significative practices and the (re)production of geographical views of the world as well as the potential to assert a particular worldview (Werlen, 1997: 378ff.).

Werlen suggests a list of six different fields of research (Werlen, 1997). With regard to exchange, the social geography of everyday regionalisations allows for the study of both geographies of production and consumption. If the spotlight is on the aspect of legitimation, geographies of 'normative appropriation' and 'political control' become evident, while if the focus is on the communicative aspect of social practice, 'geographies of information' and 'geographies of symbolic appropriation' can be observed. With these fields of research Werlen (1997) effectively proposes three separate programmes: one for an economic geography rooted in the social sciences; a second for political geography;

and a third for cultural geography. Terminologically, he subsumes these three different areas of geography within the label of social geography, which in Germany is frequently used as a synonym for human geography.

Overall Werlen's work represents a social constructivist attitude and with this orientation offers points of contact with other theories of social practice, for example, the arguments of **Pierre Bourdieu** and **Michel de Certeau** (Lippuner, 2005). Furthermore, Antje Schlottmann (2005) and Tilo Felgenhauer (2007) have shown how Werlen's action theory approach can be linked to models of speech act theory and analytical philosophy or the theory of communicative action (e.g., the work of Jürgen Habermas). His work has inspired younger geographers to examine the social construction of space from the perspective of Luhmann's theory of social systems (Lippuner, 2005; Redepenning, 2006). The wide range of empirical studies that apply Werlen's theory is documented in a number of collections of essays representing work produced under Werlen's supervision or using his concepts and models (Werlen, 2008; Werlen and Gäbler, 2008a; 2008b), ranging from studies of housing and neighbourhood design through the effects of regional forms of consumption and the production of space in the media to the problems of socio-spatial segregation and the regionalist or nationalist rhetoric of political movements.

KEY ADVANCES AND CONTROVERSIES

Werlen has unquestionably developed an independent approach and a coherent theory (e.g., Blotevogel, 1999; Kemper, 2005; Weichhart, 2008), and in German-speaking geography his name is synonymous with the practice-centred perspective of human geography as a social science. However, his work has also been subject to intense criticism from the beginning and provoked some fierce resistance from the theoretically and methodologically conservative mainstream (see Sahr, 1999). In particular his orientation towards the social sciences was perceived by older geographers as an imposition, as it questioned their understanding of their discipline and their identity as 'universal men' or polymaths in the tradition of von Humboldt as late as in the 1980s. However, for a younger generation of German geographers aware of international debates, Werlen's work was for a long time one of the few points of connection with these debates in their own language. Although partly relying on different theoretical associations, feminist, post-colonial and critical geography, for example, benefited from the fact that a social theoretical perspective had been established with Werlen's work (e.g., Fleischmann and Meyer-Hanschen 2005; Bauriedl, 2007; Lossau, 2001; Reuber and Wolkersdorfer, 2001; Schmid, 2005; Belina, 2008). Furthermore, Werlen prepared for the *cultural turn* in German human geography which, although informed by and reflecting debates in English-speaking world, had its own independent character.

Criticisms of Werlen's approach include the subject-centredness of the action theory perspective. Gerhard Hard (1998 and 1999), for example, has pointed out that with regard to acting subjects, Werlen runs the risk of once again burdening himself with the very problems of spatialisation which he wished to eliminate with the reorientation of human geography towards the social sciences. Human subjects are not only social actors

but also biological individuals, that is, fundamentally hybrid beings. If they are made the point of reference of sociological analyses, different ontological levels and ambiguities must be addressed by the theory. However, Werlen (2000) is not only concerned to overcome the 'spatial obsession' and the banal materialism of traditional geography. Working against the 'spatial forgetfulness' that persisted for a long time in much of social theory, he wishes to remind us that acting subjects are always bodily actors who continually recreate and interlink the spatial relations of their everyday lives. His aim is both to overcome the weaknesses and elisions of disembodied social or cultural theory as well as the failings of materialist-biologistic human geography.

A further criticism has to do with the idealism of individualist perspectives, which arguably ascribes human actions to the intentions of subjects and neglects structural determinants of social practice. It can be argued indeed that social practice can only be inadequately explained by referring to intentions, aims, purposes and the rational choice of means. Werlen reacts to this weakness of classical action theory in the 'social geography of everyday regionalisations' with the expansion of his perspective in the sense of a theory of practice. In contrast to the classical action models (of Weber, Schütz or rational choice theory) the theory of practice admits that social practices often proceed via 'routines'. This explains how a reproduction of social structures occurs without a reflexive steering of actions through discursive awareness. Some critics also accuse Werlen of moving too far from the classical themes of geography and too readily abandoning their strengths, for example, the regional viewpoint and the understanding of human–nature relationships. Werlen responds to such criticism with suggestions for a reorientation of research informed by social theory. Thus, for example, he shows that regional cultures in a globalised world are a form of semantic re-embedding and can be understood as a reaction to the structural disassociation of society (Lippuner and Werlen, 2007).

Werlen's approach also indicates a way in which the central theme of traditional geography, the interest in harmony and disharmony in human–nature relations, can be reformulated: from the perspective of social theoretical human geography 'human' and 'nature' are not the central foci. Instead the focus is on the relationship between society and environment, whose major problem lies in the very fact that society can alter its environmental conditions quite autonomously, that is, independently of the environment – and, therefore, can also destroy it. In this context, social theoretical human geography is faced with the challenge of studying the social formation of the relationship between society and environment (cf. Werlen and Weingarten, 2003).

In an inter-disciplinary context, Werlen has made significant contributions to recent central debates in the social and cultural sciences. Thus his two volumes on the 'social geography of everyday regionalisations' have made an original contribution to the theory of globalisation

showing, how the 'ontology of society and space' (Werlen, 1995) unfolds through the interconnections between 'globalisation, regions and regionalisation' (Werlen, 1997) – the fundamental transformation of the spatial relations of everyday life in the second half of the twentieth century. In this discussion he builds on the work of **Anthony Giddens**, **Ulrich Beck**, and **David Harvey** and expands it at the level of subjective experience and individual action. He thereby argues that globalisation itself is a form of regionalisation, that is, a type of geography-making, and that it can be understood by acting subjects as a form of 'world bonding' (*Weltbindung*) or 'relating the world to oneself' (Werlen, 1999a).

Werlen's publications, and ongoing efforts to further develop social theoretical human geography by authors who build on his ideas, are also a central point of reference for the *spatial turn* in German social and cultural sciences (see Döring and Thielmann, 2008). Although Werlen regards the rediscovery of space in the social and cultural sciences critically and tends to be sceptical about the prospects for a 'sociology of space' (Werlen, 2009b), his work has made a major contribution to the fact that geography is perceived in Germany as a key science (Bachmann-Medick, 2006: 392).

WERLEN'S KEY WORKS

Werlen, B. (1987) *Gesellschaft, Handlung und Raum: Grundlagen handlungstheoretischer Sozialgeographie.* Stuttgart: Franz Steiner Verlag (also see 3rd edition 1997).

Werlen, B. (1993) *Society, Action and Space: An Alternative Human Geography.* London: Routledge.

Werlen, B. (1995) *Sozialgeographie alltäglicher Regionalisierungen, Band 1: Zur Ontologie von Gesellschaft und Raum.* Stuttgart: Franz Steiner Verlag (also see 2nd edition 1999).

Werlen, B. (1997) *Sozialgeographie alltäglicher Regionalisierungen Band 2: Globalisierung, Region und Regionalisierung.* Stuttgart: Franz Steiner (also see 2nd edition 2007).

Werlen, B. (2000) *Sozialgeographie: Eine Einführung.* Bern: Haupt Verlag Bern (also see 3rd edition 2007)

Werlen, B. (ed.) (2008) *Sozialgeographie alltäglicher Regionalisierungen, Band 3: Empirische Befunde.* Suttgart: Franz Steiner Verlag.

Werlen, B. (2009a) *Gesellschaftliche Räumlichkeit 1: Orte der Geographie.* Stuttgart: Franz Steiner Verlag.
Werlen, B. (2010) *Gesellschaftliche Räumlichkeit 2: Konstruktion geographischer Wirklichkeiten.* Stuttgart: Franz Steiner Verlag.

Secondary Sources and References

Bachmann-Medick, D. (2006) *Cultural Turns: Neuorientierungen in den Kulturwissenschaften.* Reinbek: Rowohlt.
Bauriedl, S. (2007) 'Still gender trouble in German-speaking feminist geography', in P. Moss and K. Falconer Al-Hindi (eds), *Feminisms in Geography: Rethinking Space, Place, and Knowledge.* Lanham: Rowman and Littlefield. pp 130–9.
Belina, B. (2008) 'Kritische Geographie: Bildet Banden! Einleitung zum Themenheft', *ACME: An International E-Journal for Critical Geographies,* 7 (3): 335–49.
Blotevogel, H. H. (1999) 'Sozialgeographischer paradigmenwechsel? Eine kritik des projekts der handlungszentrierten sozialgeographie von Benno "Werlen"', in P. Meusburger (ed.), *Handlungszentrierte Sozialgeographie: Benno Werlens Entwurf in kritischer Diskussion.* Stuttgart: Franz Steiner Verlag. pp. 1–34.
Döring, J. and Thielmann, T. (2008) *Spatial Turn: Das Raumparadigma in den Kultur- und Sozialwissenschaften.* Bielefeld: transcript.
Felgenhauer, T. (2007) *Geographie als Argument: Eine Untersuchung regionalisierender Begründungspraxis am Beispiel 'Mitteldeutschland'.* Stuttgart: Franz Steiner Verlag.
Fleischmann, K. and Meyer-Hanschen, U. (2005) *Stadt Land Gender: Einführung in Feministische Geographien.* Königstein/Taunus: Urike Helmer Verlag.
Hard, G. (1998) 'Eine Sozialgeographie alltäglicher Regionalisierungen', *Erdkunde,* 52: 250–-3.
Hard, G. (1999) 'Raumfragen', in P. Meusburger (ed.), *Handlungszentrierte Sozialgeographie: Benno Werlens Entwurf in kritischer Diskussion.* Stuttgart: Franz Steiner Verlag. pp. 133–62.
Kemper, F.-J. (2005) 'Sozialgeographie', in W. Schenk and K. Schliephake (eds), *Allgemeine Anthropogeographie.* Gotha: Klett-Perthes. pp. 145–212.
Lippuner, R. (2005) *Raum – Systeme – Praktiken: Zum Verhältnis von Alltag, Wissenschaft und Geographie.* Stuttgart: Franz Steiner Verlag.
Lippuner, R. and Werlen, B. (2007) 'Regionale Kulturen und globalisierte Lebensstile', *Geographische Rundschau,* 59 (7/8): 22–7.
Lossau J. (2001) *Die Politik der Verortung: Eine postkoloniale Reise zu einer ANDEREN Geographie der Welt.* Bielefeld: transcript.
Meusburger, P. (ed.) (1999) *Handlungszentrierte Sozialgeographie: Benno Werlens Entwurf in kritischer Diskussion.* Stuttgart: Franz Steiner Verlag.
Redepenning, M. (2006) *Wozu Raum? Systemtheorie, Critical Geopolitics und raumbezogene Semantiken.* Leipzig: Beiträge zur Regionalen Geographie Europas, 62.
Reuber, P. and Wolkersdorfer, G. (eds) (2001) *Politische Geographie: Handlungsorientierte Ansätze und Critical Geopolitics.* Heidelberg: Heidelberger Geographische Arbeiten 112.
Sahr, W.-D. (1999) 'Der Ort der Regionalisierung im geographischen Diskurk', in P. Meusburger (ed.), *Handlungszentrierte Sozialgeographie: Benno Werlens Entwurf in kritischer Diskussion.* Stuttgart: Franz Steiner Verlag. pp. 43–66.
Schlottman, A. (2005) *RaumSprache. Ost-West-Differenzen in der Berichterstattung zur deutschen Einheit: Eine sozialgeographische Theorie.* Stuttgart: Franz Steiner Verlag.
Schmid, C. (2005) *Stadt, Raum und Gesellschaft: Henri Lefebvre und die Theorie der Produktion des Raumes.* Stuttgart: Franz Steiner Verlag.
Weichhart, P. (2008) *Entwicklungslinien der Sozialgeographie: Von Hans Bobek bis Benno Werlen.* Stuttgart: Franz Steiner Verlag.
Werlen, B. (1984) *Grundkategorien funktionalen Denkens in Sozialwissenschaft und Sozialgeographie.* Arbeiten aus dem Geographischen Institut Freiburg/Schweiz 3.
Werlen, B. (1999a) 'Handlungszentrierte Sozialgeographie: Replik auf die Kritiken', in P. Meusburger (ed.), *Handlungszentrierte Sozialgeographie: Benno Werlens Entwurf in kritischer Diskussion.* Stuttgart: Franz Steiner Verlag. pp. 247–68.
Werlen, B. (1999b) 'Political regionalism', in L. Embree (ed.), *Alfred Schutz's Theory of Social Sciences.* Dordrecht: Kluwer Academic Publisher. pp. 1–22.
Werlen, B. (2004a) 'Globalised everyday geographies', in J. Ole and K. Simonsen (eds), *Space Odyssey.* London: Ashgate. pp. 153–67.

Werlen, B. (2004b) 'Globalization of local action: a geographical perspective', in P. Probst and G. Spittler (eds), *Between Resistance and Expansion: Explorations of Local Vitality in Africa*. Münster: Lit. pp. 159–74.

Werlen, B. (2004c) 'Region and the process of regionalisation', in H. V. Houtum, O. Kramsch and W. Zierhofer (eds), *Bordering Space*. London: Ashgate. pp. 47–60.

Werlen, B. (2009b) 'Geographie/Sozialgeographie', in S. Günzel (ed.), *Raumwissenschaften*. Frankfurt a. M.: Suhrkamp. pp. 142–58.

Werlen, B. (2009c) 'Everyday regionalisations', in R. Kitchin and N. Thrift (eds), *The International Encyclopaedia of Human Geography*. Oxford: Elsevier.

Werlen, B. and Gäbler, K. (eds) (2008a) *Geographische Praxis I: Territorialisierungen und territoriale Konflikte*. Sozialgeographische Manuskripte 3. Jena: Selbstverlag Institut für Geographie.

Werlen, B. and Gäbler, K. (eds) (2008b) *Geographische Praxis II: Symbolische Aneignungen*. Sozialgeographische Manuskripte 4. Jena: Selbstverlag Institut für Geographie.

Werlen, B. and Weingarten, M. (2003) 'Zum forschungsintegrativen Gehalt der (Sozial-)Geographie', in P. Meusburger and T. Schwan (eds), *Humanökologie. Ansätze zur Überwindung der Natur-Kultur-Dichotomie*. Stuttgart: Franz Steiner Verlag. pp. 197–216.

Roland Lippuner, Jena University

BIOGRAPHICAL DETAIL AND THEORETICAL CONTEXT

While Raymond Williams' scholarship and politics were shaped through his engagement with the issues of his time, they remained indelibly connected to his experiences of place and class. Williams' political commitments and activities, as well as his way of academic scholarship, were *aligned* – a term he used to refer to an allegiance or orientation stemming from social position, similar to class consciousness, though also connected to place. Williams saw alignment as a critical determinant of the commitments one chooses as an individual, being neither innocent nor static. Indeed, it is political and it is worked through. The particular way that Williams simultaneously connected and developed abstract theoretical concepts, specific personal experiences, and complex social history into a way of understanding the political possibilities of the world was thus distinctive, proving deeply influential in – and well beyond – geography.

Williams (1921–1988) was born in Pandy, a Welsh village near the English border. His father was a railway signalman and union activist. Williams' ideas and politics were deeply structured by the 'border world' in which he grew up. Pandy was rural, but his father was an industrial worker; the railroad forged modern connections but never fully displaced customary ways of life. Pandy was in Wales, but 'there was all the time a certain pressure from the East ... from England' (Williams, 1979b: 21). When he went to Cambridge on a scholarship, these borders deepened: he was working class in the bastion of the elite, Welsh in the heart of Englishness, and radical at the centre of conservativism. At Cambridge Williams sought out other radical students and became an influential voice in the Communist Party's 'Writers' Group' (Inglis, 1995). At the same time, Williams was deeply influenced by F.R. Leavis, who had done so much to realign the study of literature towards the study, in Williams' (1989c [1958]: 9) terms, of 'art and experience'. Despite Leavis's conservativism, Williams saw a radical potential in Leavis's method of studying literature as almost a symptom of society to become an important tool in the construction of a progressive, socialist world. These commitments were deepened during the Second World War when Williams served as a tank commander in the battles that followed the D-Day invasion. While in the British Army, Williams was an active campaigner for the Labour Left, using his role as the editor of a regimental paper to support the party (Inglis, 1995: 101–2). By this time he had left the Communist Party, though he never later sought to distance himself from his time in it (Williams, 1989c [1975]).

Following his discharge from the Army in 1945, Williams returned to Cambridge to complete his degree (he later incorporated his thesis into his first book: Williams, 1952). His goal was to become a writer of both novels and political journalism and to become a teacher of working-class people. Briefly in Cambridge and then for 15 years around Oxford, Williams worked as an itinerant teacher of adult education surveying International Relations as well as English Literature. In all his teaching he sought to show his working-class students how their own experiences allowed them to make sense of the world and to see that they had *made* a culture, not just received one from the political and cultural elite. During this period, Williams published five books of criticism and cultural analysis, his first novel, *Border Country* (1960), and innumerable essays and pieces of journalism. With **Stuart Hall** and others, he helped to found the journal *New Left Review* (NLR). His most influential works of this period were two books that became a foundation of the academic field of cultural studies, *Culture and Society, 1780–1950* (1958) and *The Long Revolution* (1961), and an essay, 'Culture is ordinary' (1989c [1958]). These three works brought a socialist and Marxist sensibility to the study of the pressures and determinations that make 'a culture'; and they launched two enduring projects: one that sought to redefine just what *counts* as 'culture;' the other exploring the role and importance of new institutions of communication in the *formation* of culture.

In 1961, Williams was appointed to a Lectureship in English at Cambridge University. In 1969 Williams submitted his work for a D.Litt, receiving it in July of that year. In 1974, Williams was promoted to a personal Chair and named Professor of Drama. During the 22 years he was at Cambridge, Williams was deeply involved

in politics, including work with the Campaign for Nuclear Disarmament, continuing involvement with the *NLR*, and, in 1967, co-authoring the influential *New Left May Day Manifesto* which sought to organise the growing dissent of the period to push Labour leftwards. In the 1970s and 1980s he was involved in left Labour politics and was active in the promotion of regionally-based arts. He responded to the election of Thatcher, and the virulent class politics it represented, by helping to found the (short-lived) Socialist Society and by aligning himself with the Socialist Environment and Resources Association.

Between 1962 and 1983, Williams was the author, editor, or co-editor of 20 scholarly and political books as well as numerous scholarly and popular articles. He served four years in the 1970s as the television critic for *The Listener*. His most influential books during this period include: *Communications* (1962), which more or less established the field of media studies in Britain; *The Country and the City* (1973), perhaps his most cited work in geography, and one that establishes the relationship between contested representations of the national landscape and its material form; *Keywords* (1976) a social etymology of theoretically and politically crucial terms; and *Marxism and Literature* (1977; see also 1980) where he develops his influential form of cultural materialism, and outlines his important concept of 'structure of feeling'. Williams describes a 'structure of feeling' as a 'cultural hypothesis' about the way peoples' practical consciousnesses ('meanings and values ... actively lived and felt') comprise a set, or structure, with internal relations of contradiction and coordination (Williams, 1977: 132). Part of this hypothesis is that structures of feeling, in formation, are 'often ... not yet recognized as social but taken to be private, idiosyncratic, and even isolating, but which in analysis (though rarely otherwise) [have their] emergent, connecting, and dominant characteristics, indeed, [their] specific hierarchies' (Williams, 1977: 132). As a conceptual tool, structure of feeling provides a way of linking experience and feeling into organised politics.

Williams examined the implications of his structure of feeling hypothesis in his novels. While at Cambridge, Williams published three novels: *Second Generation* (1964) and *The Fight for Manod* (1979a), both sequels to *Border Country*, and *The Volunteers* (1978), an occasionally bitter look at the emergent Britain and Europe (written in the midst of late 1970s decline of the Labour Party and on the eve of the authoritarianism of Thatcherism). In his novels, Williams played out the structure of feeling as experienced and lived by individuals who are structured by class, borders, and constant social and individual change.

Between retirement (1983) and his death from a heart attack, Williams completed two novels (one published posthumously), and wrote enough of a third for his wife, Joy Williams, to complete the editing and see it to publication. In addition he published two books of essays and criticism, co-edited a third, and launched an important political intervention, *Towards 2000* (1983), which addressed the politics of nuclear destruction head on, and examined the politics of spectacle at the heart of the Falklands war. In this book Williams sought 'to catch local politics in one grand theory' (Inglis, 1995: 275). Indeed, Williams' life and work can be summarised in something like this phrase. His political and theoretical work (which were really one and the same) were a constant struggle against the institutions, class structures, and massive condemnation of history that seek to exclude and oppress, to expropriate and deny, to thwart the development of what Marx

called human's 'species being' – their true creative capacity. Williams stood for an open, creative, worked culture against those hegemonic notions of culture reinforced by the dominant class, through education, structures of work, and the multiple forms of practical consciousness that permeate social existence.

SPATIAL CONTRIBUTIONS

Williams' work and ideas have been directly and indirectly influential in human geography. Indirectly, Williams is one of the founding figures of the field of Cultural Studies. *Culture and Society* served as one of the two 'founding texts' of the Birmingham Centre for Contemporary Cultural Studies (CCCS) (the other being Hoggart, 1952). Especially under its second director, **Stuart Hall**, CCCS sought to understand culture as: firstly, both ordinary and deeply political; secondly, a significant site of ongoing social struggle and the working out of power relations between 'subcultures'; and thirdly, important in the shaping of identity.

The work of CCCS began to be cited in geography during the early 1980s, but its impact was greatest as geography underwent a 'cultural turn' (Crang, 2000). The cultural turn is itself in part a result of the influence of what is called the 'new cultural geography'. With its 'radical emphasis on culture as a medium of social power' (Daniels, 1989: 196), new cultural geography clearly echoed the work of the CCCS; but it also was rooted in Williams' work more generally (e.g., **Cosgrove** 1984; Daniels, 1989; Jackson, 1989). Williams' influence is perhaps strongest in **Peter Jackson**'s landmark text *Maps of Meaning* (1989). Jackson outlines the value of cultural materialism for geography, and in the process suggests the importance of geography to cultural materialism. A citation to Williams opens the book, and a sustained explication of his ideas follows. Jackson (1989: 35) writes that 'by focusing on "specific and indissoluble real processes", Williams offers a view of determination that is thoroughly appropriate to a reconstituted cultural geography.' In part this is because 'Williams' work comprises a thorough attack on the ... culturalism' that was so central to existing cultural geography and related fields (ibid: 36). 'This is the value of Williams' definition of culture' (Jackson, 1989: 38). By seeing it 'as "a realized signifying system",' or, in other words, 'a set of signs and symbols that are embedded in a whole range of activities, relations, and institutions, only some of which are "cultural", others being overtly economic, political, or generational', Williams' theories provide a model for how *not* to artificially separate the social, political, and economic from the cultural. Coupling this model with theories of *hegemony*, Jackson promoted an 'agenda for cultural geography' that was materialist *and* deeply concerned with signification, took language and discourse seriously while never ignoring those social practices that could be called 'extra-linguistic,' and identified the social analysis of *cultural politics* as its central focus.

Simultaneous with *Maps of Meaning*, Daniels (1989) established the relevance of Williams' work to landscape geography. Daniels followed Williams to argue that landscape is not only, or perhaps even primarily, a reflection of some sort of undifferentiated culture, but rather the materialisation of a class-based and class-ridden social order. For Williams, the class-based nature of the work that produced a landscape and its representation

resulted in a duplicity: landscape seems to speak for all but really only represents the few. The point was thus to dig beneath this duplicity to bring to light the contradictions as well as the relations of power that undergird the landscape. This way of understanding the landscape subsequently became predominant in geography.

In a critique of the new cultural geography, Mitchell (2000) drew on Williams to argue that much new cultural geography was 'not materialist enough' taking issue with how earlier new cultural geographers had deployed Williams' arguments.

Mitchell both criticised geographers who had drawn on Williams while drawing on his arguments in developing a materialist theory of culture. Such debates about how best to theorise culture in geography supported one of Williams' (1976) most quoted contentions: that 'culture' is one of the two or three most complicated words in English. 'Nature' is perhaps the most complicated. Geographers are fond of quoting Williams on this point as a means of framing and legitimating their own arguments about each of the terms, and as a means of quickly developing an argument about the production – or social construction – of nature and culture. Williams' method of tracing the etymological transformation of 'keywords' over time reveals shifts in meanings as a *social* – and not just an etymological – history. Through etymology, Williams shows not only what has been gained, but also what has been lost over time. Often the losses are of communal social relations (what he called 'the common culture' (1958; 1961; 1989c; 1989c) as the individualising power of capitalism spread and deepened. Such losses are also at times gains in certain kinds of freedom, certain opportunities for a different kind of social life. This is a method and project most fully developed by Kenneth Olwig (1996; 2002) in his attempt to recover what he calls the 'substantive meaning of landscape'. This substantive meaning resides in archaic regionally-based systems of justice that have both been eroded by and yet still persist in contemporary capitalism. For Olwig (1996: 633), like Williams (1973), this substantive meaning can be reclaimed and renewed, since 'a *landskab* was not just a region, it was a nexus of law and cultural identity.' Olwig argues that recovering such a substantive meaning of landscape also implies making a substantial argument about justice: those who make a landscape have a right to participate in it and to shape the judicial form that governs it. And here Olwig's project intersects directly with that of Williams, for running through all of Williams' work was a deep and abiding sense of right and of rights (see, e.g., Williams, 1980: 1–6).

Williams' project was a prospective one: it sought to provide the grounds for an ongoing socialist struggle for social justice. But these grounds were rooted in a retrospective, historical argument about alienation, expropriation, and the uprooting of lives and landscapes – the common culture – that is so central to the success of modernising capitalism, and that must be reclaimed for socialism. This argument was most fully, if also indirectly, developed in Williams' novels. In these he makes it clear that any common culture had to have social and geographical difference in ways of life and structures of feeling at its core.

This theme was picked up in geography most obviously by **David Harvey** (1996). For Harvey, Williams' writing provided a way to articulate the complex problems of injustice and oppression, as well as the alliances and actions that could serve to reconfigure the world in a better way. Considering the world as a totality – as Williams (1958; 1961; 1977) did – together with the significance of everyday experience (as in the 'structure of feeling' hypothesis), and closely analysing the politics of loyalty and alignment, require a dialectical and geographical understanding of society: this is the lesson Harvey took from Williams. He combines his reading of Williams with an engagement with more direct theories of social justice (e.g., **Young,** 1990), to argue that any project of social justice that takes difference (including geographical difference) seriously, and that seeks to be truly transformative, must, in fact, be *common* and *emancipatory* – two terms that are central to Williams' work, but anathema to the postmodernist theories of justice that Harvey argues against. Loyalty and alignment are thus key geographical concepts, for Harvey, since one's particular positionality, based on place or on social identity, is necessarily the very foundation from which solidarity – a common culture – can be structured. Williams presented the characters in his novels as struggling to balance their allegiances to the idea of socialism in the abstract while at the same time maintaining commitments to specific places (Harvey, 2001: 163–85). Harvey argued, based on Williams' characterisations, that though there may often be a tension between the particularities of people's identities and the progressive, universalist goals of socialism or Marxism, the two sets of goals – difference and commonality – often can and do work together. Uncovering the way this happens, Harvey argued, is the task of theory.

A significant part of the task of making clear the links people have to broader, common goals is advanced by understanding geography as a system that is both made and used by capitalism, and by all the people who are caught up in it. Harvey and Williams both assert the importance of place, as constructed relationally and through scale, in providing a commonality between loyalties at different levels of abstractions. Referring to Raymond Williams' notion of 'militant particularism', Harvey (2000: 55) argued that 'the universalism to which socialism aspires has ... to be built by negotiation between different place-specific demands, concerns, and aspirations.' The geography of difference is key, since it is real material places and spatial-social relations that shape both the opportunities and constraints for the production of a socially-just world. The geography of difference is what gives form to alignment, experience, commitment and perhaps most importantly, loyalty.

KEY ADVANCES AND CONTROVERSIES

Williams' political and theoretical advances included new conceptualisations such as 'structure of feeling', a theorisation of 'common culture', a concern with the social history of keywords, important explications of theoretical arguments within Marxism, the development of tools for the analysis of media, and, probably most significantly, a body of cultural theory, developed over four decades, that retains enormous power and subtlety and remains a model for theoretical development and empirical exploration throughout the humanities and social sciences. More generally, Williams was a key figure in post-Second World War British socialism and Western leftist thinking.

His work, however, was never received uncritically. Williams (1979b) himself

admitted that he was much too blind to the difference that gender makes, and he has been criticised on this matter in a number of places. Though he was one of the first in literary studies to focus on television as an important cultural medium, later practitioners of cultural studies found him to be too pessimistic – indeed almost scornful – about the progressive potential of pop culture (see Fiske, 1989). Similarly, his cultural criticism as exemplified in *Culture and Society*, *The Long Revolution*, and *The Country and the City* sometimes seems almost anti-modern and nostalgic (see Harvey, 1996). Furthermore, some critics, such as **Edward Said** (1989; 1993) and Gilroy (1987), charged Williams with constructing an exclusionary – rather than cosmopolitan – theory of commitment and loyalty, because of his heavy reliance on the experiences of Britain's white working class. Said (1993) further suggested, perhaps inaccurately, that Williams (1973) was largely ignorant of the critical importance of the colonies and slave labour to the construction of the English countryside. Finally, Inglis (1995) takes Williams to task over his socialist politics, accusing him on several occasions of (unspecified) 'bad faith' in his theorising, implying that Williams failed to live up to Inglis's own faith in a more moderate Labourism. *Marxism and Literature* (1977) was not uniformly praised when it was published and Williams' disdain for the theories of ideology advanced by Althusser was criticised by many, including Stuart Hall who was important for promoting the importance of Althusser's theories for the study of culture and identity.

Nonetheless, two decades after his death Williams' influence in geography and other social sciences and humanities seems to be growing. Almost all of his work is still in print, and it continues to provide inspiration for new work in geography (e.g., Mitchell, 2003) and beyond (e.g., Bennett et al., 2005). Williams' own alignments and commitments created inevitable blindspots in his theorising. But at the same time, they are exactly what gives his work such force, and what gives it its abiding relevance. In the end, then, Williams' greatest advance was probably the most basic one: his life and work provided a model of what socially and politically engaged scholarship should and can be.

WILLIAMS' KEY WORKS

Williams, R. (1958) *Culture and Society (1780–1950)*. London: Chatto and Windus.
Williams, R. (1961) *The Long Revolution*. London: Chatto and Windus.
Williams, R. (1962) *Communications*. Harmondsworth: Penguin.
Williams, R. (1973) *The Country and the City*. Oxford: Oxford University Press.
Williams, R. (1976) *Keywords*. London: Fontana.
Williams, R. (1977) *Marxism and Literature*. Oxford: Oxford University Press.
Williams, R. (1979b) *Politics and Letters: Interviews with New Left Review*. London: Verso.
Williams, R. (1980) *Problems in Materialism and Culture*. London: Chatto and Windus.
Williams, R. (1981) *Culture*. London: Chatto and Windus.
Williams, R. (1983) *Towards 2000:* London: Chatto and Windus.

Secondary Sources and References

Bennett, T., Grosberg, L. and Morris M. (eds) (2005) *New Keywords: A Revised Vocabulary of Culture and Society*. Oxford: Wiley-Blackwells.
Cosgrove, D. (1984) *Social Formation and Symbolic Landscape*. London: Croom Helm.
Crang, P. (2000) 'Cultural turn', in R. Johnston, D. Gregory and D.M. Smith (eds), *The Dictionary of Human Geography*. Oxford: Blackwell. pp. 141–3.
Daniels, S. (1989) 'Marxism, culture and the duplicity of landscape', in R. Peet and N. Thrift (eds), *New Models in Geography*, Vol. 2. London: Unwin Hyman. pp. 196–220.
Fiske, J. (1989) *Understanding Popular Culture*. Boston: Unwin Hyman.
Gilroy, P. (1987) *There Ain't No Black in the Union Jack*. London: Verso.
Harvey, D. (1996) *Justice, Nature and the Geography of Difference*. Oxford: Blackwell.
Harvey, D. (2000) *Spaces of Hope*. Berkeley: University of California Press.
Harvey, D. (2001) *Spaces of Capital: Towards a Critical Geography*. New York: Routledge.
Hoggart, R. (1952) *The Uses of Literacy*. London: Chatto and Windus.
Inglis, F. (1995) *Raymond Williams*. London: Routledge.
Jackson, P. (1989) *Maps of Meaning*. London: Unwin Hyman.
Mitchell, D. (2000) *Geography: A Critical Introduction*. Oxford: Blackwell.
Mitchell, D. (2003) *The Right to the City: Social Justice and the Fight for Public Space in America*. New York: Guilford.
Olwig, K. (1996) 'Recovering the substantive nature of landscape', *Annals of the Association of American Geographers*, 86: 630–53.
Olwig, K. (2002) *Landscape, Nature, and the Body Politic: From Britain's Renaissance to America's New World*. Madison: University of Wisconsin Press.
Said, E. (1989) 'Appendix: media, margins, and modernity', in R. Williams (ed.), *The Politics of Modernism*. London: Verso.
Said, E. (1993) *Culture and Imperialism*. London: Chatto and Windus.
Williams, R. (1952) *Drama from Ibsen to Elliot*. London: Chatto and Windus.
Williams, R. (1960) *Border Country*. London: Chatto and Windus.

Williams, R. (1964) *Second Generation*. London: Chatto and Windus.
Williams, R. (1966) *Modern Tragedy*. London: Chatto and Windus.
Williams, R. (1968a) *Drama from Ibsen to Brecht*. London: Chatto and Windus.
Williams, R. (ed.) (1968b) *May Day Manifesto*. Harmondsworth: Penguin.
Williams, R. (1970) *The English Novel from Dickens to Lawrence*. London: Chatto and Windus.
Williams, R. (1971) *George Orwell*. New York: The Viking Press.
Williams, R. (1974) *Television, Technology and Cultural Form*. London: Chatto and Windus.
Williams, R. (1978) *The Volunteers*. London: Hogarth.
Williams, R. (1979a) *The Fight for Manod*. London: Chatto and Windus.
Williams, R. (1985) *Loyalties*. London: Chatto and Windus.
Williams, R. (1989a) *People of the Black Mountains: The Beginning*. London: Chatto and Windus.
Williams, R. (1989b) *The Politics of Modernism*. London: Verso.
Williams, R. (1989c) *Resources of Hope*. London: Verso.
Williams, R. (1990) *People of the Black Mountains: The Eggs of the Eagle*. London: Chatto and Windus.
Young, I. (1990) *Justice and the Politics of Difference*. Princeton: Princeton University Press.

Don Mitchell, Syracuse University and Carrie Breitbach, Chicago State University

65 Alan Wilson

BIOGRAPHICAL DETAILS AND THEORETICAL CONTEXT

Alan Wilson was born in Bradford in 1939 and educated at Queen Elizabeth Grammar School in Darlington. At University he read mathematics and graduated from Corpus Christi College, Cambridge, in 1960. After a three-year period based at the Rutherford Laboratory (where he was Chief Scientific Officer in the 'Theoretical Physics Group') he began working in the socio-economic sciences, first as a research officer at the Institute of Economics and Statistics at the University of Oxford, followed by spells at the Ministry for Transport and then the Centre for Environmental Studies in London.

The 1960s was a key period of transition in geography as the discipline began to embrace the so-called quantitative revolution. Although statistical geography dominated the literature, mathematical models were becoming more popular following the publication of a number of prominent transport/land-use models in the US (Harris, 1962; Lowry, 1964). Alan Wilson began to work on gravity or interaction models – models of flows between residential zones and various trip destinations – derived from Newtonian physics (the formula for estimating the gravitational force between two or more planets). However, Wilson was concerned about the weak theoretical foundations of the gravity model, especially if it was to become widely used in human geography. He demonstrated it was possible to derive interaction or flow models from first principles using entropy-maximising methods (models which produced the most likely outcomes based on the average or most likely set of generated trips).

In 1967 he wrote his seminal paper 'A statistical theory of spatial distribution models', which formed the basis of this argument, leading to more substantial contribution in his 1970 book, *Entropy in Urban and Regional Modelling*. Using this entropy framework he quickly derived the family of spatial interaction models which would form the heart of many of the future mathematical models of trip movement in the city. The models were conceived around four major variables. After splitting a city or region into zones (often census tracts) then the magnitude of any flow or interaction from a zone to a destination would be a function of the size of demand in that origin zone, the attractiveness of the destination, the cost of travel (negative factor) and the location and attractiveness of other destinations (also a type of negative factor). Each of these terms could be disaggregated and parameterised. Many of the early examples in the late 1960s and early 1970s were applications based on real major UK planning projects (such as the impacts of a possible major new port at Bristol and the impacts of a new airport in London – see Foot, 1981 for an excellent review).

The construction of the 'family' of models recognised that some data sources were more readily available in different subsystems and hence models needed to be constrained in different ways. In some cases better data existed on demand in a region and hence the models were used to estimate supply-side variables. The estimation of revenue in a retail model is one example of this type of model (a so-called production-constrained model). Such models were the most common and could be seen to serve as location models making them very adaptable to many urban systems. Other areas of interest had better data and more disaggregate models could be more easily calibrated. Data on the journey to work, for example, was readily available from many censuses around the world and hence journey-to-work models could be constrained at the trip origin and destination (so called doubly constrained models). The art of modelling could be seen, according to Wilson, as the process of fitting the best model given data availability.

In 1969 Wilson became the founding editor of the journal *Environment and Planning*, which remains one of the most prestigious international journals for human geography. In 1970 Wilson was appointed to be Professor of Urban and Regional Modelling at the University of Leeds. This must have been a brave move considering that there was no history of quantitative geography at Leeds. At the same time Professor Mike Kirkby was appointed to a Chair in physical geography, and he too was a skilled mathematician. Together they were to transform geography at Leeds and introduce many new undergraduate quantitative courses themed around 'geography and the environment'. During the 1970s Wilson worked on a variety of different types of entropy or spatial interaction model. The

retail model (estimating interaction patterns for shopping trips) was often used as the exemplar for new theoretical extensions and developments but he quickly opened up new possibilities for applied research. An important component to Wilson's success was the building of substantial research teams and the establishment of an internationally renowned centre at Leeds for spatial modelling.

In the late 1980s Wilson turned his attention to university administration and served as Vice-Chancellor of the University of Leeds from 1989 for 13 years. During his time the University underwent unprecedented growth and transformation. Student numbers increased from 12,000 to 31,500; turnover increased from £100m to £320m and research income increased by more than 400% to £71m. He was knighted for his services to higher education in 2001. After this period at Leeds, Wilson served as the first Director General for Higher Education in 2004. In this role, he was a key adviser to Secretaries of State, Charles Clarke, Ruth Kelly and Alan Johnson, and played a critical role in the UK Government's drive to widen participation in higher education. However, during this time Wilson remained active in quantitative geography, exploring the topic of complexity science and how this might aid the development of dynamic and comprehensive urban models. Since 2007 Wilson has returned full time to the frontline – working with Mike Batty at the Centre for Advanced Spatial Analysis in London and re-engaging with urban and regional models.

SPATIAL CONTRIBUTIONS

During his career at Leeds Wilson developed the family of spatial interaction models. In the 1970s he collaborated with colleagues to extend the models into new application areas. Working with Martyn Senior he extended the interaction modelling framework to sophisticate models for residential location, and then with Phil Rees he developed population forecasting models based on new spatial accounting procedures. John Stillwell then joined the population team working on interaction models of migration. However, despite this progress, it was in the 1970s that the first major critiques of urban modelling appeared in the literature. These critiques were primarily aimed at large-scale urban models of the sort pioneered by Ira Lowry in the US in 1964. Such models consisted of a number of sub-systems linked together to form comprehensive models of cities and regions. The criticisms were based on the problems of large-scale models in general (over ambition, data hungriness, etc.) and around the static nature of many models. Furthermore, such models were criticised for ignoring the behaviour of individual agents in the city (see Lee, 1973; Sayer, 1976).

The focus for Alan Wilson from the mid-1970s therefore shifted to urban dynamics and a concern to make models more accessible and useful. A major landmark paper in *Environment and Planning A* in 1978 by Wilson (in collaboration with the US academic Britton Harris) introduced a dynamic element into the spatial interaction modelling framework. By adding a cost term into the models the hypothesis was that an equilibrium position would only occur when costs and revenues were balanced. The retail model was used as the exemplar. The interaction model would be run to first estimate revenues at existing shopping centres or stores in the usual way. Then the revenues would be compared to the costs of operating that centre or store. If costs were greater than

revenues the centre/store would decline in size and perhaps even close if not in a good location. If revenue exceeded costs then the centre would grow, possibly at the expense of smaller stores in the vicinity. Wilson compared this kind of dynamic to the corner shop to supermarket transition in UK retailing during the 1960s in particular. Working closely with Martin Clarke in the late 1970s and early 1980s, such research led to the discovery that small changes in key parameter values could lead to major structural change in the systems being modelled. Given that such parameter change could 'flip' systems from one state to another analogies were made to bifurcation or catastrophe theory, theories again popular in the hard sciences. The 1980s saw more extensions of the dynamic models to include models of industrial and agriculture location (with Mark Birkin).

A second wave of research was begun by Wilson in the 1970s, also partly as a response to the wider critiques mentioned above. In 1976 Wilson published a paper with colleague Carol Pownall which argued that an alternative to the aggregate models used to date could be a set of micro-models. By focusing on individuals or individual households in the city these microsimulation models (as they became known) could in theory incorporate individual decision-makers such as household members, retailers, planners and others. Spatial microsimulation models are now an important and established methodology in spatial modelling (see Ballas and Clarke, 2009). In many instances the households in these models can be linked to trip end destinations thus producing a set of highly disaggregated spatial interaction models (in fact becoming very similar to the structure of discrete choice models). More recent developments of agent-based models have increased the ability to model the behaviour of agents such as planners, developers, real estate agents and so on.

The third new research area Wilson developed in the late 1970s focused on spatial optimisation. As models became more complex (as disaggregation became more common – by person type, mode of travel, type of good, etc.) then more constraints needed to be added to make the models more realistic. For a class of problems it therefore became useful to restructure the interaction models as mathematical programming or optimisation tools, where a large number of solution constraints could be handled. In addition, there was interest in using the models to evaluate possibilities for development across entire cities or regions, rather than looking at possible new service locations in a piecemeal fashion (trying one or several locations at a time). This type of optimisation model enabled planners to effectively try a number of new locations in all possible development zones in a region simultaneously. Wilson developed these techniques with colleagues Sally MacGill, Jose Coelho and Huw Williams in particular.

However, the major thrust of the Leeds modelling team in the 1980s was in applied work. Still scarred by the savage critiques of models in the rest of geography, Wilson and his team set out to try and prove the sceptics wrong. Wilson, with Martin Clarke, set out on a mission to find new application areas. Aided by Mark Birkin, and newcomer to Leeds, Graham Clarke, they began to interest potential clients in both the public and private sectors. Early forays in to the consultancy world produced interesting application areas: the impact of a new dry ski slope in West Yorkshire; the construction of simple transport routing models for the UK Post Office, and the modelling of the car repair market for Yorkshire company, 'Charlie Brown'. However, the breakthrough came when two major

companies invested in pilot studies for the retail interaction model: UK high street retailer W.H.Smith and the car manufacturer and distributor Toyota GB. Both these projects were a great success and led to full national (and eventually international) modelling systems. These modelling systems were enhanced by the development of computer graphics and the development of improved model outputs based on the design of new suites of performance indicators (outlined in the 1994 book with Clarke and Bertuglia). As the work grew then a new level of professional service was required and the University formed a subsidiary company (GMAP) to handle the growth in business. By the early 1990s GMAP had a workforce of over 120 including many geography undergraduates and postgraduates, earning revenues well in excess of £5 million per annum. Other major blue-chip clients over the years have included Ford, Exxon/Mobil, BP, Barclays, Sainsbury's, Asda (Wal-Mart), Thomas Cook, and HBOS. By comparison with any other geographical consultancy this was amongst the largest in the world. The benefits of this work (to research, the University, geography and students) have arguably been massive and led to a major new applied book by the four authors in 1996.

KEY ADVANCES AND CONTROVERSIES

Alan Wilson has been one of the key researchers on quantitative geography and has earned a place amongst the leading thinkers in the discipline of human geography. His work on mathematical geography has led to the development of a whole plethora of applied urban models ranging from subsystem models of retailing, health, industrial location, transport and population to detailed comprehensive models for entire city-regions. Given these key advances it is not surprising that he has been honoured many times in the academic world. He was elected a Fellow of the British Academy in 1994 and in May 2006 he became a Fellow of the UK Royal Society and has also received numerous awards in the disciplines of both geography and regional science.

Through his role in the formation of GMAP he has also shown the worth of spatial modelling to both public and private sector planners. This has been a major contribution to applied geography and he has shown that this type of geography can be relevant and useful to many organisations in society. That said, controversy still surrounds the value of urban models in geography and planning, and the academic discipline has largely turned its back on urban modelling since the 1970s, with qualitative approaches having become more popular and widespread. The fact that business has used these models successfully has also led to more criticism from some critical geographers given the use of techniques to help organisations make even greater profits. It is also probably fair to say that despite the success of the applications of the various subsystem models it has proved more difficult to build and operationalise a comprehensive model of the Lowry type (which have been criticised most heavily). There are certainly more factors in their favour now: better data, faster and more powerful computers and possibly better understanding of how cities work. However, the complexity of linking sectors and incorporating the behaviour of various actors (especially endogenously) has proved difficult to solve, although new frameworks and new models do appear from time to time and Wilson continues to examine this area in his most recent publications.

As such, Wilson has been at pains to remind the non-modelling community that there is a powerful counter-argument that spatial modelling should be more prevalent in contemporary academic geography departments. For example, Wilson and his colleagues (Birkin et al., 2010) have set out the benefits of nearly 30 years of applied spatial modelling. To these authors those benefits do not simply relate to increased revenues: they also point out the raft of academic publications based on applied work, the theoretical extensions to the models sometimes needed to apply models to specific problems, the large number of industry-funded PhD students (and the success of Leeds geography department in being awarded ESRC CASE awards), the design of new undergraduate and postgraduate courses that deal with the applied nature of human geography, and the success of Leeds geography undergraduates in the job market (especially in retail and business). In a time when student fees are likely to rise and students become more vocationally focused these must be important messages to send out to the discipline of human geography.

The field of spatial modelling has hence been greatly shaped by Alan Wilson over the last 40 years. Not only has he formulated a wealth of new models and new theoretical insights, he has helped to train and influence a generation of postgraduate and postdoctoral students who themselves have had distinguished careers in academia including Martyn Senior, Roger Mackett, Martin Clarke, Mark Birkin, Graham Clarke, Sally Macgill, Huw Williams, Bob Crouchley, Paul Forte, John Beaumont and Jose Coelho: all together, a huge contribution to the discipline of human geography and the conceptualisation and of space and place.

WILSON'S KEY WORKS

Bertuglia, C.S., Clarke, G.P. and Wilson, A. (eds) (1994) *Modelling the City: Performance, Policy and Planning.* London: Routledge.

Birkin, M., Clarke, G.P., Clarke, M.P and Wilson, A. (1996) *Intelligent Geographic Information Systems.* Cambridge: GeoInformation International.

Wilson, A. (1967) 'A statistical theory of spatial distribution models', *Transportation Research,* 1: 253–69.

Wilson, A. (1970) *Entropy in Urban and Regional Modelling.* London: Pion.

Wilson, A. (1974) *Urban and Regional Models in Geography and Planning.* John Wiley: Chichester and New York.

Wilson, A. and Rees, P. (1977) *Spatial Population Analysis.* London: Edward Arnold.

Wilson, A., Rees, P. and Leigh, C.M. (eds) (1977) *Models of Cities and Regions.* Chichester: John Wiley.

Wilson, A. and Harris, B. (1978) 'Equilibrium values and dynamics of attractiveness terms in production-constrained spatial-interaction models', *Environment and Planning A,* 10: 371-88.

Wilson, A. (1981) *Catastrophe Theory and Bifurcation: Applications to Urban and Regional Systems.* Berkeley: University of California Press.

Wilson, A., Coelho, J.D., Macgill, S.M. and Williams, H.C.W.L. (1981) *Optimisation in Locational and Transport Analysis.* Chichester: John Wiley.

Wilson, A. and Bennett, R.J. (1985) *Mathematical Methods in Human Geography and Planning.* Chichester: John Wiley.

Wilson, A. (2000) *Complex Spatial Systems: The Modelling Foundations of Urban and Regional Analysis.* Harlow: Prentice Hall.

Wilson, A. (2006) 'Ecological and urban systems' models: some explorations of similarities in the context of complexity theory', *Environment and Planning A,* 38: 633–46.

Wilson, A. (2008) 'Boltzmann, Lotka and Volterra and spatial structural evolution: an integrated methodology for some dynamical systems', *Journal of the Royal Society, Interface,* 5: 865–71.

Secondary Sources and References

Ballas, D. and Clarke, G.P. (2009) 'Spatial microsimulation', in A.S. Fotheringham and P. Rogerson (eds), *Handbook of Spatial Analysis.* London: Sage. pp. 277–98.

Birkin, M., Clarke, G.P., Clarke, M.P and Wilson, A. (2010) *'The benefits of applied spatial modelling',* working paper. School of Geography, University of Leeds.

Foot, D. (1981) *Operational Urban Models.* London: Methuen.

Harris, B. (1962) *Linear programming and the projection of land uses* Paper 20, PennState Transportation Study, Philadelphia.

Lee, D.B. (1973) 'Requiem for large-scale models', *Journal of American Institute of Planners,* 39: 163–78.

Lowry, I.S. (1964) *A Model of Metropolis* RM-4035-RC, Rand Corporation, Santa Monica.

Sayer, R.A. (1976) 'A critique of urban modelling: from regional science to urban and regional political economy', *Progress in Planning,* 6: 187–254.

Wilson, A.G., and Pownall, C. (1976) 'A New Representation of the Urban System for Modelling and for the Study of Micro-Level Interdependence', *Area* 8: 256–64.

Graham Clark, University of Leeds

66   Iris Marion Young

BIOGRAPHICAL DETAILS AND THEORETICAL CONTEXT

Born in New York City in 1949, Iris Marion Young gained her doctorate in philosophy in 1974 from Pennsylvania State University, focusing her thesis on Wittgenstein's later writings. Before becoming a Professor in the Political Science department of the University of Chicago, she held various academic positions in the US in philosophy and in political theory. She died in 2006 after an 18-month battle with cancer, being survived by her husband and daughter.

Young was a prolific writer and has made theoretical advances within numerous cross-disciplinary debates from the 1980s to the present. She was best known for her writings on justice and the politics of difference, though her contributions extend into many other domains within the humanities and social sciences. Young's work has been widely translated, and she has held several visiting fellowships at universities and institutes internationally. These facts, coupled with the serial reprinting of seminal essays, help explain her international reputation and the dissemination of her ideas well beyond the fields of political theory and philosophy. Young's influence within the academy is not restricted to her monographs and sole-authored essays. In her role as editor, she cemented the importance of feminist philosophy (Jeffner and Young, 1989; Jaggar and Young, 1998) and feminist ethics and social policy (DiQuinzio and Young, 1997). She was also committed to addressing policy debates and has intervened in discussions surrounding the location of hazardous waste, the treatment of pregnant addicts, residential segregation, and institutions of global law.

Young's contributions to philosophy, political theory and feminist theory have had added resonance in the context of US academic responses to the new social movements of the 1970s – movements mobilising for justice around such categories as gender, ethnicity, 'race', sexuality and nationality. Such movements challenged both traditional Marxist commitments to the primacy of class in analysing social formations, and liberalism's investment in particular models of equality, equity and democracy. For Young, taking those movements' demands seriously required opening up the category of justice beyond its usual restriction to questions of redistribution. Furthermore, Young argued, reformulating justice and democracy must be undertaken using *situated* analysis: she has described her work as engaging in 'critical theory' – in her words, 'normative reflection that is *historically and socially contextualized*' (1990b: 5, italics added).

Young's writings are underpinned by her participation in several social and environmental movements, most notably the women's movement. As Young puts it:

> My personal political passion begins with feminism, and it is from my participation in the contemporary women's movement that I first learned to identify oppression and develop social and normative theoretical reflection on it. My feminism, however, has always been supplemented by commitment to and participation in movements against military intervention abroad and for systematic restructuring of the social circumstances that keep so many people poor and disadvantaged at home.
>
> (Young, 1990b: 13)

Young also draws from a wide range of philosophical frameworks, and her writing shows its indebtedness to the liberal tradition as well as to feminism, deconstruction, phenomenology, psychoanalysis and pragmatism. Her essays have engaged with Arendt, de Beauvoir, Derrida, **Foucault**, Habermas, Irigaray, Kristeva, Lacan, Marx, Merleau-Ponty, Rawls and Sartre. Young's use of such different and often conflictual philosophical traditions makes her own work difficult to characterise with a single label. This has not, however, staved off attempts to compartmentalise her scholarship: she was described variously as a radical postmodernist, a post-socialist, a devoted Habermasian, and too great a defender of liberal humanism.

Young's earlier writings wrestled with the debates surrounding socialist feminism and with the challenge of 'gynocentrism' (the revaluation of 'female gendered experience'). In *Throwing Like A Girl and Other Essays in Feminist Philosophy and Social Theory* (1990c), Young took up various feminist political projects associated with the Reagan–Bush Sr. years. The book moved from challenging the homogeneous

public sphere elaborated by much political theory, to understanding women's embodied oppression (in essays on gendered movement, pregnancy, clothes and breasts). Young's yearning for 'heterogeneous public life' and her critique of the ideal of universal citizenship manifested her desire for a more inclusive polity: this preoccupation continues throughout her writings. The essay 'Throwing like a girl' was a phenomenological account of 'some of the basic modalities of feminine body comportment, manner of moving, and relation in space' (1990c: 143). Here Young argued that there are specific modalities of 'feminine spatiality' – modalities in which woman 'lives space as *enclosed* or confining, ... and ... experiences herself as *positioned* in [not positioning herself in] space' (Young, 1990c: 151, italics in original).

Although *Throwing Like a Girl* contains many geographical insights, it was through the publication of her groundbreaking and prize-winning book *Justice and the Politics of Difference* (also published in 1990) that she became widely known in the discipline of geography. In that book (Young, 1990b), and in an allied essay (Young, 1990a), she laid out her fundamental claims about justice, community and the politics of difference. Arguing that a conception of justice 'should begin with the concepts of domination and oppression' (Young, 1990b: 3), rather than focusing on redistribution, she elaborated 'five faces of oppression' through which to understand how structural phenomena 'immobilize or diminish' particular groups in society. These she enumerated as exploitation, marginalisation, powerlessness, cultural imperialism and violence. She jettisoned a logic in which 'liberation' is dependent upon a transcending of group difference – the ideal of assimilation – and instead proposed that 'justice in a group-differentiated society demands social equality of groups, and mutual recognition and affirmation of group differences' (Young, 1990b: 191). Central to her formulations concerning justice and difference were conceptualisations of spatio-temporal relations. For Young, the usual ideal of community privileges face-to-face relations, and in doing so, 'seeks to suppress difference in the sense of the time and space distancing of social processes, which material media facilitate and enlarge' (Young, 1990a: 314). Thus her account displaced the ideal of community with the ideal of '[c]ity life as an openness to unassimilated otherness' (Young, 1990b: 227), thereby presenting a vision of desirable social relations as 'a being together of strangers in openness to group difference' (Young, 1990b: 256).

Justice and the Politics of Difference gained an enormous readership and had an inflammatory effect in the social sciences. It served as a flashpoint for debates over the putative 'death', or at least displacement, of the hypostatised figure of the universal, male citizen of the Enlightenment. Of particular importance was the question of what it meant socially and politically to validate, as Young had done, the category of the differentiated 'group' in place of the individual. Thus Young (1997) in her third monograph, *Intersecting Voices: Dilemmas of Gender, Political Philosophy, and Policy*, was at pains to demonstrate that her account of the social group should not be equated with an essentialising 'identity politics'. In *Intersecting Voices*, she drew upon Habermas (in particular his model of communicative ethics) and Irigaray in developing the concept of 'asymmetrical reciprocity'. We cannot put ourselves in others' places, Young stressed, but we *can* communicate across difference. Asymmetrical reciprocity implies for young that every act of communication is ghosted by other temporalities: 'A condition of our

communication is that we acknowledge the difference, interval, that others drag behind them, shadows and histories, scars and traces, that do not become present in our communication' (Young, 1997: 53).

In *Inclusion and Democracy* (2000), Young reinforced her conviction that democracy is the most productive institutional frame through which to realise 'difference'. There, her analyses extended more obviously to the scale of the global and to the debates over cosmopolitanism: she argued that her interrogation of democracy must, to have any purchase, work in the context of dense and globally extensive social, economic and legal networks. Young also devoted more attention to the role of civil society; emphasised her commitment to an agonistic rather than quiescent account of the social sphere and the democratic process; and provided another elaboration of the social group. Throughout *Inclusion and Democracy* Young developed a more explicit language of spatiality and position, particularly as a means to deflect accusations that her accounts of the social group do not provide the individual *within* the group with agency or specificity of her own:

> Understanding individuals as conditioned by their positioning in relation to social groups without their constituting individual identities helps to solve the problem of 'pop-bead' identity: a person's identity is not some sum of her gender, racial, class, and national affinities. She is only her identity, which she herself has made by the way that she deals with and acts in relation to others [sic] social group positions, among other things.
>
> (Young, 2000: 102)

Young, in pointing out that '[f]ew theories of democracy ... have thematized the normative implications of spatialized social relations' (Young, 2000: 196), solidified her place as one of the few political theorists to have done so – something emphasised in her posthumously published consideration of the social connections that bind far-flung places in ways that challenge us to think of the need for global justice (Young, 2006).

SPATIAL CONTRIBUTIONS

The moment at which Young's name gained widespread visibility in geography was one in which heated discussions were taking place about which conceptual frameworks geographers might – and should – use to understand socio-spatial relations. One way to exemplify that moment is to point to the debates surrounding **David Harvey**'s (1989) *The Condition of Postmodernity* – debates preoccupied with how to understand the vexed relations between Marxist theory, feminist theory and that which sits, loosely, under the umbrella of 'postmodern' theory. In short, the geographical question of that moment was: what kind of socio-spatial theory might best account for 'difference'?

Justice and the Politics of Difference spoke directly to these debates. That the book was resolutely committed to a liberatory politics extended its appeal to a variety of theoretical domains. In addition, Young's pragmatic tendencies and her commitment to theory that did not set itself apart from practical application fitted well with geography's guiding principles. The book, with its attentiveness to relational accounts of identity and affiliation, its theorisations of oppression and domination, and its drawing together of 'culture' and political economy endorsed many of the projects characterising the

burgeoning sphere of 'critical geography'. One indication of the proximity of Young's ideas to new directions being taken in geography is the pervasive – if not always explicit – influence of her scholarship in Keith and Pile's (1993) important collection *Place and the Politics of Identity*. Likewise, Young's work has been excerpted in McDowell and Sharp's (1997) feminist reader, in Kasinitz's (1994) reader of metropolitan writings, and in Bridge and Watson's (2002) *City Reader*. These reprintings disseminated Young's ideas further within the subdisciplines of urban, feminist and social-cultural geography.

This widespread citation and excerpting of Young's writing bears testament to the fact that she contributed to conceptualisations of space and place at a variety of scales – that of the body, the city, the region and the cosmopolitan global. In relation to the first, Young's work on a 'heterogeneous public' and her privileging of the city as the locus for imagining a 'politics of difference' helped open up models of social relations beyond those indebted to the Chicago School of Sociology (with its frequent endorsement of social assimilation), and beyond Marxist accounts that seemed not adequately attentive to axes of difference aside from that of class. Young's reformulations of community and her validation of mediated urban relations resonated with geographers' desires to account for the complexity of city interactions, and the ways in which communities are fractured rather than organically unitary. Valentine has engaged with Young's ideas in her work on lesbian communities and the 'fluid, multiple and constantly … renegotiated and contested' structures of meaning that underpin them (Valentine, 1995: 109). Dunn equally found Young's 'anti-assimilationist' approach towards group difference inspiringly progressive in his study of the concentration of Indo-Chinese Australians in Sydney (Dunn, 1998). Similarly, Fincher and Jacobs's edited collection *Cities of Difference* (1998) shows the imprint of several of Young's formulations.

Young's work also contributed to debates on the geography of the body. Young's 'five faces of oppression' (exploitation, marginalisation, powerlessness, cultural imperialism and violence) moved away from a typology that alluded to named groups of 'sufferers' (as with the terms racism, ableism, heterosexism), and towards a more flexible matrix for understanding how people may be differently inhibited or constrained. In doing so, it garnered interest from geographers wanting to think the axes of gender, 'race', disability, sexuality and class together rather than simply alongside one another. **Rose** has used Young to elaborate upon female experiences of confinement in space (Rose 1993: 146); Longhurst has incorporated Young's analyses of pregnancy and the production of 'ugly' bodies into her own examination of 'corporeographies' (Longhurst 2001); **McDowell** has taken up the category of 'cultural imperialism' to help understand how women working in the financial industries in the City of London are positioned as 'inappropriate or vile bodies' (McDowell, 1997: 8); and Imrie has found the five faces of oppression a good 'heuristic device ... for situating the lived experiences of disabled people in some form of non essentialist structural context' (Imrie, 1996: 6). Nonetheless, Young's feminist reading of the ambivalences structuring the category of 'the home' (an essay included in *Throwing Like a Girl*) are perhaps less well known within human geography. Further, Young's theoretical formulations are far from static and exhibit great elasticity. Indeed, in her writing she frequently alerts the reader to how her thinking has changed. One elegant example is Young's

(1998b) auto-critique, written nearly 20 years later, of her seminal essay 'Throwing like a girl'.

In summary, Young's refocusing of questions of justice around the undermining of oppression and domination have been thought-provoking for geographers engaged in formulating just arrangements in material situations. Smith (1994), for example, endorses Young's approach in his interrogation of models of social justice, but argues that although her conceptions are appropriately spatial, they are essentially utopian. Varley (2002) found Young's interrogation of Western thought's obsession with producing stable dualisms useful in challenging the problematic divide between 'legal' and 'illegal' that underpins debates over the occupation of land by the poor in urban Mexico. Most notably perhaps, David Harvey has directly engaged with some of the theoretical implications of Young's work on justice.

KEY ADVANCES AND CONTROVERSIES

Justice and the Politics of Difference undoubtedly contributed to the setting of new agendas within social and cultural geography, feminist geography, political economy, and urban studies. It did so by demonstrating the centrality of the term 'difference' for analyses of socio-spatial relations, and by providing new theoretical 'implements' (the 'heterogeneous public' and the 'five faces of oppression') through which the term difference could be explicated. That Young's work takes seriously the challenges of a capitalist, urban landscape and of complex spatial-temporal positioning has endeared her to many geographers. At the same time, her work was subject to the following critiques: (i) her account of difference rests on an inadequate account of the social group; (ii) she does not adequately outline the mechanisms necessary for achieving the ideal of city life as an openness to unassimilated otherness (see Smith, 1994: 107); and (iii) her formulations concerning difference end up exoticising 'the other' by overemphasising an attitude of 'wonder' *in the face of* difference at the expense of accounting for shared experiences and desires *across* difference (Stavro, 2001).

David Harvey found Young's 'five faces of oppression' productive vis-à-vis his own work on justice. Though endorsing Young's critique of constrictive versions of communitarianism, he has criticised her ideal of openness to unassimilated otherness as being 'naively specified in relation to the actual dynamics of urbanization' (1996: 312). Furthermore, Harvey has countered her 'politics of difference' in the context of his own analysis of the kinds of *class-based* politics that he deems necessary to deal with such events as a horrific fire in 1991 in a US chicken processing plant that killed 25 employees, many of whom were women and/or African-American (Harvey, 1993; 1996). To summarise, for Harvey a politics of difference threatens to deflect political attention away from combating the exploitation wrought by capitalist processes. Young in turn criticised Harvey (1993; 1996) for reducing group-based social movements to identity politics, and has challenged his model according to which 'class' is able to offer a vision of commonality, whereas gender or 'race' are deemed to be mired in partiality (Young, 2000: 108; Young, 1998a).

Scholars in disciplines beyond geography have also criticised Young's formulation of 'the social group'. Some have suggested that her politics of difference cannot be clearly distinguished either from traditional interest group politics or from a simple endorsement of 'identity politics' (Squires, 2001). Mouffe (1992: 380) has argued that Young's model of the group is 'ultimately essentialist' since in Young's account, 'there are groups with their interests and identities already given, and politics is not about the construction of new identities.' Fraser (1995) has argued that Young implicitly validates a 'cultural' definition of a social group that elevates a model of an 'ethnic group' into a paradigm for *all* collectivities. This, Fraser (1995) argues, papers over the fact that there are *different* kinds of difference – and that while some should be enjoyed, others (for example, 'groups' differently positioned within the capitalist division of labour) should be undermined or eliminated. Understanding collectivities on the model of the 'ethnic group' produces a strangely *American* conceptualisation of the social group: '[w]here else but in the United States', Fraser (1995: 174) asks, 'does ethnicity so regularly eclipse class, nation and party?' Young (2000: 82) is adamant that her politics of difference is *not* equivalent to identity politics, arguing that 'groups do not have identities as such, but rather that individuals construct their own identities on the basis of social group positioning'.

Young cited both **Castells** and Harvey in her chapter on city life in *Justice and the Politics of Difference* (1990b). However, the relays between Young's work and geographical scholarship went for some time largely in one direction: that is, geographers read, took up or critiqued Young's formulations. By the late 1990s that pattern had somewhat shifted: Young has not only addressed the specifics of David Harvey's arguments (1998a; 2000), but in *Inclusion and Democracy* (2000) cites the work of other geographers (for example, **Michael Storper** and Liz Bondi). However, geographers have, arguably, engaged less with this part of Young's oeuvre. The turn in human geography in the late 1990s towards performance and performativity perhaps made aspects of Young's work – her engagement with the legacies of liberalism and with deliberate democracy – less 'translatable' into the discipline of geography. Why Young's more phenomenological essays on embodiment, female motility and the home did not become better assimilated into geography is a fascinating, and unanswered, question. Nonetheless, as Fainstein (2007: 386) summarises, 'her commitment to justice, her insights into the urban condition, and her willingness to tackle the practical questions of social change were inspiring and will be greatly missed.'

YOUNG'S KEY WORKS

DiQuinzio, P. and Young, I. M. (eds) (1997) *Feminist Ethics and Social Policy*. Bloomington: Indiana University Press.

Jaggar, A. M. and Young, I. M. (eds) (1998) *A Companion to Feminist Philosophy*. Malden, MA and Oxford: Blackwell.

Jeffner, A. and Young, I. M. (eds) (1989) *The Thinking Muse: Feminism and Modern French Philosophy*. Bloomington and Indianapolis: Indiana University Press.

Young, I. M. (1990a) 'The ideal of community and the politics of difference', in L. J. Nicholson (ed.), *Feminism/Postmodernism*. New York and London: Routledge. pp. 300–23.

Young, I. M. (1990b) *Justice and the Politics of Difference*. Princeton, NJ: Princeton University Press.

Young, I. M. (1990c) *Throwing Like a Girl and Other Essays in Feminist Philosophy and Social Theory*. Bloomington and Indianapolis: Indiana University Press.

Young, I. M. (1997) *Intersecting Voices: Dilemmas of Gender, Political Philosophy, and Policy*. Princeton, NJ: Princeton University Press.

Young, I. M. (1998a) 'Harvey's complaint with race and gender struggles: a critical response to *Justice, Nature and the Geography of Difference*', *Antipode*, 30: 36–42.

Young, I.M. (1998b) '"Throwing like a girl": twenty years later', in D. Welton (ed.) *Body and Flesh: A Philosophical Reader*. Malden, MA and Oxford: Blackwell. pp. 286–90.

Young, I.M. (2000) *Inclusion and Democracy*. Oxford: Oxford University Press.

Young, I.M. (2006) *Responsibility and Global Justice: A Social Connection Model*. Cambridge: Cambridge University Press.

Secondary Sources and References

Bridge, G. and Watson, S. (eds) (2002) *The Blackwell City Reader*. Oxford: Blackwell.

Dunn, K. M. (1998) 'Rethinking ethnic concentration: the case of Cabramatta, Sydney', *Urban Studies*, 35: 503–27.

Fincher, R. and Jacobs, J.M. (eds) (1998) *Cities of Difference*. New York and London: Guilford.

Fainstein, S.S. (2007) 'Iris Marion Young 1949–2006: a tribute', *Antipode*, 39 (2): 382–87.

Fraser, N. (1995) 'Recognition or redistribution? A critical reading of Iris Young's *Justice and the Politics of Difference*', *Journal of Political Philosophy*, 3: 166–80.

Harvey, D. (1989) *The Condition Of Postmodernity*. Oxford: Blackwell.

Harvey, D. (1993) 'Class relations, social justice and the politics of difference', in M. Keith and S. Pile (eds), *Place and the Politics of Identity*. London and New York: Routledge. pp. 41–66.

Harvey, D. (1996) *Justice, Nature and the Geography of Difference*. Oxford: Blackwell.

Imrie, R. (1996) *Disability and the City: International Perspectives*. London: Paul Chapman.

Kasinitz, P. (ed.) (1994) *Metropolis: Center and Symbol of Our Times*. New York: New York University Press.

Keith, M. and Pile, S. (eds) (1993) *Place and the Politics of Identity*. London and New York: Routledge.

Longhurst, R. (2001) *Bodies: Exploring Fluid Boundaries.* London and New York: Routledge.

McDowell, L. (1997) *Capital Culture: Gender at Work in the City.* Oxford: Blackwell.

McDowell, L. and Sharp, J. P. (eds) (1997) *Space, Gender, Knowledge: Feminist Readings.* London: Arnold.

Mouffe, C. (1992) 'Feminism, citizenship, and radical democratic politics', in J. Butler, and J.W. Scott (eds), *Feminists Theorize the Political.* New York and London: Routledge. pp. 369–84.

Rose, G. (1993) *Feminism and Geography.* Minneapolis: University of Minnesota Press.

Smith, D. M. (1994) *Geography and Social Justice.* Oxford: Blackwell.

Squires, J. (2001) 'Representing groups, deconstructing identities', *Feminist Theory*, 2: 7–27.

Stavro, E. (2001) 'Working towards reciprocity: critical reflections on Seyla Benhabib and Iris Young', *Angelaki*, 6: 137–48.

Valentine, G. (1995) 'Out and about: geographies of lesbian landscapes', *International Journal of Urban and Regional Research*, 19: 96–111.

Varley, A. (2002) 'Private or public: debating the meaning of tenure legalization' *International Journal of Urban and Regional Research*, 26: 449–61.

Felicity Callard, Queen Mary, University of London

Glossary

This glossary provides brief definitions of key terms that are not fully explained in the context of individual entries. In each case, we refer to the principal entries where these concepts are referred to.

Actor-Network Theory: A theoretical approach that holds to the indivisibility of human and non-human agents, exploring the ways that different materials are enrolled in networks. Originally developed in debates about the production of scientific knowledge, Actor-Network Theory (often abbreviated to ANT) opens up the 'black boxes' of action to explore the way that heterogeneous materials are continually assembled to allow actions to occur. See **Latour; Thrift.**

Affect: As distinct from emotion and feeling, affect arises as we interact with the world in a multisensory and engaged way. Affect is thus imbricated in various processes of space and place-making, from everyday, banalised movements in the city, shaped as they are by senses of anticipation, boredom and curiousity, through to the mobilisation of fear, terror, hope and despair at the scale of international relations. See **Ingold; Thrift**.

Behaviouralism: An outlook or system of thought that believes that human activity can best be explained by studying the human decision-making processes that shape that activity. Originally developed in psychology, largely as a reaction to the mechanistic excesses of experimental psychology, behaviouralism – and more particularly cognitive behaviouralism – came to prominence in the human geography of the 1960s and 1970s. Primarily based on methods of quantification, behavioural geography has been criticised for its adherence to positivist principles, as well as its unwillingness to explore the role of the unconscious mind, although it still underpins many research projects, particularly those based on survey research. See **Ley; Lynch; Golledge**.

Capitalism: The political-economic system in which the organisation of society is structured in relation to a mode of production that prioritises the generation of profit for those who own the means of production. Such a structuring sees a clear division in status, wealth and living conditions between those few who own or control the means of production (bourgeois) and those that work for them (proletariat). See **Castells; Davis; Gibson-Graham; Harvey; Lefebvre; Massey; Sayer; Smith; Storper; Wallerstein; Taylor**.

Consumption: In everyday use, the utilisation of a good or a service until it has no value remaining. In the social sciences, consumption is deemed to be a more complex stage in a cycle of production and consumption, whereby a commodity may be transformed or even have value added. In contemporary capitalist societies, consumption is depicted as the driving force of the economy, and, given commodity relations have penetrated into all spheres of social life, geographers have accordingly devoted increased attention to the spaces and rituals of consumption. See **Bauman; Ley; Jackson**.

Corporeality: A recognition of the importance of the body/bodily, as opposed to simply the mind, in lived experience. See **Bourdieu; Butler; Young**.

Cultural politics: The study of the ways in which the cultural is political, and how social difference and conflict is bound up in complex power relations centred on categories of identity such as race, gender, disability, sexuality. See **Bhabha; Hall; hooks; Jackson; Young**.

Cultural turn: A trend in the late 20th and early 21st centuries that has seen the social sciences and humanities increasingly focus on culture, and specifically the production, negotiation and contestation of meanings. In geography this has meant the integration of social and cultural theory into spatial analyses to create 'new' cultural geography, wherein culture is conceived as a process and the principal means through which society and space is constructed, providing people with their sense of identity at the same time that it maps out power-laden social and spatial hierarchies See **Jackson; Williams; Said**.

Culture: Defined by Raymond Williams as the most disputed term in the English language, culture has been taken by geographers to refer to both the ways of life accruing to a particular group and the placed meanings of the material objects they produce and consume. See **Bourdieu; Hall; Jackson; Williams**.

Critical geography: Though diverse in its epistemology, ontology and methodology, and hence lacking a distinctive theoretical identity, critical geography nonetheless brings together those working with different approaches (e.g. Marxist, feminist, post-colonial, post-structural) through a shared commitment to expose the socio-spatial processes that (re)produce inequalities between people and places. In other words, critical geographers are united in general terms by their *ideological* stance and their desire to study and engender a more just world. This interest in studying and changing the social, cultural, economic or political relations that create unequal, uneven, unjust and exploitative geographies is manifest in engagements with questions of moral philosophy, social and environmental justice as well as attempts to bridge the divide between research and praxis. See **Harvey; Massey; Sibley; Smith; Ó Tuathail; Young**.

Deconstruction: A method of analysis that seeks to critique and destabilise apparently stable systems of meaning in discourses by illustrating their contradictions, paradoxes, and contingent nature. See **Hall; Harley; Haraway; Jackson; Spivak**.

Development studies: A broad field of analysis that analyses processes of economic, political and social change and the mechanisms that maintain inequalities between regions and countries with particular reference to divisions between the rich North and poorer South. See **Corbridge; Escobar; Sen; Taylor; Watts**.

Dialectics/al: A form of explanation and representation that emphasises the resolution of binary oppositions. Rather than understanding the relationship between two elements as a one-way cause and effect, dialectical thinking understands them to be part of, and inherent in, each other. A dialectic approach has been an important part of structuralist accounts that seek to understand the interplay between individuals and society. See **Giddens; Harvey; Smith**.

Diaspora/diasporic: The scattering or dispersal of a population. It can also be used as a noun to refer to dispersed or scattered populations, such as the black diaspora or the Jewish diaspora. Because transnational linkages develop across diasporic communities, diaspora is also used as a theoretical concept to challenge fixed understandings of identity and place. See **hooks; Said; Spivak**.

Difference: Post-structuralist theory has emphasised the need to recognise the complexity of human social differences associated with culturally constructed notions of gender, race, sexuality, age, disability, etc. This means providing an analysis that is sensitive to the differences between individuals and avoids over-generalisations. See **Butler; hooks; Massey; Jackson; Young**.

Discourse: A set of ways of thinking about, speaking of and acting towards particular people or places. Emphasising that language and thought are in, not outside, the world, discourse analysis has been important in developing post-structural theories. In human geography, discourse analysis has been widely used to expose the importance of representation in constructing stereotypes of place and nation. On occasion, this has required geographers interrogating their own processes of knowledge production. See **Barnes; Foucault; Gregory; Harley; Said; Spivak**.

Empiricism: A philosophy of science that emphasises empirical observation over theory. In other words it assumes 'facts speak for themselves'. See **Massey; Watts**.

Ethnography: A qualitative mode of research and writing that emphasises the importance of in-depth, contextual and intensive study in excavating the relationships between people and place. See **Augé; Davis; Ingold; Ley**.

Feminism: A set of perspectives that seek to explore the way that gender relations are played out in favour of men rather than women. In human geography, such perspectives have suggested that space is crucial in the maintenance of patriarchy – the structure by which women are exploited in the private and public sphere. See **Haraway; hooks; Massey; McDowell; Rose**.

Fordism: A prevalent form of capitalism that was characterised in industrial and social practices pioneered within the factories of Henry Ford and which led to the creation in the West of mass production and mass consumption. See **Harvey; Massey**.

Genealogy: A method of creating a 'history of the present' by historically reconstructing the ways in which we produce knowledge that shapes social formations. Here, there is an emphasis on deconstructing at individual and local scales how society is constituted and how ideas became commonsense, taken-for-granted and universal. See **Foucault**.

Gentrification: The process by which working class populations are displaced from an area or neighbourhood and replaced by wealthier populations. Often associated with material and aesthetic improvements in housing stock, debates concerning gentrification in rural and urban areas in the 1980s and 1990s provided a basis for exploring the way that economic, social and political processes entwine to create particular spatial arrangements. See **Bourdieu; Ley; Smith**.

Geopolitics: The analysis of how the geographical is bound up in the theory and practice of statecraft and international relations. More recently, the development of critical geopolitics has focused on the discourses and practices that underpin statecraft and shape the relations between territories and nations. See **Taylor; Ó Tuathail**.

Globalisation: The suite of economic, social and political processes that are enabling connections to be made between people and places on a worldwide scale. Implicated in a process of time-space compression, there are nonetheless many arguments about whether globalisation is leading to increasing homogenisation or differentiation of space. Human geographers are accordingly exploring both the causes and consequences of these processes, developing new concepts of hybridity and transnationalism as they seek to develop a language and conceptual toolkit that is adequate for these 'global times'. See **Anderson; Bauman; Castells; Dicken; Giddens; Harvey; Sassen; Taylor; Urry; Virilio; Wallerstein; Watts**.

Governance: Governance does not simply refer to the practices of governments. Rather it relates to the acts and processes of governing more generally. In its broadest sense, the study of governance is therefore interested in how individuals, organisations and states govern and regulate both others and themselves. See **Foucault; Ó Tuathail; Taylor**.

Hegemony: Hegemony generally refers to a situation of uncontested supremacy. The term under the influence of Gramsci has been reworked in the social sciences, however, to refer to the power of a dominant group to persuade subordinate groups to accept its moral, political and cultural values as the 'natural' order; as desirable, inevitable, and taken-for-granted. See **Bhabha; Corbridge; Jackson; Taylor; Wallerstein; Williams**.

Humanistic geography: An approach to understanding human geography that focuses on the creativity of human beings to shape their world and create meaningful places. Focusing on human consciousness as the basis of being in the world, humanistic geography challenged the ideas of spatial science, behavioural geography and structural approaches when it came to prominence in the 1970s. Methodologically, humanistic geographers pioneered qualitative techniques that are now widespread across the discipline, and continue to highlight issues of subjectivity in research. See **Buttimer; Ley; Tuan**.

Hybridity: In the social sciences, this is a term that is used to describe the results of a meeting of two apparently distinctive cultures. In human geography, there has been significant interest in the hybrid cultures and ways of life that occur on the boundaries between different nations, as well as the hybrid cultures that emerge as international migration creates cities typified by multiculturalism. There is also widespread geographical interest in the hybridity associated with the blurring of culture/nature. See **Bhabha; Haraway; Spivak**.

Identity: Early academic understandings of identity conceptualised them in terms of coherent, social categories such as gender and class, in which identity was assumed to reflect a core or fixed sense of self. More contemporary theorisations understand identities as reflexive projects, emphasising their multiple, fluid and contested nature. See **Butler; hooks; Jackson; Williams**.

Ideology: In general terms ideology refers to a coherent set of meanings, ideas or values that underpin a particular course of action. In relation to research praxis, ideology concerns the underlying social/political reasons or purpose for seeking knowledge. Some philosophies posit that the production of knowledge should be an ideologically-neutral activity. This view implies that it is the job of a theorist to develop ideas about how the world works and it is for others to decide how to use the ideas they uncover. Others posit that it is impossible to be ideologically-neutral, and that, whether we like it or not, it is impossible to isolate personal social and political beliefs from wider theorisation. On this basis, they argue that academics should use their theories to try and change the world for the better rather than leave it to others to interpret their ideas. See **Hall; Haraway; Latour; Williams.**

Landscape: As with space and place, landscape is a key concept in human geography yet has different connotations for different commentators. For some, landscape is an area that can be mapped and explored for the traces of its making; for others, it is a distinctive way of representing and making space that involves the imbrication of knowledge and power. See **Cosgrove; Harley; Rose.**

Localism: The study of local places and communities as sites (or laboratories) of social and economic relations and how such sites relate to, are affected and affect other locations. Often criticised as ignoring the wider picture of how a specific location is situated in relation to a broad economic and political landscape. See **Massey; Sayer; Smith.**

Locational analysis: A mode of analysis that seeks to develop spatial laws and models that explain the distribution and flow of phenomena and activities across the Earth's surface. See **Berry; Hägerstrand; Haggett; Tobler; Wilson.**

Marxism: A broad perspective that holds to the primacy of capitalist relations in structuring social and economic life. Based on the ideas of Karl Marx, Marxism has been responsible for notable examples of political radicalism within geography, as well as the development of a politically-motivated Marxist human geography that seeks to expose the injustices wrought by capitalism. See **Davis; Harvey; Lefebvre; Massey; Smith; Soja; Taylor; Wallerstein.**

Mobility: Broadly defined as the movement of people, goods, ideas, and money across space. Traditionally understood through the positivist frameworks of transport geography, the 'mobilities' turn has emphasised the social production of mobility and the variegated speed and slowness of different transactions and movements. See **Urry; Virilio.**

Mode of production: A Marxist-derived term that denotes the way that relations of production are organised in specific periods. Currently, it is accepted that the world is organised so as to reproduce and maintain a capitalist mode of production, though it is emphasised that feudal, socialist and communist modes of production have been (and in some cases, still remain) dominant in some nations. See **Lefebvre; Taylor; Wallerstein.**

Modelling: A method of analysis that seeks to create a realistic model of how a system works or to predict outcomes given certain parameters. Often used extensively in locational analysis and now most often performed using a Geographic Information System. See **Berry; Haggett; Tobler; Wilson.**

Modernity: A period associated with the West from the eighteenth century onwards characterised by the reorganisation of society through a combination of the development of a capitalist economy, the political reorganisation associated with nation-states, and the pre-eminence of cultural values such as rationality and progress arising from the philosophy of Enlightenment. This gave rise to a particular social order that remained dominant in the West until the late twentieth century. See **Bauman; Beck; Giddens; Gregory; Pred; Taylor; Wallerstein.**

Multiculturalism: This recognises that different cultural or ethnic groups have a right to assert their own distinct identities rather than be assimilated into mainstream norms. See **Bhabha; Hall; hooks; Said; Watts; Young.**

Nationalism: A political ideology that promotes amongst a nation of people shared, communal feelings of belonging and ownership to a particular, bounded territory. See **Anderson; Said; Ó Tuathail.**

Neo-liberalism: Ideological project of the New Right that has grown in strength since the 1980s in the West. Neo-liberalism positions the free market, rather than the state, as the central organising feature of society. Such a positioning has had a profound effect on social formations and economic and political policy particularly with regard to welfare and overseas development and debt. See **Corbridge; Davis; Gibson-Graham; Harvey; Smith; Ó Tuathail; Watts.**

Non-representational theory: A theory that seeks to move the emphasis of analysis from representation and interpretation to practice and mobility. Emphasis is placed on studying processes of becoming, recognising that the world is always in the making, and that such becoming is not always discursively formed (framed within, or arising out of, discourse). Here, society consists of set of heterogeneous actants who produce space and time through embodied action that often lacks reason and purpose. To understand how the world is becoming involves observant participation; a self-directed analysis of how people interact and produce space through their movement and practice. See **Thrift.**

Objectivity: Used within the social sciences, objectivity refers to conducting analysis in a supposedly non-personal, disinterested fashion that makes the findings of research neutral and value-free. The pursuit of objective analysis is a central feature of much quantitative geography, particularly that which is positivist in formulation. See **Berry; Bourdieu; Haggett; Haraway; Tobler.**

Other/otherness: The 'Other' refers to the person that is different or opposite to the self. Othering is the process through which the other is often defined in relation to the self in negative ways; for example woman is often constructed as other to man, black as other to white. See **Bhabha; Hall; hooks; Jackson; Said; Sibley; Spivak; Young.**

Paradigm: The assumptions and ideas that define a particular way of thinking about and undertaking research that become the dominant way of theorising a discipline over a period of time until challenged and replaced by a new paradigm. See **Ley.**

Patriarchy/patriarchal: Literally means 'rule of the father'. This term is used to describe a social system and practices whereby men dominate women. These unequal relationships can occur at a range of scales from the household to society as a whole. See **Butler; hooks; Rose; Massey; McDowell; Young.**

Performativity: Developed within literary theory, performativity is a rhetorical device for thinking about the way in which identity is produced in non-foundational and non-essentialist ways. Most commonly associated with the writings of Judith Butler, it is argued that identities are continuously brought into being through their performance. In relation to gender, what it means to be a woman or man is produced and sustained through acts, gestures, mannerisms, clothing and so on. In other words, there are no 'natural' gendered identities, gender is what people *do* and by performing gender people reproduce the notion of what gender constitutes. See **Butler; Ingold; Rose; Thrift.**

Political ecology: An approach that entwines Marxism with cultural ecology to account for the diverse ways in which nature was produced and exploited for capital gain in an era of flexible accumulation. Here, there is a recognition that resource management and environmental regulation and stability are wedded to how communities are integrated into a global economy. In other words, the pressure brought to bear on ecosystems is often due to economic and political pressures rather than simply mismanagement or overpopulation. See **Watts.**

Political economy: Theoretical approaches that stress the importance of the political organisation of economic reproduction in structuring social, economic and political life. Associated in human geography with the influence of Marxist thinking, political economy perspectives in fact encompass a variety of approaches that explore the workings of market economies. See **Harvey; Massey; Sayer; Smith; Taylor; Wallerstein; Watts.**

Positivism: A philosophy that suggests that universal laws and explanations can be constructed through repeated scientific observations and measurements. Though different packages of positivist thought argue that the burden of scientific proof rests with the researcher in different ways, all hold to the ideal of the researcher as objective and independent. In human geography's attempt to recast itself as a spatial science, the influence of positivism was paramount, and the tenets of positivism still arguably inform the majority of geographical investigation. See **Berry; Haggett; Harvey; Tobler.**

Post-colonialism: A set of approaches that seeks to expose the ongoing legacy of the colonial era for those nations that were subject to occupation by white, European colonisers. Emphasising both the material and symbolic effects of colonialism, post-colonial perspectives are particularly concerned with the ways that notions of inferiority and Otherness are mapped onto the global south by the north, though post-colonial perspectives have also been utilised to explore the race and ethnic relations played out on different scales. See **Bhabha; Gregory; hooks; Said; Spivak; Ó Tuathail; Watts.**

Post-modernism: Often used to denote playful and self-referential styles of art, architecture and literature, post-modernism is a term that captures both the logic of a particular epoch (i.e. late capitalism) and the methods required to make sense of this era. Associated with a breakdown of order, rationality and assured progress, post-modern times are often taken to be typified by fluidity and flexibility; accordingly post-modern theorists argue that grand theories such as feminism, Marxism or positivism are no longer appropriate for exploring social life. Instead, post-modern thinkers seek to embrace difference and fluidity, adopting methods and writing styles that are in tune with post-modern times. See **Baudrillard; Davis; Dear; Harvey; Ley; Soja.**

Post-structuralism: A broad set of theoretical positions that problematises the role of language in the construction of knowledge. Contrary to structural approaches, which see the world as constructed through fixed forms of language, such approaches emphasise the slipperiness of language and the instability of text. A wide-ranging set of assertions follow from this key argument, including the assertion that subjects are made through language; the idea that life is essentially unstable, and only given stability through language; the irrelevance of distinctions between real and simulcra, ultimately, that there is nothing 'beyond the text'. In human geography, post-structural thought has provoked attempts to deconstruct a wide variety of texts (including maps) and has encouraged geographers to reject totalising and foundationalist discourses (especially those associated with structural Marxism). See **Baudrillard; Butler; Deleuze; Foucault; Gibson-Graham.**

Praxis: Praxis is how theoretical ideas are translated into the world. In relation to academia this is primarily through research, teaching, discussion and debate. See **Haraway; Harvey; Rose.**

Producer services: Those 'knowledge-rich' businesses that provide services and expertise to corporate and governmental clients, particular those transnational corporations whose activities require careful co-ordination across time and space. Examples include accountancies, lawyers, advertising and promotions agencies, and management consultancies, all of which tend to cluster in World Cities so as to be able to service their global clients. See **Castells; Dicken; Sassen; Thrift; Taylor.**

Production: The processes by which commodities are brought into being. In human geography, production has traditionally been the remit of economic geographers, who explore how space is a formative influence on, and not just an outcome of, economic activity. Latterly, an increasing focus on consumption has questioned this analytical specialisation, and encouraged study of the way consumption and production are linked through commodity chains that extend through space in complex ways. See **Dicken; Barnes; Sayer; Stoper; Thrift.**

Psychoanalysis: Narrowly defined as a mode of therapy that seeks to resolve patients' neuroses by exploring the contents of the unconscious mind. This form of therapy involves attempts to encourage people to reconcile the unconscious and conscious mind, leading to a fuller knowledge of Self. More widely, the ideas of leading psychoanalysts such as Freud, Jung and Lacan have been interpreted as providing theories of socialisation that can be used to understand how people are constructed as (repressed) subjects. In human geography, the theories – and occasionally, the practices – of psychoanalysis have been taken up in various ways, primarily by geographers exploring the relations of sexuality and space. However, the relationship between feminism and psychoanalysis remains strained in many respects. See **Butler; Sibley; Rose.**

Qualitative method: In human geography, this denotes those methods that accept words and text as a legitimate form of data, including discourse analysis, ethnography, interviewing, and numerous methods of visual analysis. Mainly tracing their roots to the arts and humanities, such methods have often been depicted as 'soft' methods, and hence described as feminist in orientation. Latterly, however, such simplistic assertions have been dismissed, and such methods proliferate across the discipline in areas including economic and political geography. See **Barnes; Rose; Ó Tuathail.**

Quantitative method: In human geography, this denotes those methods that prioritise numerical data, including survey techniques, use of secondary statistics, numerous forms of experimentation, and many forms of content analysis. Mainly derived from the natural sciences, such methods are often depicted as 'hard' methods, deriving their analytical rigour and validity by association with masculine modes of science and exploration. However, numerous critiques have exposed the subjectivity of quantitative methods, and suggested its techniques cannot be understood as objective ways of looking at and understanding the world. This has led to a reappraisal of quantitative method in areas of the discipline such as social and cultural geography where quantitative method has long been anathema. See **Barnes; Berry; Hägerstrand; Haggett; Taylor.**

Queer theory: A set of approaches and practices that expose and challenge the implict and explicit heterosexism of academic knowledge production. Sometimes allied to feminist approaches, but sometimes in sharp opposition to them, such approaches demonstrate how homophobia is embedded in both the spaces of academia and the spaces of everyday life. This approach is often associated with confrontational writing styles and modes of research that emphasise the subjectivity of the researcher. See **Butler; Foucault.**

Realism: A theoretical perspective that seeks to transcend many of the problems associated with positivism and structuralism by seeking to isolate the causal properties of things that cause other things to happen in given situations. Based on a methodological distinction between extensive and intensive research, this approach was widely embraced in human geography in the 1980s as a way of distinguishing between spurious associations and meaningful relations. See **Giddens; Massey; Sayer.**

Regional geography: The study of the various phenomena – social, political, economic, cultural – that make up a large area that is identifiably distinguished from surrounding regions. See **Massey; Thrift.**

Relational geographies: An awareness that events on different scales are not simply linked hierarchically, but that space itself exists in a non-hierarchical flat ontology which brings together the near and far. Such conceptualisations challenge ideas that places exist in the world as bounded phenomena, and demand an openness to the world. See **Massey; Urry.**

Representation: A set of media or practices through which meaning is communicated. The study of representation has become a common way for researchers to examine sense of place and how people understand, construct and relate to socio-spatial relations. See **Cosgrove; Jackson; Hall; Harley; Spivak; Ó Tuathail.**

Sense of place: A central concept in humanistic geography, intended to describe the particular ways in which human beings invest their surroundings with meaning. Sense of place is seen be an elusive concept, yet human geographers seek to find its traces in a variety of texts and representations, including paintings, poetry, prose and cinema. See **Ley; Tuan.**

Situated knowledge: In a challenge to objectivity, a situated knowledge is one where theorisation and empirical research are framed within the context within which they were formulated. Here it is posited that knowledge is not simply 'out there' waiting to be collected but is rather made by actors who are situated within particular contexts. Research is not a neutral or objective activity but is shaped by a host of influences ranging from personal beliefs to the culture of academia to the conditions of funding to individual relationships between researcher and researched, and so on. This situatedness of knowledge production needs to be reflexively documented to allow other researchers to understand the positionality of the researcher and the findings of a study. See **Haraway; Rose.**

Social justice: A set of normative approaches concerned with the fair and equitable distribution of things that people care about such as work, wealth, food and housing, plus less tangible phenomena such as systems of power and pathways of opportunity. See **Harvey; Smith; Sen; Young.**

Spatiality: A term that refers to how space and social relations are made through each other; that is, how space is made through social relations, and how social relations are shaped by the space in which they occur. See **Lefebvre; Soja.**

Spatial science: An approach to understanding human geography that holds to the idea that there can be a search for general laws that will explain the distribution of human activity across the world's surface. Associated with the precepts of positivism, and mainly reliant on quantitative method, spatial science signalled geography's transition from an atheoretical discipline to one concerned with explanation rather than mere description. Emerging in the 1950s, and bolstered by the Quantitative Revolution of the 1960s, spatial science continues to be dominant in many areas of the discipline, though in others its philosophical underpinnings and theoretical conceits have long discredited it. See **Barnes; Berry; Hägerstrand; Haggett; Tobler.**

Structuralism: A theoretical approach that suggests that life is structured by 'deep' political, economic and social structures (such as capitalism) whose existence cannot be directly observed. This approach is particularly associated with linguistics, where structuralist thinkers argue that the meaning of language cannot be understood through the analysis of the use of individual words and phrases, but through the questioning of language as a system. Methodologically, structuralism relies upon the collection of data that might be used to prove the existence of such structures: these data might give clues as to the relations between constituent elements of the system (e.g. language, practices, behaviours) and, through a process of dialectic reasoning, seek to expose their opposite and contradictory existence within that system. In human geography, Marx's ideas have been fundamental in the development of geographical accounts that highlight the role of space in perpetuating capitalist structures. See **Harvey; Massey; Smith.**

Structuration theory: The idea that there is a distinct, reciprocal relation between agency and structure and that this can be observed and understood through study not of individual actions or broad social trajectories but social practices. See **Giddens; Gregory; Pred; Sayer; Urry.**

Subaltern: The figure of the subaltern refers to the collective agency of exploited, oppressed and marginalised groups. See **hooks; Spivak.**

Territoriality: The strategies adopted by a set of people to claim and govern a particular unit of land and its contents. See **Ó Tuathail.**

Time geography: An approach to the study of space that prioritises the effects of time and temporality. Here there is an emphasis on understanding the effects of how events are sequenced in time and space, including for example patterns of home-to-work journeys and the diffusion of diseases. See **Hägerstrand; Pred; Thrift.**

Time-space convergence: The speeding up of the pace of life due to increasing time–space compression (shrinking of space by time) and time–space distanciation (the interconnectedness and interdependence of people and places across the globe). See **Castells; Giddens; Harvey; Massey; Virilio.**

Transnationalism: The ongoing economic, social, cultural and political links developed and maintained by migrants and trade across the borders of nation-states. See **Jackson.**

World Cities: Those cities in which a disproportionate amount of the world's business is carried out. Measurements of World City importance are thus normally based on numbers of company headquarters, business transactions and size of capital markets rather than cultural vitality, population size or infrastructure (meaning London, New York and Tokyo tend to be described as World Cities, but larger cities, including Tehran, Dhaka or Khartoum, are not). See **Castells; Sassen; Taylor; Thrift.**

World systems theory: Perspectives that argue that social, economic and political analysis cannot proceed on a nation-by-nation basis, but needs to explore the way the world works as an integrated (capitalist) unit. Such perspectives have been deemed to have particular relevance in an era when globalisation is seemingly undermining the sovereignity of the nation-state. See **Dicken; Taylor; Wallerstein.**

Index

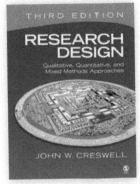

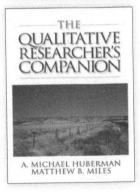

Research Methods
Books from SAGE

INTERPRETING QUALITATIVE DATA THIRD EDITION

DAVID SILVERMAN

Qualitative Research & Evaluation Methods

3 EDITION

Michael Quinn Patton

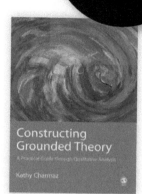

Constructing Grounded Theory

Kathy Charmaz

EVALUATION A Systematic Approach SEVENTH EDITION

PETER H. ROSSI MARK W. LIPSEY HOWARD E. FREEMAN

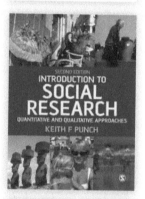

SECOND EDITION INTRODUCTION TO SOCIAL RESEARCH QUANTITATIVE AND QUALITATIVE APPROACHES

KEITH F PUNCH

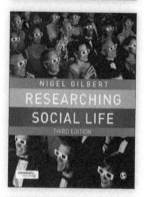

NIGEL GILBERT RESEARCHING SOCIAL LIFE THIRD EDITION

Sixth Edition INVESTIGATING THE Social World THE PROCESS AND PRACTICE OF RESEARCH

Russell K. Schutt

AN INTRODUCTION TO QUALITATIVE RESEARCH UWE FLICK EDITION 4

DEVELOPING EFFECTIVE RESEARCH PROPOSALS Keith F Punch SECOND EDITION

www.sagepub.co.uk

SAGE